Release 13 for Windows

AutoCAD
and its applications
Advanced

by

Terence M. Shumaker
Manager
Autodesk Premier Training Center
Clackamas Community College, Oregon City, OR

David A. Madsen
Chairperson
Drafting Technology
Autodesk Premier Training Center
Clackamas Community College, Oregon City, OR
Former Board of Director
American Design Drafting Association

A Autodesk.
Registered Author/Publisher

Publisher
The Goodheart-Willcox Company, Inc.
Tinley Park, Illinois

Library of Congress Catalog Card Number 96-23891
International Standard Book Number 1-56637-183-X

1 2 3 4 5 6 7 8 9 10   96   00 99 98 97 96

Library of Congress Cataloging-in-Publication Data
Shumaker, Terence M.
  AutoCAD and its applications–advanced: release 13 for
Windows / by Terence M. Shumaker, David A. Madsen.

    p. cm.
  Includes index.
  ISBN 1-56637-183-X
  1. Computer graphics. 2. AutoCAD for Windows

I. Madsen, David A. II. Title.
T385.S54613 1997
620' .0042' 02855369--dc20   96-23891
                                           CIP

Materials used for the cover art courtesy of Arthur Baker, CalComp, Moraine Valley Community College,
David Ward, and FLIR Systems Inc.

INTRODUCTION

AutoCAD and its Applications—Advanced, Release 13 for Windows is a write-in text that provides complete instruction in mastering the AutoCAD Release 13 for Windows 3D modeling commands and various customizing techniques. These topics are covered in an easy-to-understand sequence, and progress in a way that allows you to become comfortable with the commands as your knowledge builds from one chapter to the next. In addition, *AutoCAD and its Applications—Advanced, Release 13 for Windows* offers the following features:

- Step-by-step use of AutoCAD commands.
- In-depth explanations of how and why commands function as they do.
- Extensive use of font changes to specify certain meanings. These are fully explained in the next section, *Fonts used in this text*.
- Examples and discussions of industrial practices and standards.
- Actual screen captures of AutoCAD and Windows features and functions.
- Professional tips explaining how to use AutoCAD effectively and efficiently.
- Over 200 exercises involving several tasks to reinforce the chapter topics. These exercises also build on previously learned material.
- Chapter tests for review of commands and key AutoCAD concepts.
- A large selection of modeling and customizing problems supplement each chapter. Problems are presented as 3D illustrations, actual plotted drawings, and engineering sketches.

With *AutoCAD and its Applications—Basics, Release 13 for Windows*, you not only learn AutoCAD commands, but you also become acquainted with:

- Constructing models using different 3D coordinate systems.
- 3D object construction and layout techniques.
- User coordinate systems.
- Model space viewports.
- 3D editing and display techniques.
- 3D text and dimensioning.
- Surface modeling and rendering.
- Solid model construction and editing.
- AutoCAD's structured query language (SQL) functions.
- Customizing the AutoCAD for Windows environment.
- Customizing toolbars, pull-down menus, and image tiles.
- Customizing screen, button, and tablet menus.
- The basics of AutoLISP and dialog box (DCL) programming.
- Advanced AutoCAD for Windows features such as OLE and DDE.

The most important factor in learning advanced AutoCAD techniques is to find a reference that:

- Answers all your questions.
- Presents the commands in an easy-to-understand, logical sequence.
- Applies AutoCAD for Windows to typical drafting and design tasks.
- Provides proper drafting standards.
- Reduces the fear of using AutoCAD for Windows.

AutoCAD and its Applications—Advanced, Release 13 for Windows does this... and even more!

Fonts used in this text

Different typefaces are used throughout each chapter to define terms and identify AutoCAD commands. Important terms always appear in ***bold-italic face, serif*** type. AutoCAD menus, commands, variables, dialog box names, and tool button names are printed in bold-face, sans serif type. Filenames, directory names, paths, and keyboard-entry items appear in the body of the text in Roman, sans serif type. Keyboard keys are shown inside of square brackets [ ] and appear in Roman, sans serif type. For example, [Enter] means to press the enter (return) key. In addition, commands, menus, and dialog boxes related to Microsoft Windows appear in Roman, sans serif type.

Prompt sequences are set apart from the body text with space above and below, and appear in Roman, sans serif type. Keyboard entry items in prompts appear in **bold-face, sans serif** type. In prompts, the [Enter] key is represented by the ↵ symbol.

Checking the AutoCAD reference manuals

No other reference should be needed when using this text. However, the authors have referenced relevant topic areas to the *AutoCAD User's Guide* and the *AutoCAD Customization Guide*. In the margin next to many heads in this text, you will find a "book" icon. This tells you where to look in the AutoCAD reference manuals to find more information about the topic being discussed.

AutoCAD Custom Guide **5**

For example, the icon in the margin here means that the topic is discussed in Chapter 5 of the *AutoCAD Customization Guide*. The AutoCAD software is also delivered with the *AutoCAD Command Reference*. Commands and variables are presented in alphabetical order in this manual.

Other text references

For additional information, standards from organizations such as ANSI (American National Standards Institute) and ASME (American Society of Mechanical Engineers) are referenced throughout the text. These standards are used to help you create drawings that follow industrial, national, and international standards.

Also for your convenience, other Goodheart-Willcox textbooks are referenced. Textbooks that are referenced include **AutoCAD and its Applications** (Releases 10, 11, and 12), **AutoLISP Programming—Principles and Techniques**, and **AutoCAD AME—Solid Modeling for Mechanical Design**. All of these textbooks can be ordered directly from Goodheart-Willcox.

Introducing the AutoCAD commands

There are several ways to select AutoCAD for Windows drawing and editing commands. Selecting commands from a toolbars or pull-down menu is slightly different than entering them from the keyboard. All AutoCAD commands and related options in this text are presented using a variety of command entry methods.

Unless otherwise specified, command entries are shown as if typed at the keyboard. This allows the text to present the full command name and the prompts that appear on-screen. Commands, options, and values you must enter are given in bold text, as shown in the following example. Pressing the [Enter] (return) key is indicated with the ↵ symbol. (Also, refer to the earlier section *Fonts used in this text*.)

Command: **3DFACE**↵
First point: **2,2**↵
Second point: **4,2**↵
Third point: **4,6**↵
Fourth point: **2,6**↵

General input such as picking a point or selecting an object is presented in italic, serif font, as shown below.

> Command: **3DFACE**↲
> First point: *(pick a point)*
> Second point: *(pick another point)*
> Third point: *(pick a third point)*
> Fourth point: *(pick the last point)*

Other command entry methods presented throughout the text are toolbars and pull-down menus. When a toolbar button can be used to execute a command, it is illustrated in the margin next to the text reference. The text will indicate where the button is located. A grayscale button is an AutoCAD-related button. A green button is a Windows-related button. Experiment with all command entry methods to find the most convenient way for *you* to enter commands.

Flexibility in design

Flexibility is the key word when using *AutoCAD and its Applications—Advanced, Release 13 for Windows*. This text is an excellent training aid for individual, as well as classroom instruction. *AutoCAD and its Applications—Advanced, Release 13 for Windows* teaches you AutoCAD in the Windows environment and how to apply AutoCAD to common modeling and customizing tasks. It is also an invaluable resource for any professional using AutoCAD.

When working through the text, you will see a variety of notices throughout. These notices include Professional Tips, Notes, and Cautions that help you develop your AutoCAD skills.

PROFESSIONAL TIP	These ideas and suggestions are aimed at increasing your productivity and enhancing your use of AutoCAD commands and techniques.

NOTE	A note alerts you to important aspects of a command function, menu, or activity that is being discussed. These aspects should be kept in mind while you are working through the text.

CAUTION	A caution alerts you to potential problems if instructions or commands are used incorrectly, or if an action can corrupt or alter files, directories, or disks. If you are in doubt after reading a caution, always consult your instructor or supervisor.

AutoCAD and its Applications—Advanced, Release 13 for Windows provides several ways for you to evaluate your performance. Included are:

- **Exercises.** Each chapter contains in-text Exercises. These Exercises allow you to perform tasks that reinforce the material just presented. You can work through the Exercises at your own pace.
- **Chapter Tests.** Each chapter includes a written test at the end of the chapter. Questions require you to give the proper definition, command, option, or response to perform a certain task.
- **Drawing Problems.** There are a variety of drawing, design, and customizing problems at the end of each chapter. These are presented as real-world CAD drawings,

3D illustrations, and engineering sketches. The problems are designed to make you think, solve problems, use design techniques, research and use proper drawing standards, and correct errors in the drawings or engineering sketches.

Each drawing problem deals with one of six technical disciplines. Although doing all of the problems will enhance your AutoCAD skills, you may be focusing on a particular discipline. The discipline that a problem addresses is indicated by a text graphic in the margin next to the problem number. Each graphic and its description is as follows:

| Mechanical Drafting | These problems address mechanical drafting and designing applications, such as manufactured part designs. |

| Architecture | These problems address architectural and structural drafting and design applications, such as floor plans, furniture, and presentation drawings. |

| Civil Drafting | These problems address civil drafting and design application, such as plot plans, plats, and landscape drawings. |

| Graphic Design | These problems address graphic design applications, such as text creation, title blocks, and page layout. |

| Piping | These problems address piping drafting and design applications, such as piping flow diagrams, tank drawings, and pipe layout. |

| General | These problems address a variety of general drafting and design applications. These problems should be attempted by everyone learning advanced AutoCAD techniques for the first time. |

NOTE

Some problems presented in this text are given as engineering sketches. These sketches are intended to represent the kind of materials a drafter is expected to work from in a real-world situation. As such, engineering sketches often contain errors or slight inaccuracies, and are most often not drawn according to proper drafting conventions and applicable standards. Errors in these problems are *intentional* to encourage the user to apply appropriate techniques and standards in order to solve the problem. As in real-world applications, sketches should be considered preliminary layouts. Always question inaccuracies in sketches and designs, and consult the applicable standards or other resources.

DISK SUPPLEMENTS

To help you develop your AutoCAD skills, Goodheart-Willcox offers a disk supplement package to use with *AutoCAD and its Applications—Advanced, Release 13 for Windows*. The Autodesk software AutoCAD Release 13 for Windows is required for Goodheart-Willcox software to operate properly.

The *Student Work Disk* contains additional AutoCAD pull-down menus with a variety of activities. These activities are intended to be used as a supplement to the exercises and activities found in the text. The *Work Disk* activities correspond to Chapter 1 - Chapter 14 of the text. These activities allow you to progress at your own pace.

ABOUT THE AUTHORS

Terence M. Shumaker is Manager of the Autodesk Premier Training Center, and a Drafting Technology instructor at Clackamas Community College. Terence has been teaching at the community college level since 1977. He has commercial experience in surveying, civil drafting, industrial piping, and technical illustration. He is the author of Goodheart-Willcox's *Process Pipe Drafting*, and is coauthor of the *AutoCAD and its Applications Release 13* series, *AutoCAD and its Applications* (Release 10, 11, and 12 editions), and *AutoCAD Essentials*.

David A. Madsen is the Chairperson of Drafting Technology and the Autodesk Premier Training Center at Clackamas Community College. David has been an instructor/department chair at Clackamas Community College since 1972. In addition to community college experience, David was a Drafting Technology instructor at Centennial High School in Gresham, Oregon. David also has extensive experience in mechanical drafting, architectural design and drafting, and construction practices. He is the author or coauthor of several Goodheart-Willcox drafting and design textbooks, including *Geometric Dimensioning and Tolerancing*, the *AutoCAD and its Applications Release 13* series, *AutoCAD and its Applications* (Release 10, 11, and 12 editions), and *AutoCAD Essentials*.

NOTICE TO THE USER

AutoCAD and its Applications—Advanced, Release 13 for Windows covers the advanced AutoCAD for Windows applications mentioned in this introduction. For a text that covers the basic AutoCAD for Windows applications, please refer to *AutoCAD and its Applications—Basics, Release 13 for Windows*. The *Basics* text is also available for the AutoCAD Release 13 for DOS format. Copies of any of these texts can be ordered directly from Goodheart-Willcox.

ACKNOWLEDGMENTS

The authors and publisher would like to thank the following individuals and companies for their assistance and contributions:

Contributing authors

The authors are indebted to Rod Rawls for his professional expertise in providing in-depth research and testing, technical assistance, reviews, and development of new materials for Chapter 16 - Chapter 23. Rod is an AutoCAD consultant and principal instructor at the AutoCAD Premier Training Center, Clackamas Community College. He is also the coauthor of *AutoLISP Programming Principles and Techniques* published by Goodheart-Willcox.

Jackie McAninch is the ATC Manager at the Unified Technical Education Campus of Mesa College in Grand Junction, Colorado. She contributed valuable information for Chapter 9, and Chapter 13 - Chapter 15.

Technical assistance and contribution of materials

Rachel Cederdahl, student at Clackamas Community College
Margo Bilson of Willamette Industries, Inc.
Fitzgerald, Hagan, & Hackathorn
Dr. Stuart Soman of Briarcliffe College
Gil Hoellerich of Springdale, AR

Contribution of materials

Cynthia B. Clark of the American Society of Mechanical Engineers
Marty McConnell of Houston Instrument, A Summagraphics Company
Grace Avila of Autodesk, Inc.
Dave Hall of the Harris Group, Inc.

Contribution of photographs or other technical information

Amdek Corporation
Applications Development, Inc.
Arthur Baker
Autodesk, Inc.
CADalyst magazine
CADENCE magazine
CalComp
Chris Lindner
Computer-Aided Design, Inc.
Digital Equipment Corp.
EPCM Services Ltd.
Far Mountain Corporation
FLIR Systems Inc.
Gateway 2000
GTCO Corporation
Harris Group, Inc.
Hewlett-Packard
Houston Instrument, A Summagraphics
     Company
International Source for Ergonomics

IOLINE Corporation
JDL, Inc.
Jerome Hart
Jim Armstrong
Jim Webster
Kunz Associates
Matt Slay
Mark Stennfeld
Mitsubishi Electronics America, Inc.
Microsoft Corporation
Mouse Systems Corporation
Myonetics Inc.
NEC Technologies, Inc.
Norwest Engineering
Schuchart & Associates, Inc.
Summagraphics Corporation
The American Society of Mechanical Engineers
The Xerox Engineering Systems Company
Weiser, Inc.
Willamette Industries, Inc.

Technical assistance and reviews

Michael Jones, Autodesk Premier Training Center, Clackamas Community College
J.C. Malitzke, Autodesk Premier Training Center, Moraine Valley Community College
Kevin DeVoll, Margaret Burke, Earl Larson, Paul Masterson

Hardware contributions

CalComp for use of the inkjet plotter.
Moraine Valley Community College for use of their laboratory, computer, monitor, and
     digitizer.

TRADEMARKS

CONTENTS

Chapter 1

Introduction to Three-Dimensional Drawing

AutoCAD R13

Learning objectives

After completing this chapter, you will be able to:

- ❍ Describe the nature and function of rectangular 3D coordinate systems.
- ❍ Describe the "right-hand rule" of 3D visualization.
- ❍ Construct extruded and wireframe 3D objects.
- ❍ Display 3D objects from any viewpoint.

The use of three-dimensional (3D) drawing and design as a tool is becoming more prevalent throughout industry. Companies are discovering the benefits of 3D modeling in design, visualization, testing, analysis, manufacturing, assembly, and marketing. Three-dimensional models also form the basis of computer animations and *virtual worlds* used with virtual reality systems. Persons who can design objects, buildings, and "worlds" in 3D are in demand for a wide variety of positions both inside, and outside of the traditional drafting and design disciplines. The first twelve chapters of this book provide you with a variety of skills and techniques for drawing and designing 3D wireframes, surfaces, and solids. These skills provide you with the ability to construct any object in 3D, and prepare you for entry into an exciting aspect of graphic communication.

To be effective creating and using 3D objects, the drafter or designer must first have good 3D visualization skills, including the ability to see an object in three dimensions and to visualize it rotating in space. These skills can be obtained by using 3D techniques to construct objects, and by trying to see two-dimensional sketches and drawings as 3D models. This chapter provides an introduction to several aspects of 3D drawing and visualization. Subsequent chapters expand on these aspects and provide a detailed examination of 3D drawing, editing, visualization, and display.

RECTANGULAR 3D COORDINATES

In two-dimensional drawing, you see one plane defined by two dimensions. These dimensions are usually located on the X and Y axes. However, in 3D drawing, another plane and coordinate axis is added. The additional plane is defined with a third dimension located along the Z axis. If you are looking at a standard AutoCAD screen, the positive Z axis comes directly out of the screen toward your face. A computer can only draw lines in 3D if it knows the X, Y, and Z coordinate values of each point on the object. For 2D drawing, only two of the three coordinates are needed.

Compare the 2D coordinate system and the 3D coordinate system shown in Figure 1-1. Notice that the positive values of Z in the 3D system come up from the XY plane of a 2D drawing. Consider the surface of your screen as the XY plane. Anything behind the screen is negative Z and anything in front of the screen is positive Z. The object in Figure 1-2A is a 2D drawing showing the top view of an object. The XY coordinate values of each point are shown with the lower-left corner as the origin (0,0). Think of the object as being drawn directly on the surface of your screen. To convert this object to its three-dimensional form, Z values

Figure 1-1.
A comparison of 2D and 3D
coordinate systems.

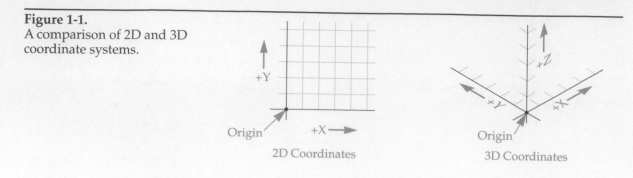

2D Coordinates

3D Coordinates

Figure 1-2.
A—The corners of a 2D object only need two coordinates. B—Each corner of a 3D object must have
an X, Y, and Z value.

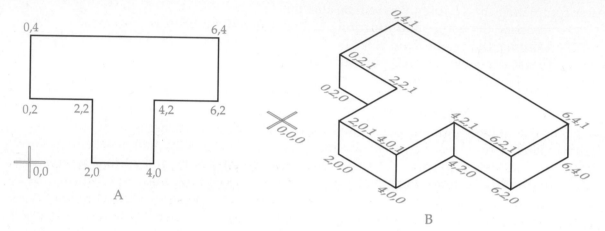

A

B

are given to each corner. Figure 1-2B shows the object pictorially with the XYZ values of each point listed. Positive Z coordinates are used. Therefore, the object comes out of your screen. The object can also be drawn using negative Z coordinates. In this case, the object extends behind, or into, the screen.

Study the nature of the 3D coordinate system. Be sure you understand Z values before you begin constructing 3D objects. It is especially important that you carefully visualize and plan your design when working with 3D constructions.

Three-dimensional objects can be drawn in AutoCAD using two additional coordinate systems—spherical and cylindrical. These two systems allow you to work with point locations using distances and angles in order to draw a variety of shapes. A complete discussion of spherical and cylindrical coordinate systems is provided in Chapter 2.

PROFESSIONAL TIP

Although the sign of the Z value (positive or negative) makes no difference to AutoCAD, it can be time-consuming to use negative values.

EXERCISE 1-1

❑ Study the multiview sketch below.
❑ Freehand sketch the object pictorially on the 3D coordinate axes.
❑ Each tick mark is one unit. Use correct dimensions as given in the multiview sketch.
❑ When you complete the freehand sketch, draw the object in AutoCAD with the **LINE** command by entering XYZ coordinates for each point.
❑ Save the drawing as A:EX1-1 and quit.

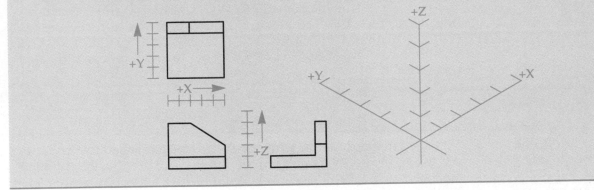

CREATING EXTRUDED 3D SHAPES

Most shapes drawn with AutoCAD are extruded shapes. *Extruded* means that a 2D shape is given a base elevation and a thickness. The object then rises up, or "extrudes" to its given thickness. The **ELEV** command is used to extrude an object. **ELEV** does not draw, it merely sets the base elevation and thickness for the next object drawn. To use this command, type ELEV at the **Command:** prompt, pick **Object Creation...** from the **Data** pull-down menu, or pick **DDemode:** from the **DATA** screen menu. When selected from the pull down or screen menu, the **Object Creation Modes** dialog box is displayed, Figure 1-3. The current elevation and thickness can be set using this dialog box.

Figure 1-3.
The **Object Creation Modes** dialog box allows you to set the current elevation and thickness.

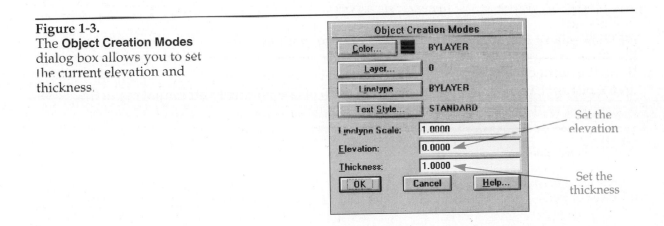

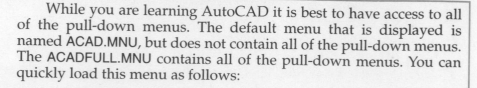

NOTE

While you are learning AutoCAD it is best to have access to all of the pull-down menus. The default menu that is displayed is named ACAD.MNU, but does not contain all of the pull-down menus. The ACADFULL.MNU contains all of the pull-down menus. You can quickly load this menu as follows:

Command: **MENU.⏎**

The **Select Menu File** dialog box is displayed. Change the selection to *.MNU and pick the file named ACADFULL.MNU in the **File Name:** list box. Then, pick **OK**. The menu is loaded and you will see the ten pull-down menus displayed. For the remainder of this text, you should have the ACADFULL.MNU menu loaded, unless indicated otherwise.

NOTE

Keep in mind that the current elevation established by the value set using the **ELEV** command or entered in the **Object Creation Modes** dialog box is the level that the next object is drawn on. Therefore, if you set the elevation at 1.0, then draw the bottom of a machine part, the bottom of that part is now sitting at an elevation of 1.0 units above the zero elevation.

On the other hand, the setting of the *thickness* is the value that determines the height of the next object you draw. Therefore, if you want to draw a part one unit high with the bottom of the part resting on the zero elevation plane, set elevation to 0.0 and thickness to 1.0.

To draw the "T"-shaped object shown in Figure 1-4A, first use the **ELEV** command as follows:

Command: **ELEV ⏎**
New current elevation ⟨0.0000⟩:⏎
New current thickness ⟨0.0000⟩: **1**⏎

After you have entered this command sequence, nothing happens on-screen. However, an elevation of 0 and thickness of 1 are now the current settings. Next, use the **LINE** command to draw the outline. Although it appears that you are drawing lines, you are actually drawing X and Y planes. Each plane has a height (thickness) of one unit that you cannot see in this view.

Figure 1-4.
A—The basic object.
B—Two hexagons and a circle are added to the basic object.

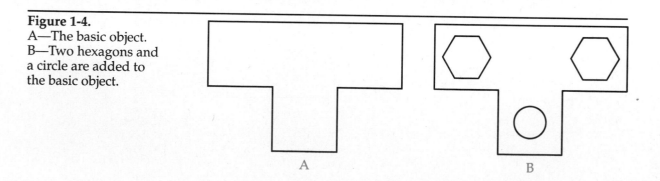

Now, use the following instructions to add two hexagons and a circle, as shown in Figure 1-4B. The hexagons should sit on top of the "T" and extend .25 units above. The circle should appear to be a hole through the leg of the "T." Since the circle has the same elevation and thickness as the "T," draw it first. This way you will only need to use the **ELEV** command when drawing the hexagons. To draw the hexagons, set the base elevation and thickness (height) using the **ELEV** command as follows. The base elevation is set to the top surface of the "T." These values can also be set in the **Object Creation Modes** dialog box, as shown in Figure 1-5.

```
Command: ELEV↵
New current elevation ⟨0.0000⟩: 1↵
New current thickness ⟨2.0000⟩: .25↵
```

Figure 1-5.
The elevation and thickness values can be set in the **Object Creation Modes** dialog box.

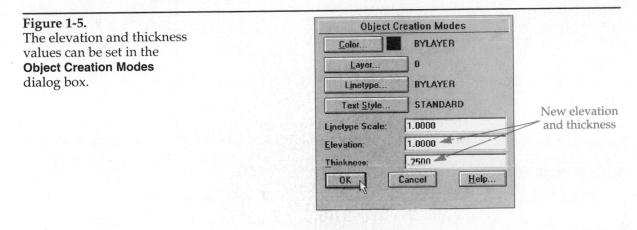

New elevation and thickness

The value of 1 is entered for the elevation because the hexagons sit on top of the "T," which is 1 unit thick. The value of .25 is the thickness, or height, of the hexagons above the base elevation. Now, draw the hexagons. With all of the elements drawn, the object is now ready to be viewed in 3D.

Displaying quick 3D views

AutoCAD has two ways to quickly display a 3D drawing. You can either select **3D Viewpoint Presets** in the **View** pull-down menu or pick the appropriate button in the **View** toolbar, Figure 1-6.

Figure 1-6.
A—The **3D Viewpoint Presets** cascading menu provides eleven different display options for the current drawing. B—The viewpoint displays can also be selected in the **View** toolbox.

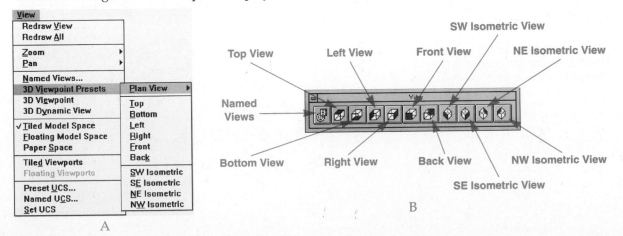

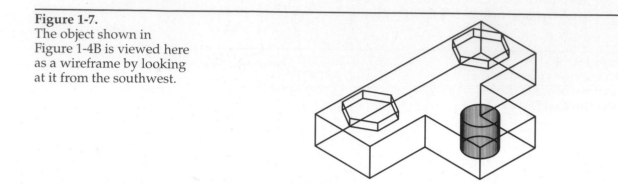

In the **View** pull-down menu, there is the **Plan View** selection not available in the toolbar. In the toolbar, there is the **Named Views** selection not available in the pull-down menu. If you pick **Plan View**, the current drawing is redisplayed in a plan view of the current user coordinate system. A plan view is shown in Figure 1-4. User coordinate systems are discussed in detail in Chapter 3. Picking the **Named Views** button in the toolbar displays the **View Control** dialog box.

Using either the pull-down menu or the toolbar, pick **SW Isometric View**. The display should look like the one shown in Figure 1-7. If you want to return to the previous 2D display, just pick **Plan View**, then **Current** in the **View** pull-down menu.

Figure 1-7.
The object shown in
Figure 1-4B is viewed here
as a wireframe by looking
at it from the southwest.

Removing hidden lines in 3D displays

In a wireframe display, every edge can be seen. This view can be confusing, especially if there are several circular features in your drawing. The best way to mask all lines that would normally be hidden is to use the **HIDE** command:

    Command: **HIDE.**↵
    Regenerating drawing
    Hiding lines 100% done

Use **HIDE** only after you have selected a 3D viewpoint. The size and complexity of the drawing, and the speed of your computer, determine how long you must wait for the lines to be hidden. The object in Figure 1-7 is shown in Figure 1-8 with hidden lines removed.

The view in Figure 1-8 may not look quite right. You probably expected the "T" to appear solid with a circle in the top representing a hole. Think back to the initial construction of the object. When drawn in the plan view, it consisted of lines, or planes. It was not drawn with a top or bottom, just sides. Then, you placed hexagons on top of the "box" and a cylinder inside. However, the object still is made up of only sides. That is why the "hidden line removed" display appears as it does.

Figure 1-8.
The hidden lines of this
object were removed using
the **HIDE** command.

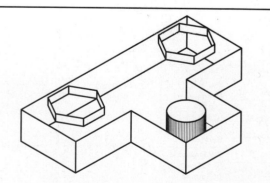

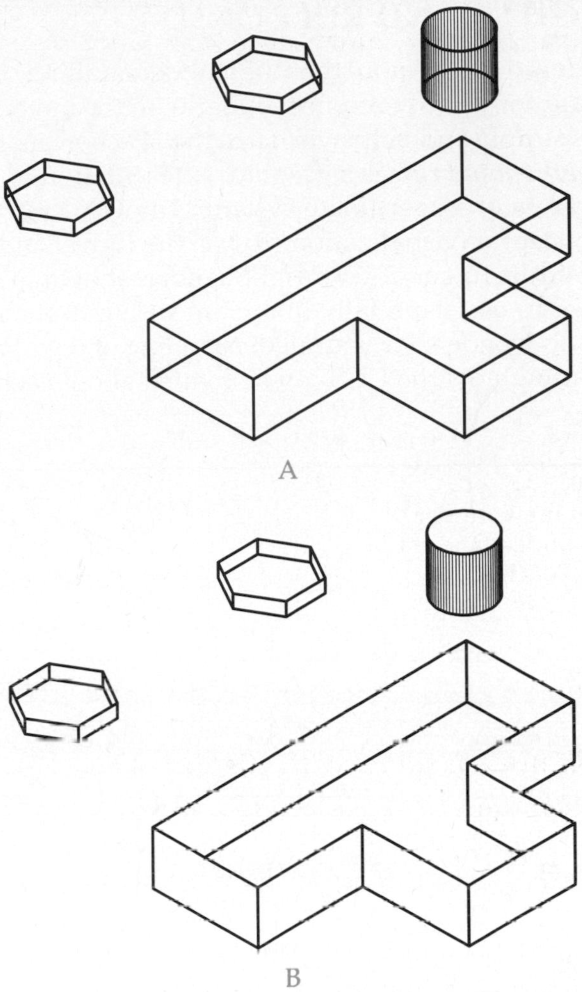

Figure 1-9.
The individual features of
the object in Figure 1-8 are
shown here as a wireframe
(A) and with hidden lines
removed (B).

A

B

The individual features that compose the object in Figure 1-7 are shown in Figure 1-9.
Both wireframe and hidden-line views are given. To redisplay the wireframe view, just select
another viewpoint or enter **REGEN** and press [Enter]. A regeneration displays all lines of the
objects.

**PROFESSIONAL
TIP**

Keep in mind that a "hole" drawn using **ELEV** and **CIRCLE** is
not really a hole to AutoCAD. It is a cylinder with solid ends. This
becomes clear when you display the objects in a 3D view with hidden lines removed, as shown in Figure 1-8.

Some 3D drawing hints

- Erasing a line drawn with the thickness set to a value other than zero erases an entire
  plane.
- Shapes drawn using the **LINE** and **ELEV** commands are open at the top and bottom.
  Shapes drawn with the **CIRCLE** and **ELEV** commands are closed at the ends.
- The **PLINE**, **POLYGON**, **RECTANG**, and **TRACE** commands give thickness to lines and
  make them appear as walls in the 3D view, similar to using the **LINE** command.

THE RIGHT-HAND RULE OF 3D

In order to gain a more thorough understanding of how AutoCAD displays 3D objects, it is important for you to become familiar with the method used to present them. The following method is simple and helps visualize the 3D coordinate system.

The *right-hand rule* is a graphic representation of positive coordinate values in the three axis directions of a coordinate system. AutoCAD's *UCS* (User Coordinate System) is based on this concept of visualization. To use the right-hand rule, position your thumb, index finger, and middle finger of your right hand as shown in Figure 1-10. Although this may seem a bit unusual to use, especially if you are sitting in the middle of a school library or computer lab, it can do wonders for your understanding of the nature of the three axes. It can also help in understanding how the UCS can be rotated about each of the axis lines (fingers).

Figure 1-10.
Try positioning your hand like this to understand the relationship of the X, Y, and Z axes.

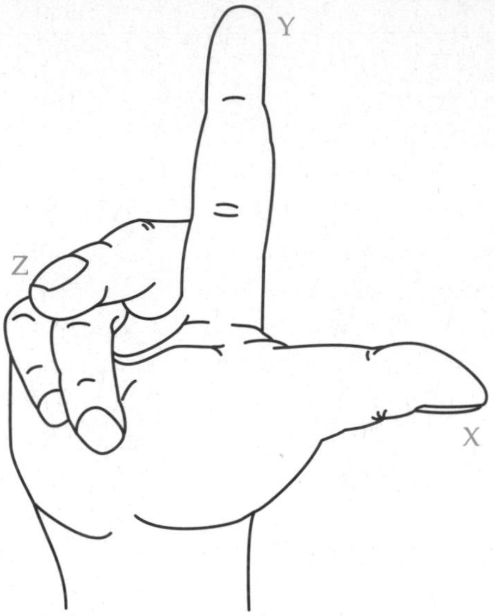

Imagine that your thumb is the X axis, your index finger the Y axis, and your middle finger the Z axis. Hold your hand directly in front of you so that your middle finger is pointing directly at you, as shown in Figure 1-10. This is the plan view. The positive X axis is pointing to the right and the positive Y axis is pointing up. The positive Z axis comes toward you, and the origin of this system is the palm of your hand.

This concept can be visualized even better if you are sitting at a computer and the AutoCAD graphics screen is displayed. If the UCS icon is not displayed in the lower-left corner of the screen, turn it on as follows:

Command: **UCSICON** ↵
ON/OFF/All/Noorigin/ORigin ⟨ON⟩: **ON** ↵

Now orient your right hand as shown in Figure 1-10 and position it next to the UCS icon on the screen. Your index finger and thumb should point in the same directions as Y and X respectively on the UCS icon. Your middle finger will be pointing out of the screen directly at you. This technique can also be used to eliminate confusion when the UCS is rotated to odd angles.

When you use the **VPOINT** command (discussed later in this chapter), a tripod appears on the screen. It is composed of three axis lines—X, Y, and Z. When you see the tripod, you should be able to make the comparison with the right-hand rule. See Figure 1-11.

Figure 1-11.
Compare the use of three fingers on the right hand and the tripod used by AutoCAD for 3D viewing.

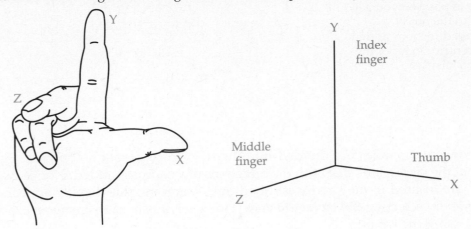

The UCS can be rotated to any position desired. The coordinate system rotates on one of the three axis lines, just like a wheel rotates on an axle. Therefore, if you want to rotate the X plane, keep your thumb stationary, and turn your hand toward or away from you. If you wish to rotate the Y plane, keep your index finger stationary and turn your hand to the left or right. When rotating the Z plane, you must keep your middle finger stationary and rotate your entire arm to the right or left.

If you discover that your 3D visualization skills are weak, or that you are having trouble with the UCS method, don't be afraid to use the right-hand rule. It is a useful technique for improving your 3D visualization skills. The ability to rotate the UCS around one or more of the three axes can become confusing if proper techniques are not used to visualize the rotation angles. A complete discussion of these techniques is provided in Chapter 3.

DISPLAYING 3D DRAWINGS

There are two ways to generate a 3D display in AutoCAD. The easiest to understand is the **VPOINT** command. This is discussed next. The second method is the **DVIEW** command. It is considerably more complex than **VPOINT**. It is discussed in detail in Chapter 6.

The **VPOINT** command allows you to display the current drawing at any angle. It may be easier to understand the function of this command as establishing your position relative to the object. Imagine that you can position yourself at a coordinate location in 3D space in relation to the object. The **VPOINT** command provides AutoCAD with the XYZ coordinates of your eyes, so the object can be positioned properly. **VPOINT** can be selected from the **View** pull-down menu by picking **3D Viewpoint** and **Tripod**, or by picking **Vpoint:** from the **VIEW** screen menu. It can also be typed at the **Command:** prompt as follows:

      Command: **VPOINT**↵
      Rotate/⟨View point⟩ ⟨0.0000,0.0000,1.0000⟩:

The three numbers reflect the XYZ coordinates of the current viewpoint. Change these coordinates to select different viewpoints. The **VPOINT** values shown above represent the coordinates for the plan view. This means that you see the XY plane. Since it is difficult to visualize a viewpoint as a number, you can display a graphic representation of the XYZ axes, and pick the desired viewpoint with your pointing device. Press [Enter] at the Rotate: prompt or select the **Axes** option from the screen menu. The screen display changes to one similar to Figure 1-12A.

As you move the pointing device, notice what happens on-screen. The XYZ coordinate tripod moves and the small crosshairs near the concentric circles also move. When the small crosshairs are inside the small circle, you are viewing the object from above. When the crosshairs are located between the two circles, you are viewing the object from below.

Figure 1-12.
A—The **VPOINT** axes display
allows you to position yourself
in relation to the object.
B—Compass directions added
to the concentric circles of the
VPOINT axes display.

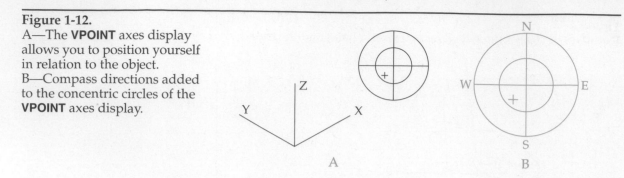

The concentric circles are divided into quarters to represent a compass. Figure 1-12B shows what the circles look like with the directions of a compass added. Notice that the small crosshairs are located in the southwest quadrant. Therefore, this display appears similar to one achieved by selecting **SW Isometric View**. However, it is hard to create an exact isometric viewpoint using the tripod.

The easiest way to locate the viewpoint is to move the cursor while observing the XYZ axes tripod movement. Pick the location where you are satisfied with the appearance of the axes. It may take some practice. Remember that in the top, or plan, view, the X axis is horizontal, Y axis is vertical, and Z axis comes out of the screen. As you move the tripod, keep track of where the crosshairs are located inside the compass. Compare their position to that of the tripod. Move the tripod until it is positioned like the one given in Figure 1-13. This is similar to picking the **SW Isometric View** button in the **View** toolbar.

The number of viewpoints you can select is endless. To get an idea of how the axes tripod and compass relate to the viewpoint, see the examples in Figure 1-14. It can be hard to distinguish top from bottom in wireframe views. Therefore, the viewpoints shown in Figure 1-14 are all from above the object and the **HIDE** command has been used to clarify the views. Use the **VPOINT** command to try each of these 3D positions on your computer.

When you are ready to return to the plan view, type PLAN at the **Command:** prompt, or type the XYZ coordinates for the plan view.

> Command: **VPOINT.⏎**
> Rotate/⟨View point⟩ ⟨*current*⟩: **0,0,1.⏎**

This returns your original top view which fills the screen. You can use the **All** option of the **ZOOM** command to display the drawing limits.

Figure 1-13.
The three axes and a 3D
view from the southwest
quadrant.

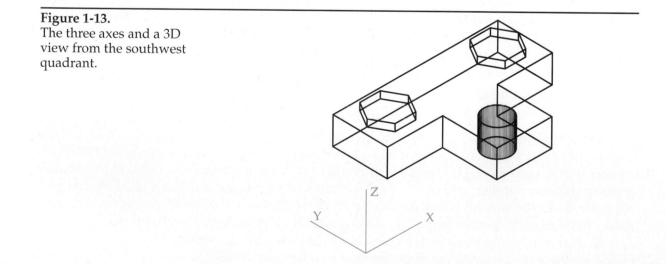

Figure 1-14.
Examples of viewpoint locations and their related axes positions.

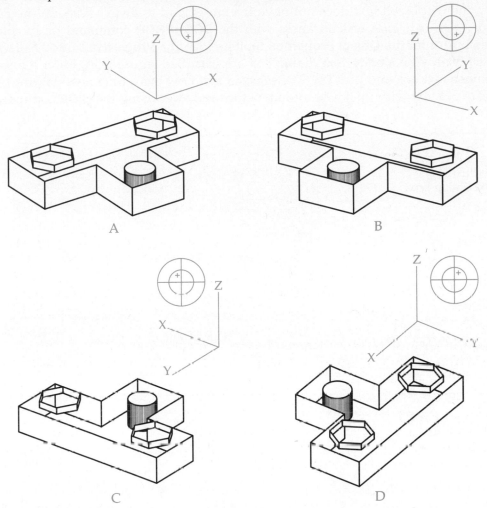

EXERCISE 1-2

❏ Set the grid spacing to .5 and snap spacing to .25.
❏ Use the **LINE** command to draw the figure in A below to the dimensions given. Do not dimension the drawing.
❏ Use the **CIRCLE** command to draw the figures in B below to the dimensions given. Do not dimension the drawing.
❏ Use the **VPOINT** command to display the 3D view of your drawing. Display it from three viewpoints using the axes tripod.
❏ Save the drawing as A:EX1-2.

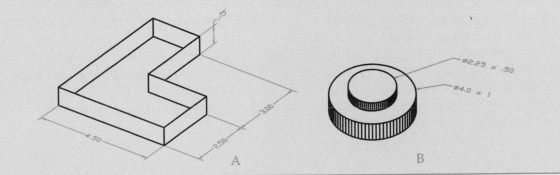

Creating extruded 3D text

Text added on the plan view is displayed in 3D when you use the **VPOINT** command. However, the displayed text does not have thickness, and it always rests on the zero elevation plane. You can give text thickness with the **DDCHPROP** command or by picking the **Properties** button in the **Object Properties** toolbar. Pick the **Properties** button, select the text, and press [Enter]. The **Modify Text** dialog box appears. See Figure 1-15. Enter a new value in the **Thickness** text box and pick **OK**. The selected text now has a thickness. Figure 1-16 shows examples of 3D text with thickness added, before and after using the **HIDE** command.

Figure 1-15.
Thickness of text can
be changed using the
Modify Text dialog box.

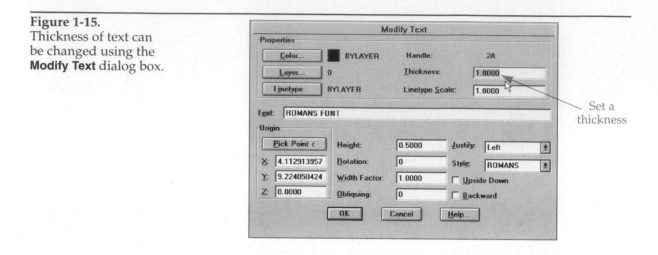

Figure 1-16.
Thickness applied to 3D
text with, and without,
the **HIDE** option.

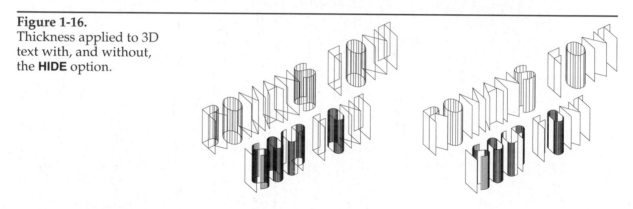

3D CONSTRUCTION TECHNIQUES

Three-dimensional objects can be drawn in three basic forms—wireframe, surface models, and solid models. The following section discusses the construction of wireframes, and the use of 3D faces to apply a surface to the wireframe. Additional information on wireframe construction is provided in Chapter 2, Chapter 3, and Chapter 4. A complete discussion of surface modeling is found in Chapter 5. Solid model construction and editing is covered in Chapter 10, Chapter 11, and Chapter 12.

A *wireframe construction* is an object that looks like it is made of wire. You can see through it. There are not a lot of practical applications for wireframe models unless you are an artist designing a new object using coat hangers. Wireframe models can be hard to visualize because it is difficult to determine the angle of view and the nature of the surfaces. Compare the two objects in Figure 1-17.

Figure 1-17.
A wireframe object may be
harder to visualize than a
surface model.
(Autodesk, Inc.)

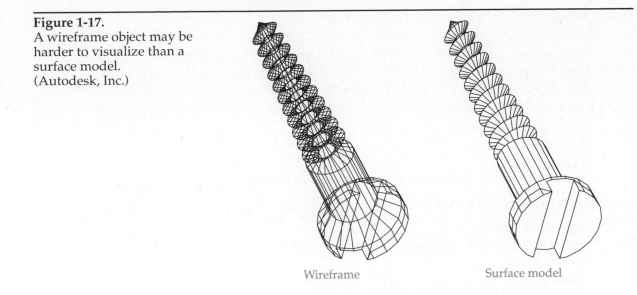

Wireframe   Surface model

Surface modeling, on the other hand, is much easier to visualize. A surface model looks more like a real object. Surface models can be used to imitate solid models. Most importantly, however, color, surface textures, lights, and shadows can be applied for realistic presentations. These "shaded and rendered" models can then be used in any number of presentation formats including slide shows, black and white or color prints, walk-arounds or walk-through animations, or animations that are recorded to videotape. A surface model can also be exported from AutoCAD for use in animation and rendering software such as Autodesk's 3D Studio. In addition, surface models are the basis for the construction of composite 3D models, often called *virtual worlds*, which are used in the field of virtual reality. These 3D rendered worlds can then be used with virtual reality software such as the Autodesk Cyberspace Developers Kit (CDK). The possibilities are endless. However, remember that their usefulness is defined by the word "presentation." This means *seeing* what the model looks like while viewing it from different angles, with different lighting, shading, and surface textures.

On the other hand, *solid modeling* more closely represents designing an object using the materials it is to be made from. This type of 3D design involves using primitive solid shapes such as boxes, cylinders, spheres, and cones to construct an object. These shapes are added and subtracted to create a finished product. The solid model can then be shaded and rendered. More importantly, they can be analyzed and tested for mass, volume, moments of inertia, and centroids. Some third-party programs allow you to perform finite element analysis on solid models.

Before constructing a 3D model, you should determine the purpose of your design. What will the model be used for—presentation, or analysis and manufacturing? This helps you determine which tools you should use to construct the model. The discussions and examples in this chapter provide an introduction to the uses of wireframe, 3D faces, and basic surfaced objects in order to create 3D constructions.

CONSTRUCTING WIREFRAMES AND 3D FACES

Wireframes can be constructed using the **LINE**, **PLINE**, **SPLINE**, and **3DPOLY** commands. There are a number of different ways to use these commands to construct wireframes, but one particularly useful method is called filters. A *filter* is an existing point, or vector in your drawing file. When using a filter, you instruct AutoCAD to find the coordinate values of a selected point, then you supply the missing value—X, Y, Z, or a combination. Filters can be used when working in two-dimensional space or when using a pictorial projection resulting from the **VPOINT** command.

Using filters to create 3D wireframe objects

When using **LINE**, you must know the XYZ coordinate values of each corner on the object. To draw an object, first decide the easiest and quickest method using the **LINE** command. One technique is to draw the bottom surface. Then, make a copy at the height of the object. Finally, connect the corners with lines. The filters can be used with the **COPY** command, or by using grips to copy. From the plan view, step through the process in this manner:

> Command: **LINE**↵
> From point: **3,3**↵
> To point: **@2,0**↵
> To point: (continue picking points to construct the shape)

Next, copy the shape up to the height of one unit.

> Command: **COPY**↵
> Select objects: (select the shape using a window or crossing box)
> Select objects:↵
> ⟨Base point or displacement⟩/Multiple: (pick a corner of the shape)
> Second point of displacement: **.XY**↵
> of (pick the same corner) (need Z): **1**↵

Since the shape is being copied straight up, the top surface has the same XY values as the bottom surface. That is why .XY was entered as the second point of displacement. This filter picks up the XY values of the previous point specified and applies them to the location of the new copy. Now, all AutoCAD needs is the Z value, which it requests. Check your progress by looking at the object using the **VPOINT** command. Enter the coordinates given below. Your display should look like that in Figure 1-18.

> Command: **VPOINT**↵
> Rotate/⟨View point⟩ ⟨current⟩: **-1,-1,0,0.75**↵

Figure 1-18.
A partially constructed
3D shape using **LINE**
and XYZ filters.

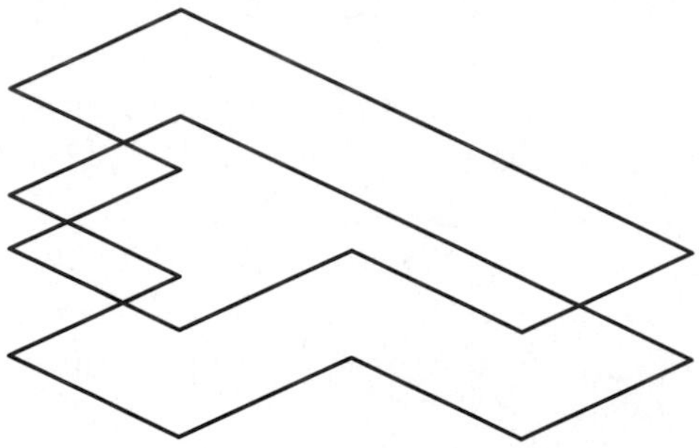

Return the drawing to the plan view and finish the object using **LINE** command and point filters. The four remaining lines are vertical and three units long.

> Command: **LINE**↵
> From point: (pick the lower-left corner)
> To point: **.XY**↵
> of (pick the lower-left corner again) (need Z): **1**↵
> To point:↵

In this example, you are instructing the computer to draw a line from the lower-left corner of the object to the same XY position one unit above. The new line connects the top and bottom planes of the object. The same process can be used to draw the other vertical lines. If you forget to enter the XY filter at the To point: prompt, AutoCAD will not ask for the Z distance. If this happens, cancel the command and start again. Use the **VPOINT** command again, and your drawing should look like Figure 1-19.

Figure 1-19.
A completed wireframe
3D object using the
LINE command.

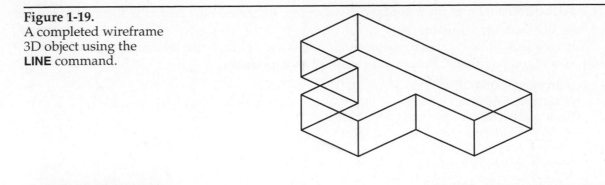

PROFESSIONAL TIP	
	If the process of drawing Z axis lines in the plan view is difficult to visualize, there is an easier option—draw them in the pictorial view. After drawing the top and bottom faces of the box, select a viewpoint and zoom in on the object. Now use the **LINE** command to construct the vertical lines using **OSNAP** modes **Endpoint**, **Midpoint**, and **Intersection**. This method allows you to see the lines in 3D as you draw them.

EXERCISE 1-3

❑ Set the grid spacing at .5, snap spacing at .25, and elevation at 0.
❑ Draw the 3D object below to the dimensions indicated.
❑ Use the **LINE** and **COPY** commands to construct the object.
❑ Construct the top and bottom planes in the plan view. Connect the vertical lines in a 3D view.
❑ Save the drawing as A:EX1-3.

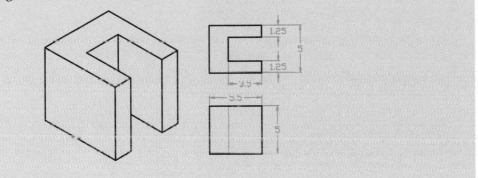

Constructing 3D faces

Surfaces that appear solid and not wireframe are called *3D faces*. They can be made with the **3DFACE** command. Its prompt structure is similar to that of the **SOLID** command, but you can specify points in a clockwise or counterclockwise manner. The **3DFACE** command is accessed and by picking the **3D Face** button in the **Surfaces** toolbar, selecting **Surfaces** in the **Draw** pull-down menu, or picking **SURFACES** in the **DRAW 2** screen menu.

A 3D face must have at least three corners, but cannot have any more than four corners. Therefore, to draw the top surface of the "T"-shaped box in Figure 1-19, two 3D faces are required. The resulting shape will look somewhat different than the one drawn as a wireframe. The steps required to draw the "T" object with 3D faces are:

1. Set the elevation to zero.
2. Draw the bottom faces.

3. Copy the bottom faces up a positive Z value (the thickness) to create the top faces.
4. Draw 3D faces on all sides.

Draw the first 3D face. Then, the second, adjoining 3D face can be drawn using the following command sequence. Refer to Figure 1-20 as you work.

Command: **3DFACE**↵
First point: **FROM**↵
Base point: **END**↵
of *(pick point A)*
⟨Offset⟩: **@2,0**↵
Second point: *(pick point 2)*
Third point: *(pick point 3)*
Fourth point: *(pick point 4)*
Third point:↵

Figure 1-20.
Draw the adjoining 3D face.

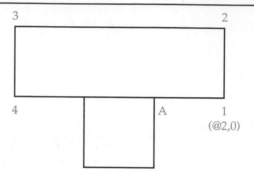

The 3D faces can be copied using the same steps taken to copy the wireframe line surface.

Command: **COPY**↵
Select objects: *(pick both 3D faces)*
Select objects:↵
⟨Base point or displacement⟩/Multiple:

Finally, draw the vertical sides of the shape. First, set a viewpoint and then connect corners of each 3D face using the running **OSNAP** mode **Endpoint** or **Intersection**.

Command: **VPOINT**↵
Rotate/⟨View point⟩ ⟨*current*⟩: **1,−1,.75**↵

The drawing should look like that shown in Figure 1-21. Zoom in if the view is too small.

Notice that you can construct a series of connected faces without exiting the **3DFACE** command. After picking the fourth point, the Third point: prompt reappears. To complete the object in Figure 1-21, first set the running **OSNAP** mode **Intersect**, then pick points 1 through 4 on the right side. Continue picking points 3 and 4 around the object until you pick the last points 3 and 4 that coincide with the original points 1 and 2. Press [Enter] to exit the command.

Figure 1-21.
The top and bottom faces of
the 3D object. The numbers
indicate the points to pick
when using the **3DFACE**
command.

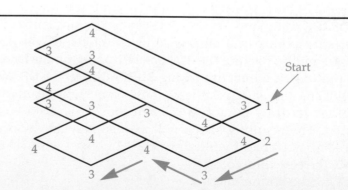

Command: **OSNAP.**↲
Object snap modes: **INT.**↲
Command: **3DFACE.**↲
First point: *(pick point 1)*
Second point: *(pick point 2)*
Third point: *(pick point 3)*
Fourth point: *(pick point 4)*
Third point: *(pick point 3)*
Fourth point: *(pick point 4)*
Third point: *(continue picking points 3 and 4 to complete the object)*
Command:

The finished box should appear similar to that in Figure 1-22.

Notice in Figure 1-22B that an intersection line is visible between the two faces on the top surface. This surface, and similar arrangements of attached 3D faces, can be drawn so that all intersecting edges are invisible. The procedure requires some planning and is discussed in Chapter 8.

How does a 3D face object differ from ones drawn using the **ELEV** and **LINE** commands? For comparison, Figure 1-23 shows boxes drawn using the **ELEV**, **LINE**, and **3DFACE** commands with hidden lines removed by **HIDE**.

Figure 1-22.
A—The completed object using **3DFACE** appears to be a wireframe construction before using **HIDE**.
B—The object after using **HIDE**.

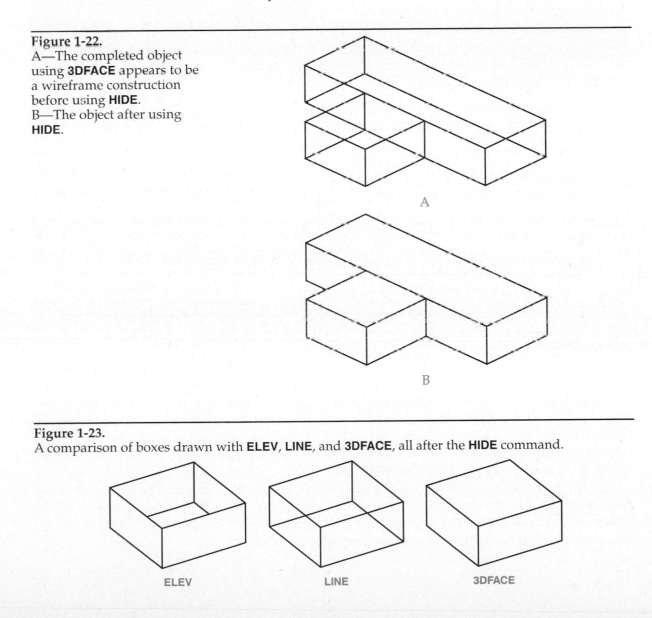

A

B

Figure 1-23.
A comparison of boxes drawn with **ELEV**, **LINE**, and **3DFACE**, all after the **HIDE** command.

ELEV   LINE   3DFACE

PROFESSIONAL TIP

When moving or copying objects in 3D space, it can simplify matters to use the displacement option to specify positioning data. This allows you to specify the X, Y, and Z movement simultaneously. For example, to copy a 3D face to a position three units above the original on the Z axis, use the following command sequence:

Command: **COPY**↵
Select objects: *(pick the 3D face)*
Select objects:↵
⟨Base point or displacement⟩/Multiple: **0,0,3**↵
⟨Second point of displacement⟩:↵

Because [Enter] was pressed at the ⟨Second point of displacement⟩: prompt, the X, Y, Z values entered are used as a relative displacement instead of a base point.

EXERCISE 1-4

❑ Set the grid spacing at .5, snap spacing at .25, and elevation at 0.
❑ Use the **3DFACE** command to construct the object shown below to the dimensions given.
❑ The front surface should be drawn with two faces shown below labeled A and B.
❑ Use the **HIDE** command when you complete the object.
❑ Save the drawing as A:EX1-4.

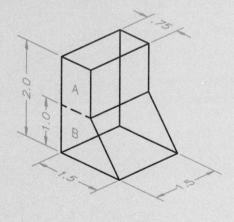

CONSTRUCTING 3D SURFACE MODELED OBJECTS

Several predrawn 3D objects can be quickly drawn by providing AutoCAD with a location and basic dimensions of the object. These objects can be selected by picking the appropriate button in the **Surfaces** toolbar. You can also select the appropriate object in the **3D Objects** dialog box, Figure 1-24. To access this dialog box, you can pick **Surfaces** then **3D Objects...** from the **Draw** pull-down menu. A list of objects can also be accessed by picking **DRAW 2** in the screen menu, then **SURFACES**.

In the **3D Objects** dialog box, notice the list box to the left. These are the names of all the objects shown. An object can be selected by picking either the name or the image. When an image or its name is selected, the image is highlighted with a box, and the name in the list box is also highlighted. Pick **OK** to draw the highlighted object.

Figure 1-24.
The **3D Objects** dialog box displays a group of 3D surface-modeled objects that can be quickly drawn by supplying a few basic dimensions. When an image or its name is selected, the image is highlighted with a box and the name is highlighted in the list box.

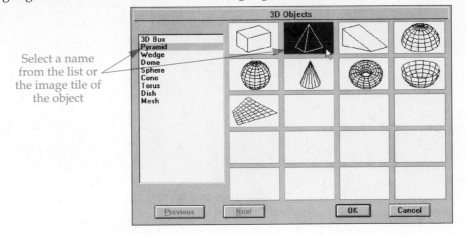

Select a name from the list or the image tile of the object

The first prompt requests a location point for the object. The remaining prompts request the length, width, height, diameter, radius, or number of longitudinal and latitudinal segments, depending on the object selected. For example, select **Dome** in the **3D Objects** dialog box. The second and following prompts are:

Center of dome: *(pick a point)*
Diameter/⟨radius⟩: *(enter a radius or pick on the screen)*
Number of longitudinal segments ⟨16⟩:↵
Number of latitudinal segments ⟨16⟩:↵

The object is drawn in the plan view, as shown in Figure 1-25A. Use the **VPOINT** command to produce a 3D view of the object, and use **HIDE** to remove hidden lines. The illustration in Figure 1-25B provides an explanation of longitudinal and latitudinal segments. Longitudinal refers to an east-west measurement, and latitudinal refers to north-south. Note that the default of 16 latitudinal segments creates only eight segments in the dome or dish, since these shapes are half of a sphere.

Remember that if the current display is a plan view, and you draw 3D objects, you must use the **VPOINT** command in order to see a 3D view. The illustrations in Figure 1-26 show all of the dimensions required to construct the predrawn 3D objects provided by AutoCAD.

Figure 1-25.
A—The plan view of a dome. B—Longitudinal segments are measured east-west, and latitudinal segments are measured north-south.

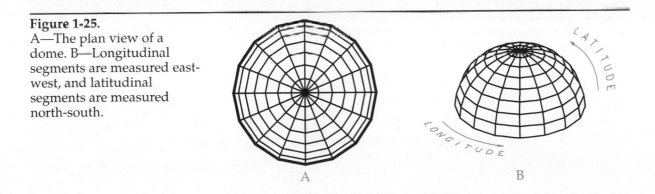

A

B

Figure 1-26.
These dimensions are required to draw AutoCAD's various 3D surface objects.

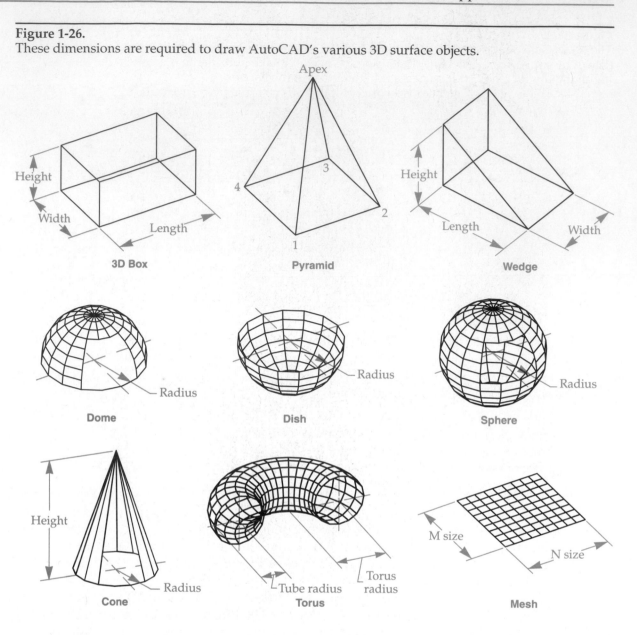

CHAPTER TEST

Write your answers in the spaces provided.

1. When looking at the screen in plan view, in which direction does the Z coordinate project? _____

   _____

2. Which command displays the **Object Creation Modes** dialog box? _____

3. Which two aspects of 3D drawing can be set in the **Object Creation Modes** dialog box?

   _____

4. Which command allows you to give objects thickness? _____

5. If you draw a line after setting a thickness, what have you actually drawn? _____

   _____

6. What is the purpose of the right-hand rule? _____

_____

_____

_____

7. According to the right-hand rule, name the coordinate axes represented by the following fingers:

Thumb— _____

Middle finger— _____

Index finger— _____

8. What is the purpose of the **VPOINT** command? _____

_____

_____

9. When the **VPOINT** command's tripod is displayed, what are the concentric circles in the upper right called? _____

10. How are you viewing an object when the little crosshairs are inside the small circle in the **VPOINT** command display? _____

11. How are you viewing an object when the little crosshairs are between the small circle and the large circle in the **VPOINT** command display? _____

12. How do you create 3D extruded text? _____

_____

13. What is the function of the **HIDE** command? _____

_____

_____

14. Define "point filters." _____

_____

_____

_____

_____

15. Compare the **3DFACE** and **SOLID** commands. _____

_____

_____

_____

16. How do you select one of AutoCAD's predrawn 3D shapes? _____

_____

_____

DRAWING PROBLEMS

*1 - 12. Draw the following objects as extruded 3D objects using the **ELEV** command. Where possible, draw additional 3D faces to enclose the object. Do not dimension the objects. Display the problems in two different 3D views. Use the **HIDE** command in one view. Do not dimension the drawings. Use your own dimensions for objects shown without dimensions. Save the drawings as **A:P1-**(problem number).*

Mechanical Drafting

1.

Mechanical Drafting

2.

Mechanical Drafting

3.

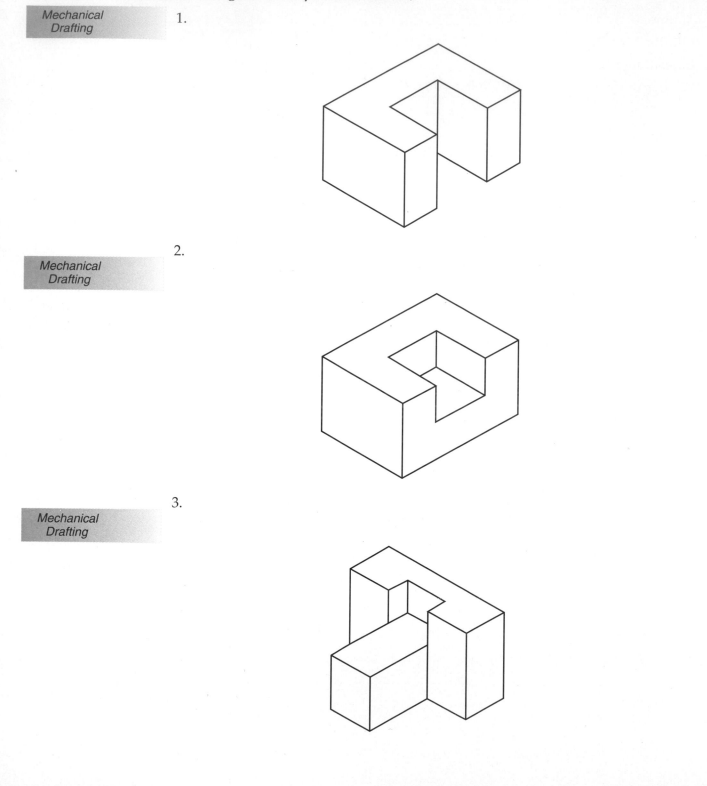

4.

5.

6.

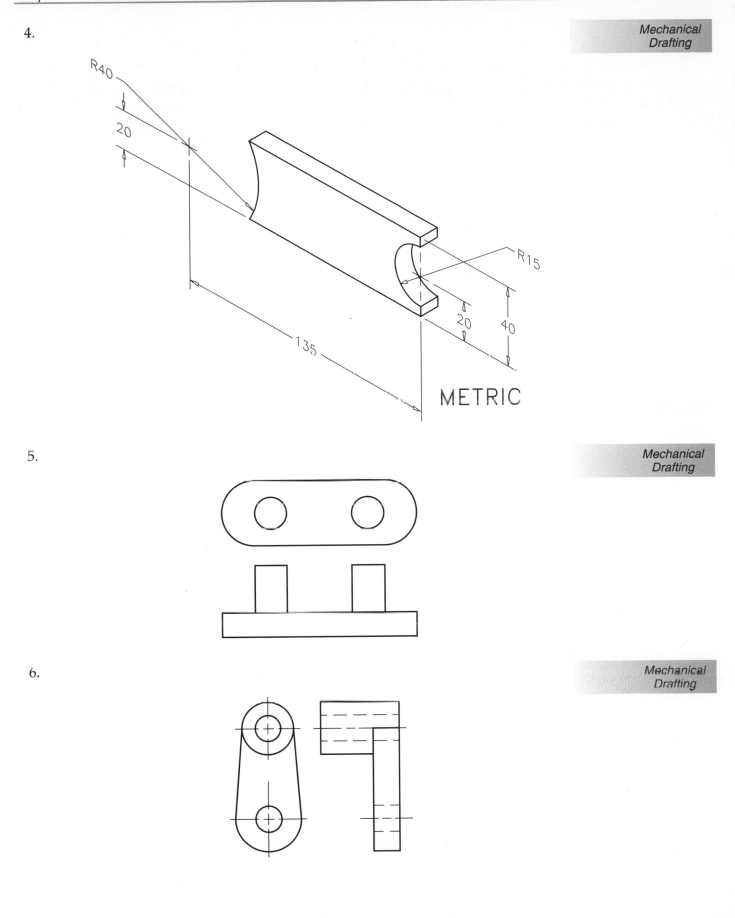

7.

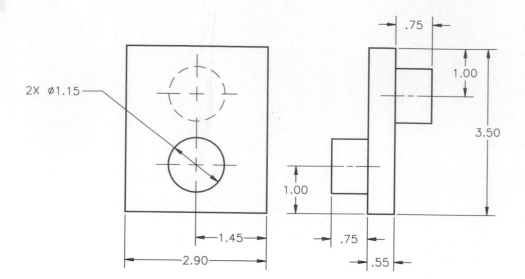

8.

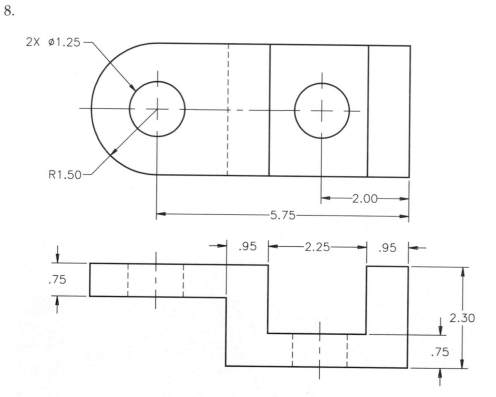

9.

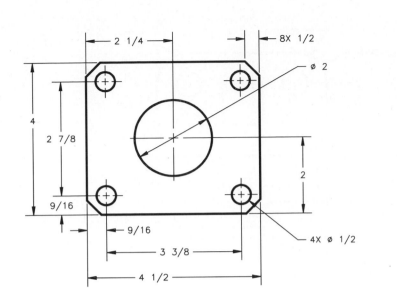

10.

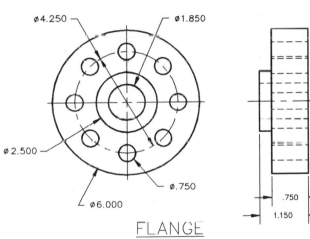

FLANGE

11.

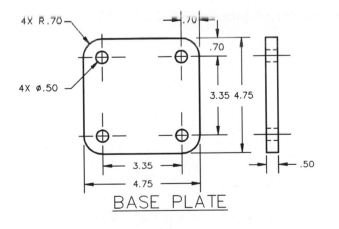

BASE PLATE

Mechanical Drafting
12.

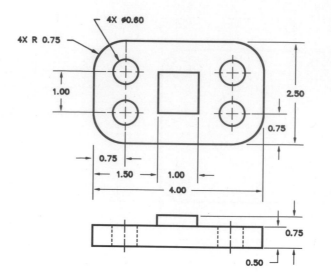

13 - 16. *Draw the following objects in 3D form. Use the* **LINE** *and* **3DFACE** *commands with the dimensions given to create the drawings. Display the drawings from three different viewpoints. Select the* **HIDE** *command for one of the views. Save the drawings as* **A:P1-** *(problem number).*

Architecture
13.

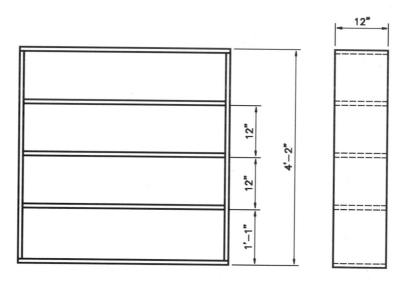

14.

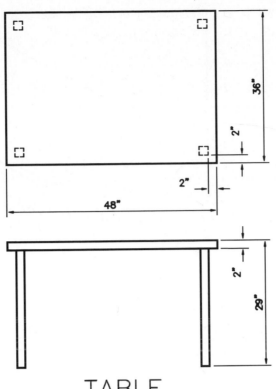

TABLE

15.

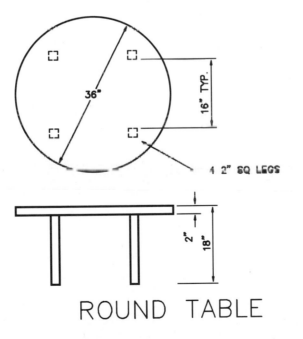

ROUND TABLE

Architecture

16.

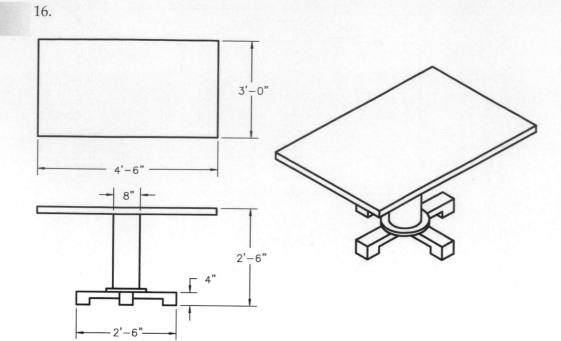

AutoCAD R13

Chapter 2

Three-Dimensional Coordinates and Constructions

Learning objectives

After completing this chapter, you will be able to:
- ○ Describe rectangular, spherical, and cylindrical 3D coordinate systems.
- ○ Explain the "right-hand rule" of 3D visualization.
- ○ Construct extruded and wireframe 3D shapes.

With AutoCAD, you can display 3D models at any angle. This gives you unlimited possibilities. However, the display and presentation of your models should always be accurate and realistic. Therefore, it is important to be familiar with a variety of coordinate entry methods that can be used with different geometric shapes. This chapter covers the three principal forms of coordinate entry. Drawing and display examples are also given for each type.

3D COORDINATE SYSTEMS

You can enter 3D coordinates in three different formats. Rectangular coordinates are the most commonly used form of 3D coordinate entry. Refer to Chapter 1 for a discussion on rectangular coordinates. Two other common coordinate systems are spherical coordinates and cylindrical coordinates. These two systems are similar, but there are some differences. The next sections cover spherical and cylindrical coordinate entry systems.

Spherical coordinates

Spherical coordinates are similar to locating a point on the Earth using longitude, latitude, and the center of the Earth as an origin. The origin value can be the default WCS (World Coordinate System) or the current UCS (User Coordinate System). Lines of longitude run between the North and South Poles. This gives an east/west measurement on the Earth's surface. The longitude measurement is the angle *in* the XY plane. The latitude measurement is the angle *from* the XY plane. Refer to Figure 2-1A. This is a measurement from the equator toward either the North Pole or the South Pole on the Earth's surface. Spherical coordinates are entered like polar coordinates. However, there is an additional angle value, as shown below and in Figure 2-1B:

7.5⟨35⟨55

Figure 2-1.
A—Latitudinal segments run from north to south. Longitudinal segments run from east to west.
B—Spherical coordinates require a distance, an angle in the XY plane, and an angle from the XY plane.

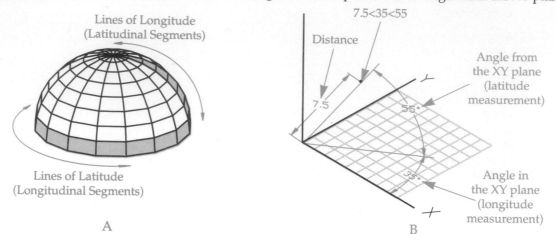

A   B

Spherical coordinates are useful for locating features on a spherical surface or model. Examples include a hole drilled into a sphere, or a feature located from a specific point on a sphere. If you are working on such a spherical object you might consider locating a UCS at the center of the sphere, then creating several different UCSs rotated at different angles on the surface of the sphere. Any time a location is required, spherical coordinates can be used.

Using spherical coordinates. Spherical coordinates are well-suited for locating points on the surface of a sphere. The first value that is entered is the radius of the sphere. The following example shows how to locate a new object on the surface of a sphere.

First, a sphere is drawn in the plan view. Then, a preset 3D viewpoint is selected. To draw a second sphere on the surface of the first, locate a node at the center of the sphere using the **POINT** command. Be sure to set an appropriate **PDMODE** value. Next, pick **Surfaces** from the **Draw** pull-down menu, and then pick **3D Objects**. Pick the sphere image, or select **Sphere** from the list, then pick **OK**. Continue as follows:

> Command: *(pick* **Sphere** *from the* **3D Objects** *dialog box or the* **Surfaces** *toolbar)*
> Center of sphere: **7,5**↵
> Diameter/⟨radius⟩: **1.5**↵
> Number of longitudinal segments ⟨16⟩: ↵
> Number of latitudinal segments ⟨16⟩: ↵
> Command:

NOTE
Create a separate layer for construction aids. For example, create a layer named CONSTRUCT and give it the color blue. Be sure this is the current layer before drawing any construction objects, such as the point used in this example.

Next, pick **3D Viewpont Presets** in the <u>**View**</u> pull-down menu, and <u>**SE Isometric**</u>. You can also pick the **SE Isometric View** button in the **View** toolbar. This displays the object in 3D. Center the object on the screen. Your drawing should look like Figure 2-2A. Pick **Sphere** again. Continue as follows. Use object snaps to assist in accurate location:

    Center of sphere: **FROM.**⏎
    Base point: **NODE.**⏎
    of *(pick the point at the center of the sphere)*
    ⟨Offset⟩ **@1.5⟨30⟨60**⏎ *(1.5 is the radius of the first sphere)*
    Diameter/⟨radius⟩: **.5**⏎
    Number of longitudinal segments ⟨16⟩: ⏎
    Number of latitudinal segments ⟨16⟩: ⏎
    Command:

The objects should now appear as shown in Figure 2-2B. The center of the new sphere is located on the surface of the original sphere. This is clear after the **HIDE** command is used. See Figure 2-2C. If you want the surfaces to be tangent, add the radius of each sphere (1.5 + .5) and enter that value as the offset (@2⟨30⟨60).

Figure 2-2.
A—A 3-unit diameter sphere shown from the SE isometric viewpoint. B—A 1-unit diameter sphere with its center located on the surface of the original object. C—The objects after using the **HIDE** command.

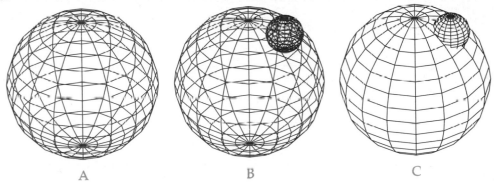

    A   B   C

Notice that the polar axis lines of both spheres in Figure 2-2C are parallel. This is because both objects were drawn with the same User Coordinate System (UCS). This can be misleading unless you are aware of how objects are constructed based on the current UCS. Test this by locating a cone on the surface of the large sphere, just below the small sphere. Pick **Cone** from the **3D Objects** dialog box or the **Surfaces** toolbar. Continue with the process as follows. Use object snaps to assist in accurate location. The result of this construction is shown in Figure 2-3.

    Base center point: **FROM.**⏎
    Base point: **NODE.**⏎
    of *(pick the point at the center of the sphere)*
    ⟨Offset⟩: **@1.5⟨30⟨30.**⏎
    Diameter/⟨radius⟩ of base: **.25.**⏎
    Diameter/⟨radius⟩ of top ⟨0⟩: ⏎
    Height: **1.**⏎
    Number of segments ⟨16⟩: ⏎
    Command:

Figure 2-3.
The axis lines of objects drawn
in the same coordinate system
are parallel. Notice that the
cone does not project from the
center of the large sphere.

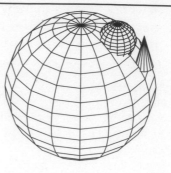

Changing the UCS. The axis of the cone is a line from the center of the base to the tip of
the cone. In Figure 2-3, the axis is tangent to the sphere, not pointing to the center. This is
because the Z plane of the large sphere and of the cone are both the World Coordinate System
(WCS). This is the default coordinate system of AutoCAD. In order for the axis of the cone to
project from the sphere's center point, the UCS must be changed. This is discussed in Chapter
3. However, here is a quick overview.

Study Figure 2-4 and the steps listed below. This describes how the UCS can be rotated in
order to draw a cone that projects from the center of the sphere. First, move the UCS icon to
the center of the sphere in Figure 2-3:

Command: **UCS.⏎**
Origin/ZAxis/3point/OBject/View/X/Y/Z/Prev/Restore/Save/Del/?/⟨World⟩: **O.⏎**
Origin point: **NODE.⏎**
of (*pick the point at the center of the sphere and press* [Enter])

Figure 2-4.
A—The World Coordinate
System must be rotated to
create a new UCS.
B—The new UCS is rotated
30° in the XY plane.
C—A line rotated up 30°
from the XY plane is the axis
of the new object.
D—The UCS is rotated 60°
about the Y axis.

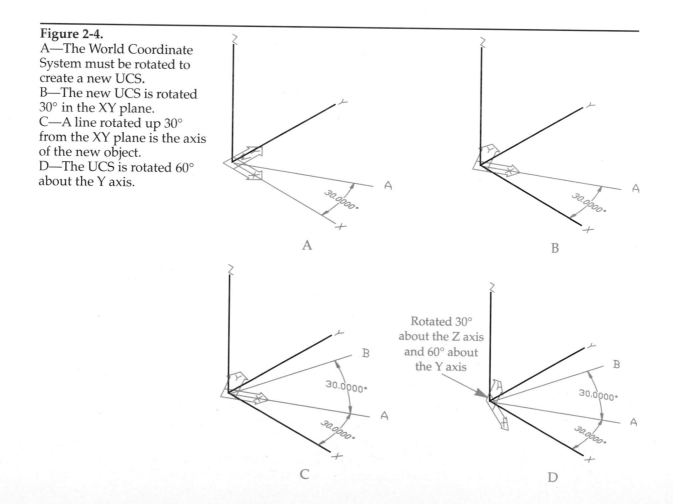

Now, continue as follows. Keep in mind that the point you are locating is 30° from the X axis and 30° from the XY plane.

> Command: **UCS**↵
> Origin/ZAxis/3point/OBject/View/X/Y/Z/Prev/Restore/Save/Del/?/〈World〉: **Z**↵
> Rotation angle about Z axis 〈0〉: **30.**↵
> Origin/ZAxis/3point/OBject/View/X/Y/Z/Prev/Restore/Save/Del/?/〈World〉: **Y.**↵
> Rotation angle about Y axis 〈0〉: **60.**↵

Save the new coordinate system with the **Save** option of the **UCS** command.

This new UCS can be used to construct a cone with its axis projecting from the center of the sphere in Figure 2-3. Figure 2-5A shows the new UCS located at the center of the sphere. Pick **Cone** from the **3D Objects** dialog box or the **Surfaces** toolbar. With the UCS rotated, rectangular coordinates can be used to locate the cone.

> Base center point: **0,0,1.5.**↵
> Diameter/〈radius〉 of base: **.25.**↵
> Diameter/〈radius〉 of top 〈0〉: ↵
> Height: **1.**↵
> Number of segments 〈16〉: ↵
> Command:

The completed cone is shown in Figure 2-5B. You can see that the axis projects from the center of the sphere. Figure 2-5C shows the objects after using **HIDE**.

Figure 2-5.
A—A new UCS is created with the Z axis projecting from the center of the sphere. B—A cone is drawn using the new UCS. C—The objects after using **HIDE**. The cone projects from the center of the sphere.

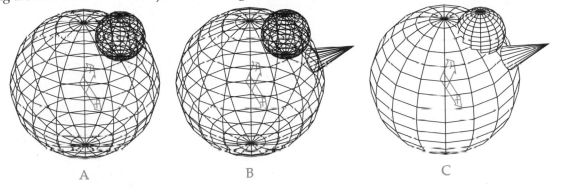

A   B   C

Constructing accurate intersections. When an object is located on a curved surface, there may be a small space between the curved surface and the object. See Figure 2-6A. In order for the model to display properly when rendered or animated, you need to make up for this space.

For example, refer to the cone and sphere in Figure 2-5. First, layout an orthographic view of the radius of the sphere. Then, draw a radial centerline for the intersecting cone. Draw a line tangent to the curve with a length equal to the diameter of the cone's base. Project a new line perpendicular from one end of the tangent through the curve. Then, move the baseline of the cone to the intersection of the projection and the curve. This is the new base. See Figure 2-6B. Next, measure the distance from the center of the sphere perpendicular to the new base. See Figure 2-6C. Use this distance when locating the cone. See Figure 2-6D.

Figure 2-7 shows the cone from Figure 2-5 and Figure 2-6 after using the **HIDE** and **SHADE** commands. Notice in Figure 2-7A and Figure 2-7B that the edge of the base can be seen as a line. This is because the cone is sitting above the surface of the sphere. In Figure 2-7C and Figure 2-7D, the edge of the base cannot be seen because it is *inside* the sphere. Therefore, the objects appear correct when rendered.

Figure 2-6.

A—A gap is created when the base of the cone is located tangent to the sphere's surface. B—Layout the base of the cone so that its edge intersects the surface of the sphere. C—Measure the distance from the center of the sphere to the base of the cone. D—The cone intersects the surface of the sphere with no gap.

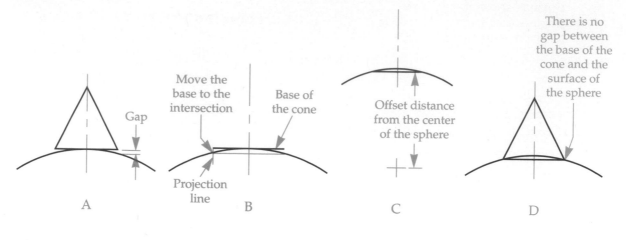

Figure 2-7.

A—A cone with the center of its base located on the surface of the sphere. B—When rendered, the edge of the base is visible. C—A cone with the edge of its base intersecting the surface of the sphere. D—When rendered, the edge of the base is not visible.

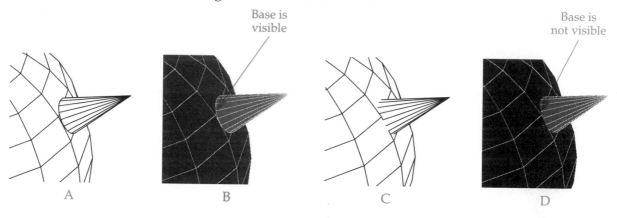

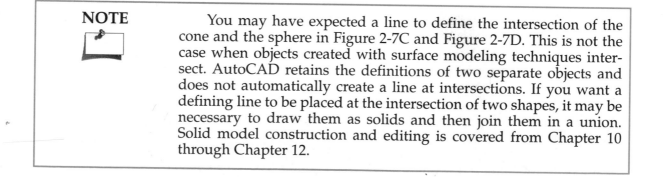

NOTE

You may have expected a line to define the intersection of the cone and the sphere in Figure 2-7C and Figure 2-7D. This is not the case when objects created with surface modeling techniques intersect. AutoCAD retains the definitions of two separate objects and does not automatically create a line at intersections. If you want a defining line to be placed at the intersection of two shapes, it may be necessary to draw them as solids and then join them in a union. Solid model construction and editing is covered from Chapter 10 through Chapter 12.

EXERCISE 2-1

❑ Open AutoCAD and begin a new drawing named EX2-1.
❑ Set **PDMODE** to 3. Set the color to blue and draw a point at 6,4.
❑ Set the color to white and draw a 4″ diameter sphere centered on the previous point.
❑ Set the color to red and draw two .75″ diameter spheres. Center both on the surface of the 4″ diameter sphere. For the first, use angular coordinates of 15° *in* the XY plane and 50° *from* the XY plane. For the second, use angular coordinates of –15° *in* the XY plane and 50° *from* the XY plane.
❑ Set the color to green and draw a cone with a .5″ diameter base. Center the cone on the surface of the 4″ diameter sphere using angular coordinates of 0° *in* the XY plane and 30° *from* the XY plane. Create a UCS so that you can construct a cone with a centerline projecting from the center of the sphere.
❑ Display the objects using **SE Isometric View**. Use the **HIDE** command.
❑ Save the drawing as EX2-1.

Displaying drawings using spherical coordinates. When using spherical coordinates to change the viewpoint, AutoCAD only needs the two angle values. This is because the viewpoint does not set a distance from the "center." The three values that make up a spherical coordinate are shown in Figure 2-1B. Enter spherical coordinates using the **Rotate** option of the **VPOINT** command as follows:

```
Command: VPOINT↵
Rotate/⟨View point⟩ ⟨current⟩: R↵
Enter angle in XY plane from X axis ⟨current⟩: 45↵
Enter angle from XY plane ⟨current⟩: 45↵
Regenerating drawing.
Command:
```

In Figure 2-8, the viewpoint is counterclockwise 45° from the X axis and 45° from the XY plane. Notice in the command sequence above that no "distance" value is entered.

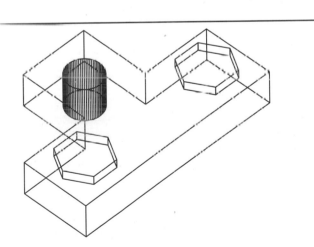

Figure 2-8.
This view was created using **Rotate** option of the **VPOINT** command. The rotation angles used are 45° in the XY plane and 45° from the XY plane.

Cylindrical coordinates

Cylindrical coordinates provide coordinate locations for a cylindrical shape. The first value is the distance from the origin of the WCS or current UCS. The second value is the angle in the XY plane. The third value is a vertical, or Z, dimension. A cylindrical coordinate is entered as follows. See Figure 2-9.

7.5⟨35,6

Figure 2-9.
Cylindrical coordinates
require a distance from the
origin, an angle in the XY
plane, and a Z dimension.

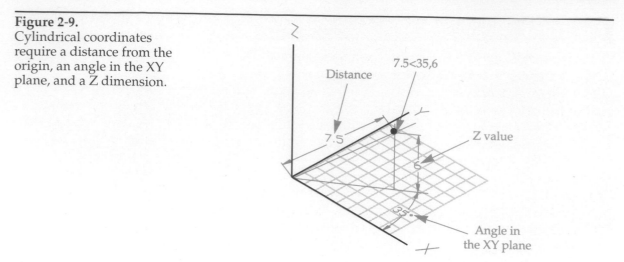

Using cylindrical coordinates. Cylindrical coordinates work well for attaching new objects to a cylindrical shape. An example is a pipe that must be attached to another pipe, a tank, or a vessel. In Figure 2-10, a pipe must be attached to a 12′ diameter tank at a 30° angle from horizontal and 2′-6″ above the floor.

An attachment point can easily be created to begin the pipe run. First, move the UCS origin to the center of the tank. Then, set an appropriate **PDMODE**. Next, locate the attachment point with cylindrical coordinates as follows:

Command: **UCS**↵
Origin/ZAxis/3point/OBject/View/X/Y/Z/Prev/Restore/Save/Del/?/⟨World⟩: **O**↵
Origin point ⟨0,0,0⟩: *(pick the center point of the tank)*

Placing the UCS origin at the center of the tank makes it easier to enter the exact coordinates of the pipe attachment location.

Command: **POINT**↵
Point: **6′⟨30,2′6**↵
Point: ↵
Command:

Look at Figure 2-10B. Notice that the point drawn with **PDMODE** set to 3 appears as two legs of an X sticking out of the tank. It is drawn in the same plane as the current UCS, which is parallel to the bottom of the tank. This is OK because the point itself is on the tank's surface. A new UCS can be established and the pipe attached at its origin. See Figure 2-10C.

Figure 2-10.
A—The plan view of a tank shows the angle of the pipe attachment. B—A 3D view from the SE quadrant shows the pipe attachment point located with cylindrical coordinates. The point was located with **PMODE** set to 3. C—The pipe is located on the tank using a new UCS.

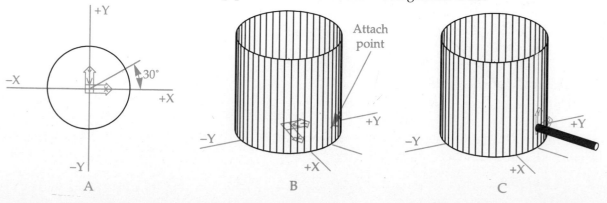

EXERCISE 2-2

❏ Open AutoCAD and begin a new drawing named EX2-2.
❏ Set the current elevation to 0 and the thickness to 3.
❏ Draw a 1.5″ diameter circle.
❏ Use the **SW Isometric View** button.
❏ Set **PDMODE** to the shape of your choice. Locate the following points on the surface of the extruded circle.
  ❏ ⟨25,1.5
  ❏ ⟨295,1.5
❏ Draw separate lines from points 1 and 2 that project from the center of the circle, and extend 2″ from the surface of the extruded circle.
❏ Project new lines from each of the previous lines at 90° angles so that they intersect, as shown in the plan view below.
❏ Save the drawing as EX2-2.

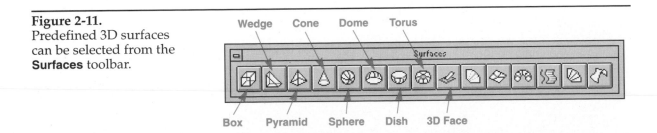

3D OBJECTS

There is a group of predefined 3D objects that come with AutoCAD. These 3D objects are box, wedge, pyramid, cone, dish, dome, sphere, torus, and mesh. You only need to enter basic dimensions and a location to draw these objects. The result is a surfaced 3D object. The **HIDE** command makes the object appear solid. Therefore, the design can be used in presentation and animation programs such as AutoVision, Animator Studio, and 3D Studio. The next sections discuss these predefined 3D objects. The box and dome are discussed further in Chapter 8.

The 3D objects can be accessed using the **Surfaces** toolbar, **Draw** pull-down menu, or **Command:** prompt. The **Surfaces** toolbar displays buttons for all of the 3D objects, Figure 2-11. Notice the six additional buttons on the toolbar. These are discussed in Chapter 6 and Chapter 8. Picking **3D Objects...** from the **Surfaces** cascading submenu displays the **3D Objects** dialog box, Figure 2-12. You can type 3D at the **Command:** prompt to access the 3D objects, then type the name of the object you want to draw. The objects are all options of the **3D** command.

Since each object is created as a 3D mesh, it is a single entity. If you wish to edit any part of the object, first use the **EXPLODE** command. After exploding, each object is made up of 3D faces.

AutoCAD
User's
Guide **2**

Figure 2-11.
Predefined 3D surfaces can be selected from the **Surfaces** toolbar.

Wedge Cone Dome Torus

Surfaces

Box Pyramid Sphere Dish 3D Face

Figure 2-12.
Predefined 3D surfaced objects can be selected from the **3D Objects** dialog box.

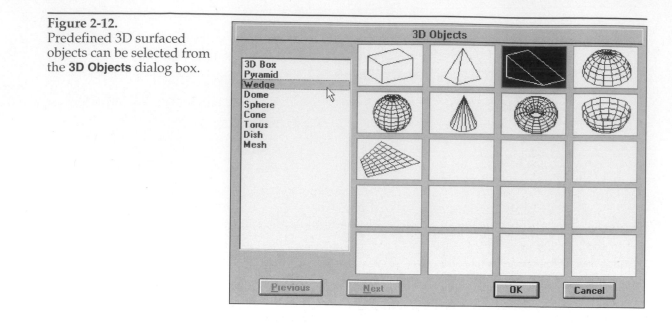

NOTE

AutoCAD creates two types of 3D shapes—solid primitives and surfaced wireframes. They are:

Solid Primitives	Surface Wireframes
Box	Box
Cone	Cone
Cylinder	Dome
Sphere	Dish
Torus	Mesh
Wedge	Pyramid
	Sphere
	Torus
	Wedge

If you type the name of one of the solid primitives listed above at the **Command:** prompt, the solid model version of that shape is created. If you want to use the surfaced wireframe version, use the **Surfaces** toolbar, **3D Objects** dialog box, or type 3D at the **Command:** prompt. You can also enter the following:

Command: **AI_CONE.**↵

The "AI" refers to an "Autodesk Incorporated" AutoLISP command definition that is found in the 3D.LSP file. When you select an object from either the dialog box or the toolbar, you will notice this entry on the command line. The underscore character (_) is used in the ACAD.MNU file of Release 13 for Windows to allow commands to be automatically translated in foreign language versions of AutoCAD.

Box

The **BOX** command lets you construct a 3D box or cube. You must provide the location of one corner, the box dimensions, and the rotation angle about the Z axis with the first corner as the base. Enter the values using the keyboard or pick them with your pointing device.

> Command: *(pick the* **Box** *in the* **3D Objects** *dialog box or from the* **Surfaces** *toolbar)*
> Command: ai_box
> Corner of box: **3,3**↵
> Length: **1**↵
> Cube/⟨Width⟩: **C** ↵
> Rotation angle about Z axis: **0**↵

If you select the **Cube** option, AutoCAD applies the value entered at the Length: prompt to the width and height. Figure 2-13 shows an example of a box.

Figure 2-13.
The **BOX** command requires a location, length, width, height, and rotation angle.

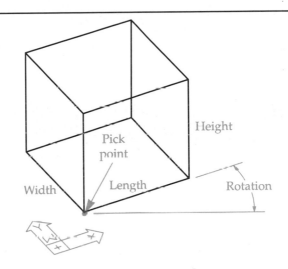

Wedge

A right-angle wedge can be drawn using the **WEDGE** command. Locate a corner of the wedge, then enter the length, width, height, and rotation angle. A wedge and its values are shown in Figure 2-14.

> Command: *(pick the* **Wedge** *in the* **3D Objects** *dialog box or from the* **Surfaces** *toolbar)*
> Command: ai_wedge
> Corner of wedge: **0,3**↵
> Length: **3**↵
> Width: **2**↵
> Height: **2**↵
> Rotation angle about Z axis: **15**↵
> Command:

Figure 2-14.
The **WEDGE** command requires a location, length, width, height, and rotation angle.

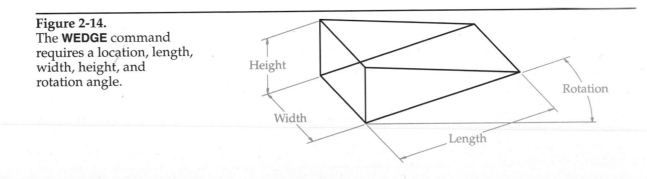

Pyramid

The **PYRAMID** command allows you to draw five different shapes. You can draw three types of four-sided pyramids, Figure 2-15. You can also draw two types of three-sided pyramids, Figure 2-16. AutoCAD calls these three-sided pyramids *tetrahedrons*.

To draw a pyramid, first draw the base. When you have located the third point, you can draw a tetrahedron or the fourth point of the base. If you draw the fourth point on the base, the options **Ridge**, **Top**, and **Apex** appear. The default is **Apex**. When drawing the apex, use XYZ filters or enter an XYZ coordinate. The following example shows how to draw a four-sided pyramid with an apex:

> Command: *(select **Pyramid** from the **Surfaces** toolbar or **3D Objects** dialog box)*
> Command: ai_pyramid
> First base point: **2,6**↵
> Second base point: **@2,0**↵
> Third base point: **@0,2**↵
> Tetrahedron/⟨Fourth base point⟩: **@–2,0**↵
> Ridge/Top/⟨Apex point⟩: **.XY**↵
> of **3,7**↵
> (need Z): **3**↵
> Command:

The **Ridge** option requires two points to define the ridge. After you draw the fourth point on the base, select **Ridge**. The last line drawn on the base is highlighted. This indicates that the first point of the ridge will begin perpendicular to the highlighted line. However, the first point does not have to touch the highlighted line.

> Ridge/Top/⟨Apex point⟩: **R**↵
> First ridge point: **.XY**↵
> of *(pick a point inside the highlighted line)*
> (need Z): **3**↵
> Second ridge point: **.XY**↵
> of *(pick a point inside the second highlighted line)*
> (need Z): **3**↵

The **Top** option creates a *truncated* (flattened) top. This option works similar to **Ridge**. However, a rubber band line is attached from the first corner of the pyramid to the crosshairs. Then, the First top point: prompt appears. Use filters to or XYZ coordinates to locate the top points. After the first top point is located, the rubber band line is attached to the second base point, and so on. When the fourth top point is located, the pyramid is complete.

Figure 2-15.
The **PYRAMID** command allows you to create an apex, ridge, or truncated pyramid.

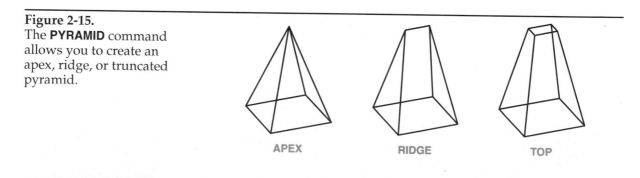

APEX   RIDGE   TOP

PROFESSIONAL TIP

Try constructing pyramids in the plan view, using XYZ coordinates or filters. Your constructions will be more accurate, and you can easily see the symmetry or asymmetry required.

A tetrahedron has a three-sided base. A tetrahedron can have an apex or flattened top. The following example illustrates how to construct a tetrahedron. Refer to Figure 2-16.

> Command: *(select* **Pyramid** *from the* **Surfaces** *toolbar or* **3D Objects** *dialog box)*
> Command: ai_pyramid
> First base point: **2,2**↵
> Second base point: **@3,0**↵
> Third base point: **@0,3**↵
> Tetrahedron/⟨Fourth base point⟩: **T**↵
> Top/⟨Apex point⟩: **.XY**↵
> of *(pick P1 in the middle of the triangle)* (need Z): **3**↵
> Command: **VPOINT**↵
> Rotate/⟨View point⟩ ⟨*default*⟩: **–1,–1,1**↵
> Command:

A truncated (flattened) top can be given to a tetrahedron by selecting the **Top** option. Refer to Figure 2-16B.

> Tetrahedron/⟨Fourth base point⟩: **T**↵
> Top/⟨Apex point⟩: **T**↵
> First top point: **.XY**↵
> of *(pick P1)* (need Z): **2.5**↵
> Second top point: **.XY**↵
> of *(pick P2)* (need Z): **2.5**↵
> Third top point: **.XY**↵
> of *(pick P3)* (need Z): **2.5**↵
> Command:

Figure 2-16.
A—A tetrahedron has a three-sided base. Tetrahedrons are special types of pyramids. B—A truncated tetrahedron requires three pick points for the top surface.

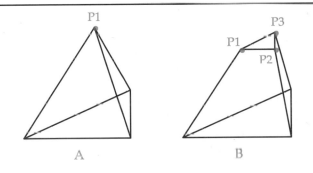

Cone

The **CONE** command draws both pointed and truncated cones. Three dimensions are required for a cone—the base diameter, the top diameter, and the height. A pointed cone has a zero top diameter. A truncated cone has a top diameter other than zero. Pick **Cone** from the **3D Objects** dialog box, from the **Surfaces** toolbar, or type the following:

> Command: **AI_CONE**↵
> Base center point: **3,3**↵
> Diameter/⟨radius⟩ of base: **1**↵
> Diameter/⟨radius⟩ of top ⟨0⟩: **.15**↵
> Height: **2**↵
> Number of segments ⟨16⟩: ↵
> Command:

If you want a pointed cone, simply press [Enter] at the Diameter/⟨radius⟩ of top: prompt. The two types of cones are shown in Figure 2-17.

Figure 2-17.
The **CONE** command can be
used to draw a truncated or
pointed cone.

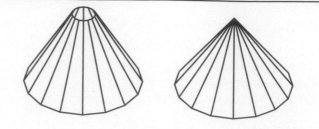

Dome and dish

Think of a dome or a dish as half of a sphere, or a hemisphere. If a dome is placed on top
of a dish, a sphere is formed. The top of the dome is the north pole. The bottom of the dish is
the south pole. Longitudinal segments run east and west around the circumference.
Latitudinal segments run north and south. See Figure 2-1A. Pick either **Dome** or **Dish** from
the **3D Objects** dialog box or **Surfaces** toolbar. You can also type the following:

    Command: **AI_DOME.↵** (or **AI_DISH** to draw a dish)
    Center of dome: (pick a point)
    Diameter/⟨radius⟩: **2.↵**
    Number of longitudinal segments ⟨16⟩: (enter a value or press [Enter])
    Number of latitudinal segments ⟨8⟩: (enter a value or press [Enter])
    Command:

> **NOTE**   The more segments you use, the longer drawing regeneration
> takes. Use as few segments as possible.

Sphere

A sphere requires the same information as a dish or dome. Since the sphere is a complete
globe, the default values for latitudinal and longitudinal segments are the same. Pick **Sphere**
from the **Surfaces** toolbar or **3D Objects** dialog box. You can also enter the following:

    Command: **AI_SPHERE.↵**
    Center of sphere: (pick a center point)
    Diameter/⟨radius⟩: (pick or type a radius, or type D and press [Enter] to provide
      a diameter)
    Number of longitudinal segments ⟨16⟩: (type number of segments and press [Enter])
    Number of latitudinal segments ⟨16⟩: (type number of segments and press [Enter])
    Command:

Figure 2-18 shows three spheres composed of 8, 16, and 32 segments.

Figure 2-18.
The more segments in a
sphere the smoother it
appears, but the longer it
takes to regenerate.

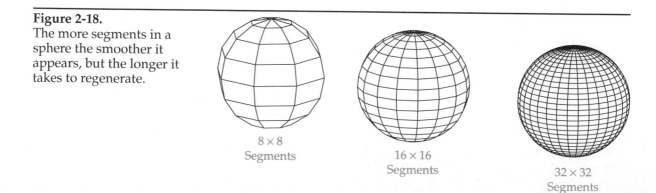

8 × 8
Segments

16 × 16
Segments

32 × 32
Segments

Torus

A *torus* looks like an inflated inner tube. See Figure 2-19. To draw a torus, you need to enter the diameter (or radius) of the torus and the tube. You also need to enter the number of segments around the torus circumference and around the tube circumference. Pick **Torus** from the **3D Objects** dialog box or **Surfaces** toolbar, or type the following:

> Command: **AI_TORUS**↵
> Center of torus: *(pick the center point)*
> Diameter/⟨radius⟩ of torus: **2**↵
> Diameter/⟨radius⟩ of tube: **.5**↵
> Segments around tube circumference ⟨16⟩: ↵
> Segments around torus circumference ⟨16⟩: ↵
> Command:

Figure 2-19.
To draw a torus, you must specify the radius (or diameter) of the torus and of the tube. You must also specify the number of segments around each.

Torus radius

Tube diameter

3D CONSTRUCTIONS

AutoCAD User's Guide 2

There are several different 3D constructions. These include 3D arrays, 3D polylines, and 3D faces. These constructions are covered in the next sections.

Arraying 3D objects

The **3DARRAY** command lets you array an object in 3D space. This works in much the same as the **ARRAY** command, but with a third dimension. You need to enter the number of rows and columns, as with the **ARRAY** command. However, *levels* give the third (Z) dimension. There are two types of 3D arrays—rectangular and polar.

The command sequence is the same as the 2D array command, with two added prompts. To create a 3D array, select **3D Array** from the **Construct** pull-down menu, and then either **Rectangular** or **Polar** from the cascading submenu. You can also select the **3D Rectangular Array** or **3D Polar Array** button in the **Modify** toolbar. Or, type 3DARRAY at the **Command:** prompt. The following example creates a rectangular array of a pyramid. See Figure 2-20.

> Command: **3DARRAY**↵
> Initializing… 3DARRAY loaded.
> Select objects: *(pick the pyramid)*
> Select objects: ↵
> Rectangular or Polar array (R/P): **R**↵
> Number of rows (---) ⟨1⟩: **2**↵
> Number of columns (¦¦¦) ⟨1⟩: **3**↵
> Number of levels (…) ⟨1⟩: **3**↵
> Distance between rows (---): **1.5**↵
> Distance between columns (¦¦¦): **1.5**↵
> Distance between levels (…): **1.5**↵
> Command: **VPOINT**↵
> Rotate/⟨View point⟩⟨*current*⟩: **−2,−4,1**↵
> Regenerating drawing.
> Command:

Figure 2-20.
A rectangular 3D array is
made up of rows, columns,
and levels.

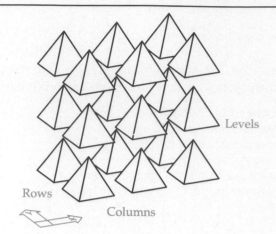

Levels

Rows

Columns

Notice that you need to enter a Z axis rotation, Figure 2-21. The Z axis of a 3D polar array can be different than the current UCS. Create a 3D polar array as follows:

    Command: **3DARRAY**↵
    Select objects: *(pick the pyramid)*
    Select objects: ↵
    Rectangular or Polar array (R/P): **P**↵
    Number of items: **5**↵
    Angle to fill ⟨360⟩: **–180**↵
    Rotate objects as they are copied? ⟨Y⟩: **N**↵
    Center point of array: *(pick P1)*
    Second point on axis of rotation: *(pick point on new Z axis)*
    Command:

If you enter the command from the toolbar or pull-down menu, the Rectangular or Polar array (R/P): prompt does not appear. A positive number entered at the Angle to fill: prompt rotates the array counterclockwise. A negative angle rotates it clockwise.

In Figure 2-21, the 3D array is tilted 90° to the current UCS. This is because the Z axis defined for the 3D array is parallel to the XY plane of the current UCS.

Figure 2-21.
The Z axis of a 3D polar
array can be different from
the current UCS.

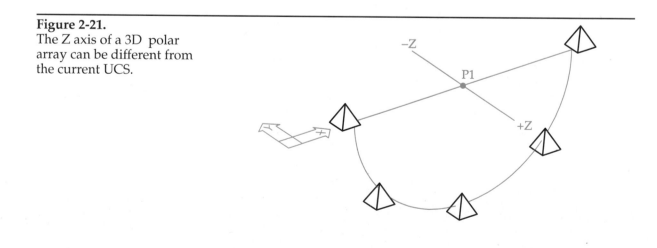

EXERCISE 2-3

❏ Open AutoCAD. Start a drawing named EX2-3.
❏ Set the limits to 34,22, the grid to 1, and snap to .5.
❏ Draw the following 3D objects using the sizes indicated. Space them evenly in your drawing.

❏ Box	$2 \times 3 \times 1.5h$
❏ Wedge	$3 \times 1 \times 1.25h$
❏ Pyramid (apex)	$2 \times 2 \times 2.5h$
❏ Pyramid (ridge)	$2 \times 2 \times 2.5h$
❏ Pyramid (top)	$2 \times 2 \times 2.25h$
❏ Tetrahedron (apex)	$2 \times 2 \times 1.5h$
❏ Tetrahedron (top)	$2 \times 2 \times 1.5h$
❏ Cone (apex)	$\varnothing2 \times 1.5h$
❏ Cone (truncated)	$\varnothing2 \times 1.5h$
❏ Dome	$\varnothing2$
❏ Dish	$\varnothing2$
❏ Sphere	$\varnothing2.5$
❏ Torus	$\varnothing3$ torus, $\varnothing.5$ tube

❏ Display the completed objects in three different 3D viewpoints. Use the **HIDE** command in each.
❏ Save the drawing as EX2-3.

3D polyline

A *3D polyline* is drawn using the **3DPOLY** command. To access this command, pick **3D Polyline** in the **Draw** pull-down menu or the **3D Polyline** button in the **Draw** toolbar. You can also type 3DPOLY at the **Command:** prompt. A 3D polyline is the same as a regular polyline with an added third (Z) dimension. Any form of coordinate entry is valid for drawing 3D polylines.

```
Command: 3DPOLY ↵
From point: 4,3,6 ↵
Close/Undo/⟨Endpoint of line⟩: @2,0,1 ↵
Close/Undo/⟨Endpoint of line⟩: @0,2,1 ↵
Command:
```

The **Close** option is used to draw the final segment and create a closed shape. The **Undo** option removes the last segment without cancelling the command.

The **PEDIT** command can be used to edit 3D polylines. The **Spline** option of **PEDIT** is used to fit a B-spline curve to the 3D polyline. Figure 2-22 shows a regular 3D polyline and the same polyline fit with a B-spline curve. The **SPLFRAME** system variable controls the display of the original polyline frame, and is either on (1) or off (0).

Figure 2-22.
A regular 3D polyline and the B-spline curve version after using the **PEDIT** command.

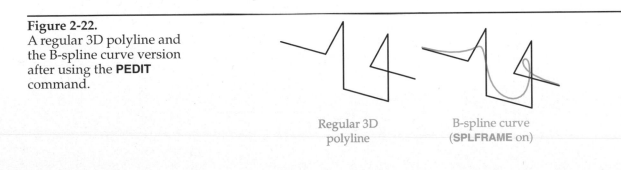

Regular 3D
polyline

B-spline curve
(**SPLFRAME** on)

3D Faces

Surfaces that appear solid and not as wireframes are called 3D faces. These are created using the **3DFACE** command. This command was introduced in Chapter 1.

You may recall that a 3D face can only have three or four straight edges. In Chapter 1, you created a "T"-shaped box using 3D faces. When the **HIDE** command was used, the edge between the faces was visible. Refer back to Figure 1-21B. This line can be made invisible. The next section briefly describes the procedure. It is discussed in more detail in Chapter 8.

Invisible 3DFACE edges. The **3DFACE** command allows you to remove, or hide, edges that should not appear as lines on a surface. This is done with the **Invisible** option. Before picking the first point of the invisible edge, enter the **Invisible** option. The following example shows how to do this. See Figure 2-23.

> Command: **3DFACE**↵
> First point: *(pick P1)*
> Second point: *(pick P2)*
> Third point: **I**↵ *(pick P3)*
> Fourth point: *(pick P4)*
> Third point: **I**↵ *(pick P5)*
> Fourth point: *(pick P6)*
> Third point: ↵
> Command: ↵
> 3DFACE First point: *(pick P6)*
> Second point: *(pick P7)*
> Third point: *(pick P8)*
> Fourth point: **I**↵ *(pick P5)*
> Third point: ↵
> Command:

If the **SPLFRAME** system variable is set to its default value of 0, invisible edges are *not* shown. If **SPLFRAME** is set to 1, invisible edges *are* shown. When screen menus are configured to display, **SPLFRAME** can be set using the **ShowEdge** and **HideEdge** options that appear in the **3Dface:** menu, Figure 2-24. Their functions are as follows:

- **ShowEdge.** **SPLFRAME** is set to 1 and hidden edges *are* shown. This option displays the following message:

> Invisible edges will be SHOWN after next Regeneration.

- **HideEdge.** **SPLFRAME** is set to 0 and edges drawn with the **Invisible** option are *not* shown. This option displays the following message:

> Invisible edges will be HIDDEN after next Regeneration.

Figure 2-23.
The **Invisible** option of the **3DFACE** command hides edges that are normally visible.

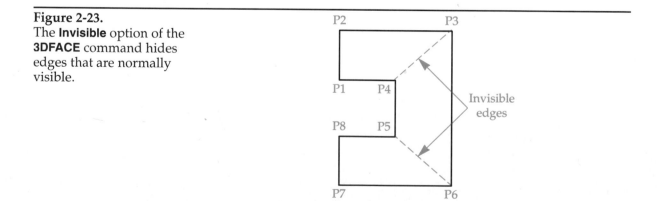

Figure 2-24.
When AutoCAD is
configured to display screen
menus, the **ShowEdge** and
HideEdge options can be
used to control visibility
of invisible edges.

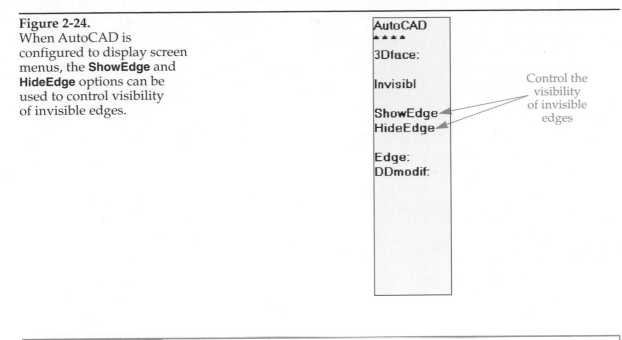

Control the
visibility
of invisible
edges

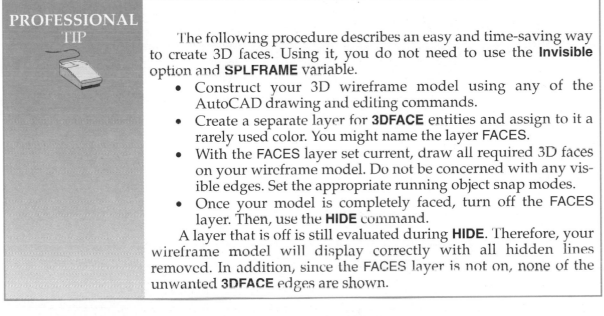

PROFESSIONAL TIP

The following procedure describes an easy and time-saving way to create 3D faces. Using it, you do not need to use the **Invisible** option and **SPLFRAME** variable.

- Construct your 3D wireframe model using any of the AutoCAD drawing and editing commands.
- Create a separate layer for **3DFACE** entities and assign to it a rarely used color. You might name the layer FACES.
- With the FACES layer set current, draw all required 3D faces on your wireframe model. Do not be concerned with any visible edges. Set the appropriate running object snap modes.
- Once your model is completely faced, turn off the FACES layer. Then, use the **HIDE** command.

A layer that is off is still evaluated during **HIDE**. Therefore, your wireframe model will display correctly with all hidden lines removed. In addition, since the FACES layer is not on, none of the unwanted **3DFACE** edges are shown.

THINGS TO CONSIDER WHEN WORKING WITH 3D

Working in 3D, like working with 2D drawings, requires careful planning to get the desired results efficiently. Use the following suggestions when working in 3D.

Planning

✓ Determine the type of final drawing you need. Then, choose the method of 3D construction that best suits your needs.

✓ Isometric is quickest and most versatile for objects needing only one pictorial view. Ellipses and arcs are easy to work with.

✓ Objects and layouts that need to be viewed from different angles for design purposes are best constructed using the 3D commands.

✓ Construct only the details needed for the function of the drawing. This saves space and time, and makes visualization much easier.

✓ Use Osnap modes **Midpoint**, **Endpoint**, and **Intersection** with the **LINE** and **3DFACE** commands.

✓ Keep in mind that the grid appears at the current elevation and viewpoint angle.

✓ Create layers having different colors for different entities. Turn them on and off as needed, or freeze those not being used.

Editing

✓ Use the **CHPROP** command to change color, layer, linetype, or thickness of 3D objects.

✓ Use the **STRETCH** command or grips in the 3D view to change only one dimension of the object. Use the **SCALE** command in the 3D view to change the size of the entire object proportionally. See Chapter 5.

✓ Do as much editing as possible in a 3D viewpoint. It is quicker and the results are seen immediately.

Displaying

✓ The **HIDE** command can help you visualize complex drawings.

✓ For quick viewpoints use the 3D viewpoint presets in the **View** toolbar or **View** pull-down menu.

✓ Use the **VIEW** command to create and save 3D views for quicker pictorial displays. This avoids having to use the **VPOINT** or **DVIEW** commands.

✓ Freeze unwanted layers before displaying objects in 3D, and especially before using **HIDE**. Also, remember that AutoCAD still regenerates layers that are off.

✓ Before using **HIDE**, zoom in on the part of a drawing to display. This saves time in regenerating the view because only the entities that are visible are regenerated.

✓ Objects that touch or intersect may have to be moved slightly if the display removes a line you need to see or plot.

CHAPTER TEST

Write your answers in the spaces provided.

1. When looking at the screen, in which direction does the Z coordinate project? _____

   _____

2. Explain the differences between spherical and cylindrical coordinates. _____

   _____

   _____

   _____

3. A new point is to be located 4.5″ from the last point. It is to be at a 63° angle in the XY plane, and at a 35° angle from the XY plane. Write the proper spherical coordinate notation.

   _____

4. Write the proper cylindrical coordinate notation for the point in question 3, but instead of a 35° angle from the XY plane, the point should be located 3.6″ from the last point in the Z axis. _____

5. How do you select one of AutoCAD's predrawn 3D shapes? _____

   _____

   _____

6. When using the **3DFACE** command, how do you indicate that an edge is to be invisible?

   _____

   _____

7. What predrawn 3D shapes are available? _____

   _____

8. How many different types of pyramids can you draw with the **PYRAMID** command (*not* including the tetrahedrons)? _____

9. How does **SPLFRAME** affect the **3DFACE** command? _____

   _____

   _____

10. Define "longitudinal segments" in reference to a dome or dish._____

    _____

11. What command allows you to draw surfaced 3D objects? _____

12. What command can you enter at the keyboard to draw a surface modeled cone?_____

13. Which 3D shape is used to draw a tetrahedron? _____

14. What two measurements are required to draw a torus? _____ _____

    _____

15. Name the system variable and value that is used to control the following functions of **3DFACE** display.

    ShowEdge _____

    HideEdge _____

16. Name the five different shapes that can be constructed with the **PYRAMID** command.

    _____

    _____

DRAWING PROBLEMS

*Problems 1 - 4. Draw each of these objects as wireframes. Then, use the **3DFACE** command to place surfaces on all sides of the objects. Measure the objects directly to obtain dimensions. Use A-size limits. Plot the drawings at a 3:1 scale with hidden lines removed. Save the drawings as P2-1, P2-2, etc.*

General

1.

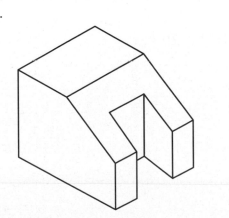

2.

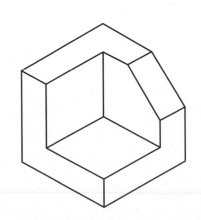

3.

4.

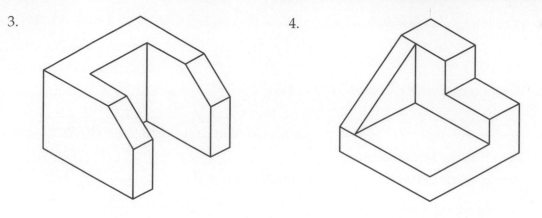

Problems 5 - 9. Draw each of these objects using the dimensions given. Use 3D objects to create the models. Use grips and editing commands to aid in constructions. Do not dimension the objects. Save the drawings as P2-5, P2-6, etc.

5.

6.

7.

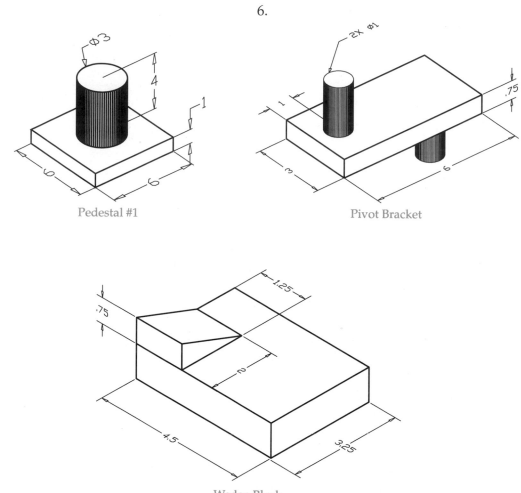

Pedestal #1

Pivot Bracket

Wedge Block

8.

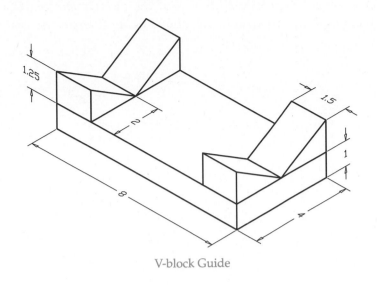

V-block Guide

9.

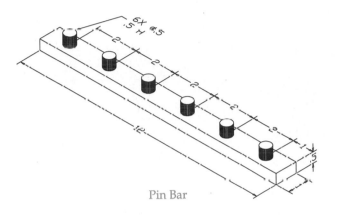

Pin Bar

10. Draw the Ø8" pedestal .5" thick. Four Ø.75" feet are located 7" between centers and are .5" high. Use elevation and thickness to assist in creating this model. Save the drawing as P2-10.

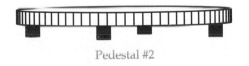

Pedestal #2

11. Four wedges, each 3" long, 1" wide, and 1" high, support this Ø10" globe. Each wedge sits .8" away from the center of the Ø12" circular base. The base is .5" thick. Save the drawing as P2-11.

Globe

Problems 12 - 17. Construct 3D models of each of the objects shown. Use only 3D objects found in the Surfaces toolbar. Construct each object using the specific instructions given.

12. **Table 1.** Table legs (A) are 2″ square and 17″ tall. Table top (B) is 24″ × 36″ × 1″.

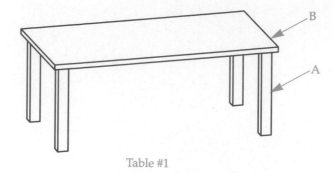

Table #1

13. **Table 2.** Table legs (A) are ∅2″ and 17″ tall. Table top (B) is 24″ × 36″ × 1″. Table legs (C) are ∅2″ and 11″ tall. Table top (D) is 24″ × 14″ × 1″.

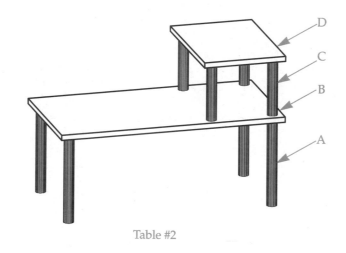

Table #2

14. **Dumbbell.** Object A is ∅6″. Object B is 6″ long and ∅1.5″.

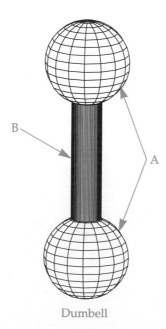

Dumbell

15. **Table lamp.** Object A is ⌀8″ in diameter at the base, ⌀7″ at the top and is 1″ tall. Object B is ⌀5″ and 7″ tall. Object C is ⌀2″ and 6″ tall. Item D is .5″ × 8″ × .125″, and there are four pieces. Object E is ⌀18″ at the base, ⌀6″ at the top and is 12″ tall.

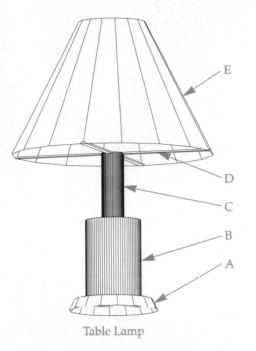

Table Lamp

16. **Garden wall.** Objects A and B are 5′ high brick walls. The walls are two courses of brick thick. Research the dimensions of standard brick and draw accordingly. Wall B is 7′ long and wall A is 5′ long. Lamps are placed at each end of the walls. Object C is ⌀2″ and 8″ tall. Object D is ⌀10″.

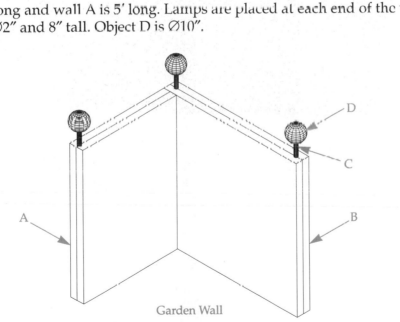

Garden Wall

17. **Floor lamp.** Object A is Ø18″ and 1″ tall. Object B is Ø1.5″ and 6′ tall. Object C is Ø6″ and .5″ tall. Object D is a Ø10″ sphere. Object E (four items) is an L-shaped bracket to support the shade to object C. Draw these an appropriate size. Object F has a base of Ø22″ and is 12″ tall.

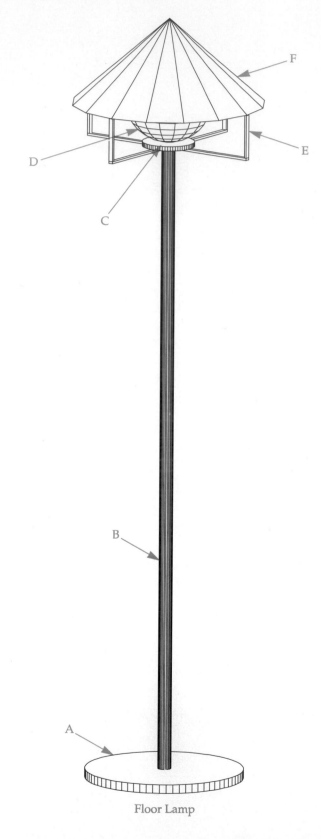

Floor Lamp

AutoCAD R13

Chapter 3

Understanding User Coordinate Systems

Learning objectives

After completing this chapter, you will be able to:

- ○ Describe the function of the world and user coordinate systems.
- ○ Move the coordinate system to any surface.
- ○ Rotate the coordinate system to any angle.
- ○ Change the coordinate system to match the plane of a geometric object.
- ○ Save named user coordinate systems.
- ○ Restore and use named user coordinate systems.

The flexibility of 3D construction with AutoCAD is the ability to create and use different 3D coordinate systems. All drawing and editing commands can be used in any coordinate system that you create. Objects that are drawn will always be parallel to the plane, or coordinate system, that you are working in. Therefore, you must be able to change your point of view so it is perpendicular to the plane you want to draw on. Your view is then said to be "plan" to that plane. This chapter provides you with detailed instructions in constructing and working with coordinate systems. This will allow you to draw any type of 3D shape that you need.

INTRODUCTION TO USER COORDINATE SYSTEMS

AutoCAD
User's
Guide
9

All points in a drawing or on an object are defined with XYZ coordinate values measured from the 0,0,0 origin. Since this system of coordinates is fixed and universal, AutoCAD refers to it as the *World Coordinate System (WCS)*. The *User Coordinate System (UCS)*, on the other hand, can be defined at any orientation desired. The **UCS** command is used to change the origin, position, and rotation of the coordinate system to match the surfaces and features of an object under construction. Changes in the UCS are reflected in the orientation and placement of the UCS icon symbol at the lower-left corner of the graphics window. The available options for creating and managing a UCS, as well as the UCS icon symbol, are found under **Set UCS** in the **View** pull-down menu, Figure 3-1.

Figure 3-1.
The UCS options can be accessed from the **View** pull-down menu.

```
View
  Redraw View
  Redraw All

  Zoom                    World
  Pan                     Origin
                          Z Axis Vector
  Named Views...          3 Point
  3D Viewpoint Presets    Object
  3D Viewpoint            View
  3D Dynamic View         X Axis Rotate
                          Y Axis Rotate
√ Tiled Model Space       Z Axis Rotate
  Floating Model Space    Previous
  Paper Space
                          Restore
  Tiled Viewports         Save
  Floating Viewports      Delete

  Preset UCS...           List
  Named UCS...
  Set UCS            ▶
```

Displaying the UCS icon

The symbol that identifies the orientation of the coordinate system is called the *UCS icon.* It is located in the lower-left corner of the viewport. The display of this symbol is controlled by the **UCSICON** command. If your drawing does not require viewports and altered coordinate systems, turn the icon off.

```
Command: UCSICON↵
ON/OFF/All/Noorigin/ORigin ⟨ON⟩: OFF↵
Command:
```

The icon disappears until you turn it on again using the **UCSICON** command.

Changing the coordinate system

To construct a three-dimensional object, you must visualize shapes at many angles. Different planes are needed to draw features on angled surfaces. It is easy to rotate the UCS icon to match any surface on an object. The following example illustrates this process.

The object in Figure 3-2 has a cylinder on the angled surface. The first step in creating this model is to draw the base in the plan view. See Figure 3-3A. Now, display the object in a 3D view.

```
Command: VPOINT↵
Rotate/⟨View point⟩ ⟨0.0000,0.0000,1.0000⟩: 1,-1,1↵
Regenerating drawing.
Command: ZOOM↵
All/Center/Dynamic/Extents/Left/Previous/Vmax/Window/⟨Scale(X/XP)⟩: .8X↵
Command:
```

Figure 3-2.
This object can be constructed by changing the orientation of the coordinate system. You will construct this object in this chapter.

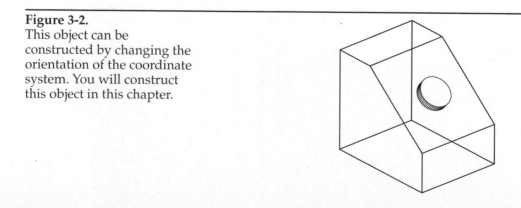

Figure 3-3.
A—The base of the object is
constructed in the plan view
of the WCS. B—The UCS
icon is rotated 90° on the X
axis to draw the sides.
Notice how the UCS icon
has changed.

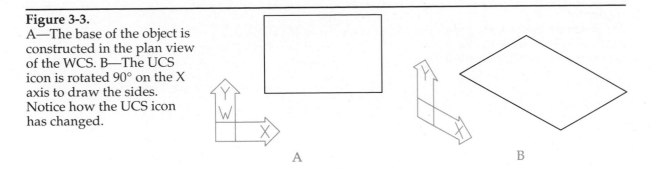

A   B

With the base of the object constructed, draw the vertical lines. You can draw the vertical lines using XYZ filters. However, it is easier to rotate the UCS so you can draw the vertical lines as if you are drawing a front view. To do so, first rotate the UCS so that the Y axis is pointing up from the bottom surface of the object and the X axis is pointing to the right side. When this happens, the Z axis is pointing out of the screen to the left. Rotate the UCS on the X axis as follows:

```
Command: UCS↵
Origin/ZAxis/3point/OBject/View/X/Y/Z/Prev/Restore/Save/Del/?/⟨World⟩: X↵
Rotation angle about X axis ⟨0⟩: 90↵
Command:
```

The UCS icon changes to reflect the new UCS. See Figure 3-3B. The next step is to draw the front face of the object, Figure 3-4A.

```
Command: LINE.↵
From point: END↵
of (pick the left end of the line)
To point: @0,5↵
To point: @0,1↵
To point: ↵
Command: ↵
From point: (pick the right end of the front edge)
To point: @0,1↵
To point: END↵
of (pick the right end of the short horizontal line)
To point: ↵
Command:
```

The lines just drawn represent the front face of the object. First, copy them to the back edge. Then, lines connecting the two surfaces can be drawn. See Figure 3-4B and Figure 3-4C. Set the running object snap **Endpoint** to help.

```
Command: OSNAP↵
Object snap modes: END↵
Command: COPY↵
Select objects: (select the lines just drawn)
Select objects: ↵
⟨Base point or displacement⟩/Multiple: ↵
of (pick P1)
Second point of displacement: ↵
of (pick P2)
Command:
```

Figure 3-4.
A—The front surface of the wedge is added using the **LINE** command. B—The front surface is copied on the Z axis to create the back surface. C—The base of the object is completed by connecting the front and back surfaces with lines.

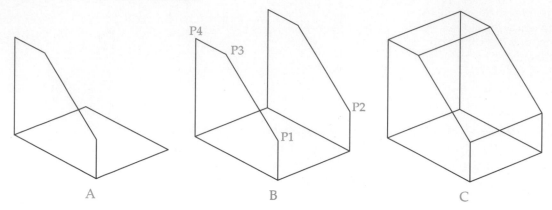

A   B   C

Use grips to quickly copy the new line to two other locations. Pick the line and pick the grip at P1 to make it hot. Press [Enter] to activate the **MOVE** command as follows:

⟨Stretch to point⟩/Base point/Copy/Undo/eXit: ↵
MOVE
⟨Move to point⟩/Base point/Copy/Undo/eXit: **C**↵

Pick points P3 and P4 then press [Enter] and [Esc] twice to remove the grips. The base of the object is complete. It should look similar to Figure 3-4C.

Aligning the UCS and UCS icon with an angled surface

The cylinder in Figure 3-2 needs to be drawn on the angled surface. In 2D drafting, an angled surface is seen in its true shape and size only when projected to an auxiliary view. An auxiliary view places your line of sight perpendicular to the angled surface. This means that you see the angled surface as a "plan" view.

AutoCAD always draws objects aligned with the plan view of the current UCS. For the construction in Figure 3-4, the plan view of the UCS looks like Figure 3-5. A plan view is always perpendicular to your line of sight. Use the **PLAN** command as follows:

Command: **PLAN**↵
⟨Current UCS⟩/Ucs/World: ↵
Regenerating drawing.
Command:

Figure 3-5.
In any UCS, horizontal lines in the plan are parallel to the X axis and vertical lines in the plan are parallel to the Y axis.

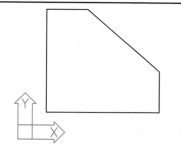

Notice that the UCS icon has exactly the same orientation as the vertical and horizontal lines of the object. The UCS and the front surface are parallel, and your line of sight is perpendicular to those planes. Therefore, if you draw the cylinder with this UCS, it will be perpendicular to this view. You must align the UCS with the angled surface of the object.

The 3point option of the UCS command changes the UCS to any angled surface. This option requires that you locate a new origin, a point on the positive X axis, and a point on the positive Y axis. Refer to Figure 3-6 for pick points as you use the following command sequence. Remember, the osnap **Endpoint** is already set.

> Command: **UCS↵**
> Origin/ZAxis/3point/OBject/View/X/Y/Z/Prev/Restore/Save/Del/?/⟨World⟩: **3↵**
> Origin point: ⟨0,0,0⟩: ↵
> of *(pick P1)*
> Point on positive portion of the X-axis ⟨10.0000,0.0000,−2.0000⟩: ↵
> of *(pick P2)*
> Point on positive-Y portion of the UCS XY plane ⟨9.0000,1.0000,−2.0000⟩: ↵
> of *(pick P3)*
> Command:

Figure 3-6.
A new UCS can be established by picking three points. P1 is the origin, P2 is the positive X axis, and P3 is the positive Y axis.

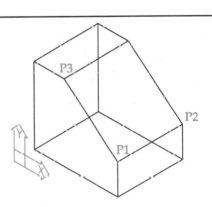

After you pick P3, the UCS icon changes its orientation to align with the angled surface of the wedge. However, it is still located at the lower-left corner of the view. To help you visualize the drawing, move the icon to the origin of the new UCS. Use the **UCSICON** command as follows:

> Command: **UCSICON↵**
> ON/OFF/All/Noorigin/ORigin/⟨ON⟩: **OR↵**
> Command:

The icon is now located on the origin of the User Coordinate System. Any coordinate locations you enter will be relative to the new origin.

The cylinder can be drawn in 3D view or "plan" to the current UCS. For this example, the current 3D view is used. First set the elevation and thickness. Then, draw the cylinder using the **CIRCLE** command.

> Command: **ELEV↵**
> New current elevation ⟨0.0000⟩: ↵
> New current thickness ⟨0.0000⟩: **.35↵**
> Command: **CIRCLE↵**
> 3P/2P/TTR/⟨Center point⟩: **2.125,2.3↵**
> Diameter/⟨Radius⟩: **.75↵**
> Command: ↵

The circle appears in its correct orientation on the angled surface. All edges and features can be seen, Figure 3-7A. The cylinder appears solid when **HIDE** is used, Figure 3-7B.

Figure 3-7.
A—The completed
wireframe wedge shows the
properly placed cylinder.
B—When **HIDE** is used, the
cylinder is solid while the
rest of the object is a
wireframe.

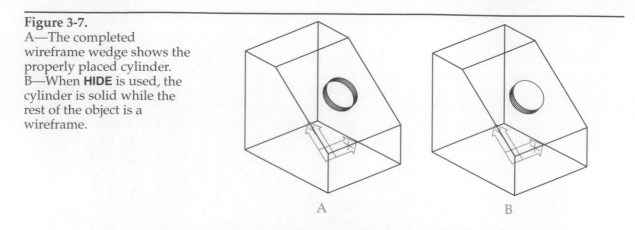

A   B

EXERCISE 3-1

❏ Load AutoCAD for Windows and begin a new drawing named EX3-1.
❏ Construct the 3D object shown using the techniques discussed in this section. Do not include dimensions. Rotate the UCS as needed.
❏ Save the drawing as A:EX3-1.

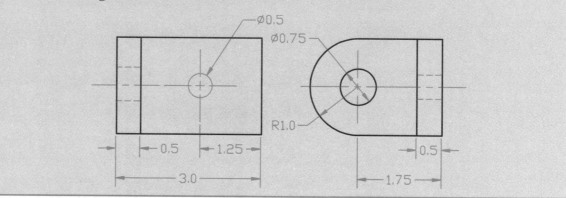

Drawing wireframe "holes"

Wireframe holes can be created by drawing a circle and copying it to new location. To add a hole to the lower surface of the object in Figure 3-2, first move the UCS. Use the **3point** option of the **UCS** command. Place it on the lower-right vertical surface of the object. Use the pick points shown in Figure 3-8A.

Set the elevation and thickness to zero before you draw any objects. Then, draw the first circle as follows:

> Command: **CIRCLE**⏎
> 3P/2P/TTR/⟨Center point⟩: **2.125,1**⏎
> Diameter/⟨Radius⟩: **.5**⏎
> Command:

Figure 3-8B shows the new circle. Since the UCS is aligned with the lower-right vertical surface, the circle can be copied using a negative Z value. This produces the appearance of a wireframe "hole." To do this, first pick the circle to display grips. Select one of the grips to make it hot, then copy the circle as follows:

Figure 3-8.
A—Use the **3point** option to set the UCS parallel to the lower vertical surface. B—The first circle representing the hole is drawn. C—The completed wireframe hole.

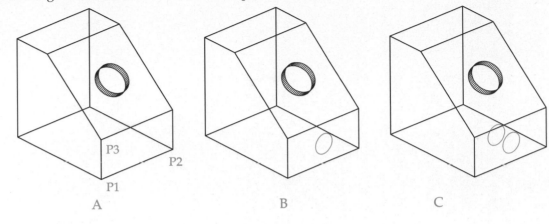

```
**STRETCH**
⟨Stretch to point⟩/Base point/Copy/Undo/eXit: ↵
⟨Move to point⟩/Base point/Copy/Undo/eXit:C↵
**MOVE (multiple) **
⟨Move to point⟩/Base point/Copy/Undo/eXit:@0,0,–1↵
**MOVE (multiple) **
⟨Move to point⟩/Base point/Copy/Undo/eXit: ↵
Command:
```

The wireframe hole is shown in Figure 3-8C.

ADDITIONAL WAYS TO CHANGE THE UCS

There are other ways to change the UCS. These options include selecting a new Z axis, picking a new origin for the UCS, rotating the Y and Z axes, and setting the UCS to an existing entity.

Selecting a new Z axis

The **ZAxis** option of the **UCS** command allows you to select the origin point and a point on the positive Z axis. Once the new Z axis is defined, AutoCAD sets the new X and Y axes. Figure 3-9A shows the current UCS on the model from Figure 3-8. The command sequence is as follows. Remember, the osnap **Endpoint** has already been set.

```
Command: UCS↵
Origin/ZAxis/3point/OBject/View/X/Y/Z/Prev/Restore/Save/Del/?/⟨World⟩: ZA↵
Origin point ⟨0,0,0⟩: ↵
of (pick P1 in Figure 3-8A)
Point on positive portion of Z-axis ⟨current⟩: ↵
of (pick P2)
Command:
```

The UCS icon now appears as shown in Figure 3-9B.

The same option can be used to quickly move the UCS to the front plane of the wedge, Figure 3-9C. Select point P2 as the origin and press [Enter] to accept the default coordinates of the second prompt.

```
Command: UCS↵
Origin/ZAxis/3point/OBject/View/X/Y/Z/Prev/Restore/Save/Del/?/⟨World⟩: ZA↵
Origin point ⟨0,0,0⟩: ↵
of (pick P2)
Point on positive portion of Z-axis ⟨current⟩: ↵
Command:
```

Figure 3-9.
A—The **ZAxis** option of the **UCS** command requires that you select the new origin and a point on the positive Z axis. B—The UCS icon is located at the new origin. C—The same process can be used to set the front plane as the UCS.

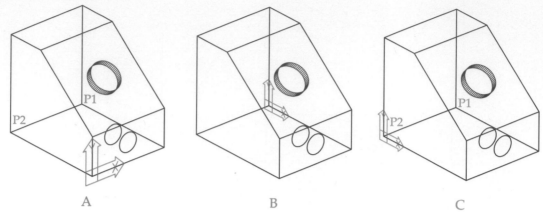

A   B   C

Selecting a new origin

The **Origin** option only asks for a new origin point. The UCS icon moves to the specified point and remains parallel to the current UCS. Figure 3-10 shows the UCS icon moved to three different origin points using the **Origin** option. Notice how all of the new locations remain parallel to the current UCS. All coordinate measurements begin at the new UCS origin.

Rotating the X, Y, and Z axes

Earlier, you rotated the current UCS about the X axis. This same technique is used to rotate the Y or Z axis. Rotating a single axis is useful when you need to rotate the UCS to match the angle of a surface on a part. Figure 3-11 shows the direction of rotation around each axis when a 90° angle is specified. You can also enter negative angles. The following sequence rotates the Z axis 90°.

```
Command: UCS↵
Origin/ZAxis/3point/OBject/View/X/Y/Z/Prev/Restore/Save/Del/?/⟨World⟩: Z↵
Rotation angle about Z axis ⟨0⟩: 90↵
Command:
```

Figure 3-10.
The UCS icon remains parallel to the current UCS when you move the origin using the **Origin** option.

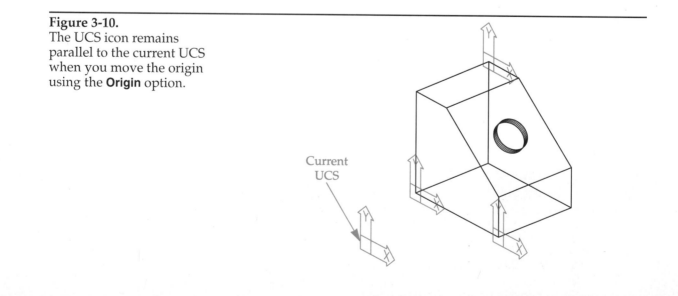

Current
UCS

Figure 3-11.
The UCS icon can be rotated around the X, Y, and Z axes by entering an angle. The angle can be positive or negative, as appropriate.

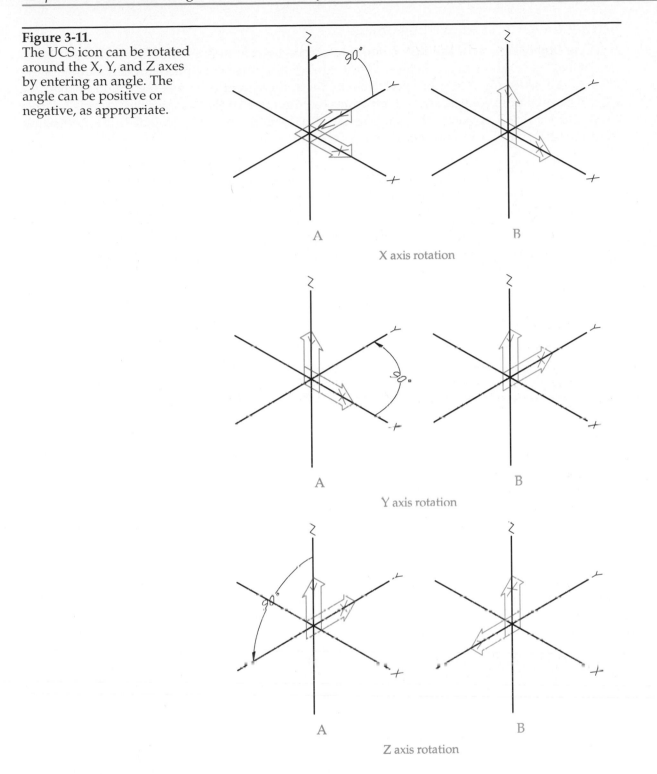

X axis rotation

Y axis rotation

Z axis rotation

PROFESSIONAL TIP

If you are having trouble visualizing the X, Y, and Z axis rotations, try using the right-hand rule. The right-hand rule is covered in Chapter 1.

Setting the UCS to an existing object

The **Object** option of the **UCS** command can be used to define a new UCS on any object, except a 3D polyline or polygon mesh. There are certain rules that control the orientation of the UCS icon. For example, if you select a circle, the center point becomes the origin of the new UCS. The pick point on the circle determines the direction of the X axis. The Y axis is relative to X, and the UCS Z axis is the same as the Z axis of the entity selected. In the following example, the cylinder in Figure 3-10 is selected for the new UCS:

```
Command: UCS↵
Origin/ZAxis/3point/OBject/View/X/Y/Z/Prev/Restore/Save/Del/?/⟨World⟩: OB↵
Select object to align UCS: (pick the top edge of the cylinder)
Command:
```

The UCS icon probably looks like the one shown in Figure 3-12A. This may not be what you expected. The X axis is determined by the pick point on the circle. In this case, the pick point was in the lower-left quadrant of the cylinder. To rotate the UCS in the current plane so the X and Y axes are parallel with the sides of the object, use the **ZAxis** option. Refer to Figure 3-12B.

```
Command: UCS↵
Origin/ZAxis/3point/OBject/View/X/Y/Z/Prev/Restore/Save/Del/?/⟨World⟩: ZA↵
Origin point ⟨0,0,0⟩: CEN↵
of (pick the cylinder)
Point on positive portion of Z-axis ⟨0.0000,0.0000,1.0000⟩: ↵
Command:
```

Figure 3-12.
A—The X axis of the UCS icon placed at the pick point of the circle. B—The UCS rotated parallel to the object with the **ZAxis** option.

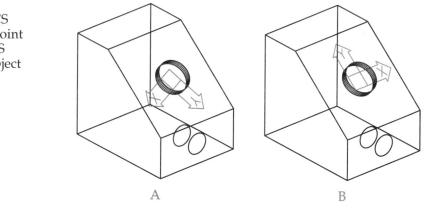

A   B

Setting the UCS perpendicular to current view

You may need to add notes or labels to a 3D drawing that appear horizontal in the current view, Figure 3-13. This is easy to do. First, select the **View** option of the **UCS** command. The UCS icon rotates to a position perpendicular to the current view.

```
Command: UCS↵
Origin/ZAxis/3point/OBject/View/X/Y/Z/Prev/Restore/Save/Del/?/⟨World⟩: V↵
Command:
```

Now, anything added to the drawing appears horizontal in the current view.

Preset UCS orientations

AutoCAD has six preset UCS orientations. To use one of these, select **UCS Preset...** from the **View** pull-down menu or pick the **Preset UCS** button from the **UCS** toolbar. The **UCS Orientation** dialog box shown in Figure 3-14 is displayed.

Figure 3-13.
The **View** option allows you to place text horizontally in the current view.

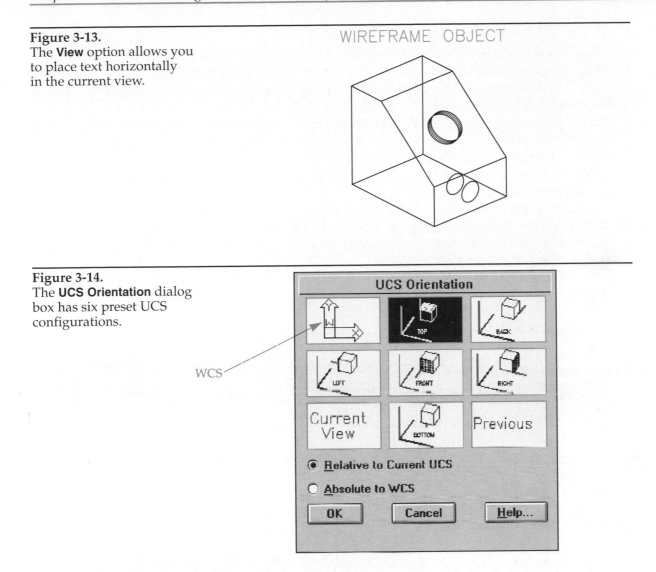

WIREFRAME OBJECT

Figure 3-14.
The **UCS Orientation** dialog box has six preset UCS configurations.

WCS

Six icons in the dialog box allow you to select a preset UCS. The icon at the upper left returns to the World Coordinate System. If you wish to restore the previous UCS you were working with, pick **Previous** in the lower-right corner. The **Current View** icon creates a UCS that is perpendicular to the current view. The two option buttons in the dialog box allow you to create a new UCS that is relative to the current UCS or absolute to the WCS.

If you have a UCS set, keep in mind that a plan view of any coordinate system can also be considered a top view. Therefore, if you select the **FRONT** icon to set a new UCS relative to the current one, you are basically rotating the UCS icon 90° around the X axis. This can be an easy way to create a new UCS. Then, move the UCS icon to a new origin using the **Origin** option of the **UCSICON** command.

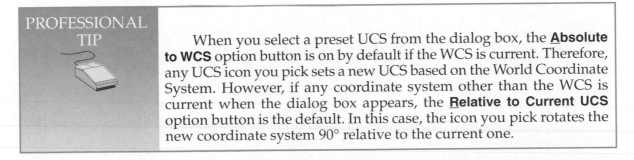

PROFESSIONAL TIP

When you select a preset UCS from the dialog box, the **Absolute to WCS** option button is on by default if the WCS is current. Therefore, any UCS icon you pick sets a new UCS based on the World Coordinate System. However, if any coordinate system other than the WCS is current when the dialog box appears, the **Relative to Current UCS** option button is the default. In this case, the icon you pick rotates the new coordinate system 90° relative to the current one.

UCS dialog boxes

User Coordinate Systems can be created, selected, and modified using dialog boxes. The **DDUCS** (dynamic dialog UCS) command activates the **UCS Control** dialog box, Figure 3-15. You can also select the **View** pull-down menu and the **Named UCS...** option or pick the **Named UCS** button in the **UCS** toolbar.

The **UCS Names** area of the dialog box contains names of all saved coordinate systems, plus *WORLD*. If other coordinate systems have been used, the word *PREVIOUS* appears in the list. The entry *NO NAME* appears if the current coordinate system has not been named. Make any of the listed coordinate systems active by highlighting the name and picking the **Current** button.

A list of coordinate and axis values of the current UCS can be displayed by picking the **List...** button. This displays the **UCS** dialog box shown in Figure 3-16.

Use the following steps to define and name a new User Coordinate System:

1. Open the **UCS Orientation** dialog box to display the preset icons.
2. Select the orientation you need and pick the **OK** button.
3. Select the **UCS** command and use the **Save** option to enter a name for the new UCS.

Figure 3-15.
The **UCS Control** dialog box allows you to rename, list, delete, and set current an existing UCS.

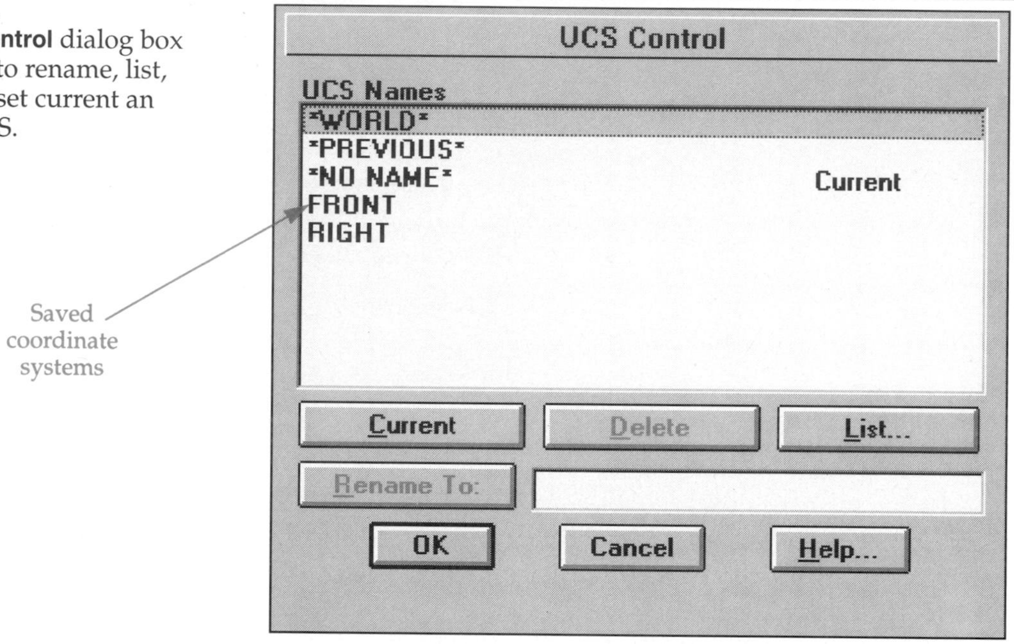

Saved coordinate systems

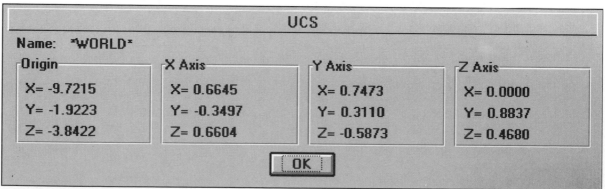

Figure 3-16.
The **UCS** dialog box displays the coordinate values of the current UCS.

UCS			
Name: *WORLD*			
Origin	X Axis	Y Axis	Z Axis
X= -9.7215	X= 0.6645	X= 0.7473	X= 0.0000
Y= -1.9223	Y= -0.3497	Y= 0.3110	Y= 0.8837
Z= -3.8422	Z= 0.6604	Z= -0.5873	Z= 0.4680

EXERCISE 3-2

❏ Load AutoCAD for Windows and begin a new drawing named EX3-2.
❏ Construct the 3D object shown below. Do not include dimensions or labels.
❏ Rotate and relocate the UCS as needed.
❏ Create and save named UCSs as follows:

Label	UCS name
A	Front
B	Right

❏ Save the drawing as A:EX3-2.

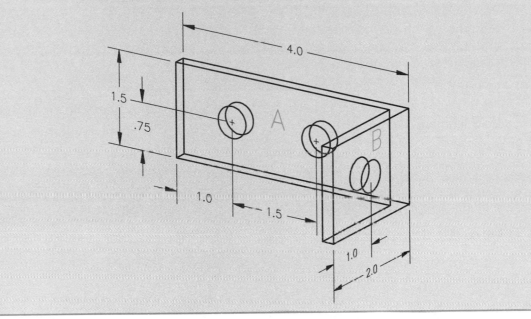

Setting an automatic plan display

Earlier, you learned how to display a plan view to the current UCS using the **PLAN** command. After changing the UCS, a plan view is often needed to give you a better feel for the XYZ directions. The plan view also allows you to visualize the object in a pictorial view. This makes it easier to decide the best viewpoint orientation to pick.

If the **UCSFOLLOW** system variable is set to 1, AutoCAD automatically generates a plan view in the current viewport when the UCS is changed. Viewports are discussed in Chapter 4. The default setting of **UCSFOLLOW** is 0 (off). The **UCSFOLLOW** variable can be set for each viewport individually. The following example sets **UCSFOLLOW** to 1 for the current viewport only.

```
Command: UCSFOLLOW↵
New value for UCSFOLLOW ⟨0⟩: 1↵
Command:
```

Working with more than one UCS

You can create as many UCSs as needed to construct your model or drawing. AutoCAD allows you to name coordinate systems for future use. Several options of the **UCS** command allow you to work with multiple coordinate systems. These are explained below.

- **?.** Switches the graphics window to the text window and displays all of the named coordinate systems. The display includes the coordinate values of the XYZ axes of each UCS relative to the current UCS. The name of the current UCS is given first. If the current UCS does not have a name and is different than the WCS, *NO NAME* appears.

- **Previous (P).** Allows you to display previously used coordinate systems. AutoCAD remembers ten previous systems in both model space and paper space, for a total of twenty. You can step back through them in the same way that **ZOOM Previous** displays previous zooms.

- **Restore (R).** Requires the name of the UCS you wish restored. If you forget the names, enter a question mark (?) to list saved coordinate systems. Only the orientation of the UCS icon will change. The views remain the same.

- **Save (S).** Save a UCS by entering a name having 31 characters or less. Numbers, letters, dollar sign ($), hyphen (–), and underscore (_) are valid.

- **Delete (D).** Enter the name of the UCS to be deleted. You can use wild card characters and a question mark (?), or delete a list by separating the names with commas.

- **World (W).** Resets the World Coordinate System (WCS) as the current UCS.

PROFESSIONAL TIP

Most drawings can be created using a single named UCS. This UCS is rotated and placed on any plane that you are working on. If the drawing is complex with several planes each containing a large amount of detail, you may wish to establish a named UCS for each detailed face. Then, to work on a different plane, just restore the proper UCS. For example, when working with architectural drawings, you may wish to establish a different UCS for each floor plan and elevation view, and for roofs that require detail work.

UCS variables

AutoCAD has a system variable that allows you to change how an object is displayed in relation to the UCS. This is the **UCSFOLLOW** variable introduced earlier. There are also variables that display a variety of information about the current UCS. These variables are explained below.

- **UCSFOLLOW.** Has an integer value of 0 or 1. When set to 1 it displays a plan view when the UCS is changed. This feature is discussed in Chapter 4.
- **UCSNAME.** (Read only) Displays the name of the current UCS.
- **UCSORG.** (Read only) Displays the XYZ origin value of the current UCS.
- **UCSXDIR.** (Read only) Displays the XYZ value of the X direction of the current UCS.
- **UCSYDIR.** (Read only) Displays the XYZ value of the Y direction of the current UCS.

CHAPTER TEST

1. Define the meaning of WCS. _____

   _____

2. What is a User Coordinate System (UCS)? _____

   _____

   _____

   _____

3. What command controls the display of the User Coordinate System icon? _____

   _____

4. What is the function of the **3point** option of the **UCS** command? _____

   _____

   _____

   _____

5. How do you create a display of the current UCS that is perpendicular to your line of sight?

   _____

   _____

6. How is the UCS icon moved to the origin of the current coordinate system? _____

   _____

   _____

7. When you use the **OBject** option of the **UCS** command, how does AutoCAD determine the X axis if you pick a circle for the new UCS? _____

   _____

   _____

8. How do you move the UCS along the current Z axis? _____

   _____

9. What is the function of the **Object** option of the **UCS** command? _____

   _____

10. When is the **View** option of the **UCS** command used? _____

    _____

    _____

11. How can you make sure that a view will always be plan to the current UCS? _____

    _____

    _____

12. How do you access the **UCS Orientation** dialog box? _____

    _____

13. What command displays the **UCS Control** dialog box? _____

    _____

14. What appears in the **UCS Control** dialog box if the current UCS has not been named?

    _____

DRAWING PROBLEMS

1 - 3. Problems 1 through 3 are engineering design sketches. They are the kinds of sketches a drafter is expected to work from in a real-world situation. Therefore, they may contain dimensioning errors and some information may be incomplete. It is up to you to supply appropriate information as needed.

Architecture

1. This is a concept sketch of a desk organizer. Create a 3D drawing, either wireframe or surfaced, using the dimensions given. Create new UCSs as needed. Length dimensions of the compartments are up to you. Plot your drawing to scale on a B-size sheet of paper. Save the drawing as P3-1.

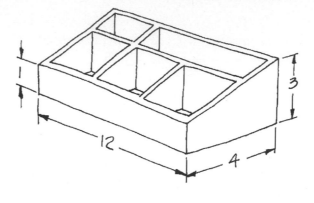

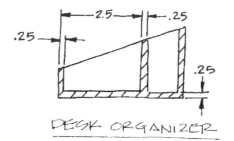

Architecture

2. This is a concept sketch of a desk pencil holder. Create a 3D wireframe drawing using the dimensions given. Create new UCSs as needed. Plot your drawing to scale on a B-size sheet of paper. Save the drawing as P3-2.

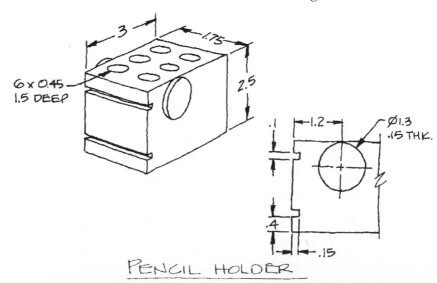

3. This is an engineering sketch of a window blind mounting bracket. Create a 3D drawing using the dimensions given. Create new UCSs as needed. Plot two views of your drawing to scale on a C-size sheet of paper. Save the drawing as P3-3.

Mechanical Drafting

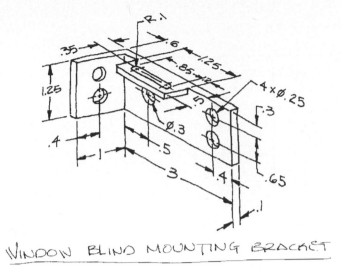

WINDOW BLIND MOUNTING BRACKET

4. This is a two view orthographic drawing of a window valance mounting bracket. Convert it to a 3D wireframe drawing. Use the dimensions given. Similar holes have the same offset dimensions. Create new UCSs as needed. Plot two views of your drawing to scale on a C-size sheet of paper. Save the drawing as P3-4.

Mechanical Drafting

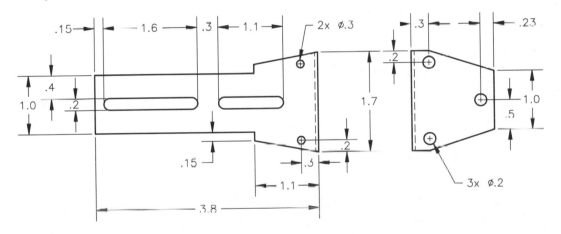

5. This is an isometric drawing of a light fixture bracket. Convert it to a 3D wireframe drawing. Use the dimensions given. Similar holes have the same offset dimensions. Create new UCSs as needed. Plot two views of your drawing to scale on a C-size sheet of paper. Save the drawing as P3-5.

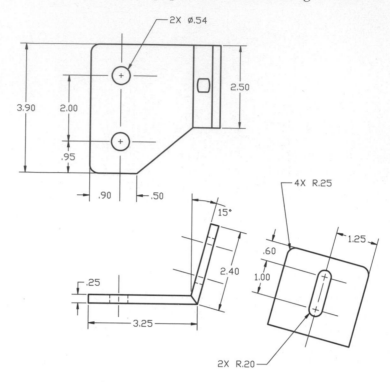

6 - 8. *Problems 6 through 8 are mechanical parts. Create a 3D wireframe drawing of each part. Do not dimension the model. Plot the finished drawings on B-size paper.*

6. Angle Bracket

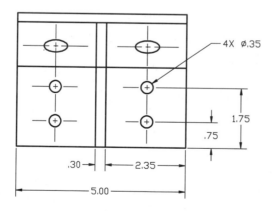

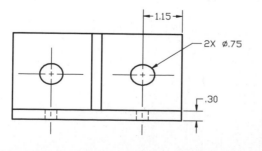

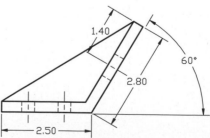

7. Guide Bracket

8. Angle Mount

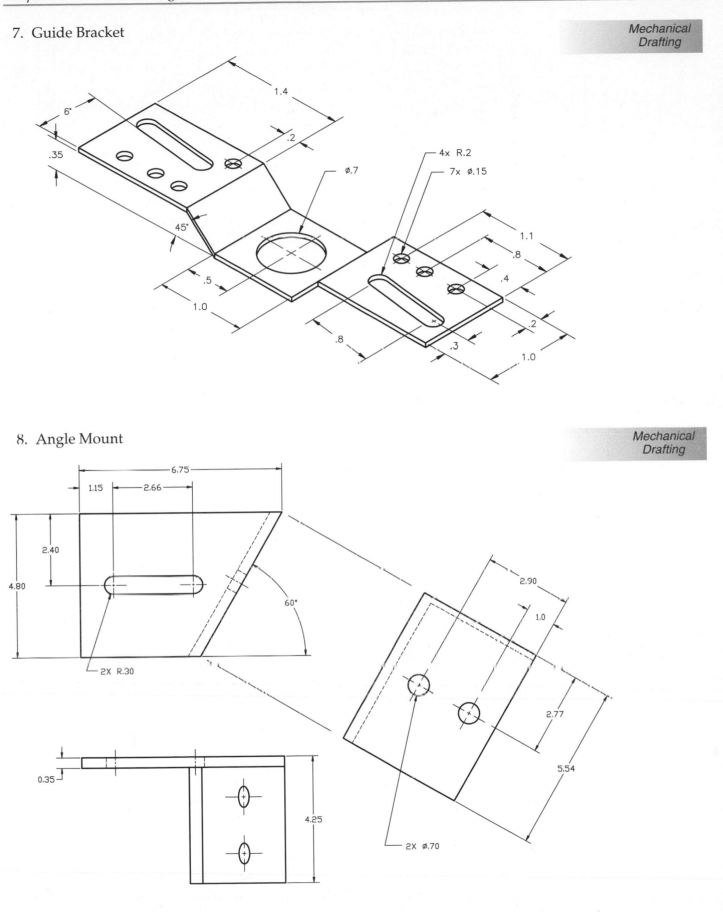

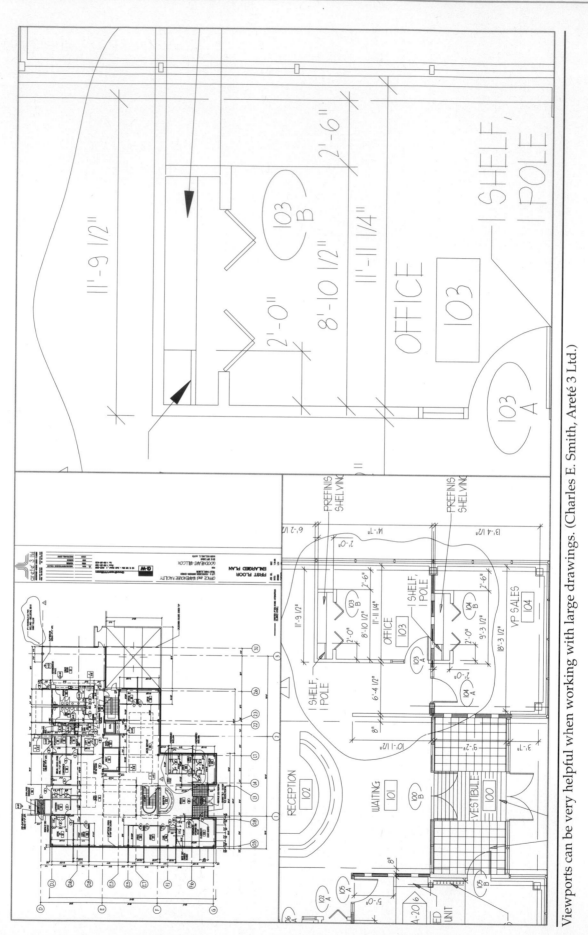

Viewports can be very helpful when working with large drawings. (Charles E. Smith, Areté 3 Ltd.)

AutoCAD R13

Chapter 4

Using Model Space Viewports

Learning objectives

After completing this chapter, you will be able to:
- ❍ Describe the function of model space viewports.
- ❍ Divide the screen into multiple viewports.
- ❍ Create and save a variety of viewport configurations.
- ❍ Alter the current viewport configuration.
- ❍ Construct a drawing using multiple viewports.

A variety of views can be displayed at one time using model space viewports. This is useful when constructing 3D models. Using the **VPORTS** command, the screen can be divided into two or more smaller screens. These smaller screens are called *viewports*. Each viewport can be configured to display a different 2D or 3D view of the model. The *active viewport* is the viewport where the model is constructed. Any viewport can be made active, but only one can be active at a time. As objects are added or edited, the results are shown in all viewports. A variety of viewport configurations can be saved and recalled as needed. This chapter discusses the use of viewports and shows how they can be used for 3D constructions.

UNDERSTANDING VIEWPORTS

The AutoCAD graphics window be divided into a maximum of 16 viewports. However, this is impractical because of the small size of each viewport. Four viewports is the maximum number practical to display at one time. The number of viewports you need depends on the model you are drawing. Each viewport can show a different view of an object. This makes it easier to construct 3D objects.

A variety of **VPORTS** command options can be found by selecting **Tiled Viewports** in the **View** pull down menu. See Figure 4-1A. Buttons for selecting model space, paper space, and floating model space can be found in the **Tiled Model Space** flyout at the right side of the standard toolbar. See Figure 4-1B. Floating model space is the area inside a paper space viewport.

Model space viewports are created with the **VPORTS** command. In order to use **VPORTS**, model space must be active. Model space is active by default when you enter AutoCAD. The **TILEMODE** system variable must also be set to the default of 1. You can have up to 16 viewports at a time. Model space viewports cannot be plotted because they are not entities. Viewports are simply a display.

Paper space viewports are used to lay out the views of a drawing before plotting. A detailed discussion of paper space viewports is found in Chapter 26 of *AutoCAD and its Applications—Basics, Release 13 for Windows.* The **MVIEW** command is used to create paper space viewports. These viewports are like "windows" cut into a sheet of paper. Paper space viewports are entities and can be edited. You can then insert, or "reference" different scaled drawings (views) into these windows. For example, architectural details or sections and details of a complex mechanical part may be referenced. These viewports can be used at the end of a project when

Figure 4-1.
A—The **VPORTS** command options can be selected from the **Tiled Viewports** cascading submenu.
B—The **VPORTS** command can be issued using the buttons found in the **Tiled Model Space** flyout in the **Standard** toolbar.

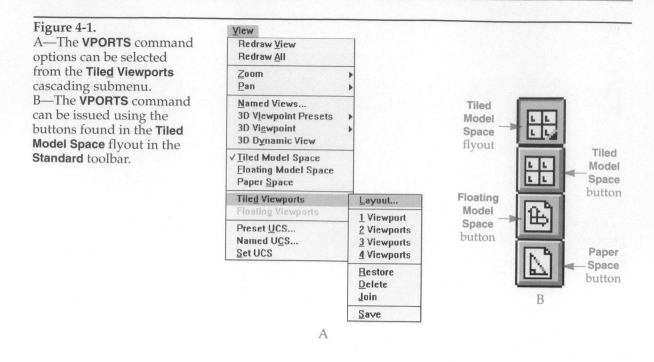

preparing the layout for plotting. Hence the name "paper space." The **TILEMODE** variable must be set to 0 to create viewports with the **MVIEW** command.

 NOTE　　　　The **MAXACTVP** (maximum active viewports) variable sets the number of paper space viewports that can be active at one time. Type MAXACTVP at the **Command:** prompt to set this value. This number depends on the operating system of your computer.

CREATING VIEWPORTS

Creating model space viewports is similar to working with a multiview layout in manual drafting. In a manual multiview layout, several views are on the same sheet. You can switch from one view to another simply by moving your pencil. With model space viewports, pick with your pointing device in the viewport you wish to work in. That viewport becomes active. Using viewports is a good way to construct 3D models because all views are updated as you draw. However, viewports are also good for creating 2D drawings.

The project you are working on determines the number of viewports needed. Keep in mind that the more viewports on your screen, the smaller they get. Small viewports may not be useful to you. Figure 4-2 shows four different viewport configurations. As you can see, when 16 viewports are displayed, the viewports get very small. Two to four viewports are normally used. You can enter a **VPORTS** value from two to sixteen to create multiple viewports:

　　　Command: **VPORTS**↵
　　　Save/Restore/Delete/Join/SIngle/?/2/⟨3⟩/4: ↵

Notice that 3 is the default value. After entering a value or accepting the default, you need to enter the configuration. For the default of three viewports, the prompt is:

　　　Horizontal/Vertical/Above/Below/Left/⟨Right⟩: ↵

The **Right** option places two viewports on the left side of the screen and a large viewport on the right. Viewports can be arranged in several ways. Selecting three viewports has the greatest number of possibilities. The options for a three-viewport layout are shown in Figure 4-3.

Figure 4-2.
A—Two vertical viewports. B—Two horizontal viewports. C—The default arrangement of three
viewports. D—The maximum of sixteen viewports.

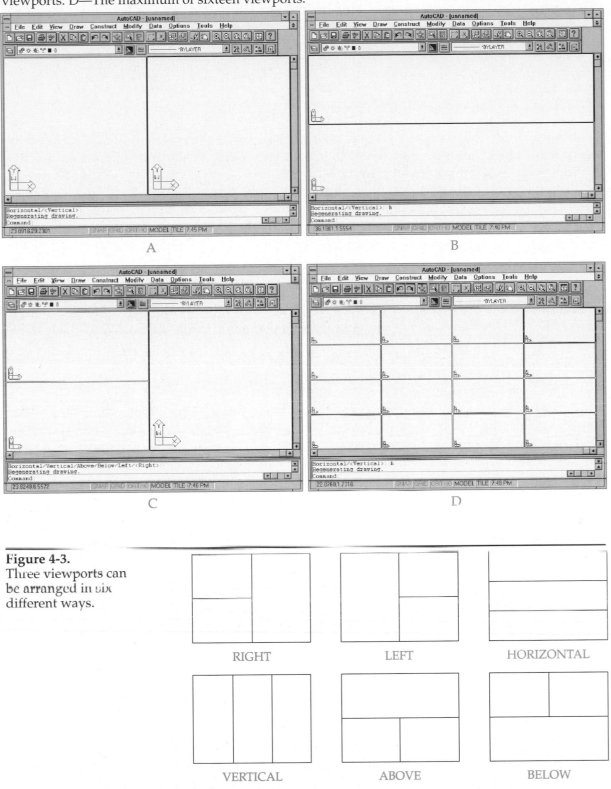

Figure 4-3.
Three viewports can
be arranged in six
different ways.

RIGHT   LEFT   HORIZONTAL

VERTICAL   ABOVE   BELOW

PROFESSIONAL TIP

Notice in Figure 4-2 that the UCS icon is displayed in all viewports. This is an easy way to tell that several separate screens are displayed, rather than different views of the drawing.

MAKING A VIEWPORT ACTIVE

Only one viewport can be active at one time. The cursor shows as crosshairs in the active viewport. A thick line also surrounds the active viewport. When moved into an inactive viewport, the cursor becomes an arrow.

Any viewport can be made active. Simply move the arrow to that viewport and pick, or press [Ctrl]+[V] to switch viewports. Viewports can also be made active by using the **CVPORT** (current viewport) command.

```
Command: CVPORT⏎
New value for CVPORT ⟨current⟩: 3⏎
Command:
```

The number is the ID number of the viewport. The ID number is automatically assigned by AutoCAD. It is discussed later in this chapter. This command is also a good way to determine the ID number of viewports.

SETTING VIEWPORTS WITH A DIALOG BOX

A layout of one to four viewports can be quickly created using a dialog box. Select **Tiled Viewports** from the **View** pull-down menu. Then, pick the **Layout...** option. This displays the **Tiled Viewport Layout** dialog box shown in Figure 4-4. There are twelve viewport configurations to choose from. You can pick the image tile or the name in the list. Pick **OK** when you are finished.

Figure 4-4.
The **Tiled Viewport Layout** dialog box. Custom configurations can be added to the blank tiles.

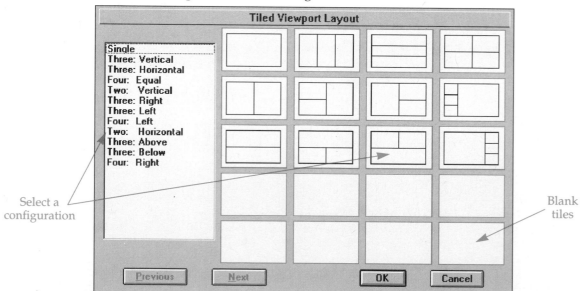

Notice that there are eight empty spaces in this dialog box. These are for additional viewport image tiles. You can create your own viewport arrangements and place new images in this menu. If you create more than eight image tiles, the **Previous** and **Next** buttons allow you to see other "pages." When there is a total of twenty or less configurations, these buttons are grayed-out. Chapter 19 details customizing image tiles.

SAVING, RESTORING, AND DELETING VIEWPORTS

Viewport configurations are not permanent. Once you change the configuration, only the previous one can be recalled. Although viewports are easy to create, it still saves time if you save individual configurations to use later. The **Save** option of the **VPORTS** command allows you to do this. Pick **Save** from the **Tiled Viewports** cascade of the **View** pull-down menu, or use the **Command:** prompt as follows:

```
Command: VPORTS⏎
Save/Restore/Delete/Join/SIngle/?/2/⟨3⟩/4: S⏎
?/Name for new viewport configuration: FIRST⏎
```

This command sequence saves the current viewport configuration with the name FIRST. This configuration can be recalled (restored) at any time. To list the configuration names, enter a question mark as follows:

```
Command: VPORTS⏎
Save/Restore/Delete/Join/SIngle/?/2/⟨3⟩/4: R⏎
?/Name of viewport configuration to restore: ?⏎
Viewport configuration(s) to list ⟨*⟩: ⏎
Current configuration:
id# 2
  corners: 0.0000,0.5000 0.5000,1.0000
id# 3
  corners: 0.5000,0.0000 1.0000,1.0000
id# 4
  corners: 0.0000,0.0000 0.5000,0.5000
Configuration FIRST:
  0.5000,0.0000 1.0000,1.0000
?/Name of viewport configuration to restore: FIRST⏎
Regenerating drawing.
Command:
```

The order that the above coordinates appear in may vary, but the values will be the same. All viewports are automatically given an ID number by AutoCAD. This number is independent of any name you might give the viewport configuration. Each viewport is also given a coordinate location with (0.0000,0.0000) as the lower-left corner of the graphics area and (1.0000,1.0000) as the upper-right corner. Look at the coordinate locations above. Can you determine the layout of the viewports by reading the coordinate values? Figure 4-5 shows the coordinate values of the viewport configuration saved as FIRST.

Unwanted viewport configurations can be removed. Select the **VPORTS** command and then enter the **Delete** option as follows:

```
Command: VPORTS⏎
Save/Restore/Delete/Join/SIngle/?/2/⟨3⟩/4: D⏎
?/Name of viewport configuration to delete: FIRST⏎ (enter ? to list the names)
Command:
```

Figure 4-5.
The viewport coordinate
values of the configuration
named FIRST. The ID
numbers are also identified.

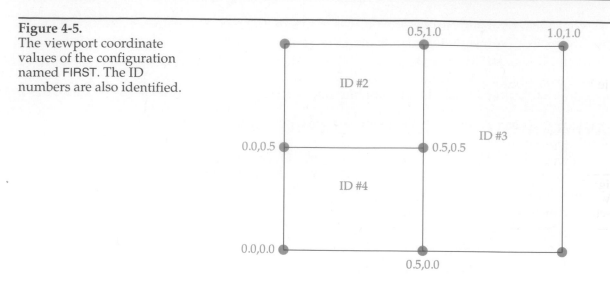

NOTE

Notice in the coordinate location listing on the previous page that the corners of only one viewport are listed under the Configuration FIRST: heading. These numbers represent the large viewport only. Previous releases of AutoCAD list the coordinates for all viewports here. The *AutoCAD Users Guide* indicates that all viewport coordinates *should* be listed here. The omission of the coordinates for the other viewports from this list may be the result of a bug in the software.

PROFESSIONAL
TIP

Each viewport can have its own viewpoint, zoom scale, limits, grid spacing, and snap setting. Specify the drawing aids in all viewports before saving the configuration. When a viewport is restored, all settings are restored as well.

ALTERING THE CURRENT VIEWPORT CONFIGURATION

You can join two adjacent viewports to form a single one. This process is quicker than trying to create an entirely new configuration. However, the two viewports must form a rectangle when joined, Figure 4-6. The **Join** option of the **VPORTS** command is used to join viewports.

When you enter the command, AutoCAD first prompts you for the *dominant viewport*. All aspects of the dominant are used in the new viewport. These aspects include limits, grid, and snap settings. Pick **Tiled Viewports** from the **View** pull-down menu, then pick **Join** to join two viewports or use the following command sequence:

        Command: **VPORTS**↵
        Save/Restore/Delete/Join/SIngle/?/2/⟨3⟩/4: **J**↵
        Select dominant viewport ⟨current⟩: (select the viewport or press [Enter])
        Select viewport to join: (select the other viewport)
        Regenerating drawing.
        Command:

The two viewports selected are eliminated and joined into a single viewport. If you select two viewports that do not form a rectangle, AutoCAD returns this message:

The selected viewports do not form a rectangle.
Select dominant viewport ⟨*current*⟩:

The screen can also be restored to a single viewport. To do so, select the **SIngle** option of the **VPORTS** command as follows:

Command: **VPORTS.**↵
Save/Restore/Delete/Join/SIngle/?/2/⟨3⟩/4: **SI**↵
Command:

Figure 4-6.
Two viewports can be joined if they will form a rectangle. If the two viewports will *not* form a rectangle, they cannot be joined.

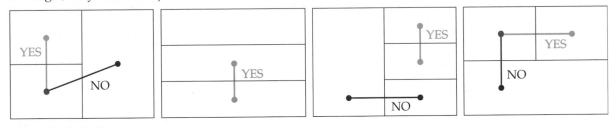

**PROFESSIONAL
TIP**

Create only the number of viewports and viewport configurations needed to construct your drawing. Too many viewports on-screen reduces the size of the images and may confuse you. It helps to zoom each view so that it fills the viewport.

EXERCISE 4-1

❐ Start a new drawing. Select the **VPORTS** command, create the following viewports, and save them with the viewport name indicated:

Number of Viewports	Configuration	Name
1		ONE
2	Vertical	TWO
3	Above	THREE-A
3	Left	THREE-L
3	Right	THREE-R
4		FOUR

❐ List the viewports to be sure all were saved.
❐ Restore each named configuration.
❐ Restore configuration THREE-A and join the two small viewports. Save the new configuration under the name TWO. Answer YES when asked if you want to replace the existing configuration named TWO.
❐ Restore configuration TWO. It should have two horizontal viewports.
❐ Delete configuration THREE-A.
❐ Restore configuration THREE-L. Set the grid and snap spacing in each viewport to different values. Save the configuration as THREE-L.
❐ Select the **SIngle** option in the **VPORTS** command and press [Enter].
❐ Restore configuration THREE-L. Check the drawing aids in each viewport to be sure they have the same values previously set.
❐ Save your work as A:EX4-1.

DRAWING IN MULTIPLE VIEWPORTS

For 2D drawings, viewports allow you to display a view of the entire drawing plus views showing portions of the drawing. This is similar to the **VIEW** command, except you can have several views on-screen at once. Adjust the zoom scale to a different area of the drawing in each viewport. Save the viewport configuration if you plan to continue working with it during other drawing sessions. You can create an unlimited number of viewport configurations.

Viewports are also a powerful aid when constructing 3D models. You can specify different viewpoints in each port and see the model take shape as you draw. A model can be constructed quicker because you can switch from one viewport to another while drawing and editing the object.

The following example gives the steps to construct a simple 3D part using two viewports. Refer to Figure 4-7 as you go through the following command sequence:

```
Command: VPORTS⏎
Save/Restore/Delete/Join/SIngle/?/2/⟨3⟩/4: 2⏎
Horizontal/⟨Vertical⟩: ⏎
Regenerating drawing.
Command: (make sure the right viewport is active) LINE⏎
From point: 3,2⏎
To point: @7,0⏎
To point: @0,5⏎
To point: @−7,0⏎
To point: C⏎
Command: CIRCLE⏎
3P/2P/TTR/⟨Center point⟩: @3.5,−2.5⏎
Diameter/⟨Radius⟩: 1⏎
Command: VPOINT⏎
Rotate/⟨View point⟩ ⟨0.0000,0.0000,1.0000⟩: −1,−1,1⏎
Regenerating drawing.
Command: ZOOM⏎
All/Center/Dynamic/Extents/Left/Previous/Vmax/Window/⟨Scale(X/XP)⟩: .9X⏎
Command: (make the left viewport active) PAN⏎
Displacement: @⏎
Second point: @6,8⏎
Command: ZOOM⏎
All/Center/Dynamic/Extents/Left/Previous/Vmax/Window/⟨Scale(X/XP)⟩: 2X⏎
Command:
```

The screen now displays two viewports. The left viewport contains a top view of the part and the right viewport displays the part in a 3D viewpoint, Figure 4-7.

The next step is to copy the shape in the left viewport up 2 units along the Z axis. This can be done using the **COPY** command and XY filters, or with grips. For this example, grips are used. Select the entire object in the left viewport so that all grips on the rectangle and circle are displayed. Pick any one of the grips to make it hot.

```
** STRETCH **
⟨Stretch to point⟩/Base point/Copy/Undo/eXit:⏎
** MOVE **
⟨Move to point⟩/Base point/Copy/Undo/eXit: C⏎
** MOVE (multiple) **
⟨Move to point⟩/Base point/Copy/Undo/eXit: @0,0,2⏎
** MOVE (multiple) **
⟨Move to point⟩/Base point/Copy/Undo/eXit:⏎
Command:
```

The screen now appears as shown in Figure 4-8. The right viewport shows the result of the copy.

Figure 4-7.
The screen is divided into two viewports. The top view appears in the left viewport and a 3D view appears in the right viewport.

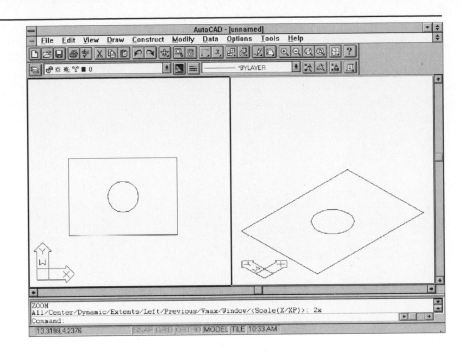

Figure 4-8.
The copied shapes appear automatically in the 3D (right) viewport.

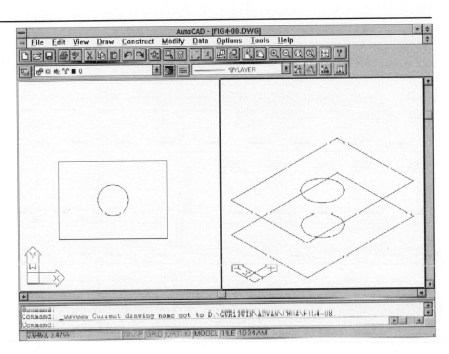

The final step is to connect the corners of the object with vertical lines. Use **LINE** command with the **Endpoint** running osnap. Draw the lines in the right viewport.

```
Command: OSNAP↵
Object snap modes: END↵
Command: MULTIPLE LINE↵
From point: (pick the corner on upper shape)
To point: (pick the adjacent corner on the lower shape)
To point: ↵
LINE From point: (continue joining the corners)
```

Press [Esc] to cancel the command when all corners have been joined. The completed object appears in Figure 4-9.

Figure 4-9.
The corners of the upper and
lower planes are connected
with lines in the right
viewport to create
the wireframe.

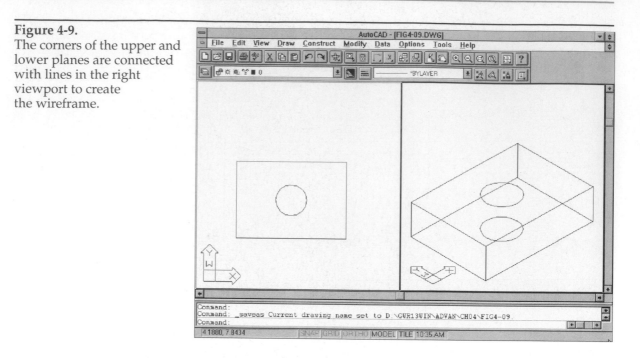

EXERCISE 4-2

❏ Start a new drawing called EX4-2.
❏ Create a viewport configuration with two ports arranged horizontally. Save it as **TWO**.
❏ Construct the object shown below. Draw a top view in the upper viewport. Display a 3D viewpoint in the lower viewport. Connect the corners in the lower viewport.
❏ Save the drawing as A:EX4-2.

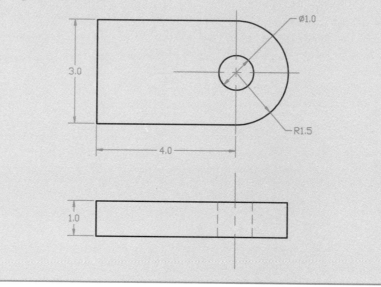

**PROFESSIONAL
TIP**

     Displaying saved viewport configurations can be automated by using custom menus. Custom menus are easy to create. If a standard naming convention is used, these named viewports can be saved with prototype drawings. This creates a consistent platform that all students or employees can use.

WORKING WITH THE UCS IN VIEWPORTS

When an object is displayed in a multiple viewport configuration, the UCS is the same in all viewports. For example, notice in Figure 4-10 that the UCS icon is the same in all views. You cannot have a variety of UCSs set in different viewports.

When working on a surface, it may help if the viewpoint is plan to the surface. Simply use the **PLAN** command in the appropriate viewport to do this. Figure 4-11 shows the upper left viewport plan to the current UCS. If you change the UCS, the viewport with the plan view has a *broken pencil* icon in the lower-left corner. See Figure 4-12. The broken pencil icon indicates that the view is plan to any UCS other than the current one.

Figure 4-10.
Only one UCS can be set at a time, and it applies to all viewports.

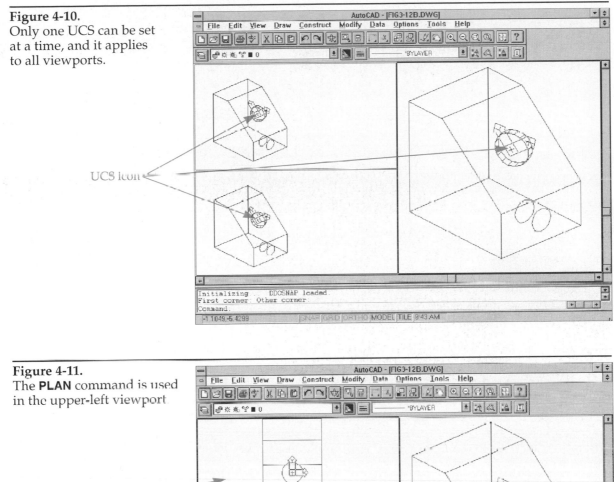

UCS icon

Figure 4-11.
The **PLAN** command is used in the upper-left viewport

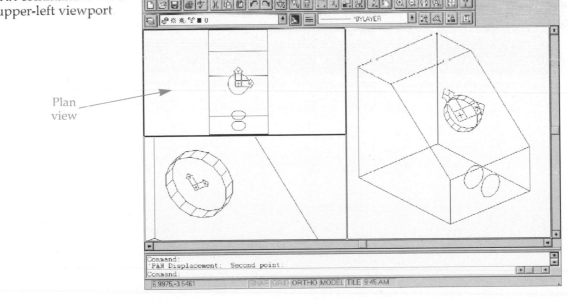

Plan view

Figure 4-12.
The broken pencil icon means that the view is plan to a UCS other than the current one.

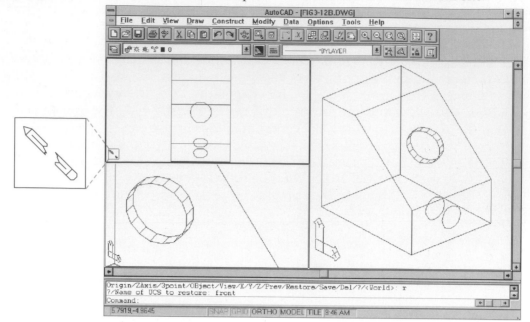

You can set up one viewport so that it is always plan to the current UCS. To do so, set the **UCSFOLLOW** variable to a value other than zero as follows:

Command: **UCSFOLLOW**↵
New value for UCSFOLLOW ⟨0⟩: **1**↵
Command:

Figure 4-13 shows the upper left viewport with **UCSFOLLOW** set to 1 after the current UCS was changed. Keep in mind that if you change the **UCSFOLLOW** variable in a viewport, the display will not change to a plan view until the UCS is changed.

Figure 4-13.
When the **UCSFOLLOW** variable is turned on in a viewport, that viewport will always display a view plan to the current UCS.

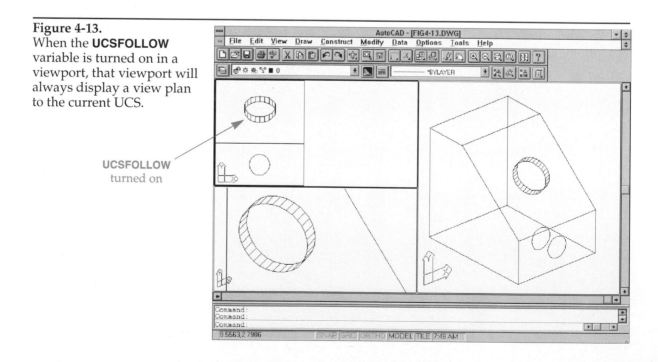

UCSFOLLOW
turned on

**PROFESSIONAL
TIP**

The **UCSFOLLOW** variable can be a very useful tool when turned on. This feature can be even more useful if the origin of the UCS is the lower-left corner, or some other meaningful reference point, of the plan surface.

REDRAWING AND REGENERATING VIEWPORTS

The **REDRAW** and **REGEN** commands affect the current viewport only. To redraw or regenerate all viewports at the same time, use the **REDRAWALL** or **REGENALL** commands. These commands can be selected from the **View** pull-down menu or typed at the **Command:** prompt. The **Redraw View** or the **Redraw All** buttons can also be selected from the **Standard** toolbar.

The **QTEXT** display feature is controlled by the **REGEN** command. Therefore, if you are working with text in viewports, be sure to use the **REGENALL** command in order for **QTEXT** to affect all viewports.

CHAPTER TEST

Write your answers in the spaces provided.

1. Identify the purpose of the **VPORTS** command. _____

_____

2. How do you name a configuration of viewports? _____

_____

3. What is the purpose of naming a configuration of viewports? _____

_____

4. Name the system variable that retains the number of viewports that can be active at one time. _____

5. What is the total number of viewports allowed with the **VPORTS** command? How many viewports are practical? _____

6. How can a named viewport be redisplayed on the screen? _____

_____

7. How can a list of the named viewports be displayed on the screen? _____

_____

8. What relationship must two viewports have before they can be joined? _____

_____

9. What is the significance of the dominant viewport when two viewports are joined? ____

_____

10. List three ways to switch active viewport. _____

_____

DRAWING PROBLEMS

General

1. Construct a prototype drawing, or edit existing prototypes, to include the following viewport configurations with the names given.

Configuration	Name
Two viewports horizontal	TWO-H
Two viewports vertical	TWO-V
Three viewports—large on right	THREE-LR
Three viewports—large on left	THREE-LL
Three viewports—large above	THREE-LA
Three viewports—large below	THREE-LB
Three viewports vertical	THREE-V

General

2. Choose one of the problems in Chapter 3 and construct it using viewports. Use one of your prototype drawings from Problem 1. Save the drawing as P4-2.

AutoCAD R13

Chapter 5

Three-Dimensional Surface Modeling Techniques

Learning objectives

After completing this chapter, you will be able to:
- ❍ Construct a 3D surface mesh.
- ❍ Create a variety of surface-modeled objects using the **EDGESURF**, **TABSURF**, **RULESURF**, and **REVSURF** commands.
- ❍ Construct a detailed surface model using multiple viewports.

There are several ways to construct surface models using AutoCAD. The method you use will depend on the object you are creating. A surface mesh, or "patch," can be created using the **3DMESH** or **PFACE** command. The **EDGESURF** command creates a surface mesh using four edges joined at the endpoints. The **RULESURF** command creates a mesh of ruled surfaces between two curves. The **TABSURF** command creates a tabulated-surface mesh using a curve and a specified direction to extend the surface. The **REVSURF** command creates a surface of revolution. A surface of revolution is a profile rotated around an axis.

3D MESH TECHNIQUES

AutoCAD User's Guide **11**

Three-dimensional face meshes are used to create surface models that cannot be constructed using surfacing commands. There are three types of 3D face meshes. These are planar mesh, 3D mesh, pface, and surface patch.

A *planar mesh* is made up of four sides. The corners can have different Z values. However, a mesh lies in a single plane. In other words, a mesh is "flat." A mesh is created with **MESH** option of the **3D** command.

A *3D mesh* is a polygon mesh composed of 3D faces. This type of mesh is not restricted to a single plane. The **3DMESH** command is used to create a 3D mesh.

A *pface mesh*, or *polyface mesh,* is a general polygon mesh of 3D faces. Each face can have an infinite number of vertices and can occupy a different plane. The **PFACE** command is used to create a polyface mesh.

The fourth type of mesh is a *surface patch.* This is created with the **EDGESURF** command. The **EDGESURF** command is discussed later in this chapter.

Constructing a 3D mesh

The **3DMESH** command creates a 3D mesh. The mesh is defined in rows and columns. The *N value* defines the number of rows. An N value of three produces two rows. The *M value* defines the number of columns. An M value of four produces three columns. See Figure 5-1. When using the **3DMESH** command, each vertex in the mesh must be given an XYZ coordinate location. The vertices of the mesh are its definition points. A mesh must have between 2 and 256 vertices in both directions.

When prompting for coordinates, the M and N location of the current vertex is indicated. See the command sequence below. The values for each vertex of the first M column must be entered. Then, values for the second, third, and remaining M columns must be entered.

Figure 5-1.
A 3D polygon mesh is similar
to a grid of XY coordinates.
M values define columns and
N values define rows. This
example has an M value of
4 and an N value of 3.

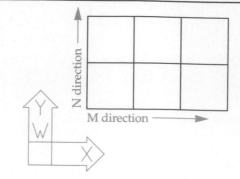

Use the following command sequence to get the feel for the **3DMESH** command. When complete, use **VPOINT** to view the mesh from different angles. The mesh should look like the one shown in Figure 5-2 after using **VPOINT**.

> Command: **3DMESH**⏎
> Mesh M size: **4**⏎
> Mesh N size: **3**⏎
> Vertex (0,0): **3,2,1**⏎
> Vertex (0,1): **3,3,1.5**⏎
> Vertex (0,2): **3,4,1**⏎
> Vertex (1,0): **4,2,.5**⏎
> Vertex (1,1): **4,3,1**⏎
> Vertex (1,2): **4,4,.5**⏎
> Vertex (2,0): **5,2,1.5**⏎
> Vertex (2,1): **5,3,1**⏎
> Vertex (2,2): **5,4,1.5**⏎
> Vertex (3,0): **6,2,2.5**⏎
> Vertex (3,1): **6,3,2**⏎
> Vertex (3,2): **6,4,2.5**⏎
> Command:

Figure 5-2.
A 3D polygon mesh. The M
value is 4 and the N value is 3.

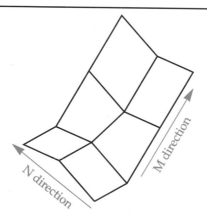

PROFESSIONAL TIP

The **3DMESH** command is not used often because it is tedious. However, AutoLISP programmers can create specialized meshes using this command.

Constructing a single-plane mesh

A *planar mesh* is a 3D mesh that lies a single plane. It has between 2 and 256 vertices in both M and N directions. To draw a planar mesh, pick **Surfaces** in the **Draw** pull-down menu. Then, pick **3D Objects...** from the cascading submenu. This displays the **3D Objects** dialog box. Pick **Mesh** from the list or pick the **Mesh** icon. You can also enter one of the following at the **Command:** prompt.

> Command: **AI_MESH**↵

or

> Command: **3D**↵
> Box/Cone/DIsh/DOme/Mesh/Pyramid/Sphere/Torus/Wedge: **M**↵

You are then asked for the four corners of the mesh and the number of vertices.

> First corner: **4,3**↵
> Second corner: **9,3**↵
> Third corner: **9,8**↵
> Fourth corner: **4,8**↵
> Mesh M size: **10**↵ *(one of the two lines representing the M direction appears as a dashed line)*
> Mesh N size: **8**↵ *(one of the two lines representing the N direction appears as a dashed line)*
> Command:

The resulting mesh is shown in Figure 5-3.

Figure 5-3.
A planar mesh has between 2 and 256 vertices in both directions.

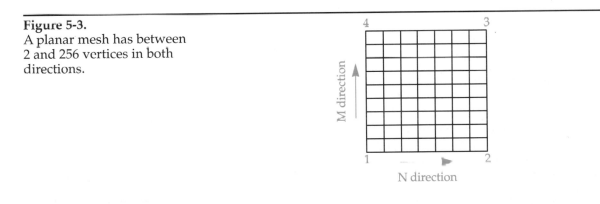

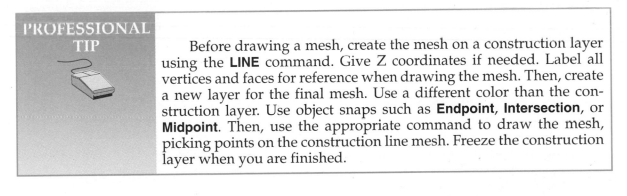

> Before drawing a mesh, create the mesh on a construction layer using the **LINE** command. Give Z coordinates if needed. Label all vertices and faces for reference when drawing the mesh. Then, create a new layer for the final mesh. Use a different color than the construction layer. Use object snaps such as **Endpoint**, **Intersection**, or **Midpoint**. Then, use the appropriate command to draw the mesh, picking points on the construction line mesh. Freeze the construction layer when you are finished.

Constructing a 3D polyface mesh

A general polygon mesh can be constructed using the **PFACE** command. This creates a mesh similar to the **3DFACE** command. However, you do not have to pick vertices twice that join another face. You can also create faces that have an infinite number of vertices, rather than the maximum of four specified by the **3DFACE** command. You can use the **PFACE** command to construct surfaces that cannot be "faced" using any of the standard surfacing commands. However, using this command is time-consuming, and is best suited for AutoLISP or ADS (Autodesk Development System) applications.

To create a pface mesh, first define all of the vertices for the mesh. Then, assign those vertices to a face. The face is then given a number and is composed of the vertices you assign to that face. While creating a pface, you can change the color, layer, or linetype by entering the **COLOR**, **LAYER**, or **LINETYPE** commands at the Face *n*, vertex *n*: prompt. The following example creates a pface mesh consisting of two faces. See Figure 5-4A. The first portion of the command defines all of the vertices of the two faces.

```
Command: PFACE↵
Vertex 1: 3,3↵
Vertex 2: 7,3↵
Vertex 3: 7,6↵
Vertex 4: 3,6↵
Vertex 5: 2,7,3↵
Vertex 6: 2,2,3↵
Vertex 7: 3,3↵
Vertex 8: ↵
```

The next sequence assigns vertices to face number 1.

```
Face 1, vertex 1: 1↵
Face 1, vertex 2: 2↵
Face 1, vertex 3: 3↵
Face 1, vertex 4: 4↵
Face 1, vertex 5: ↵
```

Now you can change the color of the second face without exiting the command.

```
Face 2, vertex 1: COLOR↵
New color ⟨BYLAYER⟩: GREEN↵
```

The last sequence assigns vertices to face number 2.

```
Face 2, vertex 1: 4↵
Face 2, vertex 2: 5↵
Face 2, vertex 3: 6↵
Face 2, vertex 4: 1↵
Face 2, vertex 5: ↵
Face 3, vertex 1: ↵
```

Now use the **VPOINT** and **HIDE** commands to view the faces.

```
Command: VPOINT↵
Rotate/⟨View point⟩ ⟨current⟩: –1,–1,.75↵
Regenerating drawing.
Command: HIDE↵
Regenerating drawing.
Command:
```

The pface mesh first appears as a wireframe. However, after using the **HIDE** command, the 3D faces can be clearly seen. See Figure 5-4B.

Figure 5-4.
A—Creating a pface mesh with two faces. B—When you use **HIDE**, you can see that each face is a surface.

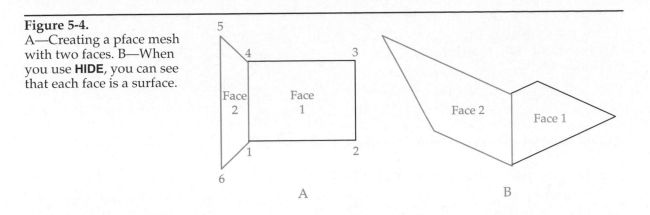

Polygon mesh variations

A polygon mesh created with **3DMESH** can be smoothed using the **PEDIT** command. The smoothness of the surface depends on the value set in the **SURFTYPE** system variable:

SURFTYPE setting	Surface type
5	Quadratic B-spline
6	Cubic B-spline
8	Bézier surface

Before smoothing a polygon mesh, set the **SURFU** (M direction) and **SURFV** (N direction) system variables larger than the M and N values. If you do not change these values, the resulting surface may have less 3D faces than the original. Figure 5-5 illustrates the different types of surfaces that can be created using **SURFTYPE** and **PEDIT** smoothing.

Figure 5-5.
A—The **SPLFRAME** variable set to 1. B—A quadratic B-spline (**SURFTYPE** = 5). C—A cubic B-spline (**SURFTYPE** = 6). D—A Bézier surface (**SURFTYPE** = 8).

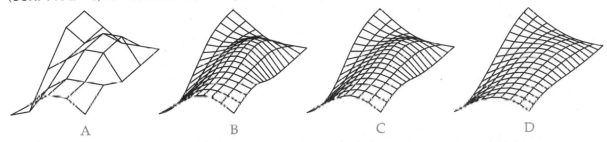

Constructing enclosed surfaces with EDGESURF

The **EDGESURF** command allows you to construct a surface mesh between four edges. The edges can be lines, polylines, splines, or arcs. The endpoints of the objects must meet precisely. However, a closed polyline *cannot* be used. The four objects can be selected in any order. The resulting surface is a smooth mesh, similar to one created with the **MESH** command. The *AutoCAD User's Guide* calls this type of surface mesh a Coons patch.

The number of faces are determined by the variables **SURFTAB1** (M direction) and **SURFTAB2** (N direction). To draw an edge surface, pick **Surfaces** and **Edge Surface** from the **Draw** pull-down menu, or pick the **Edge Surface** button in the **Surfaces** toolbar. You can also enter the following on the **Command:** line:

```
Command: EDGESURF↵
Select edge 1: (pick edge 1)
Select edge 2: (pick edge 2)
Select edge 3: (pick edge 3)
Select edge 4: (pick edge 4)
```

Figure 5-6.
A completed surface patch
with both **SURFTAB**
variables set to 12.

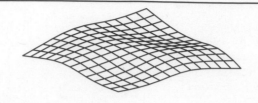

A completed surface patch with the **SURFTAB** variables set to 12 is shown in Figure 5-6.

Creating a surface mesh with RULESURF

A surface mesh can be constructed between two objects using the **RULESURF** command. This mesh is called a *ruled surface.* The two objects can be lines, arcs, circles, polylines, splines, enclosed objects, or a single plane. The two objects must both be either open or closed. A variety of constructions are shown in Figure 5-7. A point can be used with any object to create constructions such as those shown in Figure 5-8. A ruled surface is useful for surfacing holes in parts, exterior fillets (rounds), interior fillets, or flat surfaces of various shapes.

Figure 5-7.
Many different objects
can be used to create
a ruled surface.

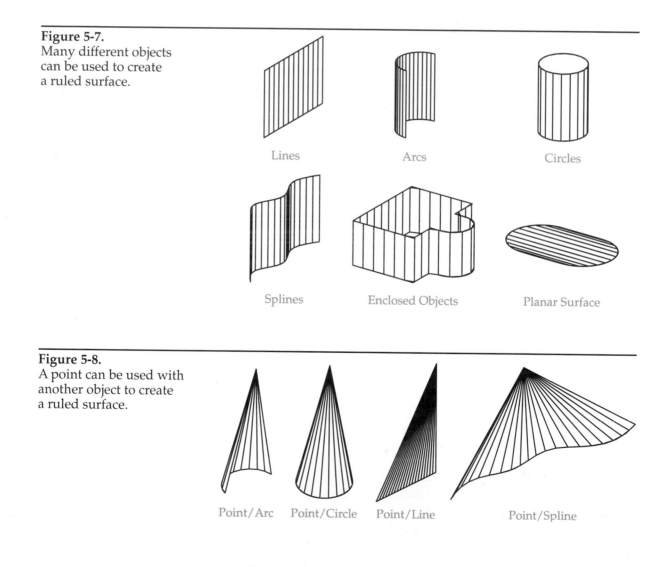

Lines   Arcs   Circles

Splines   Enclosed Objects   Planar Surface

Figure 5-8.
A point can be used with
another object to create
a ruled surface.

Point/Arc   Point/Circle   Point/Line   Point/Spline

PROFESSIONAL TIP

When constructing holes in surface modeled objects, always draw the original circles on a separate construction, or wireframe layer. After the hole has been surfaced with the **RULESURF** command, turn off or freeze the construction layer. If you do not turn off the construction layer, the inside of the hole will not be displayed when **HIDE** is used or the object is rendered.

Select **RULESURF** by picking **Surfaces** and **Ruled Surface** from the **Draw** pull-down menu, or pick the **Ruled Surface** button in the **Surfaces** toolbar. You can also use the **Command:** line as follows:

Command: **RULESURF**↵
Select first defining curve: *(pick first object)*
Select second defining curve: *(pick second object)*
Command:

When using **RULESURF** to create a surface between two objects, such as those shown in Figure 5-9A, it is important to select both objects near the same end. If you pick near opposite ends of each object, the resulting figure may not be what you want, Figure 5-9B. The correctly surfaced object is shown in Figure 5-9C.

Figure 5-9.
When creating a ruled surface, be sure to select the objects near the same end.
A—The original objects.
B—If you pick incorrectly, the surface is "twisted."
C—The surface using the correct pick points.

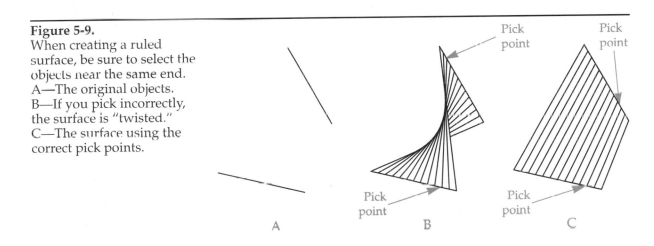

Constructing tabulated surfaces with **TABSURF**

A *tabulated surface* is similar to a ruled surface. However, only one entity is needed. This entity is called the *path curve*. Lines, arcs, circles, 2D polylines, and 3D polylines can all be used. A line called the *direction vector* is also required. This line indicates the direction and length of the tabulated surface. AutoCAD finds the endpoint of the direction vector closest to your pick point. It sets the direction toward the opposite end of the vector line. The tabulated surface follows the direction and length of the direction vector. The **SURFTAB1** system variable controls the number of "steps" that are constructed. Figure 24-10 shows the difference the pick point makes when assigning the direction.

Command: **TABSURF**↵
Select path curve: *(pick the curve)*
Select direction vector: *(pick correct end of vector)*
Command:

Figure 5-10.
The point you pick on the
direction vector determines
in which direction the
tabulated surface is
"extruded."

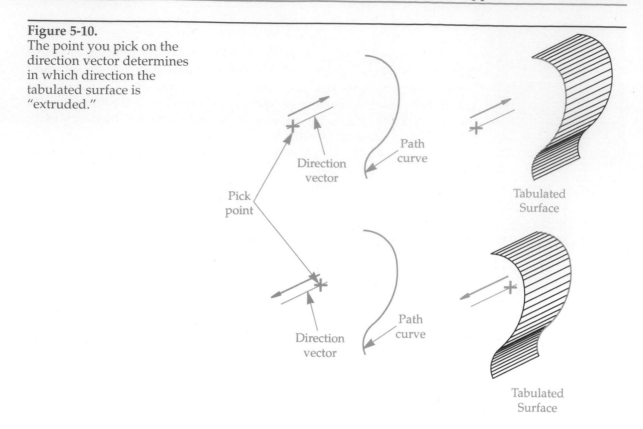

Construct revolved surfaces with REVSURF

With the **REVSURF** command, you can draw a profile and then rotate that profile around an axis to create a symmetrical object. This is a powerful tool and will greatly assist anyone who needs to draw a symmetrical three-dimensional shape. The profile, or *path curve*, can be drawn using lines, arcs, circles, 2D polylines, or 3D polylines. The rotation axis can be a line or open polyline. Notice the initial layout of the revolved surface in Figure 5-11.

Select **REVSURF** by picking **Surfaces** and **Revolved Surface** from the **Draw** pull-down menu, or pick the **Revolved Surface** button in the **Surfaces** toolbar. You can also use the **Command:** line as follows:

```
Command: REVSURF↵
Select path curve: (pick the profile)
Select axis of revolution: (pick an axis line)
Start angle ⟨0⟩: ↵
Included angle (+ = ccw, − = cw) ⟨Full circle⟩: ↵
Command:
```

Figure 5-11.
A path curve (profile) and
an axis are needed to create
a revolved surface.

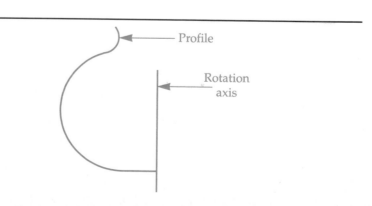

The Start angle: prompt allows you to specify an offset angle to start the surface revolution at. The Included angle: prompt lets you draw the object through 360° of rotation or just a portion of that. Figure 5-12 shows the rotated Figure 5-11 profile displayed with hidden lines removed.

The **SURFTAB1** and **SURFTAB2** system variables control the mesh of a revolved surface. The **SURFTAB1** value determines the number of segments in the direction of rotation around the axis. The **SURFTAB2** value divides the path curve into segments of equal size. The **REVSURF** command is powerful because it can create a symmetrical surface using any profile. Figure 5-13 illustrates additional examples of **REVSURF** constructions.

Figure 5-12.
The revolved surface created with the profile and axis in Figure 5-11.

Figure 5-13.
Revolved surfaces created with a variety of profiles.

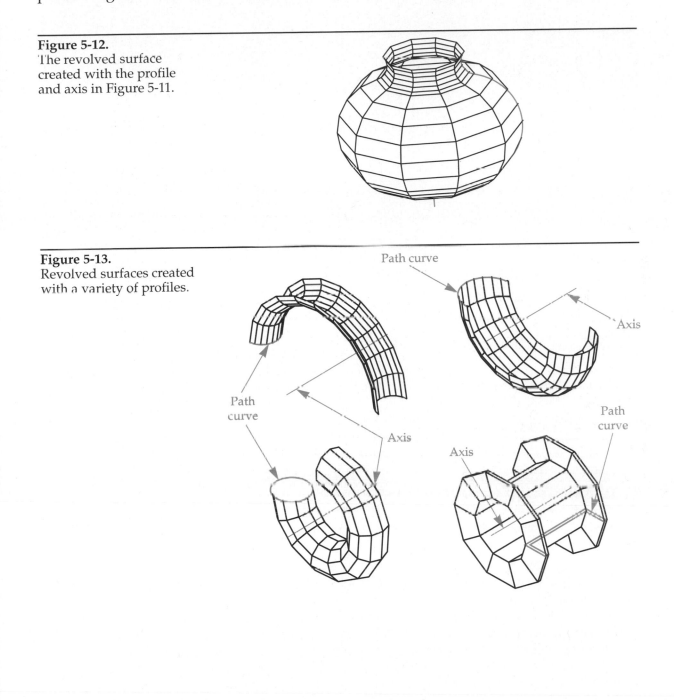

EXERCISE 5-1

❏ Begin a new drawing and name it EX5-1.
❏ Draw the objects shown below and display them in a 3D viewpoint.
❏ Set the **SURFTAB1** and **SURFTAB2** variables to values of your choice.
❏ Create the surface model constructions as indicated.
❏ Save your drawing as EX5-1.

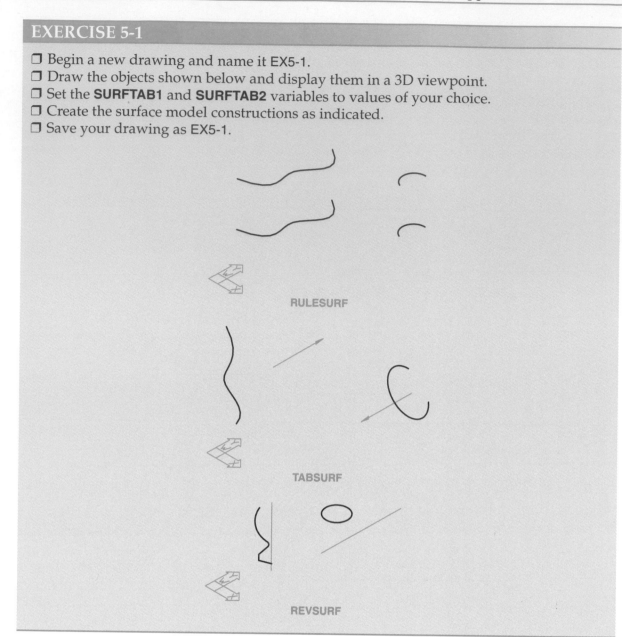

SURFACING AROUND HOLES

AutoCAD cannot automatically create surfacing around a hole. A series of steps is required to do this. A common method is to use the **RULESURF** and **3DFACE** commands to create the required surfaces.

For example, the object in Figure 5-14A must be surfaced. This object has a hole through it. To surface the hole, first construct two 180° arcs where the hole is. Use a construction layer. Next, use **RULESURF** to create the surface connecting the large arc and the hole. Use **RULESURF** again to create the surface connecting the arc and the left end of the object. The two remaining surfaces can be created using **3DFACE**. The result is shown in Figure 5-14B.

Another example is surfacing the space between two holes, as shown in Figure 5-15A. Again, create arcs where the circles are. Then, use **RULESURF** to create the surface connecting the two inside arcs. Also use **RULESURF** to create the surface between the outer arcs and the outside edges. Use **3DFACE** to surface the remaining faces. The surfaced object is shown in Figure 5-15B.

Figure 5-14.
AutoCAD cannot automatically surface a hole. To do so, you must use a combination of ruled surfaces and 3D faces.

Figure 5-15.
Surfacing an object with two holes.

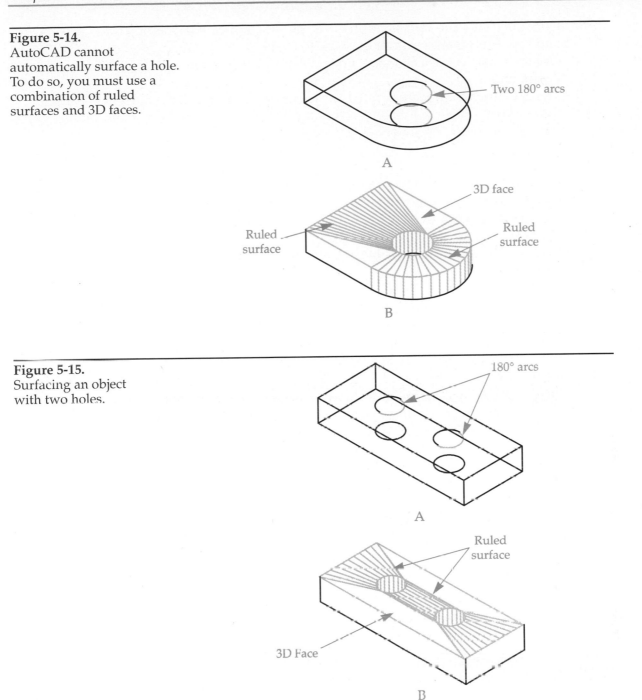

THINGS TO CONSIDER WHEN WORKING IN 3D

Working in 3D, like working in 2D drawings, requires careful planning. The following suggestions should help you work efficiently and effectively in 3D.

Planning

✓ Determine the type of finished drawing you need. Then, choose the 3D construction method that will work best.

✓ An isometric drawing is the quickest and most versatile method for objects needing only one pictorial view. Ellipses and arcs are easy to work with in isometric drawings.

✓ Objects and layouts that need to be viewed from different angles should be constructed using 3D commands.

✓ Construct only the details needed for the function of the drawing. This saves space and time, and makes the object easier to visualize.

✓ Use the osnap modes **Midpoint**, **Endpoint**, and **Intersection** with the **LINE** and **3DFACE** commands.

✓ The grid always appears parallel to the current UCS and at the current elevation.

✓ Create layers having different colors for different entities. Turn them on and off as needed, or freeze those not being used.

Editing

✓ Use **CHPROP** or **DDMODIFY** to change color, layer, linetype, or thickness of 3D objects.

✓ Use the **STRETCH** command or grips in the 3D view to change only one dimension of the object. Use the **SCALE** command in the 3D view to change the size of the entire object proportionally.

✓ Do as much editing as possible in a 3D viewpoint.

Displaying

✓ The **HIDE** command can help you visualize complex drawings.

✓ For quick viewpoints use the tablet menu RENDER/VIEW/UCS/BLOCK/LAYER section.

✓ Use the **VIEW** command to create and save 3D views for quicker pictorial displays. This avoids having to use **VPOINT** or **DVIEW** commands.

✓ Freeze unwanted layers before displaying objects in 3D, and especially before using **HIDE**. Simply turning off layers may cause invisible entities to block out portions of other objects. This is because AutoCAD regenerates layers that are off.

✓ Before using **HIDE**, zoom in on the part of a drawing to display. This saves time in regenerating the view because only the entities that are visible are regenerated.

✓ Objects that touch or intersect may have to be moved slightly if the display removes a line you need to see or plot.

CONSTRUCTING A SURFACE MODEL

The following tutorial shows how surface modeling can be used to create an object composed of several different shapes. A twelve-button digitizer puck will be constructed. See Figure 5-16. If possible, enter the commands on your workstation as you go through this example. It is not necessary to complete this tutorial in one drawing session. Complete what you can, save your work, and return when you have available time.

Figure 5-16.
A 3D surface model of
a twelve-button puck.

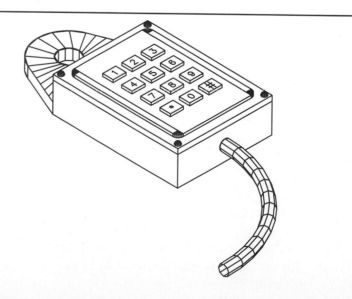

> **NOTE** Follow the instructions in this tutorial exactly. Once you are experienced with these commands, experiment on your own with different ways of using them.

Drawing setup

You should plan your work carefully before beginning any 3D drawing. Remember the basic rule for creating anything with a computer: Draw the least amount of elements that can be used to complete the project. Also, use the following guidelines.

✓ Let the computer do as much work as possible.
✓ Use predrawn shapes and create blocks when possible.
✓ Save display configurations, such as views and viewports.
✓ As an optional step, make slides of each step of your work for later reference. Slides are covered in Chapter 30 of *AutoCAD and its Applications—Basics, Release 13 for Windows.*

Begin your drawing by setting units as decimal and limits to 18,12. Set the grid spacing to .5 and snap spacing to .25. Then, create the following layers with the color indicated:

Layer Name	Color
BODY	red
BODY-CAP	white
BUTTONS	magenta
BUTTON1	magenta
BUTTON2	blue
CABLE	green
CONSTR	blue
EDGESURF	green
EYEPIECE	yellow
EYESURF	yellow
FACE1	green
FACE2	cyan
NUMBERS	cyan
SCREWS	red

Using 3D shapes

The individual parts of the digitizer puck are shown in Figure 5-17. The first step is to create a box as a basic 3D building block. This block can then be used for at least three of the parts on the puck. However, rather than drawing the box as a wireframe and adding 3D faces to it, you can use the 3D shape **Box**. Set the current layer to 0. Pick **3D Objects...** from the **3D Surfaces** submenu in the **Draw** pull-down menu. Then, pick **3D Box** in the **3D Objects** dialog box, Figure 5-18.

> **PROFESSIONAL TIP** 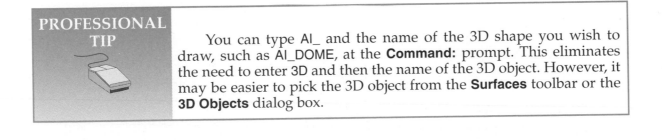 You can type AI_ and the name of the 3D shape you wish to draw, such as AI_DOME, at the **Command:** prompt. This eliminates the need to enter 3D and then the name of the 3D object. However, it may be easier to pick the 3D object from the **Surfaces** toolbar or the **3D Objects** dialog box.

Figure 5-17.
The components needed
to make the puck.

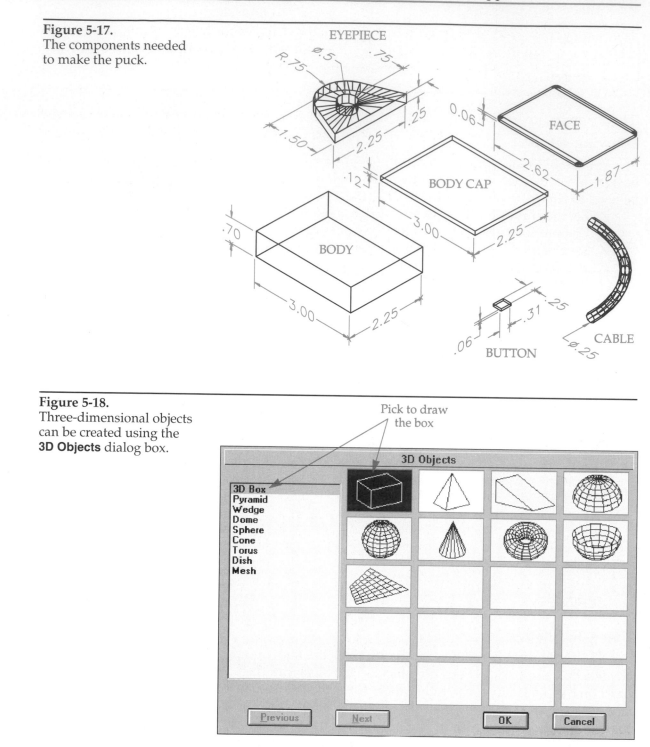

Figure 5-18.
Three-dimensional objects
can be created using the
3D Objects dialog box.

Box

The **BOX** command lets you construct a 3D box or cube. You must provide the location of one corner, the length and width of the box, and the rotation angle around the Z axis at the corner. Enter dimensions of the box at the keyboard or pick them with your pointing device.

> Command: *(pick the box in the* **3D Objects** *dialog box and pick the* **OK** *button)*
> Command: ai_box
> Corner of box: **3,3**↵
> Length: **1**↵
> Cube/⟨Width⟩: **C**↵
> Rotation angle about Z axis: **0**↵

The **Cube** option draws a cube with the dimension entered at the Length: prompt. The box is displayed in plan view after it is created. Use the **VPOINT** command to look at the box in 3D.

> Command: **VPOINT**↵
> Rotate/⟨View point⟩ ⟨*current*⟩: **–1,–1,1**↵

The box appears to be a wireframe, but it is actually a single entity composed of 3D faces. Use the **HIDE** command and you can see that it is a surface model. Figure 5-19 shows an example of a box.

　　Next, use the **BLOCK** command to make a block of the cube. Name it BOX. You can do this in the 3D display. Pick one of the corners as an insertion point using the **Endpoint** osnap, Figure 5-20.

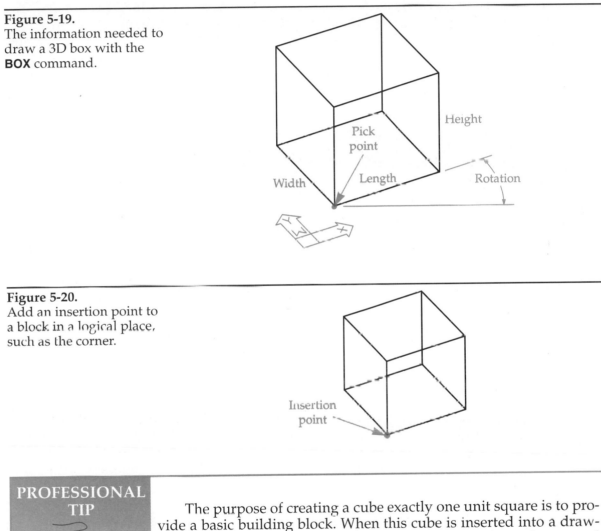

Figure 5-19.
The information needed to draw a 3D box with the **BOX** command.

Figure 5-20.
Add an insertion point to a block in a logical place, such as the corner.

PROFESSIONAL TIP

　　The purpose of creating a cube exactly one unit square is to provide a basic building block. When this cube is inserted into a drawing as a block, exact dimensions of a box or rectangle can be entered as scale factors, thus creating the required shape. This basic building block can be used for anything from mechanical parts to dimensional lumber or plywood. Use your imagination.

Inserting a 3D block

　　The block can now be inserted into the drawing to create the body of the puck. Change the current layer to BODY. Return the display to the plan view. Use the **INSERT** command as follows to insert the BOX block:

```
Command: INSERT ↵
Block name (or ?): BOX ↵
  Insertion point: (pick a point) X scale factor ⟨1⟩ / Corner / XYZ: X ↵
  X scale factor ⟨1⟩ / Corner: 2.25 ↵
  Y scale factor (default=X): 3 ↵
  Z scale factor (default=X): .7 ↵
Rotation angle ⟨0⟩: ↵
```

Now use the **ZOOM** command so the inserted block does not occupy the entire screen:

```
Command: ZOOM↵
All/Center/Dynamic/Extents/Left/Previous/Vmax/Window/⟨Scale(X/XP)⟩: .5X↵
```

The body of the puck is now in place with the required dimensions. As an alternative you can visually place and size a 3D block using the **Corner** option of the **INSERT** command. You might try it again for practice to see what the dynamic sizing of the **Corner** option provides.

Change the viewpoint back to –1,–1,1. Make layer 0 current and insert a copy of the BOX block. This time the cube is used to create a block for the puck's buttons. Insert the block as follows:

```
Command: INSERT↵
Block name (or ?) ⟨BOX⟩: ↵
  Insertion point: (pick a point) X scale factor ⟨1⟩ / Corner / XYZ: X↵
  X scale factor ⟨1⟩ / Corner: .31↵
  Y scale factor (default=X): .25↵
  Z scale factor (default=X): .06↵
Rotation angle ⟨0⟩: ↵
```

Now, make a block of the box you just inserted. Name it BUTTON and give it the same insertion point as shown in Figure 5-20. This block is used later to create an array of buttons. The next section shows how to construct a more detailed button having a curved surface.

Constructing a wireframe curved button (optional step)

The following example shows one way to create a wireframe model that you can place surface patches on using the **EDGESURF** command. A *surface patch* is a 3D mesh that creates a surface for a specified area. Begin construction of the button using the **LINE** command.

```
Command: LINE↵
From point: (pick a point)
To point: @.31,0↵
To point: @0,.25↵
To point: @−.31,0↵
To point: C↵
```

This creates the base of the button. Zoom in on the object so that it nearly fills the screen. This makes it easier to draw the vertical lines of the corners. Figure 5-21A shows what the drawing should look like. Use the **LINE** command to draw the corners as follows:

```
Command: LINE↵
From point: END↵
of (pick point 1)
To point: @0,0,.03↵
To point: ↵
Command: ↵
LINE From point: END↵
of (pick point 2)
To point: @0,0,.06↵
To point: ↵
```

The next step is to construct an arc connecting the tops of the two vertical lines. This arc represents the curved shape of the button surface. However, the UCS must be changed so that the X axis is the same direction as the line between points 1 and 2. This places the new UCS in the same plane where the arc will be drawn. See Figure 5-21B.

> Command: **UCS.**↵
> Origin/ZAxis/3point/Entity/View/X/Y/Z/Prev/Restore/Save/Del/?/⟨World⟩: **ZA.**↵
> Origin point ⟨0,0,0⟩: **END.**↵
> of *(pick point 2)*
> Point on positive portion of Z-axis ⟨defaults⟩: **@–1,0,0.**↵

If the UCS icon does not move to the new origin, use the **Origin** option of the **UCSICON** command to move the icon.

> Command: **UCSICON.**↵
> ON/OFF/All/Noorigin/ORigin/⟨ON⟩: **OR.**↵

The icon moves to the new origin. The UCS icon is a good reminder of the location of the origin of the current UCS.

Now the arc can be drawn. Refer to Figure 5-21C for the pick points of the arc. Use the **ARC** command as follows:

> Command: **ARC.**↵
> Center/⟨Start point⟩: **END.**↵
> of *(pick point 3)*
> Center/End/⟨Second point⟩: **E.**↵
> End point: **END.**↵
> of *(pick point 4)*
> Angle/Direction/Radius/⟨Center point⟩: **A.**↵
> Included angle: **20.**↵

The final steps are to copy the two vertical lines and the arc to the opposite end of the button, and to connect the top edges of the button with straight lines. The completed drawing should look like Figure 5-21D.

Figure 5-21.
Creating a wireframe of a curved button.

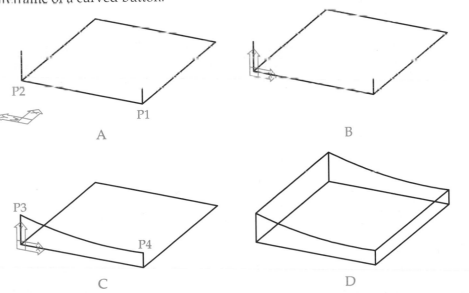

Creating edge defined surfaces

Curved surfaces having four sides can be created using the **EDGESURF** command. To use this command, select **Edge Surface** from the **Surfaces** submenu in the **Draw** pull-down menu. An *edge surface* is actually a matrix of 3D faces. The number of rows and columns of faces is controlled by the **SURFTAB1** and **SURFTAB2** system variables. Keep in mind that the greater the number of faces you have, the longer the regeneration time is, and the longer it takes to remove hidden lines using the **HIDE** command. Keep the **SURFTAB** values low for small objects.

PROFESSIONAL TIP

When working with 3D surfaces, determine the purpose of your drawing. How will you be viewing it? What other programs will you use to shade, render, or animate the object? If you will not be looking at certain sides of an object, do not apply surfacing to those sides. Also, avoid using large values for the **SURFTAB** variables.

First, set the **SURFTAB** variables. Then, set the current layer to BUTTON1 and create the first surface patch. Refer to Figure 5-22A.

```
Command: SURFTAB1↵
New value for SURFTAB1 ⟨current⟩: 6↵
Command: SURFTAB2↵
New value for SURFTAB2 ⟨current⟩: 2↵
Command: EDGESURF↵
Select edge 1: (pick edge 1)
Select edge 2: (pick edge 2)
Select edge 3: (pick edge 3)
Select edge 4: (pick edge 4)
```

The first line you pick is divided into six segments (**SURFTAB1**). The second edge is divided into two segments (**SURFTAB2**).

Next, copy the surface patch to the opposite end of the button. Your object should look like Figure 5-22C. Now, turn off layer BUTTON1 and make layer BUTTON2 current. This allows you to select the edges without the surface patch getting in the way. If you select the surface patch while defining a new surface patch, the message Entity not usable to define surface patch. appears on the command line.

Now, use **EDGESURF** to create the curved top surface of the button. Pick one of the ends that is already surfaced as the first edge. When the curved surface is completed, turn on layer BUTTON1, Figure 5-22D. Finally, use the **3DFACE** command on the two remaining sides. There is no need to use the **3DFACE** command on the bottom because it will sit on another surface.

This shape can now be saved as a block or wblocked as a file. It is also a good idea to save your drawing at this point. You will use the blocks you have created to complete the digitizer puck later.

Figure 5-22.
Surfacing the curved
button.

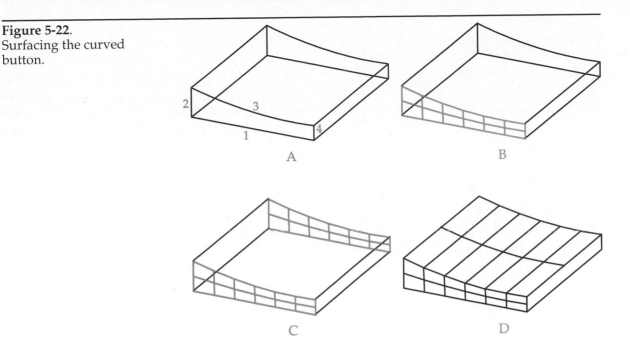

Using viewports to help create the puck

Viewports can be a great help in drawing 3D objects. Viewports will be used to help create the puck. To setup the viewports, first zoom out so that the entire body shape is displayed. Then, use the **UCS** command to return to the World Coordinate System.

Next, use the **VPORTS** command and the default options to display three views of the part, Figure 5-23. Create a pictorial view in the lower-left viewport. First, pick in the viewport to make it active. Then, continue as follows:

> Command: **VPOINT**↵
> Rotate/〈View point〉〈*current*〉: **–1,2,1**↵
> Command: **PAN**↵
> Displacement: (*pick the upper-left corner of the part*)
> Second point: (*pick at the upper midpoint of the viewport*)

Use the **ZOOM** command to magnify this view. Use **PAN** again if necessary to center the object in the viewport. Next, pick the upper-left viewport to make it active and create a plan view as follows:

> Command: **PLAN**↵
> 〈Current UCS〉/Ucs/World:↵

Figure 5-23.
Create a three-viewport
display to help you
draw the puck.

Figure 5-24.
Change the views so that
each viewport shows a
different view of the puck.

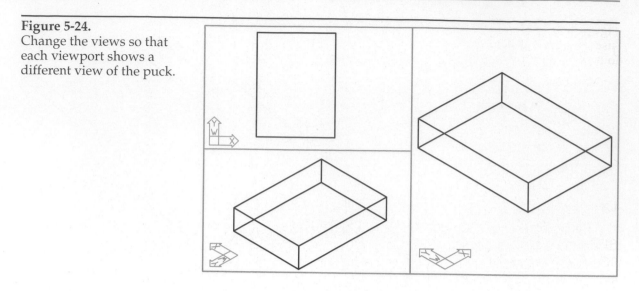

Use **ZOOM** and **PAN** to adjust all of the views as needed. The final arrangement of the viewports should be similar to Figure 5-24.

After you have adjusted all three viewports, study the orientation of the views in relation to the UCS icon. The ability to visualize the XYZ axes as they relate to the object is a must to understanding 3D construction and multiple view layouts.

An important tool when working with viewports is the ability to store a configuration. If you need the configuration again, it can simply be recalled instead of created over. Use the **Save** option of the **VPORTS** command to store a configuration. Save your current viewport configuration as follows:

> Command: **VPORTS**↵
> Save/Restore/Delete/Join/SIngle/?/2/⟨3⟩/4: **S**↵
> ?/Name for new viewport configuration: **THREE**↵

This viewport arrangement is now a named entity and can be recalled at any time. For example, use the **VPORTS** command and the **SIngle** option to return to one viewport. Then, use **VPORTS** again and the **Restore** option. Enter the name THREE for viewport configuration to restore. The configuration you just saved is restored.

Next, you need to add a "cap" to the puck body. First, set the current layer to BODY-CAP. Then, make the large viewport active. Insert the BOX block and attach it to the body at the insertion point shown in Figure 5-25A. Remember, the box is a one unit cube so you can enter the dimensions of the cap as scale factors.

> Command: **INSERT**↵
> Block name (or ?): **BOX**↵
>   Insertion point: *(pick the insertion point shown in Figure 5-25A)*
>   X scale factor ⟨1⟩ / Corner / XYZ: **X**↵
>   X scale factor ⟨1⟩ / Corner: **2.25**↵
>   Y scale factor (default=X): **3**↵
>   Z scale factor (default=X): **.12**↵
>   Rotation angle ⟨0⟩: ↵

The inserted body cap is shown in Figure 5-25B.

Figure 5-25.
Inserting the BOX block
to create the cap.

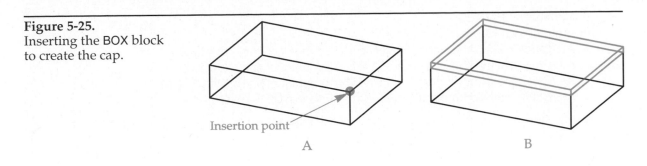

Insertion point

A   B

Using polylines in 3D

Next, you need to construct the face of the puck. Notice in Figure 5-17 that the face has filleted corners. You must construct it using a combination of polylines, ruled surfaces, and 3D faces. Since the face is placed on top of the body cap, create a UCS on that surface. Also, save the UCS for future use. Be sure the large viewport is active and use the following command sequence:

> Command: **UCS**↵
> Origin/ZAxis/3point/Entity/View/X/Y/Z/Prev/Restore/Save/Del/?/⟨World⟩: **0**↵
> Origin point ⟨0,0,0⟩: *(pick the top of the body cap above the insertion point)*
> Command: **UCSICON**↵
> ON/OFF/All/Noorigin/ORigin ⟨ON⟩: **A**↵ *(this applies the next option to all viewports)*
> ON/OFF/All/Noorigin/ORigin ⟨ON⟩: **OR**↵
> Command: **UCS**↵
> Origin/ZAxis/3point/Entity/View/X/Y/Z/Prev/Restore/Save/Del/?/⟨World⟩: **S**↵
> ?/Desired UCS name: **FACE**↵

Notice that the UCS icon is at the new origin in all three viewports. See Figure 5-26. With the UCS saved, it can be recalled at any time with the **Restore** option of the **UCS** command.

Begin drawing the puck face by making the upper-left viewport active. Change to the layer FACE1. If you return to a single viewport, the object will be larger. This may make it easier to work on. Since you have saved the three-viewport configuration, you can always go back to it later. Next, turn off any running osnaps. Then, use the **PLINE** command to draw the face. Be sure to use the **Close** option to complete the shape.

Figure 5-26.
Placing the UCS icon at the
origin helps you visualize
coordinates better.

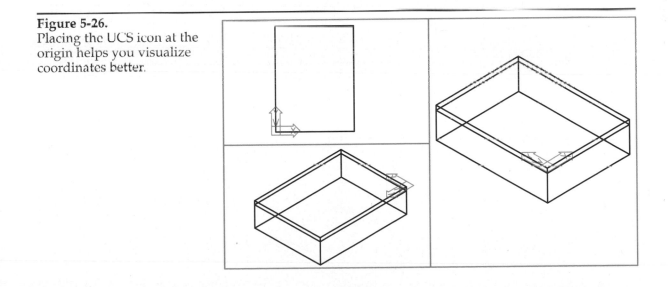

```
Command: PLINE↵
From point: .19,.19 ↵
Arc/Close/Halfwidth/Length/Undo/Width/⟨Endpoint of line⟩: @1.87,0 ↵
Arc/Close/Halfwidth/Length/Undo/Width/⟨Endpoint of line⟩: @0,2.62 ↵
Arc/Close/Halfwidth/Length/Undo/Width/⟨Endpoint of line⟩: @1.87⟨180 ↵
Arc/Close/Halfwidth/Length/Undo/Width/⟨Endpoint of line⟩: C ↵
```

If you returned to a single viewport, restore the three-viewport configuration. Your drawing should now look like Figure 5-27.

Figure 5-27.
Creating a wireframe of the face starts with drawing a closed polyline "on top" of the cap.

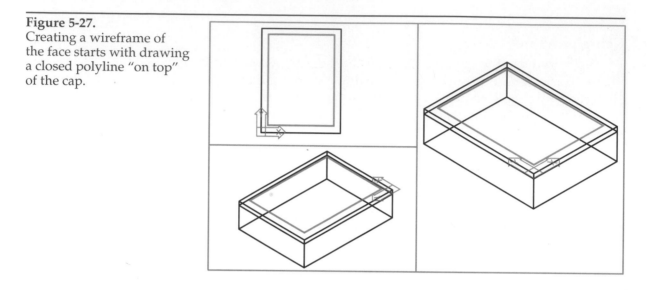

Next, place a .125 radius fillet on the corners of the polyline. Then, copy the filleted polyline on the Z axis using the following command sequence. Use the viewport that will allow you to draw most efficiently.

```
Command: COPY↵
Select objects: L↵
1 found
Select objects: ↵
⟨Base point or displacement⟩/Multiple: @↵
Second point of displacement: @0,0,.06↵ (the part is .06 units thick)
```

The result is shown in Figure 5-28.

Figure 5-28.
The face wireframe is completed by filleting the polyline and copying it on the Z axis.

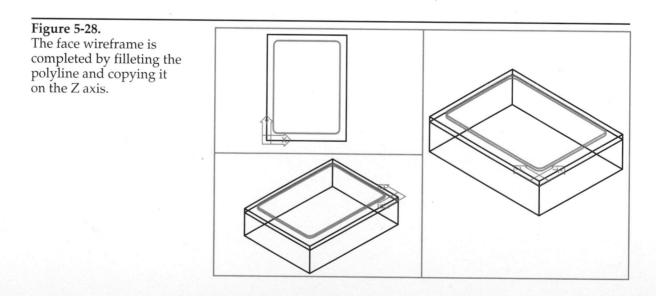

Using **RULESURF** to surface fillets

The **RULESURF** command is used on the digitizer puck to surface the round corners of the face and the top surface of the face at the corners. To do this efficiently, make a single view of the large viewport. Save this viewport configuration as ONE. Next, zoom in so that the object fills the screen. Use the **VIEW** command to save the current display as ALL. Now, zoom in on the front corner (insertion point) of the face and body cap. Save this display with the name CORNER.

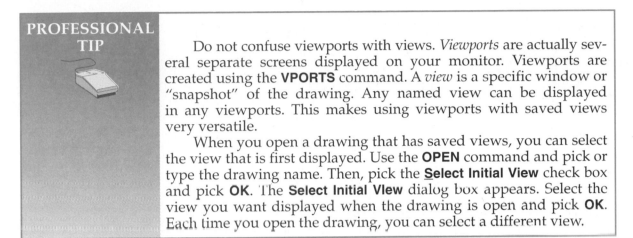

PROFESSIONAL TIP

Do not confuse viewports with views. *Viewports* are actually several separate screens displayed on your monitor. Viewports are created using the **VPORTS** command. A *view* is a specific window or "snapshot" of the drawing. Any named view can be displayed in any viewports. This makes using viewports with saved views very versatile.

When you open a drawing that has saved views, you can select the view that is first displayed. Use the **OPEN** command and pick or type the drawing name. Then, pick the **Select Initial View** check box and pick **OK**. The **Select Initial View** dialog box appears. Select the view you want displayed when the drawing is open and pick **OK**. Each time you open the drawing, you can select a different view.

Next, you need to place a point at the center of the radius on the top of the face. This point is needed to construct the ruled surface. Change to the CONSTR layer, set an appropriate value for **PDMODE**, and set **PDSIZE** to .04. In this example, a **PDMODE** value of 3 is used so that the point appears as an "X." Then, use the **POINT** command to place a point at the center of the arc, Figure 5-29A. The **Center** osnap can be quickly accessed from the right-button cursor menu to locate the center of the arc.

Use the **EXPLODE** command to break apart the two polylines that represent the face. This lets you select the corner arcs with the **RULESURF** command, Figure 5-29B. Change to the FACE2 layer, set **SURFTAB1** to 6, and select the **RULESURF** command.

```
Command: RULESURF⏎
Select first defining curve: (pick curve 1 in Figure 5-29B)
Select second defining curve: (pick curve 2 in Figure 5-29B)
```

The corner is now surfaced with six segments. See Figure 5-29C. If you want more or less segments, erase the ruled surface and redraw it with a different **SURFTAB1** setting.

Next, a ruled surface must be applied to the top of the face. This will connect the corner arc to the point at the center of the arc. You must pick the arc as the first defining curve, not the ruled surface. If you pick the ruled surface, the message Entity not usable to define ruled surface. appears on the command line. To avoid picking the ruled surface, zoom in on the arc and the point, Figure 5-29D. Notice that the ruled surface on the corner is composed of straight segments and the corner arc is smoother. Use the **RULESURF** command again to pick the top curve and the center point. After the top is surfaced, you can either erase the point or turn off the CONSTR layer. The corner should look like Figure 5-29E. Save your work before continuing.

Figure 5-29.
Surfacing the corners of the face. A—Place a point at the center of the fillets. B—Create a ruled surface using the corner arcs. C—The ruled surface on the edge of the corner. D—Zoom-in to make sure you pick the arc, not the first ruled surface, to create an edge surface on the top of the corner. E—The surfaced corner.

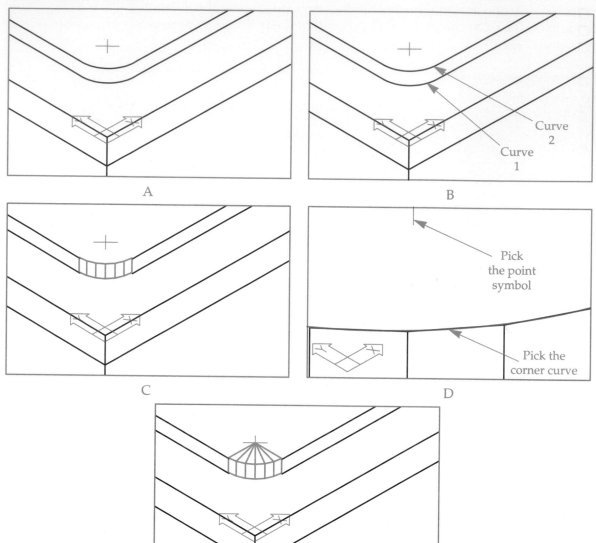

EXERCISE 5-2

❏ Begin a new drawing and name it EX5-2.
❏ Draw a circle 2″ (50.8mm) in diameter.
❏ Copy the circle up on the Z axis four units.
❏ Use the **VPOINT** command to get an isometric view (-1,-1,1) of the circles.
❏ Make two copies of the circles so that your drawing looks like the one shown below.
❏ Set the **SURFTAB1** variable to 4 and use the **RULESURF** command on the first set of circles.
❏ Set the **SURFTAB1** variable to 8 and use the **RULESURF** command on the second set of circles.
❏ Set the **SURFTAB1** variable to 16 and use the **RULESURF** command on the third set of circles.
❏ Save your drawing as A:EX5-2.

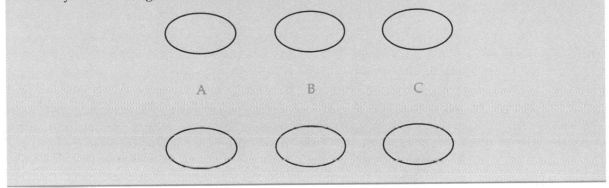

Using MIRROR and 3DFACE on a 3D object

You can repeat the above procedure for each of the three remaining corners. However, it is much faster to let AutoCAD do this for you with the **MIRROR** command. Be sure you have a single viewport and restore the ALL view. For this example, turn ortho on and reflect the surfaces along the X axis. Then reflect *both* corners along the Y axis. Use the **Midpoint** osnap to pick the mirror line. Do not delete the old objects.

Now, there are two 3D faces that must be constructed. Use the **VIEW** command to create a view of the upper-left corner. Name this view CORNER2. Next, use the **VPORTS** command to create a two-viewport vertical configuration. Save it as TWO. Restore the CORNER2 view in the left viewport and the CORNER view in the right viewport. You may also want to remake the CORNER view so that it more closely matches CORNER2. To do this, use the following command sequence:

```
Command: VIEW↵
?/Delete/Restore/Save/Window: R↵
   View name to restore: CORNER↵
Command: ↵
?/Delete/Restore/Save/Window: W↵
   View name to save: CORNER↵
First corner: (pick first window corner)
Other corner: (pick second window corner)
```

Your screen should look like Figure 5-30.

Figure 5-30.
To draw a 3D face on the edge of the puck face, create two viewports. Then, display a different corner in each.

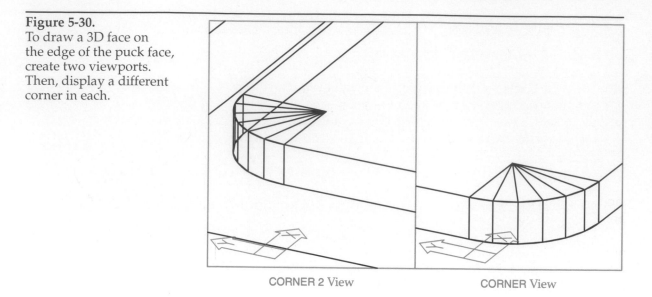

CORNER 2 View   CORNER View

Now, you can apply 3D faces to the vertical side of the puck face and the top surface between the rule-surfaced corners. Make sure the FACE2 layer is current. Set the running osnap **Endpoint**. First, draw the vertical 3D face using the pick points shown in Figure 5-31A. Then, press [Enter] to end the **3DFACE** command. Remember, to activate a viewport, simply move the cursor to the viewport and pick. Next, draw the top face between the centers of the arcs and the edge of the previous face, Figure 5-31B.

Figure 5-31.
A—Creating a 3D face on the edge of the puck face. B—Creating a 3D face on the top of the puck face. C—The finished 3D faces.

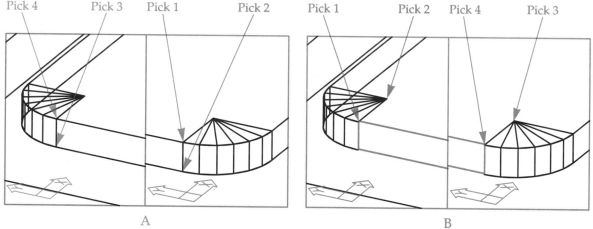

A   B

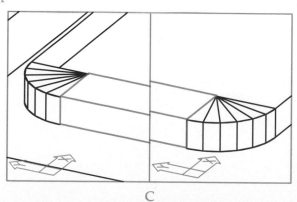

C

NOTE   You *cannot* switch viewports while inside one of the following commands:

DVIEW	SNAP	VPOINT
GRID	VPLAYER	ZOOM
PAN		

The **DVIEW** command is discussed in Chapter 7.

Restore the ONE viewport and the ALL view. Use the **MIRROR** command to copy the 3D faces and ruled surfaces to the opposite side of the face. Pick the midpoint of line 1 as the first point of the mirror line, Figure 5-32.

Next, you need to add 3D faces to the narrow vertical ends of the puck face. Then, add one large 3D face to the top of the puck face. It may be easier to change the viewpoint, or even return to a plan view, to draw the 3D face on the top. Use the **3DFACE** command and pick the four corners indicated in Figure 5-33. Use the **Endpoint** osnap to help.

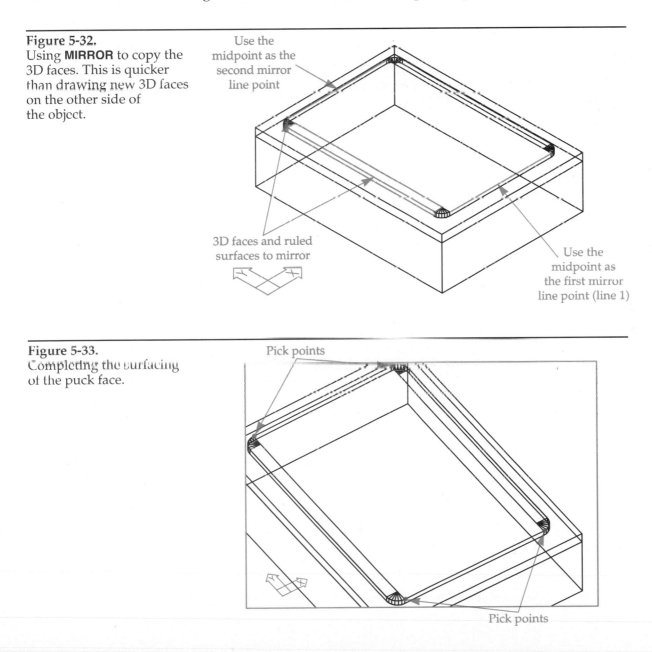

Figure 5-32.
Using **MIRROR** to copy the 3D faces. This is quicker than drawing new 3D faces on the other side of the object.

Use the midpoint as the second mirror line point

3D faces and ruled surfaces to mirror

Use the midpoint as the first mirror line point (line 1)

Figure 5-33.
Completing the surfacing of the puck face.

Pick points

Pick points

Figure 5-34.
The surfaced puck face
after using **HIDE**.

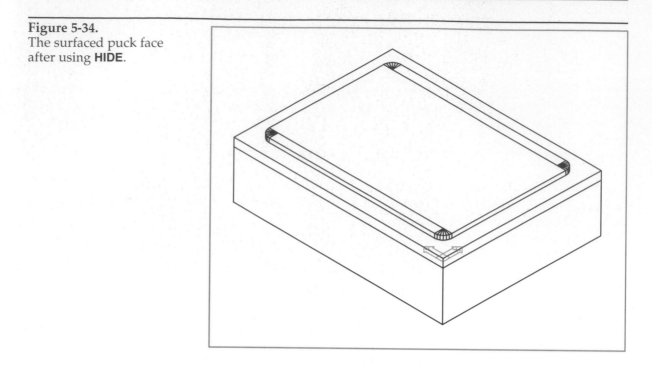

The completed face is shown in Figure 5-34 after using the **HIDE** command. Your screen display may have a line or two missing where the face rests on the body cap. This is because those two surfaces are at the same elevation and AutoCAD "thinks" some lines on the face may be hidden.

Constructing the eyepiece with **RULESURF**

To draw the eyepiece, first set the EYEPIECE layer current and restore the viewport configuration THREE. Make the upper-left viewport active and display a plan view. Then, make the large viewport active and use **VPOINT** as follows:

> Command: **VPOINT**↵
> Rotate/⟨View point⟩ ⟨*current*⟩: **–2,1.5,1**↵

Next, pick the lower-left viewport, and continue as follows:

> Command: **VPOINT** ↵
> Rotate/⟨View point⟩ ⟨*current*⟩: **–1,–1,1**↵

Your display should now look like Figure 5-35A.

Now, create a new UCS by moving the origin to where the eyepiece attaches to the body. See Figure 5-35B. Save the new UCS as EYEPIECE. Move the UCS icon to the new origin in all viewports. Save this viewport configuration as THREE. Replace the existing viewport. This new UCS allows you to enter the dimensions of the eyepiece from the origin.

To begin drawing the eyepiece, make the upper-left viewport active and return to a single viewport. Use the **CIRCLE** and **LINE** commands to draw the outline of the eyepiece as follows. Then, use the **TRIM** command to cut away the unused portion of circle.

Figure 5-35.
A—Change the views to help you draw the eyepiece. B—Place a new UCS at the bottom corner of
the puck body to help you locate coordinates better.

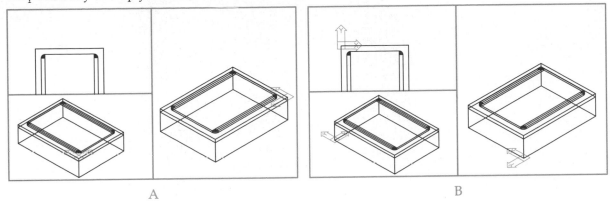

A   B

```
Command: CIRCLE↵
3P/2P/TTR/⟨Center point⟩: 1.125,.75↵
Diameter/⟨Radius⟩: D.↵
Diameter: .5↵
Command: ↵
CIRCLE 3P/2P/TTR/⟨Center point⟩: @↵
Diameter/⟨Radius⟩: .75↵
Command: LINE↵
From point: 0,0↵
To point: TAN↵
to (pick the left side of the large circle)
To point: ↵
Command: ↵
LINE From point: 2.25,0↵
To point: TAN↵
to (pick the right side of the large circle)
To point:↵
Command: TRIM↵
Select cutting edge(s)...
Select objects: (pick the two tangent lines)
Select objects: ↵
⟨Select object to trim⟩/Undo: (pick the inside portion of the large circle)
⟨Select object to trim⟩/Undo: ↵
```

Restore the viewport configuration named THREE. Use the **VIEW** command to window a
view called EYEPIECE2 in the right viewport. Window in closely on the eyepiece. Restore this
view. Your drawing should look similar to Figure 5-36A.

Activate the right viewport and copy the eyepiece outline .25″ on the Z axis. Draw a line
connecting the two ends of the top surface of the eyepiece. The 3D wireframe of the eyepiece
is complete, Figure 5-36B.

However, before you begin surfacing, it is important to determine how to surface the top
plane of the eyepiece. Remember that **RULESURF** requires two separate entities, and closed
entities, such as a circles, cannot be used. Therefore, you must redraw the circle as arcs on the
CONSTR layer before surfacing. First, set the CONSTR layer current. Then, change the UCS
origin to the top surface of the eyepiece directly above the current origin. Zoom-in on the top
circle of the eyepiece. Use the **ARC** command's **Center, Start, End** option to draw three arcs. Use
the **Center**, **Quadrant**, and **Endpoint** osnaps, as indicated in Figure 5-37A. Then, draw a point at
the quadrant between arcs two and three. Be sure **PDMODE** is set to 3 and **PDSIZE** is set to .08.

Figure 5-36.

A—First, draw the bottom of the eyepiece. B—Then, copy the objects on the Z axis to create the top.

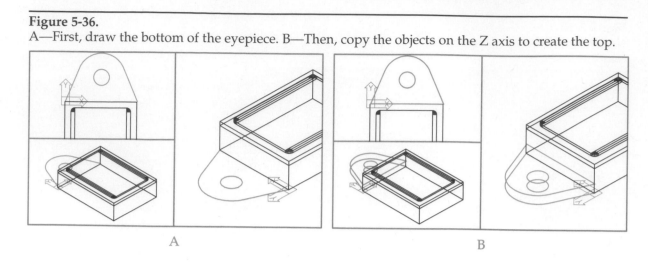

A

B

Figure 5-37.

A—Draw three arcs and a point to help you surface the top of the eyepiece. B—The pick points to use when surfacing the eyepiece.

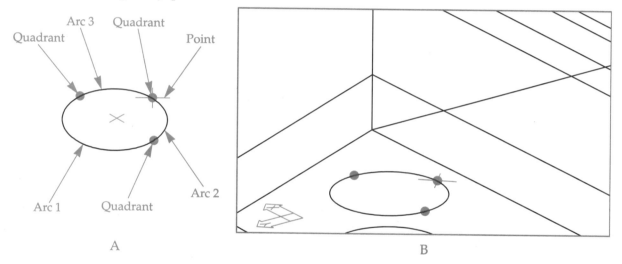

A

B

You can now use the **RULESURF** command to surface the entire eyepiece. Change the current layer to EYESURF. Then, create the following four ruled surfaces:

- The first ruled surface uses the point on the circle and the adjacent line, Figure 5-38A.
- The second ruled surface uses arc 2 and the adjacent angled line, Figure 5-38B.
- The third ruled surface uses arc 1 and the adjacent angled line, Figure 5-38C.
- The fourth ruled surface uses arc 3 and the large outside arc, Figure 5-38D.

Figure 5-38.
Use **RULESURF** four times to completely surface the top of the eyepiece.

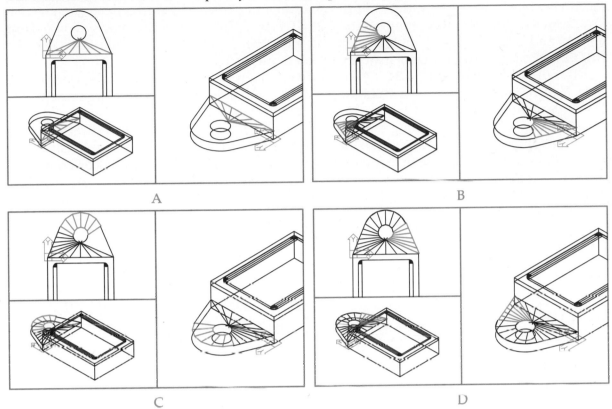

A

B

C

D

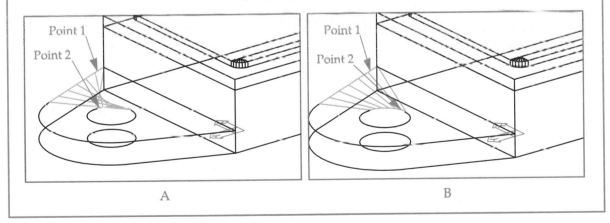

NOTE

Be sure to pick near the same end of both entities when using the **RULESURF** command. If you pick near opposite ends of the two entities, the surfacing segment lines cross over each other. For example, notice in A below that the first pick is located near the far end of the line. Pick number 2 is at the near end of the arc, diagonal to pick 1. This results in crossed segments. In B below, pick points 1 and 2 are near the same ends of the line and arc, or adjacent to each other. This creates a properly ruled surface.

Point 1

Point 2

A

Point 1

Point 2

B

The hole and the round end of the eyepiece must also be surfaced. These two surfaces are created just like the filleted corners on the puck face. Zoom-in so you can pick the original circle and not the ruled surface. Since you cannot mix open and closed paths, remove the arcs from the drawing by turning off the **CONSTR** layer. This makes sure you will not select an arc and a circle. Use a tight zoom and pick the circles, Figure 5-39. Also, use the **RULESURF** command to surface the curved end of the eyepiece.

Be sure to change **SURFTAB1** if you want more than six segments for the surface of the hole. A **SURFTAB1** setting of 8 is used for the illustration in Figure 5-40. The larger the value, the smoother the circle.

The final step in constructing the eyepiece is to create a 3D face on each vertical side. You can either draw two separate faces, or draw one face and mirror it. When you are finished, use the **HIDE** command to be sure that you have created all of the needed surfaces. See Figure 5-40.

Figure 5-39.
Zoom-in on the eyepiece to make sure you pick the circles, and not the ruled surface.

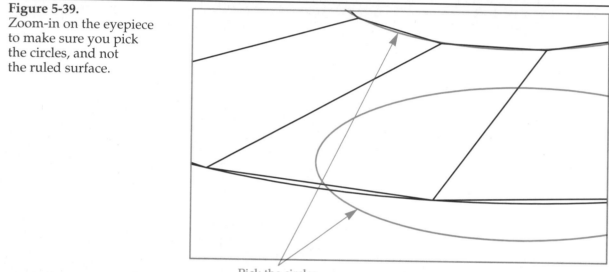

Pick the circles

Figure 5-40.
The completed eyepiece after using **HIDE**.

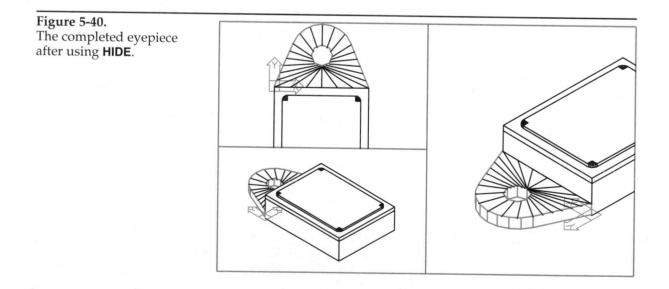

Constructing a cable with REVSURF

The **REVSURF** (revolved surface) command draws a symmetrical shape revolved around a central axis. To draw a revolved surface, you need a profile and an axis (line). The profile is the shape to be revolved. AutoCAD calls this profile the *path curve*. The *axis* is a line that the shape is revolved around. For the puck cable, the path curve is a circle. A revolved surface can be drawn to fill any angle. A 360° angle creates a full circle. For the puck cable, the circle is revolved 90°.

The **SURFTAB1** variable controls the number of segments on the surface around the axis. The **SURFTAB2** variable controls the number of segments on the path curve. Before using the **REVSURF** command, determine the number of segments needed and set the **SURFTAB** variables. For the puck cable, set **SURFTAB1** to 12 and **SURFTAB2** to 8. This creates eight segments around the circumference of the circle and twelve segments around the axis.

To draw the cable, first make the CABLE layer current. Then, use the **VPORTS**, **VPOINT**, **PAN**, and **ZOOM** commands to adjust the viewports so they look like Figure 5-41. For the lower-left viewport, you need to change the UCS. Use the **UCS** command as follows:

```
Command: UCS⏎
Origin/ZAxis/3point/Entity/View/X/Y/Z/Prev/Restore/Save/Del/?/⟨World⟩: X⏎
Rotation angle about X axis ⟨0⟩: 90⏎
Command: ⏎
Origin/ZAxis/3point/Entity/View/X/Y/Z/Prev/Restore/Save/Del/?/⟨World⟩: Y⏎
Rotation angle about Y axis ⟨0⟩: –90⏎
Command: ⏎
Origin/ZAxis/3point/Entity/View/X/Y/Z/Prev/Restore/Save/Del/?/⟨World⟩: O⏎
Origin point ⟨0,0,0⟩: END⏎
of (pick the corner shown in the large viewport of Figure 5-41)
```

Then, make the lower-left viewport active. Use the **PLAN** command to make the viewport plan to the current UCS. Once your display looks like Figure 5-41, save the viewport configuration as CABLE.

Now, create a new UCS on the end of the puck. Name this UCS CABLE. Use the **3point** and **Save** options of the **UCS** command as follows. Refer to Figure 5-42.

Figure 5-41.
Create a new viewport configuration to help draw the cable.

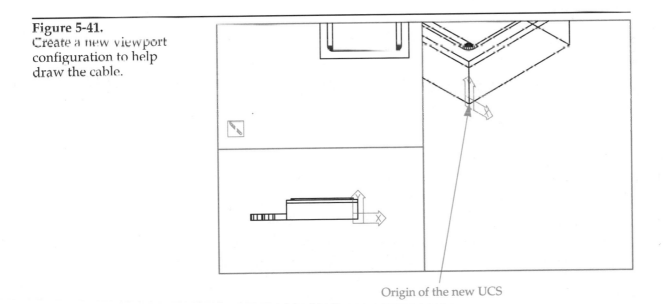

Origin of the new UCS

Figure 5-42.
Create a new UCS on the
end of the puck body. Pick
the origin, X axis, and Y
axis as shown here.

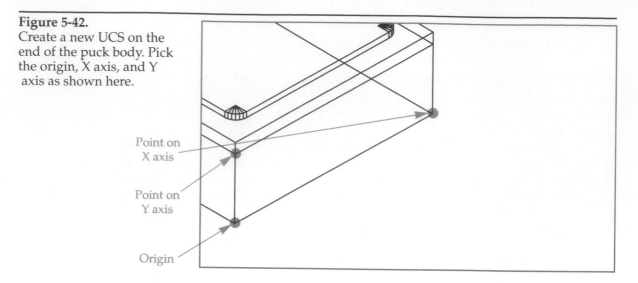

Point on
X axis

Point on
Y axis

Origin

```
Command: UCS↵
Origin/ZAxis/3point/Entity/View/X/Y/Z/Prev/Restore/Save/Del/?/〈World〉: 3↵
Origin point 〈0,0,0〉: END↵
of (pick the origin)
Point on positive portion of the X-axis 〈current〉: END↵
of (pick a point on the new X axis)
Point on positive-Y portion of the UCS XY plane 〈0.00,1.00,0.00〉: END↵
of (pick a point on the new Y axis)
Command: UCS↵
Origin/ZAxis/3point/Entity/View/X/Y/Z/Prev/Restore/Save/Del/?/〈World〉: S↵
?/Desired UCS name: CABLE↵
```

Make the large viewport active. You can now create the profile and the axis. Use the
CIRCLE and **LINE** commands as follows:

```
Command: CIRCLE↵
circle/3P/2P/TTR/〈Center point〉: 1.125,.35,0↵
Diameter/〈Radius〉: D↵
Diameter: .25↵
Command: LINE↵
From point: −1.5,1,0↵
To point: −1.5,−1,0↵
To point: ↵
```

Set the two **SURFTAB** variables and then use the **REVSURF** command to complete the cable as
follows:

```
Command: SURFTAB1↵
New value for SURFTAB1 〈10〉: 12↵
Command: SURFTAB2↵
New value for SURFTAB2 〈6〉: 8↵
Command: REVSURF↵
Select path curve: (pick the circle as shown in Figure 5-43A)
Select axis of revolution: (pick the axis as shown in Figure 5-43A)
Start angle 〈0〉: ↵
Included angle (+ = ccw, − = cw) 〈Full circle〉: −90↵
Command:
```

You can now erase the axis line. The completed cable is shown in Figure 5-43B after using the
HIDE command. Save your work before continuing.

Figure 5-43.
A—The path curve on the end of the puck and the axis of revolution. B—The completed cable.

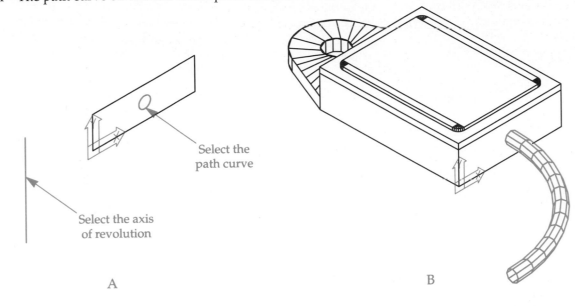

Select the
path curve

Select the axis
of revolution

A   B

Creating screw heads with the DOME command

The **3D Objects** dialog box and the **Surfaces** toolbar both contain three different spherical shapes. These are dome, dish, and sphere. The dome and the dish are simply one half of a sphere. For the puck, domes are used to represent screw heads on the face. Refer back to Figure 5-18 to see the options in the **3D Objects** dialog box.

To draw the screw heads, first set the SCREWS layer current. Then, restore the FACE UCS. It may be easiest to switch to a single viewport and zoom-in on the origin corner of the puck. Next, draw the screw heads as follows:

> Command: *(pick* **Dome** *from the* **3D Objects** *dialog box or* **Surfaces** *toolbar)*
> Center of dome: **.095,.095**↵
> Diameter/(radius): **D**↵
> Diameter: **.125**↵
> Number of longitudinal segments ⟨16⟩: **8**↵
> Number of latitudinal segments ⟨8⟩: **4**↵

This places one screw head on the face, Figure 5-44A. Now, use the **ARRAY** command to create the other three screw heads a follows:

> Command: **ARRAY**↵
> Select objects: **L**↵
> Select objects: ↵
> Rectangular or Polar array (R/P)⟨R⟩: ↵
> Number of rows (---) ⟨1⟩: **2**↵
> Number of columns (||||) ⟨1⟩: **2**↵
> Unit cell distance between rows (---): **2.81**↵
> Distance between columns (||||): **2.06**↵
> Command:

Figure 5-44B shows the array of four domes on the digitizer puck after using **HIDE**.

Figure 5-44.
Use domes to represent screw heads on the face of the puck. A—Draw one dome in the lower-left corner. B—Use ARRAY to copy the dome to the other three locations.

A   B

Inserting the button 3D block

The last to do is add the buttons. This digitizer has twelve buttons. Earlier, you created a block called BUTTON. You must insert this block on the face of the puck. First, set the BUTTONS layer current. Then, create and save a new UCS as follows:

```
Command: UCS↵
Origin/ZAxis/3point/Entity/View/X/Y/Z/Prev/Restore/Save/Del/?/⟨World⟩: O↵
Origin point ⟨0,0,0⟩: .19,.19,.06↵
Command: ↵
Origin/ZAxis/3point/Entity/View/X/Y/Z/Prev/Restore/Save/Del/?/⟨World⟩: S↵
?/Desired UCS name: BUTTON↵
Command:
```

For the insert operation, you only need a single view of the object on the screen. If you did not switch to a single view for the screw heads, switch to one now. Then, insert the buttons as follows:

```
Command: MINSERT↵
Block name: (or ?): BUTTON↵
  Insertion point: .3125,.5↵
X scale factor ⟨1⟩ / Corner / Corner / XYZ: ↵
  Y scale factor ⟨1⟩ (default=X): ↵
  Rotation angle ⟨0⟩: ↵
Number of rows (---) ⟨1⟩: 4 ↵
Number of columns (¦¦¦) ⟨1⟩: 3 ↵
Unit cell or distance between rows (---): .457 ↵
Distance between columns (¦¦¦): .457 ↵
```

The completed puck is shown in Figure 5-45.

Figure 5-45.
The completed puck
with buttons.

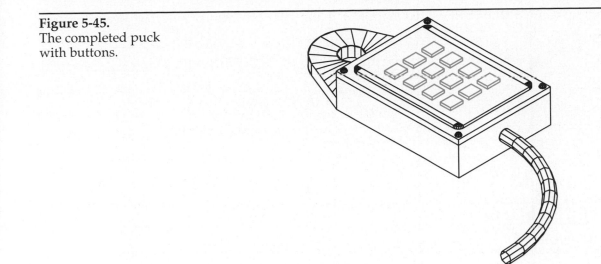

NOTE   Determine the best method for adding numbers to the buttons. If the BUTTON block had been given an attribute, the numbers can be added at insertion. However, the **INSERT** command would have to be used twelve times instead of using **MINSERT** once. If you use **DTEXT**, you first have to draw some sort of construction lines or points to define the center of the button, copy those lines to each button, then use **DTEXT** twelve times. What is the most efficient method?

CHAPTER TEST

Write your answers in the spaces provided.

1. Name three commands that allow you to create different types of meshes. _____

_____

2. What command creates a surface mesh between four edges? _____

3. How must the four edges be related when using the command in question 2? _____

4. What values does AutoCAD need to know about a 3D Mesh? _____

_____

5. AutoCAD's surface meshing commands create what type of entities? _____

6. Which surface mesh command allows you to rotate a profile about an axis to create a symmetrical object? _____

7. What object does **TABSURF** create? _____

_____

8. What do the **SURFTAB1** and **SURFTAB2** variables control? _____

_____

9. Name three entities that can be connected with the **RULESURF** command. _____

_____

10. When using **RULESURF**, what happens if the two objects are selected near opposite ends? _____

11. Why should you avoid using large numbers for the **SURFTAB** settings?_____

_____

_____

12. What objects can be used to create a ruled surface with **RULESURF**?_____

_____

Drawing Problems

*Construct 3D surfaced models of the following problems in Chapter 1. For objects without dimensions, measure directly from the text. Save them as **A:P5-**(problem number).*

Mechanical Drafting   1.

Mechanical Drafting   2.

Mechanical Drafting   3.

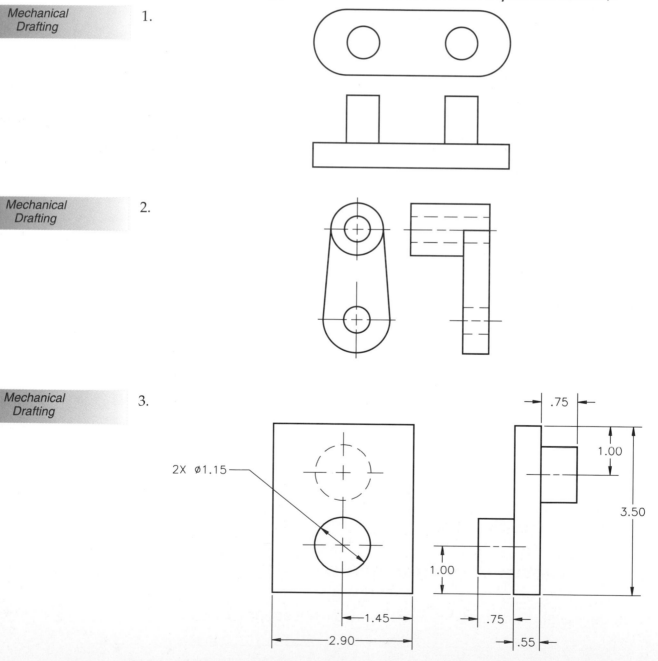

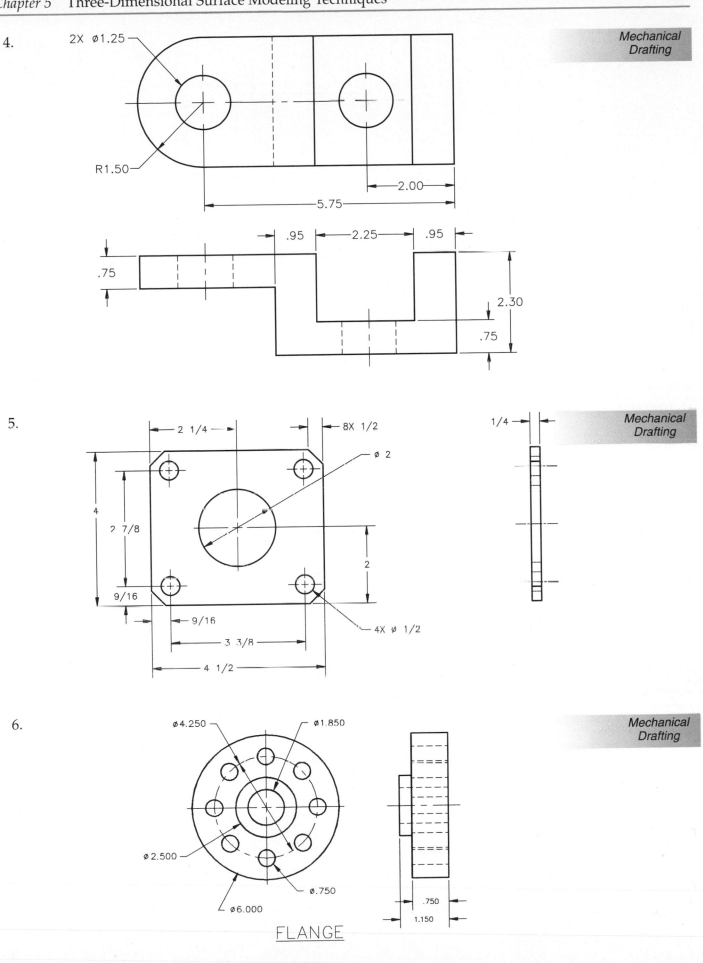

FLANGE

*Mechanical
Drafting*
7.

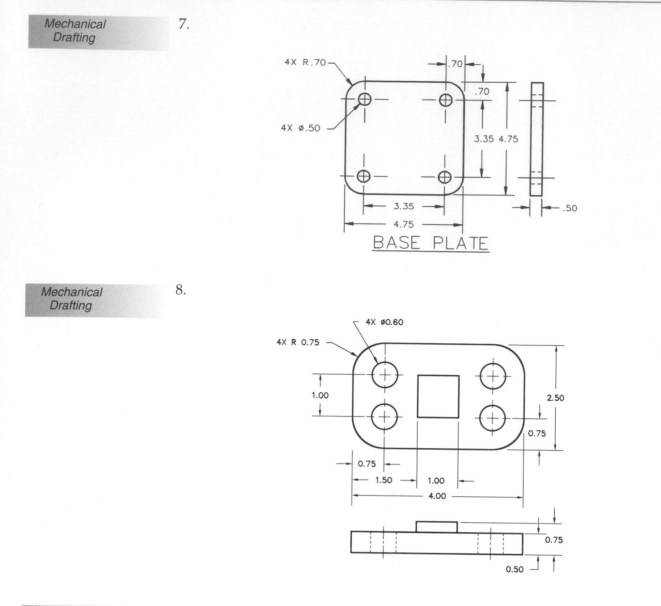

BASE PLATE

*Mechanical
Drafting*
8.

*Mechanical
Drafting*
9.

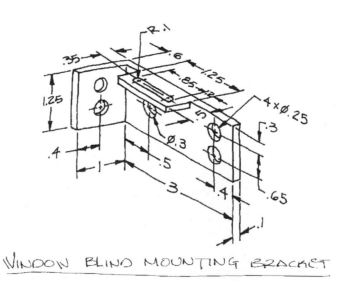

WINDOW BLIND MOUNTING BRACKET

10.

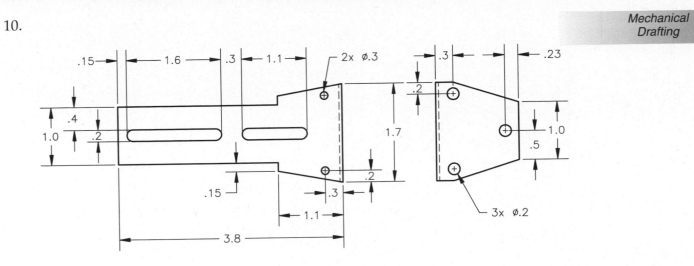

11.

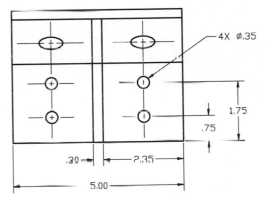

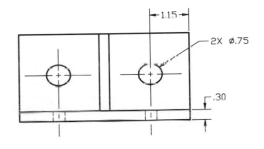

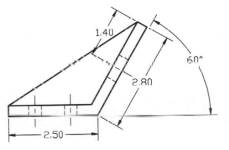

Mechanical
Drafting

12.

13.

Mechanical
Drafting

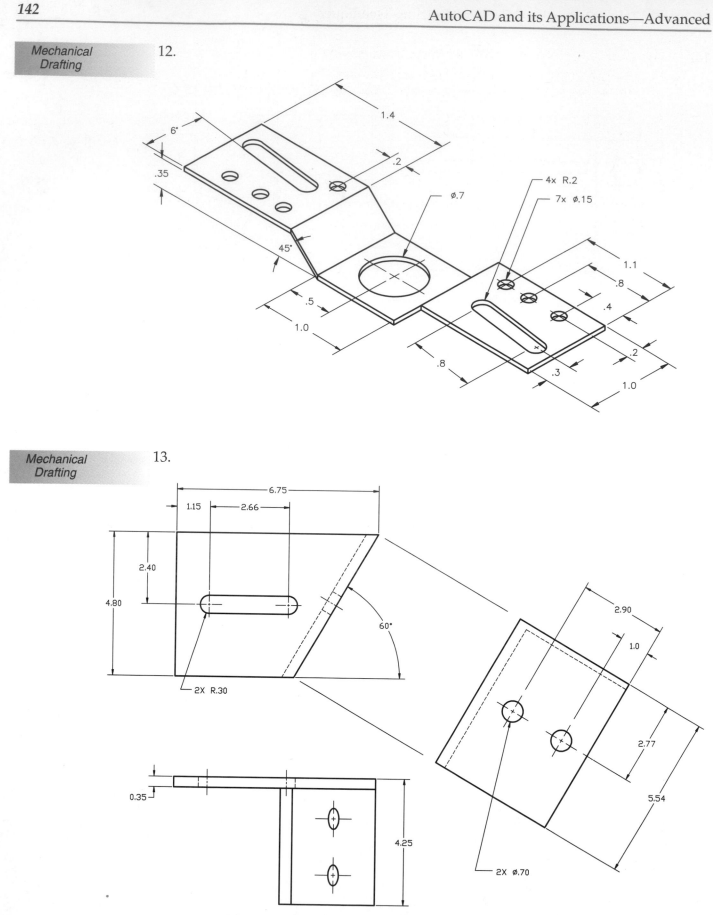

14. Create a surface model of a glass using the profile shown.

   A. Use the **REVSURF** command to construct the glass.

   B. Use the dimensions given for height and radii.

   C. Set the **SURFTAB1** variable to 16.

   D. Set the **SURFTAB2** variable to 8.

   E. Use **HIDE** to remove hidden lines.

   F. Construct the glass a second time using different **SURFTAB** settings.

   G. Plot the drawing on B-size bond both as a wireframe and with hidden lines removed.

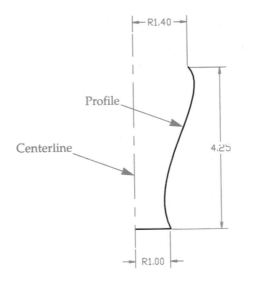

15 - 16. *Draw the following objects using the* **REVSURF** *command. Accept the default values for segments. Display the objects and use* **HIDE** *on each. Save the drawings as* **A:P5-15** *and* **A:P5-16.**

15.

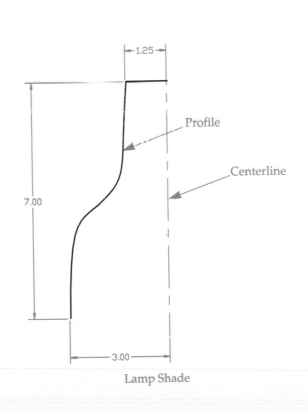

Lamp Shade

16.

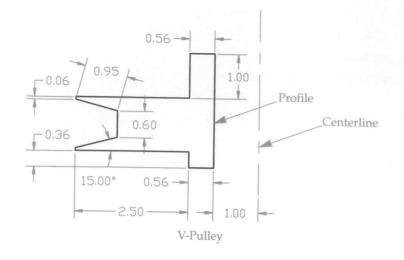

V-Pulley

17 - 19. *Problems 17 through 19 are plans of two houses and a cabin. Create a 3D model the house(s) assigned by your instructor. Use all modeling techniques covered in this chapter.*

    A. Establish multiple viewports.

    B. Create named UCSs for the floor plan and the various wall elevations.

    C. Create named viewport configurations (using one viewport) of single floors or walls so you can display the working areas as large as possible on-screen.

    D. Use the dimensions given or alter the room sizes and arrangements to suit your own design. Use your own dimensions for anything not specified.

    E. Plot the model on B-size or C-size sheet with hidden lines removed.

17.

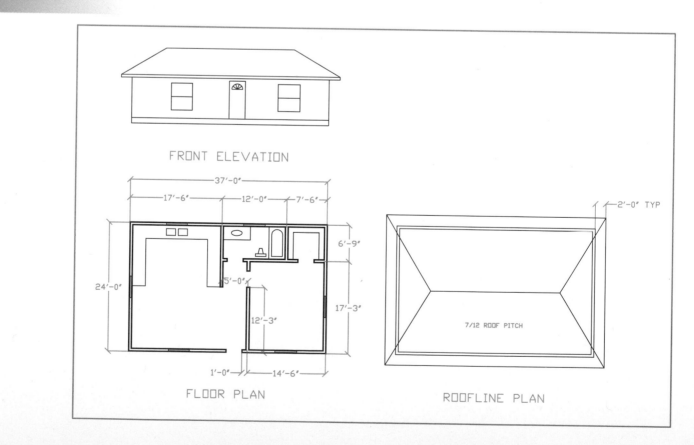

18.

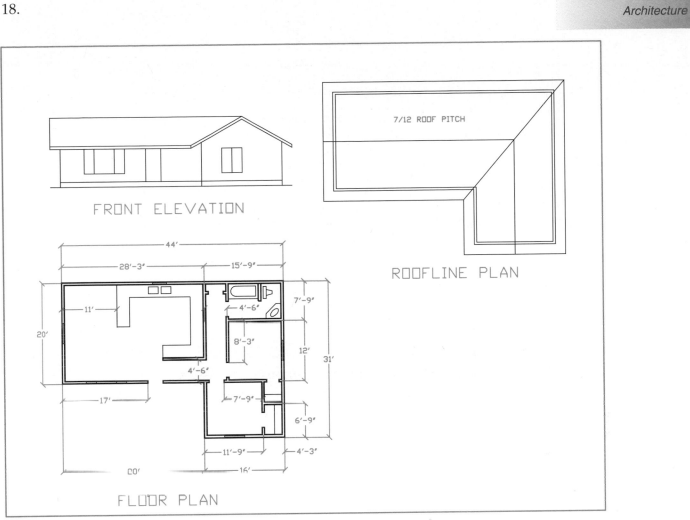

FRONT ELEVATION

7/12 ROOF PITCH

ROOFLINE PLAN

FLOOR PLAN

Architecture

19.

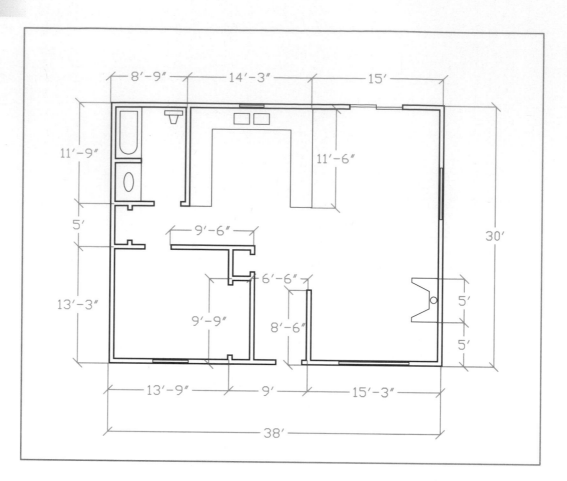

General

20. Complete the digitizer puck that was demonstrated in the tutorial.

A. Add numbers to the buttons.

B. Redraw as many 3D faces as possible using the **Invisible** option of the **3DFACE** command.

C. Delete the square buttons and insert the curved buttons.

D. Generate laser prints or pen plots on A-size or B-size paper showing the view in each of the four compass quadrants.

AutoCAD R13

Chapter 6

Editing Three-Dimensional Objects

Learning objectives

After completing this chapter, you will be able to:

- ○ Use grips to edit 3D objects.
- ○ Align, rotate, and mirror 3D objects.
- ○ Trim and extend 3D objects.
- ○ Create fillets and rounds.
- ○ Edit polygon meshes.

It is always important to use proper editing techniques and commands. This is especially true when using a variety of User Coordinate Systems (UCSs) and 3D objects. This chapter covers the correct procedures for editing 3D objects.

CHANGING PROPERTIES

The **CHANGE** command is often used to change the properties of 2D objects. However, it has some limitations when an object is not perpendicular to the Z axis of the current UCS. If you use the **CHANGE** command on this type of object, AutoCAD displays this message:

> *n* found
> *n* was not parallel with UCS.

Instead of the **CHANGE** command, use the **DDCHPROP** or **CHPROP** command. These commands can change an entity even if it is not parallel to the current UCS. The **DDCHPROP** command allows you to change properties in the **Change Properties** dialog box. If you use the **CHPROP** command, you must specify the information on the command line.

To change all aspects of the object, including the location, use the **DDMODIFY** command. This can be accessed by picking the **Properties** button in the **Object Properties** toolbar. This opens the **Modify** dialog box. In this dialog box, you can change the properties, size, and coordinate location of the object.

USING GRIPS TO EDIT 3D OBJECTS

Using grips is an efficient way to edit 3D objects. For an in-depth discussion on using grips, refer to Chapter 14 of *AutoCAD and its Applications, Basics—Release 13 for Windows.* Editing should be done in a 3D view where you can see the change dynamically. For example, to change the height of a cone using grips, first change to a 3D view.

> Command: **VPOINT**↵
> Rotate/⟨View point⟩ ⟨*current*⟩: **–1,–1,1**↵
> Command:

Next, pick anywhere on the cone and the grips appear, Figure 6-1A. Then, pick the grip at the apex of the cone so it becomes hot, Figure 6-1B. A hot grip is a red square that is filled solid. The **STRETCH** operation can be completed as follows:

    STRETCH
    ⟨Stretch to point⟩/Base point/Copy/Undo/eXit: **.XY**⏎
    of *(pick the grip at the cone apex again)* (need Z): **5**⏎
    Command:

You can move a hot grip around the screen with your pointing device. It appears that the grip is moving in all three (XYZ) directions. However, this is misleading. You are actually moving the grip in the XY plane. If you pick a point, the Z value of the grip is changed to 0. In other words, you have placed the grip on the current XY plane. Therefore, use XYZ filters or enter relative coordinates to edit 3D objects.

Figure 6-1.
Using grips to edit a 3D object. A—First, pick on the object to make the grips warm. Then, pick the grip to edit so that it becomes hot. B—Next, enter coordinates at the keyboard for the new location of the grip. C—The edited object.

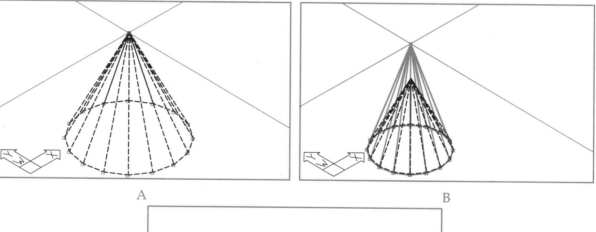

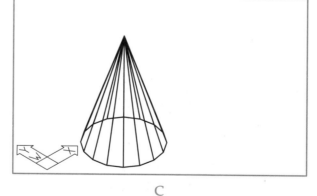

ALIGNING 3D OBJECTS

The **ALIGN** command enables you to correct errors of 3D construction, or quickly manipulate 3D shapes. **ALIGN** requires existing points (source), and the new location of those existing points (destination). The **ALIGN** command may be issued by selecting **Align** from the **Modify** pull-down menu, picking the **Align** button in the **Rotate** flyout of the **Modify** toolbar, or entering **ALIGN** at the **Command:** prompt.

For an example, refer to Figure 6-2. The wedge in Figure 6-2A is aligned in its new position as follows. Refer to the figure for the pick points.

Command: **OSNAP**↵
Object snap modes: **INT**↵
Command: **ALIGN**↵
Select objects: *(pick the wedge)*
Select objects: ↵
1st source point: *(pick P1)* 1st destination point: *(pick P2)*
2nd source point: *(pick P3)* 2nd destination point: *(pick P4)*
3rd source point: *(pick P5)* 3rd destination point: *(pick P1 again)*
Command:

The aligned object should look like Figure 6-2B.

Figure 6-2.
The **ALIGN** command can be used to properly orient 3D objects.

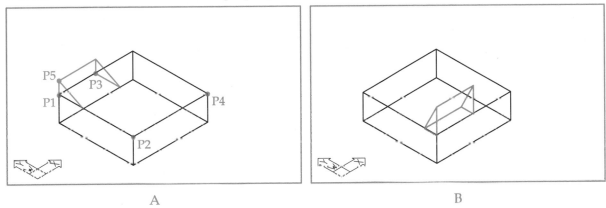

A   B

**PROFESSIONAL
TIP**

Before using 3D editing commands, set running object snap modes to enhance your accuracy and speed.

EXERCISE 6-1

❏ Load AutoCAD for Windows and start a new drawing.
❏ Draw a box and a wedge arranged like those shown in Figure 6-2A.
❏ Use the **ALIGN** command to create the arrangement shown below.
❏ Save the drawing as A:EX6-1.

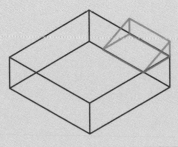

3D ROTATING

The **ROTATE3D** command can rotate objects on any axis, regardless of the current UCS. This is an extremely powerful editing and design feature. When using the default option, you must pick two points to define an axis of rotation and specify a rotation angle. The rotation angle is defined by looking down the axis from the second pick point and specifying an angle. A positive angle rotates the object counterclockwise.

To use the **ROTATE3D** command, select **3D Rotate** from the **Construct** pull-down menu, pick the **3D Rotate** button in the **Rotate** flyout of the **Modify** toolbar, or enter ROTATE3D at the **Command:** prompt. The following example rotates the wedge in Figure 6-2 –90° on a selected axis. See Figure 6-3A for the pick points.

> Command: **ROTATE3D**↵
> Select objects: *(pick the wedge)*
> Select objects: ↵
> Axis by Object/Last/View/Xaxis/Yaxis/Zaxis/⟨2points⟩: **INT**↵
> of *(pick P1)* 2nd point on axis: **INT**↵
> of *(pick P2)* ⟨Rotation angle⟩/Reference: **–90**↵
> Command:

The rotated object is shown in Figure 6-3B.

There are several different ways to define an axis of rotation with the **ROTATE3D** command. These are explained as follows:

- **Axis by Object (O).** Objects such as lines, arcs, circles, and polylines can define the axis. A line becomes the axis. The axis of a circle or arc passes through its center, perpendicular to the plane of the circle. For a polyline, the selected segment (line or arc) is used to determine the axis.
- **Last (L).** Uses the last axis of rotation defined.
- **View (V).** The viewing direction of the current viewport is aligned with a selected point to define the axis.
- **Xaxis/Yaxis/Zaxis (X, Y, or Z).** Aligns the axis of rotation with the X, Y, or Z axis and a selected point.

Figure 6-3.
The **ROTATE3D** command is used to rotate objects in 3D space.

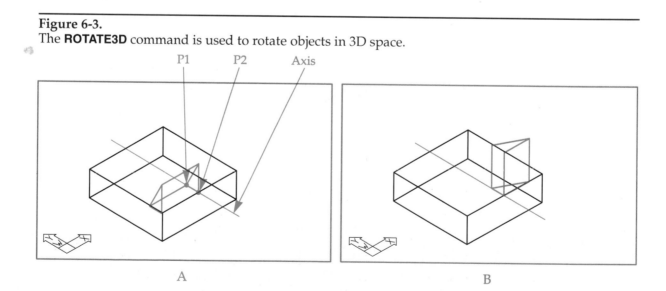

EXERCISE 6-2

❏ If drawing EX6-1 is not on-screen, begin a new drawing named EX6-2 and use A:EX6-1 as your prototype.
❏ Use the **ROTATE3D** command to rotate the wedge to the position shown below.
❏ Save the drawing as A:EX6-2.

3D MIRRORING

The **MIRROR3D** command allows you to mirror objects about any plane, regardless of the current UCS. The default option is to define a mirror plane by picking three points on that plane, Figure 6-4A. Object snap modes should be used to accurately define the mirror plane.

To use the **MIRROR3D** command, select **3D Mirror** from the **Construct** pull-down menu, pick the **3D Mirror** button in the **Copy** flyout of the **Modify** toolbar, or enter MIRROR3D at the **Command:** prompt. To mirror the wedge in Figure 6-3, use the following command sequence:

```
Command: OSNAP↵
Object snap modes: MID↵
Command: MIRROR3D↵
Select objects: (pick the wedge)
Select objects: ↵
Plane by Object/Last/Zaxis/View/XY/YZ/XZ/⟨3points⟩: (pick P1) 2nd point on plane:
    (pick P2) 3rd point on plane: (pick P3)
Delete old objects? ⟨N⟩ ↵
Command:
```

The drawing should now look like Figure 6-4B.

Figure 6-4.
The **MIRROR3D** command allows you to mirror objects on any 3D axis, regardless of the current UCS.

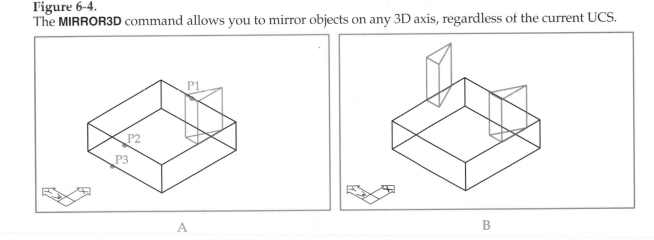

A   B

There are several different ways to define a mirror plane with the **MIRROR3D** command. These are explained as follows:

- **Plane by Object (O).** The plane that a circle, arc, or 2D polyline segment is in can be used as the mirror plane.
- **Last (L).** Uses the last mirror plane defined.
- **Zaxis (Z).** Defines the plane with a pick point on the plane and a point on the Z axis of the mirror plane.
- **View (V).** The viewing direction of the current viewpoint is aligned with a selected point to define the axis.
- **XY/YZ/XZ.** The mirror plane is placed in one of the three basic planes, and passes through a selected point.

EXERCISE 6-3

❑ If drawing EX6-2 is not on your screen, begin a new drawing named EX6-3 and use A:EX6-2 as the prototype.
❑ Use the **MIRROR3D** command to mirror the wedge to the position drawn below.
❑ Save the drawing as A:EX6-3.

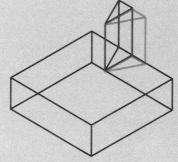

 11

CREATING A 3D ARRAY

Creating an array of 3D objects in 3D space is discussed and illustrated in Chapter 2. Refer to Figure 2-22. However, this type of construction is sometimes considered editing. Therefore, a brief discussion also appears here.

Rectangular 3D array

An example of a rectangular 3D array is the layout of structural steel columns on multiple floors of a commercial building. To use the **3DARRAY** command, select **3D Array** from the **Construct** pull-down menu, pick the **3D Rectangular Array** button in the **Copy** flyout of the **Modify** toolbar, or enter 3DARRAY at the **Command:** prompt.

In Figure 6-5A, you can see two concrete floor slabs of a building and a single steel column. It is now a simple matter of arraying the steel column in rows, columns, and levels. Use the following procedure:

```
Command: 3DARRAY↵
Initializing... 3DARRAY loaded.
Select objects: (pick the 3D object) 1 found
Select objects: ↵
Rectangular or Polar array (R/P): R↵
Number of rows (---) ⟨1⟩: 3↵
Number of columns (|||) ⟨1⟩: 5↵
Number of levels (...) ⟨1⟩: 2↵
Distance between rows (---): 10'↵
Distance between columns (|||): 10'↵
Distance between levels (...): 12'8↵
```

Figure 6-5.
A—Two floors and one steel column are drawn. B—A rectangular 3D array is used to place steel columns on both floors.

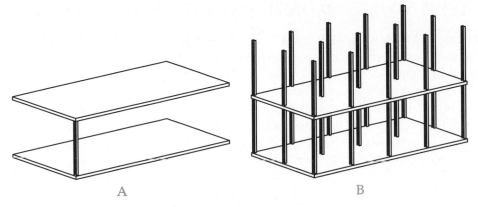

A   B

The result is shown in Figure 6-5B. Constructions like this can be quickly assembled for multiple levels using the **3DARRAY** command only once.

Polar 3D array

A polar 3D array is similar to a polar 2D array. However, you must also select a centerline axis of rotation. You can array an object in a UCS different from the current one. Unlike a rectangular 3D array, a polar 3D array does not allow you to create levels of the object. The object is arrayed in a plane defined by the object and the selected centerline (Z) axis. To use the **3DARRAY** command, select **3D Array** from the **Construct** pull-down menu, pick the **3D Polar Array** button in the **Copy** flyout of the **Modify** toolbar, or enter 3DARRAY at the **Command:** prompt.

For example, the tank nozzle in Figure 6-6A must be placed at the four quadrant points around the tank at the same elevation. Before using **3DARRAY**, an axis line must be drawn through the center of the tank. Then, continue as follows:

> Command: **3DARRAY**↵
> Select objects: *(select the object)*
> *n* found
> Select objects: ↵
> Rectangular or Polar array (R/P): **P**↵
> Number of items: **4**↵
> Angle to fill ⟨360⟩: ↵
> Rotate objects as they are copied? ⟨Y⟩: ↵
> Center point of array: *(pick center of tank base)*
> Second point on axis of rotation: *(pick top end of axis line)*
> Command:

Figure 6-6.
A—The tank and one inlet are drawn. B—A polar 3D array is used to create the three other inlets.

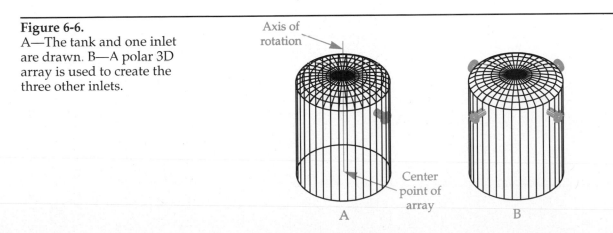

Axis of rotation

Center point of array

A   B

The completed 3D polar array is shown in Figure 6-6B. If additional levels of a polar array are needed they can be copied.

USING **TRIM** AND **EXTEND** ON 3D OBJECTS

Correct use of **TRIM** or **EXTEND** on 3D objects may be confusing at first. However, both of these commands can be powerful tools when working in 3D. This section covers using these commands on 3D objects.

Figure 6-7 shows three wireframe objects. The left viewport is a plan view of the objects. The right viewport is a 3D view. The circle is three inches directly above the ellipse on the Z axis. The bottom edge of the rectangle sits on the same plane as the ellipse. The rectangle passes through the circle at an angle. The right edge of the rectangle in the left viewport is used as the cutting edge in the following example. Use **TRIM** as follows:

```
Command: TRIM↵
Select cutting edges: (Projmode = None, Edgemode = Extend)
Select objects: (pick the bottom-right edge of the rectangle) 1 found
Select objects: ↵
⟨Select object to trim⟩/Project/Edge/Undo: P↵
None/Ucs/View ⟨Ucs⟩: N↵
⟨Select object to trim⟩/Project/Edge/Undo: (pick the right side of the ellipse)
⟨Select object to trim⟩/Project/Edge/Undo: ↵
Command:
```

Figure 6-8 shows the results.

Figure 6-7.
Three wireframe objects in 3D space that will be trimmed.

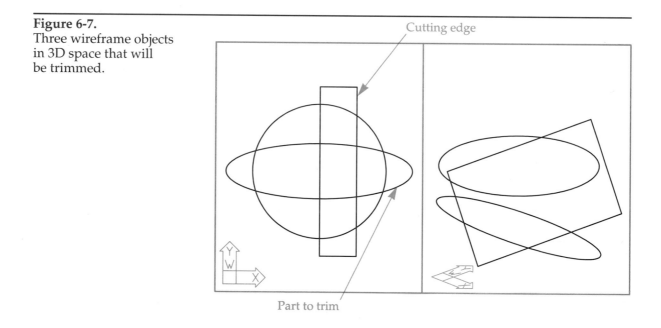

Cutting edge

Part to trim

Figure 6-8.
With the **None** suboption of the **TRIM** command **Project** option, the ellipse is trimmed where it actually intersects the rectangle.

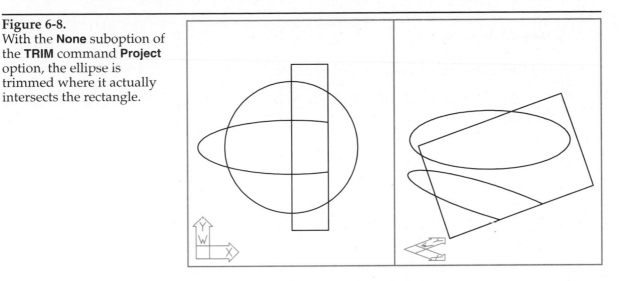

The **TRIM** command has two options—**Project** and **Edge**. The **Project** option establishes the projection method for objects to be trimmed in 3D space. This option is also controlled by the **PROJMODE** system variable. The **Project** option displays the following suboptions:

None/Ucs/View ⟨Ucs⟩:

- **None**—(**PROJMODE** = 0) No projection method is used. Objects to be trimmed in 3D space must form an actual intersection with the cutting edge. In Figure 6-8 you can see that the edge of the rectangle and the ellipse actually intersect.
- **Ucs**—(**PROJMODE** = 1) Cutting edges and edges to be trimmed are all projected onto the XY plane of the current UCS. Objects are trimmed even if they do not intersect in 3D space. See Figure 6-9.
- **View**—(**PROJMODE** = 2) Objects are projected along the current view direction and onto the current viewing plane. Objects are trimmed even if they do not intersect in 3D space. See Figure 6-10.

Figure 6-9.
With the **Ucs** suboption of the **TRIM** command **Project** option, the circle is trimmed where it intersects the cutting edge as the edge is projected to the current UCS.

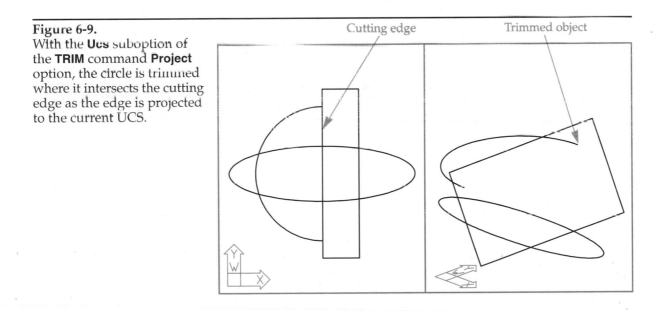

Cutting edge   Trimmed object

Figure 6-10.
With the **View** suboption of the **TRIM** command **Project** option, the rectangle is trimmed where it intersects the cutting edge as the edge is projected along the current viewing angle to the XY plane. If the objects were selected in the right viewport, more of the rectangle would have been trimmed.

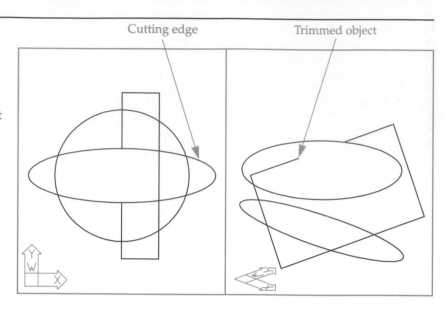

The **Edge** option of the **TRIM** command determines if an object is to be trimmed at an implied edge or at the actual intersection of an object in 3D space. This option applies specifically to the projection of an edge and *not* a plane. The **Edge** option is selected as follows:

⟨Select object to trim⟩/Project/Edge/Undo: **E** ↵
Extend/No extend ⟨No extend⟩:

- **Extend**—The cutting edge is extended into 3D space to intersect objects to be trimmed. The objects must intersect exactly when the cutting edge is extended.
- **No extend**—The cutting edge is not extended, and the object to be trimmed must intersect the cutting edge in 3D space.

CREATING FILLETS AND ROUNDS

Fillets are rounded inside corners. Rounds are rounded outside corners. Both of these are easily created with surfacing commands. **RULESURF** and **TABSURF** both produce the same results. Choose the one you prefer. Notice in Figure 6-11A that arcs have been drawn on the inside and outside corners of a wireframe object in order to create a fillet and round. The arcs are copied to the opposite side and lines are drawn connecting the tangent points of the arcs.

If you use **TABSURF**, you then only need to give direction vectors. If **RULESURF** is used, the lines connecting the arcs are not needed. Select one arc as the first defining curve and the opposite arc as the second defining curve. The result of either process is shown in Figure 6-11B.

The face of the arcs on both sides of the object must be surfaced with **RULESURF**. First, put points at the center of the arc on the round and at the intersection of the two inside edges of the part. See Figure 6-11C. Then, pick the point and the arc as the two defining curves. Now, the **3DFACE** command can be used to construct faces on the object. Three 3D faces must be drawn on the left side of the object. The completed object is shown in Figure 6-11D.

Hiding 3D face edges with the EDGE command

Notice in Figure 6-11D that the 3D face edges are visible on the left side of the object. These edges can be created as hidden edges by using the **Invisible** option of **3DFACE** while drawing them. However, you can quickly hide an existing edge with the **EDGE** command. To use this command, pick **Surfaces** from the **Draw** pull-down menu and then pick **Edge**, pick the **Edge** button in the **Surfaces** toolbar, or enter EDGE at the **Command:** prompt:

Figure 6-11.
A—To construct fillets and rounds, arcs are first drawn. The direction vectors are needed if **TABSURF** is used, but not for **RULESURF**.
B—The "edges" of the fillet and round. Now, the "faces" must be drawn.
C—Use construction points and **RULESURF** to surface the "faces" of the fillet and round.
D—Use the **3DFACE** command to complete the surfacing of the entire side of the object.

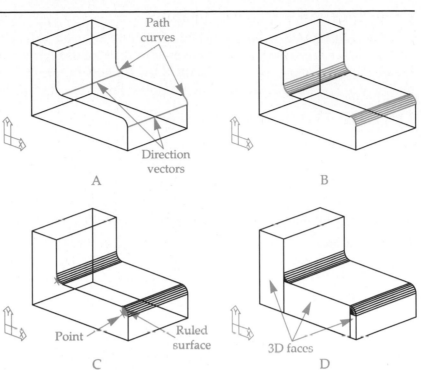

The edge is hidden and the object appears as shown in Figure 6-12. Invisible edges can be made visible using the **Display** option of the **EDGE** command as follows:

```
Command: EDGE↵
Display/⟨Select edge⟩: (pick the edge to hide)
Display/⟨Select edge⟩: ↵
Command:
```

The edge is hidden and the object appears as shown in Figure 6-12. Invisible edges can be made visible using the **Display** option of the **EDGE** command as follows:

```
Command: EDGE↵
Display/⟨Select edge⟩: D↵
Select/⟨All⟩: S↵
Select objects: (pick an edge of the 3D face) 1 found
Select objects: ↵
** Regenerating 3DFACE objects...done.
Display/⟨Select edge⟩: (pick the highlighted invisible edge)
Display/⟨Select edge⟩: ↵
Command: ↵
```

The edge is now visible. Notice that the two suboptions of the **Display** option are to **Select** a single edge or to select **All** edges.

Figure 6-12.
Notice in Figure 6-11D that the edges of the 3D faces can be seen in the middle of the object. The **EDGE** command can be used to make these edges invisible, as shown here.

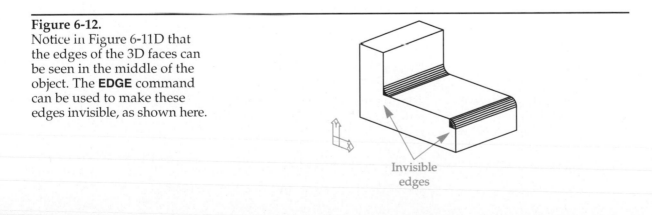

Using SPLFRAME to control visibility

The **SPLFRAME** system variable can also be used to control the visibility of **3DFACE** edges. To set this variable, pick **Display** in the **Options** pull-down menu. Then, pick **Spline Frame**. You can also type **SPLFRAME** at the **Command:** prompt. A value of 0 does not display invisible 3D face edges. A value of 1 displays invisible 3D face edges.

EDITING POLYGON MESHES

The **PEDIT** command is used to edit polygon meshes. The entire mesh can be smoothed, individual vertices can be moved, or the mesh can be closed. The following options are displayed when a polygon mesh is selected:

    Command: **PEDIT**↵
    Edit vertex/Smooth surface/Desmooth/Mclose/Nclose/Undo/eXit ⟨X⟩:

The **Edit vertex** option is used to alter individual vertices. This option is explained in detail later.

- **Smooth surface**—Applies a smooth surface to the mesh based on the value of the **SURFTYPE** variable. These types of surfaces are also discussed in Chapter 5.

SURFTYPE setting	Surface type
5	Quadratic B-spline
6	Cubic B-spline
8	Bézier surface

- **Desmooth**—Removes smoothing and returns the mesh to its original vertices.
- **Mclose**—The polylines in the M direction are closed if the M direction mesh is open.
- **Mopen**—Opens the polylines in the M direction if they are closed.
- **Nclose**—The polylines in the N direction are closed if the N direction mesh is open.
- **Nopen**—Opens the polylines in the N direction if they are closed.

Figure 6-13A shows a polygon mesh. Figure 6-13B shows the results of using the **Nclose** option on the mesh.

Figure 6-13.
A—A polygon mesh with a smoothed surface.
B—The mesh after using the **Nclose** option of **PEDIT**.

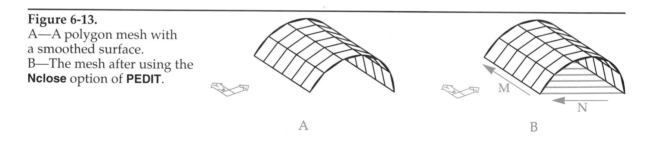

A   B

The **Edit vertex** option of **PEDIT** allows you to move individual vertices of the polygon mesh. When you select the **Edit vertex** option, you get several suboptions:

    Edit vertex/Smooth surface/Desmooth/Mclose/Nclose/Undo/eXit ⟨X⟩: **E**↵
    Vertex (0,0). Next/Previous/Left/Right/Up/Down/Move/REgen/eXit ⟨N⟩:

Notice in Figure 6-14A that an X marker appears at the first vertex. This X can be moved to the vertex you want to edit. The **Edit vertex** suboptions are explained as follows:

- **Next**—The X moves to the next vertex in the order drawn. When the end of a line is reached, the X jumps to the start of the next line.
- **Previous**—The X moves to the previous vertex in the order drawn.
- **Left**—The X moves to the previous vertex in the N direction. When the end of a line is reached, the X jumps to the start of the next line.
- **Right**—The X moves to the next vertex in the N direction. See Figure 6-14B.
- **Up**—The X moves to the next vertex in the M direction. When the end of a line is reached, the X jumps to the start of the next line. See Figure 6-14B.

Figure 6-14.
A—An X marker appears at the first vertex of a polygon mesh selected using **PEDIT**. B—Move the X marker in the N direction with the **Left** and **Right** options. Move the X in the M direction with the **Up** and **Down** options.

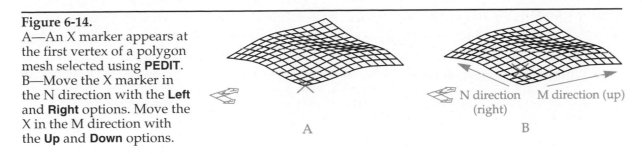

- **Down**—The X moves to the previous vertex in the M direction.
- **Move**—The vertex where the X is can be moved to a new location.

You may notice in Figure 6-14B that the **Right** option is actually moving the vertex to the left of the screen. This is because the right/left and up/down directions are determined by the order that the vertices were drawn in.

When the **Move** option is selected, the crosshairs are attached to the vertex with a rubber band line and the following prompt appears. Refer to Figure 6-15A.

Enter new location:

If a new point is picked, the mesh appears to be altered properly, Figure 6-15B. However, when the viewpoint is changed, as in Figure 6-15C, it is clear that the new point does not

Figure 6-15.
A—The crosshairs are attached by a rubber band line to the vertex to be moved and the Enter new location: prompt appears on the command line. B—A new point picked with the cursor appears correct. C—When the viewpoint is changed, you can see that using the pointing device produces inaccurate results.

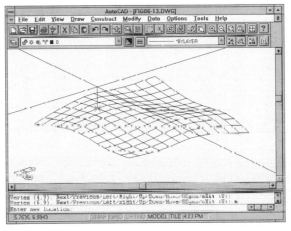

A

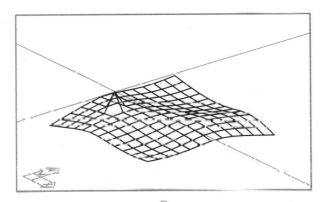

B

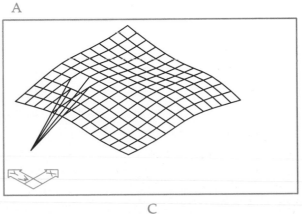

C

have the intended Z value. This is because the Z value will always be zero on the current XY plane. Therefore, do not pick a new polygon mesh location with the pointing device. Instead, enter the coordinates or use XYZ filters.

Enter new location: **@0,0,.6**↵

The new location in Figure 6-16A appears similar to Figure 6-15A. However, when viewed from another direction, it is clear that entering coordinates produced the correct results, Figure 6-16B.

Figure 6-16.
A—When coordinates are entered at the keyboard, the results at first appear the same as when using the pointing device. B—When the viewpoint is changed, you can see that entering coordinates produces correct results.

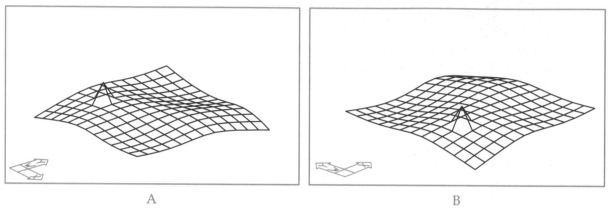

A   B

Editing polygon meshes with grips

When a polygon mesh is selected, all of its grips are displayed. See Figure 6-17A. Individual vertices can be edited by picking the grip you wish to move and entering the new coordinates at the keyboard, Figure 6-17B.

If **EXPLODE** is used on a polygon mesh, the mesh is broken into individual 3D faces. Pick any edge on the mesh and four grips appear that define the corners of the 3D face. See Figure 6-18A. The vertices of each face can be edited using grips. See Figure 6-18B. If you edit a vertex of a 3D face created by exploding a exploded polygon mesh, the vertex will no longer be attached to the original mesh. See Figure 6-18C.

Figure 6-17.
A—When a polygon mesh is selected, the grips become warm. B—Select a single grip to make it hot. This grip can then be moved.

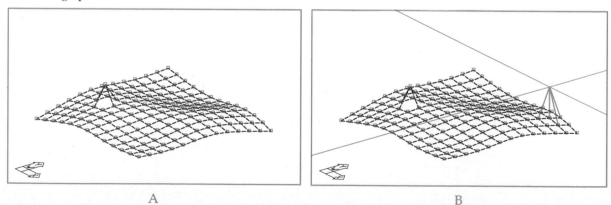

A   B

Figure 6-18.
A—When you select an edge of an exploded polygon mesh, you can see that it is made up of 3D faces.
B—A single vertex on a 3D face can be edited using grips. C—The edited 3D face vertex is
detached from the original mesh.

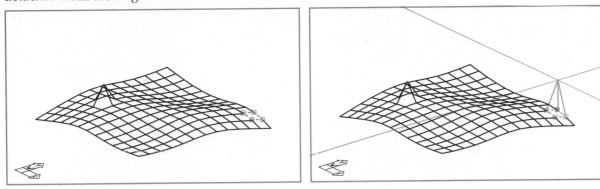

A   B

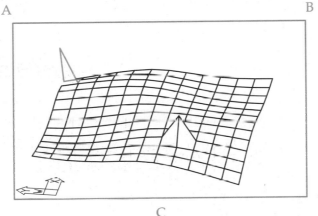

C

PROFESSIONAL TIP

    With careful planning, you can minimize the number of faces you construct. Draw only the number needed and use editing commands to create the rest. As shown in Figure 6-18, a 3D face is easily edited using grips. Use all of the grip editing functions—move, rotate, scale, and mirror—to quickly manipulate 3D faces.

CHAPTER TEST

Write your answers in the spaces provided.

1. What command allows you to both move and rotate a 3D object? _____

2. What feature do you define when using the **ROTATE3D** command? _____

3. What option of the **ROTATE3D** command allows you to use the center axis of a circle as
    the feature to rotate about? _____

4. What is the default method of picking a **MIRROR3D** mirror plane? _____

5. What are the three dimensions of a 3D array? _____

6. Indicate the **PROJMODE** values, give the name, and define the function of the three sub-options of the **Project** option of the **TRIM** command.

   PROJMODE = _____

   PROJMODE = _____

   PROJMODE = _____

7. What is the function of the **Edge** option of the **TRIM** command? _____

   _____

   _____

8. Which surfacing commands are good for creating fillets and rounds? _____

   _____

9. What is the function of the **EDGE** command? _____

   _____

10. How can invisible 3D face edges be displayed? _____

    _____

11. How can the angular faces of a polygon mesh be rounded? _____

    _____

12. Name the three types of smooth curves that can be applied to a polygon mesh, and give their **SURFTYPE** values.

    A. **SURFTYPE** = _____

    B. **SURFTYPE** = _____

    C. **SURFTYPE** = _____

13. What command, option, and suboption are used to edit a single vertex of a polygon mesh? _____

14. What is the most accurate way to move a polygon mesh vertex when using the grip method? _____

15. When a polygon mesh is exploded, what type of objects are created? _____

DRAWING PROBLEMS

Mechanical Drafting

1. Open Problem 2 from Chapter 1. If you have not done this problem, draw it in 3D wireframe using your own measurements. Then, do the following:

   A. Construct a box the exact width and depth of the slot in the object, but twice as high as the opening in the object. Draw the box sitting outside the object.

   B. Use the **ALIGN** command to place the box inside the slot.

   C. Edit the object so that the slot is moved half the distance to the left edge of the object. Move the box along with the slot.

   D. Save the drawing as P6-1.

2. Open Problem 1 from Chapter 1. If you have not done this problem, draw it in 3D wireframe using your own measurements. Then, do the following:

   A. Use **ROTATE3D** to rotate the object 90°.

   B. Use **MIRROR3D** to place a second copy at a 180° rotation using the **YZ** option.

   C. Use the **XZ** option of **MIRROR3D** to create a copy of the last operation. The final drawing should look like the one shown below.

   D. Save the drawing as P6-2.

Mechanical Drafting

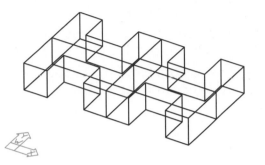

3. Open Problem 3 from Chapter 1. If you have not done this problem, draw it in 3D wireframe using your own measurements. Then, do the following:

   A. Use **ALIGN** to rotate the block that is inserted into the slot of the main body. The block should be rotated 90° so its tall side is aligned with the tall dimension of the body.

   B. Mirror and copy the body 180° so that the copy and the original fully enclose the block.

   C. Save the drawing as **P6-3**.

Mechanical Drafting

4. Draw Problem 5 from Chapter 1 as a 3D surface model using the measurements given. Use the following guidelines:

   A. Construct fillets where the two cylinders join the base.

   B. Construct chamfers at the top of each cylinder.

   C. Apply a fillet around the top edge of the base.

   D. Save the drawing as P6-4.

Mechanical Drafting

5. Draw Problem 8 from Chapter 1 as a 3D surface model using the dimensions given. Use the following guidelines:

   A. Construct a .25 radius fillet on all three inside corners.

   B. Construct a .125″ × 45° chamfer at the top of each hole.

   C. Save the drawing as P6-5.

Mechanical Drafting

6. Draw Problem 9 from Chapter 1 as a 3D surface model using the dimensions given. Use the following guidelines:

   A. Create a .25″ × 45° chamfer on the top edge of the large hole.

   B. Construct the small holes using **RULESURF**.

   C. Use **3DARRAY** to create a polar array of the four small holes.

   D. Save the drawing as P6-6.

Mechanical Drafting

7. Draw Problem 11 from Chapter 1 as a 3D surface model using the dimensions given. Use the following guidelines:

   A. Create a .25" radius fillet around the top edge of the base plate.

   B. Construct the small holes using **RULESURF**.

   C. Use **ARRAY** to create a rectangular array of the four small holes.

   D. Save the drawing as P6-7.

8. Draw Problem 9 from Chapter 2 as a 3D surface model using the dimensions given. Use the following guidelines:

   A. Draw a bar of the same dimensions to fit over the pin bar in Problem 2-9. Construct it alongside the pin bar.

   B. Use **RULESURF** to construct the holes in the new bar, and be sure to erase the original circles used to construct the holes.

   C. Use **ALIGN** to place the new bar over the pin bar.

   D. Rotate the entire assembly 90°.

   E. Save the drawing as P6-8.

9. Draw Problem 11 from Chapter 2 as a 3D surface model. Use the following guidelines:

   A. Explode the sphere mesh. Remove 20 3D faces —12 above the equator and 8 below.

   B. Draw a new sphere in the exact center of the existing one, and 1/2 its diameter.

   C. Draw a small diameter tube protruding at a 45° angle from the center of the new sphere into the northern hemisphere. It should extend out through the large sphere.

   D. Create a 3D polar array of six tubes.

   E. Save the drawing as P6-9.

10. Draw Problem 1 from Chapter 3 as a 3D surface model. Use the following guidelines:

    A. Place a .25" radius fillet on all inside vertical corners.

    B. Place a .125" radius round on all outside vertical corners.

    C. Save the drawing as P6-10.

11. Draw Problem 3 from Chapter 3 as a 3D surface model using the dimensions given. Use the following guidelines:

    A. Place a .125" radius on all exterior corners.

    B. Give the object a .25" radius bend at the "L".

    C. Save the drawing as P6-11.

12. Draw Problem 8 from Chapter 3 as a 3D surface model using the dimensions given. Use the following guidelines:

    A. Draw the 2.40 side at a 15° angle from vertical.

    B. Give the object a .25" inside radius at the bend.

    C. Save the drawing as P6-12.

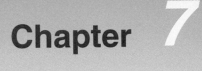
Viewing and Displaying Three-Dimensional Models

Learning objectives

After completing this chapter, you will be able to:

○ Use all options of the **VPOINT** command to display 3D models.
○ Describe how to hide lines in a variety of situations.
○ Use the **DVIEW** command to view the 3D model.
○ Apply shading to objects using the **SHADE** command.
○ Use **SHADEDGE** and **SHADEDIF** to create shading variations.
○ Use the **RENDER** command to produce quick renderings.
○ Perform "real-time" panning and zooming.

There are two different ways to select a viewpoint for 3D models. These are the **VPOINT** command and the **DVIEW** command. The **VPOINT** command, discussed in Chapter 1, is a "static" method. The viewpoint is established first, then the object is displayed. The **DVIEW** command is a "dynamic" viewing method. You can select a viewpoint as the model is being moved.

Once a viewpoint has been selected, you can enhance the display in several ways. You can pan and zoom in "real time." This means that you can see the object move as it is panned or zoomed. You can use the **HIDE** command to temporarily remove hidden lines. This command has been used in previous chapters. You can also use the **SHADE** command to create a simple rendering. A more advanced rendering is created with the **RENDER** command. This command creates the most realistic display of the model. The **RENDER** command is introduced in this chapter, but is discussed in detail in Chapter 9 and Chapter 14.

USING THE VPOINT COMMAND

The **VPOINT** command can be accessed in three different ways. It can be selected from the **View** pull-down menu by picking **3D Viewpoint** and then **Tripod**. This is covered in Chapter 1. Viewpoint angles can also be established using the **Viewpoint Presets** dialog box or the **View** toolbar. For an overview of the **VPOINT** command and the "right hand rule," refer to Chapter 1.

Using the Rotate option

Using the **Rotate** option of the **VPOINT** command, you can enter two angles to set the viewpoint. The angles are similar to spherical coordinates, but do not include a distance from the center point. Spherical coordinates can locate any point on, inside, or outside a sphere.

Figure 7-1 shows an example of a point located with spherical coordinates. Notice that the 90° angle is the angle *in* the XY plane from the X axis. The 45° angle is the angle *from* the XY plane. These are the two angles used with the **Rotate** option of the **VPOINT** command. The **Rotate** option can be selected by picking **3D Viewpoint** and **Vector** from the **View** pull-down menu, or it can be entered at the **Command:** prompt as follows:

Command: **VPOINT**⏎
Rotate/⟨View point⟩ ⟨*current*⟩: **R.**⏎
Enter angle in XY plane from X axis ⟨*current*⟩: **45.**⏎
Enter angle from XY plane ⟨*current*⟩: **45.**⏎
Regenerating drawing.
Command:

In Figure 7-2, the viewpoint in the right-hand viewport is moved counterclockwise 45° from the X axis and 45° from the XY plane.

Figure 7-1.
Spherical coordinates are made up of three values. These three values define a point on a sphere.

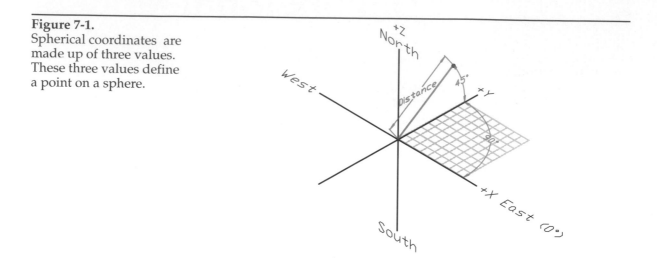

Figure 7-2.
The viewpoint in the right viewport was created using the **Rotate** option of the **VPOINT** command. Both rotation angles are 45°.

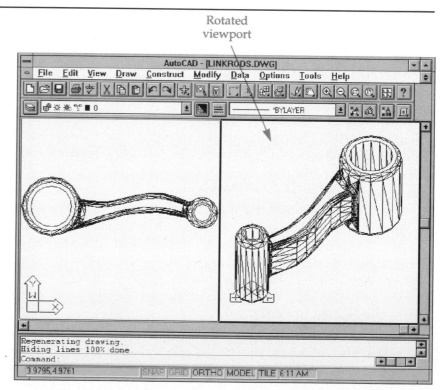

Rotated viewport

3D display options using a pull-down menu

The **View** pull-down menu provides additional options of viewpoint selection. Pick the **View** pull-down menu, then select **3D Viewpoint Presets**. A cascading submenu appears that displays viewpoint options. See Figure 7-3. This selection of preset views allows you to display six orthographic and four isometric views of the current drawing. Figure 7-4 shows how these different selections affect the drawing in Figure 7-2. The appropriate **View** toolbar button also appears next to each view.

Figure 7-3.
The **3D Viewpoint Presets** cascading submenu has several options for creating a 3D viewing angle.

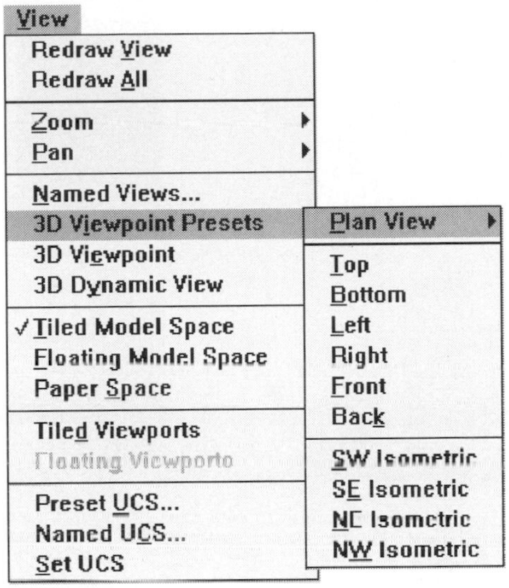

3D viewpoints using a dialog box

The **Viewpoint Presets** dialog box has a plan view on the left and an elevation view on the right. This allows you to graphically position your viewpoint. The dialog box is displayed by picking **3D Viewpoint** and then **Rotate**... from the **View** pull-down menu. See Figure 7-5. The dialog box can also be accessed by typing DDVPOINT at the **Command:** prompt.

The centers of the plan view and elevation view represent the origin on your drawing. If you pick the **Absolute to WCS** button at the top of the dialog box, the origin is based on the World Coordinate System. If you pick the **Relative to UCS** button, the origin is based on the origin of the current User Coordinate System. User Coordinate Systems are discussed in Chapter 3. Pick **OK** when you complete your settings. You can change the current view back to a plan view if you pick the **Set to Plan View** button.

In Figure 7-5, the line of sight from the X axis (0°) is indicated by the line located at the 135° mark in the plan view. The line of sight from the XY plane is indicated by the line at 30° in the elevation view. Settings of 270° and 90° create a plan view. The display shown in Figure 7-2 can be created by picking the 45° mark in the plan view and the upper 45° section inside the large arc in the elevation view.

The angle values in the **Viewpoint Presets** dialog box can be set by picking in the graphic or by entering a value in the text boxes. Picking an angle with your pointing device is not accurate. If you need a specific angle, enter it in the **From X Axis:** or **XY Plane:** text boxes. If the viewing angle does not need to be exact, it may be quicker to set the angle with the pointing device. You can select angles in 45° increments if you pick between the radial lines.

Figure 7-4.
Each of the 3D viewpoint presets applied to the LINKRODS model.

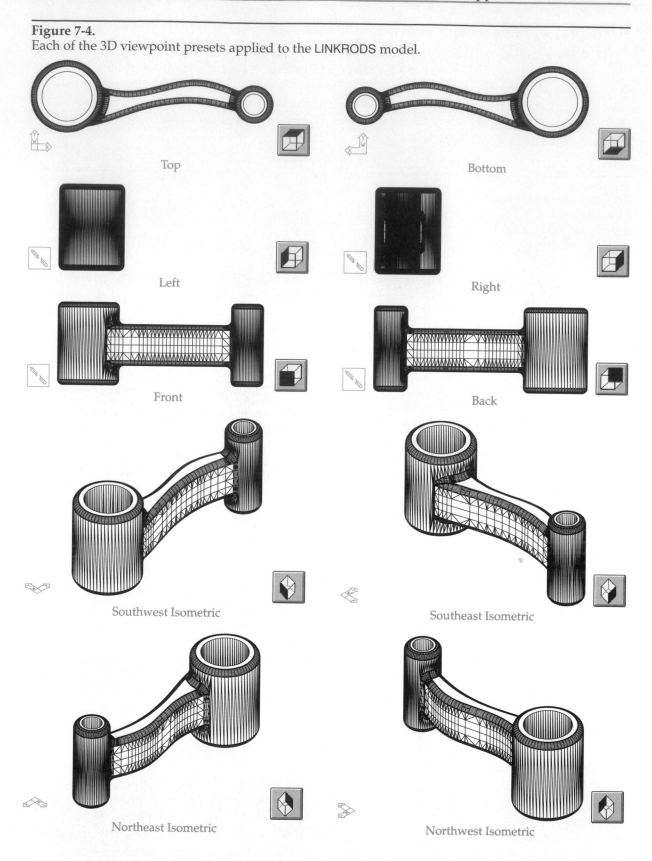

Top

Bottom

Left

Right

Front

Back

Southwest Isometric

Southeast Isometric

Northeast Isometric

Northwest Isometric

Figure 7-5.
The **Viewpoint Presets** dialog box allows you to graphically set your viewpoint.

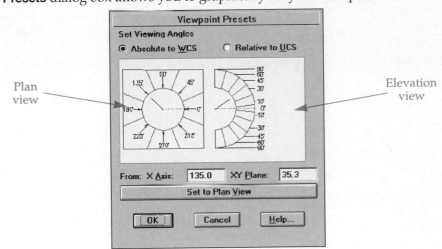

Creating a plan view

You can quickly create a plan view of any UCS or the WCS using the **PLAN** command. This command can be accessed by picking **3D Viewpoint Presets** and then **Plan View** from the **View** pull-down menu. Then, select the appropriate option in the submenu, Figure 7-6. You can also type PLAN at the **Command:** prompt. The options are explained below.

- **World**—This creates a view of the object plan to the WCS.
- **Current**—This creates a view of the object plan to the current UCS.
- **Named**—This allows you to specify a named UCS and then displays a view plan to that UCS.

You can also create a plan view by using the **VPOINT** command and typing the XYZ coordinates for the plan view.

    Command: **VPOINT**⏎
    Rotate/⟨View point⟩ ⟨*current*⟩: **0,0,1**⏎
    Regenerating drawing.
    Command:

Both the **PLAN** and **VPOINT** commands automatically **ZOOM Extents**. This fills the graphics window with the original top view. You can **ZOOM All** to display the original drawing limits, or enter a zoom scale factor less than 1 to reduce the screen display.

Figure 7-6.
Select the appropriate menu item from the **Plan View** cascading submenu to create a plan view.

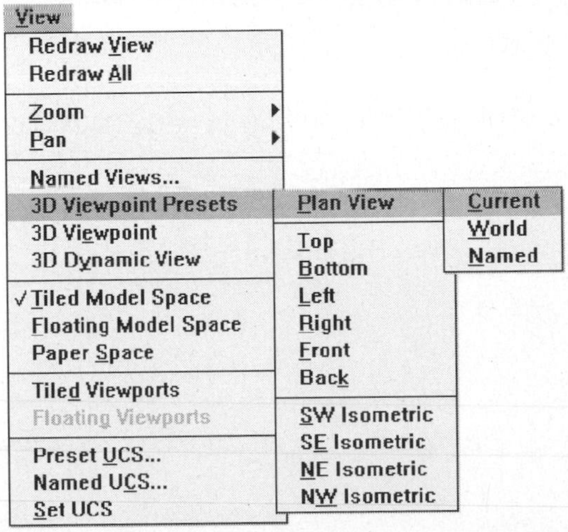

EXERCISE 7-1

❏ Begin a new drawing and name it EX7-1.
❏ Using the **3D Objects** dialog box or the **Surfaces** toolbar, draw a wedge to the size of your choice.
❏ Use the **VPOINT** command to display a 3D view of your drawing. Display it twice using the **Rotate** option.
❏ Display it again using four different views from the **View** toolbar.
❏ Select three different views from the **Viewpoint Presets** dialog box.
❏ Display the object as a plan view.
❏ Quit without saving.

USING THE DVIEW COMMAND

The **DVIEW** (dynamic view) command allows you to view a model in 3D. With this command, you can control every aspect of the display. As you alter the view, the display moves dynamically. This means that as you rotate, zoom, or pan the drawing, you can see the changes.

The viewer's eye location is called the *camera.* The focus point is the *target.* These two points form the *line of sight.* The line of sight can be adjusted to any angle. The distance from the camera to the target can be set. Also, the camera can have a telephoto or wide angle lens. These lenses allow you to create a close-up or wide field of vision. The entire image can be rotated, or *twisted,* around the center point of the display. Imaginary front and back cutting planes can be established to "clip" portions of the model you do not wish to view. Hidden lines can also be removed.

The **DVIEW** command is a powerful tool. Take time to test its options. Experiment with the various displays you can achieve. This will help you understand the command better.

Test drawings for DVIEW

The **DVIEW** command may be slow if used on a large drawing. This will depend on your computer and how much memory it has. Therefore, use a test drawing to create the view needed. Then, display your drawing using the new view settings.

AutoCAD has a test drawing named DVIEWBLOCK. This drawing is a block in the ACAD.DWG drawing file. The block is a simple house with a chimney, window, and open door, Figure 7-7. Since there are few objects in the drawing, it can be rotated, zoomed, and panned quickly. The DVIEWBLOCK drawing is displayed if you press [Enter] at the Select objects: prompt of the **DVIEW** command.

```
Command: DVIEW↵
Select objects: ↵
***Switching to the WCS***
CAmera/TArget/Distance/POints/PAn/Zoom/TWist/CLip/Hide/Off/Undo/⟨eXit⟩:
```

The house appears on the screen at the same viewpoint as the current drawing. You may not see the entire house at first, depending on the zoom magnification of the current drawing. Press [Enter] to return to the **Command:** prompt.

Figure 7-7.
The default DVIEWBLOCK drawing is a small house. This can be used to help you select a viewing angle.

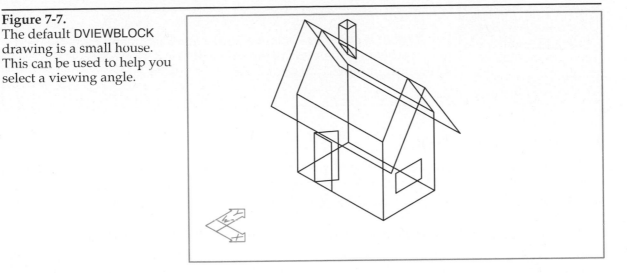

PROFESSIONAL TIP

You can create your own custom block called DVIEWBLOCK. Before you do so, make a copy of the ACAD.DWG file. It is located by default in the \R13\COM\SUPPORT subdirectory. Next, begin a new drawing. Do not place anything on the drawing except the object you will construct as your DVIEWBLOCK. Draw the block to fit into a one unit cube and keep it simple. Use the **BLOCK** command to save the object as DVIEWBLOCK, and select the lower-left corner as the origin. Return the drawing to the plan view. Save the drawing as \R13\COM\SUPPORT\ACAD.DWG. Now execute the **DVIEW** command and press [Enter] at the Select objects: prompt. Your new block should appear.

Keep the drawing simple. If you work with mechanical parts, draw an object that represents a typical part. If you work with industrial piping, draw a pipe fitting. Architects can use the default DVIEWBLOCK. Structural designers might draw a piece of wide flange. To use your custom DVIEWBLOCK, select the DVIEW command and press [Enter] in response to the Select objects: prompt.

Viewing the entire drawing

When you use **DVIEW** on a drawing for the first time, the object may fill the entire screen. If so, zoom out in order to see the object better.

```
Command: DVIEW↵
Select objects: ↵
CAmera/TArget/Distance/POints/PAn/Zoom/TWist/Clip/Hide/Off/Undo/⟨eXit⟩: Z↵
Adjust zoom scale factor ⟨1⟩: .5↵
Command:
```

The entire drawing should now be centered on-screen at half its original size. If not, select the **Zoom** option again. Enter a value less than 1.0 until the entire drawing fits within the screen borders.

PROFESSIONAL TIP

It often is easier to visualize your viewpoint (camera angle) first, before adjusting the view using other options. This is especially true if the current view is a plan view.

Specifying the camera angle

If the drawing display is a plan view after using **DVIEW**, it is best to use the **CAmera** option before any other. This option lets you locate your eye position in two directions relative to object. A vertical movement is the angle *from* the XY plane. A horizontal movement is *in* the XY plane from the X axis.

After selecting the **CAmera** option, you can move the pointing device to pick the best display. The current angle appears on the status line where the coordinates normally show. This number changes as you move the pointer. An angle value can also be entered at the keyboard.

The second prompt requests the angle of the camera in the XY plane. A 0° value results in a view looking straight down the X axis. This is looking into the window of DVIEWBLOCK. A positive value moves the camera to the right, or counterclockwise, around the house. A negative rotation angle moves the camera left, or clockwise, around the house.

    CAmera/TArget/Distance/POints/PAn/Zoom/TWist/CLip/Hide/Off/Undo/⟨eXit⟩: **CA.**⏎
    Toggle angle in/Enter angle from XY plane ⟨current⟩: **15.**⏎
    Toggle angle from/Enter angle in XY plane from X axis ⟨current⟩: **–60** ⏎

The result is shown in Figure 7-8A. The effect of these camera settings on the LINKRODS drawing is shown in Figure 7-8B.

While the **CAmera** option prompts are on the screen, you can toggle between the horizontal and vertical angle input by using the **Toggle** option. If the prompt reads Toggle angle in, you can switch to this option to input the angle *in* the XY plane by typing T and pressing [Enter]. The prompt changes to Toggle angle from. Now you can enter a camera angle in the XY plane. This allows you to try several angles while still in the **CAmera** option.

You can limit the movement of the camera to one direction by specifying an angle and pressing [Enter]. For example, if you enter 20 for the angle from the XY plane as follows, the object remains stationary at that angle and only moves clockwise or counterclockwise on the X axis.

    Toggle angle in/Enter angle from XY plane ⟨current⟩: **20.**⏎

This allows you to view the object at one vertical angle from any horizontal angle in the XY plane. You can also enter an angle in the XY plane from the X axis to limit the horizontal movement of the camera.

    Toggle angle in/Enter angle from XY plane ⟨current⟩: **T.**⏎
    Toggle angle from/Enter angle in XY plane from X axis ⟨current⟩: **30.**⏎

A plan view is 90° from the XY plane. This places your line of sight perpendicular to the XY plane of the current UCS. With the DVIEWBLOCK drawing on-screen, a 90° camera angle places your line of sight looking down onto the roof. A 0° camera angle places the line of sight looking into the door.

Figure 7-8.
A—This view was created with values of 15° *from* the XY plane and –60° *in* the XY plane.
B—The settings in A applied to the LINKRODS drawing.

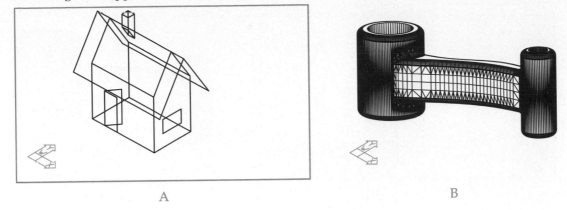

A   B

Select the target angles

Another way to change your view is with the **TArget** option. The *target* is the point where the camera looks. The target can be rotated around the camera to any angle. A 90° vertical rotation angle creates a view of the opposite side of the object, Figure 7-9.

The following angle settings for the **TArget** option create a view from below the floor of the house, Figure 7-10A. These are the same values used above for the **CAmera** option. The effect of this **DVIEW** target setting on the LINKRODS drawing is shown in Figure 7-10B.

    Command: **DVIEW**↵
    Select objects: ↵
    CAmera/TArget/Distance/POints/PAn/Zoom/TWist/CLip/Hide/Off/Undo/⟨eXit⟩: **TA.** ↵
    Toggle angle in/Enter angle from XY plane ⟨*current*⟩: **15**↵
    Toggle angle from/Enter angle in XY plane from X axis ⟨*current*⟩: **–60**↵

Figure 7-9.
The vertical rotation angle
for the target is opposite
that of the camera.

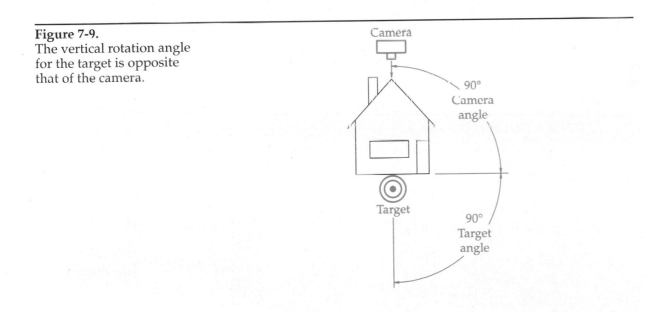

Figure 7-10.
A—When the target is moved using the values entered for the camera in Figure 7-8, the view is from under the house. B—The settings in A applied to the LINKRODS drawing.

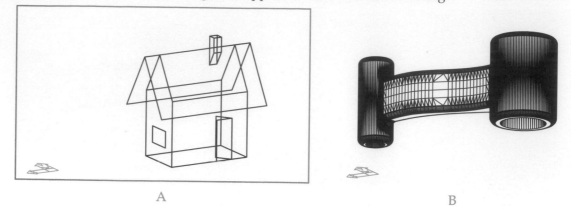

A   B

Setting a distance between camera and target (perspective)

To this point, you have created views that are parallel projections. A perspective is not a parallel projection. The **Distance** option creates a perspective by moving the camera closer or farther from the target. This is more like how your eye would actually see the object. Lines in a perspective view project to vanishing points. Therefore, lines farther from the camera appear to meet. AutoCAD indicates the perspective mode by placing a perspective icon in the lower-left corner of the screen.

CAmera/TArget/Distance/POints/PAn/Zoom/TWist/CLip/Hide/Off/Undo/⟨eXit⟩: **D**↵
New camera/target distance ⟨*current*⟩: **15**↵

The new view should look like Figure 7-11A. Press [Enter] to return to the **Command:** prompt. The effect of this **DVIEW Distance** setting on the LINKRODS drawing is shown in Figure 7-11B.

A slider bar appears when you select the **Distance** option. See Figure 7-12. It is labeled from 0× to 16×. The current distance is 1×. When you move the slider bar to 9×, the camera moves away nine times the previous distance. You can pick a distance with the slider bar or enter a distance at the keyboard. The coordinate display window constantly displays the distance. You may have to enter a distance greater than the width of your drawing to see all of the objects.

Figure 7-11.
A—The DVIEWBLOCK drawing with distance values applies. Notice the perspective icon in the lower-left corner. B—The setting in A applied to the LINKRODS drawing.

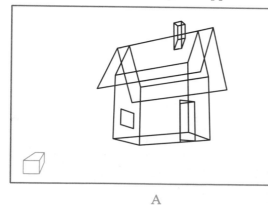
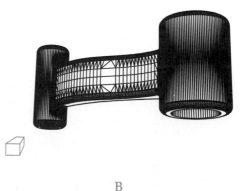

A   B

Figure 7-12.
A slider bar appears
for many of the **DVIEW**
command options.

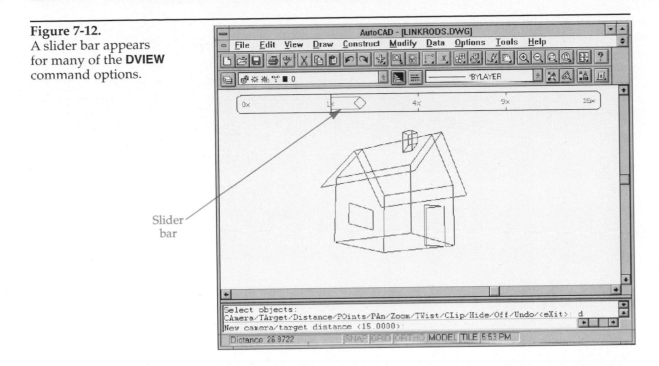

Slider
bar

The perspective view achieved with the **DVIEW Distance** option is great for display and plotting purposes, but not practical for working. Pan and zoom are not allowed in a perspective view, nor is selecting points for drawing. Therefore, turn the Distance option off as follows before continuing to work on the drawing:

CAmera/TArget/Distance/POints/PAn/Zoom/TWist/CLip/Hide/Off/Undo/〈eXit〉: **O**↵
CAmera/TArget/Distance/POints/PAn/Zoom/TWist/CLip/Hide/Off/Undo/〈eXit〉: ↵
Regenerating drawing.
Command:

Picking points for the target and camera

The **POints** option allows you to pick the target and camera locations using XYZ coordinates, filters, or osnap options. When entering XYZ coordinates, keep in mind that the coordinates are based on the current UCS. The **POints** option is best used when you have already created a display other than the initial plan view. Figure 7-13 shows target (P1) and camera (P2) pick points and the resulting view. As you select the pick points, a rubber band connects the camera and target to help you see the new line of sight. The command sequence for Figure 7-13 is:

Command: **DVIEW**↵
Select objects: *(select the objects on the screen)* ↵
CAmera/TArget/Distance/POints/PAn/Zoom/TWist/CLip/Hide/Off/Undo/〈eXit〉: **PO**↵
Enter target point 〈*default*〉: **MID**↵
of *(pick P1)*
Enter camera point 〈*default*〉: **END**↵
of *(pick P2)*

Notice in Figure 7-13B that the target and camera points are aligned. The camera point at the top of the tripod touches the target point. These two points are the line of sight. The display changes from perspective to a parallel projection to help you select camera and target points. The display then returns to perspective.

Figure 7-13.
A—The target (P1) and camera (P2) are located using the **POints** option. B—The resulting pictorial view.

A   B

PROFESSIONAL TIP

Several **DVIEW** options display a horizontal slider bar. Use this bar to visually set your display or read approximate values. The diamond in the bar indicates position. Rubber band lines are anchored to a short line in the slider bar. This short line indicates the present position of the drawing. When the diamond is centered on the short line, the current dynamic position is the same as the present drawing position. The value of the current slider setting appears in the coordinate display window.

EXERCISE 7-2

❑ Open the drawing named SEXTANT. It is located in the \R13\COM\SAMPLE subdirectory.
❑ Set **TILEMODE** to 0.
❑ Use the **DVIEW Distance** option to move your viewpoint farther away from the sextant.
❑ Use the **DVIEW Off** option to turn off the perspective display.
❑ Set the **DVIEW CAmera** and **TArget** options to both positive and negative angle values. Check each view using the **Hide** option.
❑ Set the **DVIEW POints** option to view the sextant from two different viewpoints.
❑ Close the drawing without saving.

Change the position of the drawing

The **PAn** option of **DVIEW** is similar to the **PAN** command. It allows you to move the entire drawing in relation to the graphics display area. Use the **PAn** option as follows:

CAmera/TArget/Distance/POints/PAn/Zoom/TWist/CLip/Hide/Off/Undo/⟨eXit⟩: **PA**⏎
Displacement base point: *(pick a point to move from)*
Second point: *(pick a point to move to)*

Using a zoom lens

You can change the lens on the **DVIEW** camera just as you can a real camera. Lens lengths are measured in millimeters. A zoom, or telephoto, lens is greater than 50mm. It allows you to get a close-up view while not changing the camera and target positions. A wide angle lens is less than 50mm. It takes in a wider field of vision as the lens length gets smaller. You can change lenses with the **Zoom** option.

CAmera/TArget/Distance/POints/PAn/Zoom/TWist/CLip/Hide/Off/Undo/⟨eXit⟩: **Z** ↵
Adjust lens length ⟨50.000mm⟩: **28** ↵

If your display is not in perspective, **Zoom** requests a scale factor. If the display is in perspective, **Zoom** allows you to adjust the lens length.

A 28mm lens is commonly known as a "fish-eye." This lens creates a wide field of vision. However, a fish-eye lens can distort the sides of your drawing, depending on the current distance setting. Two views of the DVIEWBLOCK drawing are shown in Figure 7-14 using a distance of 40 feet.

Figure 7-14.
A—A 28mm lens used at a distance of 40 feet. B—A 100mm lens used at a distance of 40 feet.

A   B

Rotating the drawing around a point

The **TWist** option allows you to rotate the drawing around the center point of the screen. When the twist, or *tilt angle,* is set with the pointing device, the angle appears in the coordinate display window. A rubber band line connects the center point to the crosshairs. An exact positive or negative angle can be entered at the keyboard.

Clipping portions of the drawing

Portions of a drawing can be eliminated from the display by using *clipping planes.* Think of a clipping plane as a wall that hides everything behind it. A clipping plane can also hide everything in front of it. The plane is always perpendicular to your line of sight. Lines behind the back clipping plane or in front of the front clipping plane are removed. The **CLip** option lets you dynamically place a clipping plane, or enter its distance from the target. The front and back planes are turned on by entering a distance, or turned off by selecting the **OFF** option. The camera is the default position of the front plane. The front clipping plane can be returned to the camera position with the **Eye** option.

CAmera/TArget/Distance/POints/PAn/Zoom/TWist/CLip/Hide/Off/Undo/⟨eXit⟩: **CL**↵
Back/Front/⟨Off⟩: **B**↵
ON/OFF/ ⟨Distance from target⟩ ⟨*current*⟩: *(enter a distance or use the slider bar*
  to pick)
CAmera/TArget/Distance/POints/PAn/Zoom/TWist/CLip/Hide/Off/Undo/⟨eXit⟩: **CL**↵
Back/Front/⟨Off⟩: **F**↵
Eye/ON/OFF/⟨Distance from target⟩ ⟨*default*⟩: **E**↵

When perspective is on, the front clipping plane is automatically on. The **ON** and **OFF** suboptions of the **DVIEW Front** option are available only if perspective is off. Figure 7-15 shows a drawing with front and back clipping planes.

Figure 7-15.
A—A front clipping placed in the drawing. B—A back clipping plane placed in the drawing.

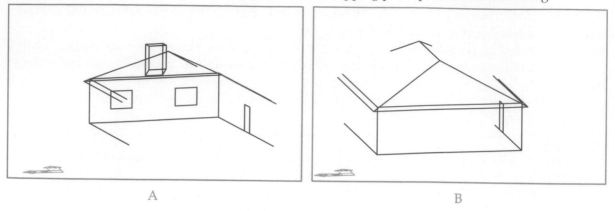

A   B

Other **DVIEW** options

The two remaining options of the **DVIEW** command are **Undo** and **Exit**. These are explained below.

- **Undo (U).** Undoes the previous **DVIEW** option. Like the **UNDO** command, this option lets you step back through previous **DVIEW** functions.
- **eXit (X).** Exits the **DVIEW** command and regenerates the drawing using the last view established.

EXERCISE 7-3

❑ Begin a new drawing called EX7-3. Draw a 3D house similar to the DVIEWBLOCK drawing in Figure 7-7.
❑ Select the **DVIEW** command to select a camera angle. Select the **Zoom** option to see the entire house.
❑ Draw a small box in the center of the house.
❑ Draw another object of your choice outside the house.
❑ Use the **POints** option of the **DVIEW** command to place the camera on the object outside the house. Place the target on a corner of the box inside the house.
❑ Select the **Distance** option to move farther away. Then, move closer to the target.
❑ Zoom to a point on, or near, the box inside the house.
❑ Select the **TArget** option. Pick an angle from the XY plane near zero. Move the pointer to several positions when picking the horizontal rotation. Notice how the house moves around you. Pick a view that allows you to see the object outside the house.
❑ Use the **CLip** option to place a back clipping plane that hides the object outside the house.
❑ Save the drawing as A:EX7-3.

AutoCAD
User's   **12**
Guide

DISPLAYING A 3D MODEL

The *display* of a 3D model is how the model is presented. This does not refer to the viewing angle. The simplest display technique is to remove hidden lines using the **HIDE** command. A simple rendered model can be created with the **SHADE** command. An advanced rendered model can be created with the **RENDER** command. This is the most realistic presentation.

Using the HIDE command

The **HIDE** command can be selected from the **Tools** pull-down menu, picked from the **Render** toolbar, or typed at the **Command:** prompt. The command regenerates the drawing and removes all lines that are behind other objects. Invisible edges of 3D faces are also removed.

Hiding lines on a plotted drawing can be done in one of two ways. These are described below:

- **Plotting**—Hidden lines are removed in a plot only if the **Hide Lines** check box is selected in the **Plot Configuration** dialog box.
- **Paper space plotting**—Hidden lines are not automatically removed in floating model space viewports when a drawing is plotted in paper space. To hide these lines, turn on the **Hideplot** option of the **MVIEW** command. Then, select the viewport to hide as follows:

```
Command: MVIEW↵
ON/OFF/Hideplot/Fit/2/3/4/Restore/⟨First Point⟩: H↵
ON/OFF: ON↵
Select objects: (pick the viewport to hide lines when plotting) 1 found
Select objects: ↵
Command:
```

When you pick the viewport, pick the border of the viewport. Do not pick the objects in the viewport.

> **CAUTION**
>
> ! Layers that are turned off are still regenerated. Frozen layers are not regenerated. Therefore, objects on layers that are turned off may block your view of objects on visible layers. On the other hand, objects on layers that are frozen will not obscure objects on visible layers.

Using the SHADE command

The **SHADE** command can be accessed by picking the **Shade** button in the **Render** toolbar, selecting **Shade** from the **Tools** pull-down menu, or typing SHADE at the **Command:** prompt. If the **Shade** button or **Command:** prompt is used, the objects are shaded using the current **SHADEDGE** value. The default value is 3. If you select the command from the **Tools** pull-down menu, a cascading submenu appears, Figure 7-16. The options in this submenu temporarily change the **SHADEDGE** variable and then shade the object. The different **SHADEDGE** settings are explained below. The corresponding **Shade** submenu options are also given.

SHADEDGE value	Explanation and Shade submenu option
0	Faces are shaded and edges are not highlighted. Pick **256 Color** in the **Shade** submenu.
1	Faces are shaded and edges are drawn in the background color. Pick **256 Color Edge Highlight** in the **Shade** submenu.
2	Faces are not shaded and edges are drawn in the object color. Pick **16 Color Hidden Line** in the **Shade** submenu.
3	Faces are shaded in the object color and edges are drawn in the background color. Pick **16 Color Filled** in the **Shade** submenu.

Figure 7-17 shows the effects of the four different **SHADEDGE** settings.

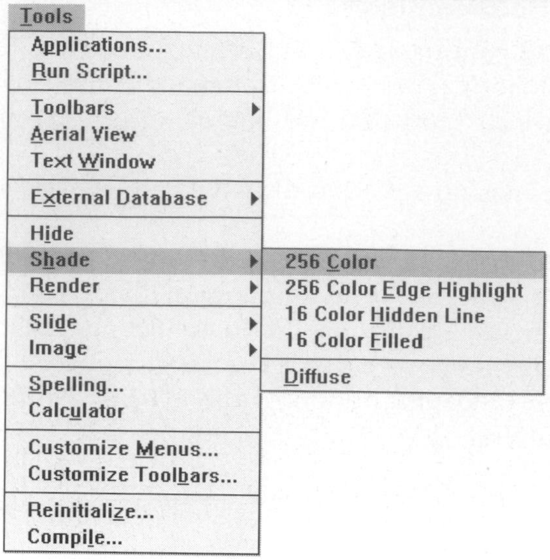

Figure 7-16.
Selecting the **SHADE**
command from the **Tools**
pull-down menu
temporarily changes the
SHADEDGE variable.

```
Tools
 Applications...
 Run Script...

 Toolbars                    ▶
 Aerial View
 Text Window

 External Database           ▶

 Hide
 Shade                       ▶     256 Color
 Render                      ▶     256 Color Edge Highlight
                                   16 Color Hidden Line
 Slide                       ▶     16 Color Filled
 Image                       ▶
                                   Diffuse
 Spelling...
 Calculator

 Customize Menus...
 Customize Toolbars...

 Reinitialize...
 Compile...
```

Figure 7-17.
The **SHADEDGE** values produce different display effects. A—**SHADEDGE** = 0. B—**SHADEDGE** = 1.
C—**SHADEDGE** = 2. D—**SHADEDGE** = 3.

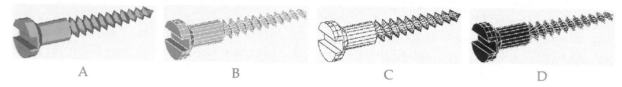

A   B   C   D

Diffuse light is light reflected off the surface of an object. The amount of diffuse light from an object is controlled by the **SHADEDIF** (shade diffuse) system variable. This value is the percent of light from the source behind your eyes that is diffused from the surface. The default value is 70, or 70%. The remaining 30% of light you see in a shaded drawing is ambient light. *Ambient light* is the natural light that surrounds you. The **SHADEDIF** value can be set by picking **Diffuse** in the **Shade** submenu, or it can be entered at the **Command:** prompt:

    Command: **SHADEDIF**↵
    New value for SHADEDIF ⟨70⟩: **100**↵

Since the SHADEDIF value is a percentage, the setting can be from 0 to 100.

The effects of several **SHADEDIF** settings are shown in Figure 7-18. All of the images in Figure 7-18 were produced with a **SHADEDGE** value of 0. This setting does not create edge highlighting.

Figure 7-18.   **SHADEDIF** can be set to values of 0 to 100. A—**SHADEDIF** = 10. B—**SHADEDIF** = 40.
C—**SHADEDIF** = 70. D—**SHADEDIF** = 100.

A   B   C   D

Producing a quick rendering

The **RENDER** command is covered in detail in Chapter 9. However, as an introduction, first open the LINKRODS drawing. Next, choose **Render** from the **Tools** pull-down menu, then pick **Render**. You can also pick the **Render** button in the **Render** toolbar. Either way, the **Render** dialog box is displayed. Use the defaults shown and pick the **Render Scene** button. A shaded and rendered image is then created, Figure 7-19.

Figure 7-19.
The **RENDER** command was used to produce this display of the LINKRODS drawing.

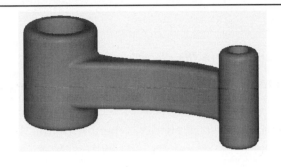

EXERCISE 7-4

❑ Open the SEXTANT drawing found in the \R13\COM\SAMPLE subdirectory.
❑ Pick each of the four shading options in the **Shade** submenu. Notice the difference in the displays.
❑ Change the **SHADEDIF** setting and select one of the shading options. Do this for three different **SHADEDIF** settings.
❑ Use the **RENDER** command to produce a shaded rendering of the sextant.
❑ Do not save the drawing.

Performing real-time pan and zoom

The **RTPAN** and **RTZOOM** commands allow you to see the model move on the screen as you pan or zoom. These commands are dynamic versions of the **PAN** and **ZOOM** commands. They are easy to use.

After typing RTPAN, press and hold the pick button and move the pointing device in the direction you wish to pan. When the drawing is where you want it, release the pick button. Then, press [Enter] or [Esc] to end the command. The **RTZOOM** command works similarly. Move the pointing device up to zoom in or down to zoom out. The prompts look like this:

```
Command: RTPAN ↵
Press pick button and move cursor to pan [Enter or ESC to exit]: ↵
Command: RTZOOM ↵
Press pick button and move cursor vertically to zoom [Enter or ESC to exit]: ↵
```

The cursor changes to a hand while in the **RTPAN** command, Figure 7-20A. The cursor changes to a magnifying glass with plus and minus signs while in the **RTZOOM** command, Figure 7-20B.

Figure 7-20.
A—The **RTPAN** cursor.
B—The **RTZOOM** cursor.

A   B

NOTE   The **RTPAN** and **RTZOOM** commands are not in versions of
AutoCAD Release 13 before the c4 maintenance release.

CHAPTER TEST

Write your answers in the spaces provided.

1. What kind of coordinates can you use with the **Rotate** option of the **VPOINT** command?
    _____

2. What two angles are needed when using the **Rotate** option of the **VPOINT** command?
    _____

3. What command produces a view that is perpendicular to the current UCS? _____
    _____

4. What does the image on the left side of the **Viewpoint Presets** dialog box represent?
    _____

5. What is the function of the DVIEWBLOCK? _____
    _____

6. How do you specify a camera angle using the **DVIEW** command? _____
    _____

7. What two values must be set to complete the **DVIEW** option in Question 6?_____
    _____

8. What point does the camera look at in the **DVIEW** command? What option is used to set it?
    _____

9. Which option of the **DVIEW** command allows you to create a perspective view?_____
    _____

10. After a perspective view is created and you are at the **Command:** prompt, which commands and activities are *not* allowed? _____
    _____

11. How is a lens length selected in the **DVIEW** command? _____
    _____

12. What portions of an object are removed when **DVIEW** clipping planes are set? _____
    _____

13. What is the function of the **MVIEW Hideplot** option? _____
    _____

14. What system variable controls the appearance of surfaces and edges when the **SHADE**
    command is used?_____

15. Which value of the variable in Question 14 produces faces that are shaded in the object
    color and edges that are drawn in the background color? _____

16. What is the function of the **SHADEDIF** system variable?_____
_____
_____
_____

17. What is the range of values that **SHADEDIF** can be set to? _____

18. What command produces the most realistic shaded image? _____

DRAWING PROBLEMS

1. Open one of your 3D drawings from a previous chapter and do the following:

    A. Use **VPOINT** to produce a display with a 30° rotation in the XY plane and a 40° rotation from the XY plane.

    B. Shade the object so that faces are shown in object colors and edges are highlighted.

    C. Produce a slide of the image. Refer to Chapter 30 of *AutoCAD and its Applications—Basics, Release 13 for Windows* for information on creating slides.

    General

2. Open one of your 3D drawings from a previous chapter and do the following:

    A. Create an arrangement of three floating model space viewports in a paper space layout.

    B. Display the drawing in a different viewpoint in each of the viewports.

    C. Set the **SHADEDGE** variable to a different value in each viewport. Create a shaded image using **SHADE** in each viewport.

    General

3. Open one of your 3D drawings from a previous chapter and perform the following:

    A. Create an arrangement of three floating model space viewports in a paper space layout.

    B. Display the drawing in a different viewpoint in each of the viewports.

    C. Set the **SHADEDGE** variable to a different value in two viewports. Set **SHADEDIF** to different values in those two viewports as well.

    D. Shade the objects in the two viewports, and use **RENDER** in the third viewport.

    General

A wireframe (top) may appear as nothing more than a mess of lines. However, when the **HIDE** command is used on this surfaced model, you can see that it is a '57 Chevy. (Autodesk)

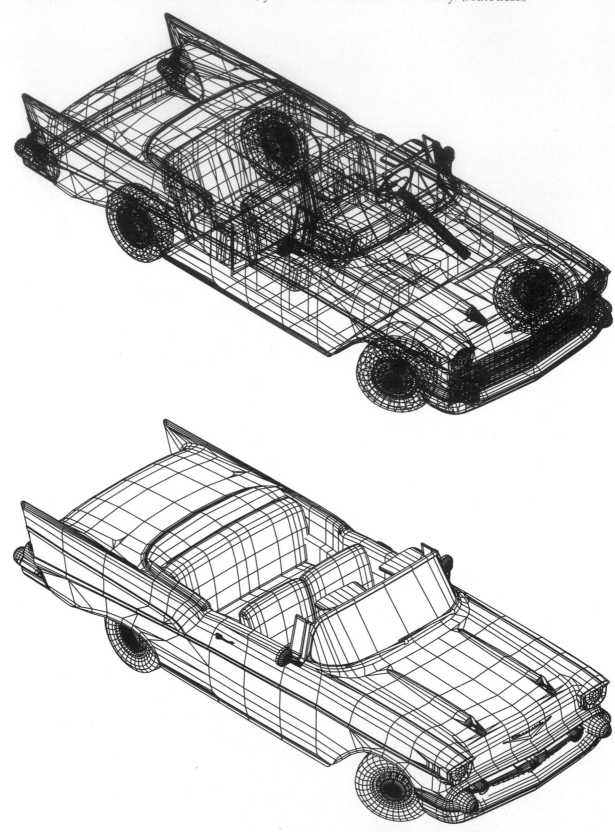

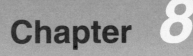
Learning objectives

After completing this chapter, you will be able to:

- ○ Create text with a thickness.
- ○ Apply horizontal text and titles to 3D views.
- ○ Rotate 3D text to a different plane.
- ○ Describe how 3D objects can hide text.
- ○ Create 3D dimensioning.
- ○ Apply leaders to different UCS planes.

CREATING 3D TEXT WITH THICKNESS

Text does not have a thickness when created. This is true even if thickness is set with the **ELEV** command before drawing text. Text must be given thickness after it is created using **CHANGE**, **DDMODIFY**, or **DDCHPROP**. Once a thickness is applied, the hidden lines can be removed by using **HIDE**. Figure 8-1 shows six different fonts as they appear after being given a thickness with hidden lines removed.

Figure 8-1.
Six different fonts with thickness after hidden lines are removed.

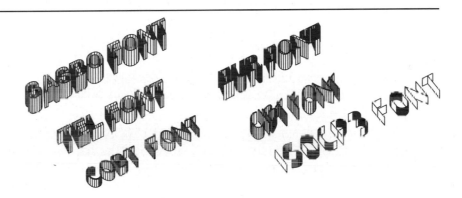

AutoCAD comes with a variety of PostScript fonts. These fonts cannot be given thickness unless they are first compiled. PostScript fonts have a .PFB file extension. To compile a font, type COMPILE at the **Command:** prompt. The **Select Shape or Font File** dialog box shown below appears. If AutoCAD was installed using default values, the directory that contains the fonts is \R13\COM\FONTS. Pick .PFB in the **List Files of Type:** list box. Next, select the font you wish to compile and pick **OK**. The font can now be given thickness.

Select Shape or Font File

File Name: eur____.pfb

cibt____.pfb
cobt____.pfb
eur____.pfb
euro____.pfb
par____.pfb
rom____.pfb
romb____.pfb
romi____.pfb

Directories: c:\r13\com\fonts

c:\
r13
com
fonts

OK
Cancel
Type It
Find File...

List Files of Type: *.pfb

Drives: c: cad

Text and the UCS

Text is parallel to the UCS that it was drawn in. Therefore, if you wish to show text appearing on a specific plane, make that plane the current UCS before placing the text. Figure 8-2 shows several examples of text on different UCS planes.

Changing the UCS of a text object

If text is placed improperly or on the wrong UCS, it can be edited using grips or 3D editing commands. For example, if the text at the upper left corner of Figure 8-2 should be "lying" on the top surface, it can be edited as follows:

        Command: **ROTATE3D**↵
        Select objects: *(pick the text object and press* [Enter])
        Select objects: ↵
        Axis by Object/Last/View/Xaxis/Yaxis/Zaxis/⟨2points⟩: **X**↵
        Point on X axis ⟨0,0,0⟩: _endp of ⟨Rotation angle⟩/Reference: **–90**↵
        Command:

After hidden lines are removed, the object appears as shown in Figure 8-3A. Since this text has a thickness, it appears to be recessed into the surface of the box with its "feet" showing through the side. To place the text on the top surface, use grips to move it the thickness of the text along the appropriate axis. The edited object is shown in Figure 8-3B.

Figure 8-2.
Text located using three different UCS planes.

Figure 8-3.
A—Text that appears recessed in the box. B—The text after being moved using grips.

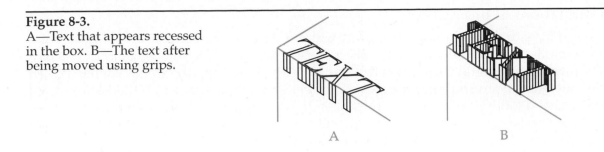

A   B

Using the UCS View option to create a text title

Text does not always have to be placed in a 3D plane. It can be drawn perpendicular and horizontal to your point of view regardless of the 3D viewpoint displayed. An application is to insert the title of a 3D view. This is done with the **View** option of the **UCS** command.

> Command: **UCS.⏎**
> Origin/ZAxis/3point/OBject/View/X/Y/Z/Prev/Restore/Save/Del/?/⟨World⟩: **V⏎**

A new UCS is created that is perpendicular to your viewpoint. However, the view remains a 3D view. Name and save the UCS if you will use it again. Since inserted text is placed parallel to the new UCS, it will be horizontal (or vertical) in the current view. See Figure 8-4.

Figure 8-4.
Titles can be placed correctly using the **View** option of the **UCS** command.

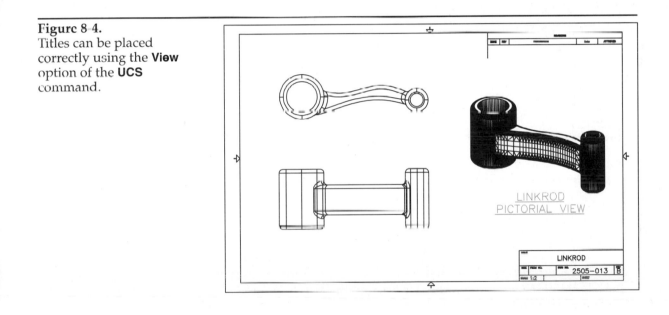

EXERCISE 8-1

❑ Begin a new drawing and name it EX8-1.
❑ Draw a 3D wedge to the dimensions of your choice.
❑ Display the wedge in a 3D viewpoint so that the angled surface points in the southeast direction.
❑ Construct a UCS for the front profile of the wedge and one for the angled surface.
❑ Place lines of text at two different angles on both of the UCS planes. Use a thickness on one text object on each surface.
❑ Place the title of 3D WEDGE below the object and perpendicular to your viewpoint.
❑ Save your drawing as EX8-1.

The limitations of hiding text

Text that is drawn without a thickness will not be properly hidden by the **HIDE** command, even if it is placed behind a 3D object. In order for text behind a 3D object to be hidden, it must be given a thickness. Text that has a thickness will appear correctly when placed inside, outside, or protruding through a 3D object. If you want text to be hidden but not appear to have a thickness, give it a thickness of .001. Figure 8-5A shows a variety of text placements in and around a 3D box. The two text objects at the upper left are sitting outside the box. Figure 8-5B shows the display after **HIDE** is used.

Figure 8-5.
A—Text objects placed in, and around, a 3D box.
B—The display after **HIDE** is used.

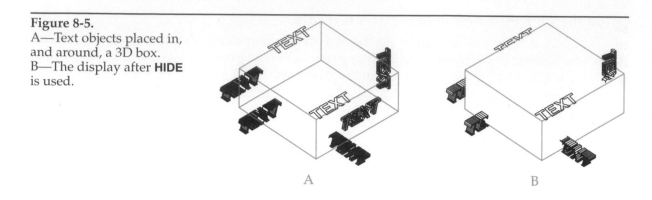

A   B

3D DIMENSIONING

Dimensioned 3D objects are seldom used for manufacturing, but may be used for assembly. Most often dimensioned 3D drawings are used for some sort of presentation, such as displays, illustrations, parts manuals, or training manuals. Therefore, dimensions shown in 3D must be clear and easy to read. The most important aspect of applying dimensions to a 3D object is planning. That means following a few basic guidelines.

Create a 3D dimensioning prototype drawing

If you often create dimensioned 3D drawings, make a prototype drawing. The prototype does not have to contain drawing entities, but should contain a few 3D display settings. These are outlined below:

- Create named dimension styles with appropriate text heights. See Chapter 20 - Chapter 22 of *AutoCAD and its Applications — Basics, Release 13 for Windows* for detailed information on dimensioning and dimension styles.
- Establish several named UCSs that match the planes where dimensions will be placed. See Figure 8-6 for examples of standard named UCSs.
- Establish several 3D viewpoints that can be used for different objects. These viewpoints will allow you to select a display that is best for reading dimensions. Name and save these views.

Figure 8-6.
Three named UCSs that can be used for dimensioning.

Placing dimensions in the proper plane

To create dimensions that display properly, it may be necessary to create more than one UCS for a single plane. Notice in Figure 8-7A that the left dimension is inverted. Note the orientation of the UCS. A second UCS is created and the dimension is redrawn correctly in Figure 8-7B.

The location and plane where dimensions are placed is often a matter of choice. For example, Figure 8-8 shows several options for placing a thickness dimension on the object. All of these are correct. However, several of the options can be eliminated when other dimensions are added. This illustrates the importance of planning.

The key to good 3D dimensioning is to avoid overlapping dimension and extension lines in different planes. A freehand sketch can help you plan this. As you lay out the 3D sketch, try to group information items together. Dimensions, notes, and item tags should be grouped so that they are easy to read and understand. This technique is called *information grouping.*

Figure 8-9A shows the object from Figure 8-8 fully dimensioned using the aligned technique. Notice that the location dimension for the hole is placed on the top surface. This avoids dimensioning to hidden points. Figure 8-9B shows the same object dimensioned using the unilateral technique.

Figure 8-7.
More than one UCS may be needed for a given plane to properly create dimensions. A—The left-hand dimension is inverted. B—The left-hand dimension drawn correctly using a different UCS.

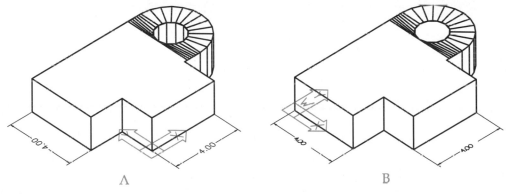

A   B

Figure 8-8.
The thickness dimension can be located in many different places. All of the locations shown here are correct.

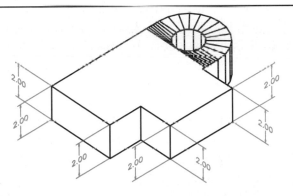

Figure 8-9.
A—An example of a 3D object dimensioned using the aligned technique. B—The object shown in A dimension with unilateral dimensions.

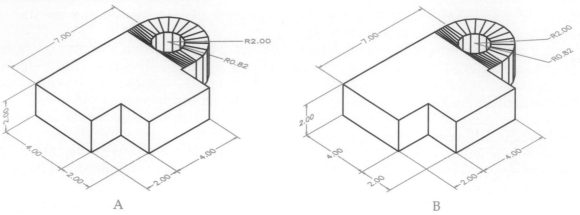

PROFESSIONAL
TIP

Prior to placing dimensions on a 3D drawing, you should determine the purpose of the drawing. What will it be used for? Just as dimensioning a drawing for manufacturing purposes is based on the function of the part, 3D dimensioning is based on the function of the drawing. This determines whether you use chain, datum, arrowless, architectural, or some other style of dimensioning. It also determines how completely the object is dimensioned.

Placing leaders and radial dimensions in 3D

Although standards such as ASME Y14.5M-1994 should be followed, the nature of 3D and the requirements of the project may determine how dimensions and leaders are placed. Remember, the most important aspect of dimensioning a 3D drawing is its presentation. Is it easy to read and interpret?

Leaders and radial dimensions can be placed in, or perpendicular to, the plane of the feature. Figure 8-10A shows the placement of leaders in the plane of the object's top surface. Figure 8-10B illustrates the placement of leaders and radial dimensions in a UCS that is perpendicular to the top surface of the object.

In Figure 8-10B, notice the arrowhead on the R2.00 dimension. The bottom half is missing. That is because it is below the top surface of the object and will not be visible when **HIDE** is used. Keep this in mind when choosing a plane for 3D dimensions.

Figure 8-10.
A—Leaders placed in the plane of the object's top surface. B—Leaders placed in a UCS perpendicular to the object's top surface. Notice the arrowhead on the radius dimension is half hidden.

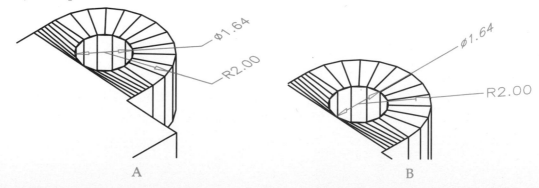

Remember that text, dimensions, and leaders are always placed in the XY plane of the current UCS. Therefore, to create the layout in Figure 8-10B, you must use more than one UCS. Figure 8-11A and Figure 8-11B show the UCS icon orientations for the two radial dimensions.

Figure 8-11.
A—The UCS for drawing the diameter dimension. B—The UCS for drawing the radius dimension.

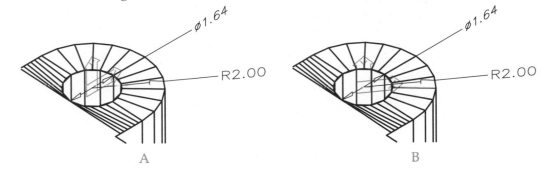

NOTE   AutoCAD does not fill in the arrowheads of 3D dimensions and leaders.

EXERCISE 8-2

❑ Begin a new drawing and name it EX8-2.
❑ Draw the object shown in Figure 8-9 using the dimensions given. Create as many different UCSs needed to draw and dimension the object.
❑ Place dimensions and leaders to achieve the best presentation.
❑ Save the drawing as EX8-2.

CHAPTER TEST

Write your answers in the spaces provided.

1. How does the **ELEV** command affect the thickness of text? _____

2. What commands are used to alter text thickness? _____

3. What file extension is used for PostScript font shape files? _____

4. How can PostScript fonts be used for 3D text with thickness? _____

_____

5. If text is placed using the wrong UCS, how can it be edited to appear on the correct one?

_____

_____

6. How can text be placed horizontally in your viewpoint if the object is displayed in 3D?

_____

_____

7. How can text be made to appear hidden when it is behind a 3D object and **HIDE** is used?

8. What is the most common use of dimensioned 3D drawings?

9. Give three items that should be a part of a 3D dimensioning prototype drawing.

10. What is information grouping?

DRAWING PROBLEMS

General

1. Construct a 4″ cube. Create a named UCS for each of the six sides. Name them FRONT, BACK, RIGHT, LEFT, TOP, and BOTTOM. Place a text label with a .75″ thickness centered on each face of the cube. Use PostScript fonts for at least two faces. Save the drawing as P8-1.

Create a fully dimensioned 3D drawing of the following problems. Save the drawings as **P8-2**, **P8-3**, *and so on.*

General	2. Chapter 2, Problem 1.	*Mechanical Drafting*	7. Chapter 2, Problem 7.
General	3. Chapter 2, Problem 2.	*Mechanical Drafting*	8. Chapter 2, Problem 8.
General	4. Chapter 2, Problem 3.	*Mechanical Drafting*	9. Chapter 2, Problem 9.
General	5. Chapter 2, Problem 4.	*Architecture*	10. Chapter 2, Problem 12.
Mechanical Drafting	6. Chapter 2, Problem 6.		

Create a fully dimensioned 3D drawing of the following problems. Place a text label below each drawing. The text should be horizontal in the current viewpoint. Use a label such as **3D VIEW**, *or the name of the object such as* **GUIDE BRACKET**. *Save the drawings as* **P8-11**, **P8-12**, *and so on.*

Architecture	11. Chapter 3, Problem 1.	*Mechanical Drafting*	15. Chapter 3, Problem 5.
Architecture	12. Chapter 3, Problem 2.	*Mechanical Drafting*	16. Chapter 3, Problem 6.
Mechanical Drafting	13. Chapter 3, Problem 3.	*Mechanical Drafting*	17. Chapter 3, Problem 7.
Mechanical Drafting	14. Chapter 3, Problem 4.	*Mechanical Drafting*	18. Chapter 3, Problem 8.

AutoCAD R13

Chapter 9

Introduction to Shading and Rendering

Learning objectives

After completing this chapter, you will be able to:

- ◯ Shade a 3D model.
- ◯ Display a model using the **SHADEDGE** system variable.
- ◯ Display a model using the **SHADEDIF** system variable.
- ◯ Render a 3D model.
- ◯ Render individual objects in a 3D model.

In previous chapters, you used the **HIDE** command to make it easier to visualize a 3D model. The **SHADE** command displays the model more realistically than the **HIDE** command. The **SHADEDGE** and **SHADEDIF** system variables control how the shaded object appears. The **RENDER** command produces the most realistic image with highlights and shading. An example of a 3D model after using **HIDE**, **SHADE**, and **RENDER** is shown in Figure 9-1. This chapter discusses the **SHADE** command and the default settings of **RENDER**.

Figure 9-1.
A—Hidden lines removed. B—Shaded. C—Rendered. (J.P. Pond, Unified Technical Education Center, Grand Junction, CO)

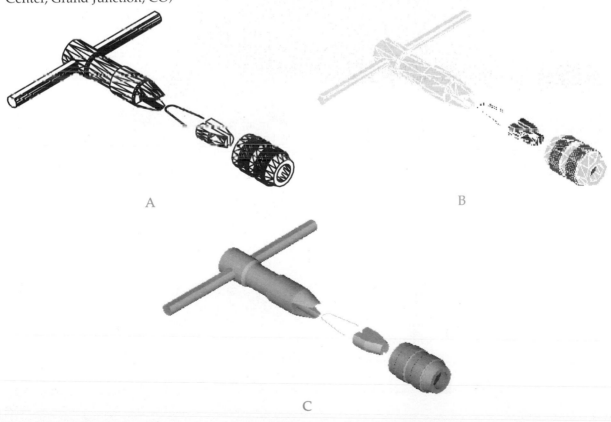

A

B

C

SHADING A MODEL

· The **SHADE** command is used to shade an object. The color of the shaded image is controlled by the color of the model. A single light source located behind the viewer points at the object. The **SHADEDGE** variable controls how the object is displayed. The **SHADEDIF** variable controls the intensity of the light.

An object can be shaded from any viewpoint. A shaded model *cannot* be selected until the screen is regenerated. You cannot plot a shaded image. However, you can copy a shaded image to the Windows Clipboard. The image can then be "pasted" into Windows Paintbrush or other software. The image can then be edited, printed, and saved in different file formats. See Chapter 13 and Chapter 23 for more detailed information on working with images using the Clipboard.

EXERCISE 9-1

❐ The 3D model created in this exercise is used in the remainder of the chapter. You can use this model, or substitute one of your own surfaced or solid models.
❐ Begin a new drawing and name it SHADING.
❐ Set units to decimal and limits to 12, 9. **ZOOM All**.
❐ Create the following layers and colors:

Layer name	Color
BOX	red
CONE	yellow
CYLINDER	magenta
TORUS	blue
SURFACES	white

❐ Make the SURFACES layer current. Use the **3DFACE** command to draw a square floor surface with the coordinates (0,0), (8,0), (8,8), and (0,8). Draw a backdrop surface with the coordinates (0,8), (8,8), (8,8,8), and (0,8,8).
❐ Set a viewpoint of (–3,–2,2).
❐ Use solid primitives to draw the following objects.
❐ Make the BOX layer current. Draw a 3D primitive box with the corner at (5.5,6,2). Select the **Cube** option with a length of 2.
❐ Make the CONE layer current. Draw a 3D primitive cone with the center at (4,4), a diameter of 3 and a height of 6.
❐ Make the TORUS layer current. Draw a 3D primitive torus with the center at (7,1,2), a diameter of 3 and a tube radius of 1.
❐ Make the CYLINDER layer current. Draw a 3D primitive cylinder with the center at (1,7), a diameter of 1.5 and a height of 6.
❐ Save the drawing as SHADING. Leave AutoCAD open. Your drawing should look like the one shown below.

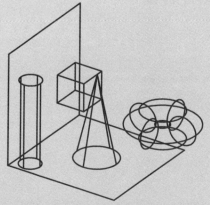

Performing a quick shade

The quickest way to display a shaded image is to select the **Shade** button in the **Render** toolbar. See Figure 9-2. You can also select **Shade** from the **Tools** pull-down menu or type SHADE at the **Command:** prompt. Using the **SHADE** command on the objects created in Exercise 9-1 produces the image shown in Figure 9-3A. Notice the difference between the **HIDE** image in Figure 9-3B and the shaded version. The model is shaded using the colors of the objects. The default settings of **SHADEDGE** = 3 and **SHADEDIF** = 70 were used in Figure 9-3. These variables are discussed in the next section.

Figure 9-2.
The **Shade** and **Render** buttons are found in the **Render** toolbar.

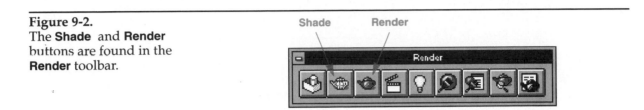

Figure 9-3.
A—The **SHADE** command used on the objects created in Exercise 9-1.
B—Hidden lines removed from the objects.

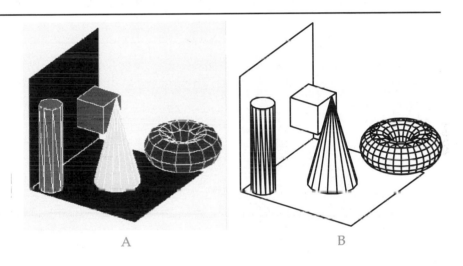

A   B

The SHADEDGE system variable

The **SHADEDGE** system variable controls how edges are displayed and how the faces are shaded. The four **SHADEDGE** options can be set at the **Command:** prompt. The options can also be selected from the **Shade** cascading submenu in the **Tools** pull-down menu, Figure 9-4. If you set the variables using the **Command:** prompt, the settings stay until you change them. If you select an option from the **Shade** submenu, the variable is only temporarily set.

The **SHADEDGE** options are explained below. The corresponding pick in the **Shade** cascading submenu is also given. You need a display with at least 256 colors using the standard AutoCAD 256 color map to see the full effect of values 0 and 1.

SHADEDGE	Value
0	Faces are shaded and edges are not highlighted. Pick **256 <u>C</u>olor**.
1	Faces are shaded and edges are drawn in the background color. Pick **256 Color <u>E</u>dge Highlight**.
2	Faces are not shaded but are displayed in the background color, and edges are drawn in the object color. Pick **16 Color <u>H</u>idden Line**.
3	Faces are shaded in the object color with no lighting effect, and edges are drawn in the background color. Pick **16 Color <u>F</u>illed**.

Figure 9-5 shows the effects of the four different **SHADEDGE** settings.

Figure 9-4.
The **SHADE** command can be selected from the **Tools** pull-down menu.

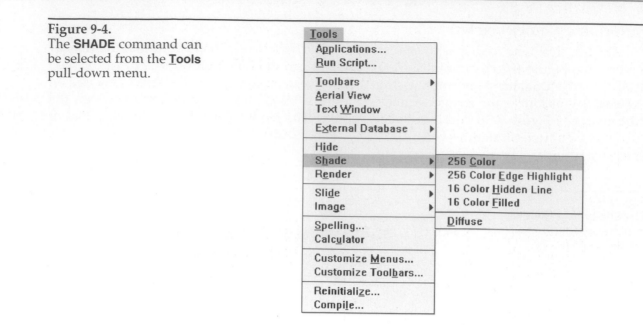

Figure 9-5.
Different **SHADEDGE** values produce different display effects. A—**SHADEDGE** = 0. B— **SHADEDGE** = 1. C— **SHADEDGE** = 2. D— **SHADEDGE** = 3. (R. Steven Wallace, Unified Technical Education Center, for the Skate Park, Grand Junction, CO)

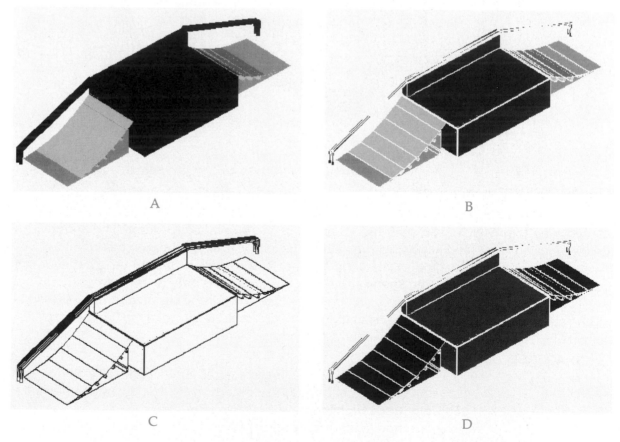

EXERCISE 9-2

❏ Open the drawing named SHADING if it is not displayed on your screen.
❏ Type SHADEDGE and enter the value 0. Use the **SHADE** command to shade the model.
❏ Set **SHADEDGE** to 1. Shade the model.
❏ Set **SHADEDGE** to 2. Shade the model.
❏ Set **SHADEDGE** to 3. Shade the model.
❏ How did each display differ?
❏ Do not save the drawing.

Using **SHADEDIF** to control lighting

The amount of diffuse light reflection from the surfaces of the object is controlled by the **SHADEDIF** (shade diffuse) system variable. The **SHADEDIF** value is the percent of light from the source behind your eyes that is reflected, or diffused, from the surface of the object. The higher the diffused value, the higher the contrast between surfaces in the image. The default value of **SHADEDIF** is 70. This means that 70% of the light striking the object is reflected. The remaining 30% is ambient light. *Ambient light* is the light that surrounds you, such as from a lamp or the sun. All surfaces receive the same amount of ambient light. Ambient light cannot create highlights.

The **SHADEDIF** value can be set by picking **Shade** then **Diffuse** in the **Tools** pull-down menu, or it can be entered at the **Command.** prompt:

        Command: **SHADEDIF**↵
        New value for SHADEDIF 〈70〉: **100**↵

The effects of several **SHADEDIF** settings are shown in Figure 9-6. All of the images in Figure 9-6 have a **SHADEDGE** value of 0. This creates no edge highlighting.

Figure 9-6.
The **SHADEDIF** variable controls the amount of diffuse light reflected from surfaces. A—**SHADEDIF** = 0. B—**SHADEDIF** = 70. C—**SHADEDIF** = 100.

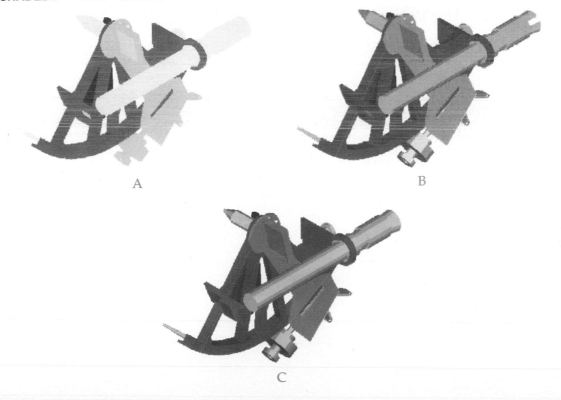

A

B

C

EXERCISE 9-3

❏ Open the drawing named SHADING if it is not displayed on your screen.
❏ Set the **SHADEDGE** variable to 0 and the **SHADEDIF** variable to 0. Shade the model. Observe the results.
❏ Change **SHADEDGE** to 1 and shade the model again.
❏ Set **SHADEDIF** to values of 30, 70, and 100 and shade the model after each setting.
❏ Experiment with combinations of **SHADEDGE** and **SHADEDIF**.
❏ Do not save the drawing.

RENDERING A MODEL

The **RENDER** command creates a realistic image of a model. However, **RENDER** takes longer than **SHADE**. There is a variety of settings that you can change with the **RENDER** command to allow you to fine-tune renderings. These include scenes, lights, materials, and preferences. These can all be changed in dialog boxes. The **RENDER** settings are discussed in detail in Chapter 14. This chapter covers the default settings of **RENDER**.

The **RENDER** default settings display an image that is rendered in only the current viewport using a single light source located behind the viewer. The light intensity is set to 1 and the material is steel. All of these options are discussed in Chapter 14.

To render a model, select **Render** from the **Tools** pull-down menu. Then, pick **Render** in the cascading submenu. You can also pick the **Render** button in the **Render** toolbar or type RENDER at the **Command:** prompt. The **Render** dialog box appears, Figure 9-7. Pick the **Render Scene** button to render the model.

Figure 9-7.
Basic rendering options are set in the **Render** dialog box.

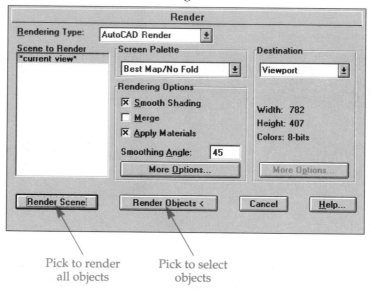

Pick to render all objects   Pick to select objects

EXERCISE 9-4

❏ Open the drawing named SHADING if it is not displayed on your screen.
❏ Change the viewpoint to the SW isometric.
❏ Render the drawing.
❏ The image should look like the one shown below.

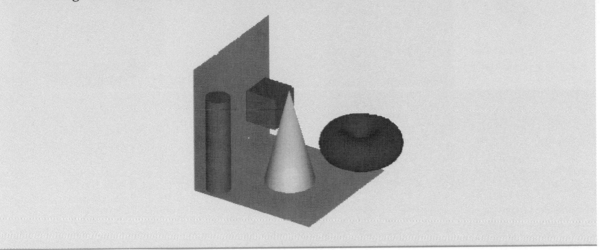

A smooth shaded rendering

Notice in Figure 9-7 that the **Smooth Shading** check box is active. This produces a rendering where individual polygon faces are smoothed to create a more realistic image. However, this is a more complicated process and takes longer to display. Figure 9-8 shows a model that is smooth shaded and the same model with no smooth shading.

Rendering individual objects

A time-saving option in the **Render** dialog box is the **Render Objects**⟨ button. This feature allows you to render individual objects in the model. Only the selected objects are rendered. Three of the objects from Exercise 9-1 are rendered in Figure 9-9. Notice how the other objects are not displayed, even as wireframes.

Figure 9-8.
A—A rendering without smooth shading. B—A rendering with smooth shading applied.

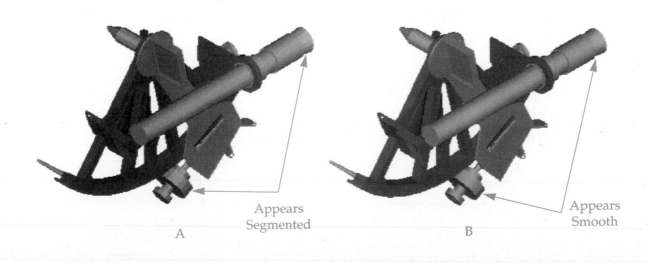

Appears
Segmented

Appears
Smooth

A   B

Figure 9-9.
When individual objects are
selected for rendering, only
those objects are displayed.

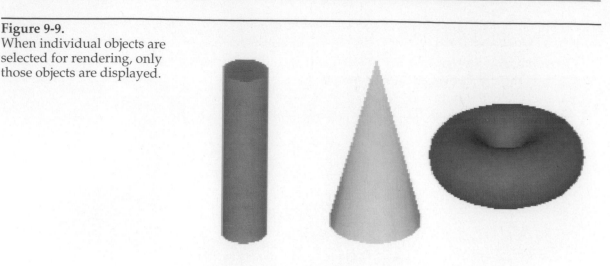

EXERCISE 9-5

❑ Open the drawing named SHADING if it is not displayed on your screen.
❑ Set the viewpoint to (3.5,–2.7,1.3).
❑ Create a rendered display of only the cone, torus, and cylinder.
❑ Change the color of the torus. Render only the torus.
❑ Do not save the drawing.

CHAPTER TEST

Write your answers in the spaces provided.

1. What is the difference between the commands **HIDE** and **SHADE**? _____

    _____

    _____

2. What affects the color of the objects to be shaded? _____

    _____

    _____

3. What is the purpose of the **SHADEDGE** system variable? _____

    _____

4. What does a **SHADEDGE** value of 2 do?_____

    _____

5. What hardware do you have to have for the **SHADEDGE** values of 0 and 1 to be effective?

    _____

6. What system variable controls the lighting effects in the **SHADE** command? _____

    _____

7. What is ambient light? _____
_____
_____
_____

8. What is diffused light? _____
_____
_____
_____

9. The default setting for **SHADEDIF** is 70. What does this mean? _____
_____

10. What is the function of the **RENDER** command? _____
_____
_____
_____

11. What is the difference between the **Render Scene** and **Render Objects**⟨ buttons? _____
_____
_____
_____

12. What are the benefits of the **Render Objects**⟨ option? _____
_____
_____
_____

DRAWING PROBLEMS

1. Open one of your 3D drawings from a previous chapter. Set the **SHADEDIF** to 30. Shade the drawing. Set **SHADEDIF** to 70 and **SHADEDGE** to 1. Shade the drawing.

   General

2. Open one of your 3D drawings from a previous chapter.

   General

   A. Create a 4 viewport configuration.
   B. Set **SHADEDGE** to 3. Shade the objects in the upper-left viewport.
   C. Set **SHADEDGE** to 2. Shade the objects in the upper-right viewport.
   D. Change **SHADEDGE** variable to 1 and shade the lower-left viewport. If you do not have a 256 display, you do not need to do this step.
   E. Shade the objects in the lower-right viewport after changing **SHADEDGE** to 0. If you do not have a 256 display, you do not need to do this step.

3. Using a 3D drawing from the last chapter, **RENDER** the current scene.

   General

General

4. Begin a new drawing, call it PR9-1.

   A. Make a BOX layer with a color yellow. Make a CONE layer with a color blue. Make a TORUS layer with a color of green. Make the TORUS layer current.

   B. Create a TORUS with a center point at (3,3,3), a diameter of 5, and a tube diameter of 1.

   C. Make the CONE layer current. Create a 3D solid cone. Place the center of the cone at (7,9,1) with a diameter of 2 and height of 7.

   D. Make the BOX layer current. Create a solid box. Place the first corner at (1,6,8) and make the box a 2 unit cube.

   E. Make 2 vertical viewports. In the left viewport, set your viewpoint to the SW isometric. In the right viewport, set the viewpoint to the SE isometric.

   F. Shade the right viewport. Render the left viewport.

   G. Experiment with different **SHADEDGE** and **SHADEDIF** settings.

Learning objectives

After completing this chapter, you will be able to:

- ○ Create regions that can be analyzed.
- ○ Construct 3D solid primitives.
- ○ Create complex solids using the **UNION** command.
- ○ Remove portions of a solid using the **SUBTRACT** command.
- ○ Create a new solid from the common intersection of two or more solids.
- ○ Verify for interference between two solids and create a new solid from the interference volume.

WORKING WITH REGIONS

A *region* is a closed two-dimensional solid. It can be extruded into a 3D solid object. A region can also be analyzed for its mass properties. Therefore, they are useful for 2D applications where area and boundary calculations must be quickly obtained from a drawing. In addition, a 2D section view can be converted to a region, then extruded into a 3D solid model.

Constructing a 2D region model

The **REGION** command allows you to convert closed two-dimensional entities into regions. A region has all of the 3D solid model properties, except for thickness (Z value). When regions are added to, subtracted from, or intersected with other regions, a *composite region* is created. A composite region is also called a *region model*. A region can be given a thickness, or *extruded*, quickly and easily. This means that you can convert a 2D shape into a 3D solid model in just a few steps.

The following example creates a base for a support bracket. First, set your limits to 18,12 and zoom all. Next, use the **RECTANG, CIRCLE,** and **ARRAY** commands to create the profile geometry. Then, convert the profile into a 2D composite region model.

```
Command: RECTANG↵
First corner: 3,3↵
Other corner: 11,11↵
Command: CIRCLE↵
3P/2P/TTR/⟨Center point⟩: 4,4↵
Diameter/⟨Radius⟩: D↵
Diameter: .75↵
Command: ARRAY↵
Select objects: L↵
1 found
Select objects: ↵
Rectangular or Polar array (R/P) ⟨R⟩: ↵
Number of rows (---) ⟨1⟩: 2↵
Number of columns (¦¦¦): 2↵
Unit cell or distance between rows (---): 6↵
Distance between columns (¦¦¦):6↵
Command:
```

This creates the AutoCAD entities that can now be converted into regions. See Figure 10-1. Convert the rectangle and circles to regions as follows. You can enter the command at the **Command:** prompt or select the **Region** button in the **Polygon** flyout of the **Draw** toolbar.

> Command: **REGION**↵
> Select objects: *(pick the rectangle and circles)*
> Select objects: ↵
> 5 loops extracted.
> 5 Regions created.
> Command:

The rectangle is now a region and each circle is a region. In order to create the surface of the rectangle, the circles must be subtracted from it. You can enter the command at the **Command:** prompt or select the **Subtract** button from the **Explode** flyout in the **Modify** toolbar.

> Command: **SUBTRACT**↵
> Select solids and regions to subtract from...
> Select objects: *(pick the rectangle)*
> Select objects: ↵
> Select solids and regions to subtract...
> Select objects: *(pick the four circles)*
> Select objects: ↵
> Command:

Now if you select the rectangle or any of the circles, you can see that all five objects have been changed into one region.

Figure 10-1.
These 2D objects can be made into a region. The region can then be made into a 3D solid.

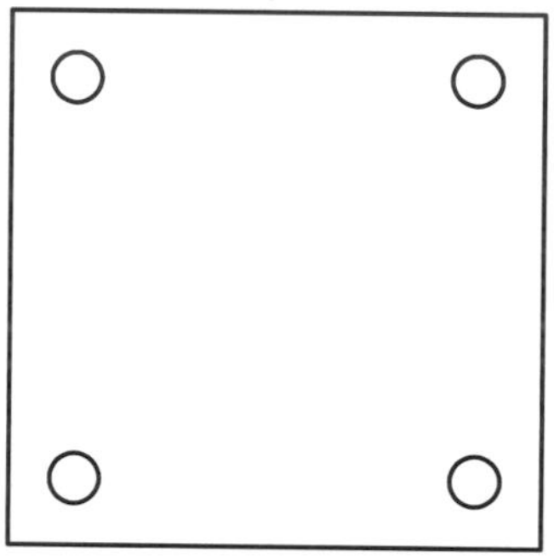

Using the BOUNDARY command to create a region

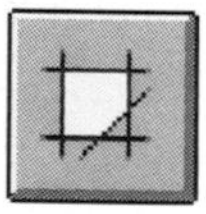

The **BOUNDARY** command is often used to create a polyline for hatching or an inquiry. In addition, **BOUNDARY** can be used to create a region. To do so, pick **Bounding Polyline** from the **Construct** pull-down menu, pick the **Boundary** button from the **Polygon** flyout of the **Draw** toolbar, or type BOUNDARY at the **Command:** prompt. The **Boundary Creation** dialog box is displayed. See Figure 10-2.

To create a region, pick the **Object Type:** pop-up menu, then pick **Region**. Next select the **Pick Points** ⟨ button. You are returned to the graphics display and prompted to select an internal point. Pick a point inside the object you wish to convert to a region. Press [Enter] when you are finished and the region is created. You can always check to see if an object is a polyline or region by using the **LIST** command.

Figure 10-2.
Regions can be created
using the **Boundary Creation**
dialog box.

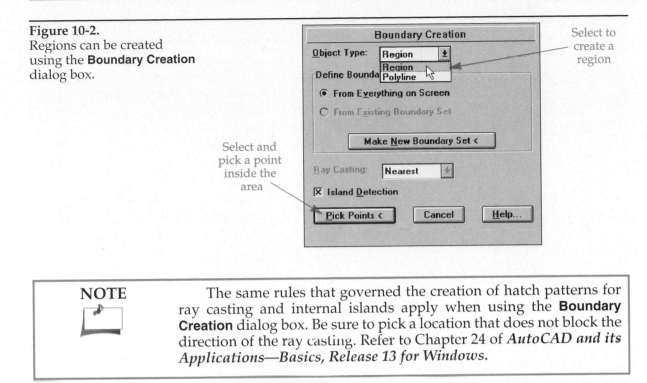

Select to
create a
region

Select and
pick a point
inside the
area

NOTE   The same rules that governed the creation of hatch patterns for
ray casting and internal islands apply when using the **Boundary Creation** dialog box. Be sure to pick a location that does not block the
direction of the ray casting. Refer to Chapter 24 of *AutoCAD and its
Applications—Basics, Release 13 for Windows.*

Extruding a 2D region into a 3D solid

The final step in creating a 3D solid model from a 2D region is to apply a thickness to the
region. The **EXTRUDE** command is used for this. A 2D region can be extruded in either a positive or negative Z direction. Enter the command at the **Command:** prompt or select the
Extrude button in the **Solids** toolbar.

    Command: **EXTRUDE**↵
    Select objects: *(pick anywhere on the region)*
    Select objects: ↵
    Path/⟨Height of Extrusion⟩: **1**↵

At the next prompt, you can enter an angle value. A positive angle tapers the extruded
solid. Press [Enter] to accept the default of 0 for no taper.

    Extrusion taper angle ⟨0⟩: ↵

The base is now a 3D solid object. A 3D solid object is called a *primitive.*
Use the **VPOINT** or **DVIEW** command to see a 3D view of the extruded solid. Notice that the
holes are shown with four lines connecting the circles. See Figure 10-3. These lines are used to
represent the wire frame outline of the objects. This feature is discussed in Chapter 12.

Figure 10-3.
The extruded 3D solid.
Notice the wireframe
display of the holes.

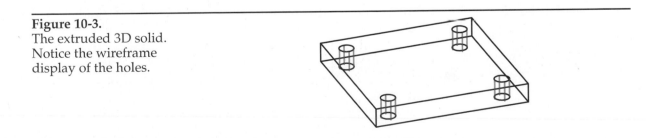

EXERCISE 10-1

❑ Start a new drawing and name it EX10-1.
❑ Using the **RECTANG** and **CIRCLE** commands, draw a two-dimensional top view of the object shown below. Use the dimensions given, but do not dimension the object.
❑ Using the appropriate commands, create a 2D composite region.
❑ Extrude the region model into a 3D solid with the given thickness.
❑ Save the model as A:EX10-1.

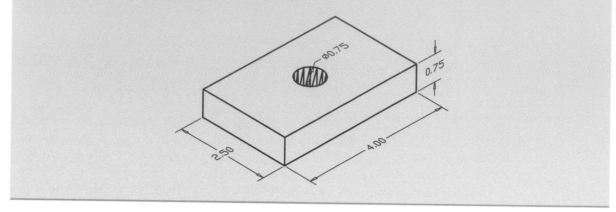

Calculating the area of a region

A region is not a polyline. It is an enclosed area called a *loop.* Certain values of the region, such as area, are stored as a value of the region primitive. The **AREA** command can be used to determine the length of all sides and the area of the loop. This can be a useful advantage of using a region.

For example, suppose a parking lot is being repaved. You need to calculate the surface area of a parking lot to determine the amount of material needed. This total surface area excludes the space taken up by planting dividers, sidewalks, and light posts. This is because you will not be paving under or over these items. If the parking lot and all objects inside it are drawn as a region, the **AREA** command can give you this figure in one step. If a polyline is used to draw the parking lot, all internal features must be subtracted each time the **AREA** command is used.

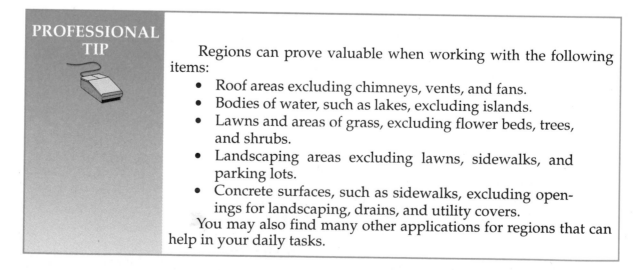

PROFESSIONAL TIP

Regions can prove valuable when working with the following items:
- Roof areas excluding chimneys, vents, and fans.
- Bodies of water, such as lakes, excluding islands.
- Lawns and areas of grass, excluding flower beds, trees, and shrubs.
- Landscaping areas excluding lawns, sidewalks, and parking lots.
- Concrete surfaces, such as sidewalks, excluding openings for landscaping, drains, and utility covers.

You may also find many other applications for regions that can help in your daily tasks.

CONSTRUCTING SOLID PRIMITIVES

Solid primitives are basic 3D geometric shapes such as box, sphere, cylinder, cone, wedge, and torus. Unlike 3D surfaced objects, they have the mass properties of a solid. Solid primitives can also be used as building blocks for complex solid models. To create a solid primitive, pick **Solids** from the **Draw** pull-down menu, pick the appropriate button in the **Solids** toolbar, or type the primitive name at the **Command:** prompt. The pull-down menu and toolbar are shown in Figure 10-4.

Figure 10-4.
A—The **Solids** cascading submenu. B—The **Solids** toolbar.

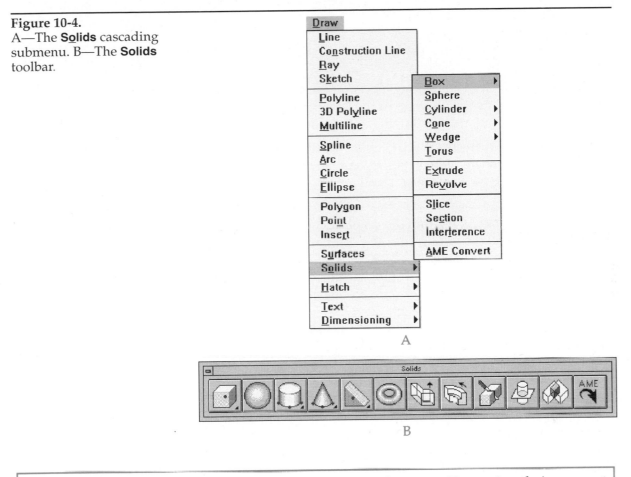

NOTE   All of the solid primitives can be created by typing their name at the **Command:** prompt. To construct a *surfaced* 3D object by entering commands at the keyboard, you must first type 3D and then enter the object name.

Box

A box can be constructed from an initial corner or the center. These options are available by picking **Solids** then **Box** in the **Draw** pull-down menu or by picking either the **Center** or **Corner** box button in the **Solids** toolbar. The two options can also be selected at the **Command:** line. Refer to Figure 10-5.

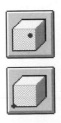

    Command: **BOX.⏎**
    Center/⟨Corner of box⟩ ⟨0,0,0⟩: *(pick a corner or type C for the* **Center** *option)*
    Cube/Length/⟨other corner⟩: *(pick the diagonal corner, or type L and press [Enter]*
       to provide a length)
    Height: **2.⏎**

If the **Cube** option is selected, the length value is applied to all dimensions.

Figure 10-5.
A—A Box created using the **Cube** option. B—A box created by selecting the center point.

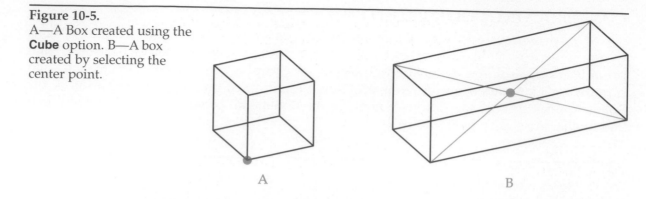

A   B

Sphere

A sphere is drawn by picking its center point then entering a radius or diameter. To draw a sphere, pick **Solids** then **Sphere** in the **Draw** pull-down menu, pick the **Sphere** button in the **Solids** toolbar, or enter the following at the **Command:** prompt:

Command: **SPHERE**↵
Center of sphere ⟨0,0,0⟩: *(pick a point or enter coordinates)*
Diameter/⟨Radius⟩ of sphere: *(pick a point or enter coordinates)*
Command:

Notice in Figure 10-6A that the display is a wire frame with few lines defining the shape. The lines that form the wire frame of a solid are called *isolines.* Isolines are controlled by the **ISOLINES** system variable.

Also, notice in Figure 10-6A that there is no outline or silhouette. The **DISPSILH** system variable controls the display of wire frame silhouettes. This variable is set to 0 by default. When **DISPSILH** is set to 1, the silhouette shown in Figure 10-6B is displayed. The sphere is shown with hidden lines removed and **DISPSILH** set to a value of 0 in Figure 10-6C. System variables that affect display are discussed in detail in Chapter 12.

Figure 10-6.
A—The basic wire frame display of spheres. B—The **DISPSILH** variable is set to 1. C—The **DISPSILH** variable is set to 1 and the **HIDE** command used. D—Spheres displayed after using **HIDE** with **DISPSILH** is set to 0.

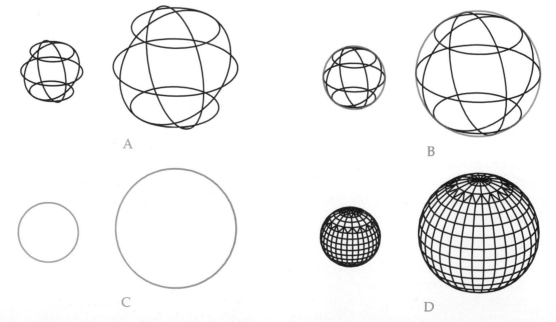

A   B

C   D

> **NOTE**
>
> If **DISPSILH** is set to a value of 1 when **HIDE** is used, the display will not show *tessellation lines.* These are lines that define the curved shape of the object. The object will just appear as a solid with hidden lines removed.

Cylinder

A cylinder can be drawn circular or elliptical. From the **Draw** pull-down menu, pick **Solids** then **Cylinder**. Next, pick either **Center** or **Ellipse**. You can also pick the **Elliptical** or **Center** cylinder button in the **Solids** toolbar.

    Command: **CYLINDER**↵
    Elliptical/⟨center point⟩⟨0,0,0⟩: *(pick a center point)*
    Diameter/⟨Radius⟩: **1**↵
    Center of other end/⟨Height⟩: **3**↵

The cylinder shown in Figure 10-7A is displayed.

You can draw an elliptical cylinder two different ways. The default method prompts you to specify the two endpoints of the first axis and the second axis distance. This prompt sequence is as follows:

    Elliptical/⟨center point⟩⟨0,0,0⟩: **E**↵
    Center/⟨Axis endpoint⟩: *(pick the first axis endpoint)*
    Axis endpoint 2: *(pick the second axis endpoint)*
    Other axis distance: *(pick the other axis distance)*
    Center of other end/⟨Height⟩: **3**↵

The cylinder in Figure 10-7B is created. The second option allows you to select the center point.

    Elliptical/⟨center point⟩⟨0,0,0⟩: **E**↵
    Center/⟨Axis endpoint⟩: **C**↵
    Center of ellipse ⟨0,0,0⟩: *(pick the center of the ellipse)*
    Axis endpoint: *(pick the axis endpoint)*
    Other axis distance: *(pick the other axis distance)*
    Center of other end/⟨Height⟩: **3**↵

To set the height, pick two points with the cursor or enter a value at the keyboard. When setting the height, you have the option of picking the center point of the opposite end of the cylinder. This is useful if you are placing a cylinder inside another object to create a hole. The cylinder can then be subtracted from the other object to create a hole. Refer to Figure 10-8 as you go through the following sequence:

    Center of other end/⟨Height⟩: **C**↵
    Center of other end: **CEN**↵
    of *(pick the top end of the cylinder)*
    Command:

Figure 10-7.
A—A circular cylinder.
B—An elliptical cylinder.

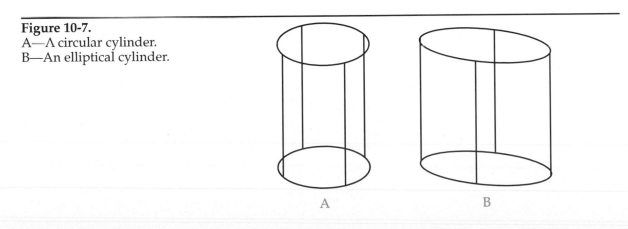

A   B

Figure 10-8.
A—A cylinder is drawn inside another cylinder using the **Center of other end** option. B—The large cylinder appears to have a hole after **SUBTRACT** is used.

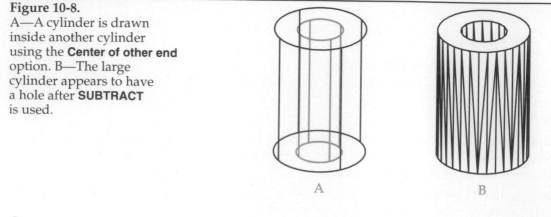

A

B

Cone

The cone can also be drawn circular or elliptical. From the **Draw** pull-down menu, pick **Solids** then **Cone**. Next, pick either **Center** or **Elliptical**. You can also pick either the **Center** or **Elliptical** cone button in the **Solids** toolbar.

> Command: **CONE**↵
> Elliptical/⟨center point⟩⟨0,0,0⟩: *(pick the center point)*
> Diameter/⟨Radius⟩: **1**↵
> Apex/⟨Height⟩: **3**↵

The cone in Figure 10-9A is displayed. An elliptical cone can be created as follows:

> Elliptical/⟨center point⟩⟨0,0,0⟩: **E**↵
> Center/⟨Axis endpoint⟩: *(pick the axis endpoint)*
> Axis endpoint 2: *(pick the other axis endpoint)*
> Other axis distance: *(pick the other axis distance)*
> Apex/⟨Height⟩: **3**↵
> Command:

The cone shown in Figure 10-9B is displayed. Just as with a cylinder, you can select the center of the cone at the following prompt:

> Center/⟨Axis endpoint⟩:

Figure 10-9.
A—A circular cone.
B—An elliptical cone.

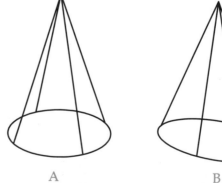

A

B

The **Apex** option is similar to the **Center of other end** option for drawing a cylinder. This option allows you to orient the cone at any angle, regardless of the current UCS. For example, to place a tapered cutout in the end of a block, locate the cone base and give a coordinate location of the apex. Refer to Figure 10-10. A diagonal line was first drawn. Then, the midpoint of the diagonal line is used for the center of the cone's base. Next, continue as follows:

> Apex/⟨Height⟩: **A**↵
> Apex: **@2,0,0**↵

Figure 10-10 illustrates the construction of the cone and its appearance after being subtracted from the box.

Figure 10-10.
A—Cones can be positioned relative to other objects using the **Apex** option. A construction line was added to help locate the base. B—The cone is subtracted from the box.

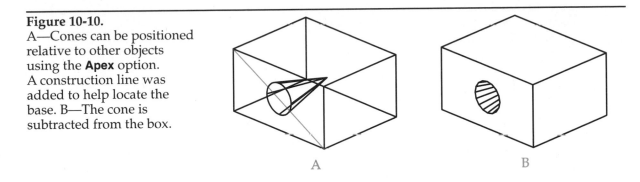

A   B

Wedge

A wedge can be constructed by picking corners or by picking the center point. The center point of a wedge is the middle of the angled surface. From the **Draw** pull-down menu, select **Solids** and **Wedge**. Then, select either **Center** or **Corner**. You can also select either the **Center** or **Corner** wedge button in the **Solids** toolbar.

> Command: **WEDGE**↵
> Center/⟨Corner of wedge⟩⟨0,0,0⟩: *(pick a corner location)*
> Cube/Length/⟨other corner⟩: *(pick the diagonal corner location)*
> Height: **2**↵

See Figure 10-11A. You can also specify the length, width, and height instead of picking the diagonal corner.

> Cube/Length/⟨other corner⟩: **L**↵
> Length: **3**↵
> Width: **2**↵
> Height: **2**↵

The **Center** option is used as follows. Refer to Figure 10-11B.

Figure 10-11.
A—A wedge drawn using the **Corner** option. B—A wedge drawn using the **Center** option. Notice the location of the center.

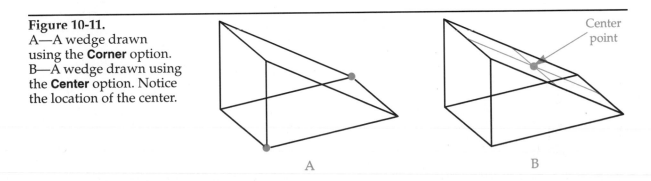

Center point

A   B

Center/⟨Corner of wedge⟩⟨0,0,0⟩: **C.**↵
Center of wedge ⟨0,0,0⟩: *(pick the center point)*
Cube/Length/⟨corner of wedge⟩:

You can pick a corner of the wedge or use the **Length** option to specify length, width, and height. The **Cube** option uses the length value for all three sides.

Torus

Although there is only one menu selection for a torus, it can be drawn in three different ways. Refer to Figure 10-12. To draw a torus, pick **Torus** from the **Solids** cascading submenu in the **Draw** pull-down menu. You can also pick the **Torus** button in the **Solids** toolbar.

Command: **TORUS.**↵
Center of torus ⟨0,0,0⟩: *(pick the center point)*
Diameter/⟨Radius⟩ of torus: **1.**↵
Diameter/⟨Radius⟩ of tube: **.4.**↵

The basic torus shown in Figure 10-12A is drawn. Notice that you can enter either a diameter or a radius.

A torus with a tube diameter that touches itself has no center hole. See Figure 10-12B. This type of torus is called *self-intersecting.* To create a self-intersecting torus, the tube radius must be greater than the torus radius.

The third type of torus looks like a football. It is drawn by entering a negative torus radius and a positive tube diameter of greater value. See Figure 10-12C.

Figure 10-12.
A—Wireframes of the three different types of tori. B—The three types with hidden lines removed.

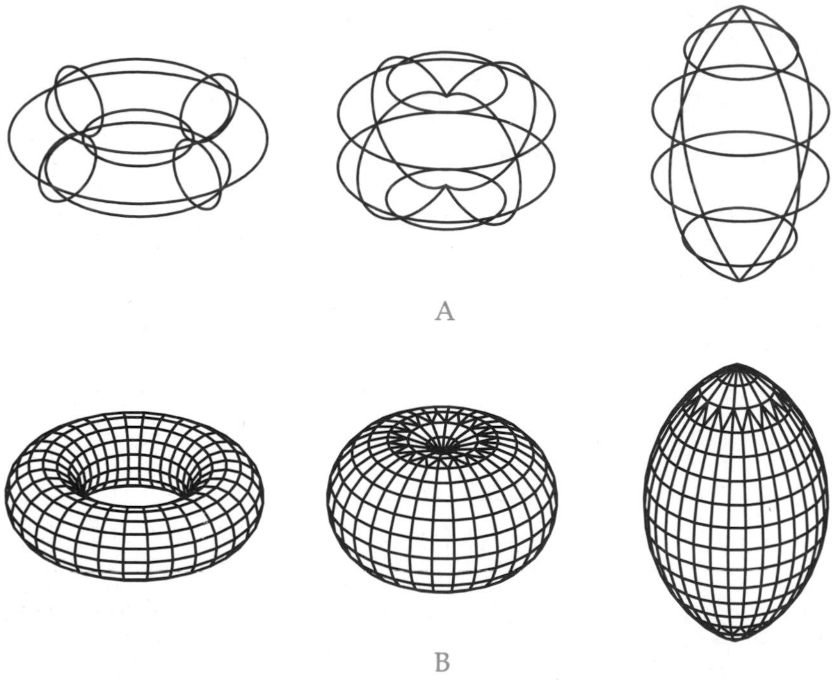

A

B

EXERCISE 10-2

❏ Begin a new drawing and name it EX10-2.
❏ Construct the following solid primitives:
  ❏ A sphere 1.5″ in diameter.
  ❏ A box 3 × 2 × 1.
  ❏ A cone 2.5″ high with a base diameter of 1.5.
  ❏ An elliptical cone 3″ high with a major base diameter of 2″ and a minor diameter of 1″.
  ❏ A wedge 4″ long, 3″ wide, and 2″ high.
  ❏ A cylinder 1.5″ in diameter and 2.5″ high.
  ❏ An elliptical cylinder with a major axis of 2″, a minor axis of 1″, and 3″ high.
  ❏ A basic torus with a radius of 2″ and a tube diameter of .75″.
  ❏ A self-intersecting torus.
  ❏ A football-shaped torus.
❏ Save your drawing as EX10-2.

CREATING COMPOSITE SOLIDS

A *composite solid* is a solid model constructed of two or more solid primitives. Primitives can be subtracted from each other, joined to form a new solid, or overlapped to create an intersection or interference. When primitives are joined, it is called a *union*. These commands are found in the **Construct** and **Draw** pull-down menus. See Figure 10-13.

Figure 10-13.
Boolean commands are located in the **Construct** and **Draw** pull-down menus. They are shown here highlighted.

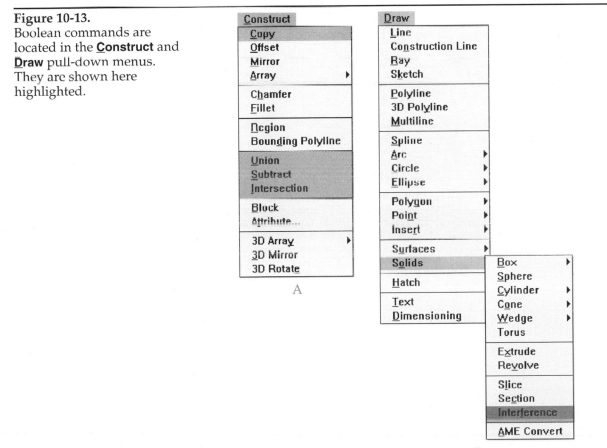

These commands perform *Boolean operations* . George Boole (1815 - 1864) was an English mathematician who developed a system of mathematical logic where all variables have the value of either one or zero. Boole's two value logic, or *binary algebra,* is the basis for the mathematical calculations used by computers, and specifically for those required in the construction of composite solids.

Subtracting solids

The **SUBTRACT** command allows you to remove the volume of one or more solids from another. The first object selected is the object to be subtracted *from*. The next object is the object to be subtracted from the first. You can select **Subtract** from the **Construct** pull-down menu. You can also pick the **Subtract** button in the **Explode** flyout of the **Modify** toolbar.

Command: **SUBTRACT**⏎
Select solids and regions to subtract from...
Select objects: *(pick the object)*
Select objects: ⏎
Select solids and regions to subtract...
Select objects: *(pick the objects to subtract)*
Select objects: ⏎
Command:

Several examples are shown in Figure 10-14.

Figure 10-14.
A—Solid primitives shown here have areas of intersection and overlap. B—Composite solids after using the **SUBTRACT** command.

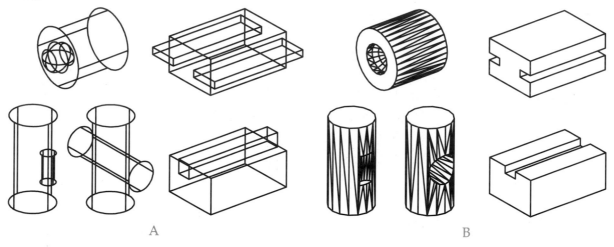

A   B

Joining two or more objects

Composite solids can be created using the **UNION** command. The primitives do not need to intersect. Therefore, locate the primitives accurately when drawing them. To create a union, select **Union** from the **Construct** pull-down menu. You can also select the **Union** button in the **Explode** flyout of the **Modify** toolbar.

Command: **UNION**⏎
Select objects: *(select all primitives to be joined)*
Select objects: ⏎
Command: ⏎

Notice in the examples shown in Figure 10-15B, that lines, or edges, are shown at the new intersection points of the joined objects.

Figure 10-15.
A— Solid primitives shown here have areas of intersection and overlap.
B—Composite solids after using the **UNION** command.

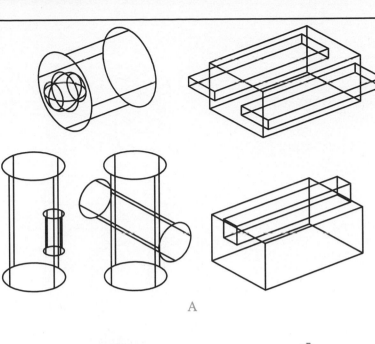

A

B

Creating solids from the intersection of primitives

When solid primitives intersect, they form a common volume. This is an area in space that both primitives share. This shared space is called an *intersection.* An intersection can be made into a composite solid using the **INTERSECT** command. To do so, select **Intersection** from the **Construct** pull-down menu. You can also select the **Intersection** button in the **Explode** flyout of the **Modify** toolbar.

> Command: **INTERSECT**↵
> Select objects: *(select the objects that form the intersection)*
> Select objects: ↵
> Command:

Figure 10-16 shows several examples.

Figure 10-16.
A—Solid primitives shown
here have areas of
intersection and overlap.
B—Composite solids after
using the **INTERSECT**
command.

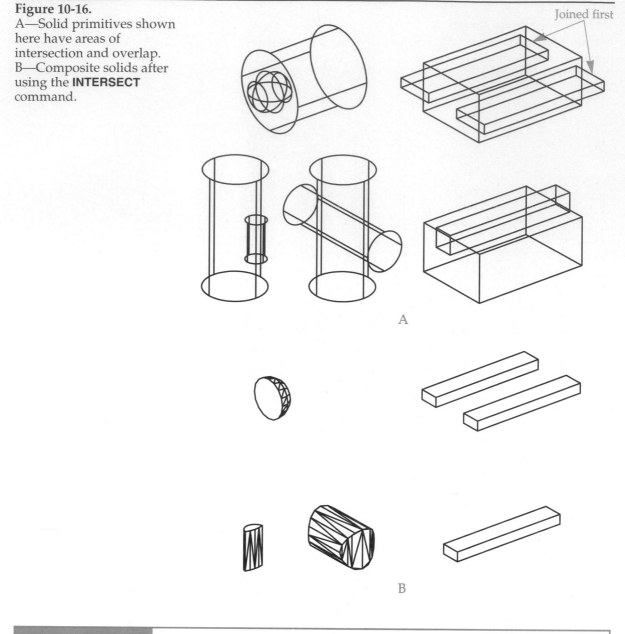

A

B

The **INTERSECT** command can also be useful in 2D drawing. For example, if you need to create a complex shape that must later be used for inquiry calculations or hatching, draw the main object first. Then, draw all intersecting or overlapping objects. Next, create regions of the shapes. Finally, use **INTERSECT** to create the final shape. The shape now has solid properties and can be used as a region.

EXERCISE 10-3

❏ Begin a new drawing and name it EX10-3.
❏ Construct objects similar to those shown in Figure 10-14A using your own dimensions. Be sure the objects intersect and overlap. Make two copies of all objects.
❏ Perform subtractions on all of the objects and observe the results.
❏ Perform unions on the copy of the objects and observe the results.
❏ Use the **INTERSECT** command on all of the objects and observe the results.
❏ Save your drawing as EX10-3.

Creating new solids using the INTERFERE command

When you use the **SUBTRACT**, **UNION**, and **INTERSECT** commands, the original solid primitives are deleted. They are replaced by the new composite solid. The **INTERFERE** command does not do this. A new solid is created from the interference, however, the original objects remain. To use the **INTERFERE** command, select **Interference** from the **Solids** submenu in the **Draw** pull-down menu. You can also select the **Interference** button in the **Solids** toolbar. Refer to Figure 10-17 as you go through the following sequence.

Command: **INTERFERE**↵
Select the first set of solids:
Select objects: *(select the first solid)*
Select objects: ↵
Select the second set of solids: *(select the second solid)*
Select objects: ↵
Comparing 1 solid against 1 solid.
Interfering solids (first set): 1
 (second set): 1
Interfering pairs: 1
Create interference solids? ⟨N⟩: **Y**↵

Figure 10-17.
A—Two solids form an area of intersection.
B—After using **INTERFERE**, a new solid is defined and the original solids remain.
C—The new solid can be moved or copied.

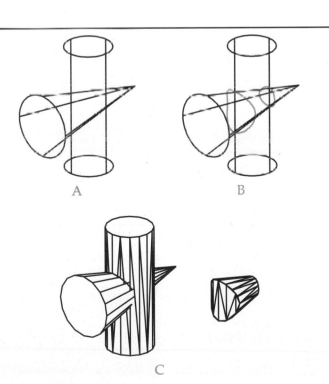

The result is shown in Figure 10-17B. Notice that the original solids are intact, but new lines indicate the new solid.

The new solid is a separate object. It can be moved, copied, and manipulated just like any other object. Figure 10-17C shows the new object after it has been moved and **HIDE** used.

AutoCAD compares the first set of solids with the second set. Any solids that are selected for both the first and second sets are automatically included as part of the first selection set, and are eliminated from the second. If you do not select a second set of objects, AutoCAD calculates the interference between the objects in the first selection set. You can do this by pressing [Enter] instead of picking the second set.

It can be confusing if there are more than two new solids created. However, you can highlight each new solid individually before ending the command.

```
Create interference solids? ⟨N⟩: Y↲
Highlight pairs of interfering solids? ⟨N⟩: Y↲
eXit/⟨Next pair⟩: ↲
eXit/⟨Next pair⟩: (press [Enter] for next pair, or E and [Enter] to exit)
Command:
```

EXERCISE 10-4

❏ Begin a new drawing and name it EX10-4.
❏ Construct objects similar to those shown in Figure 10-17A using your own dimensions. Be sure the objects intersect and overlap.
❏ Use the **INTERFERE** command on the objects and observe the results. Be sure to make a solid of the interference. Use the **HIDE** command.
❏ Make a copy of the new solid and move it to a new location.
❏ Save your drawing as EX10-4.

CHAPTER TEST

Write your answers in the spaces provided.

1. What is a region? _____

2. How can a 2D section view be converted to a 3D solid model? _____

3. What is created when regions are added to or subtracted from?_____

4. What command allows you to remove the area of one region from another?_____

5. What are two types of objects that can be created with the **BOUNDARY**? _____

6. Why is it useful to create a region instead of a pline if an object's area must be calculated?

_____

_____

_____

7. What is a solid primitive? _____

_____

_____

8. How is a solid cube created? _____

_____

_____

9. Name two system variables that control the display of lines in the wireframe view of a solid. _____

_____

10. How is an elliptical cylinder created? _____

_____

_____

11. What is the function of the **Apex** option of the **CONE** command? _____

_____

_____

_____

12. Where is the center of a wedge located? _____

_____

13. A torus can be drawn in how many different shapes? _____

_____

14. What is a composite solid? _____

_____

_____

15. What type of mathematical calculations are used in the construction of solid models?

_____

_____

16. How are two or more solids combined to make a composite solid? _____

_____

_____

17. What is the function of the **INTERSECT** command? _____

_____

_____

18. How does the **INTERFERE** command differ from **INTERSECT** and **UNION**? _____

_____

_____

_____

DRAWING PROBLEMS

Mechanical Drafting
1. Construct a solid model of P1-1.

Mechanical Drafting
2. Construct a solid model of P1-2.

Mechanical Drafting
3. Construct a solid model of P1-3.

Mechanical Drafting
4. Construct a solid model of P1-4.

Mechanical Drafting
5. Construct a solid model of P1-5.

Mechanical Drafting
6. Construct a solid model of P1-6.

Mechanical Drafting
7. Construct a solid model of P1-7.

Mechanical Drafting
8. Construct a solid model of P1-8.

Architecture
9. Construct a solid model of P3-1.

Architecture
10. Construct a solid model of P3-2.

Mechanical Drafting
11. Construct a solid model of P3-3.

Mechanical Drafting
12. Construct a solid model of P3-4.

Mechanical Drafting
13. Construct a solid model of P3-5.

Mechanical Drafting
14. Construct a solid model of P3-6.

Learning objectives

After completing this chapter, you will be able to:
- ❍ Create solid objects by extruding closed 2D profiles.
- ❍ Revolve closed 2D profiles to create symmetrical 3D solids.
- ❍ Apply fillets to solid objects.
- ❍ Apply chamfers to solid objects.
- ❍ Construct a variety of detailed solid shapes and features.

Complex shapes can be created by applying a thickness to a two-dimensional profile. This is called *extruding* the shape. Two or more profiles can be extruded to intersect. The resulting union can form a new shape. Objects having symmetry can be created by revolving a 2D profile about an axis to create a new solid. Rounded and angular corners can be constructed using the **FILLET** and **CHAMFER** commands.

CREATING SOLID EXTRUSIONS

An *extrusion* is a closed two-dimensional shape that has been given thickness. The **EXTRUDE** command allows you to create extruded solids using closed objects such as plines, polygons, splines, regions, circles, or donuts. Extrusions can be created along a straight line or along a path curve. A taper angle can also be applied as you extrude an object.

Create an extruded solid by picking **Solids** then **Extrude** from the **Draw** pull-down menu or pick the **Extrude** button in the **Solids** toolbar. You can also enter EXTRUDE at the **Command:** prompt.

> Command: **EXTRUDE**⏎
> Select objects: *(pick object to extrude)*
> Select objects: ⏎
> Path/⟨Height of Extrusion⟩: **.35**⏎
> Extrusion taper angle ⟨0⟩: ⏎
> Command:

Figure 11-1 illustrates a polygon that is extruded into a solid.

The taper angle can be any value between +90° and –90°. A positive angle tapers to the inside of the object from the base. A negative angle tapers to the outside of the object from the base. See Figure 11-2.

NOTE	The height of extrusion is always applied in the Z direction. A positive value extrudes above the XY plane. A negative value extrudes below the XY plane.

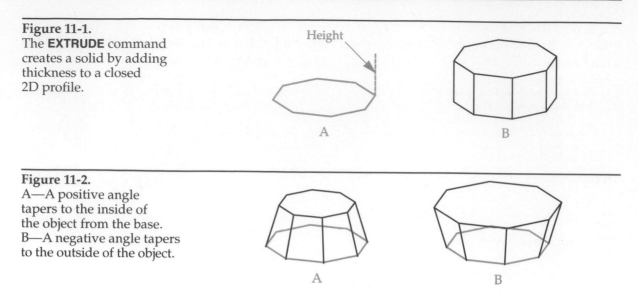

Figure 11-1.
The **EXTRUDE** command creates a solid by adding thickness to a closed 2D profile.

Figure 11-2.
A—A positive angle tapers to the inside of the object from the base.
B—A negative angle tapers to the outside of the object.

Extrusions along a path

A closed 2D shape can be extruded along a path to create a 3D solid. The path can be a line, circle, arc, ellipse, polyline, or spline. Line segments and other objects can be joined to form a polyline path. The corners of angled segments are mitered. See Figure 11-3A.

Figure 11-4B shows an object extruded along a line that angles from the base object. Notice that the plane at the end of the extruded object is perpendicular to the path. Also notice that the length of the extrusion is the same as that of the path.

> Command: **EXTRUDE.**⏎
> Select objects: *(pick object to extrude)*
> Select objects: ⏎
> Path/⟨Height of Extrusion⟩: **P**⏎
> Select path: *(pick the path)*

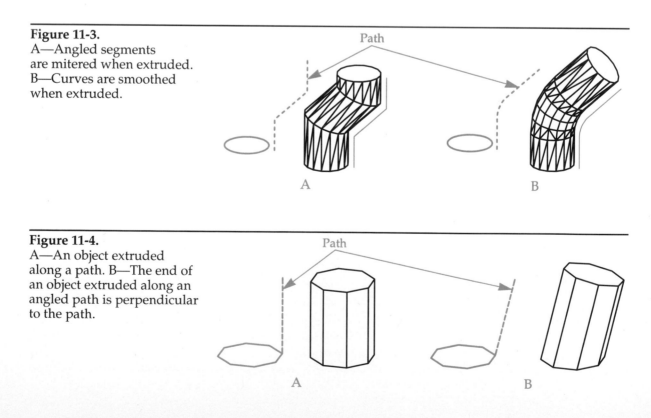

Figure 11-3.
A—Angled segments are mitered when extruded.
B—Curves are smoothed when extruded.

Figure 11-4.
A—An object extruded along a path. B—The end of an object extruded along an angled path is perpendicular to the path.

The path does not need to be perpendicular to the object. However, the new solid is created so its base is perpendicular to the path. Also, one of the endpoints of the path should be on the plane of the object to be extruded. If it is not, the path is temporarily moved to the center of the profile. The following prompts may appear after the path is selected:

> Select path: *(pick the path)*
> Path was moved to the center of the profile.
> Profile was oriented to be perpendicular to the path.
> Command: ↵

An example is shown in Figure 11-5.

Figure 11-5.
When the path is not perpendicular to the 2D profile (both shown here in color), the base profile is rotated to be perpendicular to the path.

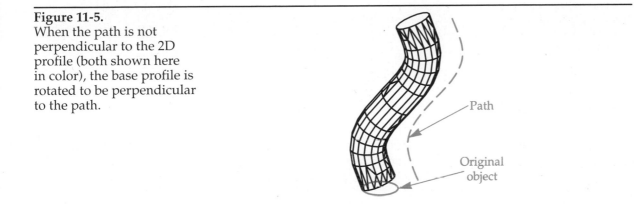

Path

Original object

Creating features with EXTRUDE

You can create a wide variety of features with the **EXTRUDE** command. With some planning, you can use regions and **SUBTRACT** to construct solids. Study the shapes shown in Figure 11-6. Those detailed solid objects were created by drawing a profile then using **EXTRUDE**. The objects in Figure 11-6C and Figure 11-6D must first be constructed as regions before they are extruded. For example, the five holes in Figure 11-6D must be removed from the base object using the **SUBTRACT** command.

Figure 11-6.
Detailed solids can be created by extruding the profile of an object. The profiles are shown here in color.

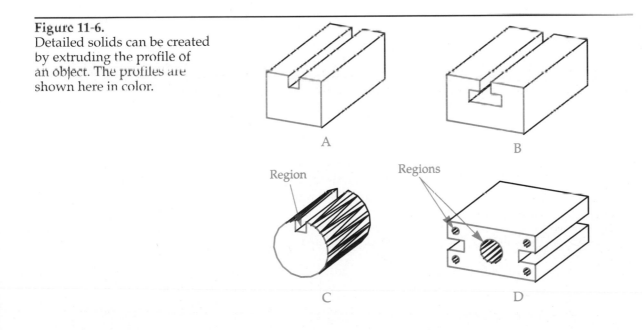

A

B

Region

Regions

C

D

EXERCISE 11-1

❑ Begin a new drawing and name it EX11-1.
❑ Construct a hex head bolt (excluding threads). Make the bolt body 5/16" diameter and 2" long. Make the hex head 1/2" across the flats and 3/16" thick.
❑ Construct the bolt oriented vertically with the head at the top.
❑ Construct a second bolt oriented vertically with the head at the bottom.
❑ Construct a flat-head wood screw (excluding threads). Make the body 3/16" diameter at the base of the head, 7/8" long, and taper to a point. Make the head 3/8" in diameter, taper to the 3/16" diameter body, and 1/8" thick.
❑ Construct the wood screw so the head faces to the left of the screen at a 90° angle to the bolts.
❑ Save the drawing and name it EX11-1.

CREATING REVOLVED SOLIDS

The **REVOLVE** command allows you to create solids by revolving closed shapes such as circles, ellipses, polylines, closed splines, regions, and donuts. The selected object can be revolved at any angle up to 360°. Choose **Solids** then **Revolve** from the **Draw** pull-down menu or pick the **Revolve** button in the **Solids** toolbar. The default option is to pick the two endpoints of an axis of revolution. This is shown in Figure 11-7.

    Command: **REVOLVE**↵
    Select objects: *(pick the objects to revolve)*
    Select objects: ↵
    Axis of revolution - Object/X/Y/⟨Start point of axis⟩: *(pick P1)*
    ⟨End point of axis⟩: *(pick P2)*
    Angle of revolution ⟨full circle⟩: ↵
    Command:

Figure 11-7.
Points P1 and P2 are selected as the axis of revolution.

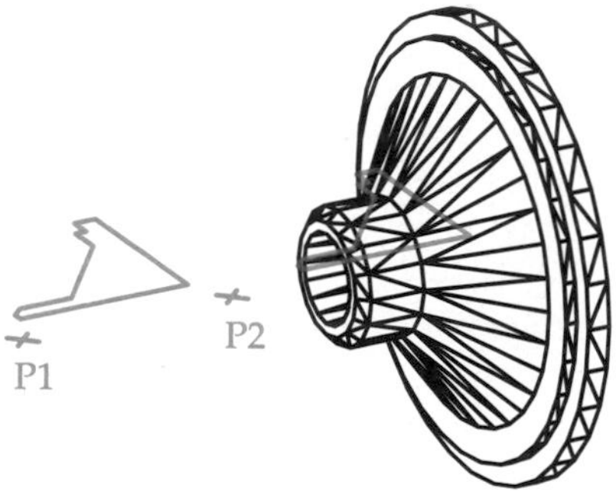

Revolving about an axis line object

You can select an object, such as a line, as the axis of revolution. Figure 11-8 shows a solid created using the **Object** option of the **REVOLVE** command. Both a full circle (360°) revolution and a 270° revolution are shown.

    Axis of revolution - Object/X/Y/⟨Start point of axis⟩: **O**↵
    Select an object: *(pick the axis line)*
    Angle of revolution ⟨full circle⟩: ↵

Figure 11-8.
An axis of revolution
can be selected using the
Object option of **REVOLVE**.
Here, the line is selected
as the axis.

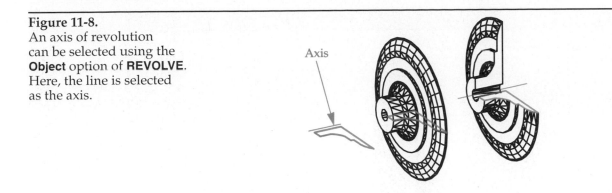

Revolving about the X axis

The X axis of the current UCS can be used as the axis of revolution by selecting the **X** option of **REVOLVE**. The origin of the current UCS is used as one end of the X axis line. Notice in Figure 11-9 that two different shapes can be created by changing the UCS origin point of the same 2D profile. No hole appears in the object in Figure 11-9B because the profile was revolved about an edge that coincides with the X axis.

```
Axis of revolution - Object/X/Y/⟨Start point of axis⟩: X↵
Angle of revolution ⟨full circle⟩: ↵
```

Figure 11-9.
A—A solid is created using
the X axis as the axis of
revolution. B—A different
object is created by changing
the UCS origin.

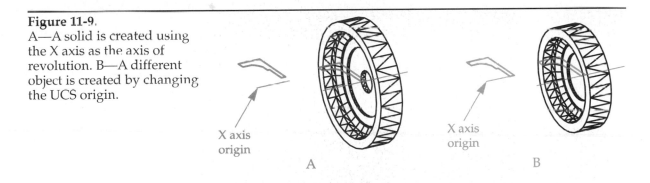

Revolving about the Y axis

The Y axis of the current UCS can be used as the axis of revolution by selecting the **Y** option of **REVOLVE**. The UCS origin determines the shape of the final object. See Figure 11-10. Notice the different shapes created by revolving the same profile with different UCS origins.

```
Axis of revolution - Object/X/Y/⟨Start point of axis⟩: Y↵
Angle of revolution ⟨full circle⟩: ↵
```

Figure 11-10.
A—A solid is created
using the Y axis as the
axis of revolution.
B—A different object is
created by changing
the UCS origin.

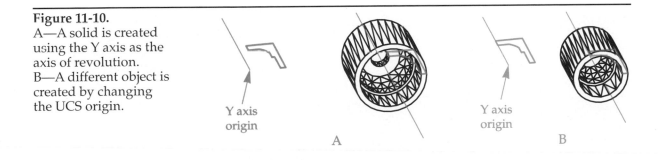

EXERCISE 11-2

❏ Begin a new drawing and name it EX11-2.
❏ Examine the object shown below. Determine the shape of the closed profiles revolved to create the solids. The dimensions of the objects are not important.
❏ Draw the profiles and revolve them to create a solid.
❏ Use the **RENDER** command to see if your objects match those shown.
❏ Save the drawing as EX11-2.

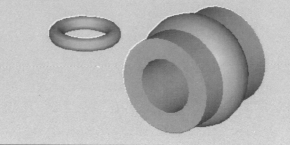

FILLETING SOLID OBJECTS

Before a fillet is created between two solid objects, the objects need to be joined as one solid using the **UNION** command. Then, use the **FILLET** command. See Figure 11-11. Since the object being filleted is actually a single solid and not two objects, only one edge is selected.

    Command: **FILLET**↵
    (TRIM mode) Current fillet radius = 0.0000
    Polyline/Radius/Trim/⟨Select first object⟩: **R**↵
    Enter fillet radius ⟨*current*⟩: **.25**↵
    Command: ↵
    FILLET
    (TRIM mode) Current fillet radius = 0.2500
    Polyline/Radius/Trim/⟨Select first object⟩: *(pick edge to be filleted)*
    Enter radius ⟨*current*⟩: ↵
    Chain/Radius/⟨Select edge⟩: ↵ *(this fillets the selected edge, but you can also select other edges at this point)*
    1 edges selected for fillet.
    Command:

Examples of fillets and rounds are shown in Figure 11-12.

Figure 11-11.
A—Pick the edge where two unioned solids intersect to create a fillet. B—The fillet after using **HIDE**.

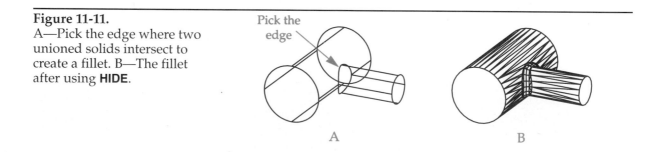

Figure 11-12.
Examples of fillets
and rounds.

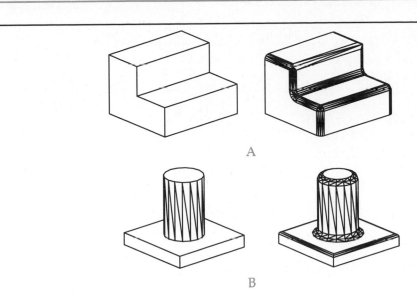

CHAMFERING SOLID OBJECTS

To create a chamfer on a 3D solid, use the **CHAMFER** command. Just as when chamfering a 2D line, there are two chamfer distances. Therefore, you must tell AutoCAD which surfaces to apply the first and second distances to. If you are chamfering a hole, the two objects must first be subtracted. If you are chamfering an intersection, the two objects must first be unioned.

After you enter the command, you must pick the edge you want to chamfer. The edge is actually the intersection of two surfaces. One of the two surfaces is highlighted when you select the edge. The highlighted surface is the one AutoCAD applies the first chamfer distance to. The surface that the first chamfer distance is applied to is called the *base surface.* If the highlighted surface is not the one you want as the base surface, enter N at the Next/〈OK〉: prompt and press [Enter]. This highlights the next surface. When the proper base surface is highlighted, press [Enter] for **OK**. Chamfering a hole is shown in Figure 11-13A.

```
Command: CHAMFER↵
(TRIM mode) Current chamfer Dist1 = 0.0000, Dist2 = 0.0000
Polyline/Distance/Angle/Trim/Method/〈Select first line〉: (pick edge 1)
Select base surface.
Next/〈OK〉: N↵
Next/〈OK〉: ↵
Enter base surface distance 〈0.0000〉: .125↵
Enter other surface distance 〈0.1250〉: ↵
Loop/〈Select edge〉: (pick edge 2, the edge of the hole)
Loop/〈Select edge〉: ↵
Command:
```

The end of the cylinder in Figure 11-13B is chamfered by first picking one of the vertical isolines, then picking the top edge.

NOTE	An edge is created by two surfaces. Therefore, when you enter N for the next surface, AutoCAD cycles through only two surfaces.

Figure 11-13.
A—A hole is chamfered by picking the top surface, then the edge of the hole.
B—The end of a cylinder is chamfered by first picking the side then the end. Both ends can be chamfered at the same time, as shown here.

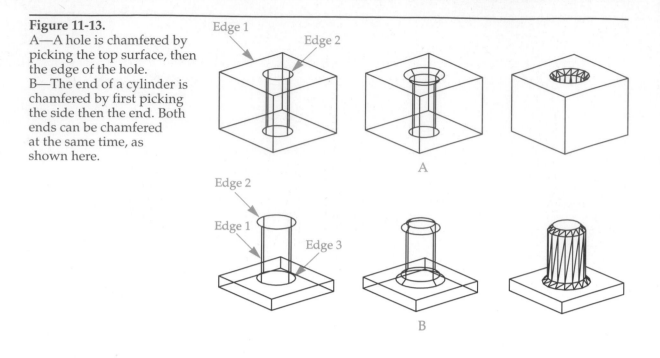

PROFESSIONAL TIP

Solids cannot be edited to change their shape using DDMODIFY, grips, or standard editing commands. Only properties, such as color, layer, and linetype, can be changed on a solid. Therefore, if you create a solid that is incorrect or edit it improperly using FILLET or CHAMFER, it is best to undo or erase and try again.

EXERCISE 11-3

❏ Begin a new drawing and name it EX11-3.
❏ Draw the locking pin shown below using the appropriate solid modeling and editing commands.
❏ The pin is 3″ long and .5″ diameter.
❏ The two cotter pin holes are .2″ diameter and .35″ from each end.
❏ The chamfer on each end is .1″ and the fillet on each hole has a .02″ radius.
❏ When you complete the object use **HIDE** then **RENDER**.
❏ Save the drawing as EX11-3.

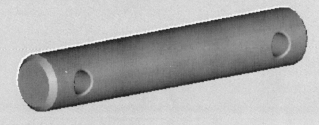

CONSTRUCTING SOLID DETAILS AND FEATURES

A variety of machining, structural, and architectural details can be created using some basic solid modeling techniques. The features discussed in the next sections are just a few of the possibilities.

Counterbore and spotface

A *counterbore* is a recess machined into a part, centered on a hole, that allows the head of a fastener to rest below the surface. Create a counterbore as follows:
1. Draw a cylinder representing the diameter of the hole, Figure 11-14A.
2. Draw a second cylinder the diameter of the counterbore and center it at the top of the first cylinder. Move the second cylinder so it extends below the surface of the object, Figure 11-14B.
3. Subtract the two cylinders from the base object, Figure 11-14C

A *spotface* is similar to a counterbore, but is not as deep. It provides a flat surface for full contact of a washer or underside of a bolt head. Construct it in the same way as a counterbore. See Figure 11-15.

Figure 11-14.
A—Draw a cylinder to represent a hole.
B—Draw a second cylinder to represent the counterbore.
C—Subtract the two cylinders from the base object. The object is shown here with hidden lines removed.

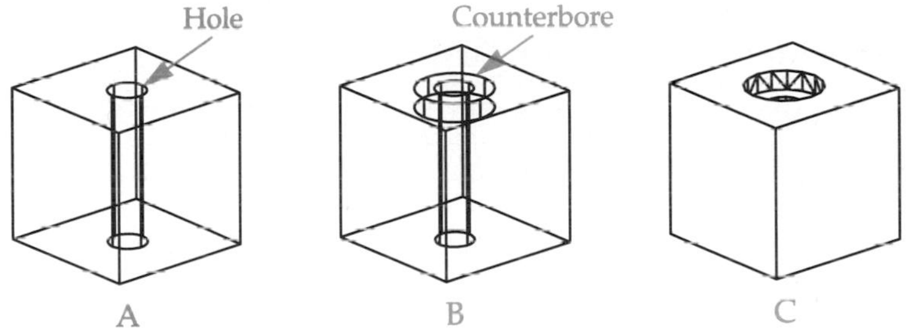

Figure 11-15.
A—The bottom of the second cylinder should be located at the exact depth of the spotface. However, the height may extend above the surface of the cube. Then, subtract the two cylinders from the base.
B—The spotface is much shallower than a counterbore.

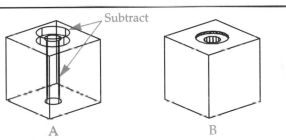

Countersink

A *countersink* is like a counterbore with angled sides. The sides allow a flat head machine screw or wood screw to sit below the surface of an object. A countersink can be drawn in one of two ways. You can draw an inverted cone centered on a hole, or you can chamfer the top edge of a hole. The chamfering technique is the quickest.
1. Draw a cylinder representing the diameter of the hole, Figure 11-16A.
2. Subtract the cylinder from the base object.
3. Select the **CHAMFER** command and enter the chamfer distance(s).
4. Select **CHAMFER** again and pick the top edge of the base object, then pick the top edge of the hole.

Figure 11-16.
A—Subtract the cylinder from the base.
B—Chamfer the top of the hole to create a countersink. The object is shown here with hidden lines removed.

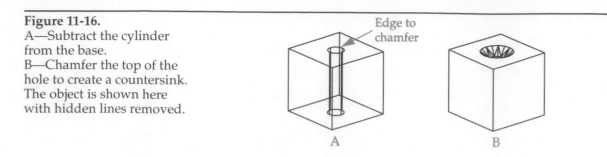

Boss

A *boss* does the same thing as a spotface, but is an area raised above the surface of an object. Draw a boss as follows:

1. Draw a cylinder representing the diameter of the hole. Extend it above the base object higher than the boss is to be, Figure 11-17A.
2. Draw a second cylinder the diameter of the boss. Place the base of the cylinder above the top surface a distance equal to the height of the boss. Give the cylinder a negative height value so that it extends inside the base object, Figure 11-17B.
3. Union the base object and the second cylinder. Subtract the hole from the new unioned object, Figure 11-17C.
4. Fillet the intersection of the boss with the base object, Figure 11-17D.

Figure 11-17.
Creating a boss.
A—Draw a cylinder for the hole extending above the surface of the object.
B—Draw a cylinder the height of the boss on the top surface of the object.
C—Union the large cylinder to the base. Then, subtract the small cylinder (hole) from the unioned objects.
D—Fillet the edge to form the boss. The final object is shown here with hidden lines removed.

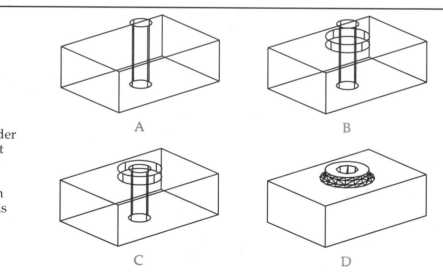

O-ring groove

An *o-ring* is a circular seal that resembles a torus. It sits inside a groove so that at least half of the o-ring is above the surface. The groove can be constructed by placing the center of a circle on the outside surface of a cylinder. Then, revolve the circle around the cylinder. Finally, subtract the extrusion from the cylinder.

1. Construct the cylinder to the required dimensions, Figure 11-18A.
2. Rotate the UCS on the X axis.
3. Draw a circle with a center point on the surface of the cylinder, Figure 11-18B.
4. Revolve the circle 360°, Figure 11-18C.
5. Subtract the revolved object from the cylinder, Figure 11-18D.

The object is shown after using **HIDE** and **RENDER** in Figure 11-18E.

Figure 11-18.
Creating an o-ring groove. A—Construct a cylinder. B—Draw a circle centered on the surface of the cylinder. C—Revolve the circle 360°. D—Subtract the revolved object from the cylinder. E—The completed o-ring groove.

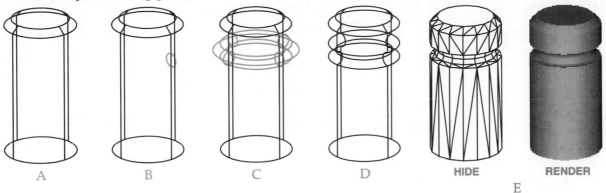

Architectural molding

Architectural details that contain molding can be quickly constructed using extrusions. The procedure is as follows:
1. Construct the profile of the molding as a closed shape, Figure 11-19A.
2. Extrude the profile the desired length, Figure 11-19B.

Figure 11-19.
A—The molding profile.
B—The profile extruded to the desired length.

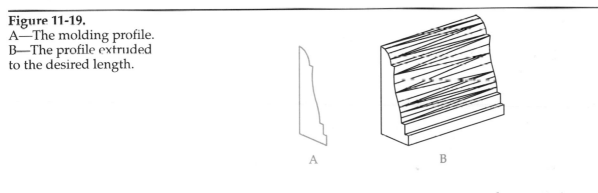

Molding intersections at corners can be quickly created by extruding the same shape in two different directions, then joining the two objects.
1. Copy and rotate the molding profile to orient the Z axis in the direction desired for the second extrusion, Figure 11-20A.
2. Extrude the copied profile the desired length, Figure 11-20B.
3. Union the two extrusions to create the new mitered corner molding, Figure 11-20C.
4. A quick rendering of this corner molding clearly displays the features, Figure 11-20D.

Multiple intersecting extrusions

Many solid objects have complex curves and profiles. These can often be constructed using two or more extrusions joined by intersection. The resulting solid is a combination of only the intersecting volume of the extrusions. The following example shows the construction of a coat hook.
1. Construct the first profile, Figure 11-21A.
2. Construct the second profile located on a common point with the first, Figure 11-21B.
3. Construct the third profile located on a common point with the first two, Figure 11-21C.
4. Extrude each profile the required dimension into the same area. Be careful to specify positive or negative heights for each extrusion, Figure 11-21D and Figure 11-21E.
5. Use **INTERSECT** to join the extrusions into a composite solid, Figure 11-21F.

Figure 11-20.
Creating corner molding. A—Copy and rotate the molding profile. B—Extrude the copied profile to the desired length. C—Union the two extrusions to create the mitered corner. D—A rendered view of the molding.

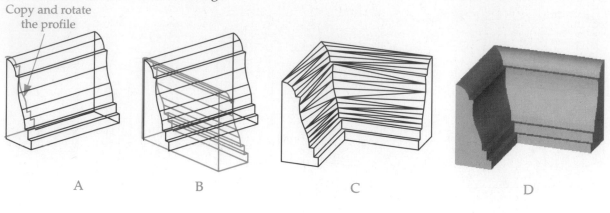

A   B   C   D

Figure 11-21.
Creating a coat hook. A—Draw the first profile. B—Draw the second profile. C—Draw the third profile. All three profiles should have a common origin. D—Extrude each profile so that the extruded objects intersect. E—Use **INTERSECT** to create the composite solid. The final solid is shown here with hidden lines removed.

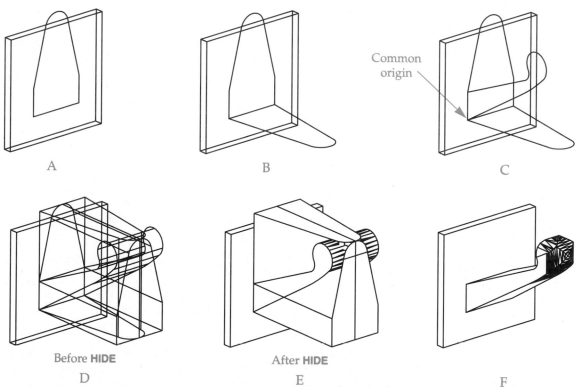

EXERCISE 11-4

❏ Begin a new drawing and name it EX11-4. Set architectural units.
❏ Construct a closed profile of a piece of corner molding that is 2″ wide by 1.5″ deep. Create your own design with arcs and corners.
❏ Copy the profile and rotate it 90°.
❏ Extrude the first molding profile to a length of 12″.
❏ Extrude the rotated molding profile to a length of 8″.
❏ Union the two pieces of molding.
❏ Alter your viewpoint to get different views of the molding.
❏ Use the **RENDER** command to create a quick rendering of the molding.
❏ Save your drawing as EX11-4.

CHAPTER TEST

Write your answers in the spaces provided.

1. What is an extrusion? _____

2. How can an extrusion be constructed to extend below the current UCS? _____
   _____

3. What is the range that a taper angle can vary in? _____

4. How can a curved extrusion be constructed? _____

5. If an extrusion is created as indicated in question 4, how is the base of the extruded object oriented? _____
   _____

6. What are the four different options for creating a revolved solid? _____
   _____

7. How can a profile be revolved twice (or more) about the same axis and create different shaped solids? _____

8. Why must only one edge of a solid be selected when using **FILLET**? _____
   _____

9. When you are chamfering a solid, how can you select the proper surface if the wrong surface is highlighted when you select an edge? _____
   _____

10. What can be edited on a solid? _____

DRAWING PROBLEMS

Piping

1. Construct an 8″ diameter tee pipe fitting using the dimensions shown below.
   A. Use **EXTRUDE** to create two sections of pipe at 90° to each other, then **UNION** the two.
   B. Use **FILLET** and **CHAMFER** to finish the object. The chamfer distance is .25″.
   C. The outside diameter of all three openings is 8.63″ and the pipe wall thickness is .322″.
   D. Save the drawing as P11-1.

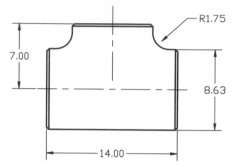

Piping

2. Construct an 8″ diameter 90° elbow pipe fitting using the dimensions shown below.
   A. Use **EXTRUDE** to create the elbow.
   B. Use **CHAMFER** to finish the object. The chamfer distance is .25″.
   C. The outside diameter is 8.63″ and the pipe wall thickness is .322″.
   D. Save the drawing as P11-2.

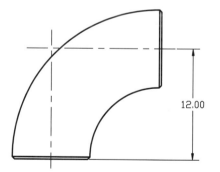

Architecture

3. Construct a 12′ long section of wide flange structural steel as shown below. Use the dimensions given. Save the drawing as P11-3.

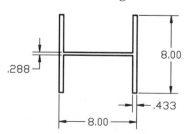

4 - 13. *These problems require you to use a variety of solid modeling functions to construct the objects. Use* **EXTRUDE, REVOLVE, FILLET,** *and* **CHAMFER** *to assist in construction.*

4. Spring clip

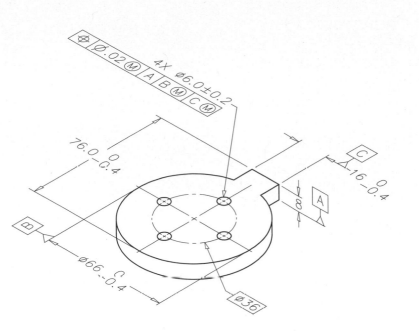

5. Thrust washer

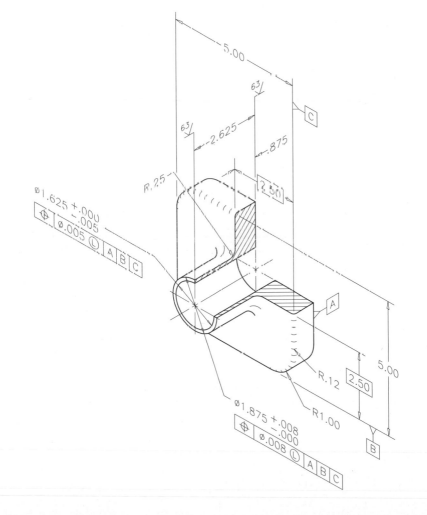

6. Valve pin

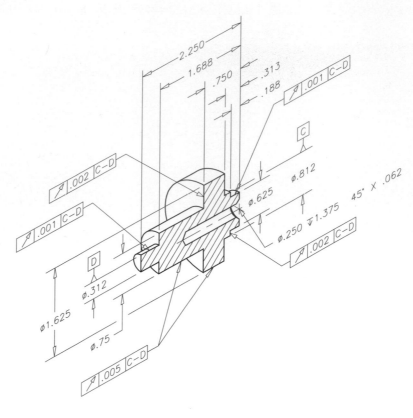

7. Spline

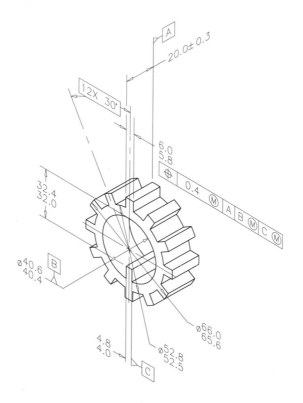

8. Flange

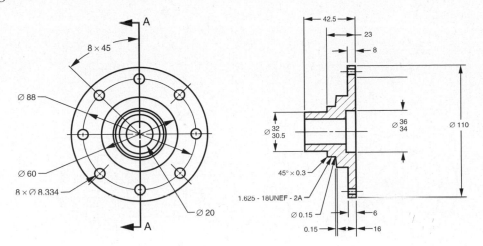

9. Collar

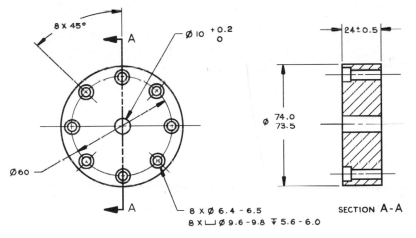

10. Diffuser

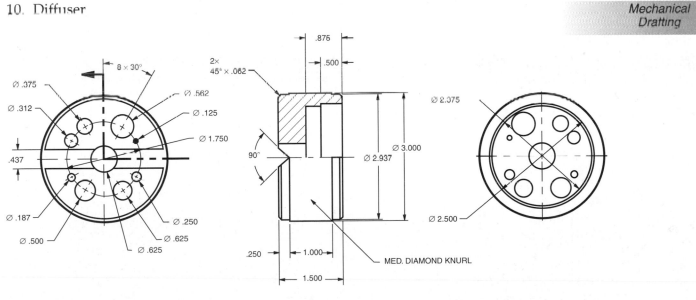

11. Bushing

12. Nozzle

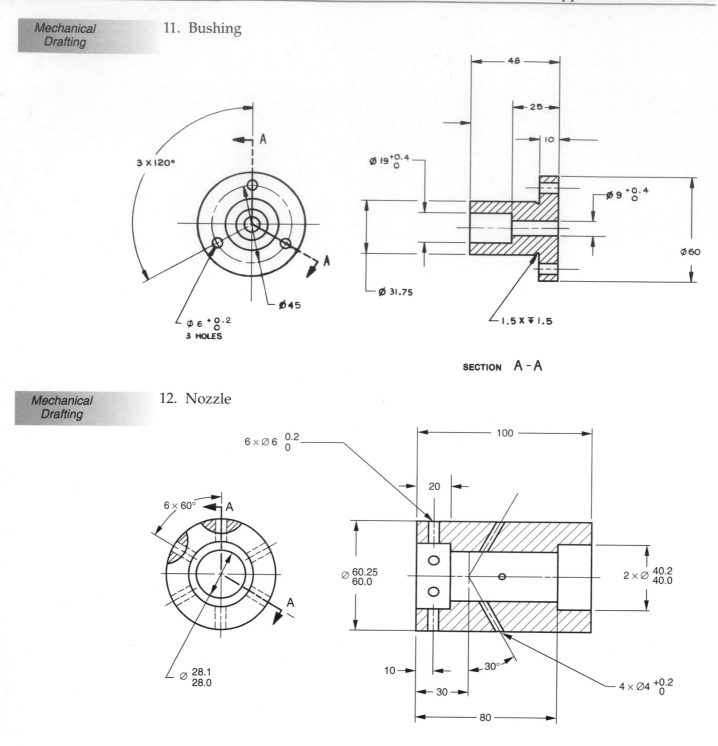

SECTION A-A

SECTION A-A

13. Hub

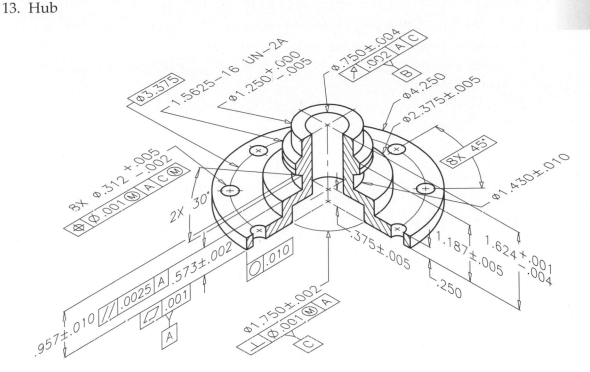

14. Construct picture frame moldings using the profiles shown below.

A. Draw each of the closed profiles shown. Use your own dimensions for the details of the moldings.

B. The length and width of A and B should be no larger than 1.5″ × 1″.

C. The length and width of C and D should be no larger than 3″ × 1.5″.

D. Construct 8″ × 12″ picture frames using moldings A and B.

E. Construct 12″ × 24″ picture frames using moldings C and D.

F. Save the drawing as P11-14.

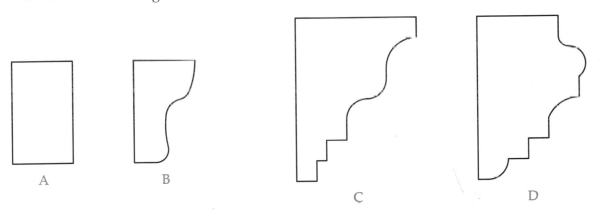

15. Construct a solid model of the faucet handle shown below.

   A. Create three UCSs. Use a common origin for each UCS.
   B. Draw each profile using the dimensions given.
   C. Extrude each profile into a common space. Be sure to use the proper Z value when extruding.
   D. Create an intersection of the three profiles to produce the final solid.
   E. Save the drawing as P11-15.

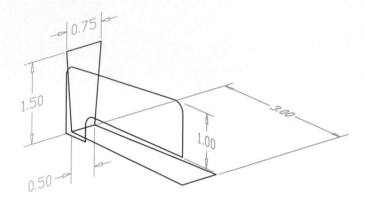

A

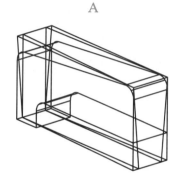

B

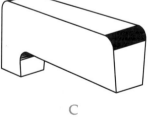

C

Chapter 12

AutoCAD R13

Solid Model Display and Analysis

Learning objectives

After completing this chapter, you will be able to:

- ○ Control the appearance of solid model displays.
- ○ Construct a 2D section through a solid model.
- ○ Construct a 3D section of a solid model.
- ○ Create a multiview layout of a solid model using **SOLVIEW** and **SOLDRAW**.
- ○ Construct a profile of a solid using **SOLPROF**.
- ○ Perform an analysis of a solid model.
- ○ Export and import solid model files and data.

The appearance of a solid model is controlled by the **ISOLINES**, **DISPSILH**, and **FACETRES** system variables. Internal features of the model can be shown using the **SLICE** and **SECTION** commands. This chapter looks at how these sections can be combined with 2D projections created with **SOLVIEW** and **SOLDRAW** to create a drawing layout for plotting. This chapter also covers how a profile of a solid can be created using the **SOLPROF** command.

> **NOTE** The **SOLPROF**, **SOLVIEW**, and **SOLDRAW** commands are not available in Release 13 before the R13c4 maintenance release. They are also available in Release 12.

CONTROLLING SOLID MODEL DISPLAY

AutoCAD User's Guide **12**

AutoCAD solid models can be displayed as a wireframe, with hidden lines removed, shaded, or rendered. A wireframe is the default display and is the quickest to create. The hidden, shaded, and rendered displays require a longer regeneration time.

Isolines

The appearance of a solid model in wireframe form is controlled by the **ISOLINES** system variable. An *isoline* is a line that connects points of equal value. In other words, all points on a horizontal isoline have the same Z value. All points on a vertical isoline have the same X or Y values.

The default value for **ISOLINES** is 4. It can have a value from 0 to 2047. All solid objects in the drawing are affected by changes in the **ISOLINES** value. Change the **ISOLINES** setting as follows:

```
Command: ISOLINES↵
New value for ISOLINES ⟨4⟩: 12↵
```

Figure 12-1 illustrates the difference between **ISOLINES** set to 4 and 12.

Figure 12-1.
Isolines define curved
surfaces. A—**ISOLINES** = 4.
B—**ISOLINES** = 12.

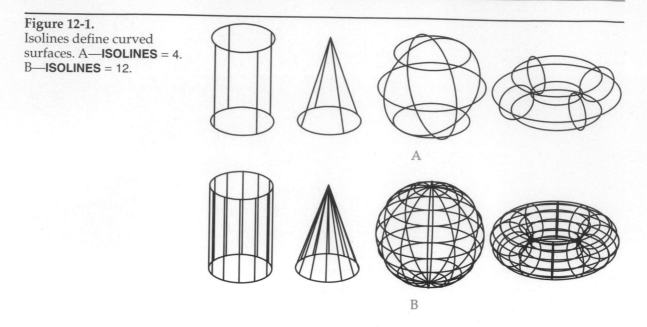

Creating a display silhouette with DISPSILH

Solids can appear in two forms when the **HIDE** command is used. The default form shows the model as if it is composed of many individual faces. These faces are defined by tessellation lines. The number of tessellation lines is controlled by the **ISOLINES** variable for wireframes and by the **FACETRES** variable in all other displays. The other way for the model to appear is smooth with no tessellation lines on the surface. This is controlled by the **DISPSILH** (display silhouette) system variable. Figure 12-2 shows solids with **DISPSILH** set to 1 after using **HIDE**.

Figure 12-2.
Solids appear as smooth
objects with no facets when
DISPSILH is set to 1.

Controlling surface smoothness with FACETRES

The smoothness of shaded or rendered images is controlled by the **FACETRES** system variable. This variable determines the number of polygon faces that are applied to the solid model. The default value is .5. Values can range from 0.01 to 10.0. The illustrations in Figure 12-3 show the differences in hidden line removed and rendered images between two different **FACETRES** settings.

CAUTION

AutoCAD's solid modeling module is called the ACIS modeler. This module may produce errors displayed in a prompt as ACIS error. Some of these errors may be encountered when trying to plot ACIS files with hidden lines removed and **FACETRES** set to a high value. These errors occur in the R13c4 maintenance release. Therefore, avoid setting **FACETRES** any higher than necessary.

Figure 12-3.
A—The **FACETRES** setting of 0.5 produces these images. B—The **FACETRES** setting of 5.0 produces smoother surfaces.

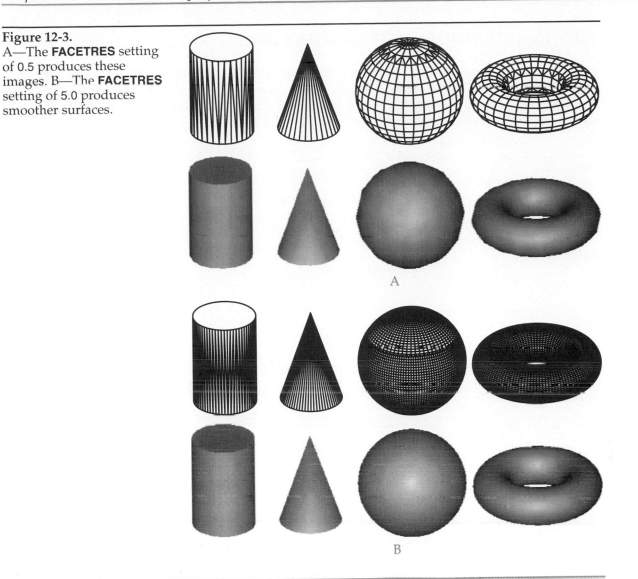

A

B

EXERCISE 12-1

☐ Begin a new drawing and name it EX12-1.
☐ Construct the object shown below using the dimensions given.
☐ Change **ISOLINES** to 6, 8, and 12, and observe the results.
☐ Use the **HIDE** command.
☐ Change **DISPSILH** to 1 and use **HIDE**. Observe the difference.
☐ Set **FACETRES** to .1, .5, 1, and 2 and use **HIDE** after each setting. Observe the results.
☐ Save the drawing as EX12-1. This drawing is used in the remainder of the chapter exercises.

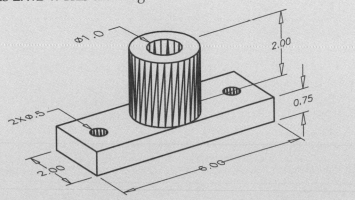

VIEWING 3D MODEL INTERNAL FEATURES

You can "cut" through a 3D solid model to view its internal features and profiles. The **SECTION** command allows you to create a 2D region of the model that is cut through. The **SLICE** command allows you to create a 3D cutaway view of the model. These commands can be selected by picking **Solids** from the **Draw** pull-down menu. See Figure 12-4.

Figure 12-4.
The **SECTION** and **SLICE** commands can be executed by picking **Solids** from the **Draw** pull-down menu. The commands are shown here highlighted.

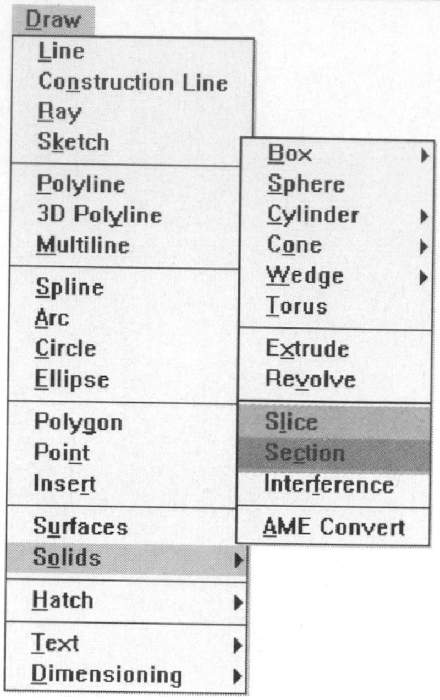

Draw
Line
Construction Line
Ray
Sketch
Polyline
3D Polyline
Multiline
Spline
Arc
Circle
Ellipse
Polygon
Point
Insert
Surfaces
Solids ▶
Hatch ▶
Text ▶
Dimensioning ▶

Solids submenu
Box ▶
Sphere
Cylinder ▶
Cone ▶
Wedge ▶
Torus
Extrude
Revolve
Slice
Section
Interference
AME Convert

Creating a 3D solid model section

The **SECTION** command places a cutting plane line through your model in the selected location. The default option of **SECTION** is to select three points to define the cutting plane. To access the command, pick **Section** from the **Solids** cascading submenu, pick the **Section** button in the **Solids** toolbox, or type SECTION at the **Command:** prompt. The following example selects two quadrant points and one center point on the object in Figure 12-5 to define the cutting plane.

```
Command: SECTION.↵
Select objects: (pick the solid to be sectioned)
Select objects: ↵
Section plane by Object/Zaxis/View/XY/YZ/ZX/⟨3points⟩: (pick the quadrant at point 1)
2nd point on plane: (pick the center at point 2)
3rd point on plane: (pick the quadrant at point 3)
Command:
```

The section created is a 2D region. It has no section lines and is created on the current layer. See Figure 12-5B. If you wish to use the new region as the basis for a 2D, hatched section view of the model, do the following:

1. Move or copy the region to a new location. See Figure 12-6A.
2. Explode the region. This creates individual regions if there were two or more separate areas in the section.
3. Explode each separate region again. This breaks the region into objects. These individual objects can be used by AutoCAD to create a boundary for hatching purposes.

4. Use **BHATCH** to draw section lines inside the areas. See Figure 12-6B. Be sure that the UCS is set to the plane of the area to be hatched. If not, a boundary definition error will appear when an object is selected.
5. Draw any connecting lines required to complete the section view. See Figure 12-6C.
    Additional options of the **SECTION** command enable you to specify sectioning planes in a variety of ways. These are explained below.

- **Object.** The section plane is aligned with a selected object such as circle, arc, ellipse, 2D spline, or 2D polyline.
- **Zaxis.** Select a point on the new section plane, then pick a point on the positive Z axis of that plane.
- **View.** Select a point on the new section plane and AutoCAD aligns the section perpendicular to the viewpoint in the current viewport.
- **XY.** The new section plane is aligned with the XY plane of the current UCS. The point selected specifies the location of the plane.
- **YZ.** The new section plane is aligned with the YZ plane of the current UCS. The point selected specifies the location of the plane.
- **ZX.** The new section plane is aligned with the ZX plane of the current UCS. The point selected specifies the location of the plane.

Figure 12-5.
A—Three points are picked to define a cutting plane.
B—The section is drawn as a region without section lines.

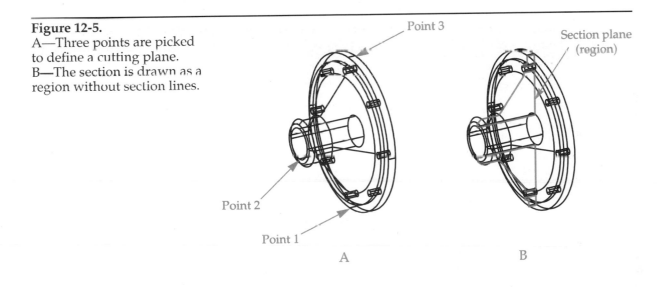

Figure 12-6.
Using a region as a new section view. A—First move the region. B—Add section lines. C—Add any other needed lines to complete the section view.

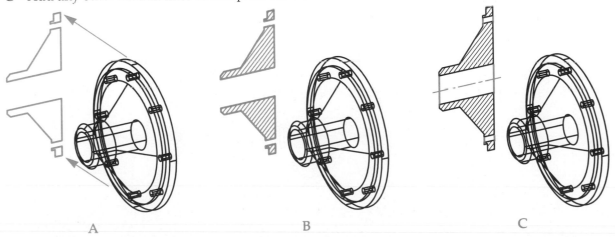

Slicing a solid model

A true 3D sectioned model is created with the **SLICE** command. You can create a new solid by discarding one side of the cut, or both parts of the sliced object can be retained. **SLICE** does not draw section lines or create regions.

Pick **Slice** from the **Solids** cascade of the **Draw** pull-down menu, pick the **Slice** button from the **Solids** toolbar, or type SLICE and the **Command:** prompt. The options of the **SLICE** command are the same as those of **SECTION**. In the following example, the **YZ** option of **SLICE** is used to define the cutting plane. Refer to Figure 12-7.

> Command: **SLICE.**↵
> Select objects: *(pick the solid)*
> Select objects: ↵
> Slicing plane by Object/Zaxis/View/XY/YZ/ZX/⟨3points⟩: **YZ.**↵
> Point on YZ plane ⟨0,0,0⟩: ↵
> Both sides/⟨Point on desired side of the plane⟩: *(pick point 1 to keep the far side of the object)*

Both sides of the slice can be kept if desired. To do so, select the **Both sides** option at the following prompt:

> Both sides/⟨Point on desired side of the plane⟩: **B.**↵

The slice plane appears the same as the section plane shown in Figure 12-7B, but the solid is now two separate objects. Test this by picking one side to display grips. Either side can be moved, copied, or rotated. See Figure 12-8.

Figure 12-7.
A—Specify the cutting plane and pick the side of the object to keep.
B—The completed slice.
C—The sliced object after **HIDE**.

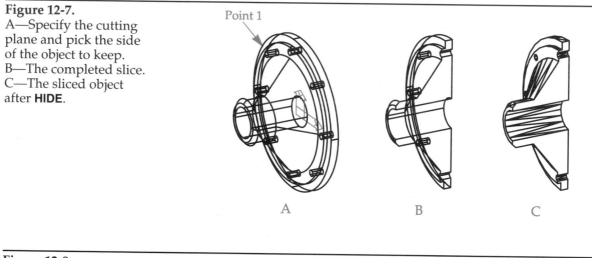

Point 1

A   B   C

Figure 12-8.
A—The slice plane appears as a section when both sides are kept. B—Each part of the sliced object can be moved, copied, or rotated.

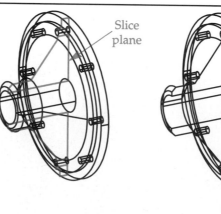
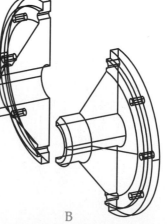

Slice plane

A   B

Creating special sections with SLICE

You are not limited to a single slice through an object. For example, you can create a half section of the object in Figure 12-9 by using the **SLICE** command a second time to cut away the top half of the object nearest to you. The example shown in Figure 12-9A shows the use of the **3 point** option of **SLICE** to remove one quarter of the original object. The results are shown in Figure 12-9B and Figure 12-9C.

Figure 12-9.
A—A cutting plane is selected to remove one quarter of the original object. B—The cutaway view in wireframe. C—A rendered view of the cutaway.

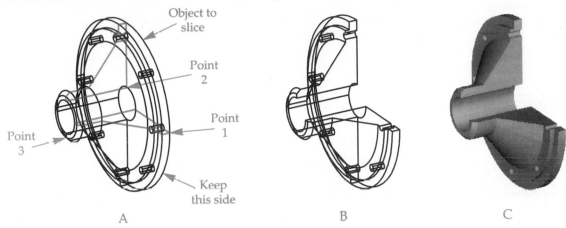

EXERCISE 12-2

- ☐ Open drawing EX12-1 if it is not on your screen.
- ☐ Create a full section that cuts through the centers of all three holes.
- ☐ Move the section region outside the object. Add section lines and connect the section areas with lines to complete the view.
- ☐ The completed section should look like A shown below.
- ☐ Create a slice through the object on the same plane as the previous section.
- ☐ Retain both sides of the slice and move both sides apart.
- ☐ Slice through the large hole on the near side and remove one half of the side.
- ☐ The completed objects should look like B shown below.
- ☐ Save the drawing as EX12-2.

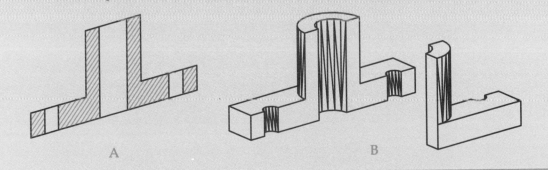

CREATING AND USING MULTIVIEW LAYOUTS

Once a solid model has been constructed, it is easy to create a multiview layout using the **SOLVIEW** command. This command allows you to create a paper space layout containing orthographic, section, and auxiliary views. The **SOLDRAW** command can then be used to complete profile and section views. **SOLDRAW** must be used after **SOLVIEW**. The **SOLPROF** command can be used to create a profile of the solid in the current view.

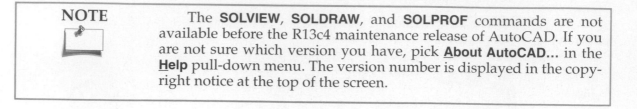

> **NOTE**
>
> The **SOLVIEW**, **SOLDRAW**, and **SOLPROF** commands are not available before the R13c4 maintenance release of AutoCAD. If you are not sure which version you have, pick **About AutoCAD...** in the **Help** pull-down menu. The version number is displayed in the copyright notice at the top of the screen.

Creating views with **SOLVIEW**

To use **SOLVIEW**, first restore the WCS. This will help avoid any confusion. Then, display a plan view. See Figure 12-10. It helps to have additional UCSs created prior to using **SOLVIEW**. This allows you to construct orthographic views based on a specific named UCS.

Next, create an initial view that others can project from. This is normally the top or front. In the following example, the top view is constructed first. The top view is created by using the plan view of a UCS named Left.

Figure 12-10.
Before using **SOLVIEW**, display the plan view of the WCS.

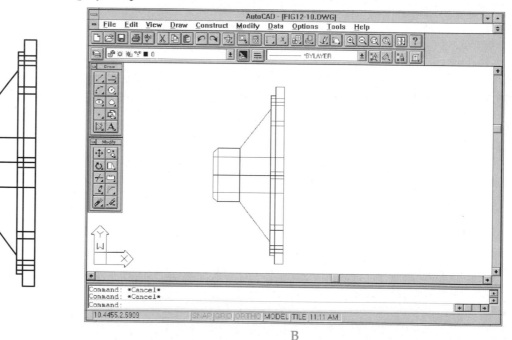

A   B

```
Command: SOLVIEW.↵
Entering Paper space. Use MVIEW to insert Model space viewports.
Regenerating drawing.
Ucs/Ortho/Auxiliary/Section/⟨eXit⟩: U↵
Named/World/?/⟨current⟩: N↵
Name of UCS to restore: LEFT↵
Enter view scale⟨1.0000⟩: .5↵
View center: (pick the center of the view)
View center: ↵
Clip first corner: (pick the first corner of a paper space viewport outside the object)
Clip other corner: (pick the opposite corner of the viewport)
View name: TOP↵
```

You must provide a name for the view in order to continue using **SOLVIEW**. The view shown in Figure 12-11 is displayed.

Figure 12-11.
The initial view named TOP is created with the **UCS** option of **SOLVIEW**.

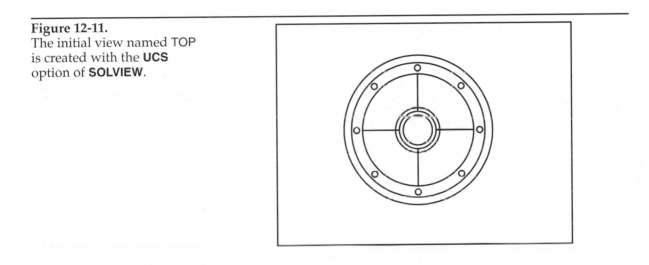

The **SOLVIEW** command remains active until you use the **eXit** option or press the [Esc] key. If you exit **SOLVIEW** at this time, you can still return to the drawing and create additional orthographic viewports. Continue and create a section view to the right of the top view as follows:

```
Ucs/Ortho/Auxiliary/Section/⟨eXit⟩: S↵
Cutting Plane's 1st point: (pick the quadrant of point 1 in Figure 12-12)
Cutting Plane's 2nd point: (pick the quadrant of point 2)
Side to view from: (pick point 3)
Enter view scale⟨0.5000⟩: ↵
View center: (pick the center of the new section view)
View center: ↵
Clip first corner: (pick one corner of the viewport)
Clip other corner: (pick the opposite corner of the viewport)
View name: SECTION↵
Ucs/Ortho/Auxiliary/Section/⟨eXit⟩: ↵
```

Notice in Figure 12-12 that the new view is shown as a wireframe and not as a section. This is normal. **SOLVIEW** is used to create the views. The **SOLDRAW** command draws the section lines. **SOLDRAW** is discussed later in this chapter.

Figure 12-12.
The section view created
with **SOLVIEW** (shown on
the right in both A and B)
does not show section lines.

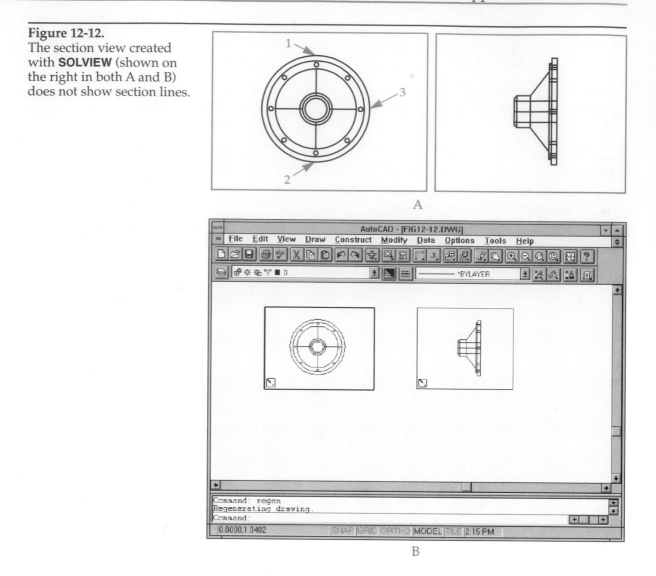

A

B

NOTE   The View center: prompt remains active until [Enter] is pressed.
This allows you to adjust the view location if necessary.

A standard orthographic view can be created using the **Ortho** option of **SOLVIEW**. This is illustrated in the following example:

Ucs/Ortho/Auxiliary/Section/⟨eXit⟩: **O.**↵
Pick side of viewport to project: *(pick the bottom edge of the left viewport)*
View center: *(pick the center of the new view)*
View center: ↵
Clip first corner: *(pick one corner of the viewport)*
Clip other corner: *(pick the opposite corner of the viewport)*
View name: **FRONT.**↵

The new orthographic view is shown in Figure 12-13.

The **SOLVIEW** command creates new layers that are used by **SOLDRAW** when profiles and sections are created. The layers are used for the placement of visible, hidden, dimension, and section lines. Each layer is named as the name of the view with a three letter tag. The layers are:

Layer name	Object
view name-VIS	Visible lines
view name-HID	Hidden lines
view name-DIM	Dimension lines
view name-HAT	Hatch patterns (sections)

The use of these layers is discussed in the next section.

Figure 12-13.
An orthographic front
view is created with the
Ortho option of **SOLVIEW**.
This is the view shown
at the lower left.

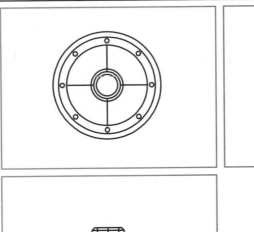
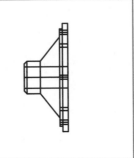
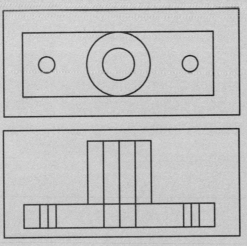

EXERCISE 12-3

❏ Open drawing EX12-1 if it is not on your screen.
❏ Return the display to a plan view of the WCS.
❏ Use **SOLVIEW** to create a top view of the solid. Locate the view near the top of the screen.
Name the view TOP.
❏ Use **SOLVIEW** to create a front section view of the solid located below the top view.
Name the view SECTION.
❏ The drawing should look similar to the one shown below.
❏ Save the drawing as EX12-3.

Creating finished views with SOLDRAW

SOLVIEW saves information specific to each viewport when a new view is created. This information is used by **SOLDRAW** to construct a finished profile or section view. **SOLDRAW** first deletes any information currently on the *view name*-VIS, *view name*-HID, and *view name*-HAT layers for the selected view. Then, visible, hidden, and section lines are automatically placed on the appropriate layer. Therefore, you should avoid placing objects on any layer other than the *view name*-DIM layer.

The **SOLDRAW** command automatically creates a profile or section in the selected viewport. If you select a viewport that was created using the **Section** option of **SOLVIEW**, the **SOLDRAW** command uses the current values of the **HPNAME**, **HPSCALE**, and **HPANG** system variables to construct the section. These three variables control the angle, boundary, and name of the hatch pattern.

If a view is selected that was not created as a section in **SOLVIEW**, the **SOLDRAW** command constructs a profile view. All new visible and hidden lines are placed on the *view name*-VIS or *view name*-HID layer. All existing objects on those layers are deleted. Use the **SOLDRAW** command as follows:

Command: **SOLDRAW**⏎
Select viewports to draw: (*pick the viewport edge*)
Select objects: 1 found
Select objects: ⏎
One solid selected.

After the profile construction is completed, lines that should be a hidden linetype are still visible (solid). This is because the linetype set for the *view name*-HID layer is CONTINUOUS. Change the linetype to HIDDEN and the drawing should appear as shown in Figure 12-14.

Figure 12-14.
The new front profile view shows hidden lines after the linetype is set to dashed for the FRONT-HID layer.

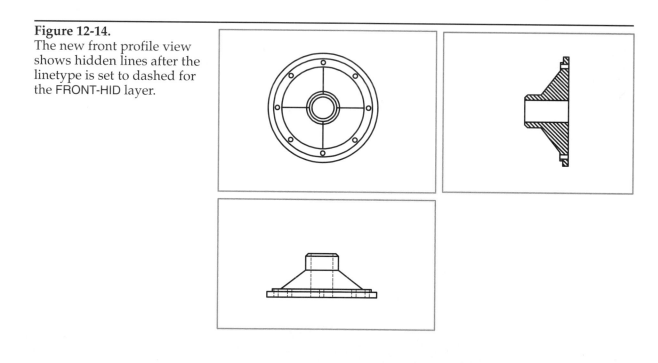

PROFESSIONAL TIP   If you wish to dimension views created with **SOLVIEW** and **SOLDRAW**, use the view-specific DIM layers. These layers are created for that purpose and are only visible in one view. **SOLDRAW** does not delete information on the DIM layers when it constructs a view.

Adding a 3D viewport to the drawing layout

If you want to add a viewport that contains a 3D view of the solid, use the **MVIEW** command. Create a single viewport by picking the corners. The object will appear in the viewport. Next use **VPOINT** to achieve the desired 3D view. Pan and zoom as necessary. If you want hidden lines removed on the 3D view when the drawing is plotted, use the **MVIEW Hideplot** option and select the 3D viewport. See Figure 12-15. Remember the following points when working with **SOLVIEW** and **SOLDRAW**:

- Use **SOLVIEW** first then **SOLDRAW**.
- Do not draw on the *view name*-HID and *view name*-VIS layers.
- Place dimensions for each view on the *view name*-DIM layer for that specific view.
- After using **SOLVIEW**, use **SOLDRAW** on all viewports in order to create hidden lines or section views.
- Change the linetype on the *view name*-HID layer to DASHED or HIDDEN.
- Create 3D viewports with the **MVIEW** command. Remove hidden lines when plotting with the **MVIEW Hideplot** option.
- Plot the drawing in paper space at the scale of 1:1.

Figure 12-15.
Create a 3D viewport with **MVIEW** and hide the lines with the **MVIEW Hideplot** option. This view is shown at the lower right.

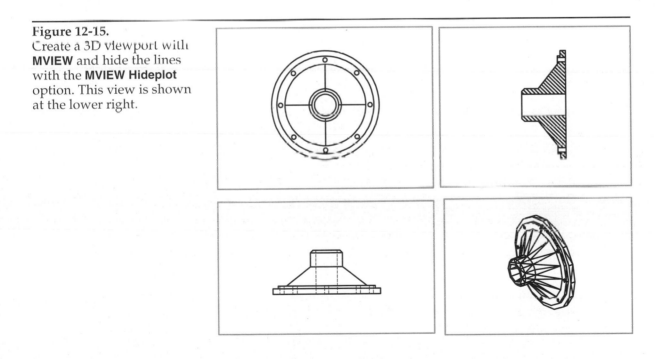

EXERCISE 12-4

❏ Open drawing EX12-3 if it is not on your screen. If you have not completed any of the exercises in this chapter, complete EX12-1 now and then complete EX12-3.

❏ Use **SOLDRAW** to create profile and section views of the two views on your screen. Adjust layer linetypes so hidden lines show properly.

❏ Add a 3D view to the right of the first two. The drawing should look similar to the one shown below.

❏ Save the drawing as EX12-4.

NOTE	The only documented help available for the **SOLPROF** command is found in the AutoCAD Documentation electronic file. This is accessible only if you have the AutoCAD Release 13 CD.

Creating a profile with SOLPROF

The **SOLPROF** command creates a profile view from a 3D solid model. This is similar to the **Profile** option of the **SOLVIEW** command. **SOLPROF** is limited to creating a profile view of the solid for the current 3D view only.

SOLPROF creates a block of all lines forming the profile of the object. It also creates a block of the hidden lines of the object. The original 3D object is retained. Each of these blocks is placed on a new layer with the name of PH-*view handle* and PV-*view handle*. A *view handle* is a name composed of numbers and letters that is automatically given to a viewport by AutoCAD. For example, if the view handle for the current viewport is 2C9, the **SOLPROF** command creates the layers PH-2C9 and PV-2C9. **SOLPROF** is used as follows:

```
Command: SOLPROF⏎
Select objects: 1 found
Select objects: ⏎
Display hidden profile lines on separate layer? ⟨Y⟩: ⏎
Project profile lines onto a plane? ⟨Y⟩: ⏎
```

If you answer yes to this prompt, the 3D profile lines are projected to a 2D plane and converted to 2D objects. This produces a cleaner profile.

```
Delete tangential edges? ⟨Y⟩: ⏎
```

Answering yes to this prompt produces a proper 2D view by eliminating lines that would normally appear at tangent points of arcs and lines.

One solid selected:
Command:

The original object and the profile created with **SOLPROF** are shown in Figure 12-16.

Figure 12-16.
A—The original solid.
B—A profile created with
SOLPROF.

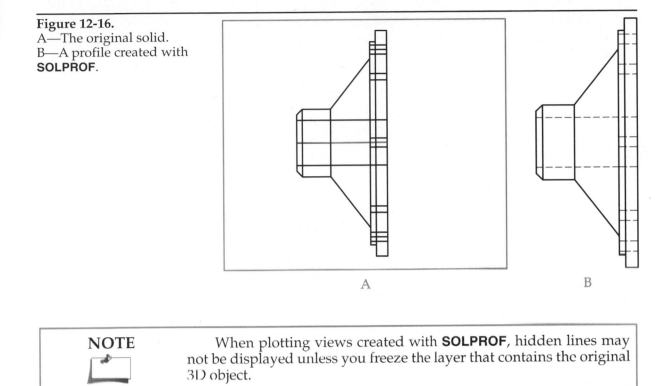

A   B

> **NOTE**   When plotting views created with **SOLPROF**, hidden lines may
> not be displayed unless you freeze the layer that contains the original
> 3D object.

SOLID MODEL ANALYSIS

The **MASSPROP** command allows you to analyze a solid model for its physical properties. There is only one material in R13 and that is mild steel.

The data obtained from **MASSPROP** can be retained for reference by saving it to a file. The default filename is the drawing name. The file is an ASCII text file with the extension of .MPR (mass properties). The analysis can be used for third party applications to produce finite element analysis, material list, or other testing studies.

Select the **MASSPROP** command by picking **Inquiry** in the **Edit** pull-down menu and then picking **Mass Properties**, Figure 12-17. You can also pick the **Mass Properties** button in the **Inquiry** flyout of the **Standard** toolbar or type MASSPROP at the **Command:** prompt:

Command: **MASSPROP**↵
Select objects: *(pick the solid model)*
Select objects: ↵

AutoCAD analyzes the model and displays the results on the text screen. See Figure 12-18. Each of the items you see displayed is explained below:
- **Mass.** A measure of the inertia of a solid. In other words, the more mass an object has, the more inertia it has. Note: Mass is *not* a unit of measurement of inertia.
- **Volume.** The amount of 3D space the solid occupies.
- **Bounding box.** A 3D box that fully encloses the solid.
- **Centroid.** A point in 3D space that represents the geometric center of the mass.
- **Moments of inertia.** A solid's resistance when rotating about a given axis.

Figure 12-17.
The **MASSPROP** command
is found in the **Inquiry**
cascade of the **Edit**
pull-down menu.

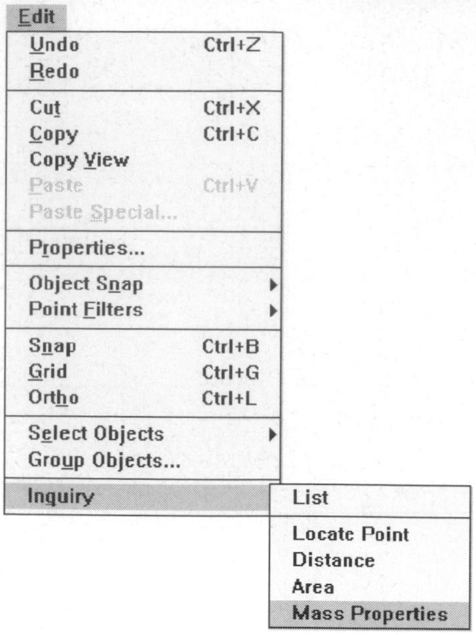

Edit	
Undo	Ctrl+Z
Redo	
Cut	Ctrl+X
Copy	Ctrl+C
Copy View	
Paste	Ctrl+V
Paste Special...	
Properties...	
Object Snap	▶
Point Filters	▶
Snap	Ctrl+B
Grid	Ctrl+G
Ortho	Ctrl+L
Select Objects	▶
Group Objects...	
Inquiry	

List
Locate Point
Distance
Area
Mass Properties

Figure 12-18.
The **MASSPROP** command displays a list of solid properties in the text screen. Each of these
properties is explained in the text.

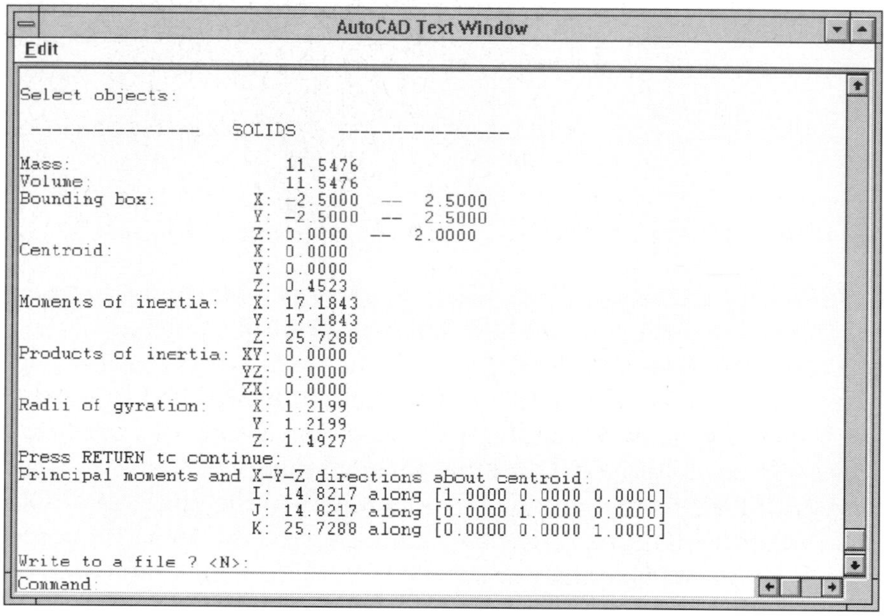

```
AutoCAD Text Window

Edit

Select objects:

-----------------    SOLIDS    -----------------

Mass:                   11.5476
Volume:                 11.5476
Bounding box:       X: -2.5000  --  2.5000
                    Y: -2.5000  --  2.5000
                    Z: 0.0000  --  2.0000
Centroid:           X: 0.0000
                    Y: 0.0000
                    Z: 0.4523
Moments of inertia: X: 17.1843
                    Y: 17.1843
                    Z: 25.7288
Products of inertia: XY: 0.0000
                    YZ: 0.0000
                    ZX: 0.0000
Radii of gyration:  X: 1.2199
                    Y: 1.2199
                    Z: 1.4927
Press RETURN to continue:
Principal moments and X-Y-Z directions about centroid:
                    I: 14.8217 along [1.0000 0.0000 0.0000]
                    J: 14.8217 along [0.0000 1.0000 0.0000]
                    K: 25.7288 along [0.0000 0.0000 1.0000]

Write to a file ? <N>:
Command:
```

- **Products of inertia.** A solid's resistance when rotating about two axes at a time.
- **Radii of gyration.** Similar to moments of inertia. Specified as a radius about an axis.
- **Principal moments and X-Y-Z directions about a centroid.** The axes about which the
  moments of inertia are the highest and lowest.

PROFESSIONAL TIP

Advanced applications of solid model design and analysis are
possible with Autodesk's Designer and Mechanical Desktop software. These products allow you to create parametric designs and
assign a wide variety of materials to the solid model.

SOLID MODEL FILE EXCHANGE

AutoCAD drawing files can be converted to files that can be used for testing and analysis with the **ACISOUT** command or **Export Data** dialog box. This creates a file with the .SAT extension. These files can be imported into AutoCAD with the **ACISIN** command or by using the **Import File** dialog box.

Solids can also be exported for use with stereo-lithography software. These files have the .STL extension. The **STLOUT** command is used for this. However, the **Export Data** dialog box *cannot* be used for .STL files.

Release 13 solids use the ACIS modeling language. Release 12 uses the AME modeling language. However, solids created in Release 12 can be converted to Release 13 ACIS models with the **AMECONVERT** command.

Importing and exporting solid model files

A solid model is frequently used with analysis and testing software or in the manufacturing of the part. The **ACISOUT** command allows you to create this type of file. You can type ACISOUT at the **Command:** prompt. This displays the **Create ACIS File** dialog box. See Figure 12-19A. You can also use the **Export Data** dialog box by picking **Export...** from the **File** pulldown menu or typing EXPORT. Pick the .SAT selection in the **List Files of Type:** list box in the **Export Data** dialog box. See Figure 12-19B.

An .SAT file can be imported into AutoCAD and automatically converted into a drawing file by entering ACISIN at the **Command:** prompt. This displays the **Select ACIS File** dialog box. See Figure 12-20A. You can also use the **Import File** dialog box by picking **Import...** from the **File** pull-down menu or typing IMPORT. Pick the .SAT selection in the **List Files of Type:** list box in the **Import File** dialog box. See Figure 12-20B.

Figure 12-19.
A—The **Create ACIS File** dialog box. B—Pick .SAT in the **Export Data** dialog box to create a solid model export file.

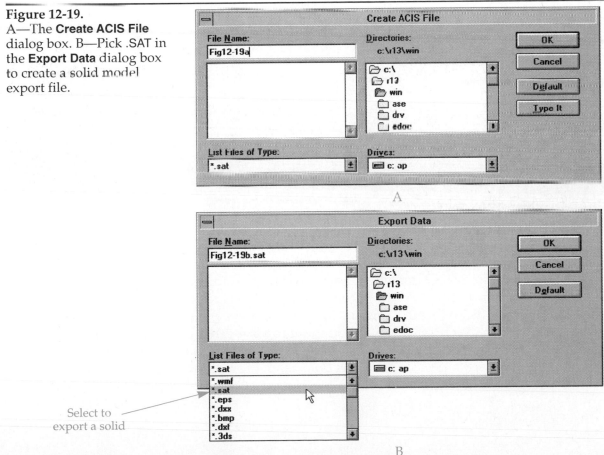

Figure 12-20.
A—The **Select ACIS File** dialog box. B—Pick .SAT in the **Import File** dialog box to import a solid model file.

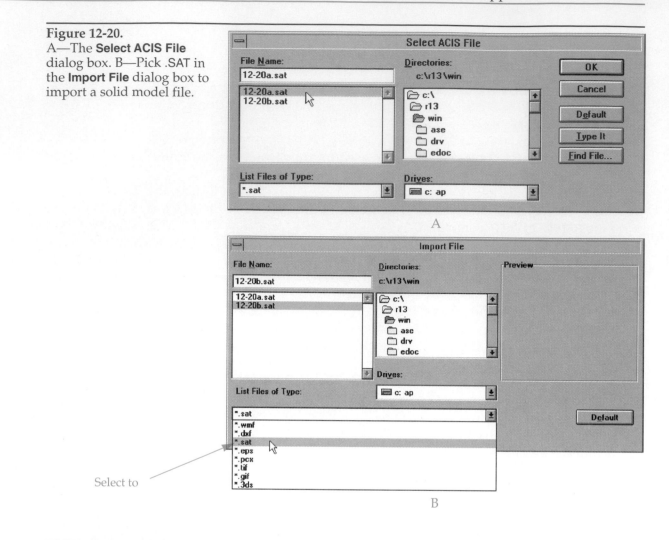

Select to

PROFESSIONAL TIP

Solid model drawing files can be saved as .SAT files for archive purposes. These files require far less disk space than .DWG files, and may be a good option when you have limited storage space.

Stereolithography files

Stereolithography is a technology where a plastic prototype 3D model is created using a computer-generated solid model, a laser, and a vat of liquid polymer. This technology is also called *rapid prototyping.* This is because a prototype 3D model can be designed and formed in a short amount of time without using standard manufacturing processes.

Most software used to create a stereolithograph can read an .STL file. AutoCAD can export a drawing file to the .STL format, but *cannot* import an .STL file. Also, the solid model must be located in the current UCS so that the entire object has positive XYZ coordinates.

Unlike exporting other types of files, you *cannot* use the **Export Data** dialog box to export an .STL file. You *must* type STLOUT at the **Command:** prompt as follows:

    Command: **STLOUT**↵
    Select a single solid for STL output:
    Select objects:

You can only select a single object. If you select more than one object, AutoCAD prompts you with the following:

> Only one solid per file is permitted.

Select one object and press [Enter]. You are then asked if you want to create a binary .STL file. If you answer no to the prompt, an ASCII file is created. Keep in mind that a binary .STL file may be at least five times smaller than the same file in ASCII format. After you choose the type of file, the **Create STL File** dialog box is displayed. Type the filename in the **File Name:** edit box and pick **OK** or press [Enter].

Converting Release 12 AME solids

The **AMECONVERT** command allows you to convert AutoCAD Release 12 AME solids into Release 13 ACIS solids. The solids must be either AME Release 2 or 2.1 regions or solids. First load the Release 12 drawing into AutoCAD. Then, pick **Solids** and **AME Convert** from the **Draw** pull-down menu or pick the **AME Convert** button in the **Solids** toolbar. You can also type AMECONVERT at the **Command:** prompt. Select all solids to be converted. Then, press [Enter] to convert the solids.

EXERCISE 12-5

❏ Open drawing EX12-4 if it is not on your screen.
❏ Perform a mass properties analysis of the solid.

  ❏ What is the mass? _____

  ❏ What is the volume? _____

  ❏ What is the bounding box?

  ❏ X: _____

  ❏ Y: _____

  ❏ Z: _____

  ❏ What is the centroid?

  ❏ X: _____

  ❏ Y: _____

  ❏ Z: _____

❏ Export an .SAT file and name it EX12-5.
❏ Begin a new drawing. Import the .SAT file named EX12-5.
❏ Export an .STL file and name it EX12-5.
❏ Do not save the drawing.

CHAPTER TEST

Write your answers in the spaces provided.

1. What is the function of the **ISOLINES** variable? _____
   _____
   _____

2. What variable controls the display of a solid primitive silhouette? _____

3. What is the function of **FACETRES**? _____
   _____
   _____

4. What command creates a 2D region that represents a cutting plane through the solid?
   _____

5. What command can display the true 3D shape of internal features and object profiles?
   _____

6. Which command should be used first, **SOLDRAW** or **SOLVIEW**? _____

7. What command allows you to create a multiview layout from a 3D solid model? _____
   _____

8. Which option of the command in question 7 is used to create an orthographic view?
   _____

9. Name the layer(s) that the command in question 7 automatically creates. _____
   _____

10. Which layer(s) in question 9 should you avoid drawing on?_____
    _____

11. What command can automatically complete a section view using the current settings of
    HPNAME, **HPSCALE**, and **HPANG**? _____

12. When plotting, how are hidden lines removed in a viewport that contains a 3D view?
    _____

13. Which command creates a profile view from a 3D model? _____

14. What is the function of the **MASSPROP** command? _____
    _____

15. What is the extension of the ASCII file that can be created by **MASSPROP**? _____

16. What is a centroid? _____
    _____

17. What commands export and import solid models?_____

18. What kind of file has an extension of .STL?_____

19. What command creates the file in question 18? _____

20. How can AutoCAD Release 12 solids be converted into AutoCAD Release 13 solids?
    _____

DRAWING PROBLEMS

1. Open one of your solid model problems from a previous chapter and do the following:

   General

   A. Set the **DISPSILH** variable to 1 and use **HIDE**.

   B. Set the **FACETRES** variable to .5 and produce a shaded model. Set **FACETRES** to 1 and shade the model again.

   C. Change the **SHADEDGE** and **SHADEDIF** variables, set **FACETRES** to 2 and shade the model.

   D. Create a rendering of the model.

   E. Save the drawing as P12-1.

2. Open one of your solid model problems from a previous chapter and do the following:

   General

   A. Construct a section through the model. Cut through as many features as possible.

   B. Move the new section region to a space outside the 3D solid.

   C. Explode the resulting regions as needed and place section lines in the appropriate areas. Add lines to complete the section.

   D. Cut a slice through the original solid in the same location as the previous section.

   E. Retain the piece of the solid that is the same side as the section.

   F. Remove the other side of the slice.

   G. Save the drawing as P12-2.

3. Open one of your solid model problems from a previous chapter and do the following:

   General

   A. Create a paper space multiview layout of the model. One of the views should be a section view. Create a minimum of three 2D views.

   B. Use **SOLVIEW** and **SOLDRAW** to create the views. Be sure that section lines and hidden lines are displayed properly.

   C. Create a fourth viewport that contains a 3D view of the solid. Label the view PICTORIAL VIEW.

   D. Plot the drawing so the 3D view is displayed with hidden lines removed.

   E. Save the drawing as P12-3.

4. Open one of your solid model problems from a previous chapter and do the following:

   General

   A. Display the model in a plan view.

   B. Use **SOLPROF** to create a profile view. Wblock the profile view to a file named P12-2PLN.

   C. Display the original model in a 3D view.

   D. Use **SECTION** to construct a front-view section of the model. Delete the original 3D solid.

   E. Display the section as a plan view.

   F. Insert the wblock P12-2PLN above the section view. Adjust the views so that they align properly.

   G. Save the drawing as P12-4.

General

5. Choose five solid model problems from previous chapters and copy them to a new directory on the hard drive. Then, do the following:

A. Open the first drawing, then export it as an .SAT file to the new directory.

B. Do the same for the remaining four files.

C. Compare the sizes of the .SAT files with the .DWG files. Compare the combined sizes of both types of files.

D. Begin a new drawing and import one of the previous .SAT files.

E. Do not save the drawing.

AutoCAD R13

Chapter 13

Introduction to Presentation Graphics

Learning objectives

After completing this chapter, you will be able to:

- ○ Import and export raster files using AutoCAD.
- ○ Set raster file variables to create a variety of displays.
- ○ Import and export vector files using AutoCAD.
- ○ Import and export PostScript files using AutoCAD.
- ○ Use PostScript fonts in AutoCAD drawings.

This chapter introduces using AutoCAD to work with presentation-quality graphics. This includes importing and exporting raster files into and out of AutoCAD. Several different types of vector files can also be imported and exported. PostScript fonts and creating PostScript files for printing are also covered in this chapter.

The Windows Clipboard can be an important part of creating presentation graphics. In addition, object linking and embedding (OLE) can be used to incorporate AutoCAD graphics into electronic presentations. Both of these topics are covered thoroughly in Chapter 23.

WORKING WITH RASTER FILES

AutoCAD drawing files are composed of vectors. A *vector* is defined by XYZ coordinates. *Pixels* (picture elements) are the "dots" or "bits" that make up your display screen. There is no relationship between the physical pixels in your monitor and a vector object. Pixels simply show the object at the current zoom percent.

Many illustrations created with drawing, painting, and presentation software are saved as raster files. A *raster file* defines objects by the location and color of the screen pixels. Raster files are usually called *bitmaps*. There are several types of raster files used for presentation graphics and desktop publishing. The most common types are covered in the next section.

Raster file types

You can work with four of the most common raster files using the **Import** and **Export** dialog boxes. These file types are:

- **.GIF (Graphics Interchange Format).** A file format developed by CompuServe to exchange graphic images over an on-line computer service.
- **.PCX (Personal Computer Exchange).** A file format developed by Z-Soft Corporation.
- **.TIF (Tagged Image File Format).** A file format developed by Aldus Corporation and Microsoft Corporation.
- **.BMP (Bitmap).** A file format developed by Microsoft Corporation.

There are many more raster file formats in use. If you have a raster image that is not one of the types listed above, you will need to first import it into a paint or draw program. Then, export the image in one of the above formats.

The Windows Clipboard can also be used to import file types not listed here into AutoCAD. This feature is discussed in Chapter 23.

NOTE   There are no .GIF, .PCX, or .TIF files shipped with Release 13. However, thousands of these types of files are easily found on computer on-line services, such as CompuServe or America Online. The mouse used in this chapter is from the AutoCAD Release 12 Bonus CD.

Importing raster images

Three commands allow you to insert raster files into an AutoCAD drawing. These commands are **GIFIN**, **PCXIN**, and **TIFFIN**. The prompts for these commands are the same. When entering the file name, you must give the complete path to the file. An easier way to import .GIF, .PCX, and .TIF files is to pick **Import...** in the **File** pull-down menu, Figure 13-1A. This displays the **Import File** dialog box. Select the file type from the **List Files of Type** pop-up menu. Then, select the file from the file list. See Figure 13-1B. Finally, pick **OK** to import the selected file.

After you have selected a file, you are prompted for an insertion point and scale factor:

    Insertion point ⟨0,0,0⟩: *(pick a point)*
    Scale factor: **5**↵

The image appears as a box with the filename inside until you pick the insertion point and scale factor. Then, the image is displayed on the screen. See Figure 13-2.

AutoCAD cannot manipulate raster files. Therefore, it converts the outlines of different color raster data to solids. The colors now appear as if created with the **SOLID** command. You can see this by turning **FILL** off and using the **REGEN** command, Figure 13-3.

Figure 13-1.
A—The **IMPORT** command can be selected from the **File** pull-down menu. B—Specify the file type and select a file.

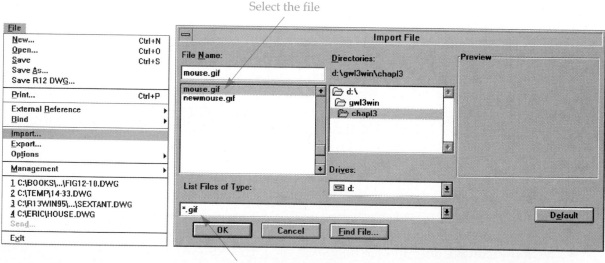

A

B

Figure 13-2.
A .GIF file is displayed using
the **GIFIN** command.

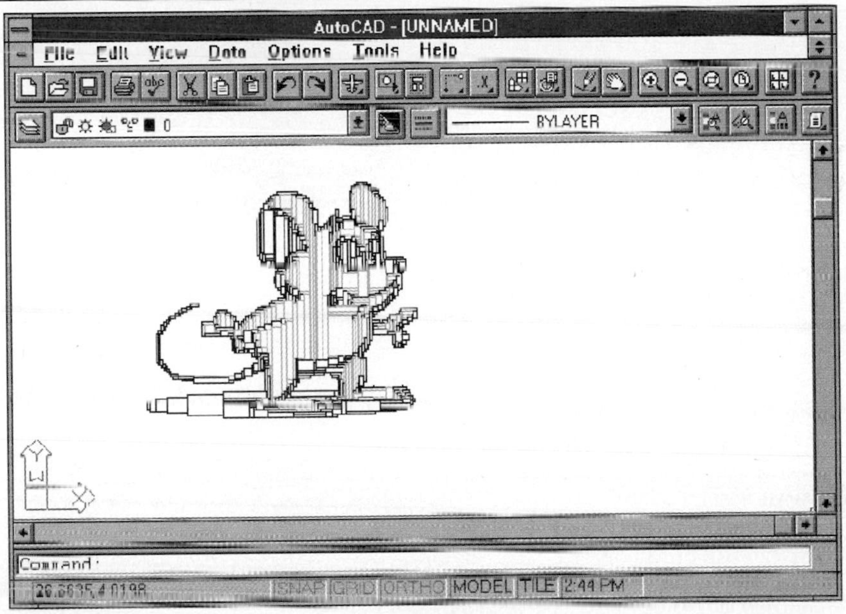

Figure 13-3.
The different raster colors
are converted to solids
in AutoCAD.

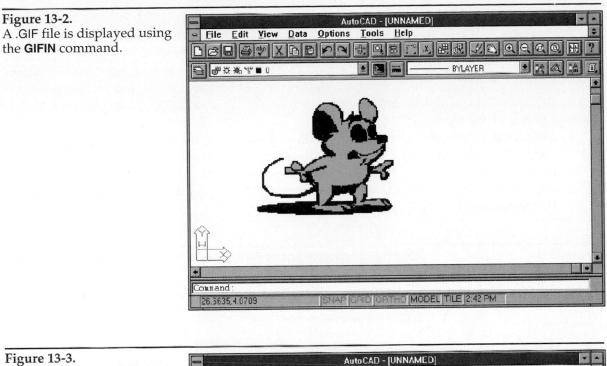

> **NOTE**
>
> The background color of the graphics window affects the background color of imported graphics. Change the graphics window background color by picking **Preferences...** from the **Options** pull-down menu. Then, pick the **Color** button in the **System** panel. Set the color that you want and close the dialog box.

Raster image system variables

Six variables allow you to control the appearance of an imported raster file. These variables are explained below:

- **RIASPECT.** Controls the aspect ratio (width to height) of the image. Use this when inserting .GIF and .TIF files. The aspect ratio of the image on the left in Figure 13-4 is 0. However, the aspect ratio of the image on the right is 0.8333. Notice the width difference of the mouse.
- **RIBACKG.** Controls the background color of your display device. The default is 0. In Figure 13-5 the AutoCAD graphics window background color is set to 7 (White) and the **RIBACKG** is set to 0 (Black). Notice the color of the eyes. Compare this to Figure 13-2 where the AutoCAD graphics window background is set to 7 (White) and **RIBACKG** is set to 7 (White).

Figure 13-4.
The aspect ratio can be used to change the appearance of the image.

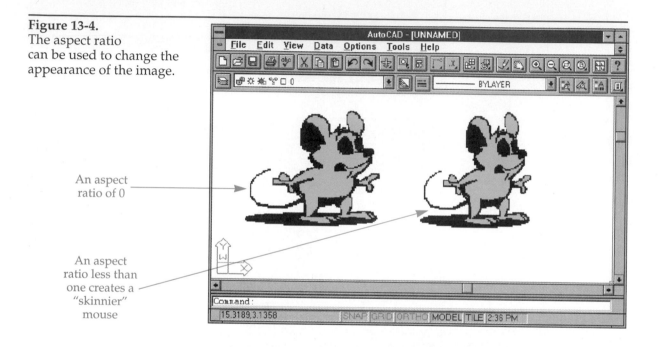

An aspect ratio of 0

An aspect ratio less than one creates a "skinnier" mouse

Figure 13-5.
The **RIBACKG** variable controls the color of the background.

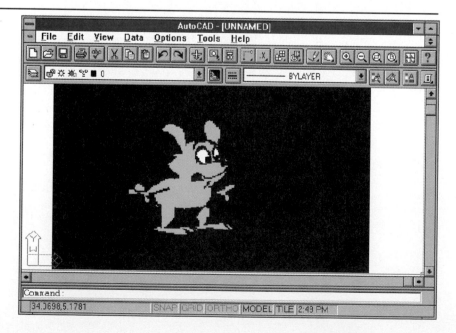

- **RIEDGE.** If set to a value other than 0, edges of the image are displayed. Use this setting if you need to trace the object. The larger the setting (up to 255), the more defined an edge must be to display. The image in Figure 13-6 has **RIASPECT** set to 0 and **RIEDGE** set to 25.
- **RIGAMUT.** Controls the range of colors used to display the image. The default is 256. If your display device uses only 8 or 16 colors, set **RIGAMUT** to that value. Reducing the number of colors can create a much smaller imported file.
- **RIGREY.** Converts the imported image to grayscale. AutoCAD has only a few gray shades. Therefore, this may not greatly reduce the size of the imported file.
- **RITHRESH.** Controls the display of an image based on brightness. By setting a value greater than 0, you establish a *threshold filter.* Only colors with a brightness value greater than the **RITHRESH** setting are displayed. Colors that are dropped out are not included in the drawing. **RITHRESH** is set to 50 for Figure 13-7.

Figure 13-6.
Edges of the raster file can be displayed by setting the **RIEDGE** variable.

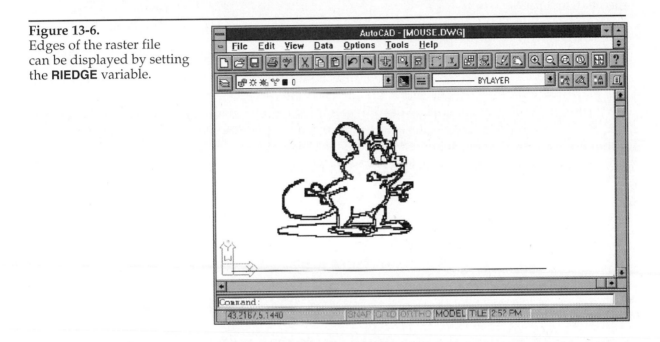

Figure 13-7.
Colors can be filtered out by using the **RITHRESH** variable.

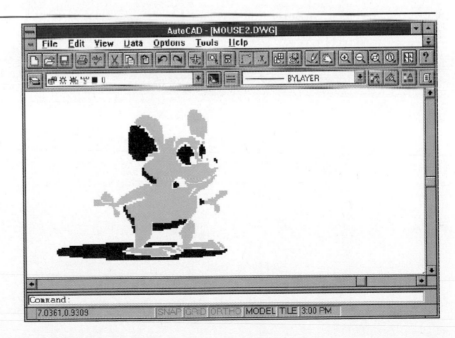

PROFESSIONAL TIP
Depending on the image, it is often easier to trace a raster display by leaving **RIEDGE** set to 0 (off). As you can see when comparing Figure 13-7 and Figure 13-3, it may be easier to see details when the original colors are displayed.

Exporting raster files

You can save or export raster files in one of four formats. These formats are .TGA, .TIF, .GIF, and .BMP. The **SAVEIMG** command is used to save .TGA, .TIF, and .GIF files. To access the command, pick **Files** and **Save Image...** from the **Render** pull-down menu or type **SAVEIMG** at the **Command:** prompt. This displays the **Save Image** dialog box. Use the dialog box to save the image. This process is discussed in detail in Chapter 14. Saving a .BMP file is discussed in the next section.

Working with bitmap files

A raster image is often called a bitmap. A bitmap is simply a record of colored pixels, rather than geometric objects. When you draw a line, the pixels between the endpoints of the line are filled in. However, the pixels are not associated with one another and do not form a single object. A bitmap file is often used by paint style programs such as Windows Paintbrush.

To create a bitmap image file, select **Export...** from the **File** menu or type EXPORT at the **Command:** prompt. Then, select .BMP in the **List Files of Type:** pop-up list of the **Export Data** dialog box. You can also type BMPOUT at the **Command:** prompt to display the **Create BMP File** dialog box. In this case, the file type is automatically selected. See Figure 13-8.

Figure 13-8.
The **Export Data** and **Create BMP File** dialog boxes.

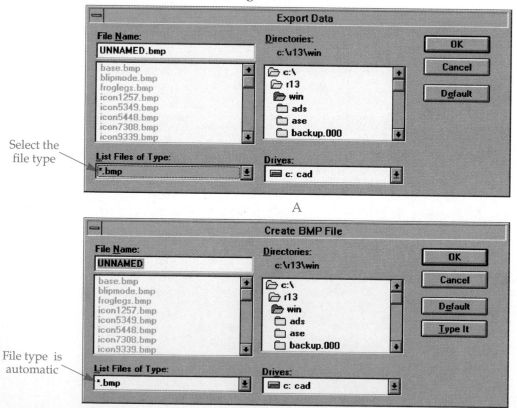

After you enter a filename, you must select the objects you want in the bitmap. The image file is a rectangular area that represents the current viewing area in AutoCAD. However, only selected objects are placed in the bitmap. Unselected objects are not placed in the bitmap file.

The current screen resolution affects the appearance of the image in the bitmap. The bitmap background size is the size of the AutoCAD graphics screen when the bitmap is created. The color is always white.

PROFESSIONAL TIP

The BMPOUT command creates a *compressed* BMP file by default. This type of file uses less disk space, but cannot be read by many Windows applications. To create an uncompressed bitmap, you need to edit the ACAD.INI file. In the [General] section, there is a line that says BmpOutCompression=1. Change the line to read BmpOutCompression=0. If the line does not exist, add the line BmpOutCompression=0 at the end of the [General] section. Save the file and exit. The next time you start AutoCAD, the changes will take effect. The R13c0 and R13c1 maintenance releases *always* write compressed .BMP files.

Uses of raster files in AutoCAD

One use of raster images is sketching or tracing. For example, you may need a line drawing of an image that is only available as a .GIF file. After importing the raster image, use the appropriate commands to sketch or trace the image. After the object is sketched, the original raster image can be deleted or frozen to produce a drawing much like Figure 13-9A. This can be further enhanced with AutoCAD to produce any type of drawing that is required by the project. An example of a refined drawing is shown in Figure 13-9B.

PROFESSIONAL TIP

A raster image is inserted as a block. If you explode it, the block reverts to entities as if created with the **SOLID** command. These can then be manipulated in any way you wish.

Figure 13-9.
A—Raster images can be traced using the **SKETCH** command.
B—Raster images can be combined with AutoCAD objects to create a drawing that you might not be able to with other software.

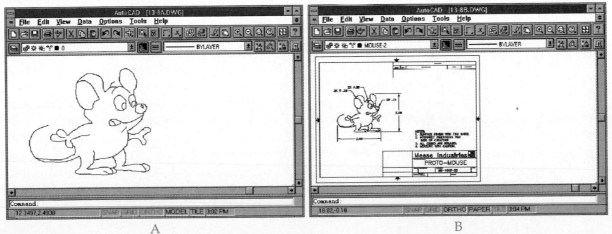

A   B

You can also add features to raster files that may not be possible in other software you are using. For example, you can import a raster file, dimension or annotate it, or even add special shapes to it. Then, export it as the same type of file with a command such as **SAVEIMG**. Now you can use the revised file in the original software in which it was created. As with any creative process, let your imagination and the job requirements determine how you use this capability of AutoCAD. Refer to Chapter 14 for a discussion on the **SAVEIMG** command.

EXERCISE 13-1

❏ Start a new drawing and name it EX13-1.
❏ Find a raster file with the extension of .GIF, .PCX, or .TIF. It can be a sample file from other software or a file downloaded from a computer on-line service such as CompuServe or America Online.
❏ Use the proper command to import the image into your drawing.
❏ Explode the image. Then, zoom-in close to examine the entities that make up the drawing.
❏ Make two new layers. Name one IMAGE and the other LINES.
❏ Make the LINES layer current. Use commands such as **SKETCH**, **PLINE** and **SPLINE** to trace a portion of the image.
❏ Make the IMAGE layer current, freeze the LINES layer, then erase all of the entities on the IMAGE layer.
❏ Thaw the LINES layer and save the drawing as A:EX13-1.

WORKING WITH VECTOR FILES

A vector file contains objects that are defined by XYZ coordinates. AutoCAD allows you to work with several different vector files using the **Export Data** and **Import File** dialog boxes. The most common is the AutoCAD drawing file (.DWG). Other vector file types are .DXF, .3DS, .WMF, and .SAT.

The .DXF file is an ASCII version of the drawing data. The .3DS file exports AutoCAD objects to the native format of Autodesk's 3D Studio. Both .DXF and .3DS files are discussed in Chapter 17 of *AutoCAD and its Applications—Basics, Release 13 for Windows.*

The .SAT file format is used with solid models and statistical analysis. Refer to Chapter 12 of this text for a discussion on .SAT files.

The .WMF file format is a Windows metafile. This file format is often used to exchange data with desktop publishing programs. The next section covers using Windows metafiles with AutoCAD.

Creating vector files using AutoCAD

The Windows metafile format works best for importing into object-based drawing programs. An object-based program creates objects such as lines, arcs, and circles like the AutoCAD software. This means that a line is drawn as a single object, rather than a collection of colored pixels on the screen. The .WMF file format is an object-based format.

To save a .WMF file, select **Export...** from the **File** menu or type EXPORT at the **Command:** prompt. This displays the **Export Data** dialog box. Select .WMF in the **List Files of Type:** pop-up list. You can also type WMFOUT at the **Command:** prompt. This displays the **Create WMF File** dialog box. In this dialog box, the .WMF file type is automatically selected. See Figure 13-10.

After specifying the filename and directory location in either dialog box, you must select the objects to place in the file. Press [Enter] once all of the objects are selected and the .WMF file is saved.

Figure 13-10
The **Export Data** and **Create WMF File** dialog boxes.

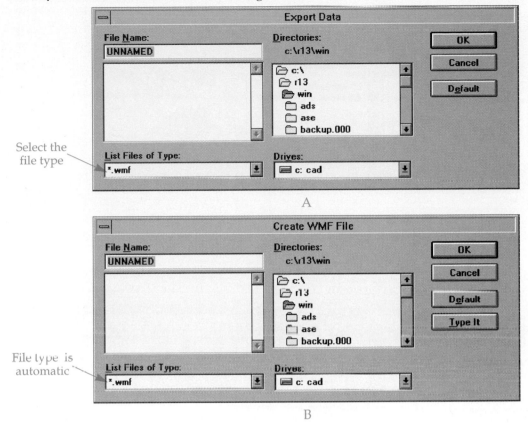

Only the portions of selected objects visible on-screen are written into the file. If part of a selected object goes off of the screen, only the visible part is written to the file. For example, if a selected circle is partially off of the screen, it appears as an arc in the .WMF file. This is because a Windows metafile is a vector format translated from a raster image.

Also, the current view resolution affects the appearance of a Windows metafile. For example, when **VIEWRES** is set low, circles in your AutoCAD drawing may look like polygons. When saved to a Windows metafile, the objects are polygons and not circles.

To import a Windows metafile, select **Import...** from the **File** menu or type IMPORT at the **Command:** prompt. This opens the **Import File** dialog box. Select WMF in the file type list and then select a file. You can also type WMFIN at the **Command:** prompt. This displays the **Import WMF** dialog box. Both of these dialog boxes have a preview window where you can see the image before you import it. See Figure 13-11.

A Windows metafile is imported as a block made up of all the objects in the file. You can explode an imported Windows metafile if you need to edit the objects within it. All of the non-filled objects in a Windows metafile are created as polylines when they are brought into AutoCAD. This includes arcs and circles. Filled objects are created from solid fill objects, as if created using the **SOLID** command.

There are two settings used to control the appearance of Windows metafiles imported into AutoCAD. Type WMFOPTS at the **Command:** prompt or select **WMF Options...** from the **Options** cascade of the **File** menu. The **WMF Import Options** dialog box is displayed, Figure 13-12. The dialog box contains the following two check boxes:

- **Wire Frames (No Fills).** When checked, filled areas are imported only as outlines. Otherwise, filled areas are imported as filled objects.
- **Wide Lines.** When this option is checked, the relative line widths of lines and borders in WMF are maintained. Otherwise, they are imported using a zero width.

Figure 13-11.
The **Import Data** and **Import WMF** dialog boxes display the highlighted file in the preview windows.

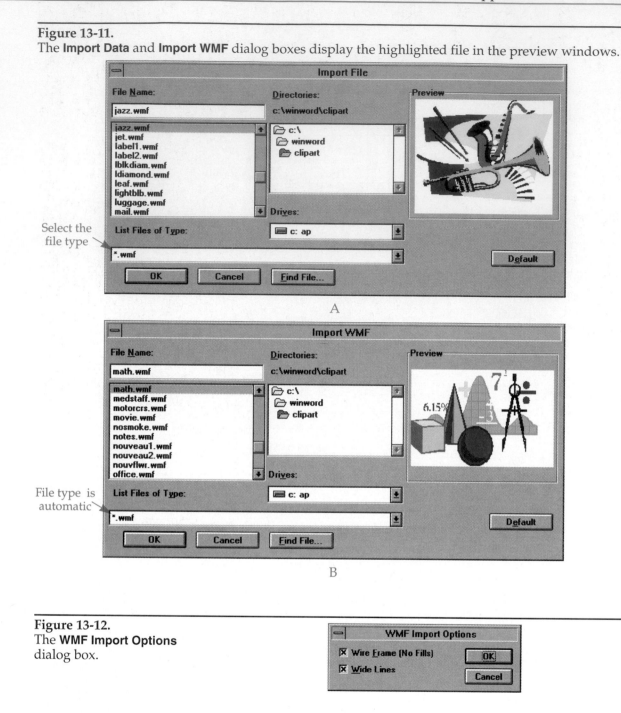

Figure 13-12.
The **WMF Import Options**
dialog box.

WORKING WITH POSTSCRIPT FONTS AND FILES

PostScript is a copyrighted page description language developed by Adobe Systems. PostScript files are widely used in desktop publishing. AutoCAD can import and export PostScript files and use PostScript fonts. This allows you to work with raster or vector files to create presentation-quality graphics and then save the graphics in a format that most desktop publishing software can read.

The **PSIN** and **PSOUT** commands are used to import and export PostScript files. The **IMPORT** and **EXPORT** commands can also be used. The **PSDRAG** command controls the visibility of the imported image as it is being inserted. The quality, or resolution, of the displayed image is controlled with the **PSQUALITY** command. The pattern that fills the graphic is set with the **PSFILL** command.

Adding fill patterns to an object

Using the **PSFILL** command, you can add PostScript fill patterns to a closed polyline. The types of fill patterns available are shown in Figure 13-13. To access the command, pick **Hatch** and then **PostScript Fill** from the **Draw** pull-down menu, pick the **PostScript Fill** button in the **Hatch** flyout of the **Draw** toolbar, or type PSFILL at the **Command:** prompt.

Each pattern prompts for different values. For example, you can enter a value from 0 to 100 when using the GRAYSCALE pattern. In this case, the value is a percentage of black. To fill an area with a grayscale value of 15 (15% black), enter the following:

> Command: **PSFILL.**↵
> Select polyline: *(pick the polyline to be filled)*
> PostScript fill pattern (. = none) 〈.〉/?: **GRAYSCALE.**↵ *(type ? to see the available fill patterns)*
> Grayscale 〈50〉: **15.**↵

Notice that no change appears on the screen. However, the pattern is included in the file when you use the **PSOUT** command.

The **RADIALGRAY** fill pattern displays a highlight in the center of the selected polyline, and darkens toward the outer edges. You can control the brightness of the highlight (ForegroundGray), and the darkness of the edges (BackgroundGray).

Figure 13-13.
The fill patterns available with the **PSFILL** command.

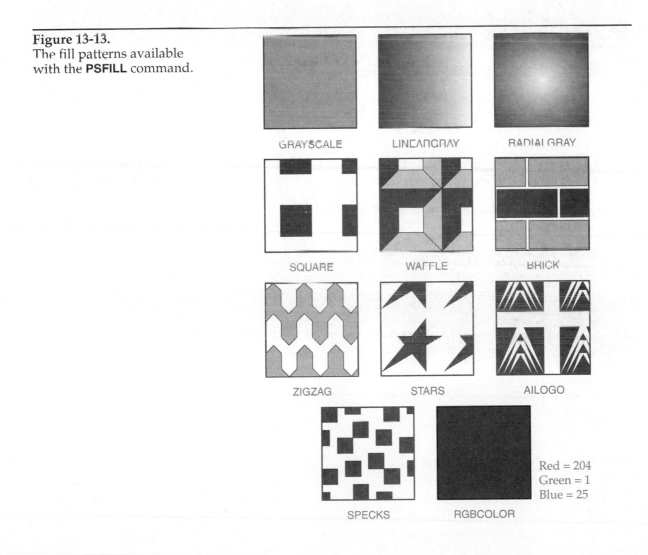

Command: **PSFILL**↵
Select polyline: (*pick the polyline to be filled*)
PostScript fill pattern (. = none) ⟨.⟩/?: ***RADIALGRAY**↵
Levels ⟨256⟩: ↵
ForegroundGray ⟨0⟩: ↵
BackgroundGray ⟨100⟩: ↵

The appearance of several RADIALGRAY settings are shown in Figure 13-14.

When the **PSOUT** command is used, any **PSFILL** patterns are automatically surrounded by a polyline. This polyline shows on the final print. If you do not want a polyline to surround the fill, place an asterisk (*) in front of the pattern name like this:

PostScript fill pattern (. = none) ⟨.⟩/?: ***GRAYSCALE**↵

You can remove a fill pattern from a polyline by entering a period at the PostScript fill pattern: prompt.

PostScript fill pattern (. = none) ⟨.⟩/?: **.**↵

AutoCAD
Custom
Guide
3

Custom fill patterns can be added to the ACAD.PSF file. This is an ASCII text file and can be edited with any text editor. However, the proper PostScript language must be used. See the *AutoCAD Customization Guide* for the correct procedures.

Figure 13-14.
Changing the value of the RADIALGRAY **PSFILL** pattern creates different effects.

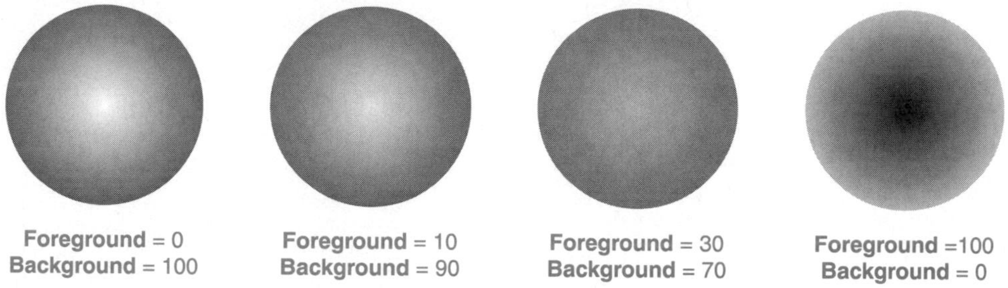

Foreground = 0 **Background** = 100	**Foreground** = 10 **Background** = 90	**Foreground** = 30 **Background** = 70	**Foreground** =100 **Background** = 0

EXERCISE 13-2

❏ Begin a new drawing named EX13-2.
❏ Draw four rectangles, each measuring 1 × 2 units.
❏ Use the following **PSFILL** patterns to fill the rectangles.
 ❏ LINEARGRAY (2 cycles)
 ❏ RADIALGRAY
 ❏ WAFFLE
 ❏ STARS (**BackgroundGray** = 20, **ForegroundGray** = 85)
❏ Save the drawing as A:EX13-2.

Exporting a PostScript image

Any drawing created in AutoCAD can be converted to a PostScript file using the **EXPORT** or **PSOUT** commands. A PostScript file is usually created if PostScript fonts or images are added to the drawing, or if the **PSFILL** command is used to add patterns. Remember, an .EPS file can only be printed by a PostScript printer. The command prompt is as follows:

Command: **PSOUT**↵

> **NOTE**
>
> If you use the **EXPORT** command to export a PostScript file, all prompts are automatically answered with the defaults. You are not given the opportunity to change any of the settings.

The **Create PostScript File** dialog box is displayed. Enter a name and pick the **OK** button. If you entered EXPORT, the **Export Data** dialog box appears. Pick .EPS in the file type list, enter a name, and pick **OK**. With the **EXPORT** command, the following prompts are automatic.

```
What to plot – Display, Extents, Limits, View or Window ⟨D⟩: ↵
Include a screen preview image in the file? (None/EPSI/TIFF) ⟨None⟩: ↵
```

A screen preview image can be included with the file. A preview is used by many desktop publishing programs. It allows an artist to see the image. If you respond with EPSI or TIFF, you are asked to select the image size. The default size of 128×128 pixels is small, so it does not slow down the software when the image is imported. The next prompt is:

```
Size units (Inches or Millimeters) ⟨Inches⟩: ↵
Output Inches=Drawing Units or Fit or ? ⟨Fit⟩: ↵
```

Enter half scale as 1 = 2. An architectural scale can be entered as 1/8″ = 1′-0″, or .125 = 12.

The text window then displays a list of standard values for output size. Several sizes are listed. You can choose from the list and type the letter listed under the size column. You can also enter a new size as follows:

```
Enter the Size or Width, Height (in Inches) ⟨USER⟩: 6,8.5↵
```

The PostScript file is created.

Printing PostScript files

After the file has been created it can be printed by a PostScript printer at the DOS prompt. The DOS prompt can be accessed by double clicking on the MS-DOS Prompt icon located in the Main program group of Program Manager. Then, type the following:

```
C:\R13\WIN⟩ COPY FILE.EPS LPT1↵
```

or

```
C:\R13\WIN⟩ PRINT FILE.EPS↵
```

> **NOTE**
>
> You cannot use the Windows "drag and drop" capability to print PostScript files. If you try to drag and drop a file to the Print Manager icon, you are prompted that there is no association with this file. If you use Associate… from the File pull-down menu, your .EPS file is associated with AutoCAD. This prints the drawing file that you select, not your .EPS file.

Importing a PostScript image

You can use the **IMPORT** or **PSIN** commands to import a PostScript file into AutoCAD. A PostScript file has the .EPS extension. **PSIN** is similar to the **INSERT** or **GIFIN** commands in that you are asked for an insertion point and a scale factor. If you use the **IMPORT** command, you must specify .EPS in the file type list of the **Import File** dialog box. If you use the **PSIN** command, .EPS is automatically selected in the **Select PostScript File** dialog box. Select the file and pick the **OK** button. It may take a few minutes to load the file, depending on its size. Then, the following prompts appear:

```
Insertion point⟨0,0,0⟩: ↵
Scale factor: (drag the image to fit and pick)
```

If **PSDRAG** is set to 0, only the outline of the box that represents the image is displayed until you set the scale factor. If you wish to see the image as you drag it, set **PSDRAG** to 1.

Now you can place additional entities or text on the drawing. You can then save it again as a PostScript file with the **PSOUT** command or save it as a .DWG drawing file.

PostScript file quality

The **PSIN** command renders an image according to the value of the **PSQUALITY** system variable. If **PSQUALITY** is set to 0, only a box representing the image is displayed with the filename inside. The default value is 75. This displays the image with 75 pixels per AutoCAD drawing unit. Higher quality values mean longer rendering time. A negative value, such as –75, renders at the same resolution but does not fill PostScript outlines.

PROFESSIONAL TIP

When you use **PSIN** to import an image into AutoCAD, a file named ACADPS.EXE is used to interpret the PostScript file into a *Ghostscript* format so the entities are compatible with AutoCAD. You can then save the drawing, edit it later, or give the drawing to someone else to work with. The ACADPS.EXE file is no longer needed.

NOTE

PostScript fonts are a copyrighted product and must be purchased from authorized dealers. Like any other software, they may be used only on the machine they were purchased for.

Using PostScript fonts

A variety of PostScript fonts are included with AutoCAD for Windows. A list is shown in Figure 13-15. These fonts are by default located in the \R13\COM\FONTS subdirectory. PostScript fonts can only be used after shape files are compiled. A *PostScript shape file* is a description of the font. Shape files have a .PFB file extension, such as SASO__.PFB. To compile a shape file, pick **Compile...** from the **Tools** pull-down menu, Figure 13-16. The **Select Shape or Font File** dialog box is displayed, Figure 13-17. Pick the shape file you want to compile from the file list and pick the **OK** button. It is immediately compiled and the compiled version is given an .SHX extension.

You can use PostScript fonts just like any other AutoCAD font. Use the **STYLE** command, enter a style name, then pick the appropriate .SHX file from the dialog box listing. Provide any additional style values you wish. Then, use the new style with the **TEXT**, **DTEXT**, or **MTEXT** commands.

Fonts that are normally filled when printed as a PostScript file appear only as an outline in AutoCAD and when the drawing is printed with the **PLOT** command. See Figure 13-18. If you use **PSOUT** and print the .EPS file, the fonts are filled.

NOTE

PostScript fonts are only printed filled if the printer you are using has the font loaded.

Figure 13-15.
Some of the PostScript fonts available with Release 13.

CIBT	The quick brown fox jumped over the lazy dog.	ABC12
COBT	*The quick brown fox jumped over the lazy dog.*	*ABC12*
ROM	**The quick brown fox jumped over the lazy dog.**	**ABC12**
ROMB	**The quick brown fox jumped over the lazy dog.**	**ABC12**
SAS	**The quick brown fox jumped over the lazy dog.**	**ABC12**
SASB	The quick brown fox jumped over the lazy dog.	ABC12
SASO	*The quick brown fox jumped over the lazy dog.*	*ABC12*
SASBO	*The quick brown fox jumped over the lazy dog.*	*ABC12*
TE	THE QUICK BROWN FOX JUMPED OVER THE LAZY DOG.	ABC12
TEL	THE QUICK BROWN FOX JUMPED OVER THE LAZY DOG.	ABC12
TEB	THE QUICK BROWN FOX JUMPED OVER THE LAZY DOG.	ABC12

Figure 13-16.
To compile a shape file, select **Compile...** from the **Tools** pull-down menu.

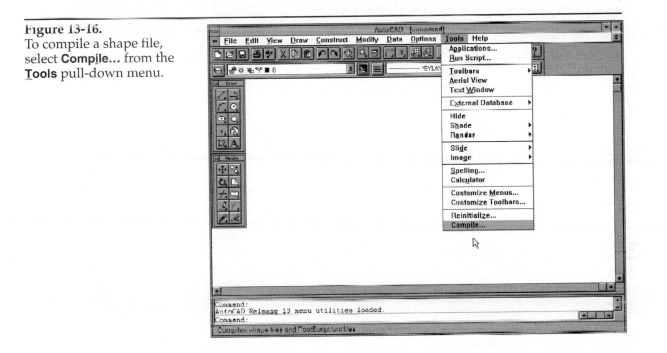

Figure 13-17.
The **Select Shape or Font File** dialog box.

Select a shape file

Select the file type

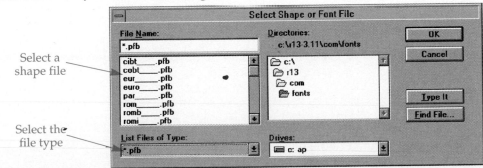

Figure 13-18.
Filled PostScript fonts
appear as an outline when
the drawing is output with
the **PLOT** command.

EXERCISE 13-3

❏ Begin a new drawing and name it EX13-3.
❏ Compile the following PostScript fonts.
    TEL__.PFB
    SAS__.PFB
    ROMB__.PFB
❏ Create a style of each of the compiled fonts. The style name should be the same as the font.
❏ Write a single line of text using **DTEXT** with each of the styles.
❏ Plot or print the drawing.
❏ Use the **PSOUT** command to create a PostScript file.
❏ Print the .EPS file if you have a PostScript printer.
❏ Save the drawing as A:EX13-3.

CHAPTER TEST

Write your answers in the spaces provided.

1. What four common formats of raster images can be imported into AutoCAD? _____
   _____

2. What command is used to insert a file that is in the CompuServe image format? _____
   _____

3. Which system variable controls the width and height of an imported raster image? ____
   _____

4. What does the **RITHRESH** variable control? _____
   _____

5. After a raster image is inserted into an AutoCAD drawing, it is composed of what type
   of AutoCAD entity? _____

6. Name two commands that allow you to export bitmap files. _____

7. Give the name and file type of the vector file that can be used to exchange files between
   object-based programs._____

8. Name the two commands that allow you to import and export the file type in Question 7.
   _____

9. Name the two commands that enable you to import and export PostScript files in
   AutoCAD._____

10. When using the **PSFILL** command, what is the numerical value range of grays that are available? _____

11. What is the three-letter extension given to PostScript files when they are exported using the proper command?_____
_____

12. What must you do to a PostScript font shape (.PFB) file so it can be used as an AutoCAD font?_____
_____

DRAWING PROBLEMS

1. Locate some sample raster files with the .GIF, .PCX, or .TIF. These files are often included as samples with software. Several can be copied from the AutoCAD Release 12 Bonus CD. They can also be downloaded from computer on-line services such as CompuServe and America Online. With the permission of your instructor or supervisor, create a subdirectory on your hard disk drive and copy the raster files there.

   Graphic Design

2. Choose one of your smaller raster files and import it into AutoCAD using the **IMPORT**, **GIFIN**, **PCXIN**, or **TIFFIN** command.

   Graphic Design

   A. Insert the image so that it fills the entire screen.

   B. Undo and insert the image again using a scale factor that fills half of the screen with the image.

   C. Experiment with different **RIASPECT** values.

   D. Create a layer named RASTER. Create a second layer named OBJECT. Give each layer the color of your choice. Set the current layer to RASTER.

   E. Import the same image next to the previous one at the same scale factor.

   F. Set the current layer to OBJECT and use any AutoCAD drawing commands to trace the outline of the second raster image.

   G. Turn off the OBJECT layer and erase all of the raster image. Turn the OBJECT layer on.

   H. Save the drawing as P13-2.

3. For this problem, you will import several raster files into AutoCAD. Then, you will trace the object in each file and save it as a block or wblock to be used on other drawings.

   Graphic Design

   A. Find as many raster files as you can that contain simple objects, shapes, or figures that you might use in other drawings. Save these to diskettes or a hard drive directory.

   B. Create a prototype drawing containing layers such as those in Problem 2.

   C. Import each raster file into AutoCAD using the appropriate command. Set a new layer and trace the shape or objects in the files using AutoCAD drawing commands.

   D. Delete the raster information, keeping only the traced lines of the object.

   E. Save the object as a block or wblock using an appropriate file-naming system.

   F. After all blocks have been created, insert each one into a single drawing and label each with its name. Include a path if necessary.

G. Save the drawing as P13-3.

F. Print or plot the final drawing.

Graphic Design

4. In this problem, you will create either a style sheet to be used for drawing standards or a presentation sheet for a detail, assembly, or pictorial drawing.

A. Begin a new drawing and name it P13-4. The drawing should be set up to A-size dimensions and the orientation should be portrait. A portrait orientation has the long side orientated vertically.

B. Create at least two new text styles using PostScript fonts.

C. Draw one or more closed shapes, such as rectangles. Use the **PSFILL** command to place a pattern of your choice inside the shapes.

D. Use the PostScript text styles to place title and related text on your drawing. See the example below. Add other graphics or text as desired.

E. Save the drawing as P13-4. Then, use the **PSOUT** command to save the file as P13-4.EPS.

F. Plot the drawing on a plotter or laser printer. If you have a PostScript printer, generate a printed copy of the .EPS file.

Graphic Design

5. Begin a new drawing named P13-5 using P13-4 as the prototype.

A. Insert the blocks you created in Problem 3 into your style sheet. Arrange them in any order you wish.

B. Add any notes you need to identify this drawing as a sheet of library shapes. Be sure each shape is identified with its filename and location (path).

C. Save the drawing with the current name (P13-5). Then, create a **PSOUT** file using the same name.

D. Print or plot the drawing.

E. If you have a PostScript printer, create a PostScript print of the file.

AutoCAD R13

Chapter 14

Rendering with AutoCAD

Learning objectives

After completing this chapter, you will be able to:
- ○ Create shaded and rendered drawings.
- ○ Place light sources.
- ○ Apply surface textures to models.
- ○ Save views and scenes.
- ○ Render and save bitmaps using Windows Clipboard.

Three-dimensional computer models can provide more information than a set of two-dimensional blueprints. The computer allows you to visualize the model from all sides, and from inside. Surface textures can be added to the model. Rendering then "colors" the model with the assigned surface. The model can also be placed in a scene with lights and shading. Views and scenes can then be saved, rendered, and placed in documents.

There are two different commands that can be used to render a model in AutoCAD. The basic command is **SHADE** and is covered in detail in Chapter 9. The **SHADE** command allows you some control over the type of display and lighting. However, the **RENDER** command gives you complete control over the lighting and surfaces of your model.

The layout in Exercise 14-1 is used throughout this chapter to illustrate aspects of rendering. This exercise can be completed in approximately 30 minutes. It combines the use of 3D shapes, user coordinate systems, and viewports.

UNDERSTANDING LIGHTS

AutoCAD uses four types of lighting. These are ambient, distant, point, and spot. See Figure 14-1. It is important to understand how each type applies light to a model.

Ambient light is like natural light. It is the same intensity everywhere. All faces of the object receive the same amount of light. Ambient light cannot create highlights. You can change the intensity of ambient light, or even turn it off, but ambient light cannot be concentrated in one area.

Figure 14-1.
AutoCAD uses ambient, spot, point, and distant light. Ambient light is an overall light and does not have an icon representation. You can see here how the other three lights strike objects.

A *distant light* is a directed light source with parallel light rays. This acts much like the sun. The intensity of distant light is the same on all objects. However, the direction that the light shines in can be changed. The intensity of a distant light can be changed. Distant light strikes all objects in your model on the same side.

A *point light* is like a lightbulb. It shines out in all directions. A point light does not cast shadows, but can create highlights. The intensity of a point light "falls off," or weakens, over distance. Other programs, such as 3D Studio, call these lights *omni lights*.

A *spotlight* is like a distant light, but projects in a cone shape. A spotlight is closer to the object than a distant light.

Properties of lights

There are different properties that affect how a light illuminates an object. These include the angle of incidence, reflectivity of the object's surface, and the distance that the light is from the object.

Angle of incidence. AutoCAD renders the faces of a model based on the angle that light rays strike the faces. This angle is called the *angle of incidence.* See Figure 14-2. A face that is perpendicular to light rays receives the most light. As the angle between the light rays and the face increases, the amount of light striking the face decreases.

Reflectivity. The "brightness" of light reflected from an object is actually the number of light rays that reach your eyes. A surface that reflects a bright light, such as a mirror, is reflecting most of the light rays that strike it. The angle at which light rays are reflected off a surface is called the *angle of reflection.* The angle of reflection is always equal to the angle of incidence.

The amount of reflection you see is called the *highlight.* The highlight is determined by the angle that you view an object in relation to the angle of incidence. Refer to Figure 14-2.

Figure 14-2.
The amount of reflection, or highlight, you see depends on the angle that you view the object from.

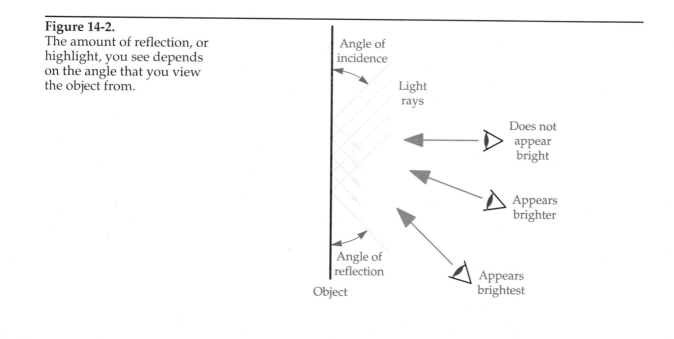

Figure 14-3.
Matte surfaces produce diffuse light. This is also referred to as a low specular factor. Shiny surfaces reflect light evenly, or have a high specular factor.

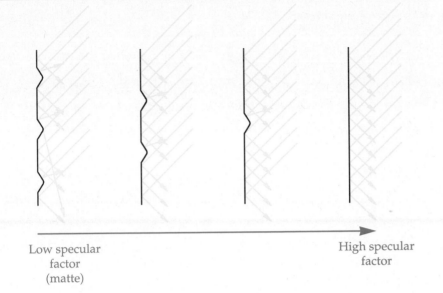

Low specular factor (matte)

High specular factor

The surface of the object affects how light is reflected. A smooth surface has a high *specular factor.* The specular factor indicates the number of light rays that have the same angle of reflection. Surfaces that are not smooth have a low specular factor. These surfaces are called *matte.* Matte surfaces *diffuse,* or "spread out," the light as it strikes the surface. This means that few of the light rays have the same angle of reflection. Figure 14-3 illustrates the difference between matte and high specular finishes. Surfaces can also vary in *roughness.* Roughness is a measure of the polish on a surface. This also affects how diffused the reflected light is.

Distance. The farther an object is from a point light or spotlight, the less light that reaches it. The intensity of light decreases over distance. This decrease is called *falloff* or *attenuation.* Attenuation only applies to point lights and spotlights. There are three different settings for attenuation. These are explained below.

- **None.** Applies the same light intensity regardless of distance. In other words, no falloff is calculated.
- **Inverse Linear.** The illumination of an object decreases in inverse proportion to the distance. For example, if an object is 2 units from the light, it receives 1/2 of the full light. If the object is 4 units away, it receives 1/4 of the full light.
- **Inverse Square.** The illumination of an object decreases in inverse proportion to the square of the distance. For example, if an object is 2 units from the light, it receives $(1/2)^2$, or 1/4, of the full light. If the object is 4 units away, it receives $(1/4)^2$, or 1/16, of the full light. As you can see, falloff is greater for each unit of distance with the **Inverse Square** option than with the **Inverse Linear** option.

EXERCISE 14-1

❏ The models created in this exercise are used throughout the rest of this chapter.

❏ Begin a new drawing named 3DSHAPES using the prototype drawing method.

❏ Set units to architectural.

❏ Set limits to 24',18'. Set the grid to 6" and snap to 2". Zoom all.

❏ Create the following layers and assign the colors indicated:

Layer	Color
FLOOR-WALL	Cyan
TABLE	Red
PYRAMID	Yellow
CONE	Green
TORUS	Blue

❏ Make the FLOOR-WALL layer current.

❏ Using the **3DFACE** command, draw the floor 8' square. Draw the wall 8' long and 6' high. You may have to change your viewpoint or UCS to draw the wall. This forms the background.

❏ Set a viewpoint of –2.5,–3,1.5.

❏ Create a UCS at the lower-front corner of the floor. Save this UCS orientation as FLOOR. Note: Depending on how you drew the floor and wall, this UCS may coincide with the WCS. If it does, you will not have to save the UCS.

❏ Create a 1" cube on layer 0 with **3DBOX**. Save the cube as a wblock named CUBE.

❏ Set the TABLE layer as current. Use the CUBE wblock to construct the table. Insert one cube for the first leg and enter the following values:

Insertion point: X = 2'10", Y = 2'

Scale factors: X = 4, Y = 4, Z = 16

Rotation angle = 0°

❏ Array the first leg using a unit cell distance of 24" for 2 rows and 2 columns.

❏ Use the CUBE wblock again for the table top as follows:

Insertion point: X = 2'10", Y = 2', Z = 16"

Scale factors: X = 28, Y = 28, Z = 2

Rotation angle = 0°

❑ Establish a new UCS at the top-front of the tabletop.
❑ Change the current layer to PYRAMID. Select **Pyramid** from the **3D Objects** dialog box. Locate the first base point of the pyramid at X = 12, Y = 10. Locate the second base point as @0,–8. Locate the third point as @8,0. Locate the fourth point as @0,8. Locate the apex point at 16,6,12. Use the **ROTATE** command or grips to rotate the pyramid 45°. Use the second point of the pyramid (closest to the UCS origin) as the rotation base point.
❑ Set the CONE layer as current and draw a cone at X = 8, Y = 20 with an 8" diameter base, 0" diameter top, and a 12" height. Leave the number of segments at 16.
❑ Set the current layer to TORUS. Set **ISOLINES** = 12. Draw a solid torus located at X = 14, Y = 14, Z = 22. The torus diameter is 18" and the tube diameter is 5".
❑ The drawing should look like the one shown below.
❑ Restore the UCS orientation named FLOOR.
❑ Save the drawing as 3DSHAPES and remain in the drawing editor. These objects are used throughout this chapter.

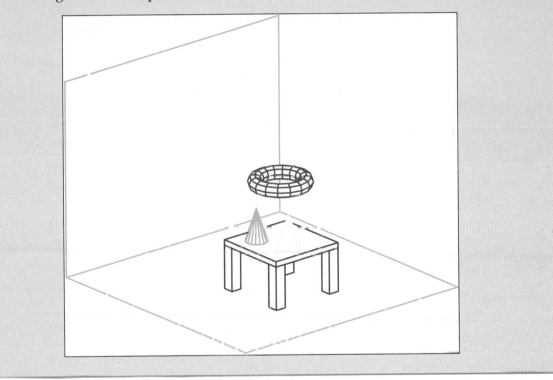

PREPARING A DRAWING FOR RENDERING

If you are creating a drawing or model that will be rendered, part of your planning should be to provide enough space around the model to place lights. Creating three viewports using the **VPORTS** command can help. The large view can be used to see a 3D view of the model. The two small viewports can be used for a plan view and a different 3D view. The lights can be placed in the plan view.

An example of this type of layout is shown in Figure 14-4. To create this layout, first use the default settings of the **VPORTS** command to create three viewports. Then, divide the two left viewports using the **2** option of the **VPORTS** command. This creates four small viewports. Now, use the **Join** option of **VPORTS** to join the two small viewports oriented vertically in the middle of the screen. Next, join the large viewport with the tall thin one in the middle. The final step is to display a plan view in the upper-left viewport and a Southeast isometric in the lower-left viewport. This gives you the arrangement shown in Figure 14-4.

Figure 14-4.
The final arrangement
of viewports for the
tutorial in the text.

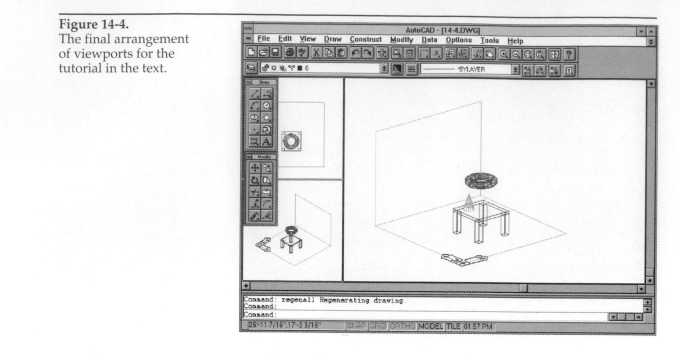

Using the **Lights** dialog box

After the objects in your model are constructed, placing lights is the first step in creating a scene for rendering. This is done with the **Lights** dialog box, Figure 14-5. Consider the properties for each type of light when choosing the lights for the model. Place as many lights as you want. When you create a scene, pick only the lights needed for that scene. You can select a different combination of lights for each scene. A *scene* is like a photograph of your model.

Figure 14-5.
The **Lights** dialog box.

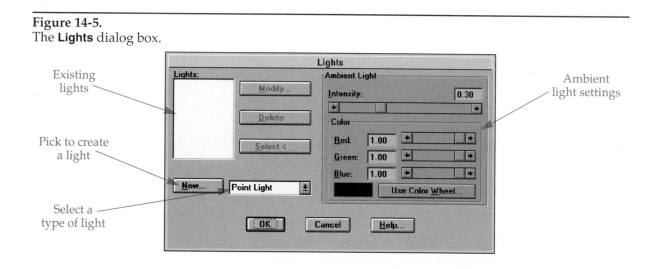

The **LIGHT** command can be accessed by picking **Lights...** and then **Render** in the **Tools** pull-down menu, picking the **Lights** button in the **Render** toolbar, or by typing LIGHT at the **Command:** prompt. The **Lights** dialog box is then displayed. Each light, other than ambient, must have a name of up to eight characters. Uppercase and lowercase letters can be used. However, light names must be different. When placing lights in a drawing, use XYZ coordinates or filters to specify a 3D location. Once a light is placed, an icon representing the light appears in the drawing editor. The icons representing point, distant, and spot lights are shown in Figure 14-6.

Ambient light is also set in the **Lights** dialog box. Use the slider bar or type a value in the text box in the **Ambient Light** section to adjust the intensity. You can also change the ambient light color adjusting the appropriate slider bar. If you pick the **Use Color Wheel...** button, you can graphically set the color. See Figure 14-7.

After lights are created, you can fine-tune them by changing their intensity, location, or color. Lights can also be turned off or deleted if needed. Once a light is selected from the list in the **Lights** dialog box, pick the **Modify...** button to adjust intensity, position, color, and falloff of the light.

Figure 14-6.
Point, spot, and distant lights appear as icons on-screen

Figure 14-7.
The color wheel lets you graphically set a color.

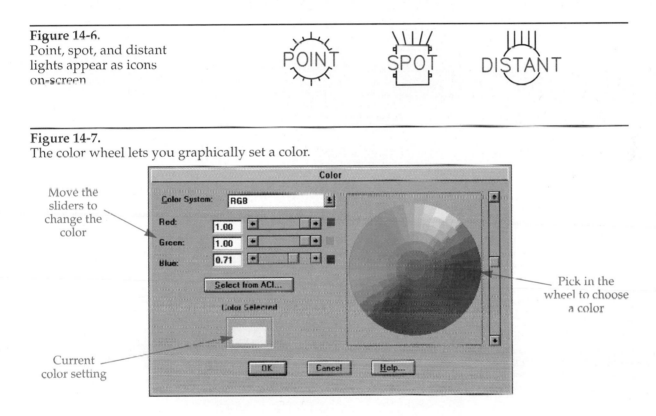

Move the sliders to change the color

Current color setting

Pick in the wheel to choose a color

Placing point lights in the model

A point light radiates light rays outward from a central point, much like a lightbulb. Other programs, such as 3D Studio, call point lights omni lights. A point light requires a location and a name. Remember, a name can have up to eight characters.

To place a point light in the 3DSHAPES drawing created in Exercise 14-1, first select **Point Light** in the pop-up list at the left of the **Lights** dialog box. Then, pick the **New...** button. This displays the **New Point Light** subdialog box shown in Figure 14-8A. Enter the name, such as P-1, in the **Light Name:** text box and pick **OK**. The **Lights** dialog box returns and P-1 is displayed and highlighted in the **Lights:** list box.

Now, pick **Modify...** and the **Modify Point Light** subdialog box shown in Figure 14-8B is displayed. Pick the **Modify** ⟨ button in the **Position** area and you are returned to the graphics window. The prompt on the command line requests a light location. You can pick the location, use filters, or enter coordinates at the keyboard as follows:

Enter light location ⟨*current*⟩: **4′,3′2″,8′**↵

The dialog box then reappears. Pick **OK** in the **Modify Point Light** and **Lights** dialog boxes to complete the command and return to the graphics window. Now, zoom all in the right viewport.

Figure 14-8.
A—The **New Point Light** dialog box. B—The **Modify Point Light** dialog box.

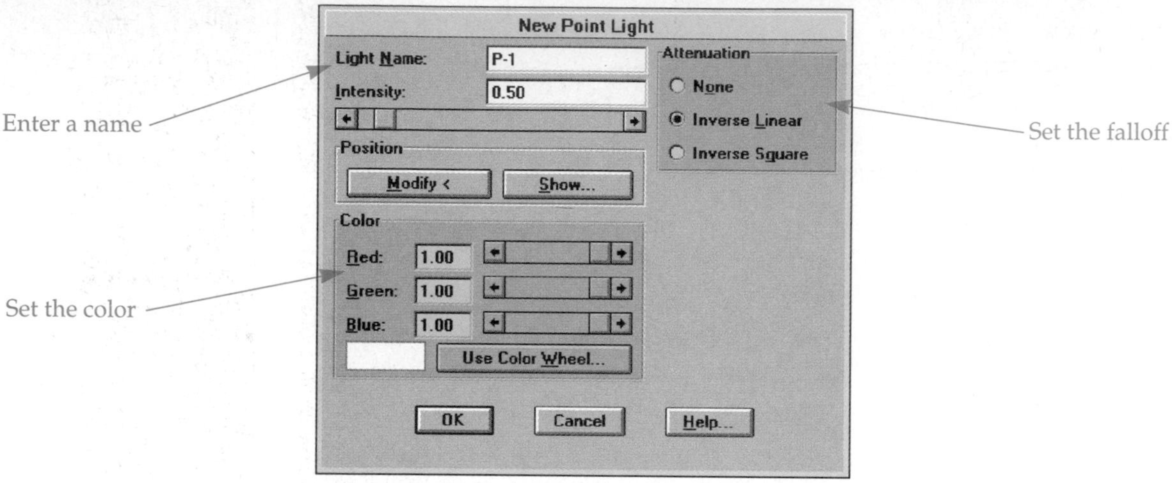

A

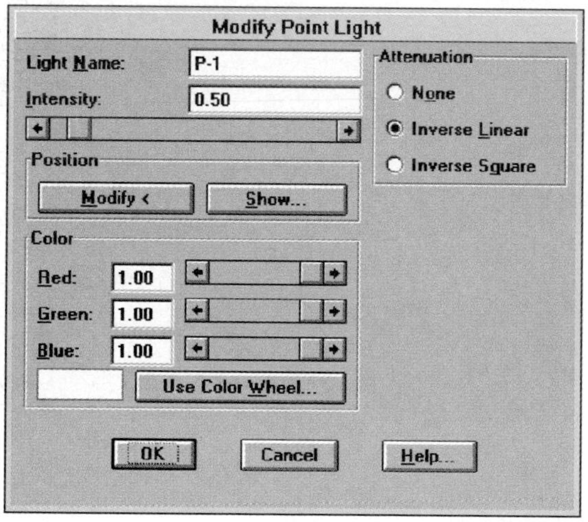

B

Setting the icon scale

After you place the point light, you should see the light icon directly above the torus. However, it is too small to see clearly. You can change the scale of icons by picking the **Preferences** button in the **Render** toolbar. You can also pick **Render** then **Preferences...** from the **Tools** pull-down menu or type RPREF at the **Command:** prompt. This displays the **Rendering Preferences** dialog box, Figure 14-9. Pick the **Icon Scale:** text box and enter 24. Pick **OK** to return to your model, Figure 14-10. The icon is now large enough to see clearly. The light name P-1 appears in the icon.

Figure 14-9.
The icon scale is set in the **Rendering Preferences** dialog box.

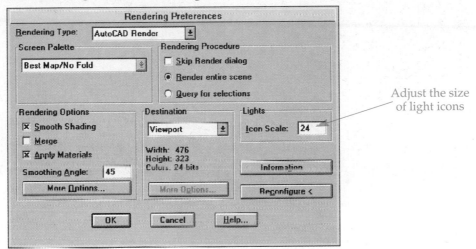

Figure 14-10.
After increasing the icon scale, the light icons are larger and can now be seen on-screen.

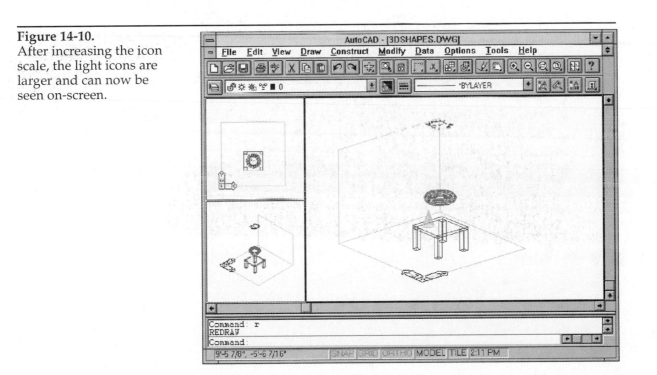

Placing distant lights in the model

Distant lights are placed in the same way as point lights. However, a target location is needed as well as a location. To place a distant light, first open the **Lights** dialog box. Then, pick **Distant Light** from the lights pop-up list. Pick the **New...** button to display the **New Distant Light** subdialog box, Figure 14-11. Notice that this dialog box is different than the **New Point Light** dialog.

Figure 14-11.
The **New Distant Light** subdialog box.

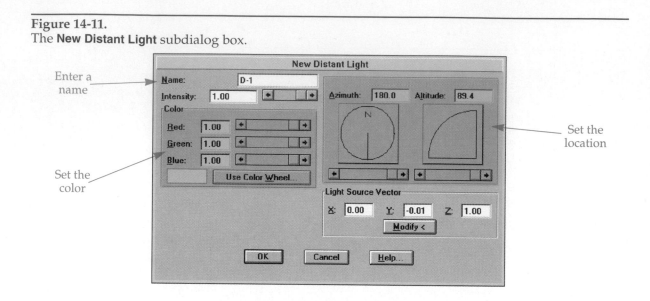

Enter a name

Set the color

Set the location

Enter a name, such as D-1, in the **Light Name:** text box. The location of the distant light can be entered as XYZ values in the **Light Source Vector** text boxes. Remember, these coordinates are relative to the origin of the current UCS. In addition, you can graphically select the location of the light using the **Azimuth:** and **Altitude:** image tiles. The *azimuth* is the angle *in* the XY plane. The *altitude* is the angle *from* the XY plane. The location can also be set by picking the **Modify ⟨** button and entering coordinates at the **Command:** prompt as follows:

> Enter light direction TO ⟨*current*⟩: **END.**↵
> of (*pick P-1 in Figure 14-12*)
> Enter light direction FROM ⟨*current*⟩: **6′,–4′,30.**↵

Figure 14-12.
The pick points for setting a distant light in the tutorial.

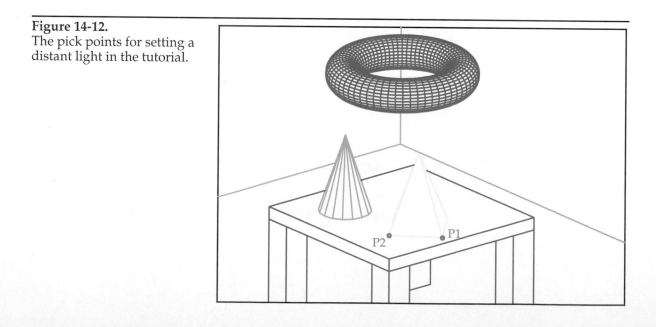

Pick **OK** to return to the **Lights** dialog box. Pick **OK** in that dialog box to return to the graphics window. The distant light is placed in the drawing.

You may not see the light in the 3D view. However, it will show in the plan view and possibly in your other view. Place one more distant light in your model using the following information:

Name:	Light direction to:	Light direction from:
D-2	Point P2 in Figure 14-12	–2',0,30

Your model should look like Figure 14-13 when you place the second distant light.

Figure 14-13.
The tutorial model with distant lights placed.

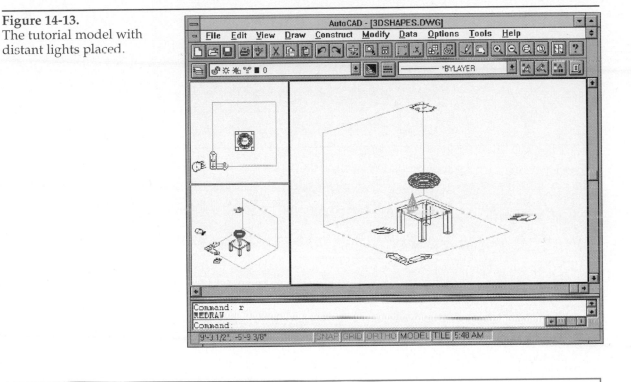

> **NOTE**
>
> When setting the location of the distant light by picking the **Azimuth:** and **Altitude:** image tiles, you may experience problems with the images on the tiles disappearing. This is a bug with the R13c4 maintenance release. The problem occurs more frequently in Windows 95, but occurs in Windows 3.1 as well. If this happens, either enter values in the text boxes or pick the **Cancel** button and start the process over.

Placing spotlights in the model

A spotlight produces a cone of light. The *hotspot* is the central portion of the cone where the light is brightest. The *falloff* is the outer portion of the cone where the light begins to blend to shadow.

Spotlights are located in the same way as distant lights. First, pick **Spotlight** in the **Lights** pop-up list of the **Lights** dialog box. This displays the **New Spotlight** dialog box. See Figure 14-14. Notice that this dialog box looks more like the **New Point Light** dialog box than the **New Distant Light** dialog box.

Notice the **Hotspot:** and **Falloff:** areas at the upper right of the dialog box. If you want the hotspot to illuminate a cone of 30° and the falloff angle to be 45°, enter 30 and 45 in the appropriate text boxes. Figure 14-15 illustrates the two cones of light and the values entered in the **New Spotlight** dialog box.

Figure 14-14.
The **New Spotlight** subdialog box.

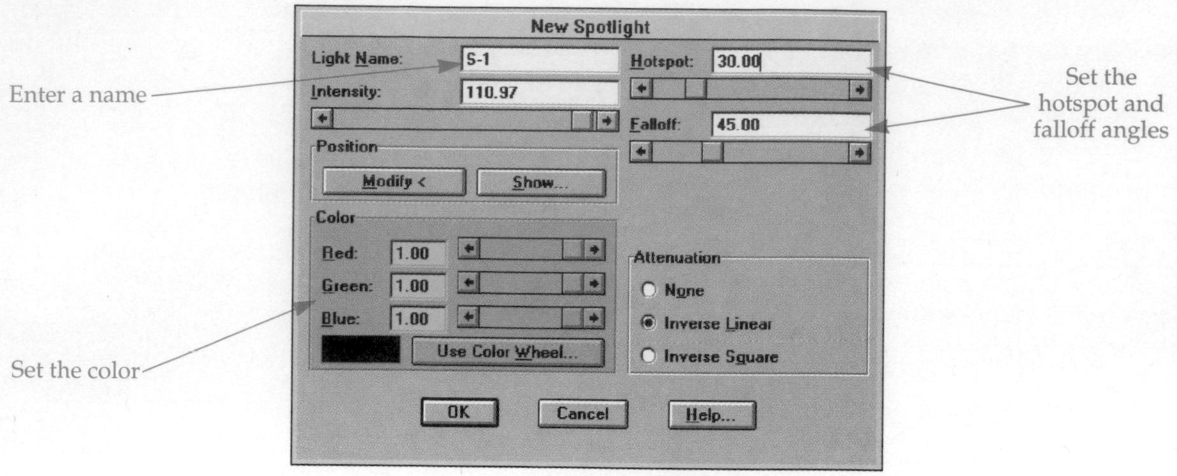

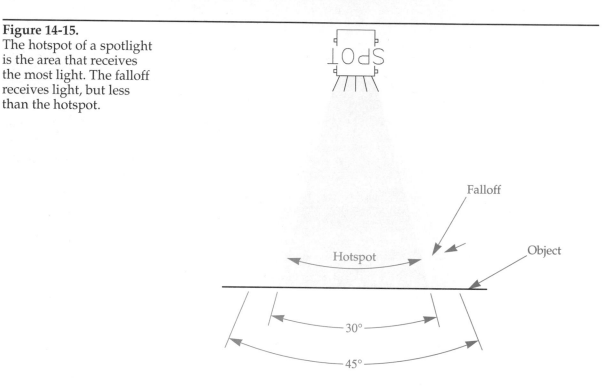

Enter a name

Set the
hotspot and
falloff angles

Set the color

Figure 14-15.
The hotspot of a spotlight
is the area that receives
the most light. The falloff
receives light, but less
than the hotspot.

Give the spotlight a name, such as S-1. Then, pick the **Modify ⟨** button to locate the light
on the graphics screen.

> Enter light target ⟨*current*⟩: **CEN**↵
> of (*pick the center of the torus*)
> Enter light location ⟨*current*⟩: **@12,12,4'**↵

The dialog box returns. Pick **OK** in both dialog boxes to complete the command and return to
the graphics window. Your drawing should look like Figure 14-16.

Figure 14-16.
The tutorial model after
the spotlight is placed.

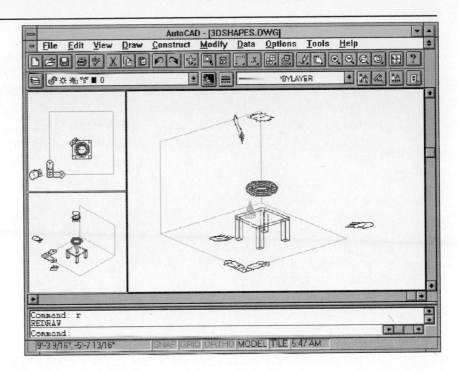

RENDERING THE MODEL

You can render your model at any time. If there are no lights in your model, AutoCAD places one behind your viewpoint. If you have placed lights in your model but have not yet constructed a "scene," AutoCAD uses all of the lights and renders the current view in the active viewport.

To render your model, type RENDER at the **Command:** prompt or pick the **Render** button from the **Render** toolbar. You can also pick **Render** and then **Render** from the **Tools** pull-down menu. All three methods open the **Render** dialog box. Pick the **Render Scene** button in this dialog box. AutoCAD then displays the rendering of your model in the current active viewport. See Figure 14-17.

Figure 14-17.
The tutorial model rendered
after the lights are placed.

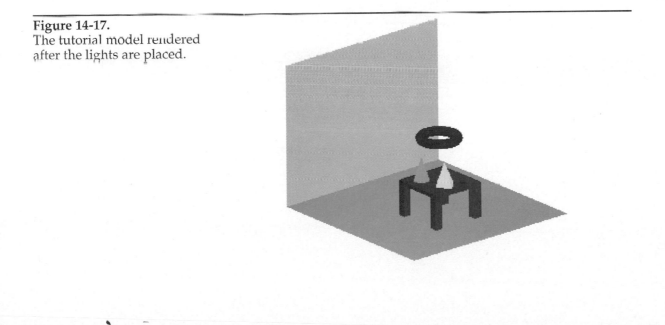

CREATING VIEWS AND SCENES

A *scene* is like a photograph. It is made up of a view and one or more lights. You can have as many scenes in a model as you want. The current view in the active viewport is used as the "camera" for the scene. You can use the **VIEW**, **VPOINT**, or **DVIEW** commands to set the viewpoints you want, then use the **VIEW** command to create named views. For the tutorial model, create the following views using the **DVIEW** command. Be sure the large viewport is active and the current UCS is FLOOR (or the WCS, depending on how you constructed the floor and walls).

```
Command: DVIEW↵
Select objects: (window the entire model)
Select objects: ↵
*** Switching to the WCS ***
CAmera/TArget/Distance/POints/PAn/Zoom/TWist/CLip/Hide/Off/Undo/⟨eXit⟩: POINTS↵
Enter target point ⟨current⟩: END↵
of (pick P2 in Figure 14-12)
Enter camera point ⟨current⟩: @–8'6",–6',4'↵
CAmera/TArget/Distance/POints/PAn/Zoom/TWist/CLip/Hide/Off/Undo/⟨eXit⟩: PAN↵
Displacement base point: (pick a point)
Second point: (pick a second point to center the drawing)
CAmera/TArget/Distance/POints/PAn/Zoom/TWist/CLip/Hide/Off/Undo/⟨eXit⟩: ↵
```

The view should look like the one shown in Figure 14-18.

Figure 14-18.
The view created and saved as VIEW1.

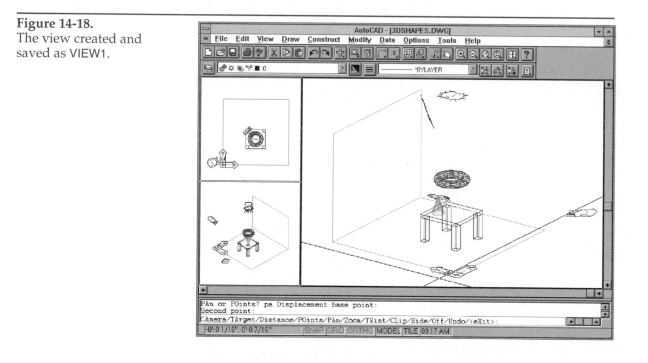

Now you can use the **VIEW** or **DDVIEW** commands and save the current display as a new view named VIEW1. Next, set up a second viewpoint with the **DVIEW** command as follows:

> Command: **DVIEW**↵
> Select objects: **P**↵
> Select objects: ↵
> *** Switching to the WCS ***
> CAmera/TArget/Distance/POints/PAn/Zoom/TWist/CLip/Hide/Off/Undo/⟨eXit⟩: **POINTS**↵
> Enter target point ⟨*current*⟩: **END**↵
> of *(pick top of cone)*
> Enter camera point ⟨*current*⟩: **@–2′,–8′6″,5′**↵

Now, turn perspective on by setting a distance.

> CAmera/TArget/Distance/POints/PAn/Zoom/TWist/CLip/Hide/Off/Undo/⟨eXit⟩: **D**↵
> New camera/target distance ⟨*current*⟩: **14′**↵
> CAmera/TArget/Distance/POints/PAn/Zoom/TWist/CLip/Hide/Off/Undo/⟨eXit⟩: ↵

Your display should look like Figure 14-19. Create another view of the current display and name it VIEW2.

Now that you have two views, make a couple of scenes by picking the **Scenes** button from the **Render** toolbar, or pick **Render** then **Scenes...** from the **Tools** pull-down menu . This displays the **Scenes** dialog box. See Figure 14-20. Pick **New...** to display the **New Scene** sub-dialog box, Figure 14-21. This dialog box lists all views and lights in the drawing.

Enter FRONT in the Scene Name: text box at the upper right. Now you need to assign a view and lights to the new scene. Pick VIEW1, then pick lights D-1 and P-1. Then, pick the **OK** button to save the scene. Pick **New...** again and make another scene named SIDE. Use VIEW2 and lights D-2 and S-1. The **Scenes** dialog box now lists the two scenes, as shown in Figure 14-20. Pick **OK**.

Figure 14-19.
The view created and saved as VIEW2.

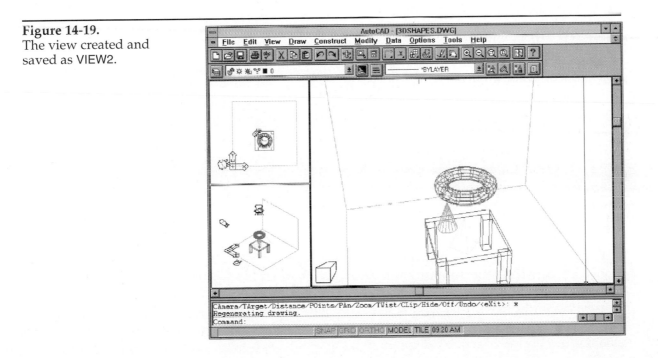

Figure 14-20.
The **Scenes** dialog box.

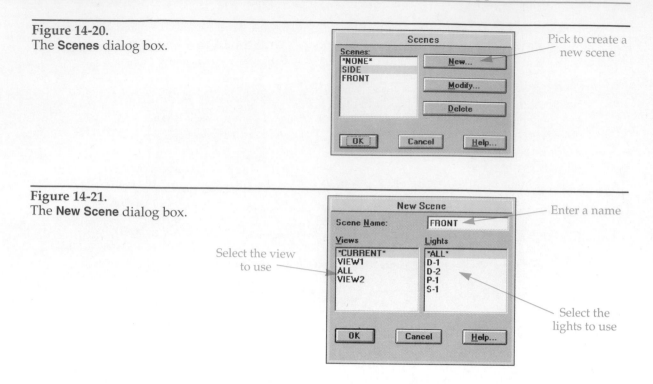

Figure 14-21.
The **New Scene** dialog box.

Render the scene with the **RENDER** command. In the **Render** dialog box, pick a scene from the list at the left and the **Render Scene** button. The **RENDER** command then renders the view used to define that scene. Therefore, the rendering may not be the same view displayed in the active viewport.

Create a third scene named SIDE2. Use the **DVIEW** command to establish a new view named VIEW3 using the same target as in VIEW1. Make the camera location X = –5′, Y = –8′6″, and Z = 12′. Set the distance in **DVIEW** to 11′6″. Use lights S-1, P-1, and D-1 for scene SIDE2.

Changing light intensities

The full intensity of point lights and spotlights should strike the first object in the model. Full intensity of any light is a value of one. Remember that spotlight falloff (attenuation) is calculated using either the **Inverse Linear** setting or **Inverse Square** setting.

In the 3DOBJECTS.DWG model you have been working with, the top of the torus is 51″ from the point light. The spotlight is approximately 40″ from the torus. Use the following calculations for each spotlight setting:

- **Inverse Linear.** If the point light is 51 units above the highest object (torus), that object receives 1/51 of the light. Set intensity to 51 so the light intensity striking the torus has a value of 1. Since the spotlight is 40″ from the nearest object, set its light intensity to 40.
- **Inverse Square.** Set light intensity to $1/51^2$, or 2601, for the point light. Set the intensity to $1/40^2$, or 1600, for the spotlight.

To change the light intensity for your model, open the **Lights** dialog box. First, set the **Ambient Light Intensity:** to 0. With ambient light at 0, you can see the effects of changing other lights. Highlight P-1 in the **Lights:** list box, then pick the **Modify...** button. Enter 51 in the **Intensity:** text box and pick **OK**. Modify S-1 and set the intensity to 40. Be sure the **Inverse Linear** radio button is active for the point light and the spotlight. Set the intensity of lights D-1 and D-2 to 1. Open the **Render** dialog box. Highlight the SIDE2 scene. Pick the **Render Scene** button to see the changes, as shown in Figure 14-22.

Figure 14-22.
The SIDE2 scene rendered.

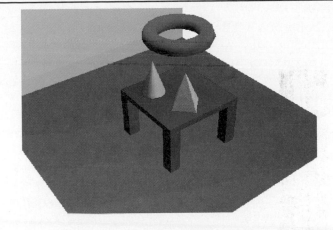

You can quickly see the effects of different light combinations. Open the **Lights** dialog box and set each distant light to an intensity of 0. The point light and spotlight are now the only ones that are on. Render the model. The top of the table is bright and the legs have no highlight. See Figure 14-23A. Now, set the ambient light to 1. Render the scene again. Notice the additional even light in the rendered scene. See Figure 14-23B.

Try turning the point light off, and turn on only one of the distant lights at a time. First, set the intensity of light D-2 to .8, then render the model. The left sides of the objects are illuminated. Now turn off D-2, give light D-1 an intensity of 1. Render the model. The front of the objects and the back wall are illuminated. The floor is dark because it is parallel to the light rays. Try additional combinations on your own.

Figure 14-23.
A—The SIDE2 scene rendered with just the point light and spotlight on. B—The SIDE2 scene rendered with the point, ambient, and spotlight on.

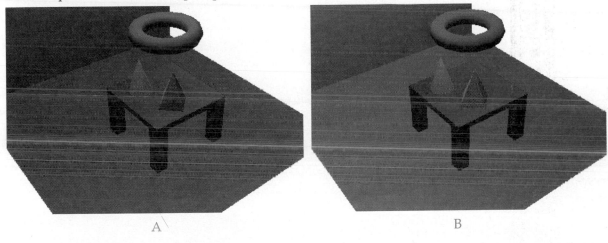

A

B

Changing light color

The color of a light can be adjusted if you want the objects in the model to appear tinted differently than they appear in white light. The amount of red, green, or blue (RGB) can be adjusted to produce any color from white to black. White is the presence of all colors. This is a setting of 1.0 for red, green, and blue. Black is the absence of all colors. This is a setting of 0.0 for red, green, and blue.

To set a color for a light, open the **Lights** dialog box. Then, highlight the light you want to adjust and pick the **Modify...** button. In the **Modify Light** dialog box pick the **Use Color Wheel...** button. This displays the **Color** dialog box, Figure 14-24. The default RGB slider bars are displayed. Notice the **Color System:** pop-up list. A selection called HLS appears in this list. HLS stands for hue, lightness, and saturation. Picking this selection displays the **Hue:**, **Lightness:**, and **Saturation:** slider bars in place of the **Red:**, **Green:**, and **Blue:** slider bars. See Figure 14-24.

- **Hue.** A single color in a range of colors.
- **Lightness**. The brightness of the color is changed by adding or removing white.
- **Saturation**. The content of black in the hue. Changes the purity of the hue by increasing or decreasing the gray.

Once you pick **OK** in the **Color** dialog box, the modified color is displayed in a color swatch to the left of the **Use Color Wheel...** button.

If you want to select a predefined color, pick the **Select from ACI...** button in the **Color** dialog box. This displays the **Select Color** dialog box shown in Figure 14-25. *ACI* stands for AutoCAD Color Index. These are the predefined colors that come with AutoCAD.

Figure 14-24.
You can set a color using either the RGB or HLS color system. The HLS system is shown here.

Select a color system

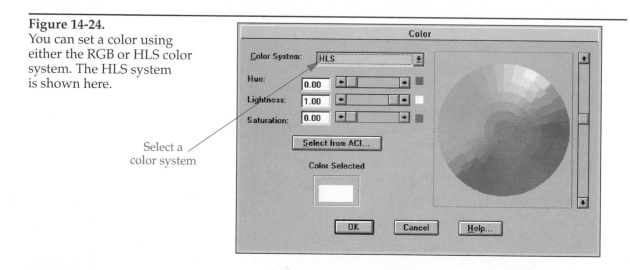

Figure 14-25.
If you use the AutoCAD Color Index, you can select a color from the presets that come with AutoCAD.

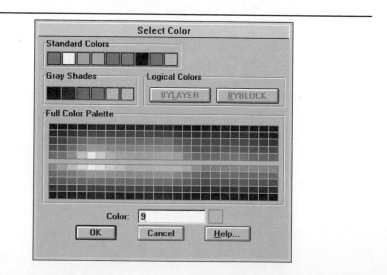

Use the ability to change the intensity and color of lights often. It can quickly provide you with a variety of rendered models before you produce the final images or prints. The best way to see how colored lights affect your model is to experiment. Remember, you can render individual objects in the model. Zoom in on an object and render. This allows you to see how light intensity and color change each object, and will save time in the process.

CREATING SURFACE FINISHES WITH MATERIALS

A *finish* in AutoCAD can be a shiny surface, dull surface, or any gradation between. You can create a variety of finishes by specifying how a surface reflects light. See the section entitled *Understanding lights* earlier in this chapter. When you create a finish, it can be assigned to an entity color that you created or to a specific AutoCAD Color Index (ACI) number. If you assign a finish to an ACI, all objects in your model with that color number are given the finish.

To create a new finish, first pick the **Materials** button in the **Render** toolbar, pick **Render** then **Materials...** from the **Tools** pull-down menu, or type RMAT at the **Command:** prompt. This displays the **Materials** dialog box, Figure 14-26A. Then, pick the **New...** button to display the **New Standard Material** dialog box, Figure 14-26B. There are four radio buttons in the **Attributes** section labeled **Color**, **Ambient**, **Reflection**, and **Roughness**. These allow you to set the attributes for the material.

- **Color.** This refers to the reflected color of the object.
- **Ambient**. This is the color of the ambient light reflected from the object.
- **Reflection**. This is the color of the highlight. The highlight is the shiniest spot on the object. This is also called the *specular* reflection or highlight.
- **Roughness**. This controls the size of the specular reflection.

Figure 14-26.
A—The **Materials** dialog box. Pick new to display the **New Standard Material** subdialog box.
B—The **New Standard Material** subdialog box.

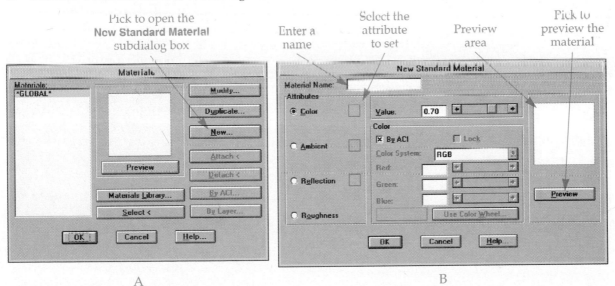

By default, the **By ACI** check box is active for color. This means that the main color is determined by the color of the object you assign the material to. Pick both the **Ambient** and **Reflection** radio buttons. Notice that the **Lock** check box is active. This means that the attribute's color is locked to the main color. You can change these colors by picking the check box to remove the lock. This activates the **By ACI** check box. Pick to remove the check and the color slider bars and the **Use Color Wheel...** button are activated.

There is also a **Value:** area in the **New Standard Material** dialog box. This represents the level, or intensity, of the attribute's color. Notice that the default **Value:** setting for **Color:** is 0.70. When combined with a 0.30 value for **Reflection:**, a matte finish is produced. A polished finish is created with a 0.30 setting for **Color:** and a 0.70 setting for **Reflection:**. The greater the value for **Ambient:**, the more pale the object appears. The default setting of 0.10 is best here, combined with a setting of 0.30 in the **Lights** dialog box. To have the brightest reflection, keep the **Color:** value low and the **Reflection:** value at least 0.70.

The **Value:** area is also used with **Roughness:**. The smaller the value, the smaller the area of highlight. A small specular highlight makes the surface appear shiny. Set a high value for **Roughness:** and a low value for **Reflection:** if you want the surface to appear rough or dull.

Preview the results of your settings by picking the **Preview** button. AutoCAD renders a sample sphere with the material the settings will create. See Figure 14-27. After you preview, you can make any changes necessary and preview again.

Figure 14-27.
A preview of the TORUS material.

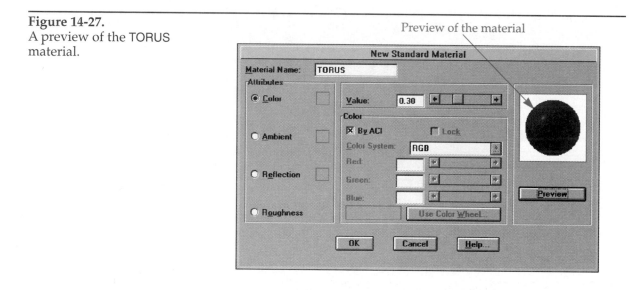

For the tutorial, enter TORUS in the **Material Name:** text box. The maximum length of a material name is 16 characters. Set the **Color:** value to 0.70, **Ambient:** to 0.10, **Reflection:** to 0.30, and **Roughness:** to 1.00. Pick **OK** to exit the **New Standard Materials** dialog box and return to the **Materials** dialog box. Now you must assign the new material to an object. Pick the **Attach ⟨** button and the following prompt appears:

> Select objects to attach "TORUS" to: *(pick the torus)*
> Select objects: ↵

The dialog box returns. Pick **OK** to exit.

To best see how the light and material changes affect the model, create a close-up view of a single object. Zoom-in close to the torus and create a new view named TORUS. Now create a new scene named TORUS. Use the TORUS view and lights S-1 and D-2. Render the scene and notice the wide area of the reflection. See Figure 14-28. Now, edit the material TORUS. Change the roughness to 0.10, color to 0.30, reflection to 0.70, and roughness to 0.10. Render the model again. Notice that the area of reflection is much smaller. There is also less diffused light indicating a smoother surface. See Figure 14-29.

Figure 14-28.
The rendered torus.

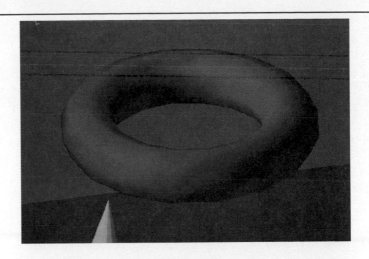

Figure 14-29.
The rendered torus after the material is modified.

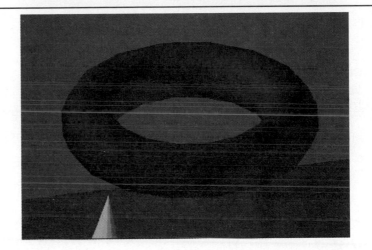

Other features of the Materials dialog box

There are several other features of the **Materials** dialog box. These help you work with materials and are explained below.

- **Preview.** Displays a sphere with the attributes of the selected material. This works the same as the preview function of the **New Standard Material** dialog box.
- **Materials Library....** Displays the **Materials Library** dialog box. This is discussed in the next section.
- **Select** ⟨. Returns to the graphics screen to allow selection of objects for application of the current material.
- **Modify....** Displays the **Modify Standard Materials** dialog box. This is the same as the **Materials** dialog box and allows you to adjust material attributes.
- **Duplicate....** Displays the **New Standard Materials** dialog box. The current material is duplicated and can be edited to create a new material.
- **New....** Displays the **New Standard Materials** dialog box.
- **Attach** ⟨. Displays the graphics screen so the current material can be attached to selected objects.
- **Detach** ⟨. Displays the graphics screen so the current material can be detached from selected objects.
- **By ACI....** Displays the **Attach by AutoCAD Color Index** dialog box. The current material will be attached to all objects in the drawing that have the selected ACI number.
- **By Layer....** Displays the **Attach by Layer** dialog box. The current material will be attached to all objects in the drawing on the selected layer.

EXERCISE 14-2

❑ Open the 3DSHAPES drawing if it is not on your screen.
❑ Zoom-in on the cone and pyramid. Create a new view named EX14-2.
❑ Create a new scene and name it EX14-2. Use light D-1 and P-1.
❑ Create a new material for the cone. Give it a dull surface by adjusting the material attributes. Name the material EX14-2.
❑ Render the new scene.
❑ Modify the material to create a shiny surface with a highlight.
❑ Render the scene.
❑ Save the drawing as EX14-2.

THE MATERIALS LIBRARY DIALOG BOX

The **Materials Library** dialog box is accessed by picking the **Materials Library** button in the **Render** toolbar, picking **R**ender then **M**aterials Library... in the **Tools** pull-down menu, or by typing MATLIB at the **Command:** prompt. In addition, you can also pick the **Materials Library** button in the **Materials** dialog box. The standard materials library is an ASCII file named RENDER.MLI. It contains a list of materials that are displayed in the **Library List:** area of the **Materials Library** dialog box. This dialog box can be used to import and export materials, and to perform housekeeping functions on the current materials list and the library list.

PROFESSIONAL TIP

You can import an AutoVision or 3D Studio material library file (.MIL) using the **Open...** button in the **Materials Library** dialog box. However, AutoCAD only displays the color, ambient, reflection, and roughness parameters of AutoVision materials. The transparency or texture mapping is *not* displayed.

For additional AutoVision information or other products that link with the AutoCAD renderer, see "Rendering and Other Applications" in the *AutoCAD User's Guide*.

Editing the materials list and materials library

The **M**aterials List: area is on the left side of the **Materials Library** dialog box. It displays a list of all the materials defined in the current drawing. See Figure 14-30. The **L**ibrary List: on the right side of the dialog displays all of the materials in the current library file. The name of the current library file appears above the list.

You can use the materials in the default RENDER.MLI library by highlighting the material name in the material library list and picking ⟨-**Import**. This copies the material from the library list to the materials list, making it available in the current drawing.

You may want to use a different library file from the default RENDER.MLI. For example, you may create several different libraries for different projects or customers. Also, if you are using the modeling capabilities of AutoCAD in conjunction with the rendering and animation capabilities of 3D Studio, you may want to have a common library used by both programs. A different library file can be used by picking the **Open...** button. This displays the **Library File** dialog box, Figure 14-31. Change to the directory where the library file is located. Then, highlight the filename and pick **OK**. The materials in that library file are now displayed in the **L**ibrary List:.

Figure 14-30.
The **Materials Library** file.

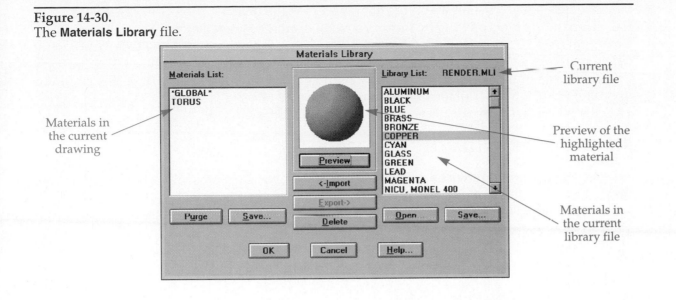

Materials in the current drawing

Current library file

Preview of the highlighted material

Materials in the current library file

Figure 14-31.
Selecting a different library file.

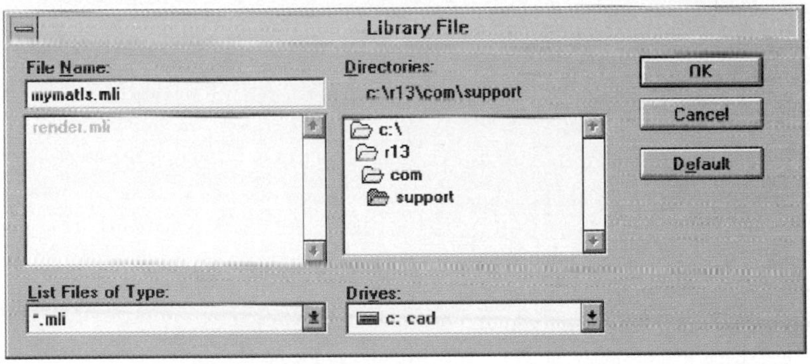

If you want to use a material that you have created in the current drawing for other applications, you need to export it to the library file. For example, highlight the TORUS material in the material list and then pick the **Export-** button. The material is added to the library list on the right side of the dialog box. Next, pick the **Save...** button to open the **Library File** dialog box. See Figure 14-31. Locate the correct directory, highlight the library file from the list or type a new name, and then pick **OK**. By default, the RENDER.MLI library file is located in the \R13\COM\SUPPORT directory.

If you make changes to the library list in the **Materials Library** dialog box and pick **OK** without saving, the **Library Modification** dialog box appears. See Figure 14-32. This gives you the chance to save the changes, discard the changes, or cancel and return to the **Materials Library** dialog box. Pick the appropriate button and continue.

Figure 14-32.
If you make changes to a library file and try to exit without saving, this dialog box appears.

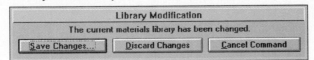

To delete a material, highlight the name and pick the **Delete** button. You can delete materials from the current drawing by picking a name from the **Materials List:**. You can also delete a material from the current library file by picking the name from the **Library List:**. You cannot delete materials that are attached to objects.

The **Purge** button deletes all unused materials from the current drawing. This is similar to typing PURGE at the **Command:** prompt to delete all unused layers, blocks, and linetypes. The current material library file is unaffected by the **Purge** button.

SPECIFYING RENDERING PREFERENCES

The **Rendering Preferences** dialog box provides several options and settings. See Figure 14-33. The following discussion outlines the function of these items.

- **Rendering Type:.** This area lists AutoCAD Render and any other installed rendering types, such as Autodesk AutoVision.
- **Screen Palette.** This pop-up list is grayed-out unless AutoCAD is configured for a continuous-color rendering driver. When available, the following options can be selected:
  - **Best Map/No Fold—** AutoCAD vector colors are not folded (blended) into colors 1 - 8. This calculates the best colors to use for rendering based on those available in your display device. The colors of entities in the other viewports may change.
  - **Best Map/Fold—** AutoCAD vector colors are folded into colors 1 - 8. This calculates the best colors to use for rendering based on those available in your display device. The colors of entities in the other viewports are changed to the closest color from 1 - 8.
  - **Fixed ACAD Map—** Uses AutoCAD's 256 colors for rendering.
- **Rendering Options**
  - **Smooth Shading—** Smoothes out the faces and blends colors across faces.
  - **Merge—** Allows you to overlay images. Available only with 24-bit, full-color display devices.
  - **Apply Materials—** Any finishes are applied to the rendering.
  - **More Options...—** This opens the **AutoCAD Render Options** subdialog box. See Figure 14-34. You can set the render quality and control how faces are rendered with the following options:
    - **Gouraud—** Calculates light intensity at each vertex and interpolates intermediate intensities. This radio button is selected by default.

Figure 14-33.
The **Rendering Preferences** dialog box.

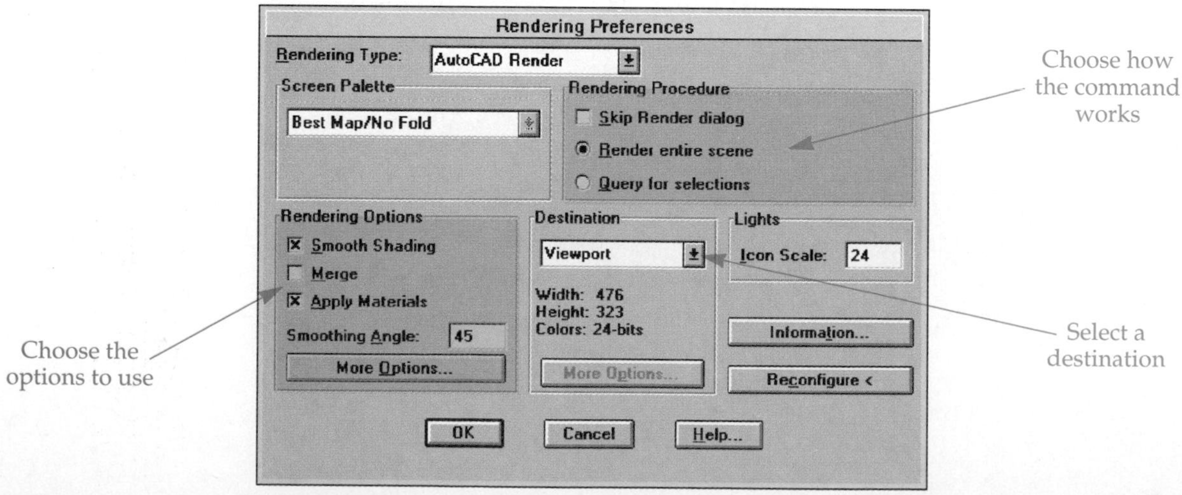

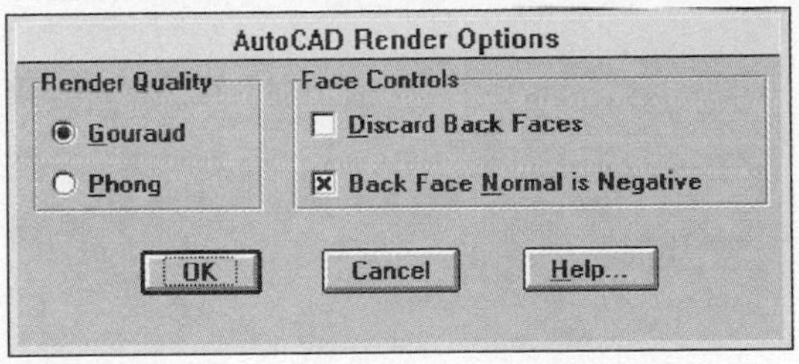

Figure 14-34.
Setting the render quality
and face controls.

- **Phong**— Calculates light intensity at each pixel to produce shading with more realistic highlights. This radio button is not selected by default.
  - **Discard Back Faces**— This check box is off by default. If on, AutoCAD does not render back faces. Saves time, but may not produce the full rendering that you desire.
  - **Back Face Normal is Negative**— This check box is on by default. A *normal* is a vector that projects perpendicular from a face. A negative normal projects away from the viewer, or into negative Z space. AutoCAD considers negative normals as *back faces* if this option is on.
- **Rendering Procedure.** This area sets the default for how the **RENDER** command works when issued.
  - **Skip Render Dialog**— Renders the objects without displaying the **Render** dialog box. The objects that are rendered depend on the settings of the following radio buttons.
  - **Render Entire Scene**— Renders all objects in a scene.
  - **Query For Selections**— Displays a prompt asking you to select the objects to render.
- **Destination.** This area controls the image output setting the selected display driver uses for the rendering. Three options are available in the pop-up list.
  - **Viewport**— Renders to the current viewport.
  - **Render Window**— Renders to the AutoCAD for Windows Render.
  - **File**— Renders to a file.
  - **More Options...**— This button is grayed-out unless **File** is selected in the pop-up list. Picking this button displays the **File Output Configuration** subdialog box. This dialog box is discussed in the *SAVING IMAGE FILES* section later in this chapter.
- **Lights**
  - **Icon Scale**— Sets the size of light and finish icons.
- **Information....** Picking this button displays the current configuration and version of AutoCAD Render.
- **Reconfigure** ⟨. Picking this button allows you to reconfigure the rendering device. The rendering configuration is saved in a file named RENDER.CFG. See Chapter 6 of the *AutoCAD Installation Guide* for information on setting the proper environment variable for this file.

Rendering statistics

The **STATS** command provides information about the last rendering performed. This command can be accessed by picking **Render** and then **Statistics...** from the **Tools** pull-down menu or by typing STATS at the **Command:** prompt. You can also pick the **Statistics** button from the **Render** toolbar. The **Statistics** dialog box displays information that cannot be altered, but can be saved to a file. See Figure 14-35.

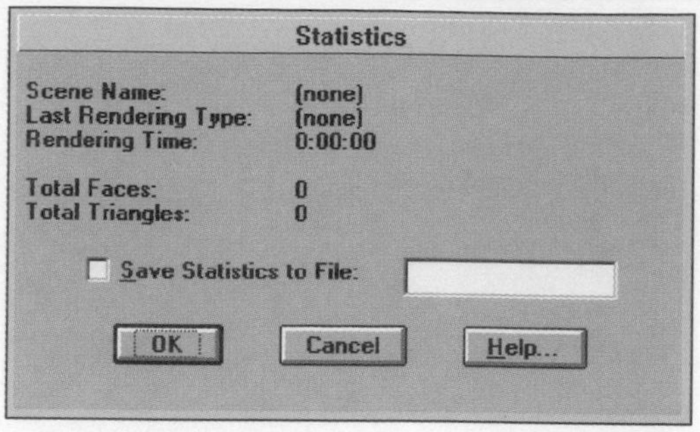

Figure 14-35.
Displaying the rendering
statistics.

SAVING IMAGE FILES

You can save a rendered image to a file in a variety of raster file formats. These images can then be used with other software programs, such as a desktop publishing program.

Rendering to file

To render an image to file, select **File** from the pop-up list in the **Destination** area of the **Render** dialog box. The **More Options...** button is activated. Pick the button and the **File Output Configuration** subdialog box is opened, Figure 14-36. Choose the file format in the **File Type** section. There are several different raster file types available, as shown in Figure 14-37. You can also render an image to a PostScript file. The default type is targa, or .TGA. Also, select the resolution, or size, for the rendered image using the second pop-up list. You can select a resolution that is higher than your display device. This is valuable when replaying the image on systems with higher resolution. If you select the **User Defined** option, you can change the aspect ratio of the output file. See Figure 14-36. Close the subdialog box and the **Rendering Preferences** dialog box. Then, render the scene. The **Rendering File** dialog box appears before the scene is rendered. This is the standard "save file" dialog box. Enter a name and location, and pick **OK**.

Raster files. A common raster file is a *bitmap* image and has a .BMP file extension. Bitmap files require a fixed amount of memory regardless of their size or complexity, and they display quickly. They can be created as standard 8-bit color images or 24-bit color images. An 8-bit color image uses 8-bits per pixel for a maximum of 256 colors (2^8). A 24-bit color image uses 24-bits per pixel for a total of 16.7 million colors (2^{24}). A display adapter capable of displaying 16.7 million colors is often called a *true-color card.* Most graphics cards have true-color capability, although many limit this to a low resolution (640×480). You can

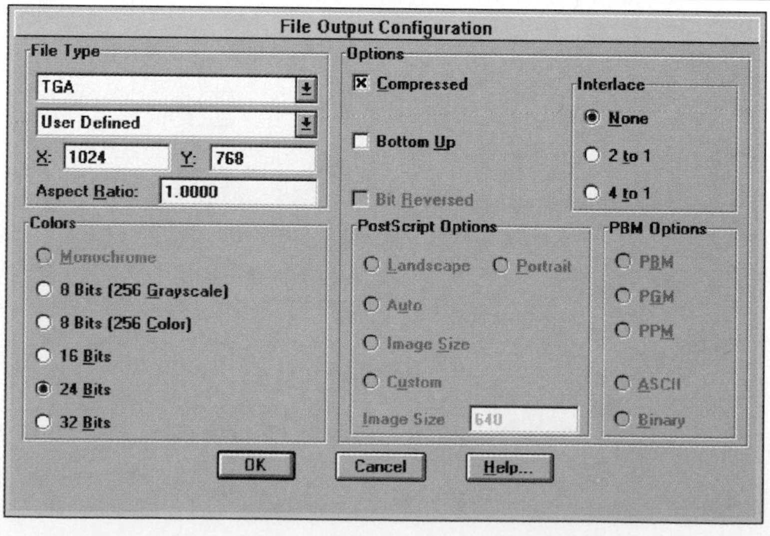

Figure 14-36.
Configuring an output
file for rendering.

Figure 14-37.
Select a file type from
the pop-up list. All of the
available file types can
be seen here.

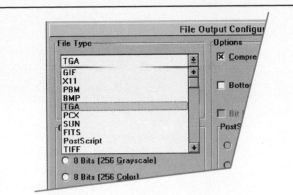

still render a 24-bit image if your system is currently configured for an 8-bit display. You can then save the rendered image as a file and display it on another computer that is configured for 24-bit color.

Keep in mind that raster files become somewhat "blocky" when scaled. This can be a major drawback when inserting the rendered image into a word processing or desktop publishing document.

Using **SAVEIMG** to save an image

Images can also be saved by picking **Image** then **Save...** from the **Tools** pull-down menu or by typing SAVEIMG at the **Command:** prompt. This displays the **Save Image** dialog box. See Figure 14-38. However, you must render the scene *before* using the **SAVEIMG** command. Also, there are only three file types available in this dialog box. The .TGA and .TIF formats can be saved as compressed files. Pick the **Options...** button to open the **TGA Options** or **TIFF Options** subdialog box. See Figure 14-39. The compressed form for .TGA files is **RLE** (Run-Length-Encoded). A .TIF file can be compressed as **PACK** for Macintosh or the standard **LZW** format. Pick **OK** to close the dialog box and the **Image File** dialog box appears. Enter a filename and pick **OK** to save the image.

Using the **Save Image** dialog box, you can crop the image by specifying the XY pixel values. The **Offset X:** and **Y:** text boxes define the lower-left corner of the image. The **Size X:** and **Y:** text boxes define the upper-right corner of the image. You can also use the pointing device and pick the two corners in the **Portion** area of the dialog box to define the image area. See Figure 14-38.

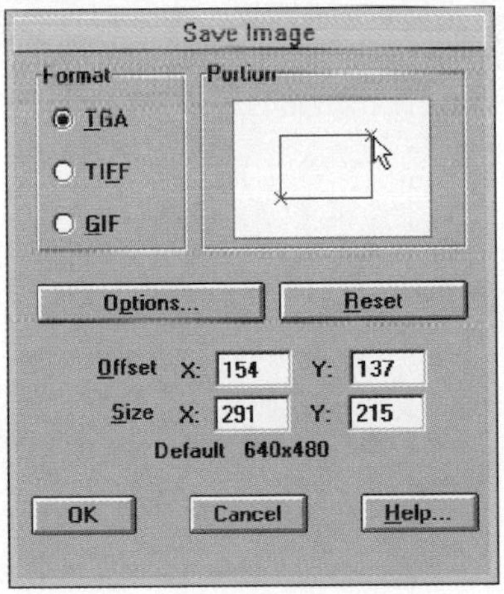

Figure 14-38.
The **Save Image** dialog box.
Notice that only three file
types are available.

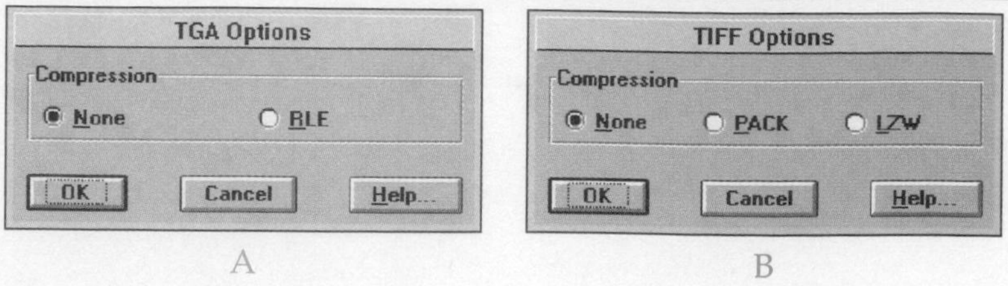

Figure 14-39.
You can specify the type of compression, or no compression, for .TGA and .TIF files.

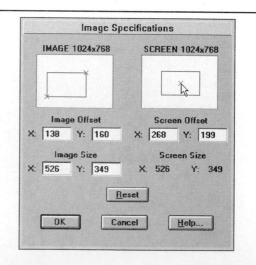

A

B

NOTE

The pixel values shown in the **Save Image** dialog box will vary depending on your current screen resolution and whether you are rendering the active viewport, the drawing area, or the full screen image. The image size represents the pixel size of the current viewport. Before saving an image, be sure that the viewport you want to save the image in is actually the current one. Click anywhere within the viewport to make it current.

Replaying image files

Images saved as .TGA, .TIF, and .GIF files can be displayed in AutoCAD with the **REPLAY** command. Access the command by selecting **Image** and then **View...** from the **Tools** pull-down menu or by typing REPLAY at the **Command:** prompt. This displays the **Replay** dialog box. Select the directory and file you want to display and pick the **OK** button. The **Image Specifications** dialog box then appears. This dialog box allows you to specify the exact portion of the image you want to display. See Figure 15-40.

The image tile on the left side of the dialog box is titled **IMAGE**. The size of the image is given in pixels just above the image tile. You can pick two points inside this tile to crop the image for display. When you do this, notice that the screen offset location of the image in the **SCREEN** image tile changes. You can also change the image size by entering the cropped size of the image in the **Image Offset** and **Image Size** text boxes. The image offset defines the lower-left corner of the image. The image size defines the upper-right corner of the image.

In addition to cropping the size of the image, you can determine where it will be displayed on the screen. Do this visually by picking a point in the **SCREEN** image tile. This point becomes the center of the image on your screen. You can also specify the location by entering **Screen Offset** values in the boxes below the tile. Notice that the **Screen Size** values cannot be changed. See Figure 14-40. The **Reset** button returns all of the image and screen values to their defaults. Pick **OK** when you are ready to display the image.

Figure 14-40.
The **Image Specifications** dialog box.

EXERCISE 14-3

❑ Load EX14-1 into AutoCAD if it is not on your screen.
❑ Save an image of the entire model in a raster file format. Save it as EX14-3.
❑ Replay the image to occupy the entire screen.
❑ Replay the image again, but display only the center of the image. Locate it in the upper-right portion of the screen.

ADVANCED RENDERING

Some of the advanced capabilities of AutoCAD Render include rendering to a separate window, copying the rendered image to the Windows Clipboard, and advanced printing options. This section discusses each of these capabilities.

The Render window

The **Render** window is made up of several elements, Figure 14-41. These elements include a menu bar, a toolbar, and a status area. The menu bar contains the **File**, **Edit**, and **Window** pull-down menus. The toolbar contains five buttons that are shortcuts to the commands in the **File** and **Edit** pull-down menus. The open area just to the right of the toolbar is the status area. Information about the currently displayed image appears in this area.

The background color for the **Render** window is determined by the color settings in Windows. To change the color, use the Control Panel in the Windows Main program group. By default, the Windows background color is white. You may want to use one color for the AutoCAD window and another color for the **Render** window. To learn more about screen color options, refer to Chapter 16 of this text.

Saving and opening a rendered image. An image rendered to the **Render** window can be saved as a bitmap (.BMP) or printed. The **Render** window can also be used to open and display a bitmap image. The **File** pull-down menu contains the **Open**, **Save**, and **Print** commands, Figure 14-42.

Figure 14-41.
The 3DSHAPES drawing rendered to the **Render** window.

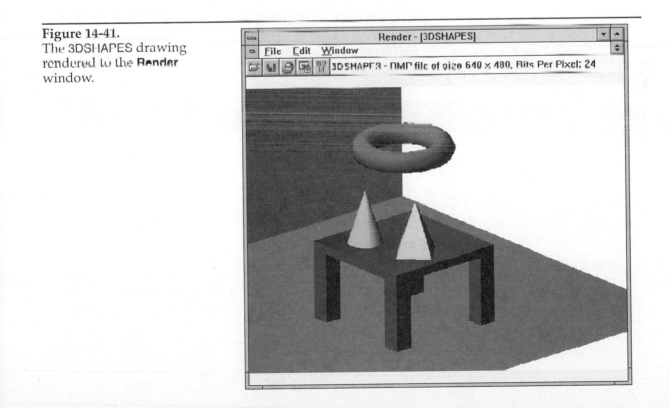

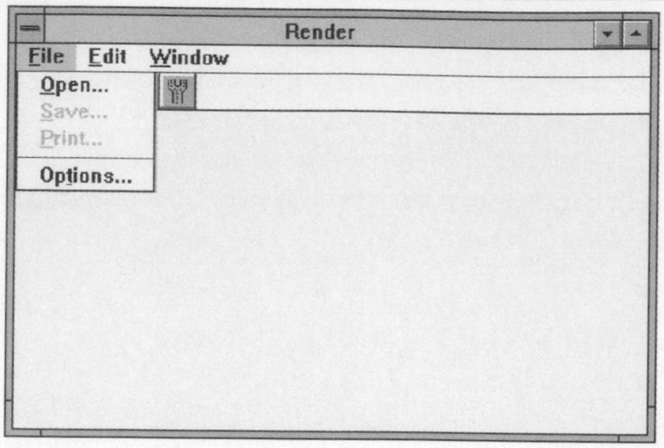

Figure 14-42.
The commands available in the **Render** window **File** pull-down menu.

The **Save** command is used to save a rendered image to a file. You can also pick the **Save** icon on the **Render** window toolbar. The default name is the name of the drawing. If you want to save the rendered image with a different filename, enter the name in the **File Name:** text box. Pick **OK** to save the image.

The **Open** command is used to open a bitmap (.BMP) image. You can also pick the **Open** icon on the **Render** window toolbar. This displays the **Render Open** dialog box, Figure 14-43. If the **Preview** check box is checked, the selected image is previewed before it is displayed in the **Render** window. In Figure 14-43, the ARCADE.BMP image is selected from the file list and previewed before loading into the **Render** window.

There is also an **Options...** selection in the **File** pull-down menu. This displays the **Windows Render Options** dialog box. This dialog box is discussed later in this chapter.

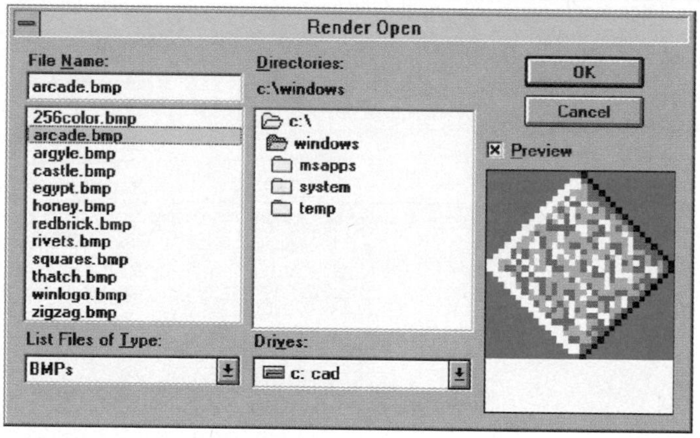

Figure 14-43.
Opening a file using the **Open...** command in the **Render** window.

NOTE

The **Render** window can display and save .BMP files *only*.

Copying a rendered image to the Clipboard

Once an image has been rendered, it can be copied to the Windows Clipboard. Think of the Clipboard as a temporary storage area for text and graphic information. Once an image is copied into the Clipboard, it can be "pasted" into another Windows application, such as a desktop publishing program. Information copied to the Clipboard stays there until something else is copied to the Clipboard, the information is deleted from the Clipboard, or you quit Windows.

To copy a rendered image to the Clipboard, pick the **Copy** icon on the **Render** window toolbar or select <u>**Copy**</u> from the <u>**Edit**</u> pull-down menu, Figure 14-44. The standard Windows key stroke of [Ctrl]+[C] also copies information to the Clipboard.

For example, suppose you want to include your 3DOBJECTS drawing as a rendered image in a memo or letter. First, render the drawing to the **Render** window. Next, copy the image to the Clipboard. Once information is on the Clipboard, start a Windows-compatible word processing program. Finally, paste the contents of the Clipboard into the document. See Figure 14-45.

Figure 14-44.
Using the <u>**Copy**</u> command in the **Render** window.

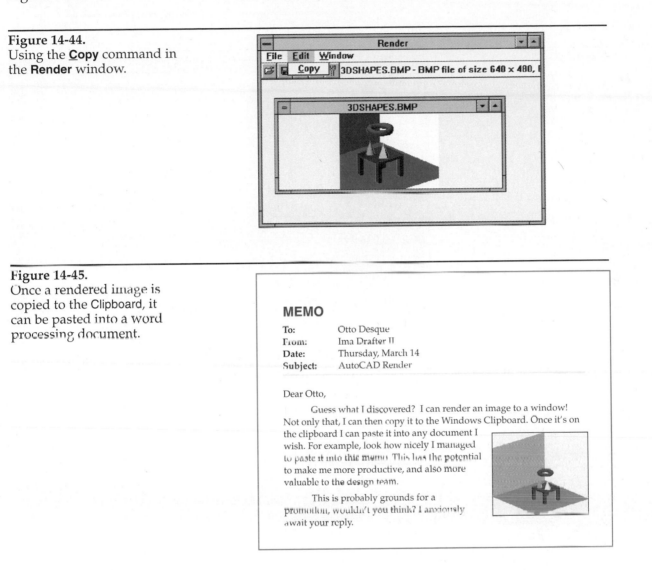

Figure 14-45.
Once a rendered image is copied to the Clipboard, it can be pasted into a word processing document.

The contents of the Clipboard can be viewed at any time by returning to the Program Manager and double-clicking the Clipboard Viewer icon in the Main program group, Figure 14-46. In Figure 14-47, the 3D shapes created in Exercise 14-2 are shown after being rendered and copied to the Clipboard.

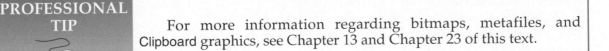

PROFESSIONAL TIP

For more information regarding bitmaps, metafiles, and Clipboard graphics, see Chapter 13 and Chapter 23 of this text.

Figure 14-46.
The Clipboard Viewer is found in the Main program group of Program Manager.

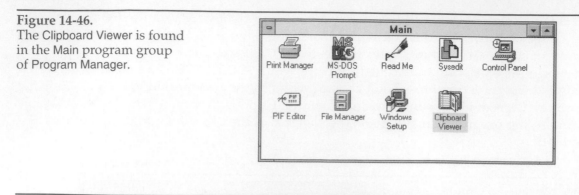

Figure 14-47.
A rendered image as it appears on the Clipboard.

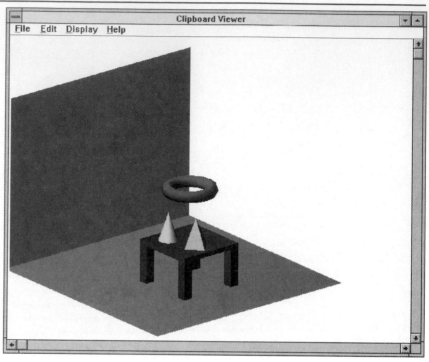

PROFESSIONAL TIP

To conserve system memory, clear the contents of the Clipboard when the copied image is no longer needed. To do so, open the Clipboard Viewer from the Main group window. Then, select Delete from the Edit pull-down menu.

EXERCISE 14-4

❏ Load EX14-3 if it is not already on your screen.
❏ Render a bitmap image to the **Render** window.
❏ Save the bitmap image with the name EX14-3.BMP. Then, copy the image to the Windows Clipboard.
❏ Return to the Program Manager and activate the Clipboard Viewer. If necessary, use the horizontal and vertical scroll bars to display different portions of your copied bitmap rendering.
❏ If you have a Windows-compatible word processing program, begin a new file and paste the contents of the Clipboard into your document.
❏ When you are finished, clear the contents of the Clipboard and exit the Clipboard Viewer. Do not close the **Render** window or exit AutoCAD.

Render window display options

The **Render** window has options that let you arrange the open display windows. These options are located in the **Window** pull-down menu, Figure 14-48. These options are explained below:

- **Tile.** This menu item arranges the open display windows so that they are adjacent to each other. Figure 14-49 shows four tiled bitmap images. Only one window can be active when multiple display windows are open. In Figure 14-49, the ARGYLE.BMP window is active, as indicated by the highlighted title bar.
- **Cascade.** This menu item arranges the open display windows so that they overlap one another, Figure 14-50. As with a tiled display, only one of the open windows can be active at a time.
- **Arrange Icons.** An open display window can be minimized to an icon. These minimized icons are usually displayed along the bottom border of a window, Figure 14-51. The **Arrange Icons** item automatically aligns minimized display windows along the bottom of the **Render** window.
- **Reuse Window.** By default, **Render** opens a new rendering window whenever a new rendering is produced. The **Reuse Window** selection clears any existing image from the active **Render** window and uses the same window for the new rendered image.

Figure 14-48.
The **Window** pull-down menu of the **Render** window.

Figure 14-49.
Four images tiled in the **Render** window. The active image is the one with the highlighted title bar.

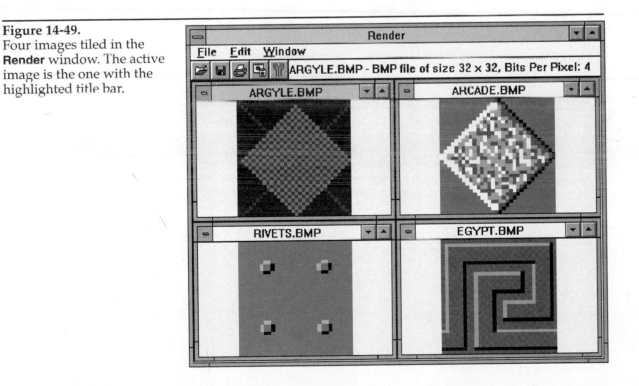

Figure 14-50.
The four images from Figure 14-49 cascaded.

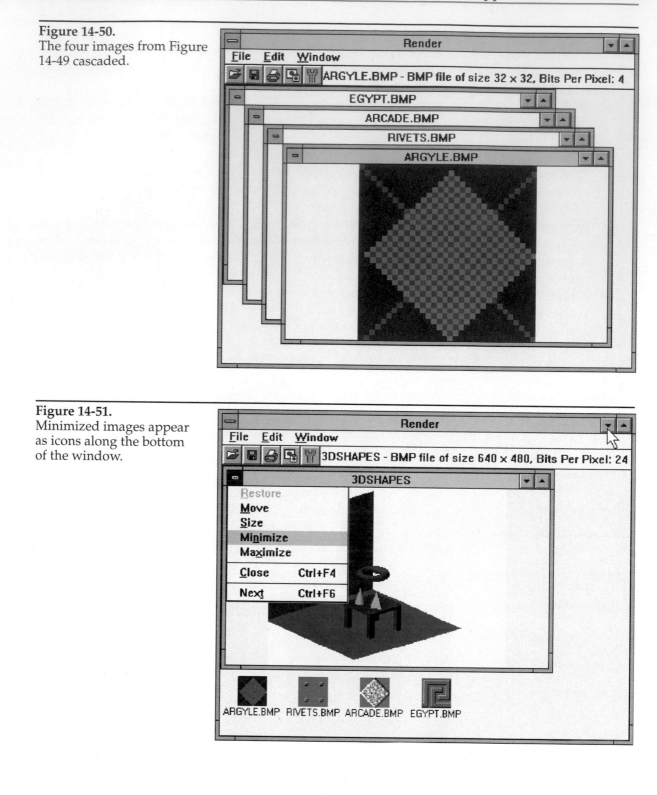

Figure 14-51.
Minimized images appear as icons along the bottom of the window.

EXERCISE 14-5

❏ Activate the **Render** window and open four bitmap files of your choice from the \WINDOWS directory.

❏ Produce a tiled display similar to that shown in Figure 14-49.

❏ Produce a cascaded display similar to that shown in Figure 14-50.

❏ Minimize each of the display windows to an icon using one of the methods described in this chapter.

❏ Align the icons at the bottom of the render window with the **Arrange Icons** option.

❏ Turn on **Reuse Window** and open EX14-3.BMP from the previous exercise.

❏ Maximize each of the icons at the bottom of the render window. Close each open display window and then close the main **Render** window.

THE **WINDOWS RENDER OPTIONS** DIALOG BOX

You can also choose pixel and color resolutions for rendered bitmap images. These settings are made in the **Windows Render Options** dialog box, Figure 14-52. To access this dialog box, pick the **Options** icon on the **Render** window toolbar or select **Options...** from the **Render** window **File** pull-down menu. Any changes made in this dialog box do not take effect until you render again.

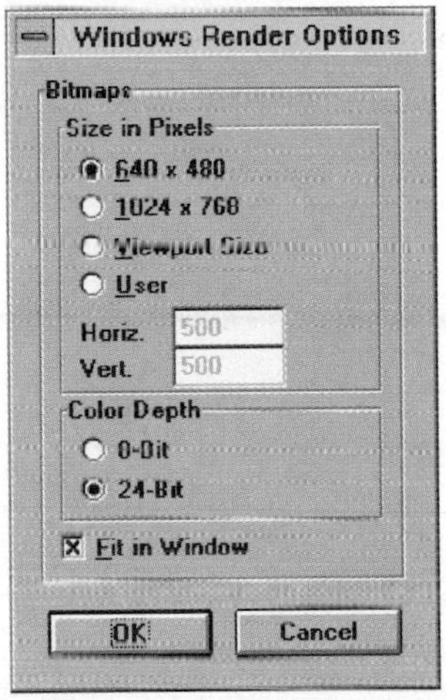

Figure 14-52.
The **Window Render Options** dialog box.

Bitmap rendering options

You can specify the screen resolution for your rendered image using one of the four radio buttons located in the **Size in Pixels** area of the **Windows Render Options** dialog box. These four radio buttons are explained below:

- **640 × 480.** This is the resolution of a standard VGA display system.
- **1024 × 768.** This is the resolution of many 17" and larger video displays.
- **Viewport Size.** This button sets the size of the bitmap to the size of the **Render** window. The larger the window, the larger the displayed image.
- **User.** This button lets you manually set the horizontal and vertical size of the bitmap. The default values are 500 pixels on both the horizontal and vertical axes. You can set a maximum size of 4096 × 4096 pixels.

Also, notice the **Fit in Window** check box at the lower left of the dialog box. This option is on by default and permits you to scale your bitmap according to the size of the display window. Therefore, the **Fit in Window** option overrides the **Size in Pixels** settings described above. As an example, suppose you have rendered an image at a given resolution and then substantially reduce the size of the **Render** window. It is likely that only a portion of your rendered image will be displayed in the reduced window. To display the entire rendered image again while maintaining the correct aspect ratio, return to the **Windows Render Options** dialog box and pick the **Fit in Window** check box. The image is then automatically rescaled to fit inside the smaller window.

In addition to the pixel size options, you can render either an 8-bit or 24-bit image. Make the setting by selecting one of the radio buttons in the **Color Depth** area of the **Windows Render Options** dialog box. Even when working on a system set up for 8-bit color display (256 colors), you can still render and save a 24-bit (16.7 million colors) image. When the image is displayed on a system set up for 24-bit color, the image displays in true color.

Printing a rendered image

You can print a rendered bitmap from the **Render** window. Select **Print...** from the **File** pull-down menu or pick the **Print** button on the toolbar. The **Print** dialog box shown in Figure 14-53 appears. The rendered image is displayed in a border that represents the paper size and orientation (portrait or landscape) currently set in the Windows Print Manager. The current system printer is used, regardless of the current printer/plotter in AutoCAD.

In Figure 14-53, the rendered 3DSHAPES drawing from Exercise 14-1 appears in the dialog box. Notice that the image is located near the top of the image area. The image area represents the paper. Where the image appears in the image area is where it will print on the paper. You can change the position of the printed image by picking anywhere on the image, holding the pick button down, and dragging the image to a new location.

Figure 14-53.
This **Print** dialog box appears when printing from the **Render** window.

Handles

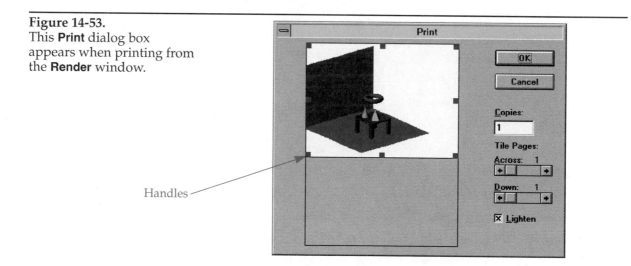

You can also change the size of the printed image. Notice the solid filled squares around the boundary of the image area. These squares are called *handles* and are used to change the size of the image both horizontally or vertically. Handles function much like a hot grip. When you move your cursor over a handle, it changes to a double-headed arrow, Figure 14-54. Simply hold down the pick button and drag the image to the desired size. If you pick a corner handle, the image is rescaled with the correct aspect ratio.

Once the image is scaled and located as needed, you can set the number of printed copies using the **Copies:** text box. You can also lighten the printed image with the **Lighten** check box. With this box checked, the entire image is printed lighter. However, darker colors are lightened more than lighter colors. When you are ready to print, pick the **OK** button.

Figure 14-54.
Adjusting an image in
the **Print** dialog box.

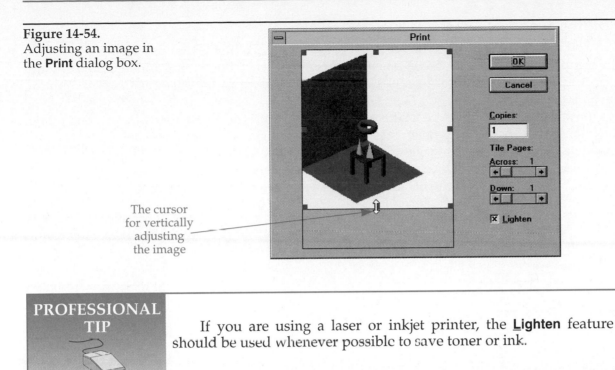

The cursor
for vertically
adjusting
the image

**PROFESSIONAL
TIP**

If you are using a laser or inkjet printer, the **Lighten** feature
should be used whenever possible to save toner or ink.

Printing across multiple pages

You can print an image that is larger than the paper using the tiling feature of the **Render**
window's **Print** dialog box. *Tiling* is printing an image on more than one sheet of paper. The
sheets are then placed together to form the completed image.

Refer to Figure 14-55. Notice the **Tile Pages: Across:** and **Down:** slider bars. These indicate that the image will print over two pages across and two pages down. This is a total of
four pages. When the four pages are printed, they can be taped or stapled together to form
one large printed image. The maximum number of pages that can be tiled depends on the
printer you are using. The image can be moved or resized across the tiled pages using the
handles.

Figure 14-55.
You can tile across many
pages using the **Tile Pages:**
sliders.

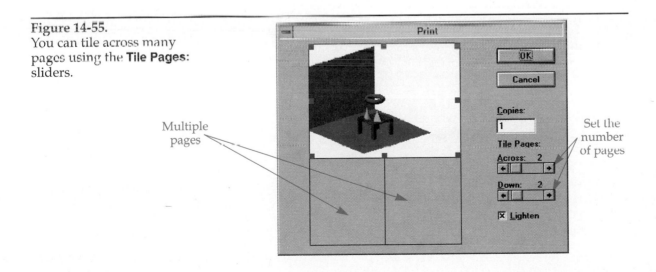

Multiple
pages

Set the
number
of pages

Printing a rendered image as a PostScript file

You can print a rendered image as a PostScript file. To do so, first use the Printers icon in the Windows Control Panel. Setup a new printer and select a PostScript printer. You can select a printer even if you do not have it since you are printing to file. Use the Connect... button and select FILE: as the port.

Next, switch to AutoCAD, set the rendering destination as the **Render** window, and render the image. Then, from the **Render** window, print the image. When the **Print** dialog box appears, change the position, size, and tiling as desired. Pick **OK** to close the dialog box. You are then prompted for a filename. Once you have given a name and path, the file is saved in PostScript format. You can then send the file to the printer as you would any other PostScript file.

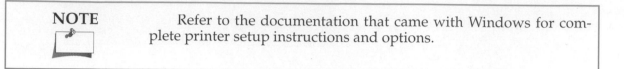

NOTE   Refer to the documentation that came with Windows for complete printer setup instructions and options.

EXERCISE 14-6

❑ If you are connected to a printer, open EX14-1 if it is not currently displayed on your screen.
❑ Set the rendering preferences to render to a window. Without changing any of the printing parameters, print the rendered image.
❑ Turn off **Lighten** in the **Print** dialog box. Print the rendered image again. Compare the two printed images. Which do you prefer?
❑ Return to the **Print** dialog box. Set the slider bars to tile 3 pages across and 3 pages down. Print the multiple page image.

CHAPTER TEST

Write your answers in the spaces provided.

1. Define the following rendering terms:
    Ambient light _____
    Distant light _____
    Point light _____
    Spotlight _____
    Roughness _____
    Diffused light _____

2. When using the **RENDER** command, what is a scene made up of? _____

    _____

3. Which dialog box allows you to specify the shininess and roughness of a surface? _____

    _____

    _____

    _____

    _____

    _____

4. What is the relationship between the numerical value of roughness and the size of the
    highlight on a shiny surface?_____
    _____
    _____
    _____

5. What command allows you to crop an image by pixels and save it as a file? What types
    of files can be saved?_____
    _____
    _____

6. What effect does selecting **Smooth Shading** have on the computer model after it has been
    rendered? _____
    _____
    _____

7. What are the advantages of rendering to a bitmap? _____
    _____
    _____

8. To produce a bitmap rendering, how should you configure the **Rendering Preferences**
    dialog box? _____
    _____
    _____
    _____

9. List the steps involved in loading a material, customizing the material, and applying it to
    a defined surface._____
    _____
    _____
    _____
    _____

10. What is the difference between point lights and distance lights when they are applied to
    a drawing? _____
    _____
    _____

11. What is attenuation? Which lights have this attribute?_____
    _____

12. What determines the background color of the **Render** window? _____
    _____
    _____
    _____
    _____

13. What is the purpose of the Windows Clipboard? What kind of files can be saved using the Clipboard? _____

_____

_____

_____

_____

14. When rendering bitmap images, the **Fit in Window** check box takes precedence over other screen resolution options. (True/False) _____

15. How can you resize the image area in the **Print** dialog box without losing the correct aspect ratio? _____

_____

16. When printing across multiple pages, what determines the maximum number of pages that can be tiled? _____

_____

DRAWING PROBLEMS

General

1. In this problem, you will draw some basic 3D shapes, place lights in the drawing, and then render it.

   A. Begin a new drawing and name it P14-1.

   B. Draw the following 3D shapes using the layer names and colors as indicated.

Shape	Layer Name	Color
Box	BOX	Red
Pyramid	PYRAMID	Yellow
Wedge	WEDGE	Green
Cone	CONE	Cyan
Dome	DOME	Blue
Dish	DISH	Magenta
Sphere	SPHERE	White

   C. Draw the shapes in a circular layout, as shown on page 321. Each shape should be one unit in size.

   D. Place a point light in the center of the objects, 3 units above them.

   E. Place two distant lights as shown on page 321, having target points in the center of the objects. Light D-1 should be located at $Z = 3$ and light D-2 should be located at $Z = 2$.

   F. Place two spotlights as shown on page 321. Light S-1 has a target of the cone apex and light S-2 has a target of the pyramid apex. Light S-1 should be located at $Z = 2.5$ and light S-2 should be located at $Z = 2$.

   G. Render the drawing.

   H. Save the image as a bitmap file named P14-1.

   I. Save the drawing as A:P14-1.

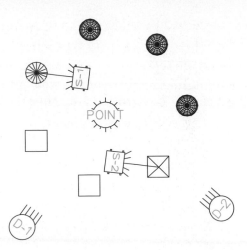

2. Open drawing P14-1. Generate the following scenes and renderings using the light values given. See the illustration below for view orientations.

General

View name	Scene name	Ambient	Point	D-1	D-2
VIEW1	ONE	.7	2	1	1
VIEW2	TWO	.3	2	0	1
VIEW3	THREE	0	5	0	0

A. Create a material for the sphere with a color of 0.3, reflection of 0.7, and roughness of 0.1. Name it SPHERE1.

B. Create a second material for the sphere named SPHERE2 with a color of 0.7, reflection of 0.3, and roughness of 1.0.

C. Create a third material for the sphere named SPHERE3 with a roughness of 0.7, color of 0.5, and a reflection of 0.5.

D. Set finish SPHERE1 as current and render scene ONE.

E. Set finish SPHERE2 as current and render scene ONE.

F. Set finish SPHERE3 as current and render scene ONE.

G. Save the drawing as A:P14-2. Create a bitmap and save it as P14-2.

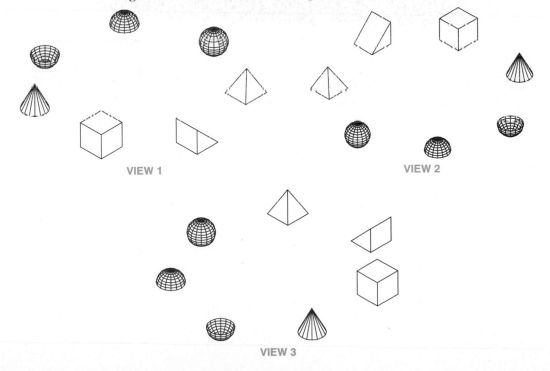

VIEW 1   VIEW 2

VIEW 3

3. This problem will place additional light to a drawing. You will then use the Windows Clipboard and place the drawing in a written document.

   A. Open the drawing P14-1.

   B. Place a new point light directly over the cone and a new distant light to one side and slightly below the "ground." Render the drawing.

   C. Send the drawing to the Windows Clipboard.

   D. Minimize AutoCAD.

   E. Open the Windows Clipboard Viewer to verify the image is there.

   F. Minimize the Windows Clipboard Viewer.

   G. Open your Windows-compatible word processor.

   H. Type the following sentence: This is an example of what AutoCAD for Windows can do for documents.

   I. Using the Edit menu of your word processor, paste the rendered drawing into the document. Save the file as P14-3.DOC.

4. Open a 3D drawing from a previous chapter. Do the following:

   A. Place two point lights around the model.

   B. Place two distant lights around the model.

   C. Place two spotlights around the model.

   D. Create three scenes of the model. Choose two different lights for each scene.

   E. Set the ambient light to a value of your choice.

   F. Render each scene once. Change the light attributes to create highlights. Render each scene again.

   G. Render one scene as a .TGA file, one as a .TIF, and one as a .GIF.

   H. Replay each image.

   I. Save the drawing as P14-4.

5. Open problem P14-4. Do the following:

   A. Configure AutoCAD to render to a window.

   B. Render each one of the three scenes.

   C. Display the rendered images in a tiled format in the **Render** window.

   D. Display the rendered images in a cascade format in the **Render** window.

   E. Minimize each of the image tiles.

   F. Open a .BMP file from the \WINDOWS directory.

   G. Print one of the images centered on a page. Reduce the image size and move it to the upper-right corner. Print it again.

   H. Copy one of the images to the Windows Clipboard.

   I. Paste the Clipboard image into a word processor document.

   J. Print the document.

   K. Save the document as P14-5.

AutoCAD R13

Chapter 15

Introduction to the AutoCAD SQL Environment (ASE)

Learning objectives

After completing this chapter, you will be able to:

- ◯ Define a database.
- ◯ List the components of a database table.
- ◯ Explain SQL and ASE.
- ◯ Describe database, SQL, and GIS applications.
- ◯ Load a database in an AutoCAD drawing.
- ◯ Initialize a database to work in an AutoCAD drawing.
- ◯ Add and edit database table rows using ASE.
- ◯ Create links between a database and an AutoCAD drawing entity.
- ◯ Use SQL to ask questions of a database.
- ◯ Add displayable attributes to the drawing.

An important aspect of any business is keeping track of information. Much of this information relates to physical objects. These objects include inventories, client and employee records, facilities, building materials, product components, and other similar items. These objects are often represented in drawings as graphical entities.

This chapter provides a look at the nature of information and how to work with it. Databases are explained in this chapter. In addition, using AutoCAD to manipulate and change databases is explained.

WHAT IS A DATABASE?

A *database* is a collection of information. "Data" is information and a "base" is a foundation where something rests. When you create a drawing in AutoCAD, you are creating a graphic database. Another common database is composed of text and numerical information. This may be as simple as a list of all the furniture in an office. A database can also be a collection of other databases. Computer software called the *Database Management System (DBMS)* is used to construct, drive, and manage the databases.

A specific database, such as the inventory of furniture, is saved in a database file with an extension of .DBF. For example, the furniture inventory might be called INVENTRY.DBF. The information in this file could include the identification number of the piece of furniture, the type, computer ID number, manufacturer, office where it is located, and employee who occupies that office. The furniture can also be represented in an AutoCAD drawing as blocks. Both the graphic and text databases must be revised when the furniture inventory changes.

Suppose the company also has database files on its employees and the computers in each office. The employee database file (EMPLOYEE.DBF) contains an employee's office number, phone extension, type of furniture in the office, and type of computer. The computer database file (COMPUTER.DBF) lists the brand, CPU and speed, memory, hard disk drive size, and input device.

Working with multiple databases

The information in the three database files from the previous section is listed below. Are there any items that are common to all of the three databases? Are there any relationships between the items in the three databases?

INVENTRY.DBF	**EMPLOYEE.DBF**	**COMPUTER.DBF**
Inventory ID No.	*Employee ID No.*	*Computer Configure No.*
Type	Last name	CPU
Description	First name	Hard drive
Manufacturer	Title	RAM
Model	*Room No.*	Graphic
Computer Configure No.	Phone extension	Input device
Price		
Room No.		
Employee ID No.		

Note the italicized items in the three lists. These items are in at least two of the files. This means that they relate to each other. If a desk is moved to another room, its room number must be changed in the INVENTRY.DBF file *and* in the EMPLOYEE.DBF file. Extra work is required to change the same piece of information twice.

The true power of a DBMS is the ability to find relationships between different database files and edit them automatically. This means time savings when maintaining the database files and drawings. A database with items in various files that are interrelated, or "linked," is called a *relational database.* In a relational database, each file contains data designed for a specific purpose. However, several files may contain data that is related to data in other database files. If a specific item is changed in one file, such as the room number, the software automatically changes that item in all other files where it appears.

For example, look at the contents of the three database files above. If these files are part of a relational database, when the computer configuration number is changed in the COMPUTER.DBF file, it is also changed in the INVENTRY.DBF file.

Retrieving information from a relational database

A request to retrieve information from a database is called a *query.* For example, you could request the database to list the names of every employee with a certain computer configuration. When you enter this query, the program first finds the computer configuration number in the COMPUTER.DBF file. The software also finds that item in the INVENTRY.DBF file. The inventory file contains the numbers of the rooms where the computers with that configuration are located. The room number is also an item in the EMPLOYEE.DBF file. Therefore, the employee names are located and then returned as the response to the initial inquiry.

The software can search between files for similar information. The manner in which queries are made is important. Structured Query Language (SQL) is the standard language used by most DBMS programs. AutoCAD has the ability to work with SQL.

STRUCTURED QUERY LANGUAGE

The *Structured Query Language (SQL)* is a standard computer programming format for querying (asking questions of) a database. SQL provides specific rules and syntax for queries. The acronym SQL is often pronounced "sequel." A newer SQL called *SQL2* is an international standard with features that enhance SQL. AutoCAD Release 13 uses SQL2. AutoCAD Release 12 uses SQL.

Computer software continues to improve and become more powerful. As it does, software that uses SQL continues to be developed with increasingly accurate and refined searches based on simpler input from the user.

AutoCAD and SQL

AutoCAD has a specific set of commands designed to work with SQL. These are called the *AutoCAD SQL Environment (ASE)*. The ASE syntax is derived from the ANSI X3.135–1989 SQL Standard.

ASE provides a vital link between graphic data created with AutoCAD and text and numerical data generated with DBMS. ASE enables you to relate and connect text and numerical databases with graphic information. You can then query ASE about that relationship.

Some examples of SQL in AutoCAD are presented in the following sections. Specific applications are covered later in this chapter.

Facilities management and SQL

For this example, there are three database files and a drawing of an office layout. The three files are the INVENTRY.DBF, EMPLOYEE.DBF, and COMPUTER.DBF files presented earlier. The office layout drawing contains blocks that are linked to the other database files.

A delivery of replacement file cabinets for some of the offices has just arrived. How do you find the offices with the file cabinets to be replaced? You can simply open the drawing in AutoCAD and query the database. The query could be "Which room numbers from the employee database file contain a type 45 file cabinet?" However, this is not the exact syntax you would use.

The query is requesting the database to indicate the room numbers of all rooms that contain a type 45 file cabinet. These rooms are automatically listed in a dialog box and can be highlighted on the AutoCAD drawing. The list of office numbers can then be printed for the delivery personnel to use.

Geographic mapping and SQL

SQL has an important application in geographic mapping. A *Geographic Information System (GIS)* is a detailed, relational database of geographic entities. This is a rapidly expanding application in any field that requires the use of maps.

One of the many applications of GIS and SQL is fighting wildfires. For example, a forest fire is beginning to burn in steep terrain. It is hot, the forest is dry, and the fire will begin to rage out of control in the next 12 hours because strong east winds are expected. It is imperative that the Forest Service get answers to the following questions quickly:

- What is the topography of the terrain?
- Are the roads in the area paved, gravel, unimproved? What size vehicles will the roads support?
- Are there any hiking trails that fire crews can use?
- Are there any streams? What size are they and what are the flow rates?
- Are there any lakes or ponds? What quantity of water do they hold and how deep are they? Are they accessible by aerial tankers, helicopters, or trucks?
- Are there any meadows, fields, or flat areas usable for helicopters, light aircraft, staging areas, and temporary encampments?
- What is the height, density, and species composition of the forest?
- What is the ground composition?
- What are the locations of any private residences, buildings, power lines, utilities?

All this information can be a part of a GIS used by the Forest Service. Using SQL, the query could be stated "Show all bodies of water within a one-mile radius that are suitable for access by helicopter with a water bucket." The computer searches the database/map and then highlights all applicable bodies of water. Based on the information returned, an initial determination can be made that dropping water by helicopter will extinguish the blaze or retard it enough to allow a ground fire crew to surround the blaze. Additional queries can be entered as the firefighting process continues, providing the fire managers with valuable information nearly instantaneously.

Another example of GIS and SQL usage is in emergency situations in rural areas. Suppose a call has been received at an emergency response center of a heart attack victim in a rural area. The dispatcher needs the following information:

- The exact location of the house.
- Current locations of paramedic and ambulance units.
- The closest area suitable for helicopter landing in case aerial transport is needed.
- The location of the nearest hospital or clinic that can handle the case.

The dispatcher can input the address of the house into the GIS and have it displayed on the screen. Then, the dispatcher can query the GIS for the location of emergency response units. These can also be displayed. A call can then be made to the nearest unit, directing them to respond. A query can then be made for the quickest route to the house. A request can also be made for alternate routes in case the primary one is blocked. The dispatcher can also request a display of the closest helicopter access and notify a medical flight center to be on standby. The map display and landing locations can be simultaneously displayed in the air rescue center allowing flight plans to be made quickly.

Mechanical applications of SQL

ASE has many mechanical applications. For example, a routine aircraft inspection determines that a bolt is defective. That particular type of bolt is used throughout the aircraft. It is possible that the manufacturer used inferior materials, or the manufacturing process was substandard. Therefore, all of the bolts in the aircraft must be located and inspected. The information required by the maintenance crew and management includes:

- The location of all such bolts in the aircraft.
- Other aircraft that use the bolts.
- The manufacturer of the bolts.
- The date of manufacture.
- The composition of materials.
- Test results from a finite element analysis.
- The cost of the bolt.
- The time required to replace all bolts.

The maintenance supervisor can initially query the system to highlight the location of all the defective bolts. Then, a printed list of the number of bolts in the aircraft, number of bolts in inventory, and possibly alternate suppliers of the bolt can be printed. In this example, it is important to know if the bolts in inventory are the same kind as the defective one. If so, the alternate supplier can be contacted for replacements.

DATABASE FILE STRUCTURE

The terminology used to describe the components in a database file can be confusing at first. Also, the appearance of database information used by ASE may not appear in an AutoCAD dialog box as you expected. This can be confusing as well. Therefore, read this section carefully. When you understand the nature of a database table, working with ASE becomes much easier.

Sample database layouts

In the simplest form, a database is a list of items. This list usually appears in a table. A *table* is data arranged in rows and columns. A *row* is a horizontal group of entries. A *column* is a vertical group of entries. Tables are commonly used in magazine articles and books.

A table based on the INVENTRY.DBF file is shown in Figure 15-1. The row across the top of the table contains the name of each column, such as TYPE and MFR. The column name tells you the type of information found in the column. A table is normally a separate database file.

Figure 15-1.
A table is an arrangement of rows and columns.

INVENTRY.DBF								
INV_ID	TYPE	DESCRIPT	MFGR	MODEL	CFG	PRICE	ROOM	EMP_ID
1	Furniture	6x3 Couch	Couches are Us	Lounge Cat	0	800.00	101	1000
6	Furniture	Adj. Chair	Chairs R Us	Comp Pro	0	200.00	102	1001
45	Furniture	2-piece Desk	Office Master	Desk 3	0	400.00	103	1030
78	Furniture	42x18 File cab.	Office Master	fc42x18d	0	40.00	104	1003

Database file components

Notice in Figure 15-2 that an entry in a row of the inventory table begins with the INV_ID number. Eight additional items complete the row. A row can also be called a *record* or *element.* A column contains some attribute of the row. For example, TYPE, DESCRIPT, and MFR are columns in the table. See Figure 15-3. A column is also often referred to as a *field*, especially for computer programming.

Figure 15-2.
A row is an element or entry in a table.

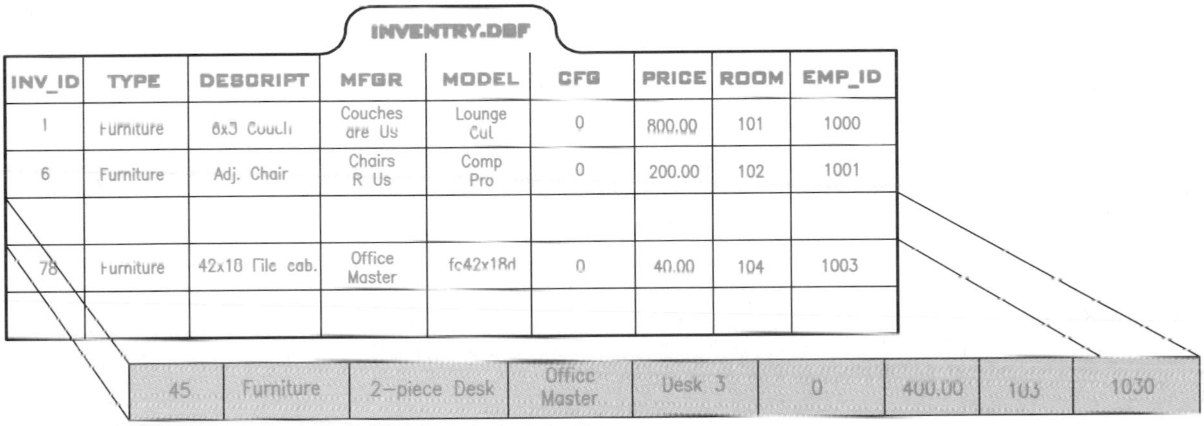

INVENTRY.DBF								
INV_ID	TYPE	DESCRIPT	MFGR	MODEL	CFG	PRICE	ROOM	EMP_ID
1	Furniture	6x3 Couch	Couches are Us	Lounge Cat	0	800.00	101	1000
6	Furniture	Adj. Chair	Chairs R Us	Comp Pro	0	200.00	102	1001
78	Furniture	42x18 File cab.	Office Master	fc42x18d	0	40.00	104	1003
45	Furniture	2-piece Desk	Office Master	Desk 3	0	400.00	103	1030

Figure 15-3.
A column contains an attribute of the row.

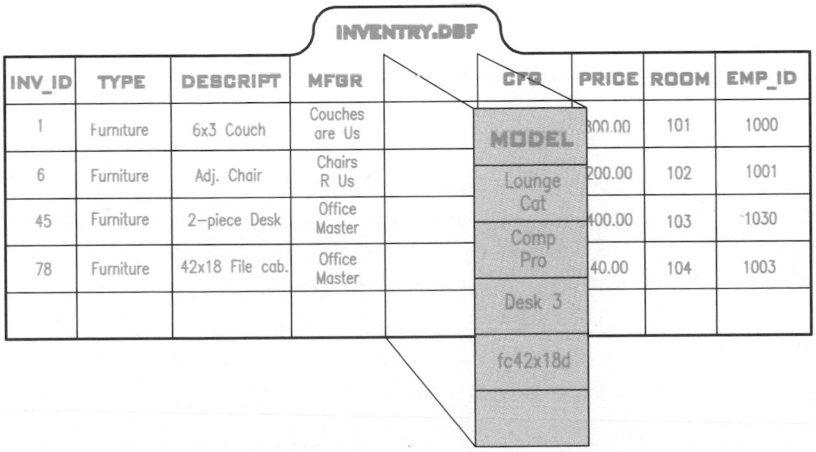

INVENTRY.DBF								
INV_ID	TYPE	DESCRIPT	MFGR		CFG	PRICE	ROOM	EMP_ID
1	Furniture	6x3 Couch	Couches are Us	MODEL		800.00	101	1000
6	Furniture	Adj. Chair	Chairs R Us	Lounge Cat		200.00	102	1001
45	Furniture	2-piece Desk	Office Master	Comp Pro		400.00	103	1030
78	Furniture	42x18 File cab.	Office Master	Desk 3		40.00	104	1003
				fc42x18d				

A table usually has a key. A *key* is a column in the table used to identify different rows in the table. The key is used as a search option. For example, the key for a sales projection table may be the MONTH column. The key can then be used to identify all of the sales projections for a certain month, such as February (the FEBRUARY row).

If more than one row can have the same value for each column, select two or more columns to be the key. This is called a *compound key.* A compound key allows a search to be more selective.

Database rows displayed in ASE

When working with ASE, you are most often using the information contained in a row. You can view the information, edit it, and link it to a graphic entity in your drawing. However, when you see a row displayed in a dialog box in AutoCAD, it does not appear horizontally. It is displayed vertically in what looks like a column. See Figure 15-4. This is an example of the **Rows** dialog box you will be working with later.

Look at the capitalized items on the left side of the list box. They may seem like different rows in a table. However, they are actually column names. The values after the | symbol are the entries in that column. Compare the information in Figure 15-4 with that in Figure 15-2.

Figure 15-4.
Row attributes are listed vertically in the **Rows** dialog box.

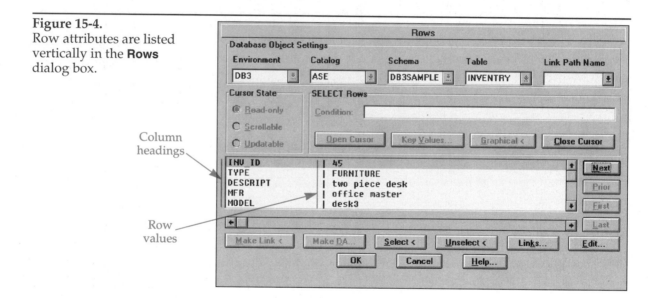

GETTING STARTED WITH ASE

Now that you are familiar with the meaning and structure of databases and their files, you can develop an understanding of how the various components of databases and AutoCAD fit together. Figure 15-5 illustrates the relationship of the DBMS, database files, and tables.

As mentioned earlier, SQL2 is a set of international standards that make up for some of the deficiencies in the original SQL standard. SQL uses databases and tables. SQL2 uses environments, catalogs, and schema. The *environment* is made up of the DBMS, the databases it can access, and the users and programs that can access those databases. The SQL2 *catalog* is like an SQL database, which contains a collection of tables with rows and columns. The catalog name points to the directory path where the database is located. A catalog is a collection of schemas. A *schema* is a single portion of the entire database. Each catalog must have a schema called the *information schema.* This schema describes the other schemas in the catalog and the tables that each schema contain.

Figure 15-5.
The relationship of the DBMS, database files, and tables.

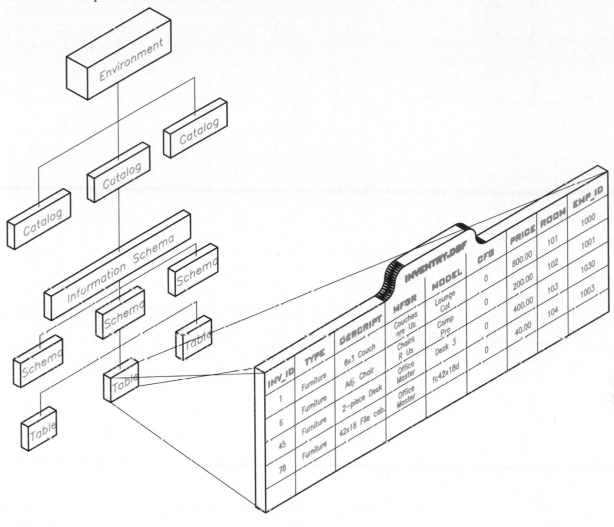

Making backup copies of the database tutorial files

Always make backup copies of database files before using them with ASE. The ASE commands can alter the content of the database files. Before you begin working through this tutorial, make copies of the following files:

        C:\R13\COM\SAMPLE\ASESMP.DWG
        C:\R13\COM\SAMPLE\DBF\COMPUTER.DBF
        C:\R13\COM\SAMPLE\DBF\EMPLOYEE.DBF
        C:\R13\COM\SAMPLE\DBF\INVENTRY.DBF

These locations are based on AutoCAD being installed on the C: drive using the R13c4 maintenance release defaults. When you want to restore the original files, simply copy them back to the original locations.

Setting the proper environment variable for ASE

AutoCAD must know which DBMS you are using and where the database files are located. This information must be specified in an environment variable. Then, when you are in AutoCAD, the ASE program must be initialized before you can work with it.

When you turn on your computer, the DOS operating system executes the instructions contained in a batch file called AUTOEXEC.BAT. A *batch file* is a group of DOS commands assembled into a text file that ends with a .BAT extension. Although batch files can be used to do any number of things, the AUTOEXEC.BAT file is used primarily to set up an environment where your software applications can run. One way this is accomplished is through the use of environment variable statements. Typically, environment variables are used to specify the directory locations of required files for your applications. These are normally set using the **PREFERENCES** command.

Before you can use ASE, you must set an environment variable that tells AutoCAD the location of the database files. This variable must be set before launching Windows and loading AutoCAD. Therefore, it is best placed in the AUTOEXEC.BAT file so that it is set as your computer boots-up. AUTOEXEC.BAT can be edited using the Windows Notepad or any other ASCII text editor. Additional information regarding Notepad and other text editors is found in Chapter 30 of *AutoCAD and its Application—Basics, Release 13 for Windows.* The following line must be added to the AUTOEXEC.BAT file:

> SET ASETUT=C:\R13\WIN\TUTORIAL\BAK

The example above assumes that AutoCAD for Windows is installed on the C: drive in a directory called R13. If your drive letter or directory name is different, be sure to substitute the parameters accordingly. Also, if you use AUTOEXEC.BAT to automatically start Windows, make sure that you add the environment variable before the statement that launches Windows. In this case the final part of your AUTOEXEC.BAT file might then look like this:

> SET TEMP=C:\WINDOWS\TEMP
> SET ASETUT=C:\R13\WIN\TUTORIAL\BAK
> WIN

Check with your instructor or supervisor if you are in doubt about how to add this environment variable to the AUTOEXEC.BAT file.

Also, be aware that if you prefer not to set the ASE environment variable in the AUTOEXEC.BAT file, the SET statement can be entered at the DOS prompt before you launch Windows. To set the environment variable at the DOS prompt, enter the following:

> C:\⟩ SET ASETUT=C:\R13\WIN\TUTORIAL\BAK↵

As with the previous example, specify the appropriate drive and directory if different from that shown above. After setting the environment variable in this manner, you can then start Windows and load AutoCAD. If you use the previous example, you must reset this variable each time you restart your computer.

SQL2 assumes everything is running on a network and handles file locking as such. If you are running in a stand-alone mode in DOS or Windows 3.11 you must run the DOS program SHARE before you start AutoCAD for DOS or before you enter Windows. Windows for Workgroups 3.11 automatically runs the SHARE program.

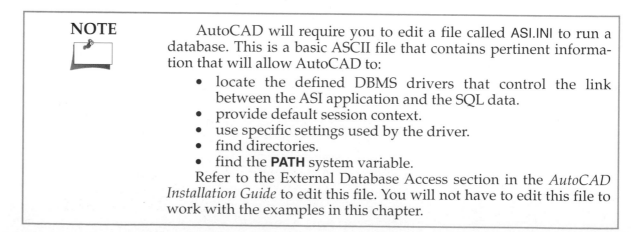

NOTE

AutoCAD will require you to edit a file called ASI.INI to run a database. This is a basic ASCII file that contains pertinent information that will allow AutoCAD to:
- locate the defined DBMS drivers that control the link between the ASI application and the SQL data.
- provide default session context.
- use specific settings used by the driver.
- find directories.
- find the **PATH** system variable.

Refer to the External Database Access section in the *AutoCAD Installation Guide* to edit this file. You will not have to edit this file to work with the examples in this chapter.

CREATING THE DATABASE ENVIRONMENT

If all files for Windows and ASE were installed properly, you should have no problem working with the examples in this text. Before you begin, the programs that run ASE must be loaded. The following procedure loads ASE, directing AutoCAD to the database information.

The administration procedure must be completed each time you work with ASE. This procedure creates a path and links to the proper database files, catalogs, schema, and tables. Once ASE is loaded into your drawing, you can work with the example that comes with AutoCAD.

> **NOTE**
>
> When a drawing is saved and AutoCAD is closed, you must reload the ASE every time you open the drawing. The catalogs, schemas, and tables are saved to the database, but AutoCAD loses the database link.

Check to be sure that the **CMDDIA** variable is set to 1, so that dialog boxes can be used with the ASE commands.

    Command: **CMDDIA**↵
    New value for CMDDIA ⟨0⟩: **1**↵

> **NOTE**
>
> If you are typing the commands at the **Command:** prompt, all of the ASE commands begin with the ASE prefix.

From the **Tools** pull-down menu, pick **Toolbars**, and **External Database**. This displays the **External Database** toolbar. Now from the toolbar, select the **Administration** button, or type ASEADMIN. The **Administration** dialog box is displayed. See Figure 15-6.

Pick the **About Env...** button. A list of defined environments will be displayed. Highlight DB3 and pick the **Connect...** button at the right side of the dialog box. The **Connect to Environment** dialog box is displayed. This example uses DBASE3 as the database management system.

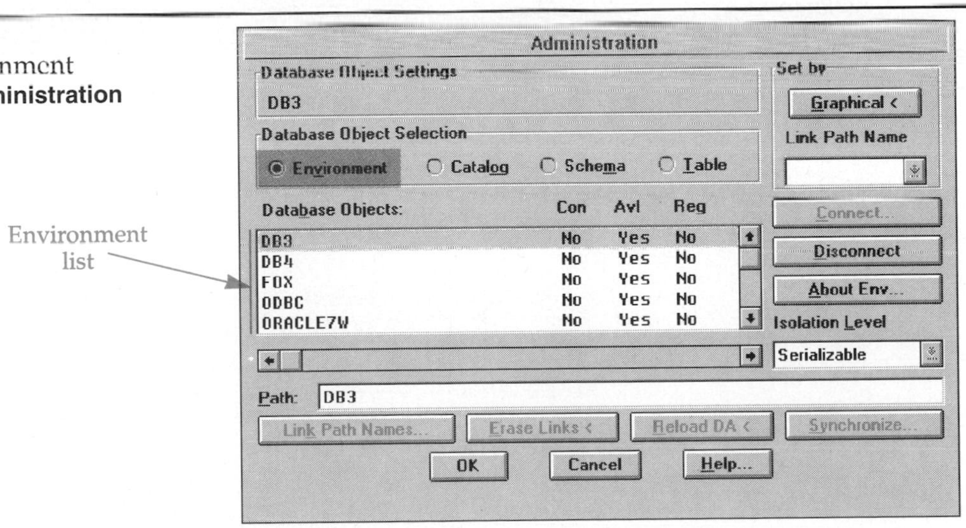

Figure 15-6.
The ASE environment is set in the **Administration** dialog box.

Environment list

If your environment requires a user name and password information, enter them. This is the network option mentioned earlier. If it does not, just select **OK**. See Figure 15-7.

Next, select **Catalog** in the **Administration** dialog box. This displays a list of available catalogs in the environment. Highlight ASE. See Figure 15-8.

Pick **Schema** next. This is the database table held in the designated location. Highlight DB3SAMPLE. See Figure 15-9.

Pick **Table**. This displays the database information, organized in rows and columns. Click on EMPLOYEE. You have loaded ASE and now have access to the EMPLOYEE database table. See Figure 15-10.

Figure 15-7.
The **Connect to Environment** dialog box.

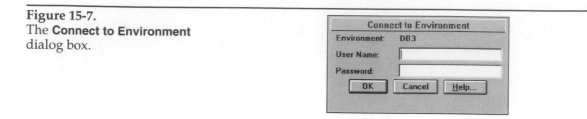

Figure 15-8.
The **Catalog** radio button displays available catalogs.

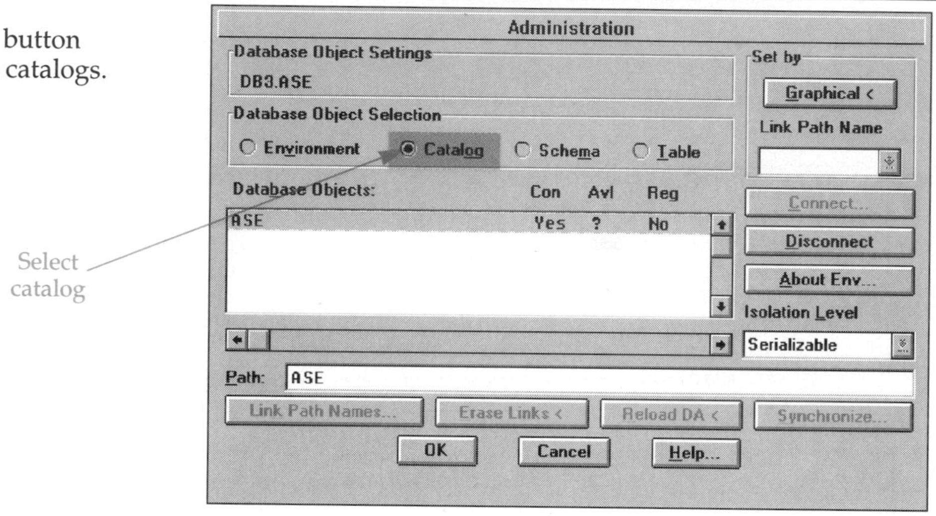

Figure 15-9.
Picking the **Schema** radio button lists the DB3SAMPLE schema.

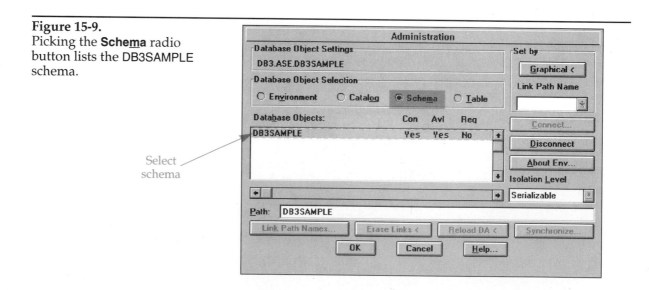

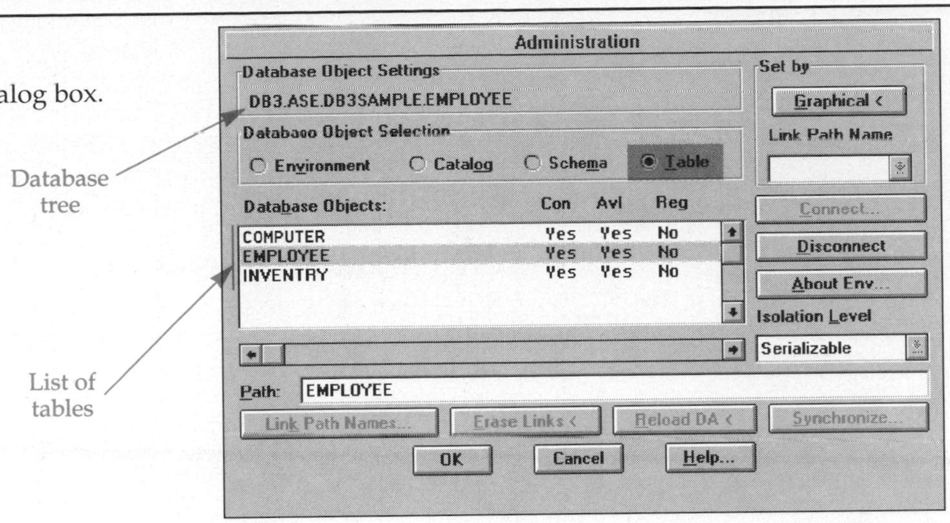

Figure 15-10.
The completed
Administration dialog box.

Database tree

List of tables

Linking a drawing to a database

After loading ASE and connecting database objects, you are able to link drawings to the database. When you highlight a table in the **Administration** dialog box, the **Link Path Names...** button is enabled. Picking this button displays the **Link Path Names** dialog box, as shown in Figure 15-11. This dialog box provides an area for key column selection.

A *key* specifies a column or set of columns whose values will be used to identify a specified row in the table. To set a column as a key, highlight the column and then pick the **On** button. More than one column can be selected as a key. Set the LAST_NAME and DEPT columns as keys.

Once the key selection items are selected, enter a new path name in the **New:** text box, then pick **New**. When you exit the dialog box, the new path name will be registered and you return to the **Administration** dialog box. Set a new path as EMPLOYEE_INFO.

There are three columns in the **Database Objects:** list: **Con**, **Avl**, and **Reg**. See Figure 15-10. **Con** indicates if a database object is connected to the DBMS that is loaded into memory. **Avl** indicates that an environment listed in the ASI.INI file has been connected and is available for use. **Reg** indicates that key columns have been registered in an associated table.

Figure 15-11.
Key columns are selected in the **Link Path Names** dialog box.

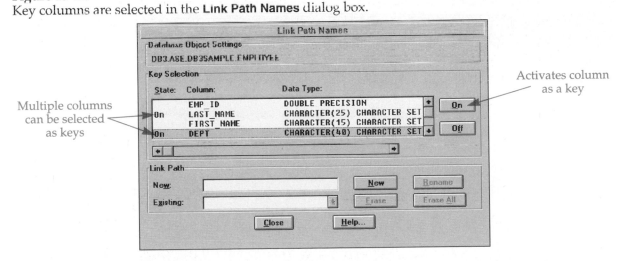

Multiple columns can be selected as keys

Activates column as a key

PROFESSIONAL TIP

You can select more than one column name to create a *compound key*. Some database tables may have rows with the same value for one or more of the columns. If so, picking only one column for the key may retrieve more than one row when you query for information. If you wish to be more selective of the row that is retrieved, pick more than one column as a key.

If you know you will need more than one table to work with on a project, it is a good idea to set them at the beginning of a drawing session. The last table that is set becomes the current one.

EXERCISE 15-1

❑ In the **Administration** dialog box, select the INVENTRY table.
❑ Use the INV_ID column as the key.
❑ Select the COMPUTER table.
❑ Use the COMP_CFG column as the key.
❑ Do *not* save the drawing.

USING SQL

The purpose of the following example and the exercises in this chapter is to illustrate the use of ASE to link graphic entities in an AutoCAD drawing with rows in a database table. The first part of this exercise steps through information that is already in the database. Then you will add a new employee to the EMPLOYEE database file (table).

Open the drawing named ASESMP.DWG located in the C:\R13\COM\SAMPLE directory. After the drawing is loaded, you need to initialize ASE, using the steps explained previously.

Set the current table to EMPLOYEE. You are now ready to edit the EMPLOYEE section of this table.

The SQL editor executes SQL statements from the user interface, from files, or from a list of previously executed commands saved in memory. Pick **External Database** then **SQL Editor** from the **Tools** pull-down menu. The **SQL Editor** dialog box appears, as shown in Figure 15-12. The dialog box can also be accessed by picking the **SQL EDITOR** button on the **External Database** toolbar or by typing ASESQLED at the **Command:** prompt.

Figure 15-12.
Queries of the database can be made in the **SQL Editor** dialog box.

SQL Editor
Database Object Settings
Environment: DB3   Catalog: ASE   Schema: DB3SAMPLE
Transaction Mode: ○ Read-only ◉ Read-write
History: select * from inventry where room = '127'
Cursor State: ☐ Scrollable
Isolation Level: Serializable
SQL Statement
SQL: select * from inventry where room = '127' ← Query
☒ Autocommit   ☐ Native   [Execute]   [File...]
[Commit] [Rollback] [Close] [Help...]

Enter the following in the **SQL Statement:** text box:

    select * from inventry where room = '127'

Pick the **Execute** button or press [Enter].

The database is queried directly. The results are displayed in the **SQL Cursor** dialog box, as shown in Figure 15-13. This is an example of how you can use an SQL query to select information. Pick **Close** to remove the dialog.

Figure 15-13.
The query result is displayed in the **SQL Cursor** dialog box.

Row information returned in response to query

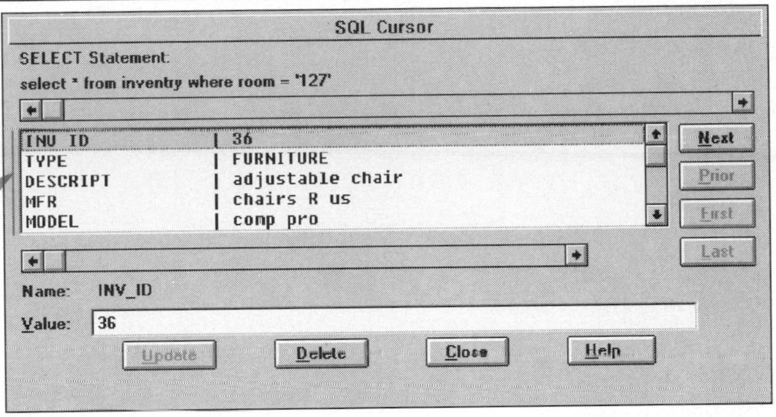

WORKING WITH ROWS

Most of your work in ASE will be with rows. You will be either viewing, editing, displaying, or linking them to a drawing entity. Remember that a row is an entry in a database file (schema) that contains several attributes. The following discussion shows you how to use rows in a variety of ways.

Understanding the Rows dialog box

The last table to be set remains the current one, and will be displayed when the **Rows** dialog box is opened. Before setting a row, be sure the correct table is current using the **Administration** dialog box as explained previously.

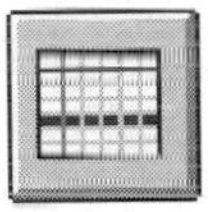

To access the **Rows** dialog box, pick **External Database** then **Rows...** from the **Tools** pull-down menu; pick the **Rows** button from the **External Database** toolbar, or type ASEROWS at the **Command:** prompt. The **Rows** dialog box is shown in Figure 15-14. Notice the three areas at the top of the dialog box.

- **Database Object Settings**—Displays the current database settings. Each setting can be changed by picking the pop-up list.
- **Cursor State**—The *cursor* is the current row that is displayed. Using the three radio buttons in this area, you can control how you work with the information in the current row.
- **SELECT Rows**—Using this area you can select a row using one of several methods.

The items displayed in the **Database Object Settings** area indicate the settings previously created in the **Administration** dialog box. Notice that the section in the center of the dialog box is blank. Row information in the current table can be displayed here.

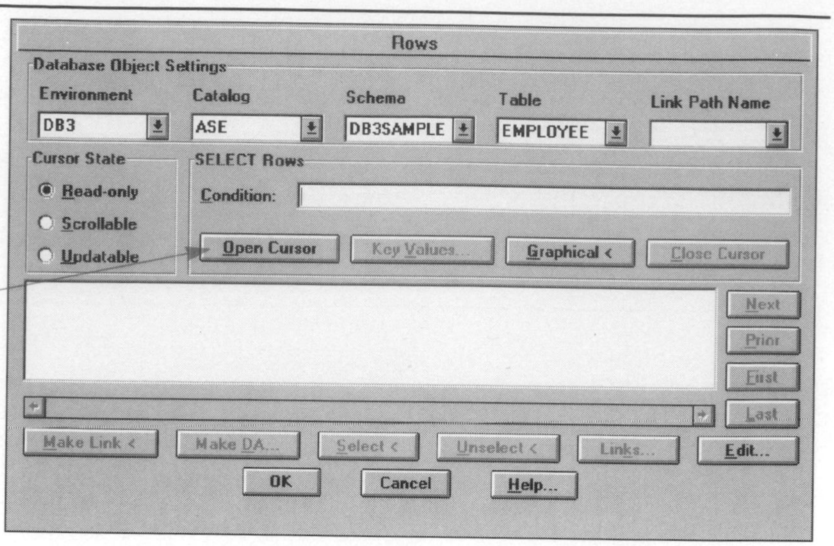

Figure 15-14.
Rows from any table can be
displayed in the **Rows**
dialog box.

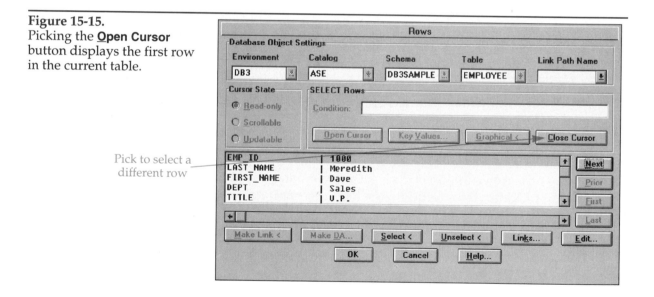

Displaying row data

The current row can be displayed by pressing [Enter] or by picking the **Open Cursor** button. This displays the columns for the first row in the EMPLOYEE table, as shown in Figure 15-15. Also notice that the row is displayed in a column fashion. The column headings are displayed on the left side of the list. You can use the scroll bar to see the remaining columns in the table. When you are finished viewing the data, pick the **Close Cursor** button.

Figure 15-15.
Picking the **Open Cursor**
button displays the first row
in the current table.

A second method for displaying row data is to write an SQL query in the **Condition:** text box. This statement must begin with a column name, then an equal sign (=), and end with the search string in single quotes. For example, if you wanted to display employees who's last name was Williams, enter the following in the **Condition:** text box, and press [Enter]:

    LAST_NAME = 'Williams'

The first row that matches your query is displayed in the list box, and all of the **SELECT Rows** options are disabled except for the **Close Cursor** button. If more than one row matches your query, pick the **Next** button to view it. See Figure 15-16. When you are finished viewing the data, pick the **Close Cursor** button. This returns to the default state of the dialog box.

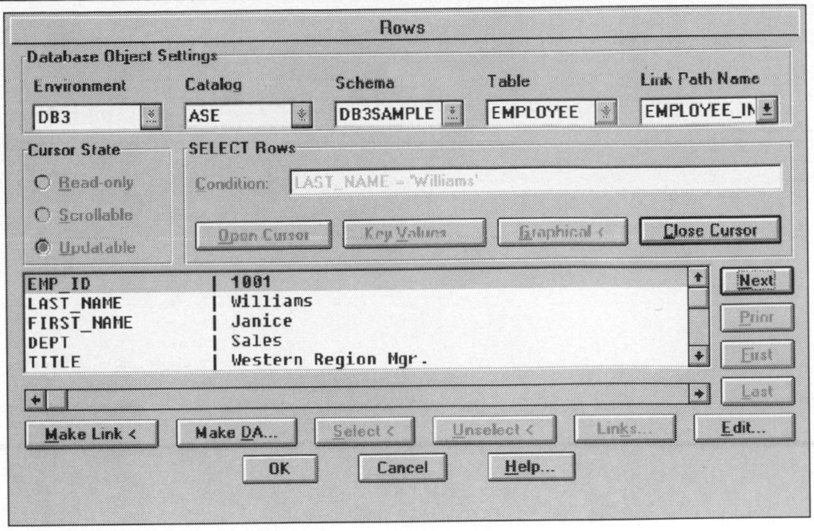

Figure 15-16.
Row data can be displayed
as a result of a query in the
Condition: text box of the
Rows dialog box.

A third method for searching out row data is to enter key values. Pick the **Key Values...** button to display the **Select Row by Key Values** dialog box. This displays the key columns that you initially selected in the **Administration** dialog box.

Begin the search by highlighting the key value in the list box that you wish to use. In this example, the DEPT key is selected. This is displayed in the **Name:** field below. Now enter the selection criteria in the **Value:** text box and press [Enter]. This value is then displayed in the list box under the **Values:** heading. See Figure 15-17. Pick **OK** to begin the search.

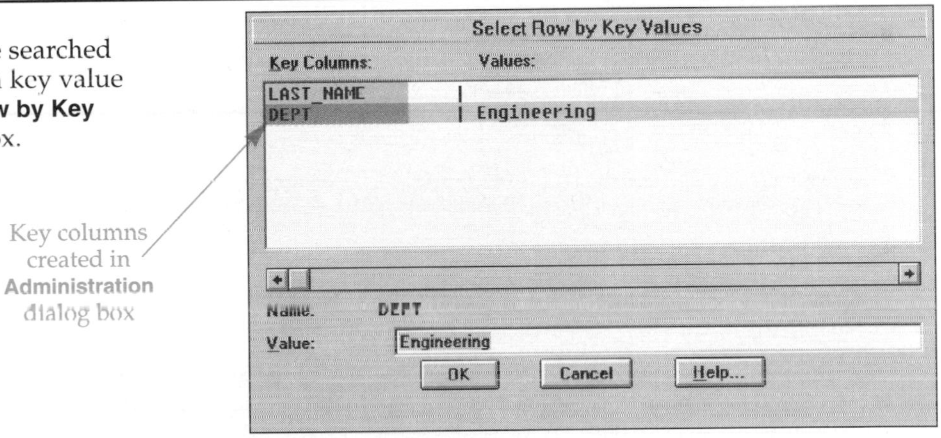

Figure 15-17.
Row data can be searched
for by entering a key value
in the **Select Row by Key
Values** dialog box.

Key columns
created in
Administration
dialog box

The first row that meets the search criteria is displayed in the **Rows** dialog box. Notice in Figure 15-18 that the search value you used is now listed in the **Condition:** text box.

The fourth method for displaying row data is to select an object in the AutoCAD drawing by picking the **Graphical ⟨** button. If this button is disabled, pick the **Close Cursor** button to remove the current row display and activate the row selection options.

Picking the **Graphical ⟨** button returns the graphic screen and issues the Select object: prompt. Pick office number 109. The **Links** dialog box is displayed with the key value of the row that is linked to your selection, as shown in Figure 15-19. In this case, the link is to employee number 1008. Pick **OK** to return to the **Rows** dialog box, which now contains the row data for employee number 1008.

Figure 15-18.
The result of a key value search. The value is displayed in the **Condition:** text box.

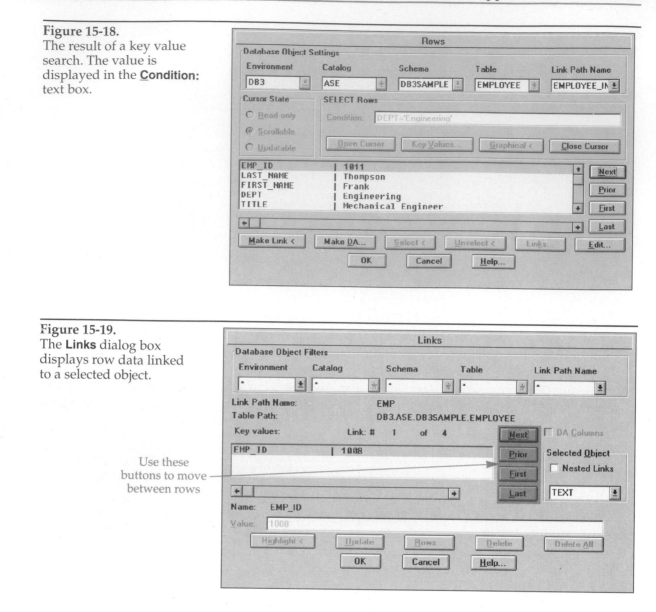

Figure 15-19.
The **Links** dialog box displays row data linked to a selected object.

Use these buttons to move between rows

When row data is displayed you can view the next row by picking the **Next** button. The remaining three scrolling buttons are disabled if the **Scrollable** radio button in the **Cursor State** area is not selected. You can activate the scrolling buttons by first picking **Close Cursor**, then pick **Scrollable** radio button. Now pick **Open Cursor**. Notice that the **Prior**, **First**, and **Last** buttons can now be used. These enable you to move through the rows quickly.

Editing a row

You can also edit the row in the database table. In the **Rows** dialog box, select the **Close Cursor** button. This temporarily clears the window, but allows you to change the **Cursor State**. Choose the **Updatable** radio button then pick the **Open Cursor** button. If you do not pick the **Updatable** radio button you will not be able to edit the row data. Use the **Next** button to find the employee 1007. Select the **Edit...** button to display the **Edit Row** dialog box. See Figure 15-20.

In the **Edit Row** dialog box, scroll to find the room number and pick it. The column name appears in the **Name:** field below the list box. The **Value:** of the current room appears, which in this case is 109. Change the room number to 121 and press [Enter]. The **Update** button becomes active. Select it and the Row is updated message is displayed in the lower-left corner. See Figure 15-21. Pick **Close** to save the change. Check the **Rows** dialog box to be sure that the room number has changed to 121.

Figure 15-20.
The **Edit Row** dialog box.

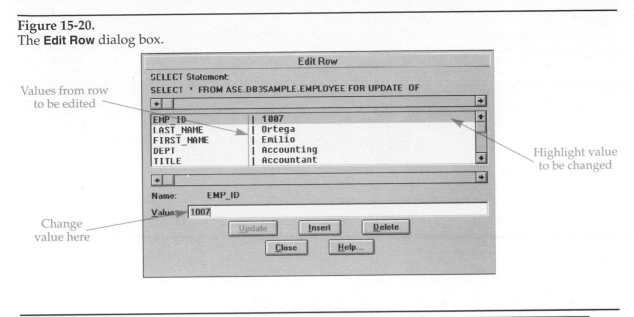

Values from row to be edited

Highlight value to be changed

Change value here

Figure 15-21.
The updated row is displayed in the **Edit Row** dialog box.

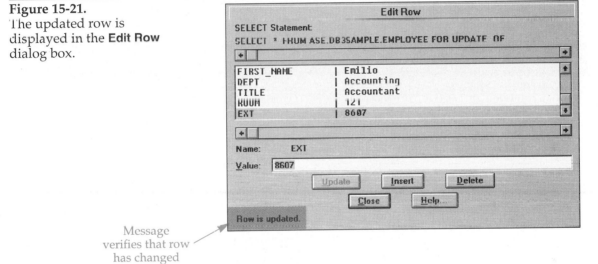

Message verifies that row has changed

Adding a row

You can also add a row using the **Rows** dialog box. To insert a new employee you must select the **Updatable** radio button, then the **Edit...** button. The **Edit Row** dialog box appears. The row data is blank. See Figure 15-22.

The column that is highlighted in the list box is displayed in the **Name:** field below. You can type a new value for this column in the **Value:** text box, then press [Enter]. This new value is entered in the list box and the LAST_NAME column is highlighted. The **Value:** text box becomes current, so type the last name and press [Enter]. Continue in this manner until all values for the new row have been entered. Type the following to create a new row:

```
EMP_ID        |2000
LAST_NAME     |Wilbourn
FIRST_NAME    |Rachel
DEPT          |CAD
TITLE         |Engineer
ROOM          |108
EXT           |0002
```

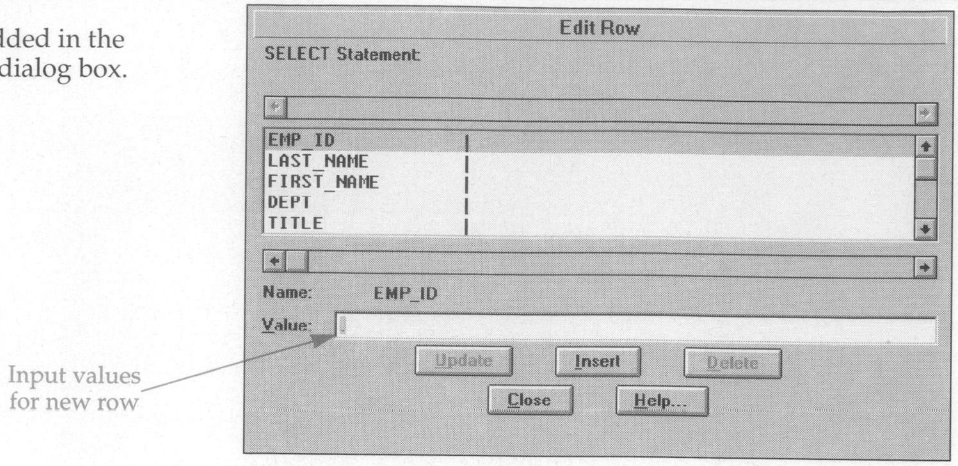

Figure 15-22.
A row can be added in the
blank **Edit Row** dialog box.

Input values
for new row

Pick the **Insert** button to insert the new row. AutoCAD displays the Row is inserted message. See Figure 15-23.

Close this dialog box and pick **OK** to exit the **Rows** dialog box. Use the SQL Editor to see if the employee has been added to the database. Open the **SQL Editor** dialog box and type the following in the **SQL:** text box:

select * from EMPLOYEE where emp_id = 2000

Pick the **Execute** button to begin the search. The **SQL Cursor** dialog box displays the results. See Figure 15-24. Close the dialog box to return to the **SQL Editor** dialog box. Your original search statement is now displayed in the **History** list box. See Figure 15-25.

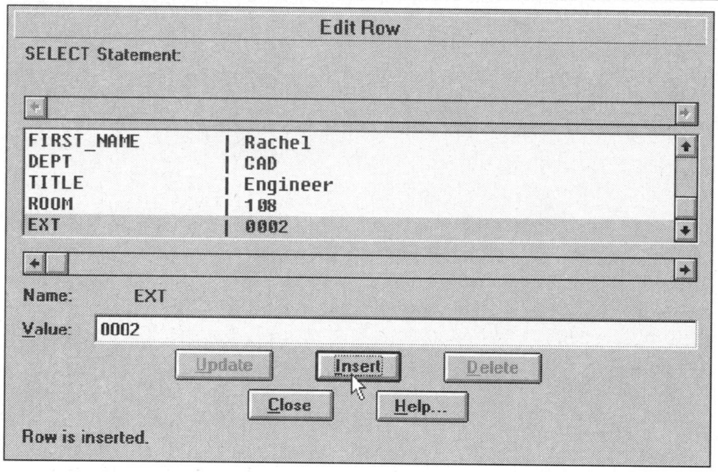

Figure 15-23.
The inserted row is
displayed in the **Edit Row**
dialog box.

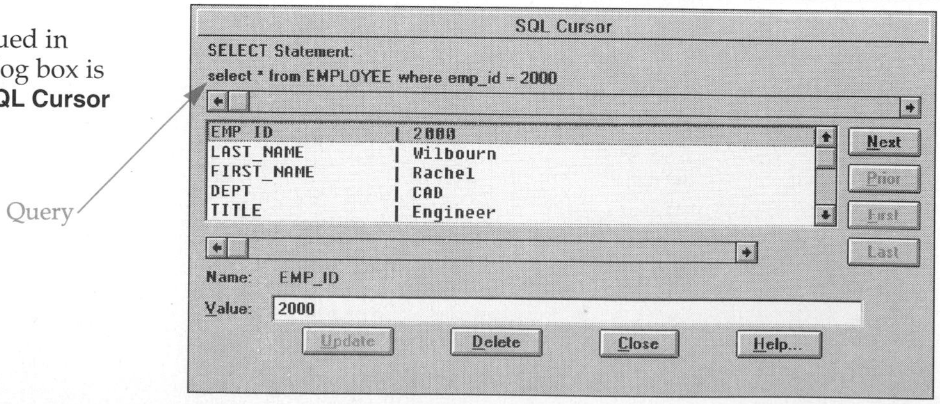

Figure 15-24.
A search query issued in
the **SQL Editor** dialog box is
displayed in the **SQL Cursor**
dialog box.

Query

Figure 15-25.
The SQL query is displayed
in the **History** list box.

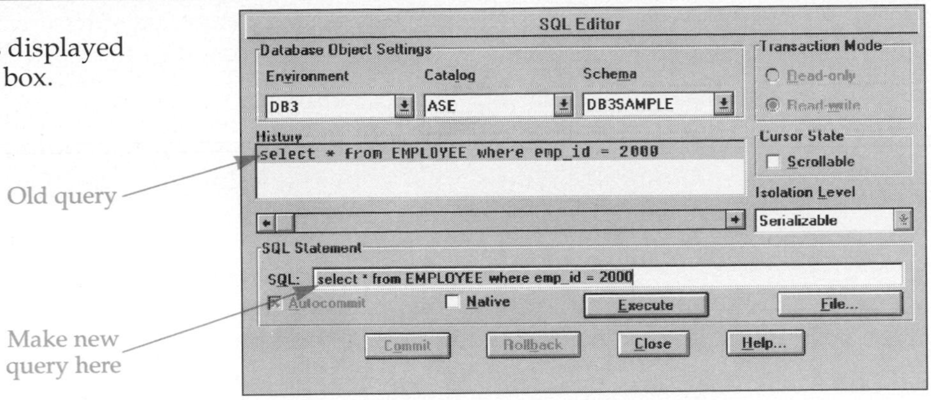

Old query

Make new
query here

EXERCISE 15-2

❑ Open the ASESMP.DWG.
❑ Open the **Administration** dialog box.
❑ Add a new row to the EMPLOYEE table. Use the following information:

Column	Value
EMP_ID	1038
LAST_NAME	Desque
FIRST_NAME	Otto
DEPT	Publications
TITLE	Graphics Specialist
ROOM	122
EXT	8627

❑ View the current row to check your work.
❑ Set the INVENTRY table as current and add a new row with the following values:

Column	Value
INV_ID	2158
TYPE	Hardware
DESCRIPT	Personal inventory
MFR	HARDWIRE HARDWARE
MODEL	cpu7
COMP_CFG	7
PRICE	4900.00
ROOM	122
EMP_ID	1038

❑ View the current row to check your work.
❑ Save the drawing as EX15-2.

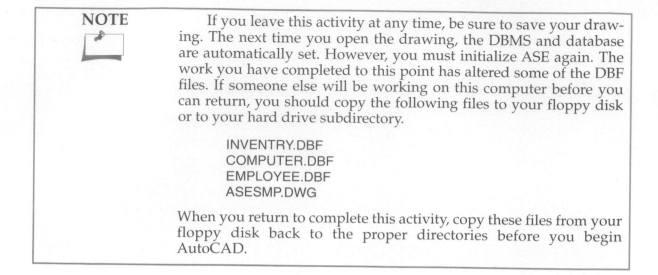

NOTE   If you leave this activity at any time, be sure to save your drawing. The next time you open the drawing, the DBMS and database are automatically set. However, you must initialize ASE again. The work you have completed to this point has altered some of the DBF files. If someone else will be working on this computer before you can return, you should copy the following files to your floppy disk or to your hard drive subdirectory.

> INVENTRY.DBF
> COMPUTER.DBF
> EMPLOYEE.DBF
> ASESMP.DWG

When you return to complete this activity, copy these files from your floppy disk back to the proper directories before you begin AutoCAD.

WORKING WITH SELECTION SETS

Simple selection sets can be created using the **Rows** dialog box. These selection sets can be used for finding and viewing objects linked to the current row data. The selected objects can be highlighted or unhighlighted, and used in editing operations.

The **ASESELECT** command allows you to create two selection sets based on textual and graphical data. These two selection sets can be combined or subtracted from each other to create a more defined set.

Using the Rows dialog box to create a selection set

In order to create a selection set in the **Rows** dialog box, row data must be shown in the list box. Display a row using any one of the methods described previously. Next pick the **Select ⟨** button. The dialog box is dismissed and all AutoCAD objects linked to the current row are highlighted. Press [Enter] and the highlighted objects are added to the selection set. A message in the lower-left corner of the dialog box indicates this. See Figure 15-26. In the example used in Figure 15-26, office number 106 was highlighted because it is the only AutoCAD object linked to the current row.

Figure 15-26.
The **Rows** dialog box can be used to create a selection set.

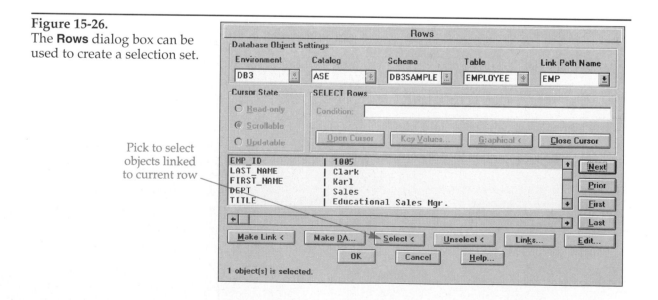

Pick to select objects linked to current row

Using the Select Objects dialog box to create a selection set

The **ASESELECT** command can create two different selection sets, A and B. Set A is composed of textual data that is specified in the **Select Objects** dialog box. Set B is composed of AutoCAD objects that are linked to selection set A.

Pick **External Database** then **Select Objects** in the **Tools** pull-down menu to display the **Select Objects** dialog box. The dialog box can also be accessed by picking the **Select Objects** button on the **External Database** toolbar, or by typing ASESELECT at the **Command:** prompt. See Figure 15-27.

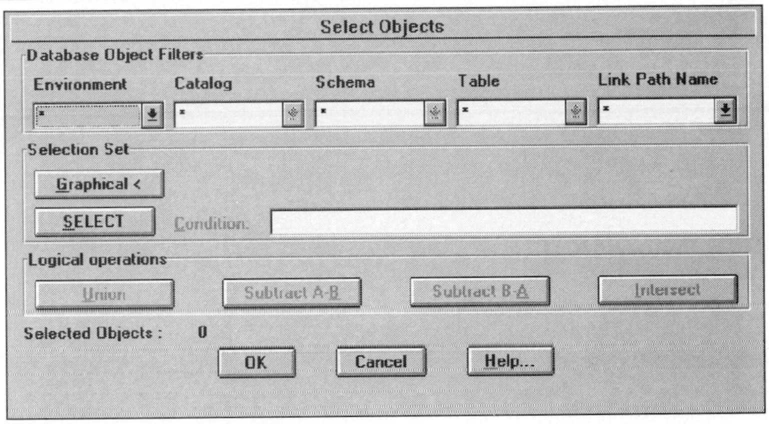

Figure 15-27.
The **Select Objects** dialog box is used to create combined selection sets.

To create a selection set you must set the **Database Object Filters** to the proper environment. These are the same settings used in the **Administration** dialog box to begin a session. The settings should look like those in Figure 15-28.

A selection set can now be created in two different ways. Objects can be selected from the graphics screen using the **Graphical** ⟨ button, or a condition statement can be used to specify the contents of the set. First type a statement in the **Condition:** text box that describes the object you wish to select, then press [Enter]:

    descript = '36x12 file cabinet'

Figure 15-28.
The **Database Object Filters** are used to create a selection set.

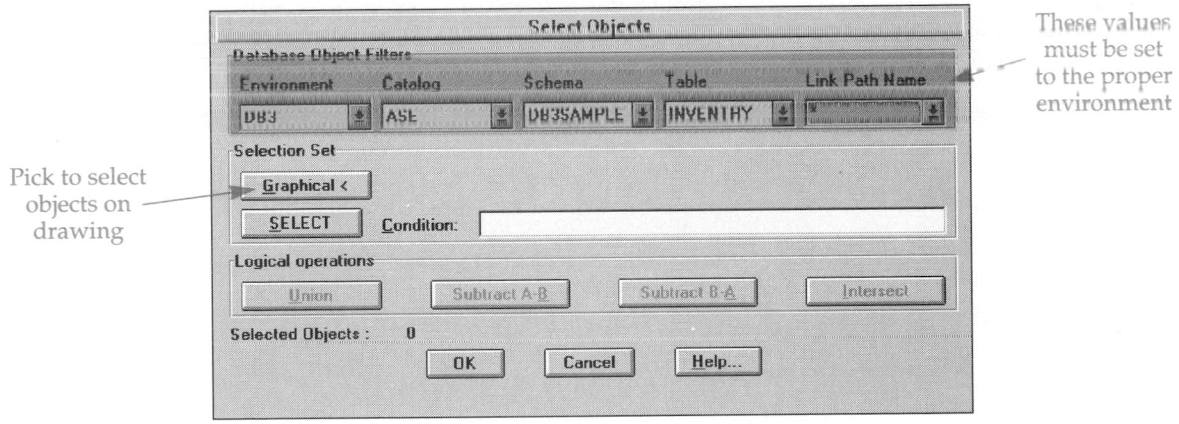

This creates set A, the textual description. Now pick the **Intersect** button to create a selection set that combines set A and set B. Next pick the **Graphical** ⟨ button. AutoCAD dismisses the dialog box for you to select the objects to be included in this selection set. Make a window selection around all of the rooms along the top of the drawing, then press [Enter]. This creates selection set B.

Even though AutoCAD reports that you selected nearly 300 objects, when the dialog box returns, a message indicates that five objects were selected. That is because you specified that the selection set was to be an *intersection* of sets A and B. Therefore AutoCAD applied the conditional specification of a 36 × 12 file cabinet to only those rooms you selected and found five objects. See Figure 15-29.

A new selection set can be created in four different ways using a union, intersection, or subtraction of sets A and B. These functions are displayed as buttons in the **Logical operations** area of the **Select Objects** dialog box.

- **Union**—Combines all criteria and objects in sets A and B to create a selection set.
- **Intersect**—Creates a selection set of only those objects defined by both set A and B.
- **Subtract A-B**—Set B is subtracted from set A to create the new selection set.
- **Subtract B-A**—Set A is subtracted from set B to create the new selection set.

The new selection set can be displayed quickly by using the **SELECT** button or any edit command and the **Previous** option.

Figure 15-29.
An intersect selection set combines textual and graphical information.

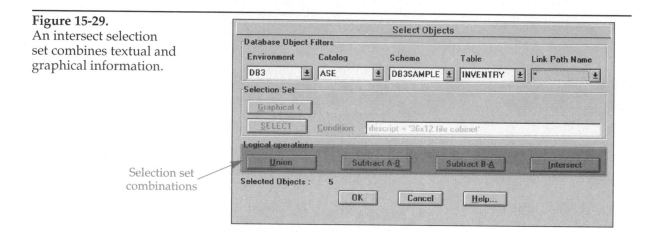

Selection set combinations

LINKING THE DATABASE TO THE DRAWING

A *link* is a connection between a graphic object in the AutoCAD drawing and a row, table, and database. You can select an object in the drawing, such as a computer, and have immediate access to all of the information stored in the database about that computer. Using ASE and the **ASELINKS** command, you can create, delete, view, and edit links.

Viewing an existing link

To initiate the **ASELINKS** command, pick **External Database** then **Links...** from the **Tools** pull-down menu, pick the **Links** button from the **External Database** toolbar, or type ASELINKS at the **Command:** prompt. The Select object: prompt appears. Zoom in to room 109 at the upper-right corner of the drawing, then pick the number 109. The **Links** dialog box is then displayed, as shown in Figure 15-30.

Figure 15-30.
The **Links** dialog box can be used to view links.

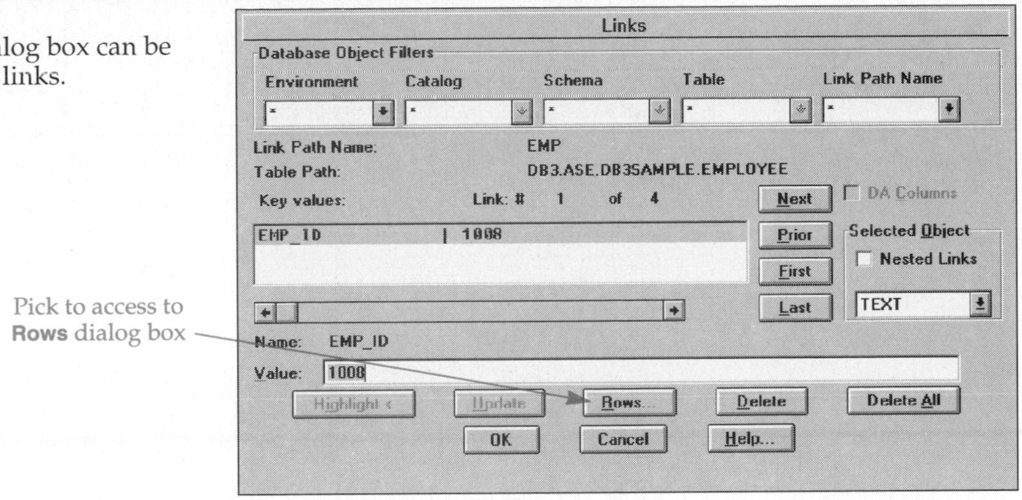

The list box displays the key values of the first row that is linked to the selected object. The **Link:** field just above the list box indicates how many links exist to the selected object. In this case there are four links. You can scroll through the links by using one of the scroll buttons to the right of the list box.

If you wish to view more than just the key values of the current link, pick the **Rows...** button. This displays the **Rows** dialog box and all of the data on the current row. You cannot use the **Next** button because only the current row is displayed in this dialog box. See Figure 15-31. Pick **OK** to return to the **Links** dialog box.

Figure 15-31.
The **Rows** dialog box displays all of the current row data in the current link.

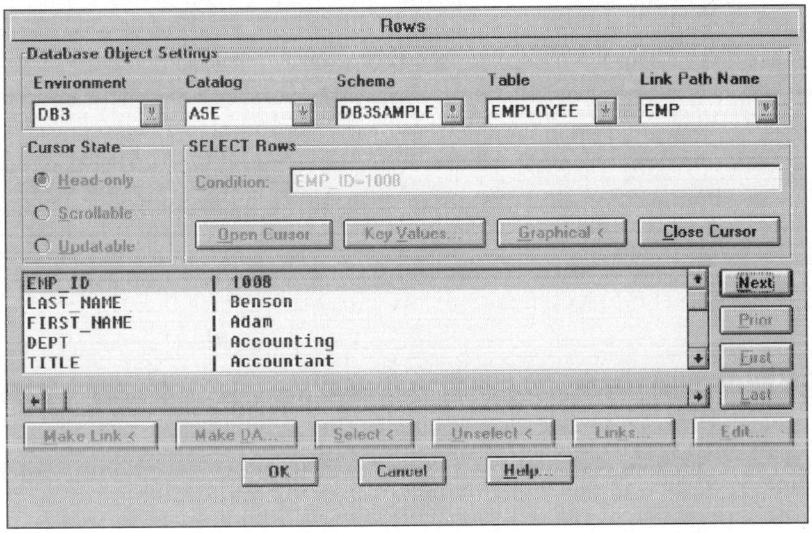

Creating a link

A link can be created between a row in a table and an AutoCAD object. An AutoCAD object can have links to more than one row in a table, and also to more than one table or database.

Links are made using the **Rows** dialog box. First, be sure that **ASEADMIN** has been used to set up the proper environment with a path link and key values. Then pick the **Make Link ⟨** button in the **Rows** dialog box. Select the objects in the AutoCAD drawing that you want to link to the current row then press [Enter]. A message in the lower-left of the dialog box indicates that the link has been made. See Figure 15-32.

Figure 15-32.
A new link is created in
the **Rows** dialog box.

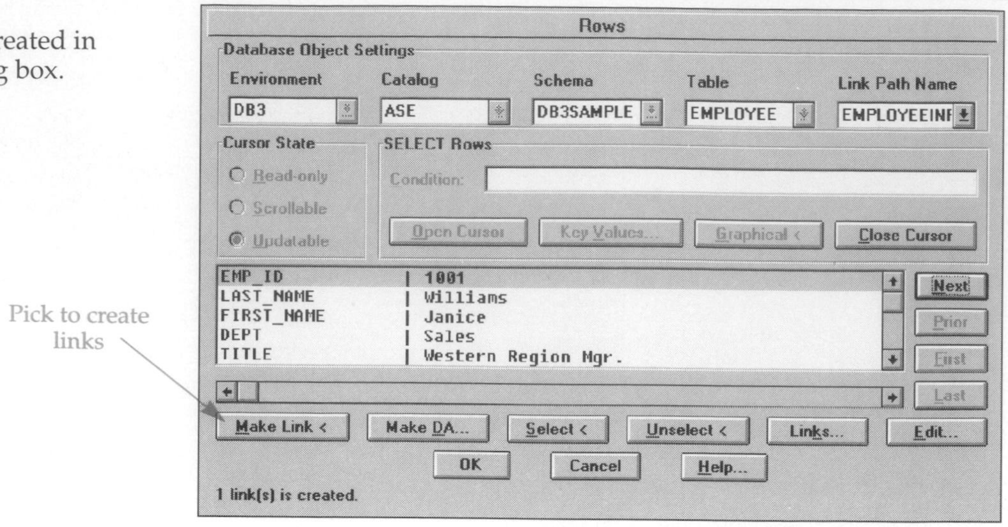

Pick to create
links

You can check to see if the link was successful by using the process described in the previous section.

Editing an existing link

Links between AutoCAD objects and database rows may have to be changed because the current data is no longer valid. This process is just as easy as creating a link. First use the **ASELINKS** command and select the object whose link must be edited. The **Links** dialog box is displayed. Check to see if there are multiple links. If so, scroll to the link you wish to edit and pick the **Rows...** button. This displays the **Rows** dialog box.

Use one of the row selection methods previously described to make the new row current. This row will become the new link after you pick **OK** to exit the dialog box.

Deleting an existing link

If an object in an AutoCAD drawing must be linked to a row, it might be important first to delete any existing links. This is quick and easy. Use the **ASELINKS** command and select the desired object(s). The **Links** dialog box displays all current links. Use the scroll buttons to display each link. Pick the **Delete** button to remove the link to the row currently displayed. A message in the lower-left indicates that the Link is deleted. Pick **OK** when you are done.

EXERCISE 15-3

❑ Open ASESMP.DWG if it is not already loaded.
❑ Use **ASEADMIN** to establish the environment and set the INVENTRY table current.
❑ View the links to the computer in the upper-right corner of room 105. Fill in the following data regarding the computer.

EMP_ID	1004
PRICE	1300
INV_ID	126
MODEL	CPU1

❑ Janice Williams and Jill Smith have exchanged rooms. They took their computers with them, but all other furniture remained. Edit all of the links associated with these two employees.
❑ Dave Meredith retired and was replaced by Rosalyn Cramer. She took his office. Delete and edit all necessary links.
❑ Save your drawing as EX15-3.

DISPLAYABLE ATTRIBUTES

A *displayable attribute* is similar to a block attribute, except it gets its text information from the database table. The text is an AutoCAD block and is composed of values from a row that you select. For example, you can select any of the column values of a row in the EMPLOYEE table to be displayed in that employee's office. The text will reflect the attribute values in the linked row. You can store the text information in the drawing near the entity it describes.

Select the **Rows** button or type **ASEROWS** at the **Command:** prompt. In the **Rows** dialog box, pick the **Updatable** radio button then pick the **Graphical** ⟨ button. This temporarily closes the dialog box to allow you to pick entities. Pick the room number 106. The dialog box is redisplayed with the linked row information in the list box. See Figure 15-33.

Figure 15-33.
The **Rows** dialog box is used to select an object for attaching a displayable attribute.

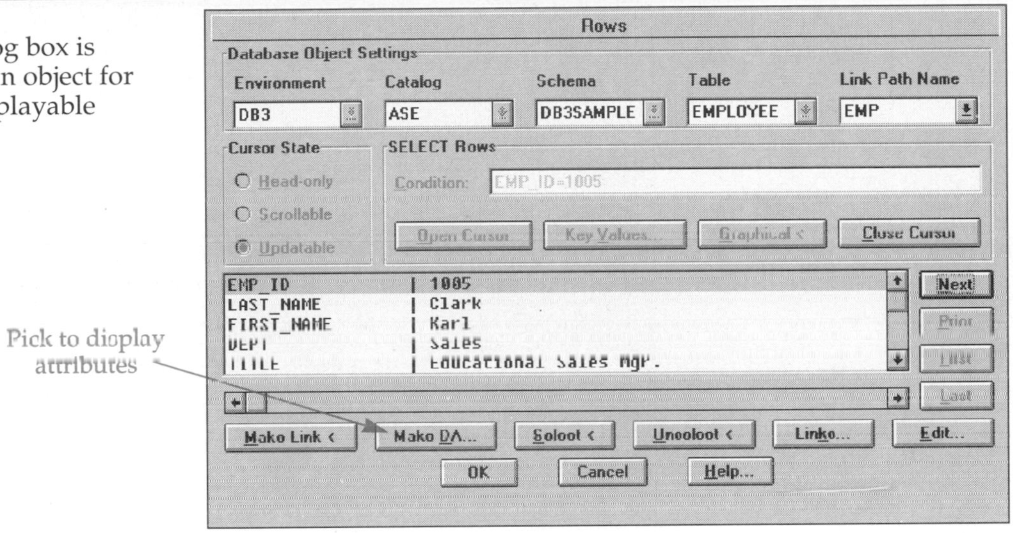

Choose the **Make DA...** button. The **Make Displayable Attribute** dialog box appears with the table columns listed on the left. Select the first column you wish displayed then pick the **Add** ⟨- button. This displays the table column in the **DA Columns:** list. Repeat this process for each column that you want to be a displayable attribute. The **Add All** ⟨- button makes all columns displayable attributes. The **Remove All** ⟨- button removes all of the entries from the **DA Columns:** list. If you wish to remove a single item from the **DA Columns:** list, highlight it and then pick the **Remove** ⟨- button.

The displayable attribute text can also be formatted. If you have predefined text styles, choose one from the **Text Style:** pop-up list. For this example, choose the **Justification** pop-up list and center the text. Change the text height to 1′ 3″. See Figure 15-34. Pick **OK**. AutoCAD prompts you to select your center point for the text. Once you do, the **Rows** dialog box reappears with the text information in the box. Pick **OK** and the attributes are displayed at the selected point, Figure 15-35.

Figure 15-34.
Displayable attributes are created in the **Make Displayable Attribute** dialog box.

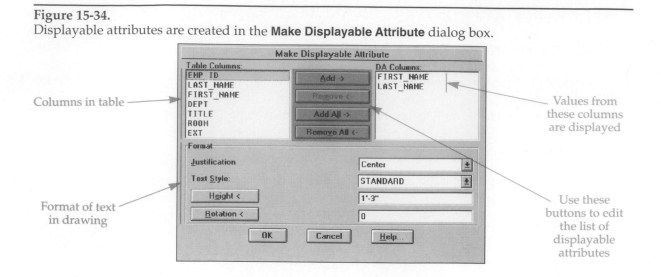

Columns in table →

Format of text in drawing →

Values from these columns are displayed

Use these buttons to edit the list of displayable attributes

Figure 15-35.
The displayable attribute appears at the pick point in the AutoCAD drawing.

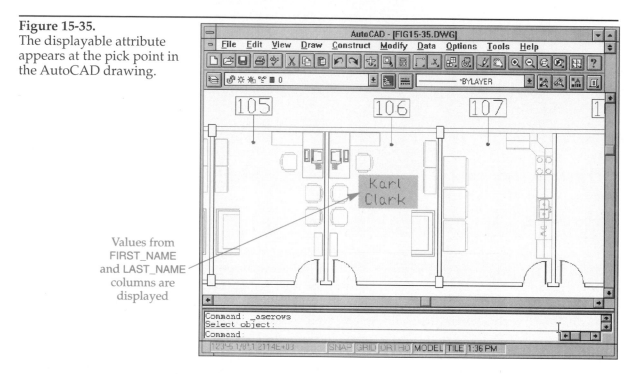

Values from FIRST_NAME and LAST_NAME columns are displayed

RESOLVING DATA AND DRAWING CONFLICTS

Errors and conflicts can creep into your drawing and database files due to several factors. Persons working on the drawing can erase or alter drawing entities, and other people using the database files can delete or alter keys or rows to linked entities. In order for the drawing and database to maintain their integrity, you can use the **ASEADMIN** command with the **Synchronize** option. This option reports invalid links within the database objects; links the existing information to a record that has been altered or deleted; and links information to entities that have been altered or deleted.

In the **Administration** dialog box, select the EMPLOYEE table. Be sure that you have a selected catalog and schema. Pick the **Synchronize...** button. See Figure 15-36. The **Synchronize Links** dialog box appears and defines any errors in the link.

If there are errors, pick the **Synchronize** button in this dialog box. AutoCAD repairs the link error and returns the table blank. Pick **Close** in this dialog box, then **OK** in the **Administration** dialog box, and the errors are repaired.

Figure 15-36.
The **Synchronize Links** dialog box defines errors in the link.

Any link errors listed in this area

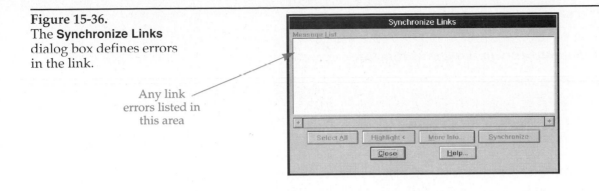

NOTE This chapter is intended to be an introduction to the capabilities of ASE. It is suggested that you go through the documentation in Chapter 13 of the *AutoCAD Users Guide*, Accessing External Databases. Begin to create your own small database and create a drawing that relates to it. This project should be a subject that is useful for you, and one that you can update and maintain easily. You will begin to see the value of working with a text and graphic relational database.

NOTE The commands from Release 12 have been consolidated into just a few Release 13 commands. The following is a list of the commands used in Release 13 and the related Release 12 commands.

Release 13 Command List	Release 12 Equivalents
	ASESETDBMS
	ASESETDB
	ASESETTABLE
	ASEERASETABLE
	ASECLOSETABLE
ASEADMIN	ASECLOSEDB
	ASEERASEDB
	ASEERASEDBMS
	ASEERASEALL
	ASEPOST
	ASERELOADDA
ASEEXPORT	{ ASEEXPORT
	ASEEDITLINK
ASELINKS	ASEVIEWLINK
	ASEDELLINK
ASESELECT	{ ASESELECT
ASESQLED	{ ASESQLED

CHAPTER TEST

Write your answers in the space provided.

1. What is a database? _____

    _____

2. What is a DBMS? _____

    _____

3. A common three-letter extension of a database file is _____.

4. Define "relational database". _____

    _____

    _____

5. What does SQL stand for, and how is it pronounced?_____

    _____

    _____

6. The letters ASE stand for_____.

7. The specialized form of SQL used in mapping applications is called_____

    _____.

8. What is a database table? _____

9. What are the two principal components of a table?_____

10. The horizontal component of a table is also known as a(n) _____.

11. The vertical component of a table is also known as a(n) _____.

12. What does the environment comprise? _____

    _____

13. What is a catalog? _____

    _____

    _____

    _____

14. What is a schema? _____

    _____

    _____

    _____

15. What command must be used before ASE can function? _____

16. What command is used to add and edit rows?_____

17. What does the **ASESELECT** command do? _____

    _____

    _____

18. Define "link". _____

    _____

19. How can you display a link you just created? _____

    _____

    _____

20. What command will make the database attributes visible? _____

    _____

21. What AutoCAD command is similar to the **Displayable Attributes** option and what is the difference between the two? _____

    _____

    _____

    _____

22. What command will fix any link errors from the entities to the database? _____

    _____

    _____

    _____

23. What is the command name for the SQL Editor? _____

24. Using the command in Question 21, what would you type to select and display the employee number (EMP_ID and Last_Name columns of all employees who work in the DEPT of sales? Assume you are working in the EMPLOYEE.DBF file.

    _____

DRAWING PROBLEMS

1. Make a copy of the ASESMP drawing and name it P15-1. Open P15-1 and set the DBMS and database used earlier in this chapter.

   General

   A. Add the following rows to each table shown below. Use **ASESQLED** to find a vacant room for the new employee, and enter that number in the proper column. For any column left blank in the lists below, find the next available number in the existing tables and use that value.

   EMPLOYEE.DBF
   EMP_ID—____
   LAST_NAME—Robinson
   FIRST_NAME—Lonnie
   DEPT—Human Resources
   TITLE—Counselor
   ROOM—____
   EXT—____
   ROOM—*(Lonnie's Room)*
   EMP_ID—*(Lonnie's EMP_ID)*

   INVENTRY.DBF
   INV_ID ____
   TYPE—Laser printer
   DESCRIPT—Personal inventory
   MFR—Quasar Lasers
   MODEL—QLP-600
   COMP_CFG—0
   PRICE—1245.00

   B. View the new rows to check for errors.

   C. Link the new employee and the new laser printer to the room number you selected in the drawing. Save the drawing as A:P15-1.

2. Open drawing P15-1 and edit the following existing rows of the tables given.

   A. COMPUTER table: Change EMP_ID 1022's last name to Wood-Jenkins, and change her TITLE to International Sales Mgr.

   B. INVENTRY table: Change the price of INV_ID 141 to 5300.00, and change the MFR to Tradewinds Computers.

   C. COMPUTER table: Change COMP_CFG 5's RAM to 16MB, and the GRAPHICS to Metheus.

   D. View each table after completion to check for errors.

3. If you have database software, create a database for each computer in your lab named COMPUTER.DBF. Columns in the table should be:

   - COMP_ID
   - CPU
   - HDRIVE
   - INPUT
   - MFR
   - RAM
   - FDRIVE
   - GRAPHICS

   A. Before constructing the database file, make a list of each computer and record the components of each according to the requirements of the database table. Then enter all of the data at one time at the computer.

   B. Generate a printed copy when you have completed the database.

4. Construct a drawing of your computer lab. Create blocks for each workstation.

   A. Set the proper database and table in order to work with the computers in your drawing.

   B. Link each one of the computers in the drawing with the appropriate row in your database table.

   C. View the links you created to check for accuracy. Edit any links that are not correct.

   D. Create displayable attributes for each workstation. The attributes should use the COMP_ID and MFR columns.

   E. Place a label in the title block, or as a general note, referring to the database name that is linked to this drawing.

   F. Save the drawing as A:P15-4 and print or plot a copy of the drawing.

AutoCAD R13

Chapter 16

Customizing the AutoCAD for Windows Environment

Learning objectives

After completing this chapter, you will be able to:

- O Interpret and modify the ACAD.INI file.
- O Enable the AutoCAD for Windows screen menu.
- O Assign colors and fonts to the text and graphics windows.
- O Set environment variables.
- O Resize and reposition the text and graphics windows.
- O Customize toolbar and toolbox buttons.
- O Modify program item properties.

AutoCAD for Windows provides a variety of options to customize the user interface and working environment. These options permit users to configure the software to suit personal preferences. These options include defining colors for the individual window elements, assigning preferred fonts to both the graphics window and text window, and customizing toolbars and buttons.

THE ACAD.INI FILE

Microsoft Windows uses initialization files that contain information that defines your Windows environment. Both Windows and Windows applications, like AutoCAD, use the information stored in these files to configure the working environment to meet your hardware needs and personal preferences.

There are two standard Windows initialization (.INI) files. The WIN.INI file primarily contains settings to customize the environment according to your preferences. The SYSTEM.INI file primarily contains settings that customize Windows to meet the hardware needs of your computer.

When AutoCAD is first installed on your workstation, the setup program adds the file ACAD.INI to the \R13\WIN directory. This file contains the environment and configuration information needed by AutoCAD each time you start a new drawing session. If AutoCAD cannot find the ACAD.INI file, it creates one. When you customize AutoCAD, your changes are saved to ACAD.INI so they are in effect each time you launch AutoCAD. As with other initialization files, ACAD.INI is an ASCII file and is very compact. This makes it easy to edit using Notepad or other text editor, Figure 16-1.

Figure 16-1.
The ACAD.INI file can be
edited with Windows
Notepad.

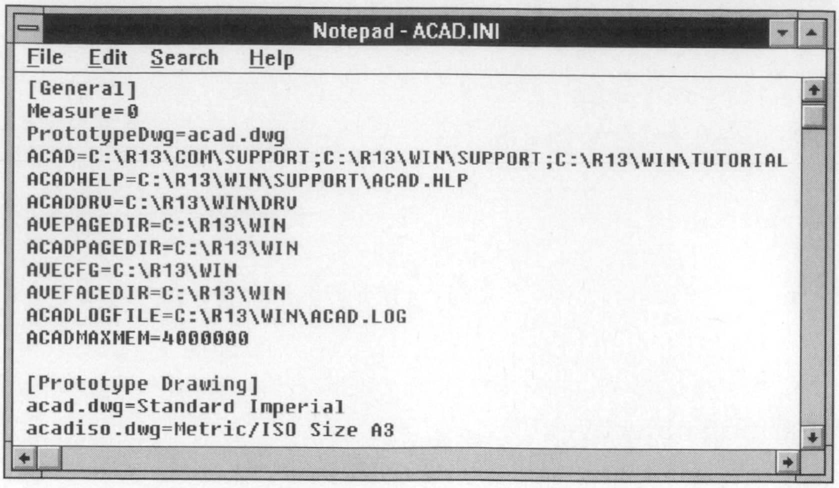

```
Notepad - ACAD.INI
File  Edit  Search  Help

[General]
Measure=0
PrototypeDwg=acad.dwg
ACAD=C:\R13\COM\SUPPORT;C:\R13\WIN\SUPPORT;C:\R13\WIN\TUTORIAL
ACADHELP=C:\R13\WIN\SUPPORT\ACAD.HLP
ACADDRU=C:\R13\WIN\DRU
AVEPAGEDIR=C:\R13\WIN
ACADPAGEDIR=C:\R13\WIN
AVECFG=C:\R13\WIN
AVEFACEDIR=C:\R13\WIN
ACADLOGFILE=C:\R13\WIN\ACAD.LOG
ACADMAXMEM=4000000

[Prototype Drawing]
acad.dwg=Standard Imperial
acadiso.dwg=Metric/ISO Size A3
```

> **NOTE**
>
> Check with your instructor or System Administrator before modifying any of the Microsoft Windows or AutoCAD initialization files. The .INI files contain information that controls not only the appearance and layout of AutoCAD, but also the manner in which the commands are displayed and function.

AutoCAD
Command
Reference

SETTING PREFERENCES

The options for customizing the AutoCAD user interface and working environment are found in the **Preferences** dialog box, Figure 16-2. This dialog box is accessed by selecting **Preferences...** from the **Options** pull-down menu, or by typing PREFERENCES at the **Command:** prompt.

Changes are not made until the **OK** button is picked. Each time you change the preferences settings, the ACAD.INI file is updated and the changes are used in subsequent drawing sessions.

Figure 16-2.
Customization of the AutoCAD working environment is done using the **Preferences** dialog box.

Digitizer
options

Pick to
change fonts

Pick to
change colors

```
Preferences

System   Environment   Render   International   Misc

AutoCAD Graphics Window          Digitizer Input
 □ Screen Menu                    ○ Digitizer              OK
 ⊠ Scroll Bars                    ● Digitizer/Mouse        Cancel
 Window Repair:                   Keystrokes               Help
 Bitmap                            ○ AutoCAD Classic
                                   ● Menu File
 Automatic Save
 ⊠ Every: 15  minutes      Font...    Color...
```

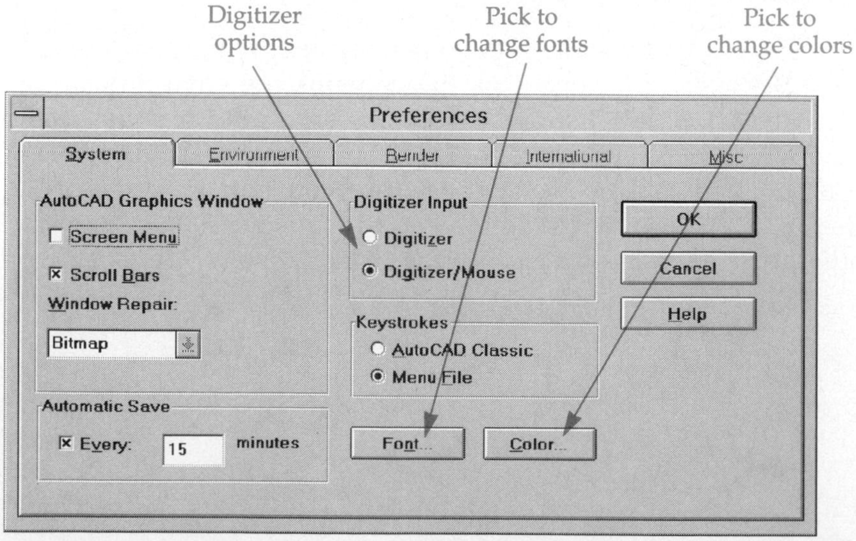

PROFESSIONAL TIP   Although ACAD.INI can easily be modified with any ASCII text editor, it is far easier to make changes and update the file using the Preferences dialog box. Regardless of the method you choose, always make a backup copy of ACAD.INI before customizing the AutoCAD for Windows environment.

Customizing the AutoCAD graphics window

Numerous options are available to customize the graphics window to your personal liking. Refer back to the **Preferences** dialog box in Figure 16-2. Look at the section titled **AutoCAD Graphics Window** at the upper-left of the dialog box. There are two check boxes, labeled **Screen Menu** and **Scroll Bars**. An "X" in either of these check boxes enables the specified options. By default, the scroll bars are turned on and the screen menus are turned off.

Located just below the check boxes is the **Window Repair:** pop-up lists. Sometimes, another window will overlay the graphics window. This option determines the mode used to "repair" the graphics window when the overlaying window is removed or closed. If you are using one of the display drivers supplied with AutoCAD, this option is set to Bitmap, and the list box does not pop up to display other choices. If you are using a third-party display driver, the pop-up list may display other choices.

NOTE   Many companies develop computer equipment or write specialized software programs that work in conjunction with AutoCAD. These companies are referred to as *third-party developers*, and the software programs they develop are called *third-party applications*. Several video card manufacturers provide a *display driver* designed to speed up video performance while working in AutoCAD.

Changing the graphics and text window colors

Most computer users would agree that one of the more satisfying aspects of software configuration is the ability to determine the colors used for the application. By customizing colors, you can add your own personal touch and make AutoCAD stand out among other active Windows applications. AutoCAD for Windows provides this capability with the **AutoCAD Window Colors** subdialog box, shown in Figure 16-3. This subdialog box is accessed by picking the **Color...** button in the **Preferences** dialog box.

The **Window Element:** pop-up list is located at the upper-right of the subdialog box. This list allows you to change color elements of graphics and text windows. These color elements include the graphics area, the screen menu and command area, the text window background, the text in the graphics window or text window, and the full-screen crosshairs. To customize the colors, do the following:

1. Pick the **Color...** button in the **Preferences** dialog box. The **AutoCAD Window Colors** subdialog box then appears.
2. If you have a monochrome display monitor, the **Monochrome Vectors** box is checked. If you have a grayscale display monitor and are experiencing problems displaying elements of AutoCAD, try checking this box.
3. Pick an area in the graphics or text window samples at the left of the dialog box, or select the element to change from the **Window Element:** pop-up list.
4. Pick the color you want from the available colors displayed in the **Basic Colors:** section. The color you select is immediately reflected in the sample area at the left of the dialog box, and in the color swatch at the bottom.

Figure 16-3.
The **AutoCAD Window Colors** subdialog box.

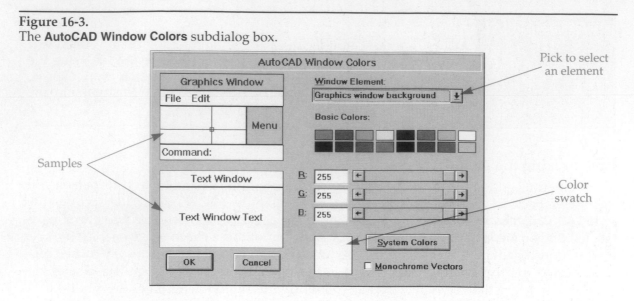

5. You can modify the selected color by using the horizontal slider controls labeled **R:**, **G:**, and **B:** to change the red, green, and blue (respectively) components of the color. Alternatively, you can type a number between 0 and 255 in the text boxes.

6. You can also customize the AutoCAD windows to match the system colors defined in the Windows Control Panel. To do so, pick the **System Colors** button just below the **R: G: B:** horizontal slider controls. Refer to the Microsoft Windows *User's Guide* for more information about the Windows Control Panel.

7. Once you have made your color selections, pick the **OK** button in the **AutoCAD Window Colors** subdialog box and pick **OK** again in the **Preferences** dialog box to implement your color changes. The graphics window regenerates and displays the color changes you made, Figure 16-4. If you modified the colors for the text window as well, press function key [F2] or select **Text Window** from the **Tools** pull-down menu to observe the color changes.

Figure 16-4.
After regenerating, the graphics window reflects the color changes made in the **AutoCAD Window Colors** subdialog box.

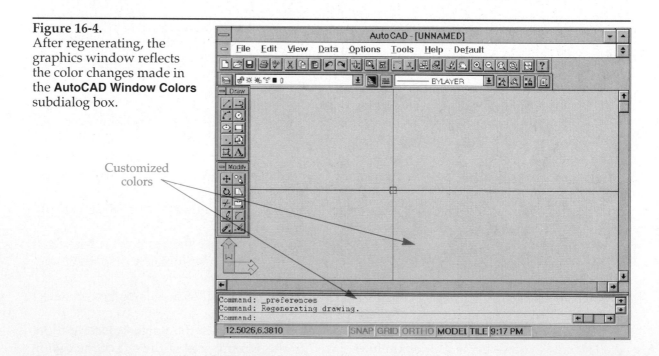

PROFESSIONAL TIP

A drawing regeneration is automatically performed whenever changes are made in the **Preferences** dialog box. To speed regeneration time and improve system performance, begin a new drawing session and customize the environment before creating objects.

Changing the graphics and text window fonts

You can also change the font used in the toolbar, command area, screen menu, and text window. The font you select has no affect on the text in your drawings, nor is the font used in the AutoCAD dialog boxes. To change the font used in the graphics and text windows, do the following:

1. Pick the **Font...** button on the **System** panel of the **Preferences** dialog box. The **Font** sub-dialog box then appears, Figure 16-5.
2. Note the two buttons at the lower-left of the dialog box in the **AutoCAD Window** section. Pick the **Graphics** button to modify the graphics window font. The **Text** button is used to modify the text window font.
3. The default font used by AutoCAD for the graphics window is MS Sans Serif. The font style for MS Sans Serif is Regular (not bold or italic), and it defaults to a size of 10 points. You can retain this font and just change the style and size.
4. To select a different font, select the new font from the **Font:** pop-up list at the upper-left of the dialog box. This file list displays each of the fonts installed in the \WINDOWS\SYSTEM subdirectory. If you have any third-party fonts, such as TrueType or Adobe Type Manager, they also appear in this list.
5. In the example shown in Figure 16-6, the Scribe TrueType font is selected from the pop-up list. The style is changed to Bold Italic in the **Font Style:** list box, and the size is changed to 12 points in the **Size:** list box. The **Sample Graphics Window Font** box at the bottom of the dialog box displays a sample of the selected font. If you are selecting a font for use in the text window, this box is labeled **Sample Text Window Font**.
6. Once you have selected the desired fonts, font styles, and sizes for the graphics and text windows, pick the **OK** button to assign the new fonts.
7. The **Preferences** dialog box is redisplayed. Pick **OK** to exit the **Preferences** dialog box and save your changes to the ACAD.INI file.

As with color modifications, changes made in font selection force a regeneration of the AutoCAD graphics window. When the regeneration is complete, the new font is displayed. You can see the Scribe TrueType font as it appears in a portion of the screen menu in Figure 16-7.

Figure 16-5.
The **Font** subdialog box sets font types, styles, and sizes used by AutoCAD's graphics and text windows.

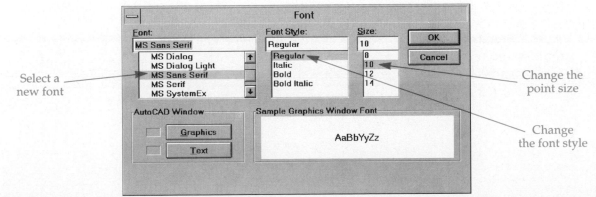

Figure 16-6.
The Scribe TrueType font is set current from the **Font:** pop-up list. The **Font Style** and **Size** are also changed.

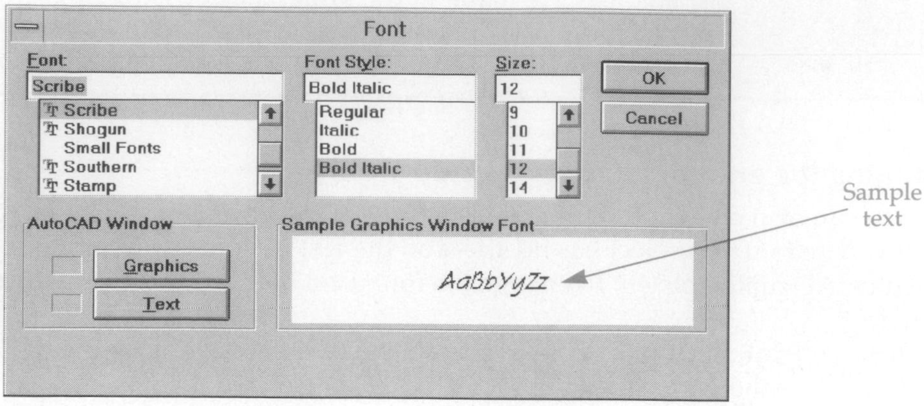

Sample text

Figure 16-7.
After regenerating, the font changes are reflected in the graphics window and menus.

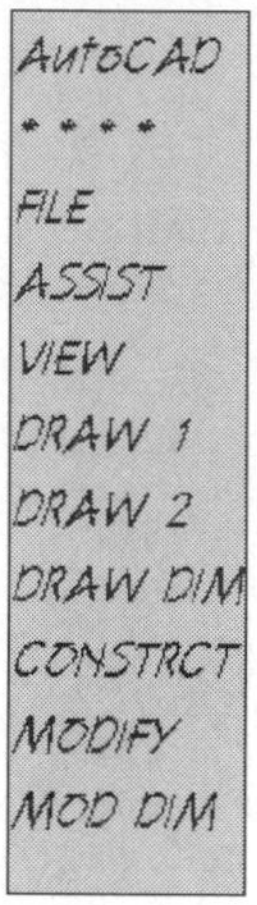

NOTE   The font changing feature is not fully functional in some maintenance releases of AutoCAD Release 13. If the changes you make
have no effect, it may be due to the particular version of the software
installed on your system.

EXERCISE 16-1

❏ Before beginning this exercise, make a backup copy of the ACAD.INI file. Keep the back-up in a separate directory or on a floppy disk.
❏ Start Windows and load AutoCAD for Windows.
❏ Use the **Preferences** dialog box to change the color elements and fonts of both the graphics and text windows to your personal liking.
❏ Once you are satisfied with your modifications, pick **OK** to save your changes.

Text window options

In addition to changing the colors and fonts used in the AutoCAD text window, there are several other options available. Select the **Misc** tab of the **Preferences** dialog box to display the **Text Window** settings. There are two options offered in this section:

- **History Lines:**. AutoCAD generates a listing of command area prompts and messages in a separate text window. This is one of the distinct advantages of running AutoCAD in the Windows environment. You can scroll through the window to see previous command input and information returned by AutoCAD. The **History Lines:** text box allows you to set the number of lines of text stored in the text window (from 25 to 2048 lines). If you do not have an abundance of RAM on your workstation, set this value to 200 lines to conserve system resources.
- **Docked Visible Lines:**. This controls the number of lines that are visible on the floating command window when it is docked. The default is 3 lines, but this value can be set higher so that more of your commands are visible. Increasing the number of lines displayed here will affect the size of your drawing area. Also, you can dynamically change the size of the floating command window (whether floating or docked) using the *resizing* cursor. Figure 16-8 shows the resizing cursor. Changing the size of the command window in this manner will automatically update the value in the **Docked Visible Lines:** edit box.

Figure 16-8.
The cursor appears like this when resizing the command window.

Digitizer input

A digitizer can be configured as both a mouse and a digitizer tablet or as a digitizer only. Refer back to the **Preferences** dialog box in Figure 16-2 and note the section labeled **Digitizer Input**. There are two option buttons in this section:

- **Digitizer.** This is the default setting. If you have a digitizer configured, AutoCAD accepts input from that device. If you have a mouse and no digitizer, AutoCAD accepts mouse input. If you have a mouse and a digitizer, the mouse pointing arrow appears in the graphics window along with the digitizer crosshairs when you pick the **Digitizer Only** button.
- **Digitizer/Mouse.** Pick this option button to accept input from whichever pointing device last moved or sent a coordinate sample back to AutoCAD.

You must configure your tablet using both the **CONFIG** and **TABLET** commands before it can be used. Refer to the *AutoCAD Installation Guide for Windows* for more information about digitizer configuration options. For detailed instructions on using your tablet as a digitizing device, see Chapter 20 of this text or *AutoCAD and its Applications, Basics—Release 13 for Windows*, Chapter 31.

Automatic Save

Picking the check box in front of the word **Every:** toggles the automatic save feature. Enabling automatic save forces AutoCAD to save a copy of the current drawing at the interval specified in the edit box in front of the label **minutes**. This adjusts the current setting of the **SAVETIME** system variable.

The automatic save feature does not overwrite the source drawing file with its incremental saves. Rather, AutoCAD creates a drawing to save temporary files. This name is specified in the configuration of AutoCAD by using the **CONFIG** command. The default name is AUTO.SV$. See Chapter 17 of *AutoCAD and its Applications—Basics, Release 13 for Windows* for information on the **CONFIG** command.

This AUTO.SV$ file can be renamed with a .DWG file extension to make it usable by AutoCAD. Having an extra backup copy of a drawing file can be useful if your system crashes or if you experience an unprotected power outage.

The interval setting you should use is based on working conditions and file size. For example, in larger drawings (1 Megabyte and above), a **SAVE** command can take a significant amount of time. If a save takes two minutes and your auto save is set to save every five minutes, then you would spend more than fifteen minutes of every hour waiting on AutoCAD to finish saving the file. So it is possible to adversely affect your productivity by setting your **SAVETIME** value too small.

Ideally, it is best to set your **SAVETIME** variable to the greatest amount of time you can afford to repeat. While it may be acceptable to redo the last fifteen minutes or less of work, it is unlikely that you would feel the same about having to redo the last hour.

PROFESSIONAL TIP

Setting and resetting the **SAVETIME** variable according to any given situation is often the best approach. The factors that should influence the current setting include not only file size, but also the working conditions. If your computer system is experiencing frequent lock-ups or crashes, your automatic saves should occur often. Weather can also be a factor. Wind or electrical storms should be an immediate cue to reduce the value of the **SAVETIME** variable.

Keystrokes

AutoCAD supports the common keystroke combinations recognized by many other Windows applications. For example, pressing [Ctrl]+[S] activates the **QSAVE** command to save your file. The [Ctrl]+[P] keystroke prints (plots) your file, [Ctrl]+[O] opens a drawing, and [Ctrl]+[N] starts a new drawing. In all releases previous to R13, the [Ctrl]+[C] is used as a **CANCEL**. However, to conform with Windows standards, this combination now starts the '**COPYCLIP** command, and the [Esc] key now cancels.

For an experienced user of AutoCAD, it may be a significant hurdle to "unlearn" several years of canceling with a [Ctrl]+[C]. For these users, AutoCAD provides a way to switch the new keystroke model with the old keystroke standards. Picking **AutoCAD Classic** enables the old-style keystroke model, and picking **Menu File** enables the new keystrokes.

SETTING AUTOCAD FOR WINDOWS ENVIRONMENT VARIABLES

There are numerous settings that control the manner that AutoCAD behaves in the Windows environment. These settings are made through the use of environment variables. The variables are used to specify which directories to search for driver or menu files, or to specify a directory for your configuration file (ACAD.CFG). The default settings created during installation are usually adequate, but changing the settings sometimes results in better performance. While several different options exist for setting environment variables, the simplest method is to use the **Environment** panel of the **Preferences** dialog box, as shown in Figure 16-9.

Specifying support file directories

The **Directories** section of the dialog box is used to specify the path AutoCAD searches to find support files and driver files. It also specifies the placement of page (swap) files. Support files include text fonts, menus, AutoLISP files, ADS files, blocks to insert, linetypes, and hatch patterns.

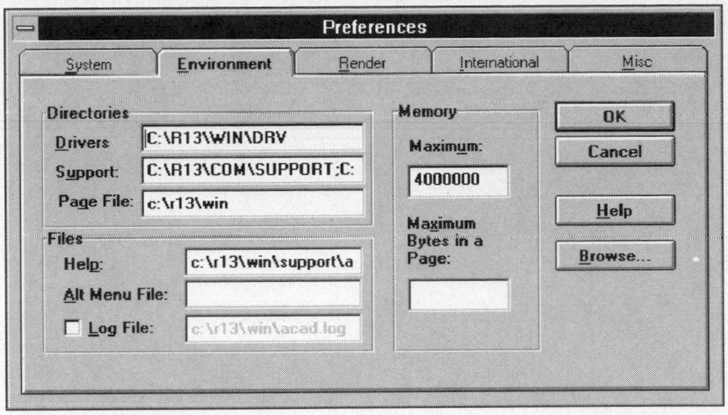

Figure 16-9.
The **Environment** panel of the **Preferences** subdialog box is an easy way of setting environment variables.

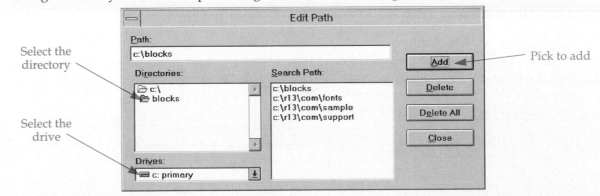

The subdirectory names shown in the **Support:** edit box of Figure 16-9 are automatically created by the AutoCAD installation procedure. These subdirectories are named SUPPORT, FONTS, and SAMPLE. You can use the **Support:** edit box to specify the path to any new directory or subdirectories you create that may contain support files.

As an example, suppose you store all of the blocks you typically use in a separate directory named \BLOCKS on the C: drive. Unless this directory name is placed in the support files search path, AutoCAD will not be able to find your blocks when you attempt to insert them.

You can add this directory to the existing search path in two ways. The first method is to type in the following directly after the \R13\COM\SUPPORT entry in the **Support:** edit box. Do not forget to use a semicolon to separate the new directory entry from those that already exist. The new setting takes effect as soon as you pick the **OK** button and close the **Environment** tab.

> **;C:\BLOCKS**

The second method is easier than the first. With this method, you simply pick the **Browse...** button in the **Environment** tab. The **Edit Path** subdialog box is then displayed, Figure 16-10. Using this subdialog box, you select the C: drive from the **Drives:** pop-up list, and then select the blocks directory from the **Directories:** list. The path C:\BLOCKS is then displayed in the **Path:** edit box at the top of the subdialog box. Pick the **Add** button to add C:\BLOCKS to the **Search Path:** list shown at the right of this subdialog box. When you are done, pick the **Close** button. You are then returned to the **Environment** tab of the **Preferences** dialog box. Pick **OK** and your new setting immediately takes effect.

Figure 16-10.
Adding a directory to the search path using the **Edit Path** subdialog box.

> **NOTE**   Using the **Environment** tab to specify the search path for support files in AutoCAD for Windows is similar to setting the **ACAD** environment variable in the DOS version of AutoCAD.

Specifying the help file

The AutoCAD for Windows help file is named ACAD.HLP. During installation, this file is placed in the \R13\WIN\SUPPORT subdirectory. You can use the **Help:** edit box to specify a different path and filename for the help file. This is particularly handy if you want to locate the help file on a network drive, or if you are using a custom help file. AutoCAD can read any Windows-format help file. It can also read the help file (ACAD.HLP) supplied with AutoCAD Release 13 for DOS.

Specifying an alternate menu file

If you have a digitizer tablet, you can use the **Alt. Menu File:** edit box to specify the path and name of an alternate menu file (.MNU) to swap with the standard AutoCAD tablet menu. This feature is typically used to load the tablet menu of a third-party application. It can also be used to load a custom tablet menu. See Chapter 20, *Customizing Tablet Menus*, for more information regarding digitizer tablet menu options.

Log file

When the **Log File:** check box is activated, AutoCAD creates a file that is, by default, named ACAD.LOG. This name can be changed by editing the value in the edit box that follows the **Log File:** label. When activated, all of the prompts, messages, and responses that appear in the text window are saved to this file. Exiting AutoCAD or turning off this check box disables the log file feature.

The log file status can also be set using the **LOGFILEON** and **LOGFILEOFF** commands. Each individual session of AutoCAD contained in a single log file is separated by a line of dashes with a date and time stamp.

This file can serve a variety of purposes. The source of drawing errors can be determined by reviewing the commands that produced the incorrect results. Additionally, log files can be reviewed by a CAD manager to determine the need for training and customization of the system. Figure 16-11 shows an example of a log file opened in the Notepad program.

Figure 16-11.
The ACAD.LOG file as it appears in Notepad.

```
────────────────────────────────────────────────────────────────
│ ≡                      Notepad - ACAD.LOG                  ▼ ▲ │
│  File   Edit   Search   Help                                  │
│ ┌──────────────────────────────────────────────────────────┐│
│ │[ AutoCAD - Sun Nov 12 12:35:33      ]--------------------↕││
│ │                                                          ││
│ │Command: rectang                                          ││
│ │                                                          ││
│ │First corner: 2,2                                         ││
│ │                                                          ││
│ │Other corner: 8,8                                         ││
│ │                                                          ││
│ │                                                          ││
│ │Command: z ZOOM                                           ││
│ │All/Center/Dynamic/Extents/Left/Previous/Vmax/Window/<Scale(X/XP)>: .5x││
│ │                                                          ││
│ │Command: dim          I                                   ││
│ │Dim: ×Cancel×                                             ││
│ │                                                          ││
│ │Command: dimlinear                                        ││
│ │                                                          ││
│ │First extension line origin or RETURN to select: int of  ││
│ │Second extension line origin: int of                     ││
│ │Dimension line location (Text/Angle/Horizontal/Vertical/Rotated):││
│ │Command:  DIMLINEAR                                       ││
│ │First extension line origin or RETURN to select:         ││
│ │Select object to dimension:                              ││
│ │Dimension line location (Text/Angle/Horizontal/Vertical/Rotated):││
│ │Command: logfileoff                                       ││
│ │                                                         ↓││
│ │←                                                        →││
│ └──────────────────────────────────────────────────────────┘│
────────────────────────────────────────────────────────────────
```

Toggle the log file open before listing any saved layers, blocks, views, UCS's, etc. You can then print the log file contents and keep a hard copy at your workstation as a handy reference. However, if you choose to save the **Log File Open** setting to the ACAD.INI file, the log file will continue to grow with each subsequent AutoCAD session. As a result, the increased size of ACAD.LOG will consume valuable hard disk space. AutoCAD does not delete or shorten this file for you. Therefore, make a point of shortening or deleting ACAD.LOG periodically to conserve disk resources. Do not be concerned about deleting this file, because AutoCAD will create another file the next time you toggle the log file open.

Memory and paging settings

The environment variables in the **Memory** section of the **Environment** panel control the way paging works. The AutoCAD pager divides the current drawing file into pages, and Windows allocates memory for the pages. When memory becomes full, the pager writes drawing data to disk.

You can specify the amount of memory (in bytes) that the pager can receive from Windows by using the **Maximum:** text box. The default value is four megabytes. This option sets the **ACADMAXMEM** variable that takes effect the next time you start AutoCAD for Windows.

This option should only be used when you need to reduce the use of physical memory for compatibility with another program. Reducing this amount causes an increase in paging to virtual memory on disk, which slows system performance. Therefore, unless you have a specific use, do not change this variable.

When memory becomes full and paging is necessary, the AutoCAD pager writes data to the first page file. A second page file is created when the first page fills. You can specify the maximum number of bytes for the first page file using the **Maximum Bytes in a Page:** text box. This option sets the **ACADMAXPAGE** variable, and takes effect the next time you start AutoCAD. It is very unlikely that you will need to specify a maximum, because the first page file is used until it is full.

Other environment settings

There are three other variables that can be set from the **Environment** panel. The first is the **ACADDRV** variable. This allows you to specify the search path for ADI (Autodesk Device Interface) drivers. The *Autodesk Device Interface* is a specification that allows dealers, manufacturers, and users to develop device drivers for peripherals that work with AutoCAD and other Autodesk products. By default, the drivers supplied with AutoCAD for Windows are placed in the \R13\WIN\DRV directory at installation. If you purchase a third-party driver to use with AutoCAD, be sure to load the driver into this directory. If the third-party driver must reside in a different directory, you should specify that directory using the **Drivers:** edit box. Otherwise, the search for the correct driver is widespread and likely to take longer. The new **ACADDRV** variable setting takes effect when you reconfigure AutoCAD for Windows.

AutoCAD is able to utilize any Windows format or platform-independent help file. This means that custom help files can be generated as needed. This can be a formidable undertaking, and is usually only done by third-party developers to supplement their software add-ons. If you are using a third-party application with AutoCAD, you may have an alternate help file.

The **Help:** edit box specifies the path and name of the help file being used. This file will typically be either ACAD.HLP or ACAD.AHP. Be warned that placing an incorrect specification in this field may make your help file inaccessible.

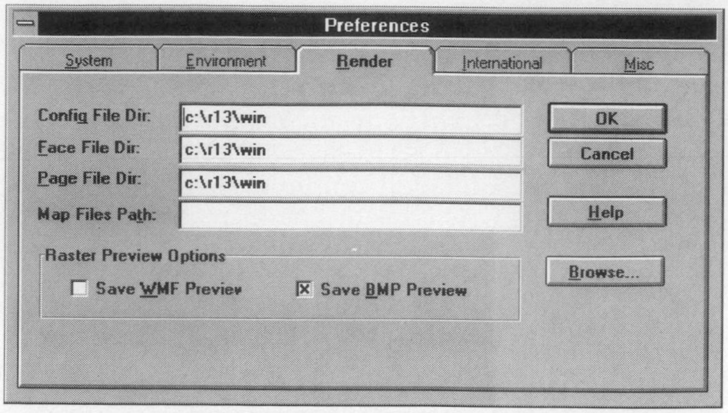

Figure 16-12.
Environment variables specific to rendering are controlled using the **Render** panel of the **Preferences** dialog box.

Variables that control the rendering environment

There are also several variables that control the rendering environment. These variables can be set using the **Render** panel of the **Preferences** dialog box, as shown in Figure 16-12.

The **Config File Dir:** edit box specifies where AutoCAD stores and locates the render configuration file. This file is named RENDER.CFG and is created in the \R13\WIN directory when you configure AutoCAD Render for your rendering display and rendering hard copy drivers. If you have several different rendering drivers, you can keep several different configurations. Since each configuration file is named RENDER.CFG, you will need to store the files in different directories. If you are in AutoCAD for Windows and want to change render configurations, first select **Render Configure...** from the **Options** pull-down menu.

The **Face File Dir:** edit box is used to specify the directory that holds the face file. The face file is one of two temporary files created on disk that hold the faces and triangles generated while rendering. By default, that face file is created in the \R13\WIN directory. If you are using a RAM disk with AutoCAD, rendering speed is increased if the face file is placed on the RAM disk. Use the **Face File Dir:** edit box to specify the RAM disk directory.

When AutoCAD runs out of memory to hold the triangles it is processing, it creates a temporary page file. As with the face file, the page file is placed in the \R13\WIN directory by default. If you are using a RAM disk, use the **Page File Dir:** text box to specify the directory location for the page file on the RAM disk to increase rendering performance. Refer to the *AutoCAD Installation Guide for Windows* for more information regarding face and page files.

The **Raster Preview Options** area allows control over the preview image generated when a drawing is saved. This preview image is displayed in the **Preview** area of the **Select File** dialog box when opening a drawing. By leaving both boxes unchecked, no preview is generated. Checking either option specifies the file format the preview is saved as within the drawing file.

Additional Environmental Settings

The **International** panel of the **Preferences** dialog box provides an option for specification of either English or Metric units of measure.

The **Prototype Drawing** box allows specification of either an English or a Metric prototype drawing. When you change this value, the text below is updated to specify the name of the prototype drawing referenced.

NOTE

In some maintenance releases of AutoCAD R13, changing this setting causes AutoCAD to crash. However, when you restart AutoCAD, the settings you made will be remembered and you can begin working without further worries.

The final panel of the **Preferences** dialog is titled **Misc** and offers controls for other features of AutoCAD. The **Options** area provides access to the following settings:

- **Text Editor.** Specifying this value as INTERNAL causes AutoCAD to use the built-in **MText Editor** to edit multiline text with. To utilize another text editor, enter the command line data required to start the desired editor. For example, if you wanted to use NOTEPAD, you would enter C:\WINDOWS\NOTEPAD.EXE in this box.
- **Font Mapping File:.** Specifies the font mapping file used by the **MText** command.
- **Maximize Application On Startup.** Check this box if you want applications started from within AutoCAD to be maximized by default. For example, if your drawing has a Microsoft Word document in it, double-clicking on the object starts Word for Windows. If this box is checked, Word for Windows is maximized (filling the entire screen) when started.
- **Maximize Drawing By Default.** Check this box if you want AutoCAD to be maximized when it starts up.
- **Plot Spooling.** This option sets the **ACADPLCMD** variable, which controls the conditions for use of a plot spooler. A plot spooler allows plotting in the background, so that you can still work while a plot is taking place.

POSITIONING THE AUTOCAD GRAPHICS AND TEXT WINDOWS

Perhaps the greatest advantage offered by the Microsoft Windows environment is the ability to have several applications displayed in separate windows simultaneously. It is then a simple matter to click anywhere within an open window and activate the application within it. Naturally, the number and size of the displayed windows is a function of the current screen resolution and monitor size.

When AutoCAD is installed, the graphics window fills the entire display screen. The text window is hidden behind the graphics window and is only brought to the front when you press function key [F2]. When you want to return to the graphics window, you simply click once more anywhere within its displayed border or press [F2] again.

By default, AutoCAD is maximized on startup. This means that it fills the entire screen. When a window is maximized, the upper right corner of the window displays two buttons, as shown in Figure 16-13A. The Minimize button closes the AutoCAD window without ending your AutoCAD session. AutoCAD is then displayed as an icon at the bottom of your screen. Double-clicking on a minimized application restores its window to the previous state. The Restore button changes the AutoCAD window to a *floating* window. When a window is floating, it can be freely adjusted and repositioned. A floating window displays the Minimize and Maximize buttons, as shown in Figure 16-13B. The Minimize button works the same as before, and the Maximize button can be used to cause the AutoCAD window to fill the screen again.

You can reposition a floating AutoCAD window by clicking within the title bar at the top of the window. Hold the pointing device button down, drag the window to the desired location, and release the pointing device button. When floating, the windows will remain at the defined locations for all subsequent AutoCAD sessions until you relocate them and save the new position settings.

Figure 16-13.
A—The **Minimize** and **Restore** buttons are located in the upper-right corner of a window. B—The **Minimize** and **Maximize** buttons found in a floating window.

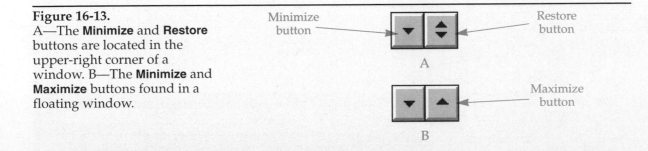

SIZING THE AUTOCAD GRAPHICS AND TEXT WINDOWS

Apart from repositioning the graphics and text windows on your display, you may also find it useful to size the windows to different values. Sizing a window can be accomplished as easily as moving its location. To stretch (or shrink) a window along its vertical axis, simply pick and hold at the top or bottom border of the window. The pointing device then assumes the shape of a double arrow, Figure 16-14. Drag the border to the desired size and release the pointing device button. For example, to stretch (or shrink) a window along its horizontal axis, pick and hold at the left or right border of the window. Then, drag the border to the desired size and release the pointing device button.

To stretch (or shrink) a window along both axes simultaneously, pick and hold one of the four corners of the window. The pointing device assumes the shape of a double arrow, but at an angle, Figure 16-15. Drag the corner to the desired position and release the pointing device button.

Figure 16-14.
Stretching the top or bottom border adjusts the vertical size of a window while stretching the right or left border adjusts the horizontal size of a window.

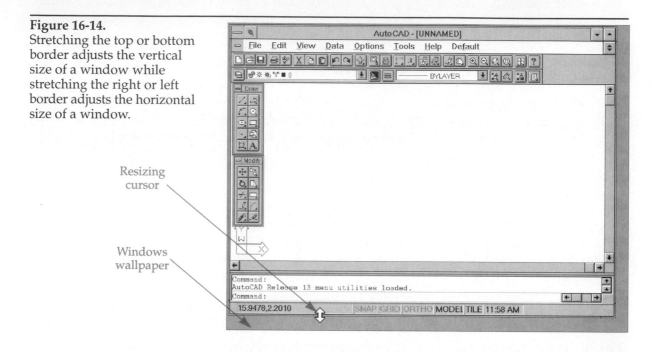

Figure 16-15.
A window is sized along both axes simultaneously by stretching one of the window corners.

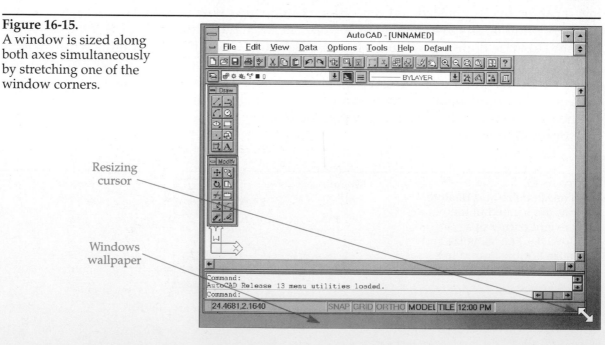

To help select the window border, you may find it useful to increase the width of the window border. To do so, return to the Program Manager and open the Main group window, Figure 16-16. Then, double-click the Control Panel icon. When the Control Panel window appears, double-click the Desktop icon, Figure 16-17.

The Sizing Grid section at the lower-left of the Desktop window contains the Border Width: drop-down list, Figure 16-18. Select a higher number from this list to increase the width of the border and a lower number to decrease the width. The border width is measured in pixels.

The AutoCAD graphics and text windows can also be minimized, maximized, or resized using the file control menu. To do so, select the appropriate command from the menu. See Figure 16-19.

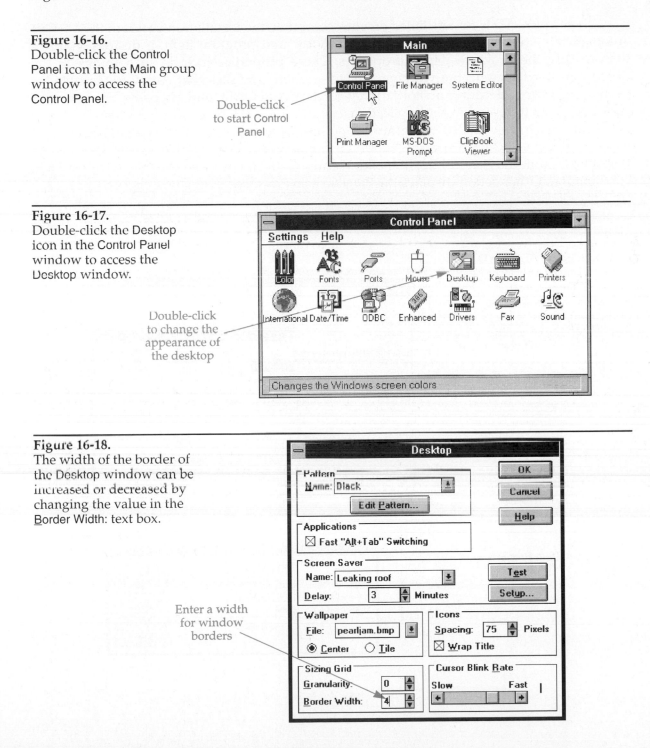

Figure 16-16.
Double-click the Control Panel icon in the Main group window to access the Control Panel.

Figure 16-17.
Double-click the Desktop icon in the Control Panel window to access the Desktop window.

Figure 16-18.
The width of the border of the Desktop window can be increased or decreased by changing the value in the Border Width: text box.

Figure 16-19.
Selecting options from the
Control menu.

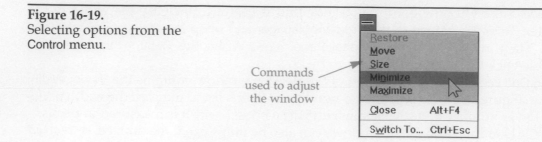

Commands
used to adjust
the window

CHANGING PROGRAM PROPERTIES

When AutoCAD is first installed on your computer, the installation program SETUP.EXE automatically creates the AutoCAD group window and program item. If desired, you can then modify the program item's properties. These properties include such things as the description for the item, the working directory where any files that AutoCAD creates (or needs) are stored, defining a shortcut key to start AutoCAD, and choosing the icon that AutoCAD uses to represent the application.

To modify the AutoCAD program properties, first return to the Program Manager and single-click the AutoCAD icon in the AutoCAD group window to highlight the icon. Next, select Properties... from the File pull-down menu, Figure 16-20. You can also use the [Alt]+[Enter] key combination. Either action displays the Program Item Properties dialog box, Figure 16-21.

Figure 16-20.
Click the AutoCAD program
item icon in the AutoCAD
group window to highlight
the icon. Then, select
Properties... from the File
pull-down menu or press
[Alt]+[Enter] to access the
Program Item Properties
dialog box.

Select to change
the properties

Highlight the icon

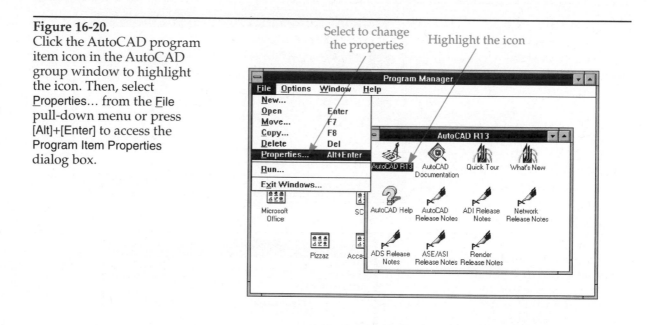

Figure 16-21.
The Program Item Properties
dialog box.

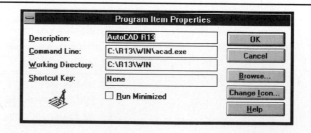

> **NOTE**   Be sure to check with your instructor or System Administrator before modifying the AutoCAD program properties.

The various elements of the Program Item Properties dialog box are described as follows:
- **Description:.** This text box is used to enter a description that uniquely identifies the application. The description becomes the label that appears under the icon. In the illustration shown, the description has been edited to read "AutoCAD R13."
- **Command Line:.** The Command Line: text box contains the name of the executable program and its path. If you change the drive or directory that contains the AutoCAD executables, be sure to edit this line accordingly. You will also need to reconfigure AutoCAD. This is because the entire path to the drivers is saved in the ACAD.CFG file.
- **Working Directory:.** This text box specifies the name of the directory where the AutoCAD program files are located. The directory specified in this text box becomes the current directory when AutoCAD is running. Any newly created files are placed here.
- **Shortcut Key:.** Microsoft Windows provides a special feature called an *application shortcut key*. This feature permits you to launch AutoCAD with a user-defined key combination. No matter where you are in Windows, or which application is currently running, you can quickly start AutoCAD by using a shortcut key. Assigning a shortcut key for AutoCAD is described later in this section.
- **Run Minimized.** When this check box is selected, AutoCAD is reduced to an icon when it starts. It is recommended that you leave this box unchecked.

When you are finished making your changes, pick the OK button to exit the Program Item Properties dialog box. Since any changes you make take effect immediately, there is no need to restart Windows.

Changing the AutoCAD program item icon

The Program Item Properties dialog box provides the option to change the program icon used by AutoCAD. To change the icon, do the following:
1. Pick the Change Icon... button at the right of the Program Item Properties dialog box.
2. The Change Icon subdialog box is then displayed, Figure 16-22.
3. Observe that there are ten icons from which to choose. Six of the icons are variations of the Release 13 calipers symbol, and two closely resemble the AutoCAD graphics window.
4. Select the icon you wish to use and pick the OK button to exit the Change Icon subdialog box.
5. Your icon selection is now displayed at the lower-left of the Program Item Properties dialog box.

Figure 16-22.
The Change Icon subdialog box offers ten different AutoCAD icons.

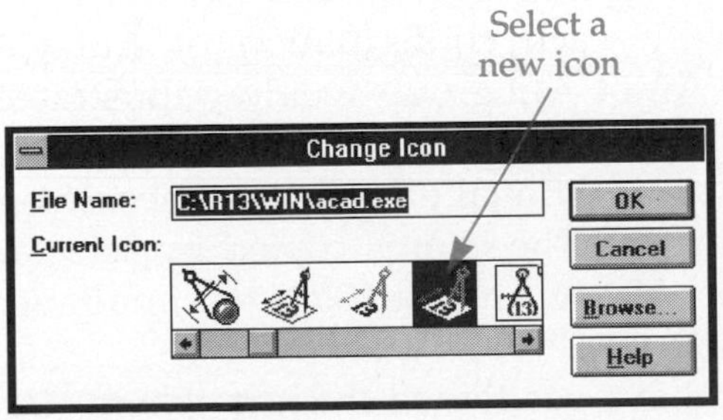

Select a new icon

Defining a shortcut key

Microsoft Windows provides the option of assigning a shortcut key that starts a new application running no matter where you are in Windows. You can use any letter, number, or special character for a shortcut key. Since AutoCAD does not use the function keys [F3], [F11], or [F12], one of these keys would make a good choice. Whichever key you choose, Windows automatically adds a [Ctrl]+[Alt] in front of it. To assign a shortcut key for launching AutoCAD, do the following:

1. Return to the Program Manager and open the AutoCAD Program Item Properties dialog box.
2. Pick within the Shortcut Key: text box. The flashing vertical cursor appears at the end of the word None.
3. Now, press function key [F12] (or whichever key you prefer).
4. The character string Ctrl + Alt + F12 appears in the text box, Figure 16-23.
5. Pick OK to exit the Program Item Properties dialog box.

You need not restart Windows to activate your new shortcut key. Now, no matter which Windows-based application is running, you can start AutoCAD with the keyboard combination [Ctrl]+[Alt]+[F12]. Refer to the Microsoft Windows *User's Guide* for more information regarding shortcut keys.

Figure 16-23.
Defining a shortcut key in the Program Item Properties dialog box.

New icon

Key combination

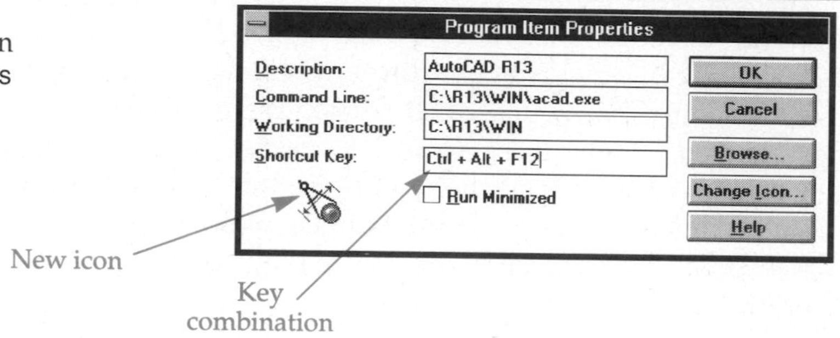

CREATING ALTERNATE AUTOCAD CONFIGURATIONS

You may find that when working with different types of drawings and designs that you change the menus and toolbars that you use. This can become a time-consuming effort if you must reload different toolbars, and customized menus each time you need them. A more efficient procedure would be to establish alternate configurations of AutoCAD. This is a simple task, and requires only that you create a new program item and a new directory for each configuration. Each alternate configuration of AutoCAD will use the same ACAD.INI and ACAD.CFG files, unless you direct AutoCAD to use different ones.

By default, these two files reside in the \R13\WIN directory. To ensure that each AutoCAD configuration uses its own ACAD.INI and ACAD.CFG files, first create a new directory and copy those files into it. In the example that follows, the new directory is named \R13\WIN\ALTCONF for alternate configuration.

Additionally, each configuration of AutoCAD uses the same program item icon. Consider the AutoCAD group window illustrated in Figure 16-24. Two separate program item icons appear in this group window and each icon is labeled differently.

To create an additional program item icon, you must copy the original AutoCAD icon in the group window. The icon is copied by selecting the AutoCAD icon, holding down the pointing device button and the [Ctrl] key simultaneously, and dragging the copied icon to the desired location.

Once you have positioned the icon where you like, highlight it and press [Alt]+[Enter] to access the Program Item Properties dialog box, Figure 16-25. You must specify the location of the separate configuration directory in the Command Line: text box. This is performed by

Figure 16-24.
Two separate AutoCAD configurations are shown in the AutoCAD group window. Note the different label used for each.

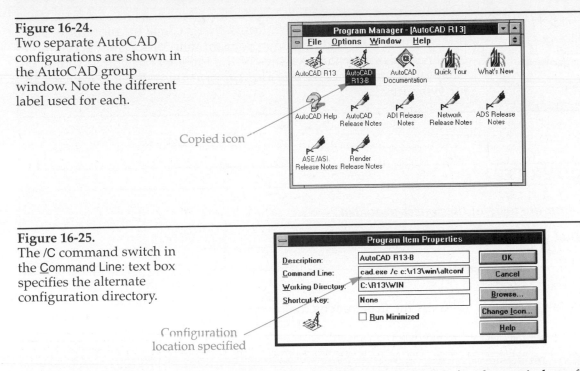

Copied icon

Figure 16-25.
The /C command switch in the Command Line: text box specifies the alternate configuration directory.

Configuration location specified

adding the /C switch, which causes the new configuration to look for the copied configuration files in the directory designated by the switch. The new text is added immediately after the line C:\R13\WIN\ACAD.EXE. In the example shown in Figure 16-25, the following line is added in the Command Line: text box:

/C C:\R13\WIN\ALTCONF

After you have added the /C switch and new path statement, select a different icon by picking the Change Icon... button. You can then edit the label of this icon in the Description: text box to distinguish it from the original icon label. To summarize the procedure:

1. Create a directory for AutoCAD's alternate configuration files.
2. Copy the files ACAD.INI and ACAD.CFG into the alternate configuration directory.
3. Hold down the [Ctrl] key and drag the AutoCAD icon to copy it.
4. Click once on the new AutoCAD icon to highlight it.
5. Press [Alt]+ [Enter] to access the Program Item Properties dialog box.
6. Add the /C switch and new path to the command line just after ACAD.EXE. For example:

C:\R13\WIN\ACAD.EXE /C C:\R13\WIN\ALTCONF

7. Select a new icon from the Change Icon subdialog box, Figure 16-22. Pick OK.
8. Pick on OK to exit the Program Item Properties dialog box.

Now when you run the alternate session, you can modify the toolbar, toolbox, and all other aspects of the AutoCAD graphics and text windows as described in this chapter. In addition, you can load different menu files for each configuration. For example, if you work with custom menus in more than one discipline, you might have program item icons named AutoCAD R13 - Piping, AutoCAD R13 - Civil, AutoCAD R13 - Structural, etc.

The first time you launch one of the new configurations, use the **MENU** command to load the appropriate menu file. Then, each time you begin one of the alternate configurations, the proper menu file is loaded, along with all other changes you may have made. When you save your changes in the alternate configuration, they are saved to the ACAD.INI and ACAD.CFG files in the alternate configuration directories.

NOTE   Refer to the Microsoft Windows *User's Guide* for more information about editing and deleting program item properties. A detailed
explanation of all characteristics of the Program Manager is found in
Chapter 32 of *AutoCAD and its Applications—Basics, Release 13
for Windows*.

CHAPTER TEST

Write your answers in the spaces provided.

1. What is the purpose of the ACAD.INI file? _____

    _____

    _____

2. List two methods to access the **Preferences** dialog box. _____

    _____

    _____

3. Fonts assigned in the **Font** subdialog box may be used in an AutoCAD drawing.
    (True/False) _____

4. How do you access the **AutoCAD Window Colors** subdialog box?_____

    _____

    _____

    _____

5. What are the advantages of toggling the log file open? The disadvantages? _____

    _____

    _____

    _____

    _____

    _____

6. Name the two commands that toggle the log file on and off. _____

    _____

7. AutoCAD for Windows resides in the C:\R13\WIN directory on your workstation. You
    have created two subdirectories under \R13\WIN named PROJECTS and SYMBOLS. You
    want to store your drawings in the projects subdirectory and your blocks in the symbols
    subdirectory. What should you enter in the **Support:** text box so that these directories
    are added to the search path? _____

    _____

8. What is a *face* file? What is a *page* file? _____

    _____

    _____

    _____

    _____

9. How do you increase the width of a window border? _____

_____

_____

_____

10. Which two files must be copied to a separate directory before creating an alternate
    AutoCAD configuration? _____

_____

_____

PROBLEMS

1. Create an alternate configuration for AutoCAD dedicated to 3D modeling and
    rendering using the methods described in this chapter. Use the following
    instructions to complete this problem:

    General

    A. Assign a different program item icon to the 3D configuration.

    B. Name the program item label: AutoCAD 3D for Windows

    C. Define a shortcut key for the configuration.

    D. Add a directory to the support path that contains 3D shapes.

2. Create another alternate configuration for AutoCAD dedicated to dimensioning.
    Use the following instructions to complete this problem:

    General

    A. Assign a different program item icon to the dimensioning configuration.

    B. Name the program item label: AutoCAD Dimensioning

    C. Define a shortcut key for the configuration.

    D. Add a directory to the support path that contains 3D shapes.

Custom toolbars and toolbar buttons can be created.

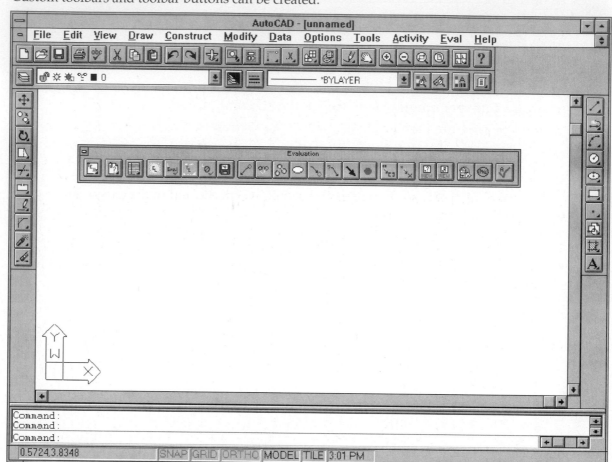

AutoCAD R13

Chapter 17

Customizing Toolbars

Learning objectives

After completing this chapter you will be able to:

- ○ Position and resize toolbars.
- ○ Display or hide toolbars.
- ○ Modify existing toolbars.
- ○ Create new toolbars.
- ○ Create new toolbar tools.
- ○ Construct new button images.
- ○ Create and modify flyout menus.
- ○ Describe the purpose and function of the AutoCAD menu files.

One of the easiest ways of altering the AutoCAD environment is to customize the toolbars. This requires no programming, and little use of text editors. Existing toolbars can be modified quickly by removing and adding buttons, or changing their shape and location. New tools can also be created and assigned to an existing toolbar. The most powerful aspect of customizing toolbars is the ability to quickly create entirely new functions and buttons to help you in your work.

WORKING WITH TOOLBARS

Toolbars provide access to most AutoCAD commands with one or two quick "picks." This graphical interface provides much flexibility. Toolbars can be quickly and easily resized, repositioned, hidden from view, or made visible.

Positioning and sizing toolbars

By default, AutoCAD shows the **Draw** and **Modify** toolbars. These are floating at the left side of the AutoCAD window. When a toolbar is *floating*, it can be adjusted and repositioned much like a window. To reposition a toolbar, place the cursor on the title bar, press and hold the pick button, and move the toolbar to the new location. The outline of the toolbar is visible while you are moving it, Figure 17-1A. Release the pick button when the toolbar is where you want it.

Unlike windows, toolbars can only be resized in one direction at a time. Moving the cursor to a vertical border changes the cursor to a horizontal resizing cursor. Again, press and hold the pick button and an outline is displayed. Move the cursor to resize the toolbar. Release the pick button to create the new size. Figure 17-1B and Figure 17-1C show the **Draw** toolbar being resized.

Toolbars can also be docked. A *docked* toolbar is positioned so that it appears as if it is part of the AutoCAD window. By default the **Standard** toolbar and the **Object Properties** toolbar are docked at the top of the screen. These toolbars can be floated, just as any other toolbar.

Figure 17-1.
A—Repositioning a floating
toolbar. B—Resizing a
floating toolbar horizontally.
C—Resizing a toolbar
vertically. Using the **Tools**
pull-down menu to display
toolbars.

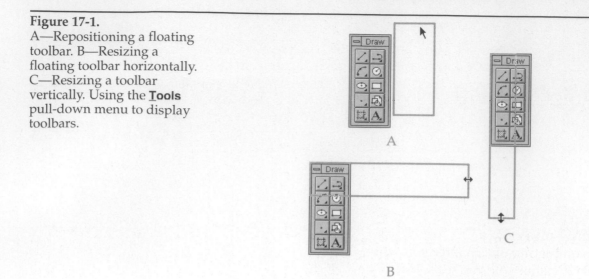

To dock a toolbar, reposition it at any edge of the AutoCAD window. A toolbar can be docked on the right, left, top, or bottom of the AutoCAD window. Figure 17-2 shows the **Draw** toolbar docked on the left side of the screen, and the **Modify** toolbar in the process of being docked on the right side. Note that the outline of the toolbar changes shape and is displayed with a thinner line when it is in position to be docked. Releasing the pick button completes the docking operation.

If you need to place a floating toolbar near the edge of the AutoCAD window, but you do not want it to dock, simply hold the [Ctrl] key down while you reposition the toolbar. This information appears on the status line as you move the toolbar, as shown in Figure 17-2. To float a docked toolbar, place your cursor anywhere on the toolbar that is not a button, then press and hold the pick button. Now, move the toolbar away from the edge and it floats. This technique can also be used to adjust the position of a docked toolbar.

Figure 17-2.
A—Toolbars can be docked on the edge of the AutoCAD window. B—Press the [Ctrl] key while moving the toolbar to prevent docking.

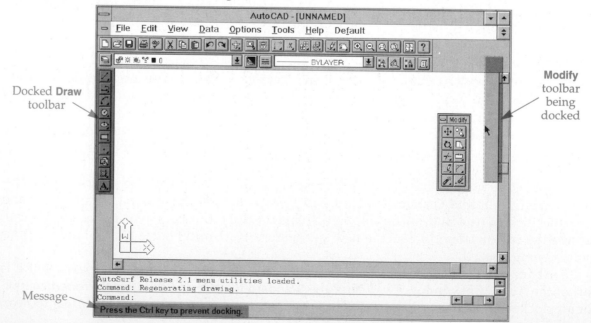

Controlling toolbar visibility

You can adjust the AutoCAD screen so that only the toolbars you need are visible. This helps conserve drawing window space. If too many toolbars are visible at one time, the drawing window can become small and crowded. When your drawing area is small, too much of your time is spent making display changes so that you can clearly see parts of the drawing. Figure 17-3 shows an example of a small and crowded drawing window.

Also, look closely at the **Attributes** toolbar docked on the left side of the window. It is partially hidden from view. When the **Draw** toolbar was docked, the combined length of the two is longer than the available space. Remember this when arranging your toolbars. You must have access to all of the buttons.

Figure 17-3.
Too many toolbars visible at once can cut down on the useful drawing area.

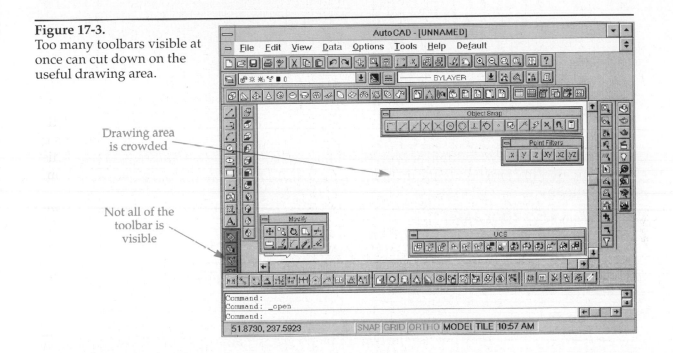

To make a toolbar visible, use the **TOOLBAR** command. This command allows you to show, hide, or position toolbars. To access the **TOOLBAR** command, pick the **Tool Windows** flyout on the **Standard Toolbar**. The default button in this flyout is **Aerial View**. You can also pick the desired toolbar name on the **Toolbars** cascade of the **Tools** pull-down menu, Figure 17-4.

To hide a floating toolbar, single-click on the menu control button. This menu button is the rectangular box in the upper left corner of the toolbar window with a horizontal dash. If you wish to hide a docked toolbar, you can first move it away from the edge to make it a floating toolbar. Then, pick the menu control button.

The **TOOLBAR** command can also be typed at the **Command:** prompt. However, you must know the name of the toolbar, as well as the menu group name it is associated with. When prompted for the toolbar name, you must combine the menu group name and the toolbar name separated by a period. For example, if you are using the ACADFULL menu, the group name is ACAD. Then, to change the position or visibility of the **Draw** toolbar, enter ACAD.DRAW. In the following example, the **Draw** toolbar is hidden using the **Hide** option of the **TOOLBAR** command:

```
Command: TOOLBAR⏎
Toolbar name (or ALL): ACAD.DRAW⏎
Show/Hide/Left/Right/Top/Bottom/Float: HIDE⏎
```

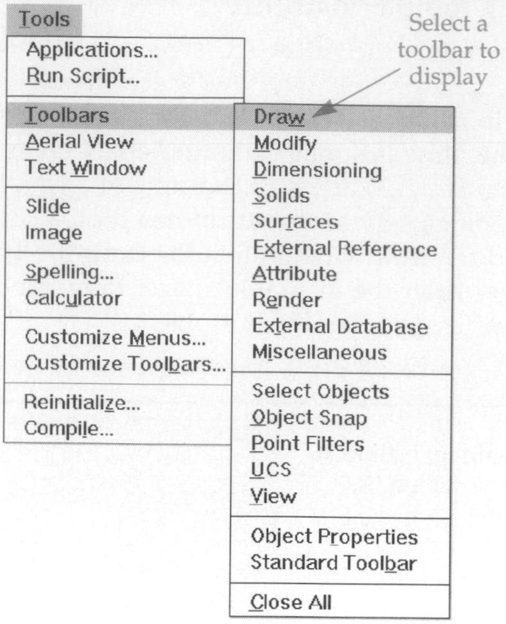

Figure 17-4.
Pick a toolbar name from
the **Toolbars** cascade of the
Tools pull-down menu.

Tools
Applications...
Run Script...
Toolbars
Aerial View
Text Window
Slide
Image
Spelling...
Calculator
Customize Menus...
Customize Toolbars...
Reinitialize...
Compile...

Select a toolbar to display

Draw
Modify
Dimensioning
Solids
Surfaces
External Reference
Attribute
Render
External Database
Miscellaneous
Select Objects
Object Snap
Point Filters
UCS
View
Object Properties
Standard Toolbar
Close All

The **Draw** toolbar is now hidden, or invisible. If the toolbar was docked, the docking area may be reformatted to compensate for the missing toolbar. To redisplay the **Draw** toolbar, use the **Show** option:

> Command: **TOOLBAR**.↵
> Toolbar name (or ALL): **ACAD.DRAW**.↵
> Show/Hide/Left/Right/Top/Bottom/Float: **SHOW**.↵

This option redisplays the toolbar in the same location before **Hide** was used.

NOTE

Modified menus or menus provided by third party developers may not use the default menu group name of ACAD. If you are using a non-standard menu, consult your instructor, CAD manager, or the third party menu documentation to determine the menu group names used.

Exact placement of toolbars is also possible by using other options of the **TOOLBAR** command. The **Left/Right/Top/Bottom/Float** options show a toolbar if it is not already visible and place it in the specified position. Specifying either Left, Right, Top, or Bottom docks the toolbar at that area of the AutoCAD window. To dock the **Modify** toolbar on the left side of the AutoCAD window, use the following command sequence:

> Command: **TOOLBAR**.↵
> Toolbar name (or ALL): **ACAD.MODIFY**.↵
> Show/Hide/Left/Right/Top/Bottom/Float: ⟨Show⟩: **LEFT**.↵
> Position ⟨0,0⟩: ↵

The Position ⟨0,0⟩: prompt is asking for a pixel value. *Pixel* stands for picture elements and refers to the smallest unit of display found on your video display. Screen resolution is described in pixels. For example, an 800×600 resolution has 800 pixels horizontally and 600 vertically. This gives a total of 480,000 pixels. Pixels used as screen coordinates are specified using the upper-left portion of the screen as 0,0. In the case of docked toolbars, the upper-left area of the docking area is considered 0,0. The previous example places the **Modify** toolbar in the upper-left corner of the toolbar docking area at the left side of the screen. Placing another toolbar in the same location (0,0) pushes the existing toolbar down on a vertical (Left/Right) configuration, or to the right on a horizontal (Top/Bottom) configuration. When docked, a horizontal toolbar is approximately 32 pixels high and a vertical toolbar is about 34 pixels wide. In the following example, notice the different toolbar placements based on the values entered:

```
Command: TOOLBAR↵
Toolbar name (or ALL): ACAD.MODIFY↵
Show/Hide/Left/Right/Top/Bottom/Float: ⟨Show⟩: HIDE↵
Command: TOOLBAR↵
Toolbar name (or ALL): ACAD.DRAW↵
Show/Hide/Left/Right/Top/Bottom/Float: ⟨Show⟩: HIDE↵
```

This hides the **Modify** and **Draw** toolbars. Now that both toolbars are hidden, use the other options to show and place them:

```
Command: TOOLBAR↵
Toolbar name (or ALL): ACAD.MODIFY↵
Show/Hide/Left/Right/Top/Bottom/Float: ⟨Show⟩: LEFT↵
Position ⟨0,0⟩: ↵
Command: TOOLBAR↵
Toolbar name (or ALL): ACAD.DRAW↵
Show/Hide/Left/Right/Top/Bottom/Float: ⟨Show⟩: LEFT↵
Position ⟨0,0⟩: ↵
```

Notice that the **Modify** toolbar is placed in the upper-left position first, then moved down to allow space for the **Draw** toolbar. The next sequence first hides the toolbars, then places the **Draw** toolbar at the 0,0 position and the **Modify** toolbar at coordinates 35,0.

```
Command: TOOLBAR↵
Toolbar name (or ALL): ACAD.MODIFY↵
Show/Hide/Left/Right/Top/Bottom/Float: ⟨Show⟩: HIDE↵
Command: TOOLBAR↵
Toolbar name (or ALL): ACAD.DRAW↵
Show/Hide/Left/Right/Top/Bottom/Float: ⟨Show⟩: HIDE↵
Command: TOOLBAR↵
Toolbar name (or ALL): ACAD.MODIFY↵
Show/Hide/Left/Right/Top/Bottom/Float: ⟨Show⟩: LEFT↵
Position ⟨0,0⟩: ↵
Command: TOOLBAR↵
Toolbar name (or ALL): ACAD.DRAW↵
Show/Hide/Left/Right/Top/Bottom/Float: ⟨Show⟩: LEFT↵
Position ⟨0,0⟩: 35,0↵
```

In this example, the **Draw** toolbar is placed to the right of the **Modify** toolbar and at the top of the docking area.

NOTE   A list of all toolbar names can be found in the **Toolbars:** list in the **Toolbars** dialog box. This is accessed through the **TBCONFIG** command discussed later in this chapter.

The last option of the **TOOLBAR** command is the **Float** option. This places the toolbar in a floating position specified in pixels at the Position ⟨0,0⟩: prompt. The anchor point of a floating toolbar is the upper-left corner. If you place the toolbar at 400,300, the upper-left corner of the toolbar is at this coordinate location, with the toolbar displayed downward and to the right of this point. You are then asked to establish the shape of the new toolbar by specifying the number of rows for the toolbar to have. For example, this sequence places the **Draw** toolbar as shown in Figure 17-5:

```
Command: TOOLBAR↵
Toolbar name (or ALL): ACAD.DRAW↵
Show/Hide/Left/Right/Top/Bottom/Float: ⟨Show⟩: FLOAT↵
Position ⟨0,0⟩: 400,300↵
Rows ⟨1⟩: 2↵
```

While using the **TOOLBAR** command is very accurate for placement, it is also time-consuming. Using the cursor is much quicker, though not as accurate. When using floating toolbars, it is also possible to overlap the toolbars to save screen space. Be sure to leave part of each toolbar showing, then to bring it to the front, simply pick somewhere on the toolbar.

Figure 17-5.
A floating toolbar.

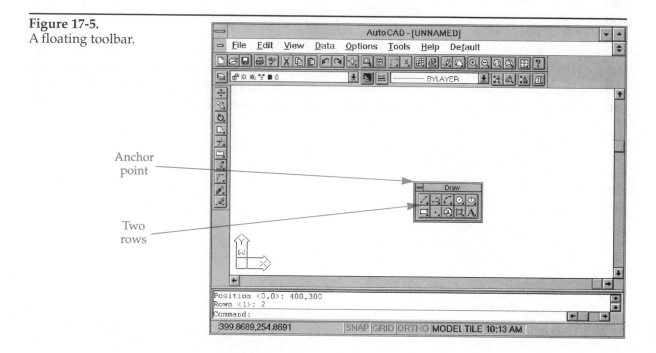

One other capability of the **TOOLBAR** command is to show or hide all toolbars at once. When prompted for the toolbar name, enter the word ALL. The only two options that appear are **Show** and **Hide**. If you use the **Hide** option, you have no toolbars displayed. Then, you can use the **Toolbars** cascade in the **Tools** pull-down menu to select the toolbars you need. The **Hide** option can also be selected in the **Toolbars** submenu by picking **Close All**. The Show option is not available in the pull-down menu. The toolbars visible by default are the **Object Properties**, **Draw**, **Modify**, and **Standard** toolbar.

| NOTE | The **TOOLBAR** command is unaffected by the **UNDO** command. This means that if you hide all of your toolbars, you cannot use **UNDO** to make them visible again. |

EXERCISE 17-1

❑ Open AutoCAD and maximize it so that it occupies the entire screen.
❑ Use the appropriate command or pull-down menu selection to display the **Draw, Modify,** and **Dimensioning** toolbars.
❑ Position the three toolbars in a floating configuration. Move them to several different floating positions around the screen.
❑ Move the **Draw** and **Modify** toolbars to a docked position at the top of the screen.
❑ Move the **Dimensioning** toolbar to a docked position at the right side of the screen.
❑ Position all three toolbars in a docked position at the right side of the screen.
❑ Position each of the toolbars in two additional docked positions on the screen.
❑ Return the screen to the original configuration.

CUSTOMIZING TOOLBARS

In addition to positioning and sizing toolbars, you can also completely customize the toolbar interface. You can add new tools or place existing tools in new locations for quick access. Infrequently used tools can be deleted or moved to a new location that is out of the way. Entirely new toolbars can be created and filled with redefined buttons, or custom button definitions can be created.

The **TBCONFIG** command is used to customize toolbars. This can be accessed by picking either the **Customize Toolbars...** option on the **Tools** menu, by *right-clicking* on any toolbar button, or by typing TBCONFIG at the **Command:** prompt. The term *right-click* means to pick using the right mouse button. On digitizer pucks, this is the same as pressing the return button.

Adding, deleting, moving and copying tools

The **TBCONFIG** command displays the **Toolbars** dialog box shown in Figure 17-6. This dialog box allows you to manipulate toolbars and toolbar buttons. One common thing to do when working with toolbars is to place an existing tool in a new location. For example, if your current project requires you to create a number of symbols using the **BLOCK** command, you may wish to place the **Rectangular Array** tool as a top level pick on a visible toolbar, such as the **Draw** toolbar.

Figure 17-6.
The **Toolbars** dialog box provides tools for customizing or creating AutoCAD toolbars.

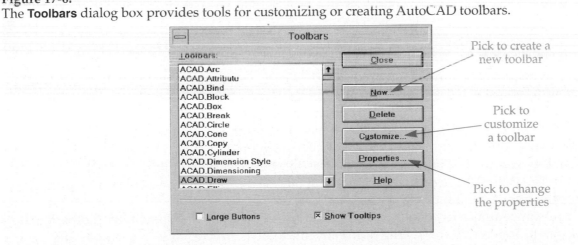

Pick to create a new toolbar

Pick to customize a toolbar

Pick to change the properties

NOTE   When modifying a floating toolbar, be sure to place it away from the center of the screen. Otherwise, when the **Toolbars** dialog box is activated, it may hide the toolbar you wish to modify.

The following sequence adds the **Rectangular Array** tool to the **Draw** toolbar. First, start the **TBCONFIG** command. The **Toolbars** dialog box is displayed. To begin customizing your toolbar, pick the **Customize...** button. This displays the **Customize Toolbars** dialog box, Figure 17-7A. The **Customize Toolbars** dialog provides access to all of AutoCAD's predefined toolbar buttons. The buttons are categorized by the top level toolbars they are associated with. A *top level* toolbar is a subset of AutoCAD toolbars that can be accessed in this dialog. Toolbars that are not top level include the flyouts. Flyouts are actually toolbars as well, but are not considered top level toolbars. Therefore, they cannot be accessed in this dialog box. Flyouts are discussed later in this chapter.

Picking the pop-up list button for the **Categories:** field provides a scrolling list of the available top level toolbars. Use this list to select the **Modify** tools where the **Rectangular Array** tool is located. The **Customize Toolbars** dialog box changes, as shown in Figure 17-7B.

Figure 17-7.
A—The **Customize Toolbars** dialog box. B—The **Modify** tools available in the **Customize Toolbars** dialog box.

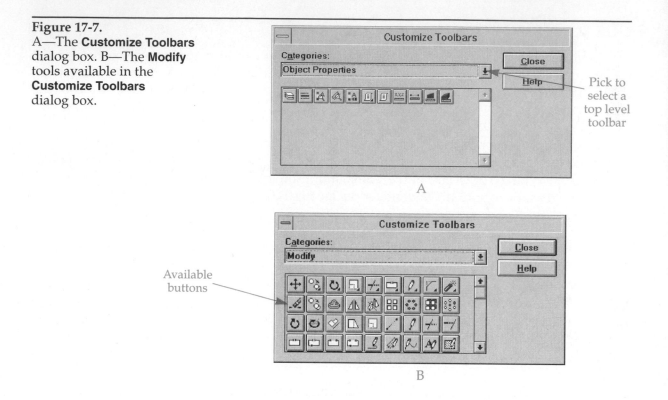

The buttons displayed under this category can now be accessed freely. If you wish to add one of these buttons to an existing toolbar, point to the button then press and hold the pick button. Now, as you move your pointing device, the outline of the selected button will be attached to your cursor. Figure 17-8A shows the button being dragged off of the **Customize Toolbars** dialog box. Note that the **Rectangular Array** button appears depressed, this shows you which button you are dragging. Drag the new button to the **Draw** toolbar, and position it where you would like it to be located. If you position it between two other buttons, it is placed between them, Figure 17-8B. The existing buttons are adjusted to accommodate the new button. When it is in the desired location, release the pick button to place it. Figure 17-8C shows the final appearance of the **Draw** toolbar after this operation.

You can continue to customize toolbars as desired while the **Customize Toolbars** dialog box is open. To remove an existing button from a toolbar, first point to the button. Then, press and hold the pick button on your pointing device. Now drag the toolbar button out to a clear area of the graphics screen and release the pick button. The toolbar button disappears and is removed from the toolbar.

Figure 17-8.
A—Dragging a button from the **Customize Toolbars** dialog box. B—Dragging a button onto an existing toolbar. C—The **Draw** toolbar after placing the new button.

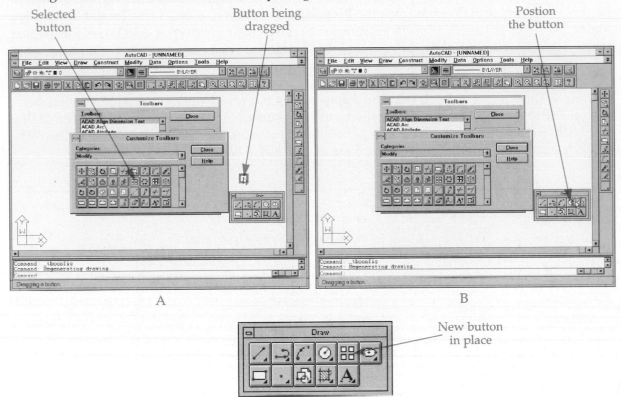

C

Moving a button to a new location is accomplished the same way. Simply drag it to the new location. This includes repositioning a button on the same toolbar, or moving it to a new toolbar. By pressing and holding the [Ctrl] key while you move a button, a small plus sign is added to the outline being dragged, Figure 17-9. This indicates that the button is being *copied* to the new location rather than being *moved*. A copied button appears in both the new and old locations.

Figure 17-9.
When dragging a button, the plus sign indicates that the toolbar button is being copied.

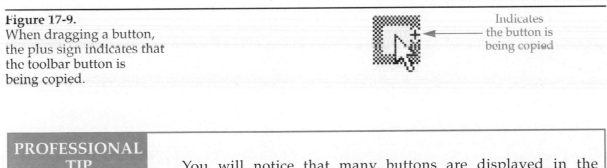

Indicates the button is being copied

PROFESSIONAL TIP

You will notice that many buttons are displayed in the **Customize Toolbars** dialog box. Some of them may be familiar and some may not. Unfortunately, ToolTips are not available for the buttons displayed in this dialog. If you are unsure of what a specific toolbar button is, pick it and drag it to an existing toolbar. Now you can point to it and get a ToolTip along with the help string on the status line. If it is not the button you wanted, simply drop it somewhere on the graphics screen to discard it.

Toolbar properties

The basic properties of a toolbar include the toolbar name, help string, and its current visibility status. Each of these properties can be adjusted in the **Toolbars** dialog box, shown in Figure 17-6. In that dialog box, pick the **Properties...** button to display the **Toolbar Properties** dialog box. This dialog box has fields for each of the toolbar properties, edit boxes for the text entry fields, and a check box for visibility. To change the name of a toolbar or the associated help string, enter the new text in the appropriate edit box. To toggle the visibility of a toolbar, pick the checkbox in front of the **Hide** label. The **Toolbar Properties** dialog box for the **Draw** toolbar is shown in Figure 17-10. The **Apply** button is grayed-out unless a change has been made. However, changes are not applied until the **Apply** button is picked. To close the dialog box without saving changes, double-click on the menu control button. The menu control button is the small box in the upper-left corner of the dialog box.

Figure 17-10.
The **Toolbar Properties** dialog box.

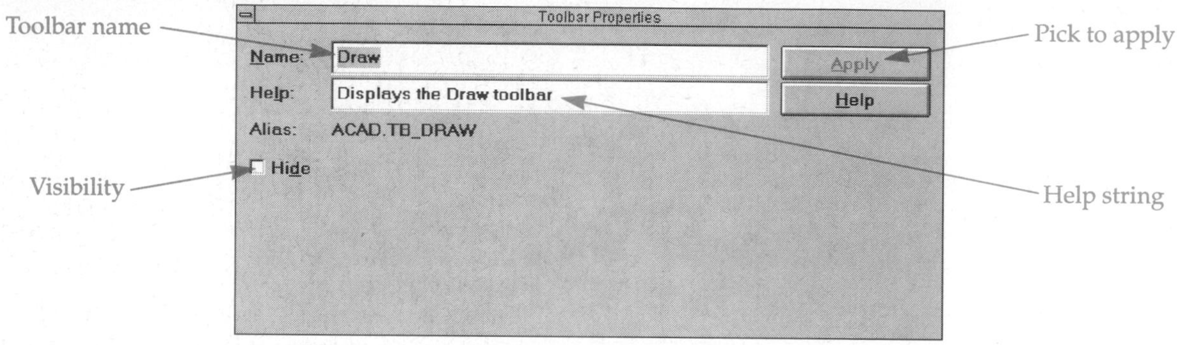

EXERCISE 17-2

❑ Begin AutoCAD. Be sure that the **Draw** toolbar is displayed in a floating position to the right or left of the screen.
❑ If you have not added the **Rectangular Array** button to the **Draw** toolbar, do so now.
❑ Copy the **Polar Array** button to the **Draw** toolbar, and place it to the right of the **Rectangular Array** button.
❑ Copy the **Mirror** button to the **Draw** toolbar, and place it to the right of the **Polar Array** button.
❑ Move the **Mirror** button to a new position to the left of the **Rectangular Array** button in the **Draw** toolbar.
❑ Remove the **Mirror, Rectangular Array,** and **Polar Array** buttons from the **Draw** toolbar.
❑ Modify the title of the **Draw** toolbar to read Draw/Construct.
❑ Modify the help string of the **Draw** toolbar to read Displays the Draw/Construct toolbar.
❑ Apply the changes you just made
❑ Change the title and help string of the **Draw** toolbar to the original wording and apply the changes.

Creating new toolbars

Use the **TBCONFIG** command to display the **Toolbars** dialog box, as shown in Figure 17-6. Pick the **New...** button to display the **New Toolbar** dialog box, Figure 17-11A. Enter the new toolbar name of Custom Tools in the **Toolbar Name:** field. Pick **OK** to create the toolbar, and the new empty toolbar appears on-screen, Figure 17-11B. The new toolbar name is also added to the listing in the **Toolbars** dialog box. It can now be customized just as any other toolbar.

Figure 17-11.
A—The **New Toolbar** dialog
box. B—A newly created
toolbar.

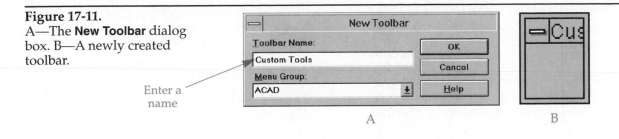

Notice that the entire title bar is not shown. You cannot resize the toolbar to show the entire
title until buttons are placed in it. Add predefined buttons by picking the **Customize...** button
and dragging the new buttons into place from the **Customize Toolbars** dialog box.

Creating new tools

New tools can be created and added to existing or new toolbars. To create a new tool,
pick the **Customize...** button from the **Toolbars** dialog box. Using the **Categories:** pop-up list,
pick the **Custom** category. This category displays a standard button and a flyout button,
Figure 17-12. Notice that both of these buttons are blank.

To begin creating your own custom button, drag a blank button to the new toolbar. Now,
point to it and right-click your mouse (or pick using the return button of a digitizer). The
Button Properties dialog box is displayed, Figure 17-13. This dialog box allows you to define
a new button.

When the **Button Properties** dialog box is open, No Name appears by default in the **Name:**
text box. The characters ^C^C appear the **Macro:** field. These represent two cancel commands.
No help string or graphic initially appears either. You can fill in all of the fields as desired. For
the purpose of this example, a macro will be created that draws an E-size rectangular border
(44″ × 34″) using a wide polyline, sets the drawing limits, and finishes with **Zoom Extents**.

First, enter a name in the **Name:** field. All buttons must have a name, or AutoCAD will
not accept the button definition. For this example, assign a name of E-Size Setup. This will
appear as the tooltip after you finish defining the button.

Figure 17-12.
The blank buttons available
in the **Customize Toolbars**
dialog box.

Figure 17-13.
The **Button Properties**
dialog box.

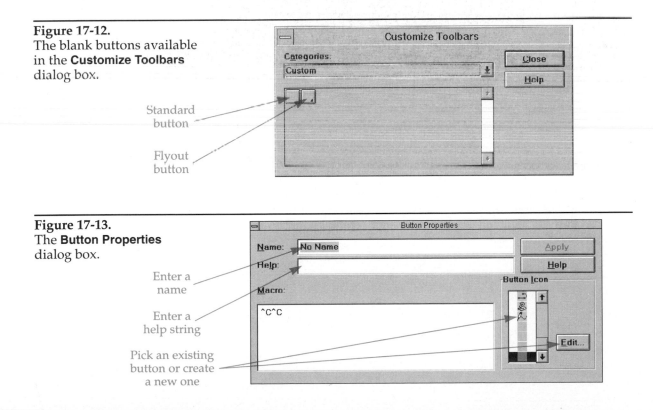

The next field is the **Help:** field. This is where you specify the help string that appears on the status line when you point to the button with your cursor. All help strings should provide a clear description of what the associated button actually does. Set this help string to read: Draws an E-Size sheet, sets and displays the limits. While help strings should be clear, they should also be brief.

Now it is time to define the macro to be performed when the button is picked. Move your cursor to the **Macro:** field. Whenever a command is not required to operate transparently, it is best to begin the macro with two cancel keystrokes (^C^C) to cancel any current command and return to the **Command:** prompt. Two cancels are required to be sure you that begin at the **Command:** prompt. If you are in the **Dim:** command and using the subcommand **Vertical**, for example, and issue one cancel by pressing the [Esc] key, you are returned only to the **Dim:** prompt. Pressing the [Esc] key a second time cancels the **Dim:** command and returns you to the **Command:** prompt.

NOTE   Previous versions of AutoCAD use the [Ctrl]+[C] key combination to issue a cancel. In Release 13, this key combination executes the **COPYCLIP** command. However, when writing a menu file, the notation of ^C is still used to indicate a cancel.

The most important thing to consider when designing a macro is that the macro information perfectly matches the requirements of the activated commands. For example, if the **LINE** command is issued, the subsequent prompt expects a coordinate point to be entered. Any other data is inappropriate and will cause an error in your macro. It is usually the best idea to walk through each step in the desired macro manually, writing down each step and the data required by each prompt. The following sequence walks through the creation of the polyline border. The polyline is set at .015 line width and is a rectangle from 0,0 to 44,34.

```
Command: PLINE↵
From point: 0,0↵
Current line-width is 0.0000
Arc/Close/Halfwidth/Length/Undo/Width/⟨Endpoint of line⟩: W↵
Starting width ⟨0.0000⟩: .015↵
Ending width ⟨0.0150⟩: .015↵
Arc/Close/Halfwidth/Length/Undo/Width/⟨Endpoint of line⟩: 44,0↵
Arc/Close/Halfwidth/Length/Undo/Width/⟨Endpoint of line⟩: 44,34↵
Arc/Close/Halfwidth/Length/Undo/Width/⟨Endpoint of line⟩: 0,34↵
Arc/Close/Halfwidth/Length/Undo/Width/⟨Endpoint of line⟩: C↵
Command:
```

Creating the menu macro involves duplicating the above keystrokes, with a couple of differences. Some symbols are used in menu macros to represent keystrokes. For example, the ^C is not entered by pressing the [Ctrl]+[C] button combination. Instead, the [Shift]+[6] is used to access the *caret* symbol, which is used to represent the [Ctrl] key in combination with the subsequent character (a 'C' in this case).

Another keystroke represented by a symbol is the [Enter] or return key. An [Enter] is shown as a semicolon (;). A space can also be used to designate [Enter]. However, the semicolon is more commonly used because it is very easy to count to make sure that the correct number are supplied. Spaces are not so easy to count.

Keeping these guidelines in mind, the following entry draws the required polyline:

```
^C^CPLINE;0,0;W;.015;.015;44,0;44,34;0,34;C;
```

Compare this with the previous command line entry example to identify each part of the menu macro. The next step is to set the limits and zoom to display the entire border. To do this at the command line would require the following entries:

```
Command: LIMITS↵
Reset Model space limits:
ON/OFF/⟨Lower left corner⟩ ⟨0.0000,0.0000⟩:↵
Upper right corner ⟨12.0000,9.0000⟩: 44,34↵
Command: ZOOM↵
All/Center/Dynamic/Extents/Left/Previous/Vmax/Window/⟨Scale(X/XP)⟩: E↵
Regenerating drawing.
```

Continue to develop this macro by entering the following sequence immediately after the previous one (shown in italics):

^C^CPLINE;0,0;W;.015;.015;44,0;44,34;0,34;C;LIMITS;;44,34;ZOOM;E

Note that an automatic carriage return is issued at the end of the macro, so it is not necessary to enter a semicolon at the end. Having completed the fields of the dialog, the **Button Properties** dialog box now appears as shown in Figure 17-14.

Next, you should create a graphic image for the button. A button can be selected from the scrolling graphic list in the **Button Icon** area of the **Button Properties** dialog box. However, having duplicate images can be a source of confusion. It is best to either modify an existing image or create a brand new one using the **Button Editor**.

Figure 17-14.
Defining the E-Size
Setup macro in the **Button Properties** dialog box.

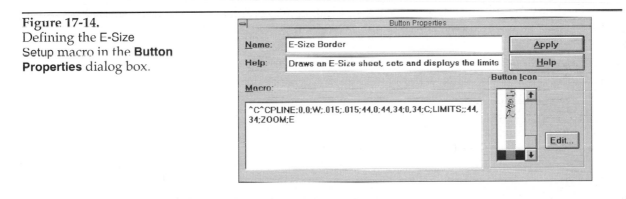

Creating button images

It is important to consider the needs of the persons who will be using your custom menu system when you design buttons. All of the standard buttons in AutoCAD show a graphic that implies something about the command that the button executes. Buttons you create will be most effective if they use this principle as well.

Simple abstract designs may be recognizable to you because you created them and you know what they do. But, when someone else uses this menu system, they may not recognize the purpose of the button.

Rather than edit an existing button in this example, an entirely new button will be created. Highlight one of the blank button icons in the **Button Icon** list of the **Button Properties** dialog box. Next, pick the **Edit...** button. The **Button Editor** dialog box is now displayed, Figure 17-15.

The **Button Editor** dialog box has basic pixel painting tools and several features to simplify the editing process. The four tools are shown as buttons at the top of the dialog box. The pencil paints individual pixels in the current color. The line tool allows you to draw a line between two points. The circle tool allows you to draw center/radius style ellipses and circles. The erase tool clears the color from individual pixels. The current color is selected from the color palette on the right side of the dialog box. Anything you draw will appear in this color.

Figure 17-15.
The **Button Editor**
dialog box.

Tools

Preview

Drawing
area

Color
palette

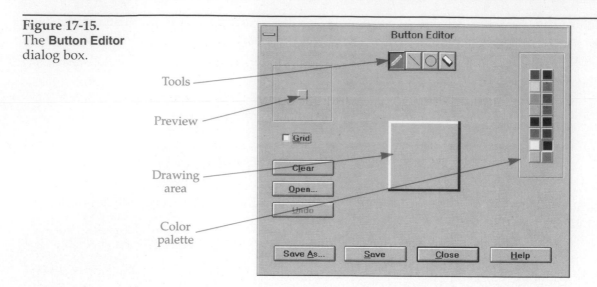

Drawing a graphic is usually much easier with the grid turned on. The grid provides outlines for each pixel in the graphic. Each square is representative of one pixel. Picking the **Grid** check box toggles the state of the grid.

The area just above the **Grid** toggle is the button preview area. The preview displays the appearance of the button in its actual size, while you draw the image.

When the toolbar buttons are set in their default size, the button editor provides a drawing area that represents 16 pixels high by 16 pixels wide. If **Large Buttons** is turned on in the **Toolbars** dialog box, then this will be a 32×32 pixel image.

Buttons require two separate images, one at 16×16 and one at 32×32. If you only create a 16×16 pixel image, your custom buttons will be blank when you switch to large buttons because they have no image defined at that size. You must create a second, 32×32 pixel image for the large button.

Figure 17-16 shows an image created at 16×16 for the **E-Size Setup** button with the **Grid** turned on. Other tools available in the **Button Editor** include:

- **Clear**—If you want to erase everything and start over, pick the **Clear** button to clear the drawing area.
- **Open...**—Use this tool to open existing bitmap files (.BMP).
- **Undo**—You can undo the last operation by picking this button. An operation that has been undone cannot be redone. Only the last operation can be undone.

Figure 17-16.
A 16×16 pixel image for the
E-Size Setup macro button.

Created
image

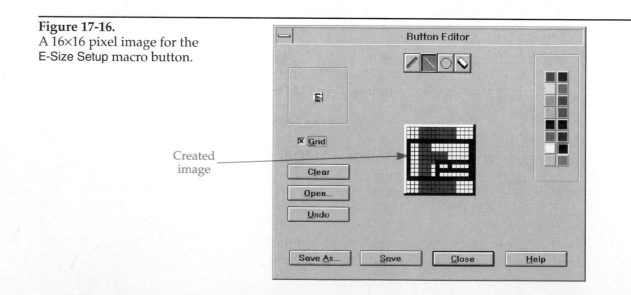

- **Save As...**—Saves a file using the **Save As** dialog box. Use this when you have opened a file and want to save it as well as keep the original on file.
- **Save**—Saves the current bitmap file. If the current image has not yet been saved, then the Save As dialog is displayed.
- **Close**—Ends the **Button Editor** session. A message is displayed if you have unsaved changes.
- **Help**—Provides context sensitive help.

After saving your button image, pick the **Close** button to return to the **Button Properties** dialog box. Your newly created image appears above the **Edit...** button, as shown in Figure 17-17. Pick the **Apply** button to apply the changes. Your button will display the new image, Figure 17-18.

PROFESSIONAL
TIP

The images defined for your custom buttons must be in a location where AutoCAD will find them. You could simply drop all of your bitmap images into one of AutoCAD's support directories, but this may not be the best choice. A better option might be to create a directory just for your bitmap images and add this directory to the support directories specified in the **Environment** panel of the **Preferences** dialog box.

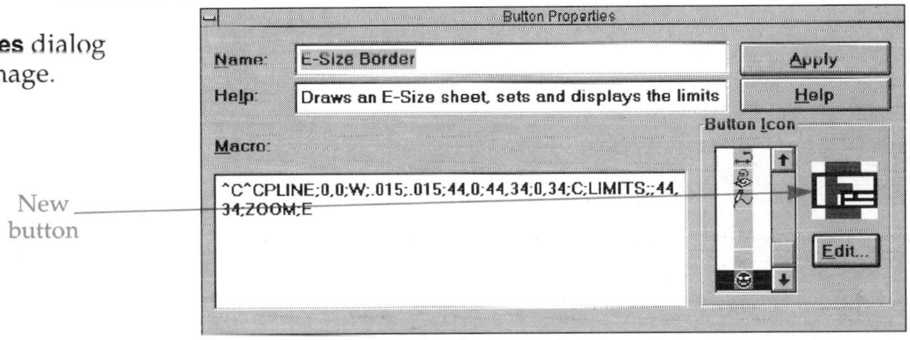

Figure 17-17.
The **Button Properties** dialog displays the new image.

New button

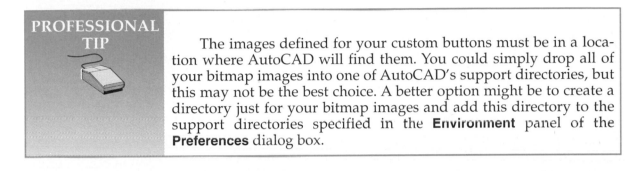

Figure 17-18.
The **E-Size Setup** button after applying the new image.

When you have completed your button, pick the menu control button in the upper left of the **Button Properties** dialog box to close it. Pick the **Close** button in the **Customize Toolbars** dialog box, then pick **Close** in the **Toolbars** dialog box.

The menu file is then recompiled, adding your new changes. More discussion of menu files is found at the end of this chapter, and in Chapter 18.

The **Toolbars** dialog box displays two check boxes at the bottom. They are toggles for the button features they represent:

- **Large Buttons**—Checking this box increases the size of your toolbar buttons from 16×16 to 32×32 pixels. At very high screen resolutions, such as 1280×1024, the smaller 16×16 buttons can be difficult to see. Setting the buttons to the larger size is easier on the eyes. But, at lower screen resolutions the large buttons take up too much of the available space in the AutoCAD window.

- **Show Tooltips**—This allows you to turn off the ToolTips feature, which displays the name of the button that you are pointing to. Unless you are very familiar with the button interface, it is usually best to leave tooltips on.

EXERCISE 17-3

❑ Begin AutoCAD and use the **TBCONFIG** command to display the **Toolbars** dialog box.
❑ If you have not created the **Custom Tools** toolbar and the **E-Size Setup** button as shown in the previous discussion, do so now.
❑ Copy the **Paper Space** button from the **Standard** toolbar into the **Custom Tools** toolbar, and place it to the left of the **E-Size Setup** button.
❑ Create a new macro that does the following:
  ❑ Executes the **MVIEW** command.
  ❑ Selects the **4** option of **MVIEW** to construct four viewports.
  ❑ Uses the **Fit** option to fit the four viewports in the current display.
❑ Test these commands at the keyboard before entering the code as a macro.
❑ Name the button **4 PS Viewports**, and enter the following as the help string: Fits 4 paper space viewports into the current drawing.
❑ Create a button icon of your own design.
❑ Place the new button to the right of the **E-Size Setup** button in the **Custom Tools** toolbar.
❑ Close each dialog box in proper order to save the new macro and toolbar configuration.
❑ The arrangement of the three icons allows you to first enter paper space, then create an E-size layout, then divide it into four paper space viewports.

WORKING WITH FLYOUTS

A flyout is a button that can display the buttons from an associated toolbar. A pick on a flyout button activates the command assigned to the currently-visible toolbar button. When you point to a flyout and hold the pick button, the buttons from the associated toolbar are displayed. Move the cursor to the desired toolbar button and release the pick button. This activates the associated command or macro, and leaves this button's image displayed as the image for the flyout.

In order to create a new flyout button, you should create the associated toolbar first. You can then associate the toolbar with the flyout using the **Flyout Properties** dialog box.

Creating a toolbar that has a tool set that you use frequently in your work can help you to save time and increase productivity. But, each new toolbar that is displayed takes up some of the available screen area. If too many toolbars are displayed at once this can become a problem, especially with lower screen resolutions.

A great way to conserve on screen space is through the implementation of flyouts. Follow through this discussion to create a customized toolbar flyout for working with 3D projects.

First, enter the **TBCONFIG** command to display the **Toolbars** dialog box. Now, select the **New...** button and name the new toolbar 3D Tools. The toolbar appears on the screen, ready to be customized. Pick the **Customize...** button, then pick the **Categories** pop-up list in the **Customize Toolbar** dialog box. Use the predefined buttons found in the **Surfaces**, **Render**, and **Standard** toolbars, and setup your new toolbar, as shown in Figure 17-19.

After you have set up your **3D Tools** toolbar, use the pop-up list to access the **Custom** category. Drag and drop a blank flyout to your **Modify** toolbar, then right-click on it to activate the **Flyout Properties** dialog box. Complete the fields for the dialog box as shown in Figure 17-20, and highlight the ACAD.3D Tools line in the **Associated Toolbar:** field.

Figure 17-19.
The customized **3D Tools** toolbar is created using a combination of buttons in existing toolbars.

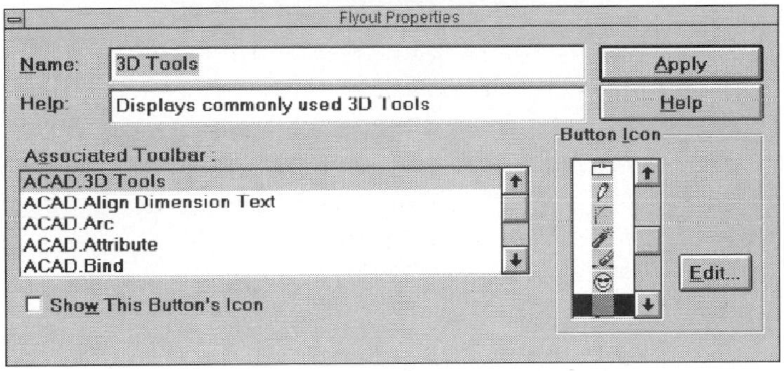

Figure 17-20.
The **Flyout Properties** dialog box for the **3D Tools** flyout button.

Picking the **Apply** button activates the changes, and the upper-left button in the **3D Tools** toolbar becomes the current image in the flyout on the **Modify** toolbar. Close the **Flyout Properties** dialog box by picking the rectangle in the upper left corner. Pick the **Close** button in the **Customize Toolbars** dialog box. Next, pick the **Close** button in the **Toolbars** dialog box and the menu is recompiled. Now when you pick the flyout, your custom **3D Tools** toolbar is displayed, as shown in Figure 17-21.

When you point at the flyout button, the name and help string you supplied in the **Flyout Properties** dialog box are not used. This is because the flyout button is defined as having no icon (or image) of its own. It assumes the identity of the most recently used button in its associated toolbar.

By picking the checkbox for **Show This Button's Icon** in the **Flyout Properties** dialog box, we can define a flyout that has its own identity and properties. If this box is checked, you need to define an icon image using the **Button Editor**.

After this is done, the assigned properties are displayed when the flyout is pointed to, as shown in Figure 17-22. The tooltip now displays the button's name, and the help string also

Figure 17-21.
The **3D Tools** flyout button placed on the **Modify** toolbar.

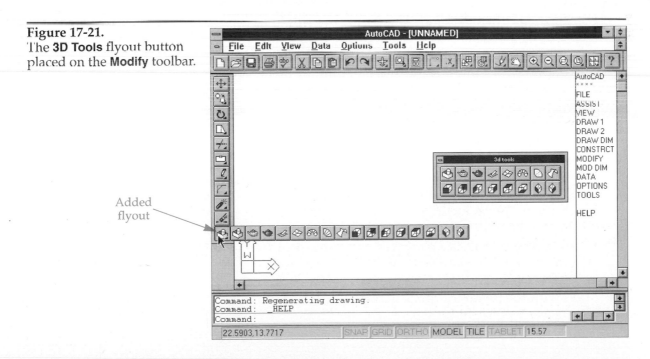

Figure 17-22.
The new flyout displays its
own tooltip and help string.

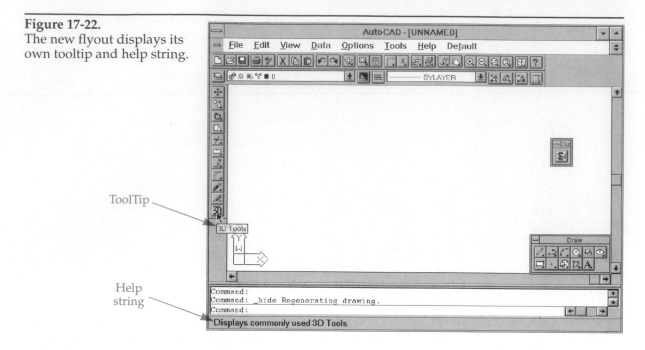

displays the information associated with this flyout. Picking this button displays its associated toolbar, but the toolbar image doesn't change to reflect the last button picked.

While both methods of creating a flyout are acceptable, it is most effective to allow the flyout to be "transparent"—or assume the identity of the most recently picked button. Commands are often used several times consecutively in a standard editing session.

For example, rarely will you only need to draw a single line. Normally, several lines must be drawn in sequence. This is generally true of many different AutoCAD commands. Therefore, having the last button picked as the default makes it more convenient to select it again. This can increase your efficiency by requiring less picks for the same amount of work.

TOOLBARS AND MENU FILES

As toolbars are adjusted and customized, the changes are stored in files. AutoCAD maintains a record of these changes in one of several files associated with the menu system. Each of these files has the same file name, but different file extensions. The two standard menus provided with the AutoCAD software are named ACAD and ACADFULL, and the files associated with these menus are located in the \R13\WIN\SUPPORT directory.

It is important to understand the handling of menu files, otherwise it is very easy for your toolbar customization work to simply disappear. The menu files associated with the ACAD menu are as follows:

- **ACAD.MNU**—This is the fully-documented *template* file. This provides the initial menu setup. If this menu is edited and then loaded using the **MENU** command, it creates a new menu *source* file.
- **ACAD.MNS**—This is the menu *source* file. Most documentation is stripped from it to reduce the file's size. All code changes to the toolbar menu are recorded into this file. (Position data is recorded in the ACAD.INI file.) This is the file that is used in the creation of a *compiled* menu file.
- **ACAD.MNC**—This is a *compiled* menu file. AutoCAD creates this optimized file to use in handling the menus in your drawing sessions.
- **ACAD.MNR**—This is the menu *resource* file. It stores all of the bitmap images associated with the menu for quick access.

As noted, the .MNS file is the location for code changes to the toolbars. However, when an .MNU file is loaded, it overwrites the current .MNS file—losing all of your changes to the toolbars. A warning to this effect is displayed whenever you attempt to load an .MNU file. In order to make your changes permanent, you should open both files with an ASCII text editor and cut and paste the new or changed data from the .MNS to the .MNU file. That way, when the .MNU file is loaded, it keeps these changes and writes them again to the new .MNS file.

Editing a menu file is done using any ASCII text editor. You will find that the menu files are too large for Notepad, but can be opened with Write. If you are using Write, be sure that you specify NO CONVERSION when you open the file. If you do not, Write will save the menu file as a Write document and will incorporate printer and text formatting codes that AutoCAD will not recognize.

Once you have opened the file, use a text search option to find the text ***TOOLBARS— this begins the toolbar data section. You can then find the listings in each file for changed toolbars and update the .MNU using the code in the .MNS file. New toolbars can be copied and pasted into the .MNU file. More information on editing menu files is found in Chapter 18.

PROFESSIONAL TIP

Other approaches to making your menu changes permanent are available. It is possible to rename or delete the .MNU file, since it is not necessary to AutoCAD. Or, you can copy the .MNS file directly over the .MNU file.

These approaches are used by AutoCAD professionals, but there is a drawback for those who are just learning to work with menus. The .MNU file is well-documented and can be a valuable tool for learning your way around the menu file. So, while you are first learning to work with menus, it may be best to keep this file on hand.

If you wish to keep the .MNU file available, you should make a copy of the .MNS file each time you modify the toolbar menus. Keep this file in an alternate directory as a backup in case you accidentally overwrite the original .MNS file. Remember, position data, show/hide status, and docked/floating status are saved only in the ACAD.INI file, not in the .MNS.

CHAPTER TEST

Write your answers in the spaces provided.

1. What two toolbars are shown by default when AutoCAD is loaded? _____

2. Describe the flexibility inherent in a floating toolbar. _____

3. How are toolbars unlike other windows? _____

4. How do you prevent a floating toolbar from being docked when repositioning it? _____

_____

5. Which command provides the means to show, hide, or position toolbars? _____

_____

6. When using the command in question 5, what name would you enter to display the **Modify** toolbar? _____

7. What option of the command in question 5 would you use to remove a toolbar from the display? _____

8. What command allows you to customize toolbars? _____

9. How can the command in question 8 be accessed using only the pointing device? _____

_____

10. In which dialog box can you find a list of the top level categories of toolbars? _____

_____

11. How do you copy an existing button from one of the top level category toolbars to another toolbar? _____

_____

12. How do you remove an existing button from a toolbar? _____

_____

_____

13. How can you copy an existing button to a new location? _____

_____

_____

14. How do you access the **New Toolbar** dialog box in order to create a new toolbar? _____

_____

15. Once the new empty toolbar is displayed on the screen, how do you place the first blank button inside it? _____

_____

_____

16. When the new toolbar is displayed on the screen with a blank button inside it, how do you access the **Button Properties** dialog box in order to create a custom macro? _____

_____

_____

17. How do you create a ToolTip for a new button? _____

_____

_____

18. How do you create a help string for a new button? _____

_____

_____

19. How should you develop and test a new macro before creating it in a new button?

    _____

    _____

20. Name two ways to specify an [Enter] or RETURN in a macro, and indicate which of the two is the safest. _____

    _____

21. What type of file (file extension), is the graphic for a new button saved as? _____

22. Name the four tools that are provided in the **Button Editor** dialog box. _____

    _____

23. What is the default size, in pixels, of the button editor drawing area? _____

24. If **Large Buttons** is turned on in the **Toolbars** dialog box, what is the size, in pixels, of the button editor drawing area? _____

25. What is the most efficient location for saving button icon graphic files? _____

    _____

26. How do you insert a flyout button into a toolbar? _____

    _____

27. How do you access the **Flyout Properties** dialog box in order to supply a tooltip and help string to a new flyout button? _____

    _____

28. Why is it more effective to allow a flyout button to assume the identity of the most recently picked button? _____

    _____

29. What is the name and extension of the AutoCAD menu file in which all code changes to the toolbar are recorded? _____

    _____

30. Which AutoCAD menu file is fully documented, and is used to create a new menu source file? _____

DRAWING PROBLEMS

Before customizing or creating any menus, check with your instructor or supervisor for specific instructions or guidelines.

General

1. Create a new toolbar using the following information:
   A. Name the toolbar **Draw/Modify**.
   B. Copy at least three, but no more than six, commonly used draw buttons into the new toolbar.
   C. Copy at least three, but no more than six, commonly used edit buttons into the new toolbar.
   D. Use only existing buttons, do not create new ones.
   E. Remove the default **Draw** and **Modify** toolbars from the current display.
   F. Dock the new **Draw/Modify** toolbar to the upper-left side of the screen.

General

2. Create a new toolbar using the following information:
   A. Name the toolbar **My 3D Tools**.
   B. Copy the following existing buttons from the **Surfaces** toolbar into the new toolbar:

Line	**3D Polyline**	**Dish**
Box	**Wedge**	**Torus**
Pyramid	**Cone**	**Sphere**
Dome		

   C. Copy the following existing buttons from the **View** toolbar into the new toolbar:

Top View	**Bottom View**	**Left View**
Right View	**Front View**	**Back View**

   D. Copy the following existing buttons from the **UCS** toolbar into the new toolbar:

Save UCS	**Named UCS**	**World UCS**
Origin UCS	**3 Point UCS**	**Previous UCS**

   E. Use only existing buttons, do not create new ones.
   F. Size the new toolbar to display two rows or columns and dock it in a location of your choice.

General

3. Create a new toolbar using the following information:
   A. Name the toolbar Paper Space Viewports.
   B. The toolbar should contain eight buttons that use the **MVIEW** command to create paper space viewports as follows:
      - 1 viewport—allow user to pick location
      - 2 viewports (horizontal)—allow user to pick location
      - 3 viewports allow user to pick orientation and location
      - 4 viewports allow user to pick location
      - 1 viewport—fit
      - 2 viewports—vertical
      - 3 viewports—right
      - 4 viewports—fit

    C. The toolbar should contain two additional buttons that do the following:
- Switch to floating model space (**TILEMODE** variable should remain 0)
- Switch to paper space from floating model space

    D. Construct new button icon graphics for the ten buttons. Save the images in a new directory that has been specified in the AutoCAD support environment.

    E. Dock the toolbar on the right side of the screen.

4. Create a new toolbar that contains eight new buttons for the insertion of a paper space border and title block drawings.

   General

    A. All buttons should use the **MVSETUP** command to either create or insert the drawings. The eight buttons should do the following:
- Insert an A-size mechanical title block
- Insert a B-size mechanical title block
- Insert a C-size mechanical title block
- Insert a D-size mechanical title block
- Insert an A-size architectural title block
- Insert a B-size architectural title block
- Insert a C-size architectural title block
- Insert a D-size architectural title block

    B. Create your own architectural title blocks and borders, or modify the mechanical versions to suit your needs. Be sure that new title blocks are added to the list that is available in the **MVSETUP** command.

    C. Construct your own button icon images for each of the eight new buttons. Save the images in a new directory that has been specified in the AutoCAD support environment.

    D. Dock the toolbar on the left side of the screen.

5. Customize the **Open** button on the **Standard** toolbar to display a flyout menu of the eight title blocks you created in problem 4. Use the following information for this problem:

   General

    A. Use the **OPEN** command for each of the buttons.

    B. The **OPEN** command should always be the default button of the flyout menu, and should not be replaced by the most recently used button.

    C. Construct your own button icon images for each of the eight new buttons, or use the same images created in problem 4. Save the images in a new directory that has been specified in the AutoCAD support environment.

Pull-down menus can be customized to suit your needs.

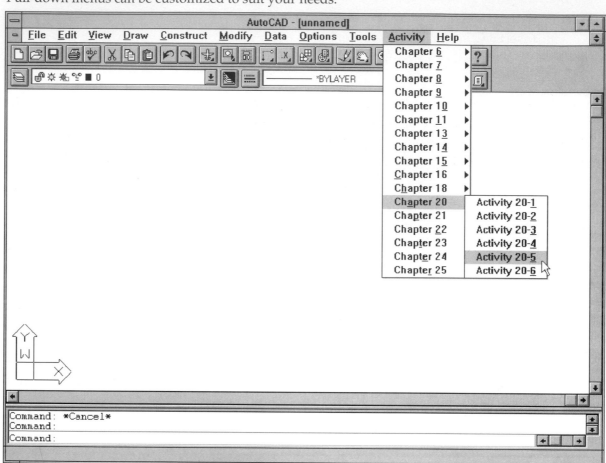

Chapter 18

AutoCAD R13

Customizing Screen and Button Menus

Learning objectives

After completing this chapter, you will be able to:
○ Describe the structure of button and screen menus.
○ Customize existing screen menus and create new ones.
○ Customize button menus.

In Chapter 16, you learned how to customize the AutoCAD working environment to suit your preferences. AutoCAD menus can also be customized to suit specific needs. Users can add special commands to the standard menus or create their own menu system from scratch. As with customized toolbar and toolbar buttons, existing commands can be used in a macro. A *macro* is a function that combines the capabilities of multiple commands and options.

All of the aspects of the menu system can be changed. This includes the cursor button functions, standard screen menus, pull-down menus, and image file menus. Study this chapter carefully to create your own menus.

AUTOCAD'S MENU STRUCTURE

Before constructing your own menus, look at AutoCAD's standard menu structure to get a feel for the layout. This will give you a better understanding of the tools and techniques you can use to build custom menus. The basic components of a menu are the main sections, submenus, item titles, and command codes.

For Chapter 18 – Chapter 21, it is assumed that you are familiar with a programmer's text editor or a word processor program. Therefore, when scrolling or paging through a file is mentioned, you must be familiar with the commands or keys in your text editor that allow you to perform such functions.

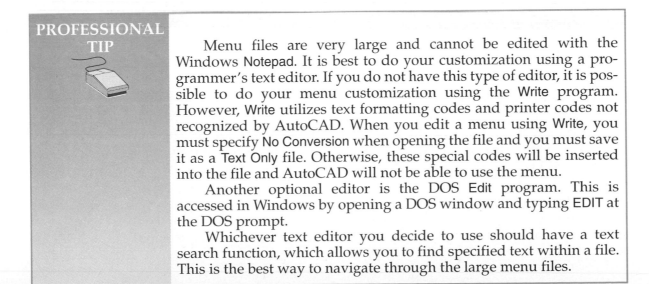

PROFESSIONAL TIP

Menu files are very large and cannot be edited with the Windows Notepad. It is best to do your customization using a programmer's text editor. If you do not have this type of editor, it is possible to do your menu customization using the Write program. However, Write utilizes text formatting codes and printer codes not recognized by AutoCAD. When you edit a menu using Write, you must specify No Conversion when opening the file and you must save it as a Text Only file. Otherwise, these special codes will be inserted into the file and AutoCAD will not be able to use the menu.

Another optional editor is the DOS Edit program. This is accessed in Windows by opening a DOS window and typing EDIT at the DOS prompt.

Whichever text editor you decide to use should have a text search function, which allows you to find specified text within a file. This is the best way to navigate through the large menu files.

AutoCAD's menu files

Several files are used to produce AutoCAD's menu system. As noted in Chapter 17, the file names may vary, but the file extensions are the same. AutoCAD comes with two primary menu files. One is named ACAD and the other is named ACADFULL. Figure 18-1 shows a screen with each of these menus loaded. Note that the ACADFULL menu offers additional selections on the menu bar.

Figure 18-1.
A—The AutoCAD screen with the ACAD menu loaded. B—The AutoCAD screen with the ACADFULL menu loaded. Notice the **Construct** pull-down menu is one of the additional menus available.

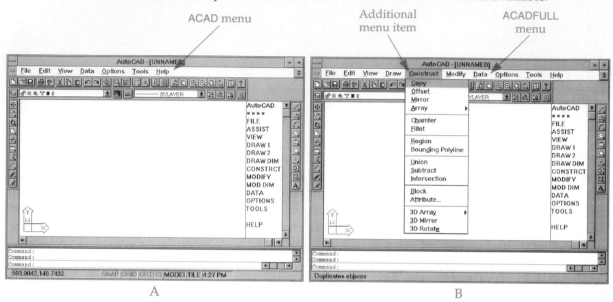

A   B

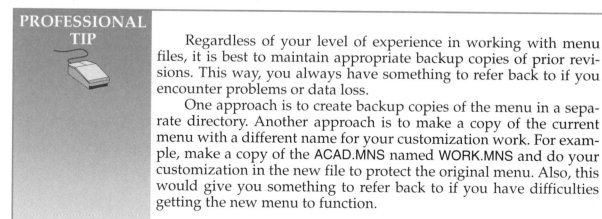

PROFESSIONAL TIP

Regardless of your level of experience in working with menu files, it is best to maintain appropriate backup copies of prior revisions. This way, you always have something to refer back to if you encounter problems or data loss.

One approach is to create backup copies of the menu in a separate directory. Another approach is to make a copy of the current menu with a different name for your customization work. For example, make a copy of the ACAD.MNS named WORK.MNS and do your customization in the new file to protect the original menu. Also, this would give you something to refer back to if you have difficulties getting the new menu to function.

The ACAD menu files are discussed in this chapter. The primary files we will be concerned with are ACAD.MNU, ACAD.MNS, ACAD.MNL, ACAD.MNC, and ACAD.MNR. The ACAD.MNL is a menu LISP file that holds the AutoLISP program code. This defines any AutoLISP functions used in the menu. The last two files, .MNC and .MNR, are automatically created and updated by AutoCAD whenever an edited .MNU or .MNS is loaded and compiled. More information on menu files is provided later in this chapter.

The menu files that you can directly edit include both the .MNU and the .MNS files. As mentioned in Chapter 17, the .MNU file is more completely documented and is, therefore, a bit easier to navigate through and understand. All work in this chapter requires the .MNU file to be edited.

Loading an edited .MNU file overwrites the existing .MNS file of the same name. Since all of your interactive toolbar modifications are written to the .MNS file, they would be overwritten and lost.

Rather than edit the current menu structure, a copy of the .MNU file should be created. This way, any changes you make to the menu will not affect your standard menu. Additionally, since the menu you will be editing will have a different name, the changes to your toolbar made previously will not be lost as you work in this chapter.

To give you a clear idea of how the two menus differ, look at the excerpts of menu code in Figure 18-2. Note that the ACAD.MNU file has documentation that explains the purpose of the code.

Figure 18-2.
The .MNU file contains helpful documentation not found in the .MNS file.

ACAD.MNU	ACAD.MNS
// // Default AutoCAD Release 13 NAMESPACE declaration: // ***MENUGROUP=ACAD // // Begin AutoCAD Button Menus // ***BUTTONS1 ; $p0=* ^C^C ^B ^O ^G ^D ^E ^T	***MENUGROUP=ACAD ***BUTTONS1 ; $p0=* ^C^C ^B ^O ^G ^D ^E ^T

Menu section labels

Using your text editing program, open the ACAD.MNU file found in the \R13\WIN\SUPPORT subdirectory. Use your keyboard cursor keys and the [Page Up]/[Page Down] buttons to page through the file.

As you look through the menu file, notice the menu section headings. Major menu headings are identified by three asterisks (***) in front of the name. Submenus are listed with two asterisks (**) in front of the name. The major menu headings are:

  ***MENUGROUP
  ***BUTTONS1
  ***BUTTONS2
  ***AUX1
  ***AUX2
  ***POP0 *through* POP7
  ***TOOLBARS
  ***image
  ***SCREEN
  ***TABLET1
  ***TABLET2
  ***TABLET3
  ***TABLET4
  ***HELPSTRINGS
  ***ACCELERATORS

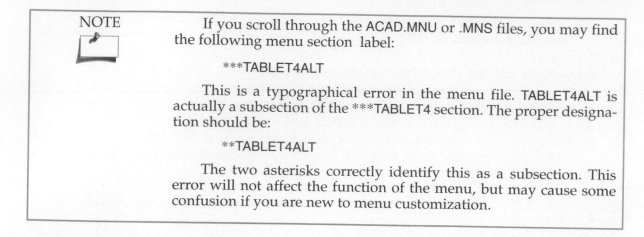

NOTE   If you scroll through the ACAD.MNU or .MNS files, you may find the following menu section label:

***TABLET4ALT

This is a typographical error in the menu file. TABLET4ALT is actually a subsection of the ***TABLET4 section. The proper designation should be:

**TABLET4ALT

The two asterisks correctly identify this as a subsection. This error will not affect the function of the menu, but may cause some confusion if you are new to menu customization.

In this chapter, you will be working with button and screen menus. Pull-down menus are discussed in Chapter 19, image tiles are discussed in Chapter 20, and tablet menus are discussed in Chapter 21. The AUX1 and AUX2 menus are used for a system mouse that comes with computers and operating systems such as Windows/NT, Macintosh, or SPARCstation.

A look at the menu layout

Before beginning any editing of the ACAD.MNU file, take a few minutes to peruse it. Load the ACAD.MNU file into your text editor and locate the line that says ***BUTTONS1. The following portion of the menu should be displayed:

```
***BUTTONS1
;
$p0=*
^C^C
^B
^O
^G
^D
^E
^T

***BUTTONS2
$p0=*

***AUX1
;
$p0=*
^C^C
^B
^O
^G
^D
^E
^T
```

This is the first page of the ACAD.MNU file. The entire file has almost 9000 lines. The first line, ***BUTTONS1, is the beginning of the button menu. The items that follow are specific assignments to the buttons on your pointing device.

Scroll down until you see the ***POP1 heading. This is the first pull-down menu, which appears at the left end of the menu bar near the top of the AutoCAD graphics window. Notice that the first word on each line is enclosed in brackets ([ ]). Any word or character string appearing inside these brackets is displayed in the pull-down menu.

Also note that the first character within the brackets is preceded by an ampersand (&). The character preceded by an ampersand in a pull-down menu title defines the keyboard shortcut key used to enable that menu. Thus, since the title of the **File** pull-down menu is defined as [&File], it can be accessed by pressing [Alt]+[F].

Once a pull-down menu is displayed, a menu item within it may be selected using a single mnemonic character key. The mnemonic keys defined for the **New** and **Open** commands in the **File** pull-down menu appear in ACAD.MNU as [&New] and [&Open]. Therefore, these menu items are enabled with the N and O keys, respectively.

PROFESSIONAL TIP

The DOS Edit program can be accessed from the MS-DOS PROMPT in the Windows Program Manager, or from the **Command:** prompt in AutoCAD. Edit the ACAD.PGP file to include a command that loads your text editor while in AutoCAD. Refer to Chapter 30 in *AutoCAD and it's Applications—Basics, Release 13 for Windows* for specific instructions on editing your ACAD.PGP file. Add the following line to the ACAD.PGP file:

ME,EDIT C:\R13\WIN\SUPPORT\ACAD.MNU,0,,4

This defines a new AutoCAD command named ME (menu edit) that starts the DOS Edit program and loads the ACAD.MNU file automatically. When you exit the editor, you are returned to AutoCAD.

Menu item titles

Learn to use the "search" function of your text editor. This function is extremely useful in moving around a file. Use the search function, or the [Page Down] key to find the ****04_DRAW1** menu. Remember, the two asterisks represent a subheading under a major section. The ****04_DRAW1** menu is the first page of the DRAW1 screen menu. In Figure 18-3, the DRAW1 submenu as seen in AutoCAD is shown on the left, and the same page is shown on the right as it appears in the ACAD.MNU file.

Figure 18-3.
On the left is the **DRAW1** screen menu as it appears on screen. On the right is the related command lines from the ACAD.MNU file.

AutoCAD Screen Menu (DRAW1)	ACAD.MNU File Menu Code
AutoCAD	
* * * *	**04_DRAW1 3
Line:	[Line:]^C^C_line
Xline:	[Xline:]^C^C_xline
Ray:	[Ray:]^C^C_ray
Sketch:	[Sketch:]^C^C_sketch
Pline:	[Pline:]^C^C_pline
3Dpoly:	[3Dpoly:]^C^C_3dpoly
Mline:	[Mline:]^C^C_mline
Spline:	[Spline:]^C^C_spline
Arc:	[Arc:]^C^C_arc
Circle:	[Circle:]^C^C_circle
Donut:	[Donut:]^C^C_donut
Ellipse:	[Ellipse:]^C^C_ellipse
Rectang:	[Rectang:]^C^C_rectang
Polygon:	[Polygon:]^C^C_polygon
Solid:	[Solid:]^C^C_solid

Notice that the command name in the menu is the same as its file listing inside the brackets ([]). A screen menu name can be up to eight characters long. You can have longer names and descriptions inside the brackets. However, only the first eight characters are displayed.

The characters to the right of the closing bracket are the command codes. Figure 18-4 shows the difference between title information and command code. Any text after the eighth character is comments.

Figure 18-4.
A—Information that can be included inside the title brackets. B—Information outside the brackets is processed by AutoCAD.

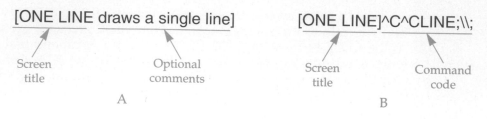

Menu command codes and syntax

When paging through the menu file, you probably noticed several characters and symbols that did not make much sense, such as $S=ACAD and \. These are menu codes, and have explicit functions in the menu. You will be using these codes to create menus.

The characters listed here can be used for button and screen menus. Special characters used in pull-down menus are described later. The following is a list of characters and their functions:

Character	Function
***	Major menu sections—Must be placed directly in front of the name of the section, for example: ***SCREEN.
**	Submenu section—Appears in front of the submenu name. The DRAW1 menu shown in the previous section has the name **04_DRAW1.
[ ]	The name of a menu item is enclosed in brackets. Only the first eight characters inside the brackets are displayed on the side screen menu in AutoCAD.
$S=	This indicates that another screen menu is to be displayed and enables AutoCAD to move between submenus. Find these in the EDIT menu discussed previously. Other similar codes are $B (BUTTONS), $T (TABLET), $I (IMAGE), $P (PULL-DOWN or POP), and $A (AUXILIARY).
^C^C	This cancels any current command. If you are in a transparent or **DIM:** command, two ^Cs are needed to get you out. Placing this in front of your commands ensures that you begin the new command cleanly by canceling any command you are in.
;	The semicolon represents pressing [Enter].
\	The backslash represents information that must be typed at the keyboard or entered with the pointing device.
+	The plus symbol is placed at the end of a long menu line and tells AutoCAD that there is more of this sequence on the next line.
=*	The current cursor, pull-down, or image tile menu is displayed.
(space)	A blank space between items is the same as pressing [Enter] or the space bar.
*^C^C	Creates a repeating command.
si	Specifies immediate action on a single item. Placed at the end of the macro; for example: Erase;si

CREATING BUTTON MENUS

Button menus control the functions of the pointing device buttons. If you use a stylus or a mouse with only one or two buttons, you will not be using button menus. If you have a pointing device with two or more buttons, you can alter the functions of the buttons to suit your needs. This can add to your drawing productivity and speed the access of commonly used commands.

Standard button menu layout

The main button menu is BUTTONS1. It is arranged for a device with nine programmable buttons. A list of this button menu and its functions is shown in Figure 18-5.

Figure 18-5.
On the left is the ***BUTTONS1 menu and on the right is the meaning of the command lines.

MENU FILE LISTING	BUTTON NUMBER AND FUNCTION
***BUTTONS1	Menu name
;	#1 Return
$p0-*	#2 Displays cursor object snap menu
^C^C	#3 Cancel
^B	#4 Snap on/off toggle
^O	#5 Ortho on/off toggle
^G	#6 Grid on/off toggle
^D	#7 Coordinate display toggle
^E	#8 Isoplane crosshair display
^T	#9 Tablet on/off toggle
	#0 Pick button—nonprogrammable

Additional button menus

You can have instant access to the four button menus, BUTTONS1 through BUTTONS4. Each of these menus can be accessed with a keyboard and pick button combination:

Action	Button Menu
pick	BUTTONS1
[Shift]+pick	BUTTONS2
[Ctrl]+pick	BUTTONS3
[Ctrl]+[Shift]+pick	BUTTONS4

Each of these button menus can contain any commands you need. For example, you can place a variety of display commands in the BUTTONS2 menu. To access these commands, simply hold down the [Shift] key on the keyboard and press the pick button. The buttons are reconfigured.

Make a copy of the ACAD.MNU before changing it

Before you edit the ACAD.MNU file, check with your instructor or supervisor to find out what procedures should be used. As discussed previously, it makes sense to first copy the ACAD.MNU file to your own subdirectory or floppy disk. Then experiment and make changes to your copy. This protects the original program. It also prevents undue frustration for students or employees who find that the revised menu does not function properly.

To avoid confusing ACAD.MNU with your menu, name the new copy MYMENU.MNU. You might also use your first name, such as NANCY.MNU. This distinguishes it from all others.

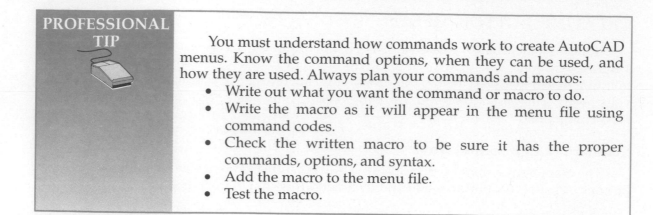

PROFESSIONAL TIP

You must understand how commands work to create AutoCAD menus. Know the command options, when they can be used, and how they are used. Always plan your commands and macros:
- Write out what you want the command or macro to do.
- Write the macro as it will appear in the menu file using command codes.
- Check the written macro to be sure it has the proper commands, options, and syntax.
- Add the macro to the menu file.
- Test the macro.

Replacing button menu items

The process of replacing button menu items is the same as editing a line in a text file. An example is replacing the existing button commands shown in Figure 18-6 with the new commands given. Place a double cancel before each command. This cancels the current command when the button is picked.

Figure 18-6.
Existing button commands can be easily replaced with new commands.

Button	Existing Command	New Command
#5	Ortho	LINE
#6	Grid	ERASE
#7	Coords	CIRCLE
#8	Isoplane	ARC

When you have finished editing, the new button menu should look like this:

```
***BUTTONS1
;
$p1=*
^C^C
^B
^C^CLINE
^C^CERASE
^C^CCIRCLE
^C^CARC
^T
```

Before testing the new menu, you must load it into memory with the **MENU** command, otherwise AutoCAD will work with the old copy. The **MENU** command displays the **Select Menu File** dialog box, Figure 18-7. Select the **List File of Type:** pop-up list to display alternate choices. Note that you can specify either .MNS/.MNC files or .MNU files.

Select the .MNU option and find your menu file using the directory windows. Then, pick your menu from the file list and select the **OK** button. A warning dialog is displayed:

Loading of a template menu file [MNU file] overwrites and redefines the menu source file [MNS file], which results in the loss of any toolbar customization changes that have been made.

Continue loading menu file?

Figure 18-7.
The **Select Menu File** dialog box is used to load the new menu file into memory.

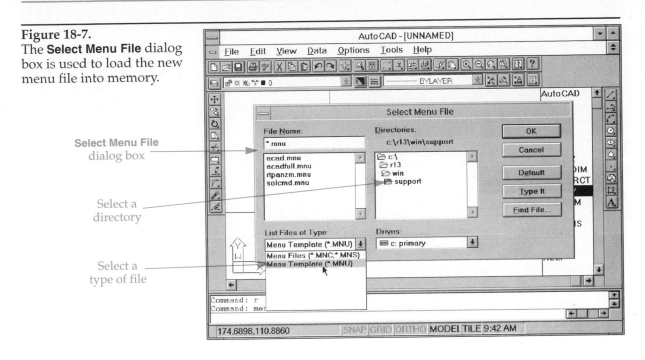

In this case, you want to load the .MNU file, so pick the **OK** button. There is a slight delay as AutoCAD compiles the .MNU file into an .MNC file. The .MNC file is written in a format that makes it usable by AutoCAD. You cannot directly edit the .MNC file.

If the system variable **FILEDIA** is turned off, load your menu file from the command line:

> Command: **MENU**↵
> Menu file name or . for none ⟨C:\R13\WIN\SUPPORT⟩ **MYMENU**↵
> Compiling menu C:\R13\WIN\SUPPORT\MYMENU.mnu…

Providing for user input

An important aspect of menu customization is having a good grasp of AutoCAD's commands and options. Most commands require some form of user input—picking a location on the screen or entering values at the keyboard.

The final action of any input is using a button on the pointing device or pressing [Enter] on the keyboard. The symbol that is used for user input is the backslash (\). A second important aspect of menu customization is inserting returns, or when the [Enter] key is pressed. This is handled with the semicolon (;).

When a command is listed in a menu file, AutoCAD automatically inserts a blank after it, which is interpreted as a return. The following command executes the **LINE** command and prompts for the From point:

> LINE

If the command is followed by a semicolon, backslash, or plus sign, AutoCAD does not insert a blank. Therefore, there is no automatic return. If you want to allow for user input, and then provide a return, you should end the line with a semicolon:

> LINE;\\;

This executes the **LINE** command, waits for the user to pick the start and end points of a line, and then terminates the command.

The button menu can do additional things with the user input symbol. If a backslash is provided after the command, the coordinates of the crosshairs on the screen are recorded when the pick button is pressed. Therefore, the following button command accepts the location of the crosshairs as the From point: for the **LINE** command when the button is pressed, and the prompt that is displayed is the To point: prompt:

    LINE;\

This instant input can be used for other applications. For example, object snaps can be set up to be transparently executed using a button menu.

Adding new button menus

You are not limited to the four button menus. You can create as many as needed. However, one of the buttons should be used to switch menus. Here are a few things to keep in mind when creating new button menus:

- There is no screen display of button names. Use brackets in your menu file to contain button labels or numbers. AutoCAD does not act on anything inside brackets. For example:

      ***BUTTONS1
      [5]^C^CLINE
      [6]^C^CERASE
      [7]^C^CCIRCLE
      [8]^C^CARC

- The letter B is used to call button menu names. The code of $B= is used to call other button submenus, just as $S= is used to call other screen submenus. For example, you could specify button 9 in the ***BUTTONS1 menu to call submenu **B1** as follows:

      [9]$B=B1

When button 9 is pressed, submenu **B1** is activated and the buttons change to reflect the new menu.

- A button menu selection can also call a screen menu in the same manner. For example, button 9 could call the **OSNAP** screen menu in addition to changing the button submenu to **B1**. The entry in the menu file would look like this:

      [9]$B=B1 $S=OSNAP

You will alter the **OSNAP** screen menu for using buttons in one of the chapter problems.

- A button menu selection can display a pull-down menu as follows:

      $P7=*

The P7 calls for pull-down menu 7 (the **Help** pull-down menu), and the =* displays it on screen.

- A space is not required after the button submenu in the file to separate it from other menus.

The following example shows revisions to the **BUTTONS1** menu. It includes a selection for button 9 that switches to the **B1** button menu and also displays the **OSNAP** screen menu. The **B1** menu provides eight object snap options, and button 9 returns to the **BUTTONS1** menu and displays the **S** screen menu.

```
***BUTTONS1
[1];
[2]$p0=*
[3]^C^C
[4]^B
[5]^C^CLINE
[6]^C^CERASE
[7]^C^CCIRCLE
[8]^C^CARC
[9]$B=B1 $S=OSNAPB
**B1
[1]ENDpoint
[2]INTersect
[3]MIDpoint
[4]PERpendicular
[5]CENter
[6]TANgent
[7]QUAdrant
[8]NEArest
[9]$B=BUTTONS1 $S=S
```

EXERCISE 18-1

❏ Copy the ACAD.MNU file into your subdirectory or onto a floppy disk. Change the name of the file to MYMENU.MNU or use your name.
❏ Create a button submenu named **B2.
❏ Include three drawing commands and three editing commands in the submenu.

CREATING STANDARD SCREEN MENUS

Once enabled, standard screen menus are located along the right side of the screen. They are created with the same techniques used for button menus. Screen menus are more versatile than button menus because you can see the command titles.

The positions of commands within the screen menu are referred to as *screenboxes*. The number of boxes available to you depends on your display device. You can find out how many boxes are available using the **SCREENBOXES** variable as follows:

```
Command: SCREENBOXES↵
SCREENBOXES = 27(read only)
```

Most people rarely use all of the commands found in AutoCAD's screen menus. In time, you will find which commands you use most often, and those you seldom use. Begin to develop an idea of what the menu structure should look like. Then start constructing custom menus, even though you may not completely know what to include. Menus are easy to change, and can be revised as many times as needed.

 NOTE   If screen menus are not enabled, the **SCREENBOXES** command returns a value of 0.

Parts of a screen menu item

A screen menu item is composed of the command name and the command code. The command name is enclosed in brackets. The code is a combination of commands, options, and characters that instruct AutoCAD to perform a function or series of functions. Take a closer look at the example in Figure 18-8. It is the same one that was introduced in Figure 18-4. The individual parts of the macro are:

- Brackets ([ ]) enclose the screen title. The first eight characters inside the brackets are displayed on the screen.
- The command name ONE LINE is displayed on the screen. Try to give descriptive names to your commands so they indicate what the command does.
- The double cancel (^C^C) cancels out any command that you are working with.
- AutoCAD commands determine what function the macro performs (**LINE**).
- A return (;) represents pressing the [Enter] key after typing LINE at the keyboard.
- The two backslashes (\\) represent user input for the From point: and To point: prompts. Remember, one backslash indicates a value entered at the keyboard or a selection made with the pointing device.
- A final return (;) represents pressing the [Enter] key to end the **LINE** command.

Figure 18-8.
The components of a screen menu item.

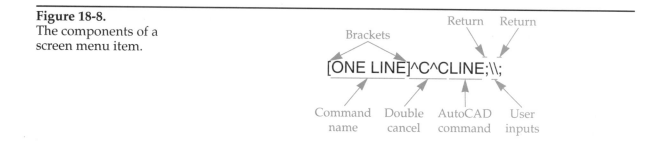

As you can see, you need to know exactly the commands, prompts, options, and entries required to perform AutoCAD functions before you can modify or create screen menus. Look at the next menu item and try to determine what it is doing.

[ERASE –1]^C^CERASE;\;

The title should give you a clue. It erases a single entity. The **ERASE** command is followed by a return, which is followed by a single backslash. This allows one pick on the screen. The second return completes the command. Here is another one.

[EXTEND 1]^C^CEXTEND;\;\;

This macro issues the **EXTEND** command, then allows for one user input to pick a boundary edge. Then a return is entered and one additional user input is allowed for the object to extend. After one object is picked, the last return completes the command automatically.

Look at one more menu item that combines two commands. What function do you think this macro performs?

[LINE T]^C^CLINE;\\;;MID;\\;

Notice that the first half of the item is exactly the same as the macro shown in Figure 18-8. It draws a single line. The return just before MID selects the **LINE** command again. MID specifies an **OSNAP** mode for the From point: prompt. The first backslash lets you pick the line on which the midpoint is needed. The second backslash is the To point: prompt. The final return ends the command.

> **PROFESSIONAL TIP**
>
> When writing menu commands and macros, write them as if you are entering the commands and options at the keyboard. Use the semicolon (;) for the [Enter] key. Use first letters where appropriate for command options.

Constructing menu commands

When you think of a useful command or function to include in a menu, the first step is to write it out in longhand. This gives you a clear picture of the scope of the command. The second step is to list the keyboard steps required to execute the new function. Third, write out the menu item as it should appear in the menu file. The following examples each utilize this three-step process:

Example 1

1. Make a menu pick called ERASE L to erase the last entity drawn.
2. **ERASE↵**
   LAST↵
3. [ERASE L]^C^CERASE;L

Example 2

1. Make a menu pick called ERASE 1 that erases one entity and returns to the **Command:** prompt.
2. **ERASE↵**
   (select entity)↵
3. [ERASE 1]^C^CERASE;\;

Example 3

1. Make a menu pick called ZOOM D that enters the **ZOOM Dynamic** display without the user having to pick the **Dynamic** option.
2. **ZOOM↵**
   DYNAMIC↵
3. [ZOOM D]^C^CZOOM;D

Example 4

1. Make a menu pick called ZOOM P that zooms to the previous display.
2. **ZOOM↵**
   PREVIOUS↵
3. [ZOOM P]^C^CZOOM;P

Example 5

1. Make a menu pick that draws as many circles as needed.
2. **MULTIPLE CIRCLE↵**
3. [M CIRCLE]^C^CMULTIPLE CIRCLE or *^C^CCIRCLE

These examples should give you the feel for the process used when creating menu items. The command items can now be written to a menu file and tested. Before doing this, though, take a look at two more examples that are a little more involved.

Example 6

1. Create a new menu pick called 25FILLET that can set a .25 fillet radius on a polyline without restarting the **FILLET** command.
2. **FILLET.**⏎
   RADIUS.⏎
   .25.⏎
   FILLET.⏎
   POLYLINE.⏎
   SELECT 2D POLYLINE.⏎
3. [25FILLET]^C^CFILLET;R;.25;;P;\

Example 7

1. Create a new menu pick called DWG AIDS that sets the grid to .5 and turns it on, sets the snap grid to .25 and turns it on, and turns **Ortho** on.
2. **GRID.**⏎
   .5.⏎
   SNAP.⏎
   .25.⏎
   ORTHO.⏎
   ON.⏎
3. [DWG AIDS]^C^CGRID;.5;;ON;SNAP;.25;;ON;ORTHO;ON

Adding macros to the menu file

The next step is to add the new macros to the menu file and then test them. Create a new submenu after the ****S** menu. Load your copy of the ACAD.MNU file into your text editor and search to find the following:

```
***SCREEN
**S
```

Listed below ****S** is AutoCAD's familiar **Root Menu**. Find the last sequential command in that menu, which is **LAST**. If you are editing the ACAD.MNU file, then just below the **[LAST]** option of the ****S** menu you will find the ****SNAP_TO** menu. It is typically preceded by 3 lines of comments. Move your cursor to the beginning of the first comment line and press the [Enter] key twice, then press the up arrow key once. Your cursor will now be on a blank line that is separated from the subsequent menu by an additional blank line.

This can be done between the end of any screen submenu and the start of the next. Remember that the first screen menu listed in the *****SCREEN** section is displayed when you enter the drawing editor. (If you insert your submenu in front of the ****S** menu, yours will be the first displayed when AutoCAD enters the drawing editor.)

Name this first submenu TEST. Type the entries in your text editor exactly as they are shown below. Be sure to press [Enter] at the end of each line. Your first entries in this menu should look like the following:

```
**TEST 3 (begins the menu on the third line from the top of the screen)
[ TEST]
[ MENU]
[ERASE L]^C^CERASE;L
[ERASE 1]^C^CERASE;\;
[ZOOM W]^C^CZOOM;W
[ZOOM P]^C^CZOOM;P
[M CIRCLE]^C^CMULTIPLE CIRCLE
[25FILLET]^C^CFILLET;R;.25;;P;\
[DWG AIDS]^C^CGRID;.5;;ON;SNAP;.25;;ON;ORTHO;ON
```

Long menu items

If a menu item occupies more than one line, instruct AutoCAD that there is more to the item. Type a plus symbol (+) at the end of the line. Do not put spaces in before or after the mark. Use the long-line technique to create a command that does the following:

- **ZOOM All**.
- Set **LIMITS** to 0,0 and 20,12.
- Set **SNAP** to 0.25.
- Set **GRID** to 0.50.
- Draw a **PLINE** border from 0.5,0.5. The border should be 17″ × 11″.
- Set **MIRRTEXT** to zero.
- Set the **APERTURE** to 3.
- Set the **ORTHOMODE** to on.
- Turn the **GRID** on.
- Set **UNITS** to three decimal places.
- **ZOOM Extents**.

The item name and code for this macro is written as follows:

```
[B-11x17]^C^CZOOM;A;LIMITS;;20,12;SNAP;.25;GRID;.5;PLINE;0.5,0.5;+
17.5,.5;17.5,11.5;0.5,11.5;C;MIRRTEXT;0;APERTURE;3;ORTHO;+
ON;GRID;ON;ZOOM;E
```

Place your menu in the root menu

You have created your first screen menu, but how do you access it from the **Root Menu** of AutoCAD? There is nothing in the **Root Menu** that calls the **TEST** menu. You need to add that item to the **Root Menu** now.

Look again at the ****S** menu and notice that only 20 lines are occupied with commands inside brackets. You can insert your menu name on the line after **HELP**. Insert the following item on the line after the **HELP** command.

```
[TEST] $S=ACAD.TEST
```

Do not press [Enter] at the end of the line or you will insert an additional line in the menu. This could push the last menu item off the screen if your monitor displays only 21 lines in the menu area.

The menu stack

The item you entered above calls your submenu **TEST**. A screen menu call is different from other menu calls because the previous menu is not removed prior to displaying the subsequent menu. Instead, the new menu is overlaid on the existing menu, with the first item being placed on the specified line.

For example, the ****TEST** menu has a 3 following the menu name. This indicates that the first two lines are to remain unchanged and the menu data placement begins on line 3 of the screen menu display area. The new items are then used to replace existing screen menu selections.

In the ****TEST** menu, ten items are defined with the menu beginning on the 3rd line. The previous menu, ****S**, has many additional lines. Since the ****TEST** menu only redefines lines 3 through 12, lines 13 and on remain unchanged. Figure 18-9A shows the ****S** menu with the addition of the **TEST** menu call, and Figure 18-9B shows the screen menu after calling the ****TEST** menu.

The standard approach to creation of screen menu submenus is to begin the submenu on the third line of the menu display area. This results in the first two lines of the ****S** menu being preserved regardless of what submenu is currently displayed. This is important because of the functions performed by these two items. The top of the ****S** menu looks like this:

```
AutoCAD
****
```

Figure 18-9.
A—The screen menu with the **TEST** menu call added below **HELP**. B—Calling the **TEST** submenu results in this display.

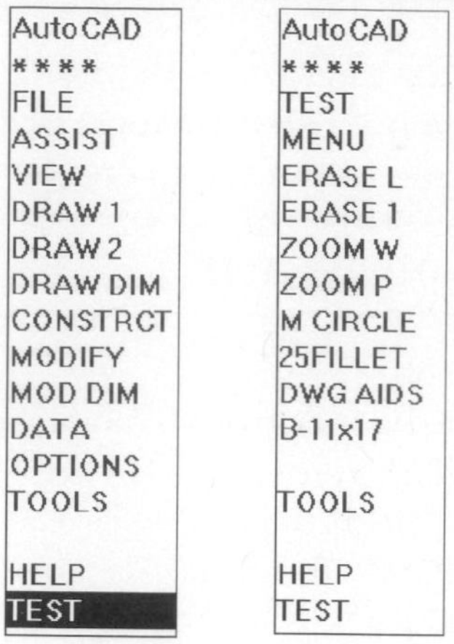

```
AutoCAD        AutoCAD
****           ****
FILE           TEST
ASSIST         MENU
VIEW           ERASE L
DRAW 1         ERASE 1
DRAW 2         ZOOM W
DRAW DIM       ZOOM P
CONSTRCT       M CIRCLE
MODIFY         25FILLET
MOD DIM        DWG AIDS
DATA           B-11x17
OPTIONS
TOOLS          TOOLS

HELP           HELP
TEST           TEST
   A              B
```

Picking the word **AutoCAD** displays the **S menu (the *root* menu), and picking the four asterisks displays an object snap menu. This way, no matter where you are in the menu system, it takes only one pick to get to these frequently needed items.

Using variables and control characters

AutoCAD system variables and control characters can be used in screen menus. They can be included to increase the speed and usefulness of your menu commands. Become familiar with these variables so you can make use of them in your menus:

- **^B. Snap** On/off toggle
- **^C. Cancel**
- **^D. Coords** On/off toggle
- **^E. Isoplane** On/off toggle
- **^G. Grid** On/off toggle
- **^H.** Issues a backspace
- **^M.** Issues a ↵
- **^O. Ortho** On/off toggle
- **^P. MENUECHO** Variable on/off toggle
- **^T. Tablet** On/off toggle
- **^V.** Switches current viewport

EXERCISE 18-2

❑ Use the three-step process to write the menu items given below.
❑ Use the spaces provided to write the macros.
  ❑ [GRID]—Turn the snap and grid on or off. _____
  ❑ [TEXT-S.1]—Set the snap at .1 and select the **TEXT** command. _____
  ❑ [MIRROR]—Turn the **MIRRTEXT** variable off and select the **Window** option of the **MIRROR** command. Do not delete the old object. This command should return the user to **Command:** prompt._____
  ❑ [BREAK @]—Break a single line into two parts. _____
  ❑ [CHMFER.5]—Set a chamfer distance of .5 and allow two lines to be picked. _____

CHAPTER TEST

Write your answers in the spaces provided.

1. The name and extension of the file that contains all of the fully-documented menus for
    AutoCAD is _____ .

2. List the names of the major sections in AutoCAD's default menu. _____

    _____

3. All interactive toolbar modifications are written to which file? _____

    _____

4. Why should you edit a copy of the ACAD.MNU file when customizing menus? _____

    _____

    _____

    _____

5. How many different button menus can you have? _____

    _____

6. What kind of symbol is used to indicate a screen submenu? _____

7. Describe the function of each of the following screen menu commands:

    A. [Layer:]$S=ACAD.10_DATA^C^CDDLMODES _____

        _____

        _____

    B. [Copy W]^C^CCOPY;W;\\ _____

        _____

        _____

    C. [CHANGE 1]^C^CCHANGE;\; _____

        _____

        _____

8. Give the function of the following menu command codes:

    [Brackets] _____

    Semicolon (;) _____

    Backslash (\) _____

    _____

    _____

    Plus sign (+) _____

    Single (si) _____

9. How many button menus can be accessed with combinations of key and button picks?

    _____

10. How would the following button menu command function? _____

    Erase;\ _____

11. What system variable gives you the number of screen menu items you can have? _____

    _____

12. List the three steps you should use when creating a new menu command. _____

    A. _____

    B. _____

    C. _____

13. Suppose you add a new menu to the ACAD.MNU file. How does the new menu get displayed on the screen? _____

_____

14. Define a menu stack. _____

_____

15. Define the use of the following control characters.

    ^B— _____

    ^G— _____

    ^O— _____

    ^V— _____

DRAWING PROBLEMS

General

1. Begin an entirely new AutoCAD menu composed of a general button section and an **OSNAP** button menu and screen menu. Name the menu P18-1.MNU. Plan your menu items before you begin. The main button menu (***BUTTONS1**) should have the following items:

BUTTON #	FUNCTION
1	Select text and allow user to reword.
2	Cancel last and activate the **LINE** command.
3	Cancel last and activate the **CIRCLE** command.
4	**ZOOM Dynamic**.
5	Leave blank.
6	Erase one object and end the **ERASE** command.
7	Cancel last and **ZOOM Window**.
8	[Enter] (return).
9	Cancel last and **ZOOM Previous**.

The ****BUTTONS2** menu is an **OSNAP** interrupt menu. All **OSNAP** items should activate the **OSNAP** mode and select a point when the button is pressed. The ****BUTTONS2** menu should contain the following items:

BUTTON #	FUNCTION
1	**Endpoint**
2	**Intersection**
3	**Perpendicular**
4	**Midpoint**
5	**Center**
6	**Tangent**
7	**Quadrant**
8	Return to main button and screen menus.
9	**Node**

Write the menus in small segments and be sure to test all items. Generate a printed copy of the menu file.

2. Add the menu given below to the P18-1.MNU file you created in Problem 1. The section name should be ***SCREEN**. The main menu name should be **S**. Plan all of your menu items before entering them in the text editor. The following items should be included.

POSITION	MENU ITEMS
1	Menu title [HOME]
2	Cancel and **ARC**.
3	Cancel and **POLYGON**.
4	Cancel and **PLINE**.
5	Cancel and **LIST**.
6	Cancel and **DIST**.
7	Cancel and **SCALE**.
8	Cancel and **OFFSET**.
9	Cancel and **ROTATE**.
10	Cancel and **STRETCH**.
11	Blank.
12	Cancel and **ZOOM**.
13	Blank.
14	Rotate crosshairs axis to user-specified angle. Allow user to set base point and leave **SNAP** on.
15	Reset crosshairs axis to zero and turn **SNAP** off.
16	Allow user to pick multiple objects and change all to a new layer.
17	Select text string and allow user to input new height.

General

Test all menu items to ensure that they are working properly before going to the next problem. Generate a printed copy of the menu file.

3. Add the following screen menu to your P18-1.MNU file. This is an editing menu and should be named **EDIT**. At position 18 in your main screen menu (see Problem 2), add an item that calls the **EDIT** menu. Place the following items in the **EDIT** menu:

General

POSITION	MENU ITEMS	
1	[ERASE-F]	Erase with **FENCE** option.
2	[COPY-WP]	Copy with **Window Polygon** option.
3	[MOVE-W]	Move with **Window** option.
4	[BREAK-F]	Activate **BREAK**, allow user to select object, then pick first and second points without entering F
5	[CHANGE-1]	Activate **CHANGE**, select object, and stop for user input.
6	[REWORD-M]	Allow user to reword one to four lines of text without restarting command.
7	[0-FILLET]	Select two lines and clean up corners with zero radius fillet. Allow selection of one to five clean-ups without restarting the command.
8	[0-BREAK]	Select line or arc and split into two parts.
9	[0-CORNER]	Select two intersecting lines at the intersection. Clean up corner using two picks.

Generate a printed copy of the menu file.

General

4. Add an item to the main button menu at button 5 that calls the **BUTTONS2** menu and a new screen menu called **OSNAP**. The line should read:

    [5]$B=BUTTONS2 $S=OSNAP

The new **OSNAP** screen menu should contain the following items:

POSITION	MENU ITEM	
1	[BUTTONS]	Label
2	[1=Endpt]	Show button assignment and activate normal **OSNAP** if picked from the screen.
3	[2=Inter]	Show button assignment and activate normal **OSNAP** if picked from the screen.
4	[3=Perp]	Show button assignment and activate normal **OSNAP** if picked from the screen.
5	[4=Middle]	Show button assignment and activate normal **OSNAP** if picked from the screen.
6	[5=Center]	Show button assignment and activate normal **OSNAP** if picked from the screen.
7	[6=Tangent]	Show button assignment and activate normal **OSNAP** if picked from the screen.
8	[7=Quad]	Show button assignment and activate normal **OSNAP** if picked from the screen.
9	[8=HOME]	Page back to main button and screen.
10	[9=Node]	Show button assignment and activate normal **OSNAP** if picked from the screen.
11	[Nearest]	Activate **Nearest OSNAP** from screen.
12	[Insert]	Activate **Insert OSNAP** from screen.

Generate a printed copy of the menu file.

General

5. Alter the **OSNAPB** menu in your copy of the ACAD.MNU file. Make it function with a button menu in the same manner as given in Problem 4. If you have not added a **BUTTONS2** menu to your ACAD.MNU file (explained earlier in this chapter), do so for this problem.

AutoCAD R13

Learning objectives

After completing this chapter, you will be able to:

- ○ Create single- or multiple-page pull-down menus.
- ○ Understand the structure of pull-down menus.
- ○ Create user-defined accelerator keys.
- ○ Describe the purpose and function of image tile menus.
- ○ Describe the purpose and the function of a slide library.
- ○ Create slides for image tile menus.
- ○ Create a slide library for an image tile menu.
- ○ Create an image tile menu file listing.

PULL-DOWN MENUS AND ACCELERATOR KEYS

AutoCAD
Custom | 4
Guide

The names of the standard pull-down menus appear in the menu bar at the top of the AutoCAD graphics window. They are selected by placing the cursor arrow over the menu item and clicking to select it.

Pull-down menus are referred to as "POP" menus in the menu file, and are listed as POP0, POP1, etc. POP0 is the cursor menu, which provides quick access to frequently used items. The cursor menu is enabled by simultaneously pressing the [Shift] key and clicking the [Enter] button on your mouse or digitizer tablet puck. By default, the cursor menu displays each of the object snap modes. When the cursor menu is active, the pull-down menus are not available.

Once you understand how pull-down menus are designed, you can customize existing menus and create your own. Some basic information about pull-down menus follows:

- You can have from 1 to 16 pull-down menus.
- The name of the pull-down menu, or "header," can be up to 14 characters long. On low resolution displays, headers should average less than five characters if all 16 POP menus are used. This will allow all of the item titles to fit on the screen.
- Menu item labels can be any length. The menu is as wide as its longest label.
- There can be at least 21 items listed in the menu, including the header.
- Each menu can have multiple cascading submenus.
- A pull-down menu, plus its cascading submenus, can have up to 999 items.
- The cursor menu, plus its cascading submenus, can have up to 499 items.
- If a pull-down menu title duplicates the title of a standard Windows pull-down menu (such as File, Edit, or Help), that section of the menu is ignored and does not appear in the menu bar.

Pull-down menu structure and codes

Many of the same codes used for writing screen menus are used for pull-down menus. The primary difference is the sequence of characters, or *syntax*, used for cascading submenus. This different syntax allows for the definition of accelerator and mnemonic shortcut keys used in the pull-down menus.

This is best seen by loading your copy of the ACAD.MNU file into your text editor. Look for the ***POP4 heading. This is the **Data** pull-down menu. The first 21 lines of this menu are shown in Figure 19-1.

Figure 19-1.

The first 21 lines of the ***POP4 **Data** pull-down menu. Note the placement of the ampersand character (&) to define accelerator and mnemonic shortcut keys.

```
***POP4
ID_Data      [&Data]
ID_Objcre    [&Object Creation...]'_ddemodes
             [--]
ID_Layers    [&Layers...]'_ddlmodes
ID_Vlc       [-)$(if,$(getvar,tilemode),~)&Viewport Layer Controls]
ID_Vlcf      [&Freeze]^C^C_vplayer _f
ID_Vlct          [&Thaw]^C^C_vplayer _t
                 [--]
ID_Vlcr          [&Reset]^C^C_vplayer _r
ID_Vlcn          [&New Freeze]^C^C_vplayer _n
ID_Vlcd          [&Default Visibility]^C^C_vplayer _v
                 [--]
ID_Vlcl          [(-&List]^C^C_vplayer _? \;
             [--]
ID_Color     [&Color]'_ddcolor
ID_Linety    [Li&netype...]'_ddltype
ID_Mlstyle   [&Multiline Style...]^C^C_mlstyle
ID_TexSty    [&Text Style]'_style
ID_DimSty    [&Dimension Style...]^C^C_ddim
ID_Shape     [&Shape File...]^C^C_load
```

A   B

Compare the appearance of the menu file syntax and the pull-down menu. A few new menu syntax characters are found in this menu. These characters are explained below. They provide a separator line, indicate where cascading submenus begin and end, and define accelerator and mnemonic shortcut keys.

Character	Function
[--]	Two hyphens are used to insert a separator line across the pull-down menu. The line is automatically drawn the width of the menu.
-⟩	Indicates this item has a cascading submenu.
⟨-	Indicates this is the last item in the cascade.
⟨-⟨-	Indicates this item is the last item in the submenu, and the last item of the previous menu (parent menu).
&c	The ampersand specifies the mnemonic key in a pull-down or cursor menu label. The "c" shown here represents any character.

PROFESSIONAL TIP

Notice in the POP4 (**Data**) pull-down menu listing in Figure 19-1 that indentation has been used to indicate cascading submenus. Indenting is not necessary to write a valid menu file, but it gives the file an appearance similar to the actual submenus. It also makes the file easier to read and understand.

Marking menu items

Menu items can be marked with a check mark (✓) or other character of your choosing. You can also have items "grayed out." The following characters are used for these purposes:

Character	Function
[~]	The tilde grays out any characters that follow.
!.	The combination of an exclamation point and a period places a check mark (✓) before the menu item.

When these marking characters are used in a menu, they mark an item permanently. This may be desirable for the separator line and for graying out specific items, but a check mark is often related to an item that is toggled on or off. Look at the following example menu file and its pull-down menu in Figure 19-2.

Figure 19-2.
An example of check mark and grayed-out character definition in a pull-down menu.

```
***POP8
[&Test]
[!.Checkmark]
[--]
[~Grayed out text]
[   ]
[~!.Grayed out checkmark]
```

A   B

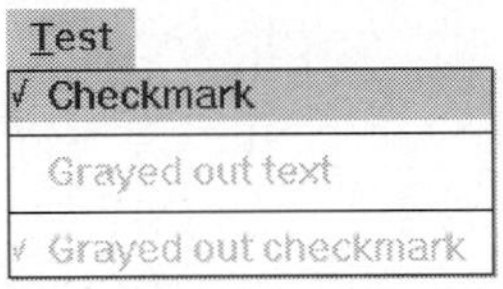

Creating "smart" pull-down menu items

A check mark is often placed by any item to indicate that it has been selected, or that it is on. You can add this capability to your pull-down menus by using a new string expression language called DIESEL. A *string* is simply a group of characters that can be input from the keyboard or from the value of a system variable. DIESEL (Direct Interpretively Evaluated String Expression Language) uses a string for its input and provides a string for output. In other words, you give DIESEL a value, and it gives something back to you.

The check mark is an excellent example of how DIESEL can be used in menu items. For example, you may want to put the **ORTHO** command in a pull-down menu, and indicate when it is on with a check mark. Use the following line in your menu:

[$(if,$(getvar,orthomode),!.)/OOrtho]^O

The first $ signals the pull-down menu to evaluate a DIESEL macro. This macro gets the value (getvar) of the **ORTHOMODE** system variable, and places the check mark by the item if the value is 1, or on. Notice that the AutoCAD command being executed is **ORTHO** (^O).

Figure 19-3 shows how two DIESEL additions to the previous **Test** menu look in the menu file and the pull-down menu. The pull-down menu shows that **ORTHO** is on.

Figure 19-3.
An example of DIESEL macros added to a pull-down menu. Note that **Ortho** is toggled on.

```
***POP8
[&Test]
[$(if,$(getvar,orthomode),!.)&Ortho]^O
[$(if,$(getvar,snapmode),!.)&Snap]^B
[!.Checkmark]
[- -]
[~Grayed out text]
[- -]
[~!.Grayed out checkmark]
```

A   B

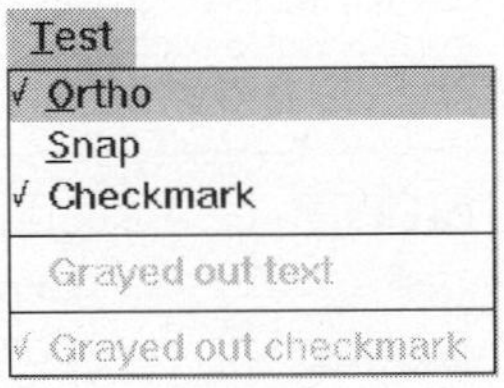

The use of DIESEL expressions in your menus can enhance their power and make them more "intelligent." See Chapters 4 and 5 of the AutoCAD *Customization Guide* for a complete discussion of the DIESEL language. A second example of using DIESEL is shown in the next section.

Referencing other pull-down menus

A pick on one menu can activate, or "reference" another pull-down menu. A menu pick can also gray out or place a marking character by another pull-down menu item. The following character codes are used for these purposes:

Character	Function
$pn=	Activates another pull-down menu, where "n" is the number of the menu.
$pn=*	Activates and displays another pull-down menu.
$pn.1=	References a specific item number on another pull-down menu.

When referencing other pull-down menus, you can combine the marking symbols to add "gray out" or place check marks. Study the following menu item examples. The first example activates POP4 and displays it.

    $p4=*

The next menu item places a check mark on item 7 of POP6.

    $p6.7=!.

NOTE   In some maintenance releases of AutoCAD R13, the **$pn=*** menu call does not display the specified menu as it should. If this feature is non-functional on your system, you may need to upgrade to a more recent maintenance release of the AutoCAD software.

Now, study these menu item examples. The first entry grays out item 3 of POP6.

    $p6.3=~

The following menu item places an X by item 2 of POP8 and grays it out.

    $p8.2=!X~

The next menu item removes all marks and gray out from item 2 of POP8.

    $p8.2=

The following examples show how these techniques can be combined in a macro.

    [Insert desk]^C^Cinsert;desk;\\\\$p2=*
    [Setup .5]^C^Cgrid;.5;snap;.25;$p2.1=!. $p2.2=!.~
    [Defaults]^C^Cgrid;off;snap;off;$p2.1= $p2.2=

NOTE   Menu item numbering begins with the first line of the pull-down menu below the title and continues to the bottom of the file. AutoCAD numbers items consecutively through all submenus, without considering submenu levels.

Creating a new pull-down menu

Scroll through your copy of the ACAD.MNU file until you find the comments preceding the ***TOOLBARS section. It is located after the last line of ***POP7 pull-down.

If you want to add an additional pull-down menu, it should be inserted before the ***TOOLBARS section. Your new pull-down menu will be located in the menu bar after the **Help** menu. Be sure to leave an empty line between pull-down menus.

Test each item of a new menu to make sure it works properly. Remember, when you return to the drawing editor, you must use the **MENU** command to reload the revised menu. If you neglect to do this, you will be working with the old version of the menu.

    Command: **MENU**⏎
    Menu file name or . for none ⟨*current*⟩: **MENUNAME.**⏎ *(or pick from the dialog box)*

PROFESSIONAL TIP

    A pull-down menu item can be as long as needed, but should be as brief as possible for easy reading. The pull-down menu width is automatically created to fit the width of the longest item.

Sample menu items

The following examples show how AutoCAD commands and options can be used to create pull-down or screen menu items. They are listed using a three-step process:

- Step 1 is a verbal description of the macro.
- Step 2 lists the keyboard strokes required for the macro.
- Step 3 gives the actual macro as it appears in the menu file.

Example 1

1. This **HEXAGON** command will display the polygon screen menu and be repeated. It should select the **POLYGON** command and request a six-sided polygon inscribed in a circle.
2.   **POLYGON**⏎
    6⏎
    SELECT CENTER⏎
    I⏎
3. [Hexagon]*^C^C$S=ACAD.polygon polygon 6 \I

As mentioned earlier, you can indicate a return in a command or macro by using either a space or a semicolon. Notice the italicized portions of the following two commands. Both commands perform the same function.

    [Hexagon]*^C^C$S=ACAD.polygon *polygon 6* \I
    [Hexagon]*^C^C$S=ACAD.polygon *polygon;6;*\I

The first example uses spaces and the second example uses semicolons to represent pressing the [Enter] key. The technique you use is a matter of personal preference, but it is recommended to use semicolons.

PROFESSIONAL TIP

    Some people prefer to use the semicolon for a return to clearly indicate that a return has been inserted. When using spaces, an extra space can slip into a menu item and go unnoticed until the item is tested.

Example 2

1. This **DOT** command should draw a solid dot, .1 inch in diameter. Use the **DONUT** command. The inside diameter is 0 (zero) and the outside diameter is .1.
2.   **DONUT.⏎**
       0.⏎
       .1.⏎
3. [&Dot]^C^Cdonut;0;.1

Example 3

1. This **X-POINT** command sets **PDMODE**=3 and draws an X at the pick point. The command should be repeated.
2.   **PDMODE.⏎**
       3.⏎
       POINT.⏎
       (*Pick the point*)
3. [&X-Point]*^C^C$S=ACAD.point pdmode;3;point

Example 4

1. This macro, named Notation, could be used by a drawing checker or instructor. It allows them to circle features on a drawing or design that requires editing, and then add a leader and text. It first sets the color to red, then draws a circle, snaps a leader to the nearest point that is picked on the circle, and prompts for the text. User input for text is provided, then a cancel returns the **Command:** prompt and the color is set to white.
2.   **COLOR.⏎**
       RED.⏎
       CIRCLE.⏎
       (*Pick center point*)
       (*Pick radius*)
       DIM.⏎
       LEADER.⏎
       NEA.⏎
       (*Pick a point on the circle*)
       (*Pick end of leader*).⏎
       (*Press* [Enter] *for automatic shoulder*)
       (*Enter text*).⏎
       (*Press* [Esc] *to cancel*)
       COLOR.⏎
       WHITE.⏎
3. [&Notation]^C^Ccolor;red;circle;\\dim;lea;nea;\\;\^Ccolor;white

Example 5

1. A repeating command named Multisquare, which draws one inch squares oriented at a 0° horizontal angle.
2.   **RECTANG.⏎**
       (*Pick lower left corner*)
       @1,1.⏎
3. [&Multisquare]*^C^Crectang;\@1,1

EXERCISE 19-1

❑ Use your text editor and create a new file named EX19-1.MNU. Put the following three commands in a new ***POP3 menu titled **Custom**.
  ❑ [Copy M]—Make multiple copies. Allow two picks.
  ❑ [Rotate45]—Rotate an object 45° counterclockwise. Should be an automatic command.
  ❑ [Fillet .5]—A repeating command that applies a .5 fillet.
❑ All commands should display their screen submenus and mnemonic keys.
❑ Use the spaces below to write out the commands before you enter them in the computer.

[Copy M]—_____

[Rotate45]—_____

[Fillet .5]—_____

Creating help strings for pull-down menus

Help strings are the brief descriptions on the status line describing the menu item currently highlighted. These can provide helpful information to those who are using your menu. It becomes very important to create appropriate help strings when you are adding new items to the menu, since these items may be unfamiliar to even experienced AutoCAD users. To get an idea of the ideal content of a help string for your menu item, carefully review some of AutoCAD's built in help strings. Help string definitions are placed in the ***HELPSTRINGS section in your menu file, but references to a help string can be placed throughout your menu file. For example, if a 0.5″ wide polyline option is added to a pull-down menu, the menu code might look like this:

    [0.5 Polyline]^C^Cpline;\w;0.5;0.5;

To create a help string for this selection, open your menu file and find the ***HELPSTRINGS section. The beginning of the ***HELPSTRINGS section looks like this:

    ***HELPSTRINGS
    ID_New [Creates a new drawing file]
    ID_Open [Opens an existing drawing file]
    ID_Close [Closes the drawing file]
    ID_Save [Saves the drawing with the current file name or a specified name]
    ID_Saveas [Saves an unnamed drawing with a file name or renames the current drawing]
    ID_SavR12 [Saves the current drawing in AutoCAD Release 12 format]
    ID_Print [Prints a drawing to a plotter, printer, or file]
    ID_Import [Imports a file into a drawing]
    ID_Export [Exports a drawing to a different file format]

The format for an entry in the ***HELPSTRINGS section is as follows:

    ID_*tagname* [Help message...]

The ID_*tagname* should be unique. Duplicate tags can cause unexpected results. Do a text search using your text editor's "find" function to see if the tag name you select is already in use. The help message should be short enough to fit along the bottom of the screen, and as clearly worded as possible. A search of the default ACAD.MNU file reveals that the ID tag name selected for the wide polyline "ID_Wpline" is not already in use. To prepare the help string for use, enter the following line in the ***HELPSTRINGS section of your menu file:

    ID_Wpline [Draws a 0.5″ wide polyline.]

Now that the help string definition has been created, any menu item referencing the ID_Wpline tag will display this help string. To place a reference to this help string, you need to precede the menu item label with the ID tag name as follows:

ID_Wpline [0.5 Polyline]^C^Cpline;\w;0.5;0.5;

When the **0.5 Polyline** menu item is highlighted, the help string Draws a 0.5″ wide polyline is displayed on the status line.

PROFESSIONAL TIP

A new help string can be placed anywhere within the help string section. Since this section is rather extensive, it can be helpful to place all of your custom help string definitions together at the bottom. This makes them easy to locate when you need to edit them.

EXERCISE 19-2

❑ Use your text editor and open the menu file EX19-1.MNU from Exercise 19-1. Alternatively you can make a *copy* of the ACAD.MNU file and name it TEST.MNU. Using this file, do the following:
  ❑ Create a ***HELPSTRINGS section in your menu file if one does not exist.
  ❑ Create a help string for each of the three new commands you developed in Exercise 19-1.
  ❑ Test each command to be sure each help string is displayed properly.
  ❑ Use the spaces below to write the notation for each help string before you insert it into your menu.

  [Copy M]— _____

  [Rotate 45]— _____

  [Fillet .5]— _____

Creating and using accelerator keys

AutoCAD Release 13 for Windows supports user-defined accelerator keys. The accelerator keys are the keystrokes available when you specify **Menu File** in the **Keystrokes** area of the **System** panel of the **Preferences** dialog box. These include [Ctrl]+[C] as **COPYCLIP**, [Ctrl]+[V] as **PASTECLIP**, [Ctrl]+[S] as **QSAVE**, and [Ctrl]+[P] as **PRINT**. If you select **AutoCAD Classic** keystrokes, the accelerator keys cannot be used. These definitions are all contained in the ***ACCELERATORS section of your menu file:

```
***ACCELERATORS
[CONTROL+"L"]^O
[CONTROL+"R"]^V
ID_Undo [CONTROL+"Z"]
ID_Cut [CONTROL+"X"]
ID_Copy [CONTROL+"C"]
ID_Paste [CONTROL+"V"]
ID_Open [CONTROL+"O"]
ID_Print [CONTROL+"P"]
ID_New [CONTROL+"N"]
ID_Save [CONTROL+"S"]
```

There are two different ways to specify an accelerator key. The first entry in the list on the previous page defines the [Ctrl]+[L] keystroke as an **Ortho** mode toggle. This method allows you to specify the keystroke as a label, followed by any menu code required. For example, to define a [Ctrl]+[I] keystroke to start the **DDINSERT** command, enter the following line into your ***ACCELERATORS section:

        [CONTROL+"I"]^C^CDDINSERT

It is also possible to create macros associated with accelerator keys. Simply enter the menu code just as you would for any other menu area. For example, to create a [Ctrl]+[A] accelerator key that automatically sets up A-size drawing limits and draws a 0.15 wide polyline border, enter the following in the ***ACCELERATORS section:

        [CONTROL+ "A"]^C^CLIMITS;;11,8.5;PLINEWID;0.15;RECTANG;0.5,0.5;10.5,8;ZOOM;A

The second way to define accelerator keys references a defined ID_*tagname* for a menu pick as the source code, followed by the keystroke definition. Any item on a pull-down menu that displays a help string can be used in this manner. For example, under the **Tiled Viewports** cascade on the **View** pull-down menu, the **4 Viewports** selection displays a help string when highlighted. Searching through the menu for this item reveals the following code for this menu pick:

        ID_TVp4 [&4 Viewports]^C^C_vports 4

The ID tag ID_TVp4 can be referenced in the ***ACCELERATORS section to execute the menu code listed for this item as follows:

        ID_TVp4 [CONTROL+"4"]

Pressing [Ctrl]+[4] now activates the **4 Viewports** menu selection. Basically, it is the same as entering the following under ***ACCELERATORS:

        [CONTROL+"4"]^C^C_vports 4

Either way works equally as well, but it is unnecessary to duplicate existing menu code if you reference the ID tag.

EXERCISE 19-3

❑ Use your text editor and open the menu file you used in Exercise 19-2. Do the following:
  ❑ Create an ***ACCELERATORS section in your menu file if one does not exist.
  ❑ Create an accelerator key for each of the three new commands you developed in Exercise 19-1.
  ❑ Test each command to be sure that each accelerator functions properly.
  ❑ Use the spaces below to write the notation for each accelerator before you insert it into your menu.
        [Copy M]— _____
        [Rotate 45]— _____
        [Fillet .5]— _____

Some notes about pull-down menus

Here are a few more things to keep in mind when developing pull-down menus.

- If the first line of a pull-down menu (the title line) is blank, that menu is not displayed in the menu bar, and all menus to the right are moved left to take its place.
- Pull-down menus are disabled during the following commands:
  - ✓ **DTEXT**, after the rotation angle is entered
  - ✓ **SKETCH**, after the record increment is set
  - ✓ **VPOINT**, during use of the tripod and compass
  - ✓ **ZOOM Dynamic**
  - ✓ **DVIEW**
- Pull-down menus that are longer than the screen display are truncated to fit on the screen.
- The cursor menu is named POP0. It can contain items that reference other pull-down and screen menus.
- The menu bar is not active while the cursor menu is displayed.

MENU GROUPS AND PARTIAL MENUS

Two additional menu file handling commands are provided, in addition to the **MENU** command. The **MENU** command loads a base menu in its default condition, and provides no flexibility. However, it is possible to load multiple menus at one time and use only the desired elements of each by using the **MENULOAD** command.

The purpose of the **MENULOAD** command is to allow loading of partial menus. This allows you to add to your base menu (e.g. ACAD or ACADFULL) additional options from a different menu. This allows you to customize your menu so that you have access to desired features from two or more different menu files.

AutoCAD menu files are assigned menu group names. For example, in the beginning of the ACAD.MNU file, you will find the line:

　　***MENUGROUP=ACAD

This assigns the group name ACAD to this menu. However, if you open the sample menu file SHAFT.MNU, which is found in the \R13\WIN\SAMPLE directory, you will find the specification:

　　***MENUGROUP=SHAFT

This identifies items in this menu as being in the SHAFT menu group. This allows you to identify items from different menus easily. For example, when working with screen menus, your calls to submenus were preceded by ACAD. This identified the group containing the desired menu. In Chapter 17, your call to the TEST screen submenu appeared as:

　　$S=ACAD.TEST

If the SHAFT menu was loaded and also had a screen submenu named TEST, your menu call would specify from which group to obtain the definition for the TEST menu.

If you try to load the ACADFULL menu with MENULOAD while the ACAD menu is already loaded, you will get an error message. This is because these two menus both use the same group name. You can force AutoCAD to replace existing group definitions with newly loaded menu data.

The **MENULOAD** command can be accessed by picking **Customize Menus...** from the **Tools** pull-down menu, or it can be typed directly at the **Command:** prompt. Entering the **MENULOAD** command displays the **Menu Customization** dialog box, as shown in Figure 19-4. There are several options available:

- **Menu Groups:**—This list shows all of the currently loaded menu groups. Items on this list can be highlighted in preparation for other actions.

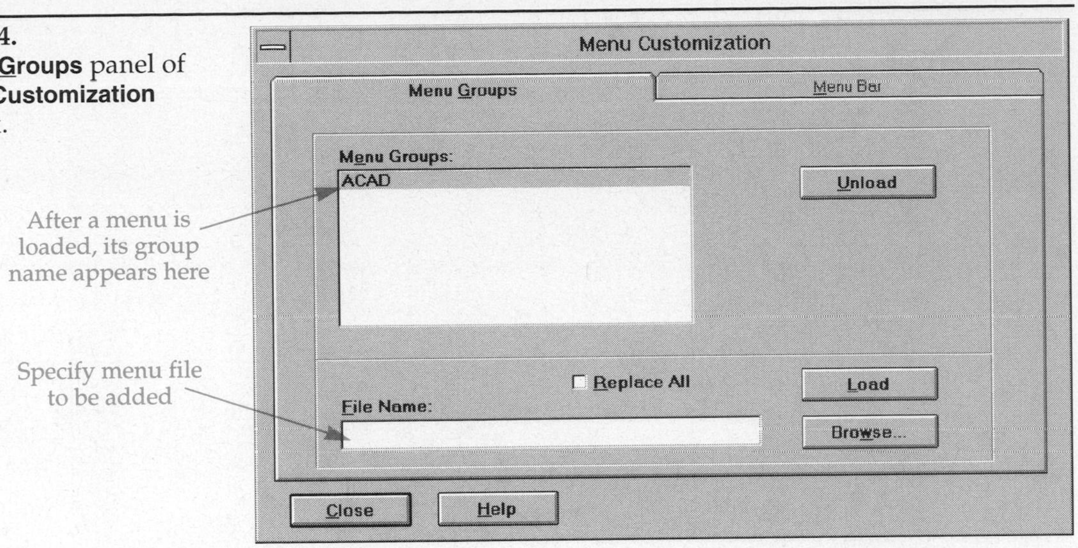

Figure 19-4.
The **Menu Groups** panel of the **Menu Customization** dialog box.

After a menu is loaded, its group name appears here

Specify menu file to be added

- **File Name:**—This edit box shows the name of the currently selected menu file.
- **Replace All**—A check in this check box forces newly loaded group names to replace existing duplicate file names.
- **Unload**—This button unloads the definition for the menu group highlighted in the **Menu Groups** list box.
- **Load**—This button loads the menu file specified in the **File Name:** edit box and places its associated group name in the **Menu Groups** list box.
- **Browse...**—This is often the easiest way to specify a new menu file name for loading. It displays the **Select Menu File** dialog box and allows you to select a menu file. This is often easier than typing the entire path and file name.

To practice loading an additional menu, use the **Select Menu File** dialog box to find the SHAFT.MNU file. Remember that you must first specify *.MNU in the **List Files of Type:** pop-up list.

After selecting the SHAFT.MNU file, you are returned to the **Menu Groups** panel of the **Menu Customization** dialog box. The SHAFT.MNU file and path name appear in the **File Name:** edit box. Pick the **Load** button to load the menu definition and the new group name will be displayed in the **Menu Groups** list box.

Now that you have loaded an additional menu definition, you can specify which menus to display. First, pick the **Menu Bar** tab, Figure 19-5. The features of this panel of the dialog are as follows:

- **Menu Group**—This pop-up list provides access to the currently loaded menu group names. The currently selected menu group name is displayed here.
- **Menus:**—All of the available pull-down menu names defined in this group are displayed here.
- **Menu Bar:**—This shows the pull-down menus that are currently available on the menu bar. The top item of the list takes a position at the far left of the menu bar, and each subsequent menu title is displayed to the right of the previous one.
- **Insert 》**—Picking this button inserts the currently highlighted menu in the **Menus:** list into the highlighted position in the **Menu Bar:** list.
- **《Remove**—Removes the currently highlighted menu title from the **Menu Bar:** list.
- **《Remove All**—Removes all menu titles from the **Menu Bar:** list.

The SHAFT menu group displays only one menu name. Other menu files may display one or more menu names. By selecting the desired group name and adjusting the various individual menu titles, you can completely customize the menu bar to have only the pull-down menus that are necessary to your current project.

Figure 19-5.
The **Menu Bar** panel of the **Menu Customization** dialog box.

Pick to see currently loaded menu groups

Menus in the selected group

Menus currently on the menu bar

PROFESSIONAL TIP

It is also possible to customize the pull-down menu bar with only one menu group loaded. You can remove unwanted menus as desired, and replace them later if needed.

IMAGE TILE MENUS

Image tile menus contain graphic symbols displayed in dialog boxes. They appear in certain dialog boxes, such as the **3D Objects** dialog box. See Figure 19-6. This dialog box is accessed by selecting **Surfaces** from the **Draw** pull-down menu.

The dialog box shown contains several small boxes. Each box contains a small image. These displays are AutoCAD slides.

Figure 19-6.
The **3D Objects** dialog box has an image tile menu.

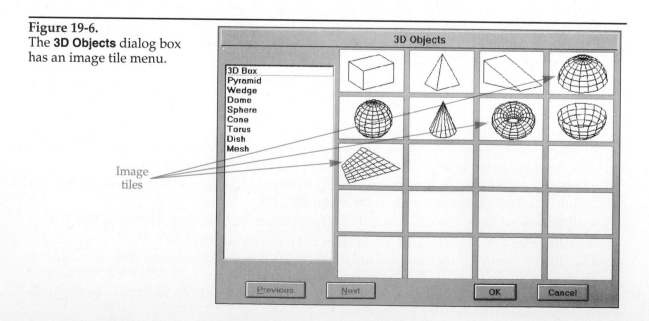

Image tiles

The slides are saved in a file created with the SLIDELIB program. This program creates a file with an .SLB extension. The slides become an image tile menu by entering them in the menu file. Chapter 30 of *AutoCAD and its Applications—Basics, Release 13 for Windows* explains the use of the SLIDELIB program.

Image tile menu creation

The addition of image tile menus can enhance the operation of AutoCAD. However, you must create images using certain guidelines:

✓ Keep images simple. This saves display time and storage space. The image can be a simplified version of the actual symbol.

✓ When making slides, fill the screen with the image to be sure the image tile is filled. Center long items on the screen using **PAN**. This centers them in the image tile.

✓ Use image tile menus for symbols only. Do not clutter your program with image tile menus of text information. This slows the system down.

✓ AutoCAD does not display solid filled areas in image tiles. If you use fills, such as arrowheads, use the shade command prior to making the slide image file.

✓ A maximum of 20 slides can be displayed in one image tile menu. The names of the images are automatically displayed in a list box to the left of the image tiles. Image names (up to 17 characters) are displayed in the list box.

✓ If you have more than 20 slides in an image tile menu, AutoCAD creates additional "pages," each containing a **Next** and a **Previous** button for changing pages. The **OK** and **Cancel** buttons are automatically provided in the image tile menu.

✓ If an item label in an image tile menu has a space before the first character, no image is displayed for that label, but the label name is shown. This can be used to execute other commands or call other image tile menus.

Making symbols and slides for the image tile menu

Image tile menus can be used for a variety of purposes, but they are most commonly used to display images of blocks. Regardless of the types of symbols used, follow these steps when making image tile menus:

1. Draw the symbol or block.
2. Center the drawing on the display screen. When the drawing appears in the image tile menu, it is displayed in a box with a 1.5:1 ratio of width to height. With your drawing on the screen, set **TILEMODE** = 0, and create a 3 × 2 viewport. Now, **ZOOM Extents** and then switch back to model space. The drawing is now at the correct ratio.
3. Make a slide of the symbol using the **MSLIDE** command.
4. Write the **SLIDELIB** file.
5. Write the image tile menu file and test it.

Draw the three shapes shown in Figure 19-7. They represent a table, desk, and chair. Draw them any size you wish. Save each one as a block, and name them TABLE, DESK, and CHAIR. Do not include text or attributes.

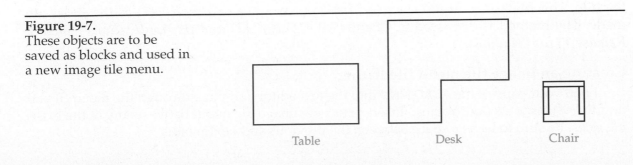

Figure 19-7.
These objects are to be
saved as blocks and used in
a new image tile menu.

Table   Desk   Chair

Now, insert into the current drawing, copies of all of the blocks you plan to include in the image tile menu; in this example, one TABLE, DESK, and CHAIR. Do not scale or rotate the blocks.

Use the **MSLIDE** command to make a slide of each one of the blocks, centering the slide as previously discussed. Give the slides the same name as the block. This completes the second step. Now you will use the SLIDELIB program to make the slide file.

Using the SLIDELIB program for an image tile menu

The SLIDELIB program operates in DOS and allows you to create a list of slide (.SLD extension) files. This list of slides can then be used for slide shows and image tile menus.

To use the SLIDELIB program, you must return to the Program Manager, open the Main group window, and launch MS-DOS Prompt. Alternatively, you can use the **SHELL** command from within AutoCAD.

The creation of a slide file called FURNITUR begins as follows:

```
Command: SHELL↵
OS Command:↵
```

You will now see the following on your screen:

> ■ Type EXIT and press ENTER to quit this MS-DOS prompt and return to Windows.
> ■ Press ALT + TAB to switch to Windows or another application.
> ■ Press ALT + ENTER to switch this MS-DOS Prompt between a window and a full screen.

```
Microsoft(R) MS-DOS(R) Version 6
  (C)Copyright Microsoft Corp 1981-1993.
C:\R13\WIN⟩ R13\COM\SUPPORT\SLIDELIB FURNITUR ↵
SLIDELIB 1.2 (3/8/89)
  (C) Copyright 1987-89 Autodesk, Inc.
  All Rights Reserved
TABLE↵
CHAIR↵
DESK↵
  ↵
  ↵
```

The second [Enter] on a blank line after the last slide name exits the SLIDELIB program. Check to see that the slide library file was created by listing all files with a .SLB extension. It should be listed as FURNITUR.SLB. Type EXIT to return to the AutoCAD graphics window.

```
C:\R13\COM\SUPPORT⟩ DIR *.SLB↵
C:\R13\COM\SUPPORT⟩ EXIT↵
```

A second method of creating a slide library involves using an existing list of slides in a text file. This method is useful if you add slide names to a text file (.TXT) as the slides are made. The method is discussed in Chapter 30 of *AutoCAD and its Applications—Basics, Release 13 for Windows*.

Creating an image tile menu file listing

Load your copy of the ACAD.MNU into the text editor and page through the file until you find the ***image section. You can insert your new image tile menu between any of the existing ones. Be sure to leave a space between the previous and next menus.

Now begin a menu called furniture below the last image tile heading, **image_vporti. The first item in the menu is used as the title. If you neglect to put a title here, the first line of the menu will be used as the title. Your new menu should look like the following:

```
**image_ furniture
[Select Furniture]
[furnitur(Table)]^C^Cinsert;table
[furnitur(Desk)]^C^Cinsert;desk
[furnitur(Chair)]^C^Cinsert;chair
[ Plants]$I=plants $I=*
```

Notice the space in the last entry, [Plants], after the left bracket. This produces a label without an image tile. This label is used to execute other commands, or as in this case, display other image tile menus.

These are called *branching* image tile menus. In this example, the Plants menu may show images of several types of plants. You can have as many branching icon menus as needed.

The new image tile menu is still not usable because there is no selection that calls this menu to the screen. The **Draw** pull-down menu is a good place to put the call for this menu. Insert the following line in the pull-down menu:

```
[Furniture]$I=furniture $I=*
```

The first part of this entry, $I=furniture, calls the new furniture menu. The second part, $I=*, displays the menu and makes the items selectable.

Save the file and use the **MENU** command to reload the menu. Test all the items in the menu and correct any problems. The new image tile menu should look like the one in Figure 19-8.

Figure 19-8.
The customized image tile menu utilizing previously created objects.

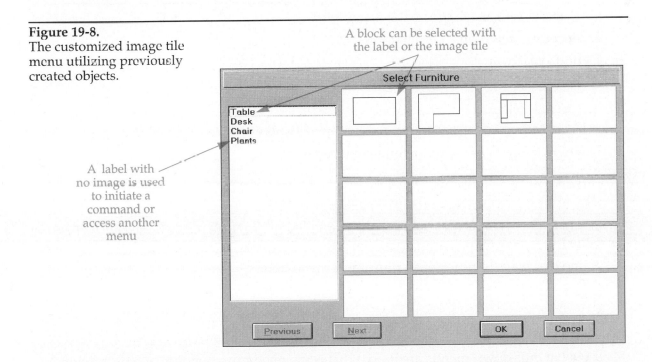

A block can be selected with the label or the image tile

A label with no image is used to initiate a command or access another menu

PROFESSIONAL TIP   Your primary goal in developing menus is to eliminate extra steps required to perform a function. The end result is that you can execute a thought or idea with one pick, rather than labor through a series of commands and options.

CHAPTER TEST

Write your answers in the spaces provided.

1. How many items can a pull-down menu contain? _____

2. Define the following pull-down menu characters.

    -⟩ _____

    ⟨- _____

    ⟨-⟨- _____

    & _____

3. Provide the character(s) required to perform the following functions:

    A. Insert a separator line across the pull-down menu. _____

    B. Gray out characters._____

    C. Place a check mark before the menu item. _____

    D. Specify a mnemonic key shortcut._____

4. Define a macro. _____

    _____

    _____

5. What code is used to make pull-down menus display and be selectable?_____

6. Describe the uses of the following menu codes:

    Asterisk [*] _____

    [–] _____

    _____

    Tilde [~] _____

7. Name two ways to represent a return in a menu item. _____

    _____

    _____

8. How many pull-down menus can be displayed on one screen? _____

9. If twelve pull-down menus are used, what is the maximum length that a pull-down menu heading should be? _____

10. How wide is a pull-down menu? _____

11. What is the function of the following DIESEL expression?

    [$(if,$(getvar,snapmode),!.)Snap]^B _____

    _____

    _____

12. What is the function of the following menu item characters?

    $p3=* _____

    $p4.1=~ _____

    $p6.7=!. _____

13. How many items can be listed in a pull-down menu? _____

14. Interpret the following menu item:

    ^C^Crectang;\@1,1 _____

    _____

    _____

15. Why is it a good idea to make a copy of the ACAD.MNU file before you begin experi-

    menting or customizing? _____

    _____

    _____

16. In the ACAD.MNU file, how is a menu group name specified in an item that calls a spe-

    cific menu? _____

    _____

17. Write the proper notation for the ***HELPSTRINGS section as it appears in the

    ACAD.MNU file. _____

18. You wish to create a new macro that executes the **PURGE** command, and uses the **Block**

    option. Write the macro as it would appear in the menu file, and the correct notation in

    the ***HELPSTRINGS section of the ACAD.MNU file.

    Menu file _____

    Help string _____

19. What is the key combination called that allows you to press the [Ctrl] key and one addi-

    tional key to execute a command? _____

20. Write the proper notation to define the type of key mentioned in question 19 using the

    [M] key to execute the **MVIEW** command.

    _____

    _____

21. What is the purpose of the **MENULOAD** command? _____

    _____

    _____

22. In the ACAD.MNU file, how is a menu group name specified in an item that calls a

    specific menu? _____

    _____

    _____

23. Which command is used to create the slide file that is used for an image tile menu? _____

_____

24. What is the first line of an image tile menu called? _____

25. List the steps required to create an image tile menu.

    A. _____

    B. _____

    C. _____

    D. _____

    E. _____

26. Write the correct syntax for executing the SLIDELIB program at the DOS prompt. The syntax should include a slide library name of CIVIL. _____

27. Describe the function of the following entry in an image tile menu file.

    [Fittings]$i=fittings $i=* _____

28. How would the title of an image tile menu named FITTINGS appear in the file listing?

_____

DRAWING PROBLEMS

General

1. Create a dimensioning pull-down menu. Place as many dimensioning commands as you need in the menu. Use cascading submenus if necessary. One or more of the submenus should be dimensioning variables. Include mnemonic keys.

General

2. Create a pull-down menu for 3D objects. Add it to your copy of ACAD.MNU. Include mnemonic keys. The contents of the menu should include the following:

        Elev
        3Dobjects
        3Dsurfaces
        3Dface
        Vpoint
        Vports
        Dview
        Hide
        Filters

3. Create a new pull-down menu named **Special**. The menu should include the following drawing and editing commands:

Line	Move
Arc	Copy
Circle	Stretch
Polyline	Trim
Polygon	Extend
Rectangle	Chamfer
Dtext	Fillet
Erase	

   Use cascading submenus if necessary. Include a separator line between the drawing and editing commands, and specify appropriate mnemonic shortcut keys.

General

4. Create a single pull-down menu that is used to insert a variety of blocks or symbols. These symbols can be for any drawing discipline that you use often. Use cascading menus and mnemonic keys if necessary. This menu should have a special group name that will enable it to be loaded with the **MENULOAD** command. This menu can be added to the existing pull-downs in the ACAD or ACADFULL menus, or it can replace one of them.

General

5. Create a single pull-down menu that is used to insert a variety of blocks, or drawing files of symbols. These symbols can be for any drawing discipline that you use often. Use cascading menus and mnemonic keys if necessary. This menu should have a special group name that will enable it to be loaded with the **MENULOAD** command. This menu can be added to the ACAD or ACADFULL menus.

General

6. Choose one of the previous four problems and create help strings for each of the new menu items. Use existing defined help strings whenever possible. When you define new help strings, always do a search of the menu file to see if the string is being used.

General

7. Refer to problem 3. Create an accelerator key for each of the drawing and editing commands in that problem. Search the menu file to see if any of the commands are currently tagged with an accelerator key to avoid duplication.

General

8. Construct an image tile menu of a symbol library that you use in a specific discipline of drafting or design. This menu can be selected from the **Draw** pull-down menu, or from a new pull-down menu of your own creation. Use as many image tiles as needed. You can call additional image tile menus from the initial one. Examples of disciplines that symbols can be created for are:

General

- Mechanical
- Architectural
- Civil
- Structural
- Piping
- HVAC
- Electrical
- Electronics
- PC board layout
- Geometric tolerancing
- 3D construction

9. Modify the existing **3D Objects** dialog box and image tile menu to include additional 3D objects of your own creation. You can insert an additional nine images to the existing dialog box. Create additional menus, or "pages," if needed.

General

General

10. Create a new image tile menu and dialog box that illustrates a variety of hatch patterns. When an image is selected, it should set a specific hatch pattern, then execute the **HATCH** command so that the user can set the scale and angle for the hatch pattern. Be sure to include the proper name of the hatch pattern in your menu file so that the user does not have to enter it when the **HATCH** command is executed.

General

11. Create a new image tile menu that provides images of a variety of dimensioning styles. When a specific image is picked, it should automatically set the appropriate dimension variables in order to achieve the appearance of the dimension in the selected image. Test each of these selections carefully before incorporating them into the file. This menu may be an excellent one for using branching image tile dialog boxes in order to display variations in different dimension styles.

AutoCAD R13

Chapter 20

Customizing Tablet Menus

Learning objectives

After completing this chapter, you will be able to:
- ❍ Configure and use the AutoCAD tablet menu template.
- ❍ Customize the AutoCAD tablet menu.
- ❍ Create a new tablet menu.

If you have a digitizer, the AutoCAD standard tablet menu is an alternative to keyboard entry or picking screen commands. The tablet menu template is a thick piece of plastic that measures 11" × 12". Printed on it are many of the commands available in AutoCAD. Some commands are accompanied by small symbols, or icons, which indicate the function of the command. The menu is helpful because it provides a clear display of various AutoCAD commands.

Like the screen menus, the tablet menu can be customized. Notice the empty spaces on it at the top of the tablet. This space is available for adding commands or symbols. You can have several overlays for this area.

Most people discover that many of the commands in the AutoCAD tablet are not used for specific types of drawings, so they construct their own tablet menus. This is similar to creating screen menus.

USING THE AUTOCAD TABLET MENU

To use a tablet menu, the digitizer must be configured for your specific hardware configuration and for the type of menu you will be using. When you initially configure AutoCAD to recognize a digitizer, the entire surface of the tablet represents the screen pointing area. The **TABLET** command allows you to configure the digitizer to recognize the tablet menu overlay. This includes informing AutoCAD of the exact layout of the menu areas and the size and position of the screen pointing area. Depending on the type of pointing device you are using with Microsoft Windows, there are additional aspects of tablet configuration to be considered.

Using the digitizer tablet for all Windows applications

If you are using your digitizer as the sole pointing device for all of your Microsoft Windows applications, you will require a driver called WINTAB. The WINTAB driver configures a digitizer to act as a mouse for Windows-based applications, but permits you to use the tablet screen pointing area and menus when running AutoCAD for Windows. This is called *absolute mode*.

You must install the WINTAB driver as your system pointing device in Microsoft Windows before starting AutoCAD. WINTAB drivers are supplied by the digitizer tablet manufacturers, not by Autodesk. If you have access to CompuServe®, you can easily download the current WINTAB driver for your particular digitizer tablet.

Tablet menu layout

The AutoCAD tablet menu presents commands in related groups. See Figure 20-1. Notice the headings below each menu area. Find the **TEMPLATE** command in the **UTILITY** section of the menu template. This command is used to load custom templates. It is also used to recognize some additional third-party applications. These third-party applications usually supply their own menu file to be compatible with AutoCAD, and the file must be installed on your hard drive before it can be used.

Figure 20-1.
The AutoCAD tablet menu template. (Autodesk, Inc.)

A— **User Area**
B— **SCREEN**
C— **DRAW/ZOOM**
D— **DISPLAY/INQUIRY/LAYER**

E— **TEXT/DIMENSION**
F— **BLOCK/XREF/SETTINGS**
G— **SNAP/TOGGLE/EDIT**
H— **UTILITY**

I— **TABLET SWAP**
J— **NUMERIC**

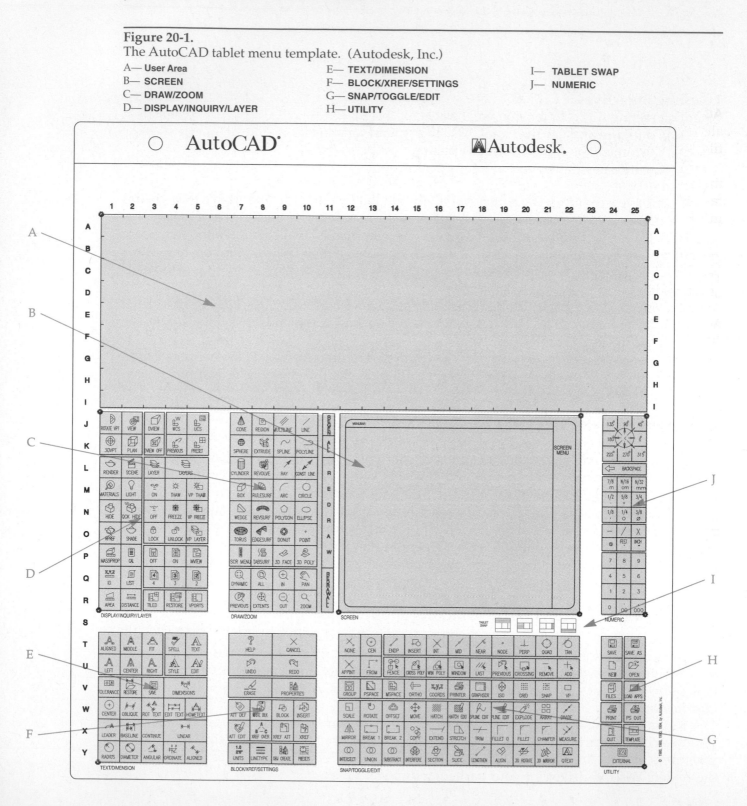

Also, you must set the environment variable **ACADALTMENU** in order for the **TEMPLATE** command to work. You may recall from Chapter 16 that environment variables may be set using the **Environment** dialog box. To access this dialog box, first select **Preferences...** from the **Options** pull-down menu. Then, when the **Preferences** dialog box appears, click the **Environment** tab.

Suppose, for example, that you have a customized alternate menu file called PIPING.MNU located in the D:\CADPIPE subdirectory. As shown in Figure 20-2, you need to add the following line in the **Alt. Menu File:** edit box:

    d:\cadpipe\piping.mnu

Next, pick the **OK** button to exit the **Preferences** dialog box. The new environment variable takes effect immediately.

When you pick **TEMPLATE** from the tablet menu, it looks for the value in the **ACADALTMENU** environment variable and loads the piping menu. Keep in mind that the alternate menu can be an entirely new menu composed of button, pull-down, screen, image tile, and tablet menus.

As previously mentioned, many third-party applications supply their own customized menu files. An example of one such application is illustrated in Figure 20-3. The custom tablet menu shown is from Design Pacifica's ANSI Mechanical™; a widely-used advanced mechanical and design annotation application for AutoCAD.

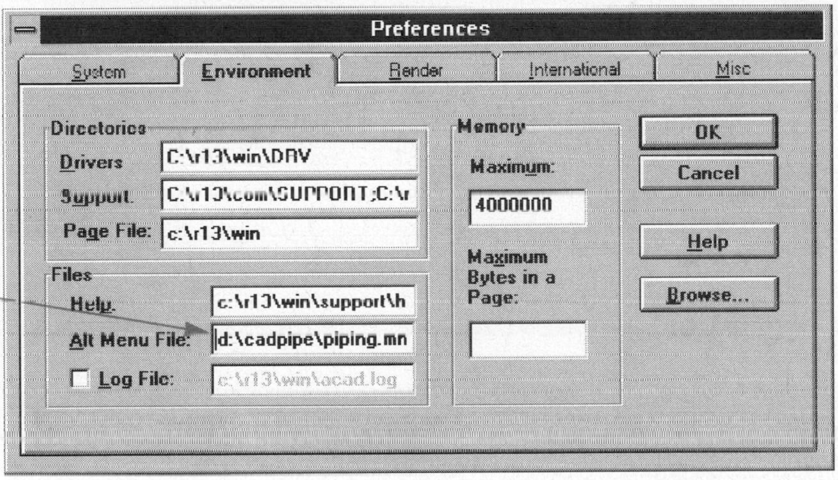

Figure 20-2.
The **Environment** panel of the **Preferences** dialog box is used to set the **ACADALTMENU** environment variable.

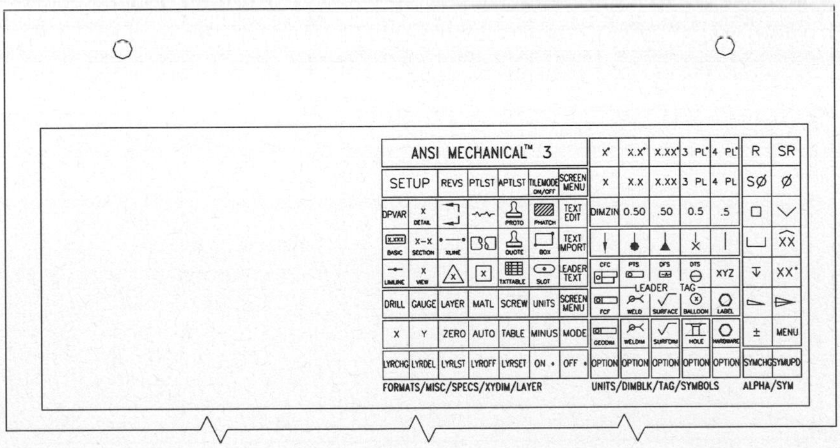

Figure 20-3.
Third-party applications, such as ANSI Mechanical™, often include their own specialized tablet menu functions. (Design Pacifica)

This program uses the available menu space for its specialized functions. This unused portion is called Menu Area 1. As you develop your own customized tablet menu, make a point of taking advantage of this unused space. Suggestions and instructions for customizing Menu Area 1 appear later in this chapter.

Configuring the tablet menu

The **TABLET** command is used to tell AutoCAD the layout of the tablet menu. It prompts for three corners of each menu area and the number of columns and rows in each area. The screen pointing area is defined by picking two opposite corners. Three corners of each menu area are marked with small doughnuts. As you read the following example, look at Figure 20-4. It illustrates how the standard AutoCAD tablet menu is configured and shows the doughnuts marking menu area corners.

Figure 20-4.
Small doughnuts mark the corners of the menu areas on the AutoCAD template. (Autodesk, Inc.)

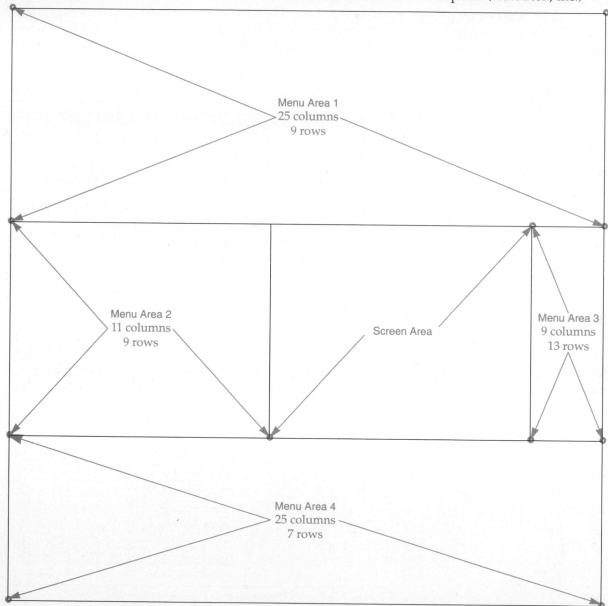

Menu Area 1
25 columns
9 rows

Menu Area 2
11 columns
9 rows

Screen Area

Menu Area 3
9 columns
13 rows

Menu Area 4
25 columns
7 rows

Command: **TABLET**↵
Option (ON/OFF/CAL/CFG): **CFG**↵
Enter number of tablet menus desired (0-4): **4**↵
Digitize upper left corner of menu area 1: *(pick the doughnut at the upper-left corner)*
Digitize lower left corner of menu area 1: *(pick the point)*
Digitize lower right corner of menu area 1: *(pick the point)*
Enter the number of columns for menu area 1, *(n-nnnn)* ⟨25⟩:↵
Enter the number of rows for menu area 1, *(n-nnnn)* ⟨9⟩:↵

You have now given AutoCAD the location of Menu Area 1 and specified the number of boxes that are available. The command continues with Menu Area 2:

Digitize upper left corner of menu area 2: *(pick the point)*
Digitize lower left corner of menu area 2: *(pick the point)*
Digitize lower right corner of menu area 2: *(pick the point)*
Enter the number of columns for menu area 2, *(n-nnnn)* ⟨11⟩:↵
Enter the number of rows for menu area 2, *(n-nnnn)* ⟨9⟩:↵
Digitize upper left corner of menu area 3: *(pick the point)*
Digitize lower left corner of menu area 3: *(pick the point)*
Digitize lower right corner of menu area 3: *(pick the point)*
Enter the number of columns for menu area 3, *(n-nnnn)* ⟨9⟩:↵
Enter the number of rows for menu area 3, *(n-nnnn)* ⟨13⟩:↵
Digitize upper left corner of menu area 4: *(pick the point)*
Digitize lower left corner of menu area 4: *(pick the point)*
Digitize lower right corner of menu area 4: *(pick the point)*
Enter the number of columns for menu area 4, *(n-nnnn)* ⟨25⟩:↵
Enter the number of rows for menu area 4, *(n-nnnn)* ⟨7⟩:↵

Next, you must locate opposite corners of the screen pointing area:

Do you want to specify the Floating Screen Pointing Area? ⟨N⟩: **Y**↵
Do you want the Floating Screen Pointing Area to be the same size as the Fixed
    Screen Pointing Area? ⟨Y⟩: *(enter* Y *or* N; *if you enter* Y, *digitize the lower-left*
    and upper-right corners of the floating screen pointing area when prompted.)
The F12 key will toggle the Floating Screen Pointing Area ON and OFF.
Would you like to specify a button to toggle the Floating Screen Area? ⟨N⟩:
    (enter Y *or* N)

If you choose to use a digitizer puck button as the toggle, press the button of your choice. Do not press the pick button.

The tablet configuration is saved in the ACAD.CFG file, which is in your \R13\WIN directory. The system reads this file when loading AutoCAD to determine what kind of equipment you are using. It also determines which menu is current. Use this same process when configuring the tablet for your custom menus.

Configuring the AutoCAD template menu can be done more simply by selecting the **Re-Cfg** option from the **TABLET:** screen menu. First enable the screen menu as explained in Chapter 16 and then pick **SETTINGS** from the AutoCAD root menu. Next, pick **TABLET:** and then select **Re-Cfg**. The **TABLET:** screen menu options are shown in Figure 20-5.

When the **Re-Cfg** option is selected, the configuration prompts appear as shown earlier. However, you do not have to enter the number of columns and rows. The **Re-Cfg** option assumes you are realigning the AutoCAD template. Therefore, it only requires the locations of the menu area and the screen pointing area. Use this screen menu option when you wish to return to the standard AutoCAD template after using a custom menu.

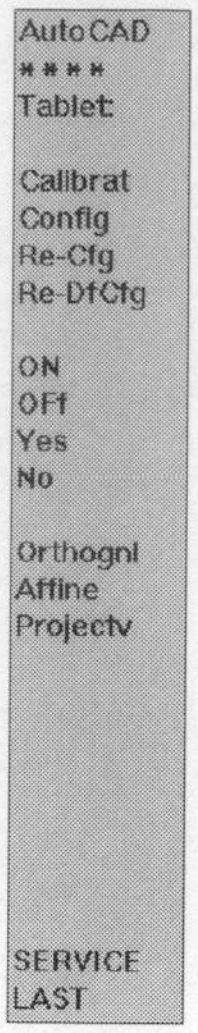

Figure 20-5.
Select **Re-Cfg** from the
TABLET: screen menu to
configure the tablet menu.

```
AutoCAD
* * * *
Tablet

Calibrat
Config
Re-Cfg
Re-DfCfg

ON
Off
Yes
No

Orthognl
Affine
Projectv




SERVICE
LAST
```

Swapping template areas

Tablet swap icons are located below the screen area on the template. These four picks allow you to swap each of the four tablet areas. The black area of each icon indicates the area that is swapped when the icon is picked. In addition, a prompt on the monitor indicates the type of swap.

For example, if you pick area 1, the entire area is available for custom commands. Customizing this area is discussed later. The following list indicates the area swapped, and the prompt.

- Area 1 prompt:

  Alternate tablet area 1 loaded.
  This area is for your personal applications and menu items.

- Area 2 prompt:

  Alternate tablet area 2 loaded.
  Zoom and other commands issue CTRL+Cs: VPOINT and DVIEW in current
      UCS mode.

  The CTRL+C referred to above is the cancel issued with the [Esc] key, not the **COPYCLIP** that is issued with the [Ctrl]+[C] key combination.

- Area 3 prompt:

  Alternate tablet area 3 loaded.
  Select Metric units from the Numeric menu.

- Area 4 prompt:

  Alternate tablet area 4 loaded.
  Object snap modes issue running modes: commands repeat.

Any of the areas can be swapped back to the default menu by picking the icon again. You can have more than one swapped menu at a time. If you are unsure if any of the tablet areas have been swapped, it is easy to check. Just pick a tablet area and the ensuing prompt will indicate if the swap area is loaded or unloaded. The following prompt is displayed when a pick on a tablet swap icon unloads the swapped area and returns to the default configuration:

  Alternate tablet area n unloaded.

The configuration of alternate tablet areas is saved in the configuration file. Therefore, when AutoCAD is loaded, or a new drawing is opened, AutoCAD displays the Alternate tablet area n loaded message for each of the swapped areas that are loaded. This provides you with an additional reminder.

The prompt that is issued after picking a swap icon can be shortened or eliminated. Use the **EXPERT** system variable to change the prompt. A value of 0 for **EXPERT** displays the entire prompt. A value of 1 or 2 displays only the first part of the prompt:

> Alternate tablet area 3 loaded.

A value of 4 for the **EXPERT** variable displays no prompt when a swap icon is picked. A value of 3 displays an abbreviated prompt. Set the variable as follows:

> Command: **EXPERT**↵
> New value for EXPERT ⟨0⟩: **3**↵

CUSTOMIZING THE AUTOCAD TABLET MENU

AutoCAD Custom Guide **4**

The empty upper portion of the AutoCAD tablet menu can be used to add custom commands. This is Menu Area 1. It contains 225 boxes that can be programmed for additional commands, macros, scripts, or blocks. It is a good place to locate often-used symbols and shapes.

An overlay containing block names and drawings can be plotted and slipped under the plastic template. Several overlays can be added for different disciplines, and can be structured to operate in different ways.

Plan the template

Before adding items to the AutoCAD template, take time to think about what the template should include. Ask yourself the following questions:
- ✓ For what kinds of drawings will the template be used?
- ✓ What kind of symbols should be placed in a template?
- ✓ What additional commands or macros should be in the template?
- ✓ Should the symbols be stored as blocks or wblocks?
- ✓ Which symbols and blocks are used most often?
- ✓ If the symbols are blocks, should they be in a prototype drawing?

After answering these questions, you will be able to lay out a quality template. The next step is to draw the overlay.

Draw the menu overlay

Part of your plan should be drawing or sketching the menu area. The quickest way to make an accurate drawing is to plot Menu Area 1 of the AutoCAD template. There is such a drawing, called TABLET.DWG, furnished with the software. It is located in the \R13\COM\SAMPLE subdirectory. The following steps should be used to create the drawing of Menu Area 1:

1. Open the drawing file named TABLET.
2. **ZOOM Window** around Menu Area 1. See Figure 20-6.
3. Freeze all layers except:

> 0
> OUTLINES
> PLINES

4. Make a new layer named AREA1, and give it the color cyan.
5. Use **PLINE** to trace over the outline of AREA1.
6. Draw a vertical line between tick marks on the right or left side and array it in 24 columns with a spacing of .4020.
7. Draw a horizontal line between tick marks at the top or bottom and array 8 rows with a spacing of .4020.
8. Erase the remaining black lines in the menu. See Figure 20-7.

Figure 20-6.
Menu Area 1 is located at the top of the AutoCAD template. It contains a grid of 225 boxes inside the menu area border.

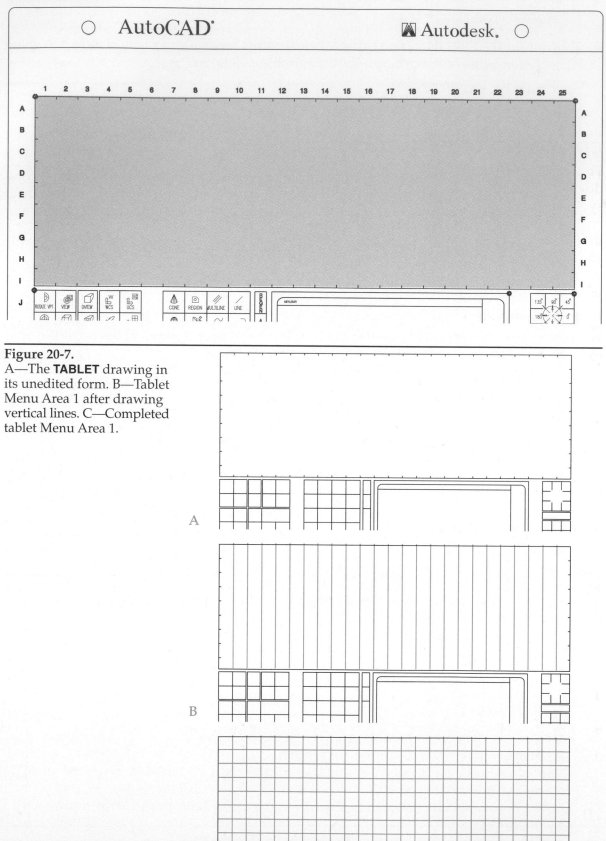

Figure 20-7.
A—The **TABLET** drawing in its unedited form. B—Tablet Menu Area 1 after drawing vertical lines. C—Completed tablet Menu Area 1.

9. Plot the menu on B-size or larger paper. A plot using 1.5 = 1 or 2 = 1 scale provides a larger drawing, which is easier to work with for initial menu design purposes.
10. Erase all unnecessary layers.
11. Save the drawing as TABAREA1 (tablet area one) for future use.

Make several copies of your drawing. Pencil in the command and symbol names. Try more than one arrangement based on some of the considerations mentioned above. Keep in mind the purpose of the template you are making. Symbols that are used frequently should be placed along the outer edges for quick selection.

Complete the menu drawing

The next step in creating your customized AutoCAD template is to draw the symbols in the menu. This should be relatively easy. Symbols should already be in the form of blocks. They can now be inserted into the boxes of the menu. You will have to scale the symbols down to make them fit. The menu should now resemble that shown in Figure 20-8. These symbols were inserted from the symbols library prototype drawing created in Chapter 25.

After drawing the menu, plot it at full scale (1 = 1). Use vellum or polyester film and wet ink. Use black rather than colored ink. This produces a good-quality plot, clearly seen when slipped under the AutoCAD template.

The menu area can be modified to suit your needs. The symbols shown in Figure 20-9 are used for isometric process piping drawings.

Figure 20-8.
Symbols (blocks) are inserted into the boxes of the menu.

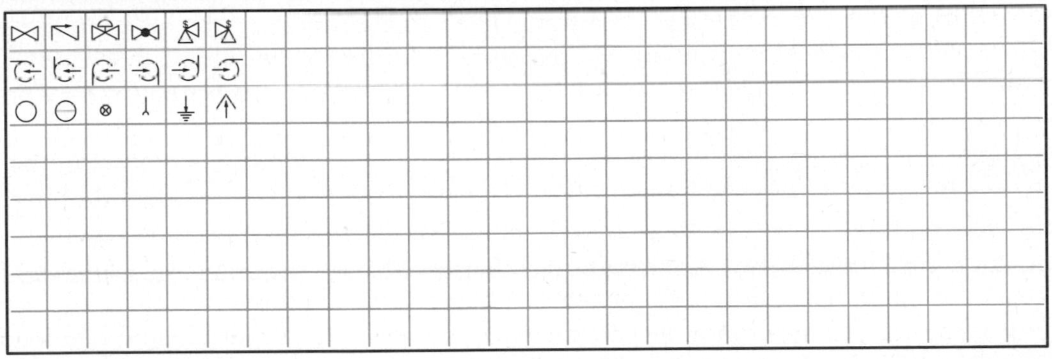

Figure 20-9.
This custom overlay for Menu Area 1 is used for isometric process piping drawings. (Willamette Industries, Inc.)

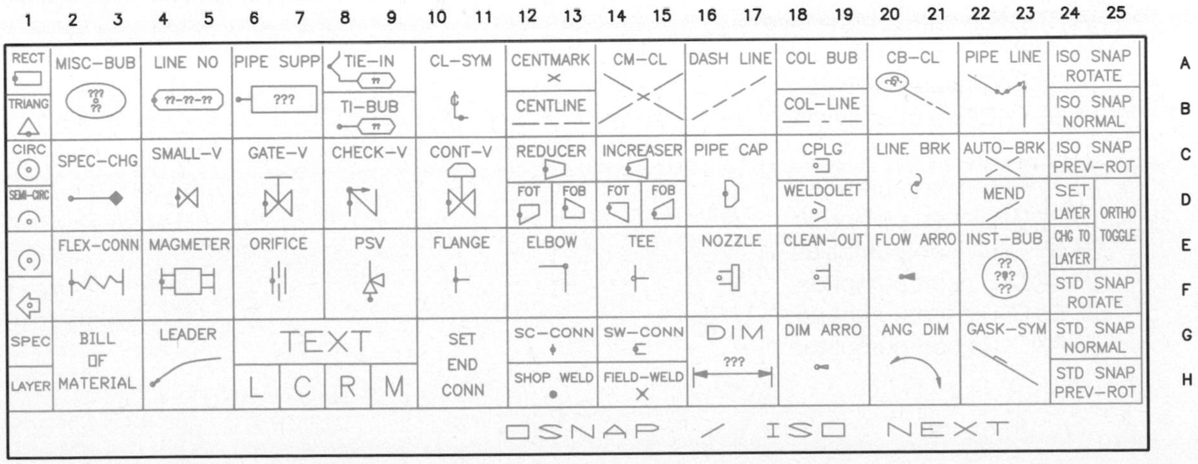

EXERCISE 20-1

❑ Open the TABLET drawing.
❑ Edit the drawing as shown in the previous discussion to create a tablet Menu Area 1 with boxes.
❑ Save the drawing of Menu Area 1 as A:EX20-1.
❑ Insert two blocks into the first two boxes of the menu area.
❑ Scale the blocks so they fit in the boxes.
❑ Save the drawing as A:EX20-1 and quit.

Write the menu file

The final step in customizing the AutoCAD template is to write the code in the ***TABLET1 section of the menu file. Load the ACAD.MNU file into your text editor and find the section label ***TABLET1. It should look like the following:

```
***TABLET1
[A-1]
[A-2]
[A-3]
[A-4]
[A-5]
```

Look at the tablet menu in Figure 20-6 and notice the row and column numbers and letters along the top and sides of the tablet. These correspond to the numbers in brackets in the ACAD.MNU file under the ***TABLET headings. Each row contains 25 boxes numbered from left to right. There are 225 boxes in all. Therefore, box number 70 would also be C-20.

Notice in Figure 20-8 that the symbols placed in the menu occupy the first six boxes of each row. The first box of each row is labeled [A-1], [B-1], and [C-1], respectively.

The code can be entered in two ways. It can replace the box numbers listed in the menu file, or it can be entered after the box numbers. The latter method is recommended because it provides you with reference numbers for the tablet box. There are no screen labels for tablet menus. Thus, anything inside brackets is not displayed, nor is it read by AutoCAD. This means that the notations inside the brackets can be left as helpful reminders.

Before making changes to the menu, make a copy of the ACAD.MNU file. Then load your copy of ACAD.MNU into the text editor. The following example shows the menu entries for the customized template shown in Figure 20-8.

```
**TABLET1STD
[A-1]^C^Cinsert;gatevalve
[A-2]^C^Cinsert;checkvalve
[A-3]^C^Cinsert;controlvalve
[A-4]^C^Cinsert;globevalve
[A-5]^C^Cinsert;safetyvalv-r
[A-6]^C^Cinsert;safetyvalv-l

[B-1]^C^Cinsert;pumpr-top
[B-2]^C^Cinsert;pumpr-up
[B-3]^C^Cinsert;pumpr-dn
[B-4]^C^Cinsert;pumpl-dn
[B-5]^C^Cinsert;pumpl-up
[B-6]^C^Cinsert;pumpl-top
```

```
[C-1]^C^Cinsert;instr-loc
[C-2]^C^Cinsert;instr-pan
[C-3]^C^Cinsert;trans
[C-4]^C^Cinsert;instr-con
[C-5]^C^Cinsert;drain
[C-6]^C^Cinsert;vent
```

After you edit or create a new menu in this manner, save the menu file and then exit the text editor. Use the **MENU** command to load your copy of the ACAD.MNU file. If your menu file is in a subdirectory, be sure to enter the proper path to the file. Pick tablet swap icon 1 to use your menu. If you will be editing your menu often, consider making a menu pick on the screen that automatically loads the menu file as follows:

```
[LOADMENU]^C^Cmenu;/cadpipe/piping
```

Alternate ways to use the menu

The method just discussed uses blocks that have been saved in a prototype drawing. In order to use the blocks, the prototype must first be inserted into the current drawing. Or, the new drawing must be started using the prototype method.

For example, suppose the piping flow diagram symbols are saved in a prototype drawing called PIPEFLOW. You may want to begin a new drawing with the name of PROJ2-05. You can use the symbols if you enter the following drawing file names for the prototype drawing method:

```
Prototype: PIPEFLOW
New drawing name: PROJ2-05↵
```

This loads the PIPEFLOW drawing into the computer and gives it the name of PROJ2-05. All of the blocks in the PIPEFLOW drawing can be picked from your new tablet menu.

There is yet another method to use the blocks located in another drawing. You can insert one drawing into another using the **INSERT** command. You may consider putting an insertion command on your tablet menu. Only the named items, such as blocks, views, and layers are inserted.

```
Command: INSERT↵
Block name (or ?): PIPEFLOW.↵
Insertion point:(press [Esc] to cancel)
```

Remember to cancel the **INSERT** command at the Insertion point: prompt. Wait for all of the named items to be inserted into the drawing.

The **insert prototype drawing** pick in your tablet menu file can be written as follows:

```
^C^CINSERT;PIPEFLOW;^C
```

This does the same thing as entering the prototype drawing name to begin a new drawing. However, it takes less time because you do not have to type in any command names or drawing files.

A third way to use the menu is to use all drawing files. This method does not require using symbol drawings. The drawing files can be on the hard disk or floppy disks. The use of drawing files as opposed to blocks is discussed in Chapter 25 of *AutoCAD and its Applications—Basics, Release 13 for Windows*. Remember that symbols stored as drawing files require more disk storage space. Disk access time also is often slower.

PROFESSIONAL TIP

Evaluate your present use of blocks and drawing files when making or modifying tablet menus. Take into account your current method of symbol creation, storage, and usage when developing tablet menus for symbols. If symbol drawings (prototypes) are working best for your application, develop your tablet menu around these, or if individual drawing files are used the menus should access these.

DESIGNING A NEW TABLET MENU

A tablet menu is somewhat inefficient because it requires you to move your eyes away from the screen to find a tablet command. However, there are advantages of tablet menus over screen menus.

- Screen menus must be "paged" or "cascaded" when looking for a command. Flipping through pages of screen menus and submenus slows down the design and drawing process.
- A tablet menu provides immediate access to most commands. If necessary, it can be paged for additional commands and symbols.
- Available tablet commands can be chosen with only one pick of the input device.
- Graphic symbols on the template make it easy to identify commands.
- Numerous commands can be printed on a tablet menu. This enables users to select commands that they might seldom select if using just screen menus.

Any technique that increases your efficiency and productivity should be investigated and incorporated as part of your operating procedures. You will find that making custom tablet menus is one such procedure. They can be used alone or together with screen menus. A tablet menu pick can display a specialized screen menu or load new tablet menus. After gaining experience and confidence in your menu-creating abilities, you will become aware of the value of tablet menus.

Plan your new tablet menu

Planning a custom AutoCAD menu was discussed earlier in the text. Planning is also needed when developing new tablet menus. The creation of a tablet menu should not be the first thing you do when customizing AutoCAD. There are several important preliminary steps that should be taken before designing a menu:

1. List the commands that you use most often.
2. Develop macros that automate your CAD work as much as possible.
3. List the different types of symbol overlays you may need.
4. List each group of symbols used in order of most-often used to least-often used.

PROFESSIONAL TIP

When designing macros, think of the commands and functions you use most often. Automate these first. Keep in mind that your goal is to create a drawing or design. This requires knowledge of the specific discipline. You want to spend more time using your knowledge and skills rather than picking the proper succession of AutoCAD commands and options. Therefore, for each function that you automate, reduce the number of picks required to complete the function. In doing so, your time spent at the computer will be more productive.

After listing the items just mentioned, begin the process of creating commands, macros, and menus.

1. Develop and test individual macros in a screen menu or tablet menu.
2. Determine major groups of commands and macros based on their frequency of use.
3. Design the tablet menu layout. Draw it larger than actual size, using a pencil. This gives you room for lettering and sketches. You can have up to four menu areas and a screen pointing area. Some common layouts are shown in Figure 20-10.
4. Draw the basic menu layout with AutoCAD. This should be a preliminary test menu. Do not add text or graphics yet. Pencil in commands on a plotted copy of the menu.
5. Write the code for the menu and test each function for convenience.
6. Add text and graphics to the menu, then plot it. Revise the menu as needed to make it more efficient.

Figure 20-10.
Some common tablet menu layouts.

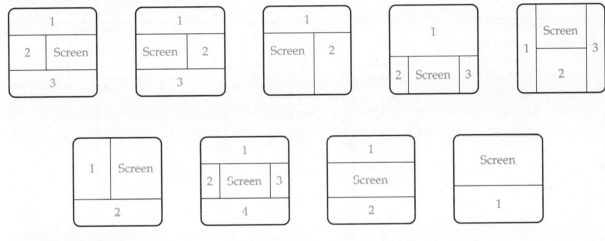

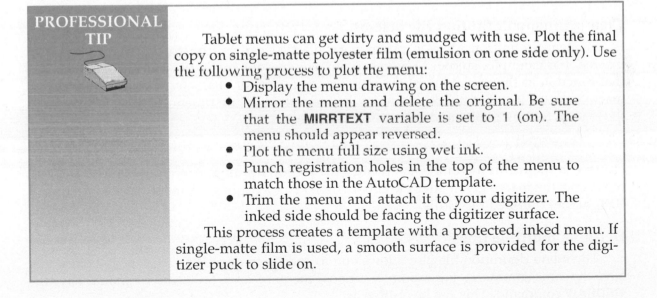

PROFESSIONAL TIP	Tablet menus can get dirty and smudged with use. Plot the final copy on single-matte polyester film (emulsion on one side only). Use the following process to plot the menu:

    Tablet menus can get dirty and smudged with use. Plot the final copy on single-matte polyester film (emulsion on one side only). Use the following process to plot the menu:

- Display the menu drawing on the screen.
- Mirror the menu and delete the original. Be sure that the **MIRRTEXT** variable is set to 1 (on). The menu should appear reversed.
- Plot the menu full size using wet ink.
- Punch registration holes in the top of the menu to match those in the AutoCAD template.
- Trim the menu and attach it to your digitizer. The inked side should be facing the digitizer surface.

    This process creates a template with a protected, inked menu. If single-matte film is used, a smooth surface is provided for the digitizer puck to slide on.

Creating a menu definition file

The process of developing your own menu is similar to customizing the AutoCAD template. Of course, it takes longer because you are creating the entire menu. But do not let this bother you. Autodesk has developed a menu definition and compiling process that can speed up the menu creation process. This capability is available in the \R13\COM\SAMPLE subdirectory.

A menu definition file is a preliminary menu file in which macros can be created to represent frequently used functions. In addition, a command located in several boxes of the menu can be defined once using a multiple line definition. The menu definition file is created with a file extension of .MND. If you are developing a menu named TEST, name the file TEST.MND.

The definition file must be compiled before it can be used by AutoCAD. This is done with the MC.EXE program. The relationship between the MC.EXE, .MND, .MNU, .MNS, and .MNC files is shown in Figure 20-11. The MND file is written first. Then the MC.EXE program, run from DOS, compiles the MND file into an MNU file. AutoCAD then reads the MNU file and further compiles it into an MNC file. This is the version used for drawing.

Figure 20-11.
The .MND file must be compiled twice before it can be used by AutoCAD for drawing purposes.

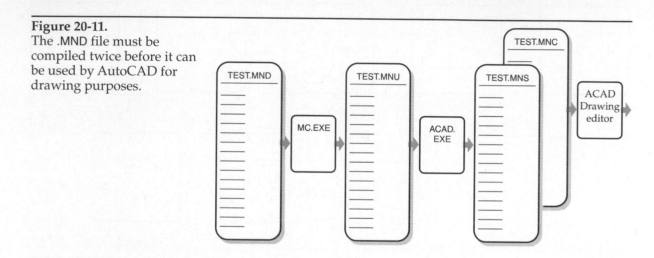

Creating menu definition file macros

A menu definition file is a preliminary file that can be constructed with the aid of macros. For example, suppose several commands in your menu use ^C^C. You can define that function at the beginning of the menu as any word or character. The menu definition macro must be listed at the beginning of the file, before the first menu section. If you assign the letter C to the double cancel, it would be written as:

    {C}= ^C^C

Put this in the menu file immediately after the section heading. Anything inside the braces represents the macro given after the equals sign. Place a {C} in your menu where you need a ^C^C in the compiled MNU file.

Defining multiple lines

The menu definition file also allows you to specify multiple lines (template boxes) that have the same command. For example, suppose menu boxes 5, 6, 30, and 31 should have the **'REDRAW** command. This can be written as:

    ⟨5,6,30,31⟩'REDRAW

This is interpreted by the MC.EXE program to mean that menu boxes 5, 6, 30, and 31 are assigned the **'REDRAW** command. Multiple definitions such as this must be entered immediately below the menu heading.

```
***TABLET1
⟨5,6,30,31⟩'REDRAW
```

This ability to specify multiple line definitions is especially useful for tablet menus. There may be several boxes on the template that represent the same thing. Look at the **BLOCK/XREF/SETTINGS** area of the AutoCAD template and notice the **HELP** box, Figure 20-12. AutoCAD does not see the **HELP** area as one large box because tablet Menu Area 4 is divided into 175 equal size boxes. The **HELP** command on the template is located across two boxes. Therefore, two lines in the menu file must have the **HELP** command.

Load ACAD.MNU into your text editor and page to the ***TABLET4 section. You should notice several lines on which there is just a semicolon (;). These specify the blank, gray space above tablet Menu Area 4. All of the gray spaces on the tablet produce a RETURN when picked. Now scroll down one page until you find two lines that read '_?. These are boxes 32 and 33. These two boxes would be defined at the beginning of the MND file as:

```
***TABLET4
⟨32,33⟩'HELP
```

Figure 20-12.
The HELP box on the
AutoCAD template is
actually composed of two
smaller boxes.

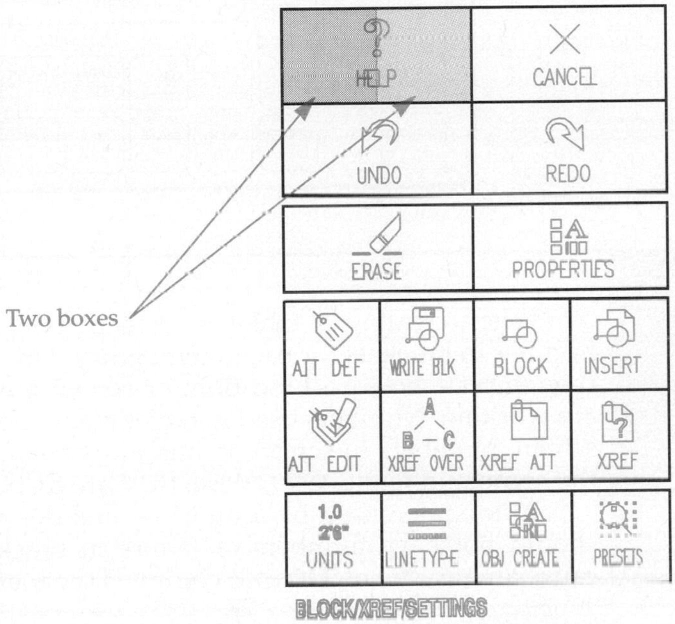

Two boxes

A sample tablet menu

An example of a custom menu is shown in Figure 20-13. It is similar to the AutoCAD template, but contains fewer boxes. The template shows a grid of numbers along the top and letters down the left side. These locations are used at the beginning of each line of code in the menu file for reference:

```
***TABLET1STD
[A-1]
[A-2]
[A-3]
```

Anything inside brackets in a tablet menu section is not displayed, and does not affect the menu code. It is only a helpful reference. The same notation is used in the ACAD.MNU. It indicates the tablet section and box number within that section.

Figure 20-13.
A sample custom menu
layout.

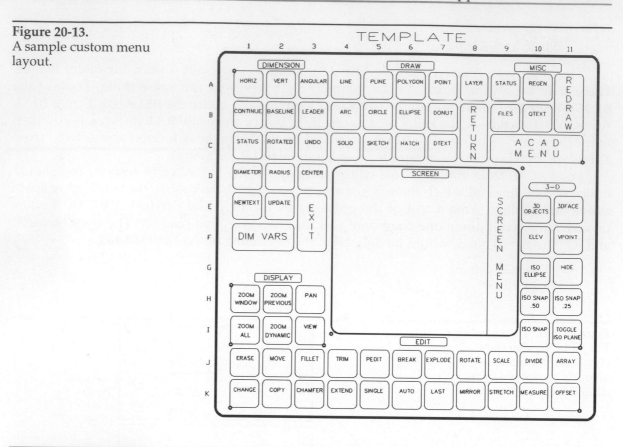

PROFESSIONAL TIP

When creating a tablet or screen menu, provide a reference number in brackets for each menu entry. This immediately tells you the template box, grid location, or screen menu line on which you are working. Numbers used in tablet menus are not displayed on the screen. Numbers in screen menus must be after the eighth space in the command name. Otherwise, they are displayed on the screen.

A line referenced by a multiple line definition in the MND file should not have numbers or letters in brackets. If it does, it will cause an error when MC.EXE compiles the menu.

In Figure 20-13, notice that often-used commands, such as **RETURN**, **REDRAW**, **ACADMENU** (loads the AutoCAD menu), **DIM VARS**, and **EXIT** (from the dimension menu) are placed inside large boxes. This allows you to pick them quickly.

The code for this menu can be written as an MNU or MND file. Remember, the menu definition (.MND) file involves less typing if you use its macro functions. Both versions are given here for comparison. As you look through the following files, compare the entries to the appropriate template boxes in Figure 20-13. Also note the codes located at the beginning of the menu and the box numbers left blank in the MND file. A blank line indicates that the function of the box was defined in one of the multiple line codes at the beginning of the tablet section. The grid locations of each menu item are indicated in brackets for quick identification. The button menu is for a 12 button cursor.

MENU1.MND	MENU1.MNU	MENU1.MND	MENU1.MNU
***BUTTONS	***BUTTONS	[D-3]{D};center	[D-3]^C^Cdim;center
;	;	[E-1]{D};newtext	[E-1]^C^Cdim;newtext
'REDRAW	'REDRAW	[E-2]{D};update	[E-2]^C^Cdim;update
^C	^C	[E-3]exit	[E-3]exit
^B	^B	[F-1]{DV}	[F-1]^C^Cdim $s=var1
^O	^O	[F-2]{DV}	[F-2]^C^Cdim $s=var1
^G	^G	[F-3]exit	[F-3]exit
^D	^D	[G-1]	[G-1]
^E	^E	[G-2]	[G-2]
^T	^T	[G-3]	[G-3]
{D}=^C^Cdim		[H-1]'zoom;w	[H-1]'zoom;w
{C}=^C^C		[H-2]'zoom;p	[H-2]'zoom;p
{MA}=^C^Cmenu;acad		[H-3]'pan	[H-3]'pan
{DV}=^C^Cdim $s=var1		[I-1]'zoom;a	[I-1]'zoom;a
		[I-2]'zoom;d	[I-2]'zoom;d
***TABLET1	***TABLET1	[I-3]{C}view	[I-3]^C^Cview
⟨11,22⟩redraw			
⟨19,29⟩"		***TABLET3	***TABLET3
[A–1]{D};horiz	[A–1]^C^Cdim;horiz	[D-10]	[D-10]
[A-2]{D};vert	[A-2]^C^Cdim;vert	[D-11]	[D-11]
[A-3]{D};angular	[A-3]^C^Cdim;angular	[E-10]$i=3dobjects $I=*	[E-10] $i=3dobjects $I=*
[A-4]{C}line	[A-4]^C^Cline	[F-11]{C}3dface	[F-11]^C^C3dface
[A-5]{C}pline	[A-5]^C^Cpline	[F-10]{C}elev	[F-10]^C^Celev
[A-6]{C}polygon	[A-6]^C^Cpolygon	[F-11]{C}vpoint;;	[F-11]^C^Cvpoint;;
[A-7]{C}line;\\	[A-7]^C^Cline;\\	[G-10]{C}ellipse;i	[G-10]^C^Cellipse;i
[A-8]{C}point	[A-8]^C^Cpoint	[G-11]{C}hide	[G-11]^C^Chide
[A-9]{C}status	[A-9]^C^Cstatus	[H-10]{C}snap;s;i;.5	[H-10]^C^Csnap;s;i;.5
[A-10]{C}regen	[A-10]^C^Cregen	[H-11]{C}snap;s;i;.25	[H-11]^C^Csnap;s;i;.25
	[A-11]'redraw	[I-10]{C}snap;s;s;;	[I-10]^C^Csnap;s;s;;
[B-1]{D};continue	[B-1]^C^Cdim;continue	[I-11]{C}^E	[I-11]^E
[B-2]{D};baseline	[B-2]^C^Cdim;baseline		
[B-3]{D};leader	[B-3]^C^Cdim;leader	***TABLET4	***TABLET4
[B-4]{C}arc	[B-4]^C^Carc	[J-1]{C}erase	[J-1]^C^Cerase
[B-5]{C}circle	[B-5]^C^Ccircle	[J-2]{C}move	[J-2]^C^Cmove
[B-6]{C}ellipse	[B-6]^C^Cellipse	[J-3]{C}fillet	[J-3]^C^Cfillet
[B-7]{C}donut	[B-7]^C^Cdonut	[J-4]{C}trim	[J-4]^C^Ctrim
	[B-8]^C^C;	[J-5]{C}pedit	[J-5]^C^Cpedit
[B-9]{C}files	[B-9]^C^Cfiles	[J-6]{C}break	[J-6]^C^Cbreak
[B-10]{C}qtext	[B-10]^C^Cqtext	[J-7]{C}explode	[J-7]^C^Cexplode
	[D-11]	[J-8]{C}rotate	[J-8]^C^Crotate
[C-1]{D};status	[C-1]^C^Cdim;status	[J-9]{C}scale	[J-9]^C^Cscale
[C-2]{D};rotated	[C-2]^C^Cdim;rotated	[J-10]{C}divide	[J-10]^C^Cdivide
[C-3]{D};undo	[C-3]^C^Cdim;undo	[J-11]{C}array	[J-11]^C^Carray
[C-4]{C}solid	[C-4]^C^Csolid	[K-1]{C}change	[K-1]^C^Cchange
[C-5]{C}sketch	[C-5]^C^Csketch	[K-2]{C}copy	[K-2]^C^Ccopy
[C-6]{C}hatch	[C-6]^C^Chatch	[K-3]{C}chamfer	[K-3]^C^Cchamfer
[C-7]{C}dtext	[C-7]^C^Cdtext	[K-4]{C}extend	[K-4]^C^Cextend
	[C-8]	[K-5]single	[K-5]single
[C-9]{MA}	[C-9]^C^Cmenu;acad	[K-6]auto	[K-6]auto
[C-10]{MA}	[C-10]^C^Cmenu;acad	[K-7] last	[K-7]last
[C-11]{MA}	[C-11]^C^Cmenu;acad	[K-8]{C}mirror	[K-8]^C^Cmirror
		[K-9]{C}stretch	[K-9]^C^Cstretch
***TABLET2	***TABLET2	[K-10]{C}measure	[K-10]^C^Cmeasure
[D-1]{D};diameter	[D-1]^C^Cdim;diameter	[K-11]{C}offset	[K-11]^C^Coffset
[D-2]{D};radius	[D-2]^C^Cdim;radius		

If you plan to try this menu, enter the code with your text editor. Assign the name MENU1.MND. After creating the menu definition file, you must compile it with the MC.EXE program. The program is found in the R13\COM\SAMPLE subdirectory. Both the MC.EXE file and your .MND file should be in the same directory, or you must provide a path for MC to find your definition file.

The MC program runs from the DOS prompt. If you are in Windows, return to the Program Manager, open the Main group window and double-click the MS-DOS Prompt icon. Be sure that the R13\COM\SAMPLE subdirectory is made current.

The MC.EXE program can now be run to compile the MENU1.MND file and create a file named MENU1.MNU. In the following example, the MC program is run after entering the **SHELL** command and changing to the R13\COM\SAMPLE subdirectory.

```
Command: SHELL↵
OS Command:↵
C:\R13\WIN⟩ CD..\COM\SAMPLE↵
C:\R13\COM\SAMPLE⟩ MC MENU1↵
AutoCAD Menu Compiler 2.71    (08/09/94)
Copyright /(c)/1985-91 Throoput, Ltd.
C:\R13\COM\SAMPLE⟩
```

Before changing back to the \R13\WIN directory, check to see that the .MNU file has been created by getting a directory listing of all files with .MNU extensions:

```
C:\R13\COM\SAMPLE⟩ DIR *.MNU↵
C:\R13\COM\SAMPLE⟩ CD \R13\WIN↵
C:\R13\WIN⟩ EXIT↵
```

The new menu cannot be used until it is loaded into AutoCAD using the **MENU** command. In the following example, the system variable **FILEDIA** is set to 0:

```
Command: MENU↵
Menu file name or . for none ⟨current⟩: SAMPLE\MENU1↵
```

The compiled version of the menu file has an .MNC extension. AutoCAD looks for the latest version of the compiled menu file when you begin a new drawing. If there is no such file, AutoCAD compiles the menu file again.

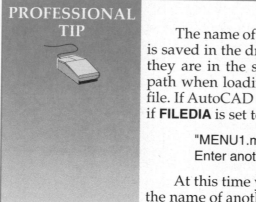

PROFESSIONAL TIP

The name of the particular menu you use to construct a drawing is saved in the drawing file. If you use different menus, be sure that they are in the same directory as the drawings, or use the proper path when loading the menu. This path is saved with the drawing file. If AutoCAD cannot find a menu, the following message appears if **FILEDIA** is set to 0:

```
"MENU1.mnu": Can't open file
Enter another menu file name (or RETURN for none):
```

At this time you can enter the proper path to the menu, or enter the name of another menu.

After loading your new menu, select the **TABLET** command and configure the new template. If you select the **TABLET** command from the screen menu, do not pick the **Re-Cfg** option. This starts the configuration routine for the ACAD tablet menu. Instead, use the **Config** option.

The configure routine asks the number of tablet menus desired. The MENU1 template requires four. You are then asked if you want to realign tablet menu areas. Answer Y (Yes). Now digitize the upper-left, lower-left, and lower-right corners of each of the four tablet menu areas. When prompted, provide the number of columns and rows in each area. The corners of MENU1 are shown in Figure 20-14. The columns and rows in each area are given in the following chart:

Menu Area	Columns	Rows
1	11	3
2	3	6
3	2	6
4	11	2

The final prompt in the configure process asks you to specify the lower-left and upper-right corners of the screen pointing area. These are also shown in Figure 20-14.

Test all of the menu items to be sure they function properly. Correct any mistakes you find. You may encounter one shortcoming if you select the **ACAD MENU** item in Menu Area 1. The AutoCAD menu will be loaded, but how do you get back to the MENU1 template? There must be a call, or item in the AutoCAD menu, that loads the MENU1 template. Load the ACAD.MNU file into your text editor and add the following line to the **S menu, or to a pull-down menu:

    [MENU1]^C^Cmenu;menu1

If you insert this entry between two existing items, do not press [Enter]. Otherwise you will insert a blank line into the menu. Examples of customized menu templates are given in the appendix.

Figure 20-14.
Digitize the corners of the tablet menu areas indicated here. Also, pick the lower-left and upper-right corners of the screen pointing area to properly configure the template.

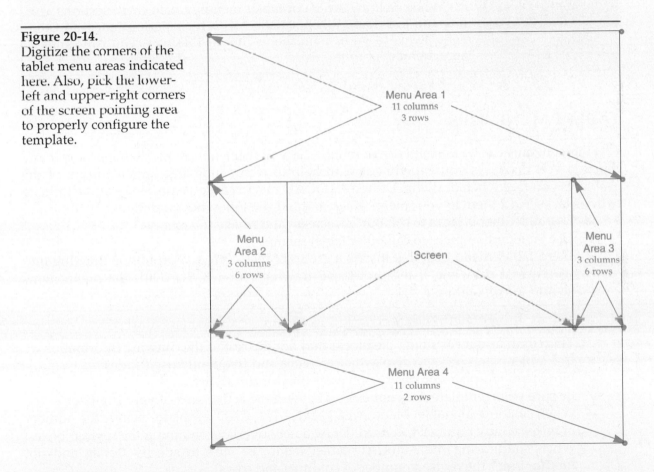

Automating the menu editing process

Modifying screen or tablet menus requires loading the text editor on a regular basis. This can become tedious. The process can be automated if you place a macro in a menu that loads the text editor and .MNU file. If you are using the **EDIT** command, in the .PGP file, add the following item to the **S or **ED section:

    [EDITMENU]^C^Cedit;menu1.mnu;menu;menu1

When picked, this item cancels the current command and executes the **EDIT** command (your text editor). The file name of the menu is entered automatically. When you exit the text editor, the revised version of MENU1 is automatically loaded into AutoCAD.

If you use a text editor other than the DOS EDIT program, just substitute its name in place of edit. For example, suppose Boris' Editor is used. The following entry is placed in the screen menu section:

> [EDITMENU]^C^Cbe;menu1.mnu;menu;menu1;

The **BE** command will not work when entered at the **Command:** prompt unless you have altered the ACAD.PGP file as discussed in Chapter 30 of *AutoCAD and its Applications— Basics, Release 13*. In order for the menu item above to work properly, you must first add a line to the ACAD.PGP file to make **BE** a valid command in AutoCAD. Edit your ACAD.PGP file by adding the following line:

> BE,BE,   0,File to edit; ,4

Be sure the second entry, BE, is the proper name of your text editor's executable file (BE.EXE).

PROFESSIONAL TIP

When creating screen or tablet menus, create small sections at a time and test them. When satisfied with their performance, add the menu items to your main menu file. In this way, you can build a large menu over time.

TABLET MENU TIPS

Tablet menus can be as simple or as complex as you want, and can contain just about any function you need. As you experiment with helpful commands and options, think of the problems you face when drawing. Design AutoCAD macros to solve problems and eliminate tedious tasks. Add them to your menu. Keep in mind the following guidelines:

✓ Use tablet menu picks to call button, screen, and image tile menus.

✓ Use tablet menu picks to call other tablet menus.

✓ Use a tablet menu pick that inserts a group of blocks from a prototype drawing into the current drawing. If the prototype drawing name is ELEC001, the menu items should look like this:

> ^C^Cinsert;elec001;^C

This command inserts only the blocks and not the rest of the drawing information.

✓ Use tablet menu picks to display help screens and frequently used slides.

✓ Plot menu templates on heavy polyester film for durability.

✓ Be sure your template does not extend beyond the active area of your digitizer.

✓ When customizing tablet Menu Area 1 of the AutoCAD template, change the number of boxes to any number you need. Draw a new overlay containing the revised boxes. When configuring the AutoCAD tablet menu, be sure to specify **Config** and not **Re-Cfg**. Enter the revised number of columns and rows.

✓ Any portion of the AutoCAD template can be changed to suit your needs. Just alter the portion of the ACAD.MNU file that you wish to change.

✓ When customizing the ACAD.MNU file, always work with a copy, not the original file.

✓ If you work at a computer that other people use, return the tablet and menu configuration to the way it was before you changed it.

✓ Build your menus in small pieces as you work.

CHAPTER TEST

Write your answers in the spaces provided.

1. How many menu areas are on the AutoCAD template?_____

2. Provide the command and option responses that allow you to initially set up the AutoCAD template.

   Command:_____

   Option (ON/OFF/CAL/CFG): _____

3. Fill in the number of columns and rows found in each of the following tablet menu areas of the AutoCAD template.

Menu Area	Columns	Rows
1	_____	_____
2	_____	_____
3	_____	_____
4	_____	_____

4. Suppose you select the **TABLET** command from the screen menu. Which option allows you to set up the AutoCAD template without entering the number of rows and columns?_____
   _____

5. How many boxes are in the user portion of the AutoCAD template? _____

6. Identify the first step you take to customize the AutoCAD template. _____
   _____

7. Describe how the tablet Menu Area 1 boxes are numbered in the ACAD.MNU file._____
   _____

8. Explain why it is a good idea to leave the box numbers in the menu file. _____
   _____

9. List two advantages of using tablet menus instead of screen menus._____
   _____
   _____

10. Which commands should you automate first when designing a screen or tablet menu?
    _____

11. Define a menu definition file. _____
    _____
    _____
    _____
    _____

12. The extension of the menu file AutoCAD uses for drawing purposes is _____.

13. How would a custom macro that represents **REDRAW** be shown in an .MND file?_____
    _____

14. Suppose boxes 25, 50, 75, and 100 are to be used for the **REDRAW** command. How would they be listed in the .MND file as a multiple line function?_____

15. Give the advantage of creating an .MND file instead of an .MNU file. _____

_____

_____

16. Explain the purpose of the MC.EXE program._____

_____

17. How do you combine different menus to form a larger menu?_____

_____

_____

18. Why is it a good idea to combine screen menus with a tablet menu?_____

_____

_____

DRAWING PROBLEMS

Drawing Problem

1. Add ten new commands or macros to the user area of the AutoCAD template. Follow these guidelines:

   A. Place the commands along the bottom line (I) of the template. They should occupy boxes I-1 through I-10.

   B. Plot a copy of the Menu Area 1 grid and sketch the commands in the boxes.

   C. Sketch graphic symbols to represent the commands.

   D. Draw the command text and graphics in a copy of the Menu Area 1 grid.

   E. Plot a final copy of the overlay on vellum or polyester film.

   F. Make a copy of the ACAD.MNU file and write the code for the new commands in it.

Drawing Problem

2. Create a menu overlay for the user area of the AutoCAD template. It should contain graphic symbols for one of the following drafting disciplines:

   - Architectural
   - Structural
   - HVAC
   - Mechanical
   - Industrial Piping
   - Electrical
   - Electronics

   A. Use existing blocks or symbols that you have on file, or create new ones.

   B. Provide a tablet pick that allows you to insert all symbols into a drawing without inserting the additional prototype drawing data.

   C. Provide a tablet pick that calls the AutoCAD menu.

3. Redesign the user area of the AutoCAD template so that it contains a complete selection of dimensioning commands, options, and variables. Follow these guidelines:

   A. Use the standard 225 boxes or change the numbers of boxes to suit your personal requirements.

   B. Provide access to dimensioning dialog boxes.

   C. Design a special section for dimensioning variables. Draw a small graphic symbol for each variable in the menu box.

   D. Plot a menu overlay on vellum or polyester film that can be slipped under the AutoCAD template.

4. Design a new tablet menu that occupies only the lower half of your digitizer. Follow these guidelines:

   A. The menu should contain a screen pointing area and two menu areas.

   B. Design the menu so it can work with the AutoCAD screen menus.

   C. Provide an area of symbols (blocks) and an area for special commands that you have created.

   D. Make a drawing of the new tablet overlay and plot it on vellum or polyester film. Plot the overlay as a mirror image of the original as discussed earlier in this chapter.

5. Design a new tablet menu that occupies the entire active area of your digitizer. Follow these guidelines:

   A. Provide four menu areas and a screen pointing area.

   B. Provide access to the AutoCAD menu.

   C. Include custom commands you have created, plus an area for symbols. Allow the user to change the symbols section of the menu to a different set of drawing symbols.

   D. Draw an overlay for the new tablet menu. Draw two separate, smaller overlays for the two sets of drawing symbols.

   E. Draw graphic symbols to represent commands and place them in the menu overlay.

   F. Insert scaled-down copies of blocks into the symbol overlays of the menu.

   G. Plot test copies of the template and two symbol overlays and use them for several days.

   H. Plot a final copy of the template on vellum or polyester film using the mirror image technique discussed in this chapter.

6. Design a custom tablet overlay for a specific drafting field, such as electronics, piping, or mapping. Follow these guidelines:

   A. Create as many menu areas as you need, between one and four.

   B. Provide space for a complete selection of symbols. These should reflect the type of drawing for which you will be designing the template.

   C. Place only those commands on the template that you will use often for this type of drawing.

   D. Place commands used less frequently in special screen menus. These should be accessed from the template.

E. Provide the ability to load a variety of prototype drawings from the template.

F. Create menu selections that allow you to do the following:

- Edit a file using the DOS text editor.
- Edit a file using your text editor or word processor.
- Edit the menu template file that you design for this problem.
- Exit to DOS.
- List all drawing files in your active subdirectories.

G. Plot the template overlay on vellum or film using the mirroring technique.

AutoCAD R13

Chapter *21*

Introduction to AutoLISP

Learning objectives

After completing this chapter, you will be able to:
- ○ Locate, load, and run existing AutoLISP programs.
- ○ Use basic AutoLISP commands.
- ○ Write screen and tablet menu macros using AutoLISP.
- ○ Write basic AutoLISP programs.

AutoLISP is a dialect of the LISP programming language. *LISP* (list processing) is a high level language used in artificial intelligence (AI). The AutoLISP dialect, or "interpreter," is specially designed by Autodesk for use with AutoCAD. It has special graphic features designed to work within the AutoCAD drawing editor. Overall, it is a flexible language that allows the programmer to create commands and functions that can greatly increase productivity and drawing efficiency.

AutoLISP can be utilized in several ways. It resides in AutoCAD and is therefore available at the **Command:** prompt. When AutoLISP commands and functions are issued inside parentheses, the AutoLISP program goes to work. AutoLISP functions incorporated into screen and tablet menu items are executed with a single pick. AutoLISP programs can also be saved as .LSP files and then "loaded" into AutoCAD at the **Command:** prompt. Frequently used AutoLISP programs can be included in a file called ACAD.LSP that is automatically loaded with AutoCAD. The programs in the ACAD.LSP file can then be used at any time without going through the "load" procedure.

The benefits of AutoLISP are endless. A wealth of third-party programs (add-on software that enhances AutoCAD) use AutoLISP to create special shapes, symbols, and functions. A person with a good knowledge of AutoLISP can create new commands and programs to satisfy specific needs. In reading this chapter, you will be able to add greater capabilities to your screen, tablet, toolbar, and toolbox macros. Examples of these new functions may include:
- Automatically creating shapes with text placed inside.
- Drawing parallel lines by specifying beginning and end points.
- Creating multiple lines of text in a preset style at a specific height and spacing.
- Deleting specific layers or changing selected entities to a new layer.

Even though you may not need, or want, to learn programming, knowing basic AutoLISP gives you a feel for how AutoCAD works. Read through this chapter slowly while you are at a computer. Type all of the examples and exercises as you read them. This is the best way to get a feel for AutoLISP.

The references such as ACG 13 given in this chapter refer to the *AutoCAD Customization Guide*. For a more detailed coverage of the AutoLISP programming language, refer to *AutoLISP Programming—Principles and Techniques* published by Goodheart-Willcox.

FINDING, STORING, AND USING AUTOLISP PROGRAMS

Most AutoLISP programs are individual files located in separate subdirectories specifically for .LSP files. These programs must first be loaded into AutoCAD before they can be used. Once loaded, entering the command or function name invokes the program.

Locating standard AutoLISP files

A variety of AutoLISP programs are supplied with the AutoCAD for Windows software. If you installed the program according to instructions in the *AutoCAD Installation Guide for Windows*, you should have LISP files located in the following two directories:

    \R13\COM\SAMPLE
    \R13\COM\SUPPORT

The standard support LISP files are located in the \R13\COM\SUPPORT subdirectory. To get a listing of just the .LSP files in this directory, first [Alt]+[Tab] to Program Manager and start File Manager. Then, highlight the \R13\COM\SUPPORT directory folder, select By File Type... from the **V**iew pull-down menu, and enter *.LSP in the **N**ame: text box. Now, only the LISP files are displayed in the directory window.

A brief description of two of the routines found in this directory is given below. Most of the support AutoLISP files work automatically when you make the appropriate AutoCAD menu selection.

- **3D.** This routine is activated when you select the **3D Objects...** option of the **Surfaces** selection in the **Draw** pull-down menu. It allows you to draw polymesh shapes such as a box, wedge, torus, sphere, and pyramid.
- **3DARRAY.** An arrangement of rows, columns, and levels of an object is possible with this routine. See Chapter 2 for a detailed explanation.

Supplied AutoLISP files

Additional AutoLISP programs are supplied with AutoCAD for Windows. These are automatically copied to the \R13\COM\SAMPLE subdirectory when AutoCAD for Windows is installed on your computer. Use File Manager again to get a listing of only the .LSP files in the \R13\WIN\SAMPLE subdirectory.

These program files must be loaded by the operator in order to use them. This can be done by first selecting **Applications...** from the **Tools** pull-down menu. Then, pick the **File...** button in the **Load AutoLISP, ADS, and ARX Files** dialog box. Select the file you want to load in the **Select AutoLISP, ADS, or ARX File** subdialog box. Finally, pick the **Load** button in the **Load AutoLISP, ADS, and ARX Files** dialog box to load the desired program file.

AutoLISP files that are used by AutoCAD should reside in a directory that is specified in the ACAD environment setting. It is good practice to keep the main \R13\WIN directory free of nonessential files, and this is true of .LSP files. However, do not remove files from the directory that they were installed to unless you add the new directory's name to the ACAD environment setting. This is easily accomplished using the **Support:** edit box located in the **Environment** panel of the **Preferences** dialog box. If AutoCAD for Windows is installed on the C: drive of your computer, the installation procedure creates the following default entry in the **Support:** edit box:

C:\R13\COM\SUPPORT;C:\R13\WIN;C:\R13\WIN\TUTORIAL

If you rename any of the directories specified above, or add new directories to store your AutoLISP programs, edit the **Support:** text box accordingly. Instructions for editing the variables specified in this dialog box are given in Chapter 16, *Customizing the AutoCAD for Windows Environment*.

The appearance of an AutoLISP file

AutoLISP programs are best created using a programmer's editor or text editor. AutoLISP files are text files, but different in appearance from any other type of file you have worked with in this text. Use your text editor to open and view one of the sample AutoLISP files found in the \R13\COM\SUPPORT directory. Figure 21-1 shows the file BMAKE.LSP opened using the Notepad text editor that comes with Windows. Use your page-up and page-down buttons or the scroll bar to view additional pages of the file.

Notice that several lines of the program begin with a semicolon (;) and a brief explanation of the line follows. The semicolon indicates everything that follows on the line is a remark and is not evaluated by AutoLISP. This is how explanations, definitions, programmer's name, and copyrights are noted.

Notice that AutoLISP statements (except remarks) are enclosed in parentheses. This is true of the statements in an AutoLISP file, a menu macro, and an AutoLISP command entered at the **Command:** prompt.

Figure 21-1.
Windows Notepad can be used to open the BMAKE.LSP file.

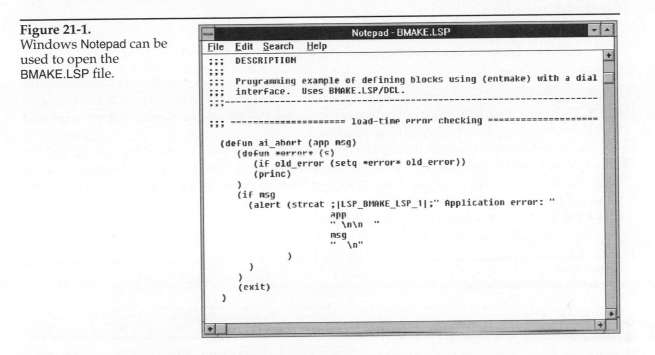

```
;;;  DESCRIPTION
;;;
;;;  Programming example of defining blocks using (entmake) with a dial
;;;  interface.  Uses BMAKE.LSP/DCL.
;;;--------------------------------------------------------------------

;;; --------------------- load-time error checking ====================

(defun ai_abort (app msg)
    (defun *error* (s)
        (if old_error (setq *error* old_error))
        (princ)
    )
    (if msg
        (alert (strcat ;|LSP_BMAKE_LSP_1|;" Application error: "
                       app
                       " \n\n  "
                       msg
                       "   \n"
               )
        )
    )
    (exit)
)
```

EXERCISE 21-1

❏ Use your text editor to open and view the first portion of the 3D.LSP file.
❏ Provide the following information about the file:

  ❏ Copyright holder's name: _____

  ❏ Year of copyright: _____

  ❏ Brief explanation of its function: _____

LOADING AND USING AUTOLISP PROGRAMS

AutoLISP programs must first be loaded into AutoCAD before they can be used. This can be done using the dialog box as explained previously in this chapter, or a program can be loaded at AutoCAD's **Command:** prompt by using the AutoLISP **LOAD** function. Remember to enclose AutoLISP commands and functions in parentheses. When loading an AutoLISP file, it is not necessary to include the .LSP extension. Also, the filename must be enclosed in quotation marks.

Begin a new drawing called LISPTEST. You will use this drawing to experiment with two AutoLISP programs. If you must quit before completing this section, save the drawing.

A program for making blocks

The BMAKE program is a sample routine that displays a dialog box for creating block definitions. To load the BMAKE.LSP file, select **Applications...** from the **Tools** pull-down menu and use the dialog box to select and load the file. You can also enter the following at the **Command:** prompt:

> Command: **(LOAD "C:\\R13\\COM\\SAMPLE\\BMAKE.LSP").**↵
> C:BMAKE loaded. Start command with BMAKE.

The AutoLISP interpreter prints a message specifying that the file was successfully loaded and indicates how to start the program. Draw two or three objects such as lines, arcs or circles before you run this application. Now, enter BMAKE at the **Command:** prompt and the dialog box shown in Figure 21-2 is displayed.

Once the **Block Definition** dialog box is displayed, the fields are fairly self-explanatory. This dialog is more flexible than entering the **BLOCK** command at the **Command:** prompt. With the dialog box, you do not need to assign a name to the block, and the objects can be retained in the drawing after the block is created. This program is provided as a sample AutoLISP routine, and it can be used as desired.

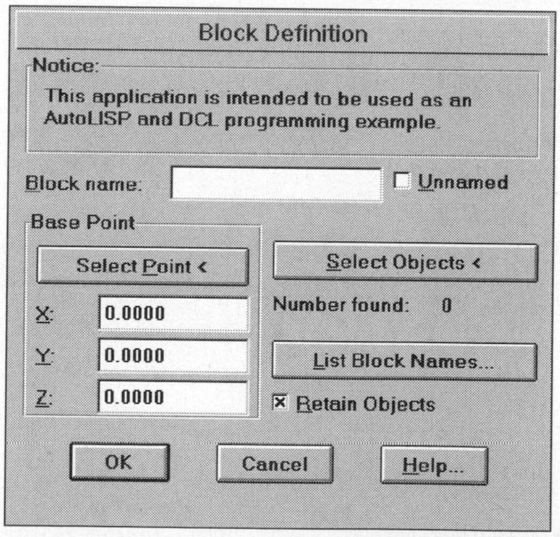

Figure 21-2.
The **Block Definition** dialog box displayed by the BMAKE.LSP program.

Block Definition
Notice: This application is intended to be used as an AutoLISP and DCL programming example.

Block name: [   ] ☐ Unnamed

Base Point

Select Point <		Select Objects <
X: 0.0000		Number found: 0
Y: 0.0000		List Block Names...
Z: 0.0000		☒ Retain Objects

[OK]   [Cancel]   [Help...]

Note

The BMAKE AutoLISP file requires the BMAKE.DCL file to create the dialog box. Therefore, you should add the \R13\COM\SAMPLE directory to the **Support:** path in the **Environment** panel of the **Preferences** dialog box. This is the directory where the BMAKE.DCL file is located.

PROFESSIONAL TIP

Backslash characters (\) are used in AutoLISP to specify special characters within text strings. Therefore, they cannot be used in path names as you would normally. One way to specify a backslash is by using *two* backslashes (\\) as in the previous example given in the text. You can also substitute a *forward* slash in place of a backslash:

Command: **(LOAD "C:/R13/COM/SAMPLE/BMAKE")**↵

Either method is correct and works exactly the same when used at the **Command:** prompt. However, if you are entering an AutoLISP **LOAD** expression into your menu file, be sure to use forward slashes *only*. Backslashes in the menu file are interpreted as a pause for user input and can prevent your file from loading properly.

Dialog test AutoLISP program file

The DLGTEST.LSP file is also found in the \R13\COM\SAMPLE subdirectory. This file is a sample program that shows how to control a dialog session. Loading the file defines two new AutoCAD commands that use dialog boxes. The first command is **DIMEN**. Entering it at the **Command:** prompt displays the AutoCAD **Dimension Controls** dialog box, Figure 21-3A. The second command is **SETCOLOR**, which displays the **Select Color** dialog box, Figure 21-3B. After loading the program file, enter DIMEN or SETCOLOR at the **Command:** prompt to use these routines.

Loading this routine returns the text TILE_RECT, which is the name of an internal function definition within the DLGTEST.LSP file. Internal functions cannot be used in the same manner as AutoLISP defined commands, so if you enter TILE_RECT at the **Command:** prompt, AutoCAD reports it as a unknown command.

Figure 21-3.
A—The AutoCAD **Dimension Controls** dialog box opened by the DLGTEST.LSP program.
B—The **Select Color** dialog box opened by the DLGTEST.LSP program.

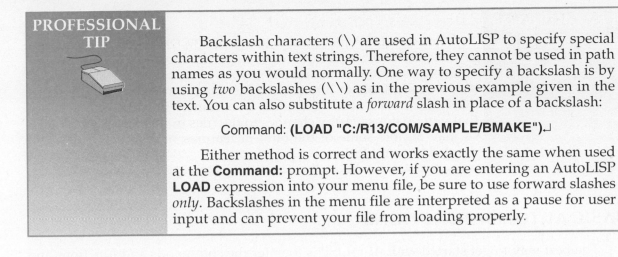

A   B

AutoCAD Custom Guide **13**

BASIC AUTOLISP FUNCTIONS

The best way to get started with AutoLISP is to enter the commands and functions and see what they do. The following discussion includes basic AutoLISP functions that are the foundation for all AutoLISP programs. Practice using the commands as you read. Then, begin using them in menus and macros. Practice using AutoLISP for at least 30 minutes, twice a week.

AutoLISP math functions

You can perform arithmetic calculations using AutoLISP. Calculations are given as either real numbers or integers. AutoLISP defines a real number as any number that contains a decimal. AutoLISP also defines an integer as any number that does not contain a decimal. These definitions may vary slightly from conventional mathematical definitions. AutoLISP keeps 16 decimal place accuracy. Note the following examples:

| 4 | integer | 0.4 | real | 25 | integer | 378 | integer |
| 4.0 | real | 0.25 | real | 25.0 | real | 378.002 | real |

Arithmetic calculations, as well as all AutoLISP commands, are given inside parentheses. The first item inside the left parenthesis is the math function. When data is "returned" by AutoLISP, it is displayed at the command line. The following functions are allowed:

Symbol	Function
+	Returns the sum of all numbers.
−	The second number is subtracted from the first and the difference is returned.
*	Returns the product of all numbers.
/	The first number is divided by the second and the quotient is returned.

The examples below illustrate math functions entered at the **Command:** prompt. Enter data in the following order: beginning parenthesis, math function, space, first number, space, next number, and so on. Close the statement with a parenthesis. If you leave out a parenthesis, AutoLISP reminds you as follows:

    Command: (+ 2 4.⌐
    1⟩

The "1⟩" indicates that you are missing one closing (right-hand) parenthesis. Enter the missing parenthesis and the function is completed.

```
1⟩ )↵
6
Command:
```

Enter the following examples at your keyboard:

```
Command: (+ 6 2)↵
8
Command: (+ 6.0 2)↵
8.0
Command: (– 15 9)↵
6
Command: (*4 6)↵
24
Command: (/ 12 3)↵
4
Command: (/ 12 3.2)↵
3.75
Command: (/ 15 6)↵
2
```

Notice that 2 is returned for the last function. The actual answer is 2.5, however, only integers were used in the calculation. Therefore, an integer is returned as the answer. Also notice that the number is not rounded. Normally, 2.5 is rounded to 3, however, 2 is the value returned. To obtain a real number answer, give at least one real number in the equation.

```
Command: (/ 15.0 6)↵
2.5
```

If using numbers less than zero, give a zero before the decimal or you will receive an error message.

```
Command: (+ .5 6)↵
error: invalid dotted pair
*Cancel*
```

The correct entry is:

```
Command: (+ 0.5 6)↵
6.5
```

EXERCISE 21-2

❑ Solve the following equations by using AutoLISP functions at the **Command:** prompt. Write down the equation you used.

❑ 57 + 12 _____   ❑ 8 × 4 _____

❑ 86.4 + 16 _____   ❑ 16 × 5 × 35 _____

❑ 24 + 12 + 8 + 35 _____   ❑ 7.3 × 22 _____

❑ 8 – 3 _____   ❑ 45 / 9 _____

❑ 29 – 17 _____   ❑ 60 / 2 / 2 _____

❑ 89.16 – 14.6 _____   ❑ 76 / 27.3 _____

Multiple calculations can be done on a single line if the functions and numbers are "nested" properly. All opening (left) parentheses must have closing (right) parentheses. Additional math functions must be enclosed in their own set of parentheses. AutoLISP evaluates the nested function first, then applies the result to the beginning function. This is shown in the following examples:

Command: **(+ 24 (* 5 4))**↵
44
Command: **(* 12 (/ 60 20))**↵
36
Command: **(/ 39 (* 1.6 11))**↵
2.2159
Command: **(– 67. (–14. (+ 3.2 6)))**↵
62.2

EXERCISE 21-3

❑ Use the proper AutoLISP format to solve the following problems. Write the AutoLISP notations and answers in the space provided.

❑ 56.3 + (12 / 3) _____

❑ 23 – (17.65 / 4) _____

❑ 14 ÷ (12 / 3.6) _____

❑ 47 / (31 – 16.4) _____

❑ 257 / (34 – 3.6) _____

❑ 123.65 + 84 – 43.8 _____

❑ 16 ÷ (46 – 23) _____

Storing values using variables

The most frequent AutoLISP function is **SETQ** (set quote). This allows you to create a variable, assign it a value, and store it. Once a variable is set, AutoLISP returns the value. Variables must begin with a letter and can be any combination of letters and numbers. They *cannot* contain the following symbols:

( )	parentheses
.	period
'	apostrophe
"	quotation marks
;	semicolon

The following examples show a legal and an illegal variable name. Notice that the statement must be placed inside parentheses.

Command: **(SETQ A 5)**↵ *(this is a legal entry)*
5
Command: **(SETQ 5 A)**↵ *(this is an illegal entry)*
error: bad argument type
(SETQ 5 A)

AutoLISP lets you know if something does not work. In the previous example, a number was entered as a variable name. This is illegal. AutoLISP displays the point where the error was found. The error message bad argument type refers to the item after the **SETQ** function name. In this example, the 5 is the item referred to. The first item after a function is called an *argument.* An AutoLISP statement that has a function, argument, and options is called an *expression.* Look at another example:

    Command: **(SETQ POINT1 6)**↵
    6

If you do not remember the value of a variable, confirm it by entering an exclamation mark and the variable name:

    Command: **!A**↵
    5
    Command: **!POINT1**↵
    6

Variables can also be assigned as the result of a mathematical calculation. Look at the following examples:

    Command: **(SETQ B (− A 1))**↵
    4
    Command: **(SETQ C (− A B))**↵
    1
    Command: **(SETQ D (* (+ A B) 2))**↵
    18

Look closely at the example illustrated in Figure 21-4. Find the three separate expressions inside parentheses. AutoLISP evaluates expression 3 first. The result is applied to expression 2, which is then evaluated. The result of expression 2 is applied to 1. The final evaluation determines the value of variable D.

Figure 21-4.
Each AutoLISP expression needs to be enclosed with parentheses.

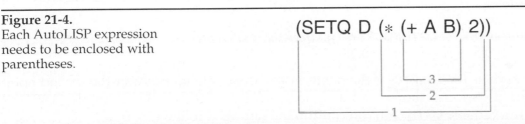

EXERCISE 21-4

❏ In the spaces provided, write the AutoLISP expressions in the proper format. After writing the expression, enter it into the computer to test your solution.

    ❏ Assign the value of 4 to the variable ONE. _____

    ❏ Assign the value of 3 + 2 to the variable TWO._____

    ❏ Assign the value of ONE + TWO to the variable THREE._____

    ❏ Assign the value of THREE + (TWO − ONE) to the variable FOUR. _____

Assigning input to variables

Variables can also be assigned values using point coordinates picked on the screen or entered at the keyboard. To do so, AutoLISP needs to be told to get the coordinate pair (X,Y) value from an input device using the **GETPOINT** function. For example:

Command: **(SETQ PT1 (GETPOINT))**↵

After pressing [Enter], no readout appears on the command line. AutoLISP is waiting for you to enter a value to be assigned to the variable PT1. Pick a point on the screen. The coordinate is then displayed on the command line. If you know the X,Y coordinates, enter them at the keyboard.

Command: **(SETQ PT1 (GETPOINT))**↵
9.5,6.3.↵

An example of how closely AutoCAD and AutoLISP work together follows. First enter the two variables P1 and P2 as shown below. Then, enter LINE and use AutoLISP notation to return the values of P1 and P2 as the From point and To point.

Command: **(SETQ P1 (GETPOINT))**↵ *(select a point on-screen)*
2,2
Command: **(SETQ P2 (GETPOINT))**↵ *(select a point on-screen)*
6.25,2
Command: **LINE.**↵
From point: **!P1.**↵
To point: **!P2.**↵
To point:↵

AutoCAD uses the values you assigned to P1 and P2 for the points. You will later see how to add AutoCAD commands, such as **LINE**, to LISP expressions.

When developing AutoLISP routines, you may need to assign the length of a line or the distance between two points to a variable. The **GETPOINT** function will not work for this because it only retrieves one point. The **GETDIST** function allows you to assign distance to a variable.

Command: **(SETQ LGTH (GETDIST))**↵ *(pick the first point)*
Second point: *(pick the point)* 8.35

Use **OSNAP** options for accuracy if the points are on existing entities. After the second point is picked, the distance is shown and assigned to the variable. In this example, 8.35 was assigned to the variable LGTH. You can confirm the setting as follows:

Command: **!LGTH.**↵
8.35

PROFESSIONAL TIP

Understanding the difference between the **GETPOINT** and **GETDIST** functions will help you determine the best way to assign a value to a variable.

DISTANCE is a function similar to **GETDIST**. However, **DISTANCE** does not require picking two points. Instead, it measures the distance between two existing points. **DISTANCE** can be used to display a distance or assign a distance to a variable.

Command: **(DISTANCE P1 P2)**↵
4.25
Command: **(SETQ D1 (DISTANCE P1 P2))**↵
4.25

The first example returns the distance between the previously defined points P1 and P2. The second example applies that distance to the variable D1. Check the value of D1 as follows:

Command: **!D1**↵
4.25

EXERCISE 21-5

❑ Use the proper AutoLISP format to write the following expressions. Use the spaces provided to write the code. Test all of the exercise examples by entering them in the computer.

❑ Assign a point picked on the screen to the variable PNT1._____

❑ Assign a point picked on the screen to the variable PNT2._____

❑ Create the variable DIS and assign it the distance between PNT1 and PNT2. _____

_____

❑ Draw a line between PNT1 and PNT2.

_____

_____

_____

❑ Use the AutoLISP **DISTANCE** command to return the distance between PNT1 and PNT2. _____

Issuing prompts and getting text

Variables can be given values other than numbers. You may need to assign a word or line of text to a variable. Use the **SETQ** command and enclose the word(s) in quotation marks as follows:

Command: **(SETQ W "What Next?")**↵
"What next?"

You can also assign a word or line of text to a variable with the **GETSTRING** function. This operates similar to the **GETPOINT** function. Look at the following example:

Command: **(SETQ E (GETSTRING))**↵

Nothing is displayed on the command line because AutoLISP is waiting for a "string" of characters. You can enter as many characters (numbers and letters) as needed. Once you press the space bar, the string is entered and displayed. To allow for spaces in the response, enter the letter T or a number after the **GETSTRING** function as follows:

Command: **(SETQ E (GETSTRING 4))**↵
hi there↵
"hi there"
Command:

Confirm the value of the variable as follows:

```
Command: !E↵
"hi there"
```

To this point, you have been told what AutoLISP needs for specific variables. Yet, under normal circumstances, a person using an AutoLISP program needs to be prompted for information. For example, suppose you want a prompt to appear asking the user to pick a point. This is done in conjunction with the **GETPOINT** function. Enter the following:

```
Command: (SETQ P1 (GETPOINT "Pick a point: "))↵
Pick a point:
```

Now the user knows what the computer needs.

The same technique can be used when assigning a distance to a variable. Place the prompt in quotation marks and leave a space before the ending quotes.

```
Command: (SETQ G (GETDIST "What is the distance? "))↵
What is the distance?
```

The **GETSTRING** function may also require a prompt to make it look like an AutoCAD command. Remember to use a number or letter after the function to allow for spaces between words. The letter "T" is used, but the number 6 achieves the same result.

```
Command: (SETQ S (GETSTRING T "Enter text: "))↵
Enter text: Using the "T" allows spaces between words.↵
```

The **PROMPT** function is used to simply display a message. It has no value and is not assigned to a variable. AutoLISP indicates this by printing "nil" after the prompt.

```
Command: (PROMPT "Select an object: ")↵
Select an object: nil
```

You can use prompts in AutoLISP programs to provide information or prompt the user.

EXERCISE 21-6

❑ Use the proper AutoLISP format to write the following expressions. Use the spaces provided to write the code. Test all of the exercise examples by entering them in the computer.

  ❑ Assign the word Void to the variable VO. _____

  ❑ Assign the text Enter text height to the variable TE. _____

  ❑ Create the variable JP as a point that is picked on the screen. Issue the prompt Pick a point:. _____

  ❑ Create the variable KP as a point that is picked on the screen, and issue the prompt Pick a point:. _____

  ❑ Set the distance between points JP and KP to the variable LP. _____

  ❑ Issue a prompt that says This is only an exercise. _____

A quick review

Before applying these newly learned commands to an AutoLISP program, take a few minutes to review the following list. These commands are used in the next section.

- **(+, −, *, /).** Math functions—Must be the first part of an expression. Example: (+ 6 8).
- **(SETQ).** Set quote—The command that allows a value to be assigned to a variable. Example: (SETQ CITY "San Francisco") sets the value of San Francisco to the variable CITY.
- **(!).** Returns the value of a variable. Example: !CITY returns San Francisco.
- **(GETPOINT).** Get point—Gets a point entered at the keyboard or pointing device. Can be applied to a variable. Example: (SETQ A (GETPOINT)) assigns a point to the variable A.
- **(GETDIST).** Get distance—Gets a distance from two points entered at the keyboard or picked with the pointing device. Can be applied to a variable, and a prompt is allowed. Example: (SETQ D2 (GETDIST "Pick two points: ")) gets a distance and assigns it to the variable D2.
- **(DISTANCE).** Distance—Returns a distance between two existing points. Example: (DISTANCE P1 P2) returns the distance between P1 and P2. Can also assign the distance to a variable. Example: (SETQ D (DISTANCE P1 P2)).
- **(GETSTRING).** Get string—Returns a word or group of characters. No spaces are allowed. Example: (GETSTRING) waits for a string of characters and displays the string when [Enter] or the space bar is pressed. Can be assigned to a variable. Spaces are allowed in the string if a letter or number follows the **GETSTRING** function. Example: (SETQ T (GETSTRING T "Enter text: ")) assigns the text entered to the variable T.
- **(PROMPT).** Prompt—Allows a prompt to be issued in a program. Example: (PROMPT "Select an entity: ") prints the Select an entity: prompt.

Using AutoCAD commands in AutoLISP

Earlier you saw how the **LINE** command can be combined with AutoLISP statements to draw a line. This combination is allowed when writing menu macros, but is not possible when developing a LISP program. To incorporate AutoCAD commands into an AutoLISP program, the **COMMAND** function is used. For example, a line is drawn as follows:

```
Command: (COMMAND "LINE").⌐
line From point: nil
From point: (pick the "from" point)
To point: (pick the "to" point)
To point:⌐
```

Notice how this sequence automatically activates the **LINE** command. Also, notice how it is executed in AutoLISP. The **LINE** command, like any AutoCAD command or option in AutoLISP, is enclosed in quotes. Try another one:

```
Command: (COMMAND "CIRCLE").⌐
circle 3P/2P/TTR/⟨Center point⟩: nil
3P/2P/TTR/⟨Center point⟩:
```

The next section shows you how to incorporate all of the previously discussed functions into a program.

CREATING AUTOLISP PROGRAMS

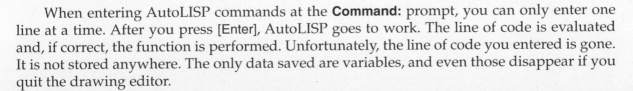

When entering AutoLISP commands at the **Command:** prompt, you can only enter one line at a time. After you press [Enter], AutoLISP goes to work. The line of code is evaluated and, if correct, the function is performed. Unfortunately, the line of code you entered is gone. It is not stored anywhere. The only data saved are variables, and even those disappear if you quit the drawing editor.

To save AutoLISP programs, create them as an ASCII text file using a word processor or text editor. Although Windows Notepad or DOS EDIT can be used, they are not designed for the task of programming. If you plan on developing menus and AutoLISP programs, invest in a good text editor.

Load your text editor and begin a new file named FIRST.LSP. Enter the following lines of AutoLISP code exactly as they appear. Be sure to press [Enter] after each line. Save the file when finished.

```
(DEFUN FIRST ( )
(PROMPT "This is my first AutoLISP program. ")
)
```

Now, examine the lines of the program. The first line uses the **DEFUN** (define function) command. This allows you to define a word that activates the AutoLISP program. Most AutoLISP programs begin with this command. The second word FIRST is the name of the new function. The parentheses ( ) after the word FIRST indicate that there are no defined variables in the program.

The second line begins with the **PROMPT** command and the text string prompt follows. The string is in quotes and a space precedes the closing quote. Parentheses enclose the entire line. The last line of the program is a single closing parenthesis. Can you find the matching left parenthesis? It is the first one in the program.

The correct use of parentheses is critical to the operation of your programs. Therefore, remember to place them in the proper locations. A technique that helps to solve this problem is indenting. Look at the FIRST.LSP program as written in its indented format:

```
(DEFUN FIRST ( )
   (PROMPT "This is my first AutoLISP program. ")
)
```

This allows you to easily see all closing parentheses.

Run the program now to see if it works. Load AutoLISP programs at the **Command:** prompt by entering LOAD and the filename inside parentheses. Also enclose the filename with quotes. You may need to include the entire path with the filename. Load the FIRST.LSP program as follows:

```
Command: (LOAD "FIRST").⏎
first
Command: (FIRST).⏎
This is my first AutoLISP program. nil
Command:
```

The name returned after entering LOAD is the name assigned to the program with **DEFUN**. This name can then be typed inside parentheses to run the program and display your prompt.

The next program combines an AutoCAD command with AutoLISP to draw a line between two points. Start a new file in your text editor named LINE1.LSP. Enter the code exactly as it appears below.

```
(DEFUN LINE1 (/ P1 P2)
   (GRAPHSCR)
   (SETQ P1 (GETPOINT "Enter first point: "))
   (SETQ P2 (GETPOINT "Enter second point: "))
   (COMMAND "LINE" P1 P2)
)
```

Take a close look at each line of the program. The word LINE1 is the defined function of the program. The program has two variables, P1 and P2. The "/" indicates that the variables will only be available for use inside this program. Once the program is completed, the values for these variables are removed. This kind of variable is called *local* because it can only be used by the program that it is defined in.

The **GRAPHSCR** command resets the screen to the graphics window. This is a good function to place at the beginning of your programs to switch the monitor from text to graphics. The two "SETQ" lines allow the user to pick or enter points for variables P1 and P2. The values are supplied by the **GETPOINT** function. A prompt is provided with each.

The "COMMAND" expression executes AutoCAD's **LINE** command. AutoLISP retrieves the value for P1 and uses it for the "From point" of the line. The value of P2 is returned and used for the "To point." The last line of the program is the closing parenthesis for the first function, DEFUN.

When finished, save the file and return to AutoCAD. Load and run the program to see how it works. The following sequence of prompts should appear.

```
Command: (LOAD "LINE1").↵
line1
Command: (LINE1).↵
Enter first point: (pick first point) Enter second point: (pick second point)
line From point:
To point:
To point: nil
To point:↵
```

Notice two things about the program. First, the prompt for the second point is on the same line as the first prompt. It might be better to have this prompt begin on a new line for clarity. Second, the **LINE** command does not end. There is still a rubber band line attached to the cursor. The program should be changed to end the line.

Return to your text editor and load the LINE1.LSP file. Add the items shown below in bold to the file:

```
(DEFUN LINE1 (/ P1 P2)
   (GRAPHSCR)
   (SETQ P1 (GETPOINT "\nEnter first point: "))
   (SETQ P2 (GETPOINT "\nEnter second point: "))
   (COMMAND "LINE" P1 P2 "")
)
```

Two prompts that follow each other in a program are displayed on the same line unless you instruct AutoLISP to terminate the line. This is done using the "\n" statement. Notice that this "n" must be lowercase. Also, the double quote added after P2 in the last line of the program indicates a return. The semicolon (;) cannot be used for a return because it represents a remark in AutoLISP. Anything after a semicolon is ignored. The return ("") ends the **LINE** command.

Save the file and return to AutoCAD. Load and run the program again. The sequence of prompts now looks like the following:

```
Command: (LOAD "LINE1").↵
line
Command: (LINE1).↵
Enter first point: (pick the first point)
Enter second point: (pick the second point)
LINE From point:
To point:
To point:
Command: nil
Command:
```

PROFESSIONAL TIP

Design your AutoLISP programs to closely resemble the way AutoCAD for Windows works. For example, it is easier for the user to read "back-to-back" prompts when the prompts appear on separate lines. Use "\n" for this.

EXERCISE 21-7

❑ Write an AutoLISP program that places NOTES: at a location that you pick on the screen. Name the file EX21-7.LSP.

❑ In the space below, write a description of the program in longhand. Then, write each line of code.

❑ Enter the program using your text editor and then test it in AutoCAD.

❑ The lines of your program should include the following:
   ❑ A remark line containing the author, date, and name of the file.
   ❑ The function defined is NOTES and has two local variables, P1 and T.
   ❑ The graphics window should be activated.
   ❑ Set the P1 variable. Provide a prompt for entering the text location at P1.
   ❑ Give the variable T the value NOTES:.
   ❑ Execute the **TEXT** command to do the following: Use P1 as the text location; enter text height of 0.25"; rotation angle of 0; and use the variable T as the text.

_____

_____

_____

_____

_____

_____

_____

_____

_____

_____

GETTING DEEPER INTO AUTOLISP

As you practice with AutoLISP, you will develop ideas for programs that require additional commands and functions. Some of these programs may require that the user pick two corners of a windowed selection set. Another program may use existing points to draw a shape. You may also need to locate a point using polar coordinate notation, or determine the angle of a line. All of these can be done with AutoLISP programs.

Getting additional input

The **GETREAL** command allows the user to enter a real number at the keyboard. Remember, as defined by AutoLISP, a real number is more accurate than an integer because it has a decimal value. The **GETREAL** command works with numbers as units. You cannot respond with a value of feet and inches. Once issued, the command waits for user input. If input is provided, a prompt is given and the real number is returned. **GETREAL** can be used to set the value of a variable as follows:

Command: **(SETQ X (GETREAL "Enter number: "))**↵
Enter number: **34.**↵
34.0

The **GETCORNER** command allows the user to pick the opposite corner of a rectangle. This is like placing a window around entities in a drawing. An existing point serves as the first corner. When positioning the opposite corner, a rubber band box appears on the crosshairs, similar to the window box. The command can also be used to set the value of a variable. The second corner can be picked with the pointing device or entered at the keyboard. To find the second corner, the first point must have been chosen. An example use of **GETCORNER** follows:

Command: **(SETQ PT1 (GETPOINT "\nPick a point: "))**↵
  Pick a point: *(pick the point)*
Command: **(SETQ PT2 (GETCORNER PT1 "\nPick the second corner: "))**↵
  Pick the second corner: *(pick the corner)*

Notice that the value of PT1 is set first. Point PT1 becomes the base point for locating PT2. The two points (corners) located in this example can be used to construct an angled line, rectangle, or other shape. It can also be applied to other functions.

Using the values of system variables

AutoCAD's system variables can be accessed with the AutoLISP **GETVAR** and **SETVAR** commands. This can be useful if an application requires you to store the value of a system variable, change the variable for your program, then reset it to its original value.

GETVAR command is commonly used to see the value of a variable. Refer to the following example:

Command: **(SETQ V1 (GETVAR "TEXTSIZE"))**↵
0.125
Command: **(SETQ V2 (GETVAR "FILLETRAD"))**↵
0. 0

The **SETVAR** command is used to change a system variable. Assign the value to a variable as follows:

Command: **(SETQ V3 (SETVAR "TEXTSIZE" 0.25))**↵
0.25
Command: **(SETQ V4 (SETVAR "FILLETRAD" 0.25))**↵
0.25

Suppose you need to save a current system variable, reset the variable, and then reset the variable to its original value after the command is executed. The **GETVAR** command can be used to supply a value to a new variable, as shown in the previous "TEXTSIZE" example. When the program is complete, the **SETVAR** command is used to reset the text size to its original value as follows:

Command: **(SETVAR "TEXTSIZE" V1)**↵
0.125

This returns the value of TEXTSIZE to the variable V1 which is the default 0.125.

EXERCISE 21-8

❑ In the spaces provided, write the following expressions in longhand using proper AutoLISP format. Enter the expressions into your computer to see if they work.

    ❑ Get the current aperture size and set it to the variable APER. _____

    ❑ Set the variable APER4 to the aperture size of four pixels. _____

    ❑ Use the **LINE** command and an **OSNAP** setting to connect the line with other entities on the screen. _____

    ❑ Reset the aperture to the original setting using AutoLISP commands and the variables previously set. _____

❑ Add the following capabilities to the EX21-7.LSP file that you created in the previous exercise:

    ❑ Create a variable V1 to hold the current text size. Insert this line after the "DEFUN" line.

    _____

    ❑ At the end of the program, reset the text size to its original size. _____

Working with lists

A list is created when you pick a point on the screen in response to the **GETPOINT** command. The list is composed of three numbers—the X, Y, and Z coordinate values. You can tell it is a list because AutoLISP returns the numbers enclosed in parentheses. A number entered in response to the **GETREAL** command returns as just a real number not enclosed in parentheses. This is because a single number is not a list. The following expression returns a list:

> Command: **(SETQ P1 (GETPOINT "Enter point: "))**↵
> Enter point: *(pick a point)*
> (5.5 2.75 0.0)

The individual values in a list are called *elements,* and can be used in an AutoLISP program to create new points to draw shapes. The **CAR** function retrieves the first element of a list (the X coordinate in the above example). The second element of a list (the Y coordinate) is retrieved with the **CADR** function. The variable P1 in the example above is composed of the list (5.5 2.75 0.0). Thus, **CAR** returns a value of 5.5. Enter the following:

> Command: **(CAR P1)**↵
> 5.5

Find the **CADR** of P1 by entering:

> Command: **(CADR P1)**↵
> 2.75

You can create a new list of two coordinates by selecting values from existing points using the **CAR** and **CADR** functions. This is done with the **LIST** function. Values returned by the list function are placed inside parentheses. The coordinates of P1 can be combined with the coordinates of a second point P2 to form a third point P3. Study the following example, and the illustration in Figure 21-5.

> Command: **(SETQ P2 (GETCORNER "Enter second point: " P1))**↵
> (6.0 4.5)
> Command: **(SETQ P3 (LIST (CAR P2)(CADR P1)))**↵
> (6.0 2.75)

In AutoLISP, a function is followed by an argument. An *argument* is the value that a function uses. An expression must be composed of only one function and at least one argument. Therefore, the functions **CAR** and **CADR** must be separated because they are two different expressions combined to make a list. Examine Figure 21-6. The **CAR** value of P2 is to be the X value of P3, so it is given first. The **CADR** of P1 is placed second because it is to be the Y value of P3. Notice the number of closing parentheses at the end of the expression.

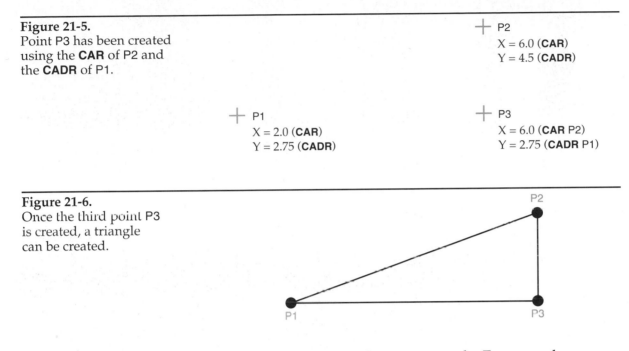

Figure 21-5.
Point P3 has been created using the **CAR** of P2 and the **CADR** of P1.

P2
X = 6.0 (**CAR**)
Y = 4.5 (**CADR**)

P1
X = 2.0 (**CAR**)
Y = 2.75 (**CADR**)

P3
X = 6.0 (**CAR** P2)
Y = 2.75 (**CADR** P1)

Figure 21-6.
Once the third point P3 is created, a triangle can be created.

Now, with three points defined, there are many things you can do. For example, you can draw lines through the points to form a triangle. To do so, use the **COMMAND** function as follows:

Command: **(COMMAND "LINE" P1 P2 P3 "C")**.⏎

The **CAR** and **CADR** functions allow you to work with 2D coordinates. The **CADDR** function allows you to get the Z value of a 3D coordinate (the third element of a list). Enter the following at your keyboard:

Command: **(SETQ B (LIST 3 4 6))**⏎
(3 4 6)

You have created a list of three elements, or coordinate values. The third element is the Z coordinate. Retrieve that value with the **CADDR** function as follows:

Command: **(CADDR B)**⏎
6

Since 6 is a single value as opposed to a list, it is not enclosed in parentheses. Now use **CAR** and **CADR** to find the other two elements of the list:

Command: **(CAR B)**⏎
3
Command: **(CADR B)**⏎
4

Try the following examples. Enter them at the **Command:** prompt exactly as shown. Press [Enter] at the end of each line.

```
(SETQ A1 (GETPOINT "Enter point: "))
(SETQ B1 (GETPOINT "Enter point: "))
(SETQ C1 (LIST (CAR A1)(CADR B1)))
(CAR A1)
(CADR A1)
(CAR B1)
(CADR B1)
(SETQ C1 (LIST (CAR A1)(CADR B1)(CAR B1)))
!C1
(CAR C1)
(CADR C1)
(CADDR C1)
```

The last function to discuss in basic list manipulations is the **CDR** function. This allows you to retrieve the second and remaining elements of a list. Therefore, suppose the list (3 4 6) is assigned to variable B, as done earlier in this section. The **CDR** function returns the list (4 6). Try it:

```
Command: (CDR B).↲
(4 6)
```

This is now a separate list that can be manipulated with **CAR** and **CADR**, just like a 2D coordinate list. Study Figure 21-7 and the following examples:

```
Command: (CAR (CDR B)).↲
4
Command: (CADR (CDR B)).↲
6
```

The first example is asking for the first element (**CAR**) of the list (4 6). It originally was the last two elements (**CDR**) of the list for variable B. In the second example, the second element (**CADR**) of the list (4 6) is returned.

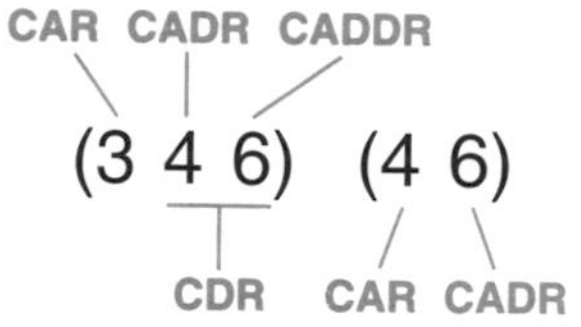

Figure 21-7.
The **CDR** consists of the second and remaining elements of a list.

```
CAR CADR CADDR
  \   |   /
(3 4 6)  (4 6)
   |      / \
  CDR  CAR CADR
```

The four functions used to manipulate lists—**CAR**, **CADR**, **CADDR**, and **CDR**—may seem confusing at first. Practice using them and discover how they work. Practice with a list of numbers, coordinate values, or text strings. Remember, text strings must be enclosed in quotes. Try the following examples to see what happens. Enter the expressions at the **Command:** prompt exactly as shown and press [Enter] at the end of each line.

```
(SETQ NOTES (LIST "DO" "RE" "MI"))
(CAR NOTES)
(CADR NOTES)
(CADDR NOTES)
(CDR NOTES)
(SETQ LAST (CDR NOTES))
(CAR (CDR NOTES))
(CADR (CDR NOTES))
(CAR LAST)
(CADR LAST)
```

Review of list-making functions

- **(CAR).** Returns the first element of a list.
- **(CADR).** Returns the second element of a list.
- **(CADDR).** Returns the third element of a list.
- **(CDR).** Returns the second and remaining elements of a list. Since the **CDR** function returns more than one element, the values it returns are always placed in a list.
- **(LIST).** Creates a list of all values entered after the function **LIST**.

EXERCISE 21-9

❑ Write an AutoLISP program that draws a right triangle. The 90° angle can be on either the left or right side.
❑ Write the program in proper AutoLISP format. Use your text editor and save it as EX21-9.LSP.
❑ Use the following items in writing the program:
  ❑ Define the function as "triangle."
  ❑ Turn the graphics window mode on.
  ❑ Set the variable P1 as the first point of the triangle. Use a prompt.
  ❑ Set the variable P2 as the endpoint of the hypotenuse (**GETCORNER**). Place the prompt on the next line.
  ❑ Set the variable P3 to the X coordinate of P2 and the Y coordinate of P1.
  ❑ Draw a line through all three points and close the triangle.
❑ Before saving the program, check for matching parentheses and quotes. Save the program and test it.

POLAR COORDINATES AND ANGLES

The ability to work with angles is vital if you plan to do much AutoLISP programming. Four functions **ANGLE**, **POLAR**, **GETANGLE**, and **GETORIENT** allow you to use angles. AutoLISP works with these commands using the radian system of angle measurement. This system of measurement is explained in the next section.

Measuring an angle

The **ANGLE** function is used to calculate the angle between two given points. The value of the angle is given in radians. *Radian angle measurement* is a system where 180° equals "pi" (π). Pi is equal to 3.14159. AutoLISP functions use radians for angular measurement, but AutoCAD commands use degrees. Therefore, to use a radian angle in an AutoCAD command, it must first be converted to degrees. Conversely, a degree angle to be used by AutoLISP must be converted to radians. The following formulas are used for those conversions.

- To convert degrees to radians:
  (* PI (/ AD 180.0)) (AD = angle in degrees)
- To convert radians to degrees:
  (/ (* AR 180.0) PI) (AR = angle in radians)

The following example illustrates how the angle between two points can be set to a variable, then converted to degrees.

```
Command: (SETQ P1 (GETPOINT "Enter first point: "))↵
Enter first point: (1.75 5.25)↵
Command: (SETQ P2 (GETPOINT "Enter second point: "))↵
Enter second point: (6.75 7.25)↵
Command: (SETQ A1 (ANGLE P1 P2))↵
0.380506
```

The angle A1 is measured in radians (0.380506). To convert this to degrees, use the following entry:

Command: **(/ (* A1 180.0) PI)**↵
21.80141

The value 21.80141 is the angle in degrees between P1 and P2. The following list gives common angles measured in degrees, the AutoLISP expressions used to convert to radian values, and the values in radians.

Angle in Degrees	AutoLISP Expression	Angle in Radians
0.0		0.0
30.0	(/ PI 6)	0.5236
45.0	(/ PI 4)	0.7854
60.0	(/ PI 3)	1.0472
90.0	(/ PI 2)	1.5708
135.0	(+ PI 4)(/ PI 2))	2.3562
180.0	PI	3.1416
270.0	(+ PI (/ PI 2))	4.7124
360.0	(* PI 2)	6.2832

EXERCISE 21-10

❑ Using AutoLISP expressions, locate the endpoints of a line and store each endpoint as a variable.
❑ Use **GETANGLE** to find the angle of the line.
❑ Use the proper formula to convert the radian value to degrees.
❑ Use the proper formula to convert the degree value back to radians.

Getting angular input

The **GETANGLE** function is for a user-input angle value. This function is often used to set a variable that can be used by another function. The **GETANGLE** function automatically issues the prompt Second point:. The following example illustrates how you can set a variable to an angle input by the user:

Command: **(SETQ A (GETANGLE "Pick first point: "))**↵
Pick first point: *(pick first point)* Second point: *(pick point)*
2.35619

The angle value is given in radians (2.35219). To convert this to degrees, use the following procedure:

Command: **(/ (* A 180.0) PI)**↵
135.0
Command: **!A**↵
2.35619

Notice that the radian value is returned, even after the conversion to degrees. The conversion did not set the angle value to a variable. Make the value permanent by assigning it to a variable using the following expression:

Command: **(SETQ A (/ (* A 180.0) PI))**↵
135.0
Command: **!A**↵
135.0

The variable A now has a value of 135°.

An important point to remember is that **GETANGLE** uses the current **ANGBASE** (angle 0 direction) and **ANGDIR** (clockwise or counterclockwise) system variables. Therefore, if you have angles set to be measured from north (**ANGBASE** = 90°), angles picked with **GETANGLE** will be measured from north. If the **ANGDIR** variable is set to measure angles clockwise, **GETANGLE** will accept input of clockwise values, but returns counterclockwise values. A companion function to **GETANGLE** is **GETORIENT**. It is used in exactly the same manner as **GETANGLE**, but always measures angles counterclockwise from east (0°).

EXERCISE 21-11

❑ Use **GETANGLE** to assign an angle to the variable ANG1.
   ❑ Convert the radian value to degrees using AutoLISP expressions.
   ❑ Convert the degree value back to radians using AutoLISP expressions.
❑ Use **GETORIENT** to find the angle in radians of any two points.
   ❑ Reset **ANGBASE** to 90.
   ❑ Use **GETORIENT** to find the angle of the two points.
   ❑ Use **GETANGLE** to find the angle of the two points.
❑ Compare the values. Explain the results.

Saving often-used functions in **ACAD.LSP**

Certain AutoLISP programs are used quite frequently. It can be time-consuming to load these programs individually when needed. Instead, you can place often-used AutoLISP functions in a common file that is loaded each time you run AutoCAD for Windows. The file is named ACAD.LSP. Two programs that should be entered into ACAD.LSP are the angle/radian conversion formulas.

Before you create the ACAD.LSP file, check to see if it already exists in the \R13\WIN subdirectory. Then, either load the existing file into your text editor or begin a new text file called ACAD.LSP. Enter the following programs exactly as they appear here:

```
; CONVERTS DEGREES TO RADIANS
(VMON)
(DEFUN DTR (A)
   (* Pi (/ A 180.0))
)
; CONVERTS RADIANS TO DEGREES
(DEFUN RTD (A)
   (/ (* 180.0) PI)
)
```

The line that reads (VMON) at the beginning of the file is not needed with the AutoCAD Release 13 for Windows or DOS versions, but is still supported for compatibility with some earlier versions. It helps to eliminate errors that occur from a lack of memory.

Any program added to the ACAD.LSP file must be loaded into AutoCAD using parentheses during the current drawing session. This is because AutoCAD is working with the old version of the file. To use the updated version of ACAD.LSP, save the drawing you are working on and simply re-open it or start a new one.

Using polar coordinates

The **POLAR** command allows you to specify the angle and distance of a point relative to another point. Two variables must first be set for **POLAR** to work properly—the point that you are locating a new point from and the distance between the two points. For example, suppose you want to specify a point P1, then locate another point P2 at a specific distance and angle from P1. Enter the following expressions:

```
Command: (SETQ P1 (GETPOINT "Enter point: ")).⌋
Enter point: (pick point or enter the coordinates at the keyboard) (4.0 4.5).⌋
Command: (SETQ D (GETDIST P1 "Enter distance: "))
Enter distance: (pick distance or enter at keyboard) 3.0.⌋
Command: (SETQ A (DTR 60)).⌋
1.0472
```

In this expression, the angle 60° is used. However, AutoLISP uses radians. Therefore, the **DTR** (degrees to radians) function is used to evaluate 60°. The resulting angle of 1.047198 is saved as variable A. A line can now be drawn from P1 at 60° using the **POLAR** command as follows:

```
Command: (SETQ P2 (POLAR P1 A D)).⌋
(5.5 7.09807)
Command: (COMMAND "line" P1 P2 " ").⌋
```

EXERCISE 21-12

❑ Write a program to draw a right triangle. If you need to, refer to EX21-9. However, use **POLAR** instead of **LIST** functions.
❑ Write the AutoLISP expressions for the program in the proper format. Save the file as EX21-12.LSP.
❑ Enter the program in your computer when you have finished writing it.
❑ Use the following items in the program:
  ❑ Define a function called POLARTRI.
  ❑ Set a variable P1 as the first corner of the triangle.
  ❑ Set a variable D as the length of one side.
  ❑ Set a variable P2 0° from P1 at a distance of D.
  ❑ Set a variable P3 90° from P2 at a distance of D.
  ❑ Use the **LINE** command to draw the triangle.

SAMPLE AUTOLISP PROGRAMS

One of the best ways to become familiar with AutoLISP is to enter expressions and programs on your computer. Look for programs in books or magazines that you read. Get a feel for how the functions and arguments go together and how they work in AutoCAD. Make a habit of reading through one of the AutoCAD journals. Experiment with AutoLISP routines printed in them. Also, refer to the *AutoCAD Customization Guide* for other samples.

The following programs are provided for you to copy and add to your ACAD.LSP file or to your menus. Practice for a few minutes a couple of times a week. This will help you begin to better understand and utilize AutoLISP. Train yourself to learn a new function every week. Before long, you will be writing your own useful programs.

Erase the entire screen

This program sets two variables to the minimum and maximum screen limits. It then erases everything within those limits and redraws the screen. Name this program ZAP.LSP.

```
; ERASES ENTIRE LIMITS
(DEFUN C:ZAP ( )
  (SETQ MIN (GETVAR "LIMMIN"))
  (SETQ MAX (GETVAR "LIMMAX"))
  (COMMAND "ERASE" "C" MIN MAX "")
  (COMMAND "REDRAW")
)
```

Set the current layer

This program asks for the user to point to a linetype or color of the layer to be set current. The program finds the layer of the entity picked and sets the layer as current.

```
; AUTHOR        : MARGO K. BILSON
; COMPANY       : WILLAMETTE INDUSTRIES, INC., PORTLAND, OR
(DEFUN C:SETLAYER (/ E)
   (SETQ E (ENTSEL "\nPoint to linetype and\or color..."))
   (SETQ E (ENTGET (CAR E)))
   (SETQ L (CDR (ASSOC '8 E)))
   (COMMAND "LAYER" "S" L "")
)
```

Inserting centerlines on circles

This program works with a block composed of equal length, vertical and horizontal centerlines that intersect at the midpoint. This type of centerline mark is used on circles (holes) and circular features. Draw the lines each 1" long. Then, when the block is inserted, it can be scaled easily. For example, suppose you need to put centerlines in a 3" circle, with .25" extensions beyond the circle. The X and Y scale factors will be 3.5. This allows for .25" on each side. Name the program CENL1.LSP.

```
; AUTHOR        : MATT SLAY
; ADDRESS       : 2475 PINSON HIGHWAY, TARRANT, ALABAMA nnnnn
; PHONE         : (nnn) nnn-nnnn
(DEFUN C:CENL1 ( )
   (COMMAND "INSERT" "CENL1" (GETPOINT)
        (GETPOINT) "" "")
)
```

Clean overlapping corners

This program allows you to trim the overlapping ends of intersecting lines. You are requested to pick the two lines that intersect and overlap. The program does the rest. Name the program TRIMENDS.LSP.

```
; AUTHOR        : GEORGE HEAD
; PRINTED IN THE JANUARY, 1988 ISSUE OF "CADENCE" MAGAZINE
(DEFUN C:CLEANC (/ O1 P1 P2)
   (SETQ O1 (GETVAR "OSMODE"))
   (SETVAR "OSMODE" 512)
   (COMMAND "FILLET" "R" 0)
   (SETQ P1 (GETPOINT "\nPick a line "))
   (SETQ P2 (GETPOINT "\nPick other line "))
   (COMMAND "FILLET" P1 P2)
   (SETVAR "OSMODE" O1)
)
```

Calculate the length of lines

This program calculates the length of all lines on a specified layer. It can be used for estimating and material takeoffs. This program works only with lines, not with polylines. Name the program LINEAR.LSP. After loading it into the AutoCAD drawing editor, respond to the first prompt by entering the name of the layer that contains the lines you wish to total. The answer is given in current drawing units.

```
; AUTHOR        : JOE PUCILOWSKI
; COMPANY       : JOSEPH & ASSOCIATES
; ADDRESS       : 7809A RIVER RESORT LANE, TAMPA, FL nnnnn
; PHONE         : (nnn) nnn-nnnn
; DATE          : 9/19/xx
; NOTE          : THIS PROGRAM FIGURES THE TOTAL NUMBER OF LINEAR
;                     UNITS (FEET, INCHES, ETC.) OF LINES ON A SPECIFIC LAYER.
; REVISED       : 10/8/xx BY ROD RAWLS
;
(DEFUN C:LINEAR ( )
  (SETQ  TOTAL     0
         E              (ENTNEXT)
         NUMLIN     0
         LAYPIK      (STRCASE
                        (GETSTRING "\nAdd up lines on layer: ")
                      )
  )
  (IF (TBLSEARCH "LAYER" LAYPIK)
    (PROGN
      (WHILE E
        (SET  ENTTYP (CDR (ASSOC 0 (SETQ EG (ENTGET E))))
              LAYNAM (CDR (ASSOC 8 EG))
        )
        (IF
          (AND
            (EQUAL ENTTYP "LINE")
            (EQUAL LAYNAM LAYPIK)
          )
          (PROGN
            (SETQ  LINLEN (DISTANCE (CDR (ASSOC 10 EG)) (CDR (ASSOC 11 EG)))
                   TOTAL (+ TOTAL LINLEN)
                   NUMLIN (1 + NUMLIN)
            )
          )
        )
        (SETQ E (ENTNEXT E))
      )
      (PRINC
        (STRCAT  "\nFound "
                 (ITOA NUMLIN)
                 " lines on layer 〈 "
                 LAYPIK
                 "〉 with a total of "
                 (RTOS TOTAL)
                 " linear units."
        )
      )
    )
    (PRINC "\nLayer does not exist.")
  )
  (PRINC)
)
```

Easy grid rotation

This program, titled S.LSP, rotates the grid to the angle of any picked line. The second routine, SS.LSP, returns the grid to zero rotation.

```
; AUTHOR      : EBEN KUNZ
; COMPANY     : KUNZ ASSOCIATES ARCHITECTS
; ADDRESS     : 38 GREENWICH PARK, BOSTON, MA nnnnn
; PHONE       : (nnn) nnn-nnnn
;
(DEFUN C:S (/ PT1 PT2)
   (SETVAR "ORTHOMODE" 0)
   (SETQ PT1 (OSNAP (GETPOINT "\nPick line to match new Grid angle: \n") "NEA"))
   (SETQ PT2 (OSNAP PT1 "END"))
   (COMMAND "SNAP" "R" PT1 PT2)
   (SETVAR "SNAPMODE" 0)
)
(DEFUN C:SS ( )
   (PROMPT "\nReturn Grid to zero.")
   (COMMAND "SNAP" "R" "" 0.0)
   (SETVAR "SNAPMODE" 0)
)
```

Move to current layer

This simple program quickly changes selected entities to the current layer.

```
; AUTHOR      : BILL FANE
; COMPANY     : WEISER, INC.
; ADDRESS     : 6700 BERESFORD ST., BURNABY, B.C.
;
(DEFUN C:CL (/ THINGS)
   (SETQ THINGS (SSGET))
   (COMMAND "CHANGE" THINGS "" "P" "1A"
       (GETVAR "CLAYER") "" )
)
```

Change to selected layer

This routine allows you to move entities to a layer by picking an entity on the destination layer.

```
; AUTHOR      : SHELDON MCCARTHY
; COMPANY     : EPCM SERVICES LTD.
; ADDRESS     : 2404 HAINES ROAD, MISSISSAUGA, ONTARIO
; PHONE       : (nnn) nnn-nnnn
;
(DEFUN C:LA ( )
   (SETQ 1A (CDR (ASSOC 8 (ENTGET (CAR (ENTSEL "Entity on destination layer: "))))))
   (PROMPT "Select objects to change:")
   (SSGET)
   (COMMAND "CHANGE" "P" "" "1" 1A)
)
```

SOLUTIONS TO CHAPTER EXERCISES

Compare these solutions to the versions you created for the exercises in this chapter. If your program works, but looks different from those given here, you do not necessarily need to change it. There are several ways to program the same function.

Exercise 21-7

```
; AUTHOR, DATE, FILENAME EX35-7.LSP
(DEFUN NOTES (/ T P1)
  (GRAPHSCR)
  (SETQ P1 (GETPOINT "\nEnter text location: "))
  (SETQ T "NOTES:")
  (COMMAND "TEXT" P1 0.25 0 T)
)
```

Exercise 21-9

```
; DRAWS A RIGHT TRIANGLE GIVEN THE LENGTH OF A SIDE
(DEFUN TRIANGLE (/ P1 P2 P3)
  (GRAPHSCR)
  (SETQ P1 (GETPOINT "\nEnter point: "))
  (SETQ P2 (GETCORNER P1 "\nPick endpoint of hypotenuse: "))
  (SETQ P3 (LIST (CAR P2)(CADR P1)))
  (COMMAND "LINE" P1 P2 P3 "C")
)
```

Exercise 21-12

```
; DRAWS A TRIANGLE USING POLAR
(DEFUN TRIANGLE2 (/ P1 P2 P3 D)
  (GRAPHSCR)
  (SETQ P1 (GETPOINT "\nPick a point: "))
  (SETQ D (GETDIST P1 "\nEnter length of a side: "))
  (SETQ P2 (POLAR P1 0.0 D))
  (SETQ P3 (POLAR P2 (DTR 90) D))
  (COMMAND "LINE" P1 P2 P3 "C")
)
```

CHAPTER TEST

Write your answers in the spaces provided.

1. The extension used for AutoLISP files is _____.
2. Why is it a good idea to make a separate subdirectory for LISP files? _____
3. A remark is indicated in an AutoLISP file with _____.
4. When in the drawing editor, how do you load an AutoLISP file named CHGTEXT.LSP?

5. Define an integer as related to AutoLISP. _____

6. Define a real number as related to AutoLISP. _____

7. Write the following arithmetic expressions in the proper AutoLISP format.

    A. 23 + 54 _____

    B. 12.45 + 6.28 _____

    C. 56 – 34 _____

    D. 23.004 – 7.008 _____

    E. 16 × 4.6 _____

    F. 7.25 × 10.30 _____

    G. 45 / 23 _____

    H. 147 / 29.6 _____

    I. 53 + (12 × 3.8) _____

    J. 567 / (34 – 14) _____

8. Explain the purpose of the **SETQ** function. _____

    _____

    _____

9. Write the proper AutoLISP notation to assign the value of (67 – 34.5) to the variable NUM1. _____.

10. What does the **GETPOINT** function allow you to do? _____

    _____

11. Write the proper AutoLISP notation to assign the values of X = 3.5 and Y = 5.25 to the variable PI1. _____

12. The AutoLISP function that allows you to get the measurement between two points is _____.

13. The AutoLISP function that allows you to find the length of a line is _____.

14. Explain the purpose of the **GETSTRING** function. _____

    _____

15. Write the proper AutoLISP notation for assigning the string This is a test: to the variable TXT. _____.

16. How do you allow spaces in a string of text when using the **GETSTRING** function?

    _____

17. Write the proper AutoLISP notation for using the **PLINE** command. _____

18. How must an AutoCAD command be handled in an AutoLISP expression? _____

    _____

19. Define a function. _____

20. Define an argument. _____

    _____

21. The AutoLISP function that describes the name of a function in a program is _____.

22. Describe why lines are indented in an AutoLISP program. _____

    _____

23. Explain the purpose of the **\n** function. _____

_____

24. The command that allows you to retrieve a decimal number is _____.

25. Which two commands allow you to work with system variables? _____

26. Define the following AutoLISP functions:

   A. **CAR** _____

   B. **CADR** _____

   C. **CDR** _____

   D. **CADDR** _____

   E. **LIST** _____

27. Write the proper AutoLISP notation to return the last two numbers of the list (4 7 3).

_____

28. Write an expression to set a variable **a** to the result of question 27. _____

29. Write an expression to select the second element of the list returned in question 28.

_____

30. Compare and contrast the **GETANGLE** and **GETORIENT** functions._____

_____

_____

31. Write an expression to set the angle between points P3 and P4 to the variable A. _____

_____

32. What system of angle measurement does AutoLISP use? _____

33. The name of the function that converts degrees to the system mentioned in question 32
   is _____.

34. What is the value of 270° in the angular system AutoLISP uses? _____

35. Explain the purpose of the **POLAR** function. _____

_____

DRAWING PROBLEMS

General

1. Add the following capabilities to the right triangle function developed in Exercise 21-9.

   A. Use **GETDIST** instead of **GETCORNER**.

   B. Allow the angle of the hypotenuse to be picked.

   C. Allow the length of a side to be picked.

General

2. Create an AutoLISP program similar to that in Problem 1, but it should draw an equilateral triangle (equal angles and equal sides). Use the **POLAR** function.

3. Write a program to draw a rectangle. Use only the **GETPOINT** function to set opposite corners of the rectangle. Follow these guidelines:

   A. Set P1 as the first corner.

   B. Set P3 as the opposite corner.

   C. Set points P2 and P4 using the list functions of AutoLISP.

   D. Use the **LINE** command to draw the rectangle.

   General

4. Revise the program in Problem 3 to draw a rectangle using the **GETCORNER** function to find the second corner.

   General

5. Create an AutoLISP command to draw a square. Follow these guidelines:

   A. Set a variable for the length of one side.

   B. Set the variable p1 as the lower-left corner of the square.

   C. Use the **LINE** command to draw the square.

   General

6. Revise the program in Problem 5 to draw a square using the **PLINE** command.

   General

7. Use the program in Problem 6 to create a new command that draws a square and allows you to change the line thickness.

   A. Use either **PLINE** or **POLYGON** commands to draw the square.

   B. Set a variable to get the line thickness input by the user.

   General

8. Add a **Fillet 0** command to your **Construct** pull-down screen menu. Use menu code and AutoLISP expressions to create the command. Follow these guidelines:

   A. Get the current fillet radius and assign it to an AutoLISP variable.

   B. Set the fillet radius to 0.

   C. Select two lines and enter a 0 fillet.

   D. Reset the fillet radius to the original value.

   E. Assign an appropriate mnemonic shortcut key to the new command.

   General

9. Add a **DISTANCE** command to any pull-down menu area. Use menu code and AutoLISP expressions to do the following:

   A. Get desired unit precision from user and store it as a variable.

   B. Store current unit precision as an AutoLISP variable.

   C. Set unit precision with a user variable.

   D. Reset unit precision to the original value.

   E. Assign an appropriate mnemonic shortcut key to the new command.

   General

10. Write an AutoLISP program to draw parallel rectangles.

    A. Use the rectangle program in Problem 3, but replace **LINE** with the **PLINE** command.

    B. Get user offset distance for the inside rectangle.

    C. Use the **OFFSET** command to draw the parallel rectangle inside the original.

    General

General

11. Write a program to draw a rectangle and place a circle having a user-specified diameter in the center of the rectangle.
    A. Incorporate the rectangle program in Problem 3.
    B. Use the **ANGLE**, **POLAR**, and **DISTANCE** functions to find the center point of the rectangle.
    C. Request the user to enter the diameter.
    D. Draw a circle at the center point of the rectangle.

General

12. Write a program to draw a leader with a diameter dimension having plus and minus tolerances.
    A. Prompt for and allow user to set **DIMTP** and **DIMTM** system variables.
    B. Activate the **DIM** command and turn **DIMTOL** on.
    C. Activate the **DIAMETER** command, select the circle, and cancel.
    D. Start the leader from the "last point" and allow two leader picks.
    E. End the leader and accept default dimension text.
    F. Turn tolerancing off and exit the **DIM** command.

General

13. Write a program to draw a leader with a bubble attached to the end.
    A. Get the start point of the leader and set it to P1.
    B. Get the endpoint of the leader and set it to P2.
    C. Ask the user for text height and set it to a variable.
    D. Ask for the text string (maximum of two characters) and set it to a variable.
    E. Calculate the circle diameter 2.5 or 3 times the text height and set it to a variable.
    F. Set the circle center point P3 to a value relative to P2 using **POLAR**.
    G. Activate the **DIMI** command and draw a leader from P1 to P2.
    H. Erase the "last" portion of the leader.
    I. Draw a circle at P3.
    J. Draw text in the center of the circle using the appropriate option in the **TEXT** command.

General

14. Develop a program that writes a line of text and places a box around it.
    A. Ask the user for the text height and set it to variable TXHT.
    B. Ask for the lower-left corner to start box.
    C. Ask for the text string from the user.
    D. Set string length to variable LG1. Use the **STRLEN** function.
    E. Set the X length of the box to: (LG1 * TXHT).
    F. Set the Y length to: (3 * TXHT).
    G. Draw box to X and Y lengths.
    H. Calculate center of the box, and set it to variable CENL1.
    I. Draw the text string inside the box. Use the **M** justification option from point CEN1.

```
(STRLEN) example:
    (setq text (getstring T "Enter Text: "))
    (setq lg1 (strlen text))
```

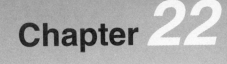
Learning objectives

After completing this chapter you will be able to:

- ○ Describe the types of files that control dialog boxes.
- ○ Define the components of a dialog box.
- ○ Write a DCL file for a basic dialog box.
- ○ Write an AutoLISP file to control a dialog box.
- ○ Associate an action with a dialog box tile.

Programmable dialog boxes can be used to completely customize the interface of your AutoLISP programs. This will allow your programs to work like many of AutoCAD's own built-in functions. Using dialog boxes improves efficiency and reduces data entry errors.

Dialog boxes minimize the amount of typing required by the user. Rather than answering a series of text prompts at the command line, the user selects options from the dialog box. Dialog box fields can be filled in by the user in any order. While the dialog is still active, the user can revise values as necessary.

AutoLISP provides basic tools for controlling dialog boxes, but the dialog box itself must be defined using *Dialog Control Language*, or *DCL*. A dialog box is defined using this language. Then, the definition is written to an ASCII file with a .DCL file extension.

DCL FILE FORMATS

A DCL file is formatted as an ASCII text file. Dialog Control Language files can have a 1 to 8 character filename. Writing with DCL is easy—many of the components of a DCL file are normal English words.

The components of a dialog box, such as edit boxes, images, and pop-up lists are referred to as *tiles*. Tiles are defined by specifying various *attribute* values. Each attribute controls a specific property of the tile being defined, such as size, location, and default values.

When writing a DCL file, you do not use parentheses (as with AutoLISP). When defining a dialog box or tile, all of the required attributes are placed within {braces}. Indentation helps to separate individual elements, making the file more readable. Comments are preceded by two forward slashes (//). Semicolons are used at the end of an attribute definition line.

To view an example of DCL code, open the ACAD.DCL and BASE.DCL files with your text editor. These two files are found in the \R13\COM\SUPPORT directory. A portion of the ACAD.DCL file is shown in Figure 22-1.

AutoCAD Custom Guide **19**

CAUTION

The BASE.DCL file contains standard prototype definitions. The ACAD.DCL file contains definitions for all of the dialog boxes used by AutoCAD. *Do not edit either one of these files!* Altering them can cause AutoCAD's built-in dialog boxes to crash.

Figure 22-1.
A portion of the
ACAD.DCL file.

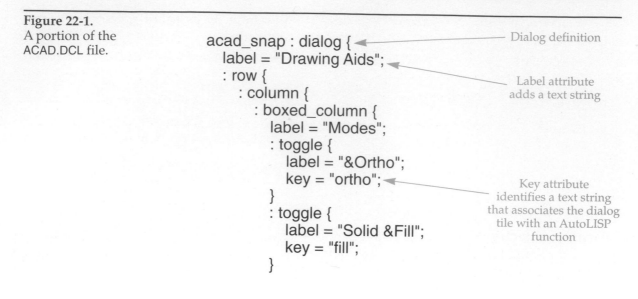

```
acad_snap : dialog {                          Dialog definition
    label = "Drawing Aids";
    : row {                                   Label attribute
        : column {                            adds a text string
            : boxed_column {
                label = "Modes";
                : toggle {
                    label = "&Ortho";
                    key = "ortho";            Key attribute
                }                             identifies a text string
                : toggle {                    that associates the dialog
                    label = "Solid &Fill";    tile with an AutoLISP
                    key = "fill";             function
                }
```

DCL tiles

Your work in AutoCAD has provided you with a good background in how dialog boxes work. By now, you should be familiar with the use of buttons, edit boxes, radio buttons, and list boxes. This will be helpful as you design dialog interfaces for your AutoLISP programs.

DCL tiles can be used individually or combined into structures known as *clusters*. For example, a series of button tiles can be placed in a column tile to control the arrangement of the buttons in the dialog box. The primary tile is the dialog box itself.

This chapter is only an introduction to DCL, and will cover basic DCL file construction and a few common tile types. For a full discussion of DCL and dialog creation and management techniques, refer to *AutoLISP Programming: Principles and Techniques*, published by The Goodheart-Willcox Co., Inc.

The best way to begin understanding the format of a DCL file is to study a simple dialog box definition. The following DCL code defines the dialog box shown in Figure 22-2.

```
main : dialog {
    label           = "Dialog Box Example 1";
    : text_part {
        value       = "This is an example.";
    }
    ok_only;
}
```

Now, let's take a closer look at the definition of this dialog box:

```
main : dialog {
    label           = "Dialog Box Example 1";
    : text_part {
        value       = "This is an example.";
    }
    ok_only;
}
```

Figure 22-2.
A sample custom
dialog box.

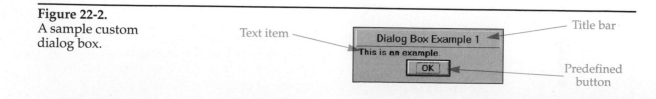

The *dialog definition* is always the first tile definition. Everything within the braces defines the features of the dialog box. The word "main" indicates the name of the dialog box. This name is referenced by the controlling AutoLISP application. A colon (:) precedes all tile callouts. In the case of a dialog tile, the colon separates the name from the tile callout.

> **label   = "Dialog Box Example 1";**

The *label* attribute of the dialog tile controls the text that appears in the title bar of the dialog box. The line is terminated with a semicolon. All attribute lines must be terminated with a semicolon.

> **: text_part {**
> **   value   = "This is an example.";**
> **}**

The *text_part* tile allows placement of text items in a dialog box. The *value* attribute is used to specify the text that will be displayed. Just as with the dialog tile, all of the attributes are defined between the braces.

> **ok_only;**

This is a call to a *predefined tile* found in the BASE.DCL file. It is not preceded with a colon because it is not a specific definition. This line is terminated with a semicolon just like an attribute. No braces are required because this is not a tile definition, but a reference to a predefined tile.

There are many predefined tiles and subassemblies. A *subassembly* is a predefined tile cluster, such as OK_CANCEL and OK_CANCEL_HELP. The OK_ONLY shown here places an **OK** button at the bottom of the dialog box.

Once you have defined a dialog box, the definition must then be saved in a DCL file. For this example, the dialog definition above is saved in the file EXAMPLE1.DCL. This is treated as any other support file, and should be found in the AutoCAD support path.

For reference, look at the **Insert** dialog box shown in Figure 22-3. Various tiles of this dialog box are identified with the corresponding portion of the ACAD.DCL file.

Figure 22-3.
Some of the tile definitions and attributes associated with the **Insert** dialog box.

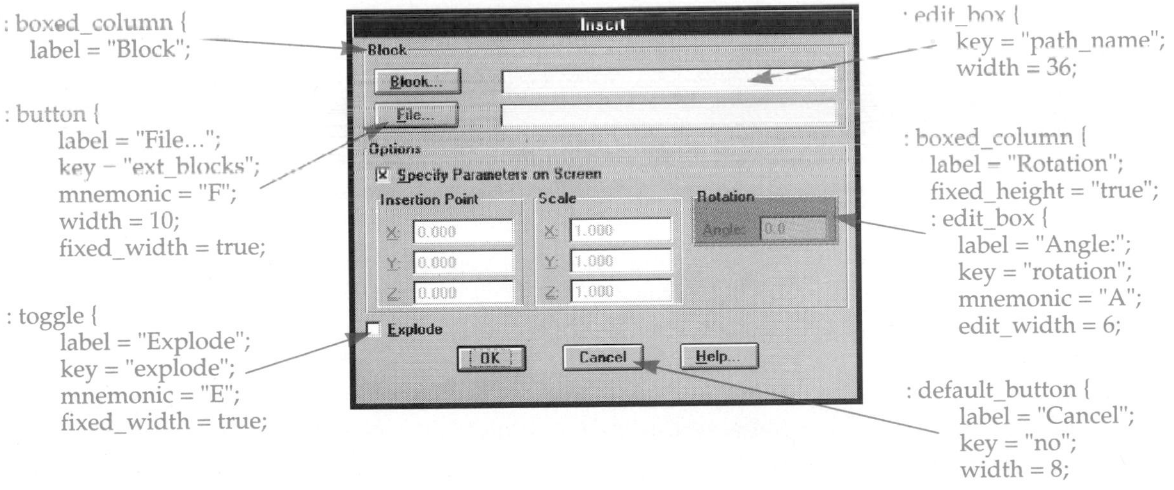

AutoLISP AND DCL

A DCL file by itself is merely a definition of a dialog box, and cannot actually do anything without a controlling application. Both ADS and AutoLISP are frequently used to control dialog sessions. While the functions provided for handling dialog boxes differ in name and usage between ADS and AutoLISP, both applications have the same basic tool set. This section shows examples using the AutoLISP dialog handling functions.

NOTE

An ADS application is written in the AutoCAD Development System (ADS) programming language. This is a C-language programming environment that requires a solid understanding of AutoCAD and AutoLISP, in addition to the standard C programming language. The AutoLISP interpreter must call an ADS application, hence it is not a stand-alone program.

ADS applications can access facilities unavailable to AutoLISP. Conversely, they are more platform-dependent and require more effort to develop and maintain. ADS is useful in applications that have intense computation requirements and those that must interact with the operating system.

In order to display a dialog box, the controlling application must first load the dialog definition. The LOAD_DIALOG function loads the specified dialog definition file:

(load_dialog *"filename*.dcl")

The filename is enclosed in quotation marks. The LOAD_DIALOG expression returns a positive integer that identifies the loaded DCL file. If the attempted load was unsuccessful, a negative integer is returned.

Once the descriptions within a specific DCL file are no longer needed, they can be removed from memory by using the UNLOAD_DIALOG function:

(unload_dialog *filename*.dcl)

CAUTION

Do not unload a dialog definition until your application is finished using the DCL file, otherwise your application may fail to function properly.

The next step is to activate a specific dialog box definition contained within the DCL file. The NEW_DIALOG function activates the dialog box specified, where *dlgname* is the name of the dialog box:

(new_dialog *dlgname* dcl_id)

This function is case-sensitive. The dialog definition used in the previous example was named main. Specifying Main or MAIN would not activate this dialog box, since the text string does not match exactly.

The dcl_id argument represents the integer value returned by LOAD_DIALOG. NEW_DIALOG also supports additional, optional arguments, which are not discussed here.

To actually begin accepting input from the user, the START_DIALOG function must be used:

(start_dialog)

This function has no arguments. It allows for input to be received from the dialog box initialized by the previous NEW_DIALOG expression.

With these basic AutoLISP functions, it is possible to display the dialog box shown in Figure 22-2. The controlling AutoLISP application named EXAMPLE1.LSP appears as follows:

```
(setq DCL_ID (load_dialog "EXAMPLE1.DCL"))
(if (not (new_dialog "main" DCL_ID))
   (exit)
)
(start_dialog)
```

Now, let's take a closer look at the controlling code for this dialog box:

(setq DCL_ID (load_dialog "EXAMPLE1.DCL"))

This expression loads the dialog definition found in EXAMPLE1.DCL and assigns the variable DCL_ID to the integer returned by LOAD_DIALOG.

(if (not (new_dialog "main" DCL_ID))
   (exit)
)

If NEW_DIALOG is unable to activate the specified dialog box for any reason, this function will exit the application. This is an important safety feature. In many cases, loading an incorrect or incomplete definition can cause your system to lock up, often requiring that the system be rebooted.

(start_dialog)

This expression starts the dialog session using the dialog box indicated by the previous NEW_DIALOG expression.

Exercise 22-1

❏ Use the examples in the text to create EXAMPLE1.DCL and EXAMPLE1.LSP. Create each file in your text editor. You may wish to position a Notepad window alongside your AutoCAD window. In this manner, you can quickly jump from one application to another while writing and testing your dialog box. Load the AutoLISP program file in AutoCAD and run the dialog session.

Associating functions with tiles

Most tiles can be associated with actions. These actions vary from run-time error checking to performing tasks outside of the dialog session. The ACTION_TILE function provides the basic means of associating tiles with actions:

(action_tile *"key"* *"action-expression"*)

The key references the attribute assigned in the DCL file. The action-expression is the AutoLISP expression performed when the action is called. Both the key and action-expression arguments are supplied as text strings.

In order to access a specific tile from AutoLISP, the key of the tile must be referenced. The key is specified as an attribute in the DCL file. Tiles that are static (unchanging) do not require keys. Any tile that must be referenced in any way—such as setting or retrieving a value, associating an action, or enabling/disabling the tile—requires a key.

This next example provides a button on the dialog box that updates the text_part value.

```
main : dialog {
  label            = "Dialog Box Example 2";
  : text_part {
    value          = "";
    key            = "time";
  }
  : button {
    key            = "update";
    label          = "Display Current Time";
    mnemonic = "C";
  }
  ok_only;
}
```

This DCL file is the same as EXAMPLE1.DCL, with the exception of the bold text. Note the addition of a key attribute to the text_part tile. This allows access by the AutoLISP application while the dialog session is running.

Another addition is the button tile. A key is provided in the button tile so that an association can be created with an action-expression. The label attribute provides the text displayed on the button. The mnemonic attribute underlines the specified letter within the label to allow keyboard access.

The AutoLISP application used to manage this dialog session is shown below.

```
(setq DCL_ID (load_dialog "EXAMPLE2.DCL"))
(if  (not (new_dialog "main" DCL_ID))
    (exit)
)
(defun UPDTILE ()
  (setq  CDVAR (rtos (getvar "CDATE") 2 16)
         CDTXT (strcat "Current Time: "
                       (substr CDVAR 10 2)
                       "."
                       (substr CDVAR 12 2)
                       "."
                       (substr CDVAR 14 2)
               )
  )
  (set_tile "time" CDTXT)
)
(UPDTILE)

(action_tile "update" "(UPDTILE)")
(start_dialog)
```

Some AutoLISP functions that are not covered in this text are used in the above programming to retrieve and display the current date. The "update" button will display the current time when the button is picked. The dialog box displayed by this code is shown in Figure 22-4.

Figure 22-4.
The dialog box defined by
EXAMPLE2.DCL and
controlled by
EXAMPLE2.LSP.

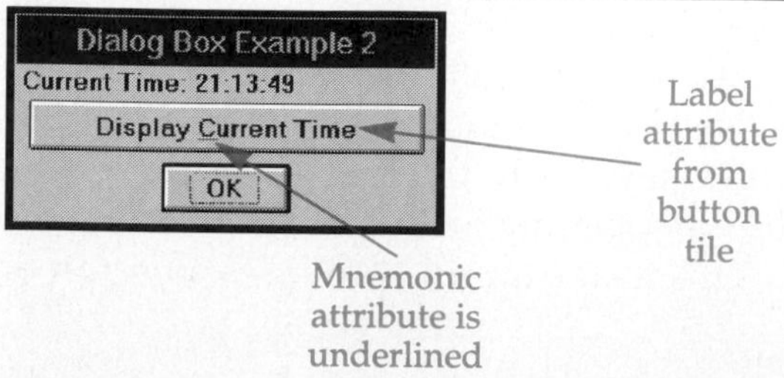

Label attribute from button tile

Mnemonic attribute is underlined

Commands that change the display or require user input (outside of the dialog interface) cannot be used while a dialog box is active. These AutoLISP functions are unavailable:

command	getangle	getpoint	grread	prompt
entdel	getcorner	getreal	grtext	redraw
entmake	getdist	getstring	grvecs	ssget (interactive)
entmod	getint	graphscr	menucmd	textpage
entsel	getkword	grclear	nentsel	textscr
entupd	getorient	grdraw	osnap	

When the desired action requires a large amount of AutoLISP code, it is best to define a function to perform the required tasks. This function is then called within the action-expression.

Exercise 22-2

❑ Use the examples in the text to create EXAMPLE2.DCL and EXAMPLE2.LSP. Load the AutoLISP program file and run the dialog session. Note the action performed when the button is picked.

WORKING WITH DCL

There are many types of DCL tiles available. You can provide edit boxes for users to enter information into directly, such as numeric or text information. You can create lists and pop-up lists to allow users to choose from preset selections. Buttons provide a simple means of initiating an action.

Images can be used to enhance dialog boxes. You can place company or personal logos on your dialog boxes. An interactive image, as shown in the **Viewpoint Presets** dialog box in Figure 22-5, can also be used. Tools such as text tiles, sliders, and clusters are used to control the layout of your tiles in a dialog box.

A wide variety of attributes are available for controlling the appearance and function of a dialog session. Additionally, several AutoLISP functions are provided to control your dialog session. You can disable or enable tiles, and change the active tile. It is even possible to change the value or state of a tile based on an entry in another tile.

The following section provides some applications that use various dialog boxes. Study these examples for additional insight into the creation of dialog sessions. Be sure to have an appropriate reference handy, such as the *AutoCAD Customization Guide*, to look up DCL and AutoLISP terms. You can adapt or modify these files to produce dialog sessions of your own.

Figure 22-5.
The **Viewpoint Presets** dialog box contains an interactive image.

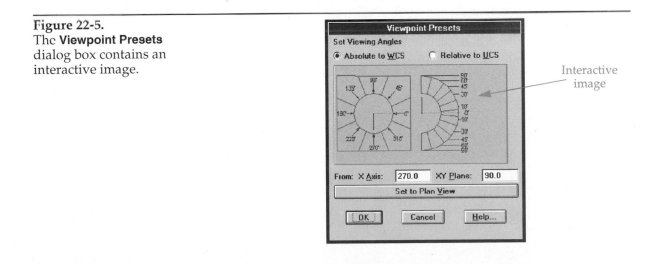

Interactive image

Dialog Example 3:

Create the following two files as shown, then load the AutoLISP file. To initiate, type DRAW at the **Command:** prompt.

```
//EXAMPLE3.DCL
//Defines a dialog box that presents three drawing options to the user.
//
draw : dialog {
  label            = "Select Drawing Option";
  :  text_part
    label          = "Select object type to draw: ";
  }
  : row {
   : button {
     key           = "line";
     label         = "Line";
     mnemonic  = "L";
     fixed_width = true;
  }
  : button {
     key           = "circle";
     label         = "Circle";
     mnemonic  = "C";
     fixed_width  = true;
  }
  : button {
     key           = "arc";
     label         = "Arc";
     mnemonic  = "A";
     fixed_width = true;
  }
  : button {
     key           = "cancel";
     label         = "Cancel";
     is_cancel    = true;
     fixed_width  = true;
  }
  }
}
;EXAMPLE3.LSP
;This file displays the dialog box defined in EXAMPLE3.DCL and begins the
; selected drawing command as specified by the user.
;
(defun C:DRAW (/ DCL_ID)
  (setq DCL_ID (load_dialog "EXAMPLE3.DCL"))
  (if (not (new_dialog "draw" DCL_ID))
    (exit)
  )
  (action_tile "line" "setq CMD $key")
  (action_tile "circle" "setq CMD $key")
  (action_tile "arc" "setq CMD $key")
  (start_dialog)
  (unload_dialog DCL_ID)
  (command CMD)
)
```

Dialog Example 4

```
//EXAMPLE4.DCL
// Presents a list of layers to the user.
fourth : dialog {
        label            = "Select Layer";
        : popup_list {
          label          = "New Current Layer:";
          mnemonic       = "N";
          key            = "lyr_pop";
          allow_accept   = true;
          width          = 32;
        }
        ok_cancel;
}
;;EXAMPLE4.LSP
;;
(defun CHECKOUT ()
  (setq LD (tblsearch "LAYER" (nth (atoi (get_tile "lyr_pop")) LL))
        LN (cdr (assoc 2 LD))
        LS (cdr (assoc 70 LD))
  )
  (if (and
        (/= 1 LS)
        (/= 65 LS)
      )
      (progn
        (setvar "CLAYER" (nth (atoi (get_tile "lyr_pop")) LL))
        (done_dialog)
      )
      (alert "Selected layer is frozen!")
) )
(defun C:GOFOR ()
  (setq DCL_ID (load_dialog "DDFOURTH.DCL"))
  (if (not (new_dialog "fourth" DCL_ID)) (exit))
  (start_list "lyr_pop")
  (setq LL '()
        NL (tblnext "LAYER" T)
        IDX 0
  )
  (while NL
        (if (= (getvar "CLAYER") (cdr (assoc 2 NL)))
          (setq CL IDX)
          (setq IDX (1+ IDX))
        )
        (setq LL (append LL (list (cdr (assoc 2 NL))))
              NL (tblnext "LAYER")
  )    )
  (mapcar 'add_list LL)
  (end_list)
  (set_tile "lyr_pop" (itoa CL))
  (action_tile "lyr_pop" "(if (= $reason 4) (mode_tile \"accept\" 2))")
  (action_tile "accept" "(CHECKOUT)")
  (start_dialog)
  (unload_dialog DCL_ID)
  (princ)
)
```

CHAPTER TEST

Write your answers in the spaces provided.

1. What are the three-letter extensions of the two types of files that must be created to construct a functioning dialog box? _____

2. When referring to a dialog box, what is a tile? _____

    _____

    _____

    _____

3. When defining a dialog or tile, inside of what are all of the required attributes for a tile definition placed? _____

4. What symbol indicates a comment inside a DCL file? _____

5. Write the appropriate notation for the first line of a DCL file that defines a dialog box named **TEST**. _____

6. Write the appropriate notation in a DCL file that defines the text in the title bar of a dialog box named **Select Application**. _____

    _____

7. Write the notation for defining a cluster of four buttons labeled **OK**, **NEXT**, **CANCEL**, and **HELP**. _____

    _____

8. What type of file controls a DCL file? _____

9. Write the notation that would appear in the file in Question 8 that loads a dialog file named PICKFILE. _____

    _____

10. What is a *key* in a DCL file? _____

    _____

    _____

11. What is the function of a *mnemonic* attribute? _____

    _____

    _____

12. Write the proper DCL file notation for the first line that identifies a button. _____

    _____

PROBLEMS

1. Create a dialog box that contains the following items. Write the required DCL and AutoLISP files.

    A. Title bar—**Dialog Box Test**

    B. Label—**This is a test.**

    C. **OK** button

2. Create a dialog box that contains the following items. Write the required DCL and AutoLISP files.

    A. Title bar—**Date**

    B. Label—**Current date.**

    C. Action button—**Display Current Date**

    D. **OK** button

3. Create a dialog box that performs the following tasks. Then, write the required DCL and AutoLISP files.

    A. Displays the current date.

    B. Displays the current time.

    C. Displays the current drawing name.

    D. Contains buttons to update current date and time.

    E. Contains an **OK** button.

General

General

General

AutoCAD drawings can be linked to or embedded in text files. This can be useful when creating presentations or proposals.

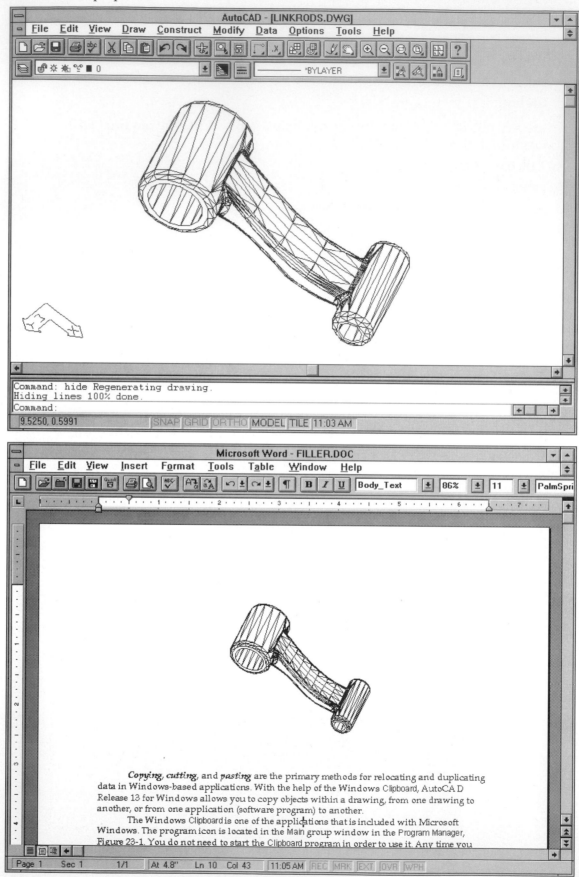

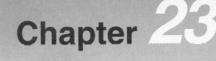

AutoCAD R13

Advanced AutoCAD for Windows Features, OLE, and DDE

Learning objectives

- ◯ Identify and use advanced clipboard text and graphics options.
- ◯ Copy and reference AutoCAD drawing data to other Windows applications using Object Linking and Embedding (OLE).
- ◯ Describe the differences between linking and embedding.
- ◯ Create a drawing file manager using the Windows Cardfile.
- ◯ Exchange drawing data with a spreadsheet using Dynamic Data Exchange (DDE).

ADVANCED CLIPBOARD SUPPORT

Copying, *cutting*, and *pasting* are the primary methods for relocating and duplicating data in Windows-based applications. With the help of the Windows Clipboard, AutoCAD Release 13 for Windows allows you to copy objects within a drawing, from one drawing to another, or from one application (software program) to another.

The Windows Clipboard is one of the applications that is included with Microsoft Windows. The program icon is located in the Main group window in the Program Manager, Figure 23-1. You do not need to start the Clipboard program in order to use it. Anytime you cut or copy data in a Windows application, it is automatically stored in the Clipboard.

Think of the Clipboard as a temporary storage area, or buffer, for text and graphic information. Once an image or some text is copied to the Clipboard, it can then be pasted as desired into any Windows program file, such as a word processor document, a spreadsheet, or even an AutoCAD drawing. Information copied to the Clipboard remains there until it is replaced by copying new information. The Windows Clipboard provides a simple means of taking information from one application into another application, or from one drawing into another.

Figure 23-1.
The Windows Clipboard program icon is located in the Main group window.

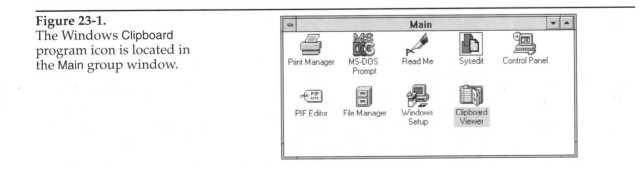

507

Copying, cutting, and pasting

Copying, cutting, and pasting represent the simplest means for transferring information from one application to another. The copy, cut, and paste features are typically found under the **Edit** pull-down menu of the Windows application you are using. Like most other Windows applications, AutoCAD has an **Edit** menu with these Clipboard based options available. See Figure 23-2.

The primary function of each option is listed here. Detailed information on the use of these features is provided using several examples throughout this chapter.

- **Cut**—Removes the selected text or graphic objects and places them on the Clipboard. In AutoCAD, this starts the **CUTCLIP** command.
- **Copy**—Copies the selected text or graphic objects and places them on the Clipboard. In AutoCAD, this starts the **COPYCLIP** command.
- **Copy View**—Copies all objects visible on the screen and places them on the Clipboard. In AutoCAD, this starts the **COPYLINK** command.
- **Paste**—Pastes the contents of the Clipboard into the current drawing. In AutoCAD, this starts the **PASTECLIP** command. Note that pasted objects are not removed from the Clipboard. They can be pasted into multiple locations in your drawing.
- **Paste Special...**—Opens the **Paste Special** dialog box where additional parameters can be set for the incoming data. In AutoCAD, this starts the **PASTESPEC** command.

These Clipboard-based options can be used in many ways in AutoCAD. They can be used to copy information within a drawing session. Both drawing data and text data can be manipulated this way to help save time and maintain accuracy.

Figure 23-2.
The **Edit** pull-down
menu in AutoCAD.

Edit	
Undo	Ctrl+Z
Redo	
Cut	Ctrl+X
Copy	Ctrl+C
Copy View	
Paste	Ctrl+V
Paste Special...	
Properties...	
Object Snap	▶
Point Filters	▶
Snap	Ctrl+B
Grid	Ctrl+G
Ortho	Ctrl+L
Select Objects	▶
Group Objects...	
Inquiry	▶
Links...	
Insert Object...	

Copying, cutting, and pasting in an AutoCAD drawing session

Typically, when you need to copy or move drawing objects in AutoCAD, you use the **COPY** and **MOVE** commands. For most drawing requirements, these commands will serve you better than **COPYCLIP**, **CUTCLIP**, and **PASTECLIP**. When using these features, it is important to understand how each of the available commands works.

Both the **Cut** and the **Copy** options place drawing information on the Clipboard in the same manner. The difference is similar to the relationship between the **MOVE** and the **COPY** commands in AutoCAD. **Cut** works like **MOVE**, it removes the drawing information from its original location and places it on the Clipboard. **Copy**, however, places the same information on the Clipboard but leaves the original objects in place. Deciding which one to use depends on whether or not you require the original objects to remain in place.

The **Paste** option takes the information from the Clipboard and inserts it into the current drawing session. Note that the pasted objects come in as an ***unnamed block***, a block that AutoCAD has named through an automated process. Unnamed blocks typically have names similar to A$C57. Because the pasted objects are assembled into a block, you will need to explode it if you wish to edit the objects you have pasted.

The primary advantages of using the Clipboard for copying and moving objects in a drawing session are speed and convenience. By pressing the [Ctrl]+[C] keystroke or a menu pick, you enter the **COPYCLIP** command and can select objects to be copied. When using this command, there is no need to indicate a base point for the copy operation. To place the objects or copies in the desired location, press [Ctrl]+[V] or pick **Paste**. From this point, the **PASTECLIP** command works just like the **INSERT** command, asking for an insertion point, scale factors, and rotation angles.

The following sequence shows an example of the steps followed to copy and paste objects in a drawing:

```
Command: (press [Ctrl]+[C])
Command: '_copyclip
Select objects: (select the desired objects)
# found
Select objects: (continue selecting as desired)
Select objects: ↵
Command: (press [Ctrl]+[V])
Command: '_pasteclip
Insertion point: (select the insertion point)
X scale factor ⟨1⟩ / Corner / XYZ: ↵
Y scale factor (default=X): ↵
Rotation angle ⟨0⟩: ↵
Command:
```

It is important to remember that the new copy is actually a block and must be exploded to be directly edited. Also, this pasting example uses the default scale factors and rotation angles, but these values can be adjusted as required for any given situation.

The clipboard-based features can be very useful when editing dialog box text in AutoCAD. Text objects in your drawing are treated like any other drawing object and become a block object when pasted. However, in an edit box within a dialog session, the text is copied, cut, and pasted as text only. This is true within any edit box in any dialog session, as well as the text-editing area of the **Edit MText** dialog box.

The following example shows the **Edit Attributes** dialog box while editing attributes in a drawing title block. In this example, the drawing was completed, checked, and approved on the same date. Observe how a quick copy and paste operation can be used to reduce typing requirements.

In Figure 23-3, the text listed in the **Date Drawn** edit box has been highlighted. The entire contents of an edit box can be highlighted by using the [Tab] key to set the keyboard focus, or you can double-click in the target edit box. After highlighting the text to be copied, press [Ctrl]+[C] to copy it to the clipboard. Now, move your cursor to the edit box that you are copying the text to, as shown in Figure 23-4. Press [Ctrl]+[V] to paste the copied text to its destination.

The previous example shows the entire contents of the edit box being copied, but it could just as well be only a portion of the contents. An example of this more specialized editing technique is demonstrated here using the **Edit MText** dialog box to copy part of one mtext object into another. In this example, the customized portion of the text defined for a dimension object is cut and moved to another dimension.

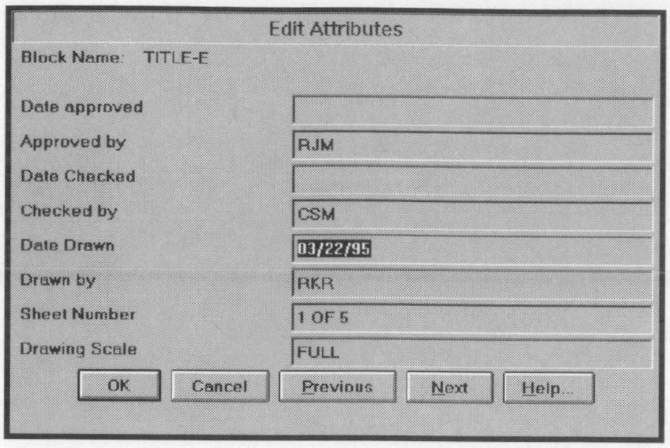

Figure 23-3.
Within the edit box,
highlight the text
to be copied.

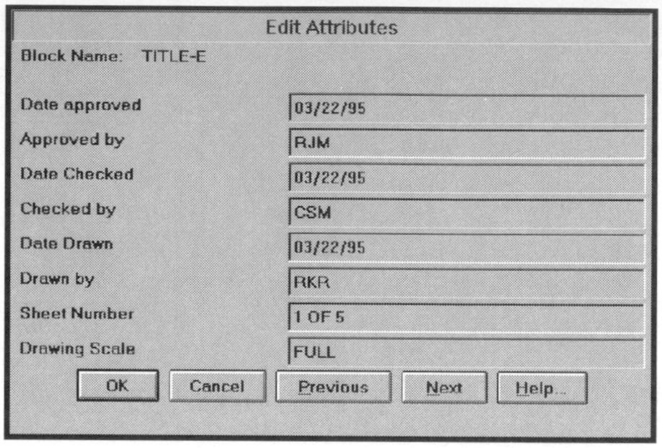

Figure 23-4.
Use the **Paste** option to
paste the copied text into
each location you are
copying it to.

Figure 23-5 shows the **Edit MText** dialog box after a dimension object has been selected for editing with the **DDEDIT** command. Highlighting the text is done by pointing to the start, pressing and holding the pick button, then dragging the cursor to the end of the text to be copied before releasing the pick button.

In Figure 23-6, a second dimension object is selected for editing with the **DDEDIT** command. In this illustration, the dimension text is the default value, as specified by the "⟨⟩" symbols.

Position the cursor where the Clipboard text is to be pasted and press the pick button. Next, press [Ctrl]+[V] to paste the Clipboard contents, see Figure 23-7.

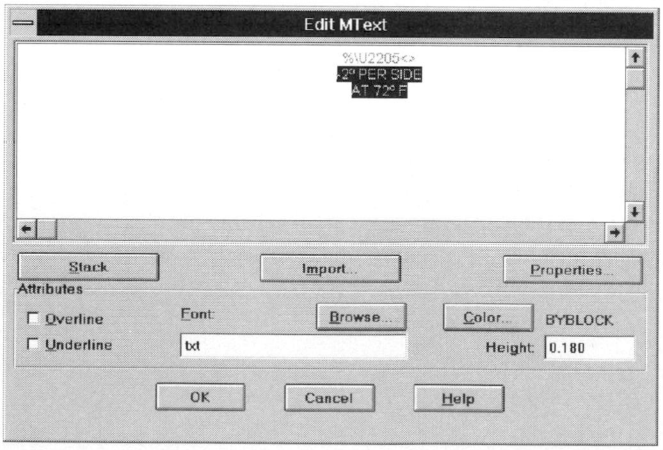

Figure 23-5.
The text in the **Edit MText**
dialog box can be copied to
the Clipboard using [Ctrl]+[C].

Figure 23-6.
The default dimension text value is shown for this dimension object.

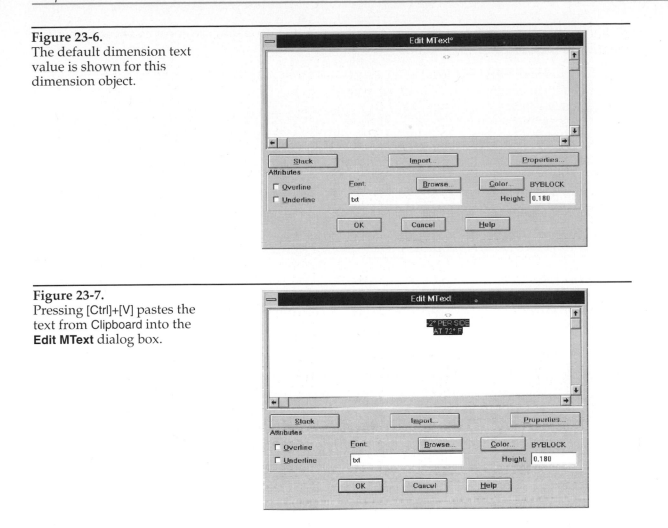

Figure 23-7.
Pressing [Ctrl]+[V] pastes the text from Clipboard into the **Edit MText** dialog box.

Copying information between drawings

The Windows 3.1 and Windows for Workgroups 3.11 operating systems only allow one session of AutoCAD to be active at a time. This represents a special challenge for bringing partial drawing information from one drawing to another.

Using conventional methods for earlier releases of AutoCAD, you would use the **WBLOCK** command to write the desired information to a drawing file for temporary storage. Then, you would open the next drawing and use the **INSERT** command to bring in the stored drawing information. Finally, good disk management practices would require deleting the temporary storage file. The Windows copy, cut, and paste features allow you to transfer information with much greater convenience.

The following sequence shows an example of how to copy drawing information from one drawing to another using **COPYCLIP** and **PASTECLIP**. First, open the drawing you wish to copy objects *from*. Now do the following:

    Command: **COPYCLIP**↵
    Select objects: *(select the desired objects)*
    # found
    Select objects: *(continue selecting as desired)*
    Select objects: ↵
    Command:

Next, use the **OPEN** command to open the drawing that you are copying the information *to.* Enter the **PASTECLIP** command:

Command: **PASTECLIP**↵
Insertion point: *(select the insertion point)*
X scale factor ⟨1⟩ / Corner / XYZ: ↵
Y scale factor (default=X): ↵
Rotation angle ⟨0⟩: ↵
Command:

NOTE

In some maintenance releases of AutoCAD, when picked from the toolbar or the **Edit** pull-down menu, or by using the available accelerator keys, the **COPYCLIP**, **CUTCLIP**, and **PASTECLIP** commands are entered using a leading apostrophe. This implies that the commands can be entered transparently, but these are not actually transparent commands. Attempting to enter one of these commands while another AutoCAD command is active has no effect. The leading apostrophe has no adverse effects when entered at the **Command:** prompt.

PROFESSIONAL TIP

When pasted objects that include associative dimensions are exploded, the dimension objects are automatically updated to the current dimension variable settings. If you explode a pasted object containing associative dimensions, be sure to verify all included dimensions for correct formatting.

Using the Clipboard Viewer

Once a graphic image or an item of text is copied to the Clipboard, it remains there until something new is copied or until you exit Windows. This means that the contents of the Clipboard can be available for use long after you have copied them. The application provided for you to work with the Clipboard contents is called the Clipboard Viewer.

The Clipboard Viewer allows you to examine the current contents of the Clipboard. Additionally, you can clear the Clipboard or even save the contents to a file for later use. The Clipboard icon is typically located in the Main group window of the Program Manager. Double-click on the icon to start the viewer.

When the viewer is launched, it will display the currently stored data. If you cannot see all of the image or text, use the scroll bars. In Figure 23-8, several AutoCAD objects have been copied and are displayed in the Clipboard Viewer window.

The contents of the Clipboard can also be saved to disk for later use. Regardless of the type of information contained in the Clipboard, when saved to disk using the viewer it will be saved in a .CLP file. This file can then be opened later using the Clipboard Viewer. To save a .CLP file, select Save As from the File pull-down menu in the Clipboard Viewer. A Save As dialog box will be displayed where you can specify the directory location and filename for the saved data. To open the saved file, select Open from the File menu and specify the file to open in the Open dialog box. When a .CLP file is opened, the contents of the file are copied to the clipboard, and are then ready to be pasted into other applications.

If you have copied a very large image or many pages of text to the clipboard and no longer need the data, you can clear the contents of the Clipboard. This is useful when you are running low on memory and need to free up some resources. To clear the contents of the Clipboard, select Delete from the File menu in the Clipboard Viewer.

Figure 23-8.
The Windows Clipboard
Viewer displays the current
contents of the Clipboard.

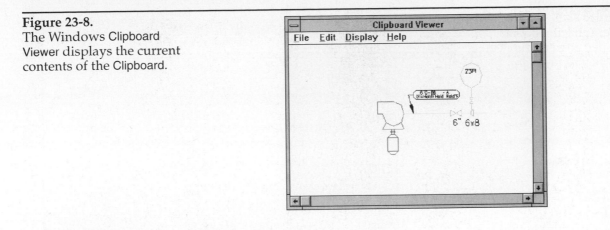

OBJECT LINKING AND EMBEDDING (OLE)

Object linking and embedding, or OLE, is a feature of the Windows operating system that allows data from many different source applications to be combined into a single document. A technical document will often present data in several forms to ensure effective communications. For example, the technical documentation for a product might include formatted text from a word processor, technical drawings from AutoCAD, charts and graphs from a spreadsheet program, and even graphic images from a paint program. Understanding the use of OLE will help you to produce high quality documentation to communicate your ideas effectively.

As implied by the name, there are two distinct aspects to OLE. One is *linking* and the other is *embedding*. Both linking and embedding allow you insert data from one application into another, but they differ in the way that they store the information. The following terms are used in the OLE process:

- **Object**—A piece of data created by a Windows application that supports OLE server functions. Such data could be text from a word processor, an AutoCAD drawing, or a graphic image.
- **OLE Server**—A source application. For example, when using OLE to bring an AutoCAD drawing into your word processor, AutoCAD becomes the OLE server.
- **OLE Client**—A destination application. AutoCAD is an OLE client when you use OLE to bring an object into AutoCAD from another application.

Embedding objects in AutoCAD

The term *embedding* refers to storing a copy of an OLE object in a client document. Embedding differs from importing because an imported object maintains no association with its source application. An embedded object is edited by using the source application, or server. For example, if a Corel Photo-Paint picture (.PCX) was embedded in an AutoCAD drawing, double-clicking on the picture would start the Corel Photo-Paint application and load the selected picture. Using the **Import** command to bring a .PCX file into AutoCAD would bring in the graphic image, but it would have no association with the original application.

To embed an OLE object in an AutoCAD drawing, first copy it to the Clipboard from the source application. Return to AutoCAD and paste the Clipboard contents using **PASTECLIP**. When the contents of the Clipboard is non-AutoCAD data and contains OLE information, it will be embedded in the AutoCAD drawing.

One application for using embedded graphics is using a Paintbrush picture in a title block for a logo design. In Figure 23-9, the Paintbrush program has been used to design a logo graphic. Selecting the graphic image and pressing [Ctrl]+[C] copies the selected image to the Clipboard.

Figure 23-9.
A graphic image can
be designed in the
Paintbrush program.

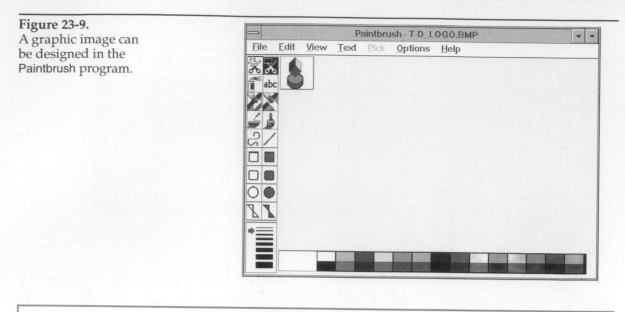

NOTE

While working through these examples, you will be switching between applications in Windows. One convenient means of switching applications is using the [Alt]+[Tab] keystroke. Or, you may find it more convenient to have both windows visible at once on your desktop. Another option is to press [Ctrl]+[Esc] and select the application you need to be active.

Once you have copied the image to the Clipboard, return to AutoCAD. Now press [Ctrl]+[V] to paste the Clipboard contents into the AutoCAD drawing. A pasted image will appear in the upper left corner of the graphics screen, see Figure 23-10. Moving your cursor to point at the pasted image changes your cursor into a four-way arrow, similar to the one displayed when Move is picked from the Windows menu. Press and hold the pick button to move the image, release the pick button when the image is in the desired location.

Figure 23-10.
Pasted image appears in
the upper left corner.

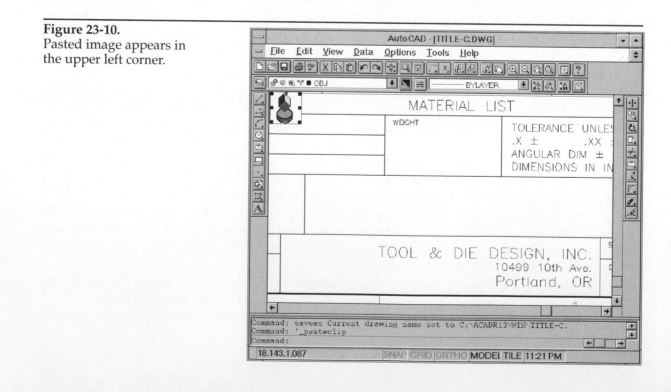

Once the image is positioned correctly, pick anywhere on the screen that is not on the image and the grips will disappear. Figure 23-11 shows the image in its final position within the title block.

Note that the filled squares surrounding the image are just like AutoCAD's own grips, and can be used to adjust the size and proportions of the image. Pointing to the grips changes the cursor to the appropriate resizing cursor. Press and hold the pick button to move the grip. Release the pick button when you are finished adjusting the image. The illustration in Figure 23-12 shows the function of each of the grip points, as well as the appearance of the cursor when moving an image.

Because the image is embedded, it maintains an association with the original application. You can use the original application whenever you need to edit the image. The application can be initiated by double-clicking on the image, or this and additional options are available on the **OLE Object Menu**. To display the **OLE Object Menu**, point to an image and right-click. This displays the menu shown in Figure 23-13.

Figure 23-11.
Picking anywhere outside
the image removes the grips
from the screen.

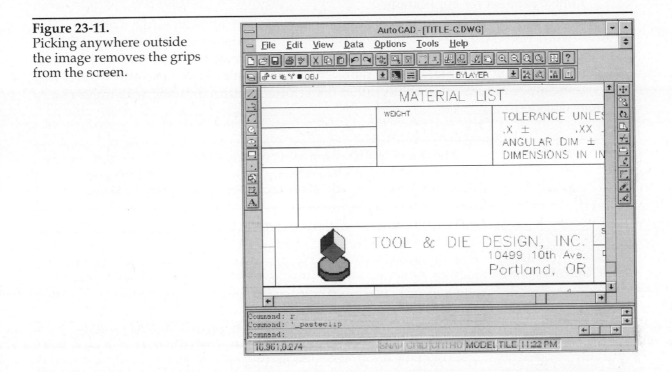

Figure 23-12.
The resize and move cursor
shapes for pasted images.

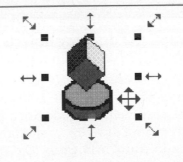

Figure 23-13.
The **OLE Object Menu**.

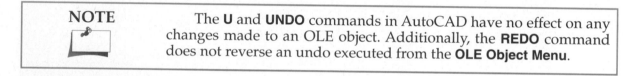

The bottom line on this menu indicates the type of object and the application that will be used to edit it. In this case, the Windows Paintbrush program is the server application. The other menu items function as follows:

- **Cut**—Removes the OLE object and copies it to the Clipboard.
- **Copy**—Copies the object to the Clipboard.
- **Clear**—Removes the object from the drawing without copying it to the Clipboard.
- **Undo**—Reverses the last action performed with this menu. Similar to AutoCAD's **U** command, this can be used repeatedly. Note that this will not undo object updates done by the server application.

It is possible to embed virtually any OLE object into an AutoCAD drawing. This includes word processing documents, charts, graphs, spreadsheets, audio clips, and video clips. Using these various OLE data types can transform a standard technical drawing into a complete multimedia presentation. As you use these techniques, try to use only objects that have significant communication value, rather than cluttering up a drawing with unnecessary bells and whistles.

NOTE

The **U** and **UNDO** commands in AutoCAD have no effect on any changes made to an OLE object. Additionally, the **REDO** command does not reverse an undo executed from the **OLE Object Menu**.

PROFESSIONAL TIP

OLE objects that are linked or embedded in an AutoCAD drawing only print on printers or plotters that use the Windows System Printer driver. They will still be displayed on screen, but cannot be printed using non-Windows drivers.

Additionally, only the Windows version of AutoCAD will display the OLE objects. The OLE objects will not appear in DOS AutoCAD and other non-Windows versions of AutoCAD.

Embedding AutoCAD drawing objects in other documents

AutoCAD Release 13 provides both client and server OLE functions. This means that in addition to using embedded OLE objects, AutoCAD can provide objects for other applications. A common use for this feature is to combine technical drawings and illustrations with text in a technical document created with a word processing program.

If you already have a drawing created that you need to embed in another document, first open the drawing in AutoCAD. Press [Ctrl]+[C] or select **Copy** from the **File** menu, and select the desired objects. This places the selected objects on the Clipboard. For this example, the entire AutoCAD drawing shown in Figure 23-14 has been copied to the Clipboard.

For the purposes of this example, the Windows Write word processing program will be used as the client application. The OLE client concepts demonstrated with this application will be similar for most other Windows based word processors as well. In this next step, the Write application is opened with the destination document for the AutoCAD drawing, Figure 23-15.

Figure 23-14.
To prepare to embed
a drawing, copy it to the
Clipboard using [Ctrl]+[C] or
by picking **Copy** from
the **File** menu.

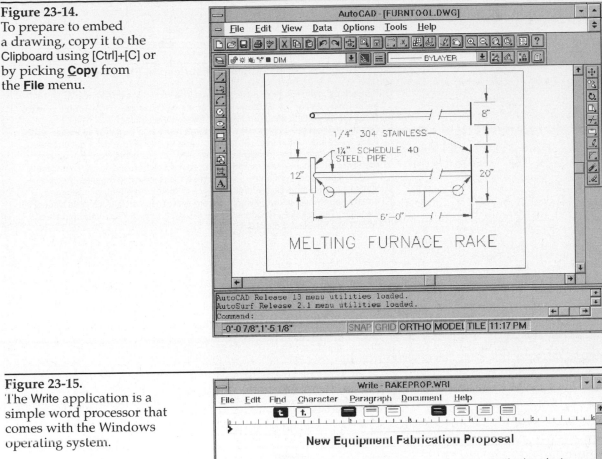

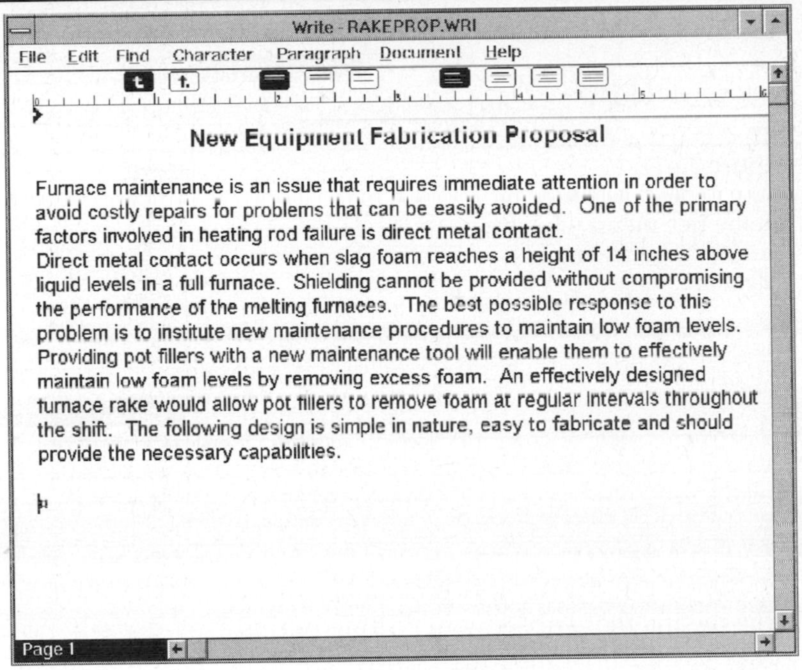

Figure 23-15.
The Write application is a
simple word processor that
comes with the Windows
operating system.

After opening the document, select the <u>E</u>dit menu and pick the <u>P</u>aste option to embed the AutoCAD drawing. Note that the embedded drawing will be placed at the current cursor location. You are not prompted for a location or a size. If you need to change either the location or the size, you can do so by clicking once on the drawing to highlight it and then select either <u>M</u>ove Picture or <u>S</u>ize Picture from the <u>E</u>dit menu. Figure 23-16 shows the document with the drawing embedded, resized, and moved to the center of the document.

Embedding an OLE object in an application also modifies the menu to display new options when the object is highlighted. The <u>E</u>dit menu in the Write program appears as shown in Figure 23-17 after highlighting the embedded drawing.

Figure 23-16.
The AutoCAD drawing
has been embedded in
the Write document.

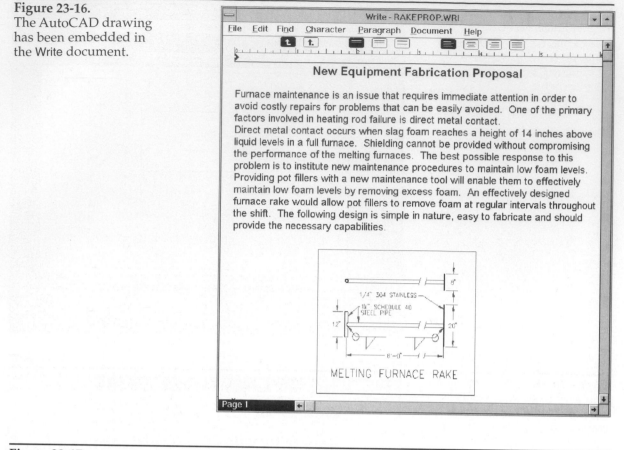

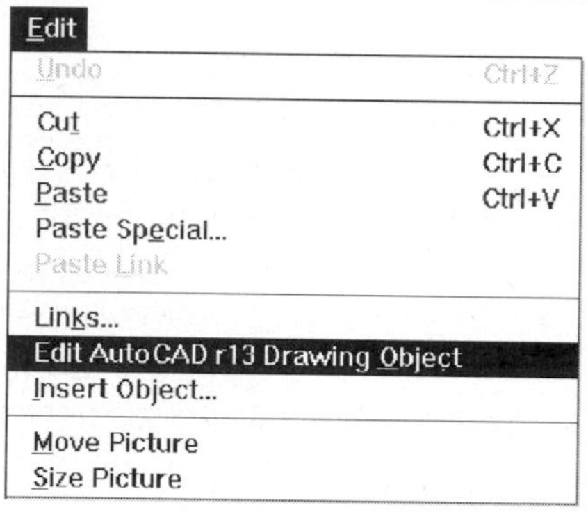

Figure 23-17.
New choices are displayed
on the Edit menu when the
embedded drawing is
selected.

Once the drawing is embedded, it loses all connection with the original drawing file. This means that subsequent editing of this drawing will not affect the original source file. In order to edit the embedded drawing, highlight the image and select Edit AutoCAD-r13 Object from the Edit menu or simply double-click on the drawing. When the AutoCAD window opens, examine the title bar and note the specified filename. In Figure 23-18, the filename shows up as A$CF149.DWG. This is a temporary name assigned to the drawing while it is being edited, and may change from one editing session to another.

Updating refers to recording your changes to the embedded object within the client document. There are two ways to update the file when you have finished editing it. Picking the Edit menu displays a new option, in this case the new option reads: Update RAKEPROP.WRI. The text RAKEPROP.WRI represents the client document filename, and selecting this option replaces the currently embedded drawing with the revised version. You can simply exit AutoCAD. If changes have been made, the dialog box shown in Figure 23-19 will be displayed. Selecting the **Yes** button updates the client document.

Figure 23-18.
An embedded drawing is edited using a unique, temporary filename.

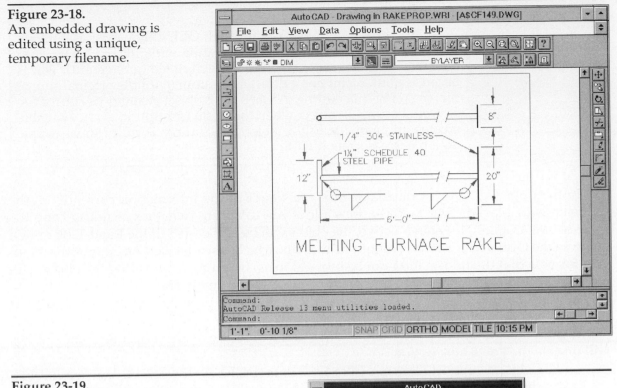

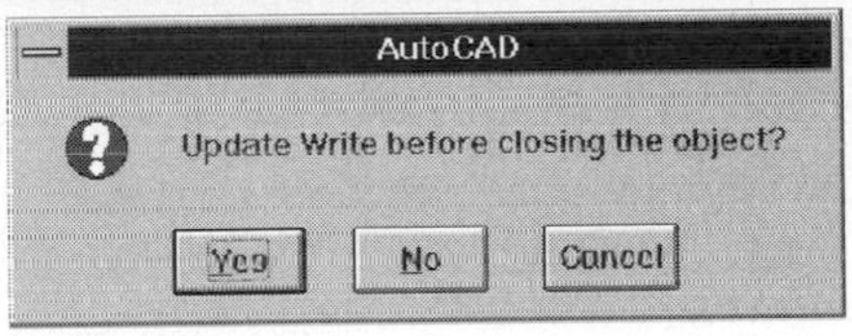

Figure 23-19.
If there are unsaved changes in your drawing, this dialog box is displayed.

Linking objects in AutoCAD

Linking is similar to embedding, in that objects from one application are brought into another application. With linking, however, a direct link is maintained between the source data and the OLE object in the client application.

To link an object within AutoCAD, first it must be copied to the clipboard. When bringing the object into AutoCAD, select the **Paste Special...** option from the **Edit** menu. Using this option activates the **Paste Special** dialog box, see Figure 23-20.

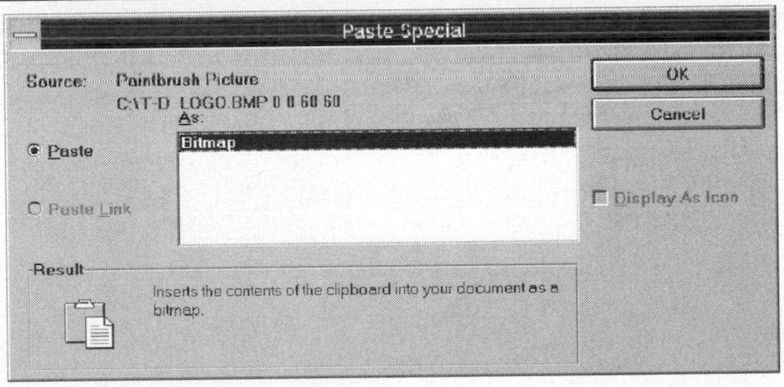

Figure 23-20.
The **PASTESPEC** command starts the **Paste Special** dialog box.

Objects can only be linked through OLE if they exist as a file on disk. If you copy data from an application without first saving it to disk, the Paste Link radio button will be disabled (grayed out). This is because a link maintains a direct association with the original source file, meaning that editing a linked OLE object changes its source file as well. Pasting an object when the Paste Link option is not available creates an embedded OLE object since there is no original source data file to associate it with.

In the upper left area of the dialog box, the source of the information currently on the Clipboard is displayed. Two radio buttons allow you to specify whether or not to copy the information as a link. If **Paste** is active, the object will be embedded. If the **Paste Link** option is active the OLE object will be brought in as a link. The list box labeled **As:** shows the available formats that the information can be brought in as. If you are embedding the object, you may have several options, depending on the type of data being pasted.

A linked object comes in as the file type that is associated with the server application. For example, in Figure 23-21, text from Microsoft Word has been copied to the Clipboard. Item A shows the available options when embedding, and item B shows that selecting some options will disable the **Paste Link** option.

Linked objects support Dynamic Data Exchange (DDE). As the source data is modified, the link in the client application is updated. To see how this works, follow this sequence.

Figure 23-21.
A—Inserting an object enables the **Paste Link** option. B—Some data types cannot be linked.

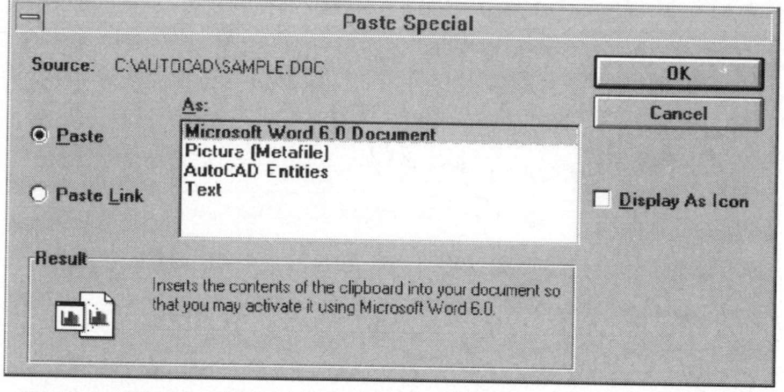

A

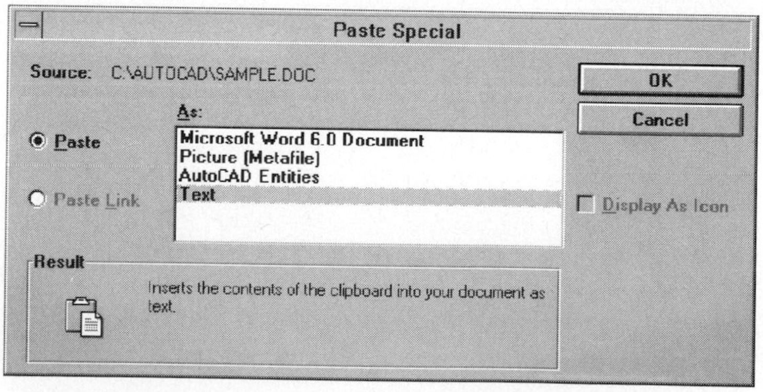

B

First, open both AutoCAD and the Microsoft Paintbrush program. Now, create a simple image in Paintbrush and save the file. Next, use one of the cutout tools (Scissors icon) to select all or part of the Paintbrush drawing, and press [Ctrl]+[C] to copy the data to the Clipboard. In the AutoCAD window, select **Paste Special...** from the **Edit** menu. In the **Paste Special** dialog box, be sure to pick the **Paste Link** radio button, then pick **OK**. A copy of the Paintbrush drawing will appear in the upper left corner of the graphics screen area. Now, close the Paintbrush program.

To edit the linked OLE object, double-click on it. This opens Paintbrush, the server applications. For the best visibility, arrange the desktop so that both windows are visible at once, see Figure 23-22. Notice that any changes you make to the image are immediately updated in the OLE object. Also, by examining the title bar of the Paintbrush program, you will note that the original file was opened for editing.

Figure 23-22.
If both the client and the server of an OLE link are visible, you will see the dynamic updates.

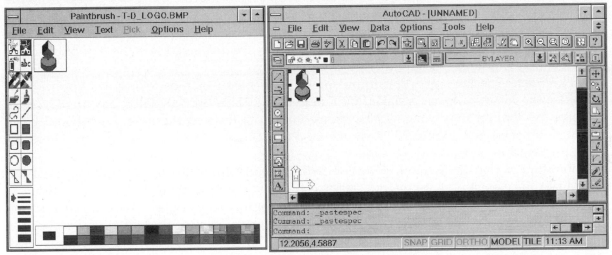

Any linked OLE object will behave in much the same manner as the previous example. In certain applications, the updates may be slower, but they are still automatic. To change the way that a link is updated or to adjust current links in a drawing, select the **Links...** option from the **Edit** menu. This opens the **Links** dialog box as shown in Figure 23-23. If no links are present in the current drawing, picking this option has no effect.

The **Links:** list box displays all of the active links in the current drawing. The filename of the link and the update method are also shown, Figure 23-23. By default, a link is automatically updated. In the lower left area of this dialog are two radio buttons that allow you to adjust this feature. If you do not want the updates to be automatic, pick the **Manual** radio button. To force an update manually, select the **Update Now** button in the lower left area of the dialog. The **Cancel Link** button removes link information from the OLE object and removes any association with the source file— effectively converting a linked object into an embedded object. Select the **Change Link...** button to change the source file that the link is associated with; specify the new file in the **Change Link** file dialog box.

The names of the **Activate** and **Edit** buttons may vary in the **Links** dialog box according to the object type that has been linked. For example, a video clip would show a **Play** and an **Edit** button. The status of these buttons is dependent on the link data type as well as the availability of an associated application. For example, there is no way to "activate" a bitmap or a word processing document, so the activate button is shown grayed-out, as in Figure 23-23. In the case of a video clip, the **Play** button is only enabled if an associated application for playing the clips is available.

Figure 23-23.
The **Links** dialog box
displays all active links.

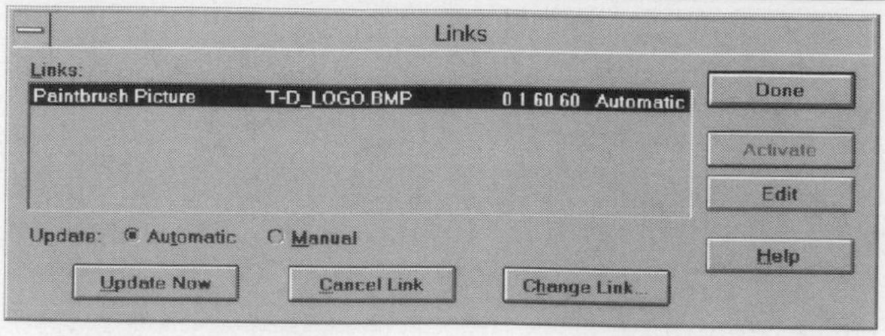

Linking AutoCAD drawings in other applications

As with linking OLE objects from other applications within AutoCAD, the data to be linked is first copied to the Clipboard, then pasted into the client application using the **Paste Special** option. Just as with the procedure for embedding AutoCAD drawings, you can use **COPYCLIP** to place the desired information on the Clipboard. Alternately, you can use the **COPYLINK** command.

COPYLINK can be typed at the **Command:** prompt, or you can select **Copy View** from the **Edit** pull-down menu in AutoCAD. Using **COPYLINK** differs from **COPYCLIP** in that there is no selection process. All currently visible objects are automatically selected as they appear on screen. Also similar to **COPYCLIP**, the selected objects are displayed in a client application in the view that was active when the copy was made.

The Paste Special... selection found on the **Edit** menu of most Windows applications provides the means to paste a linked OLE object. The Paste Special dialog box displayed by picking this option may vary slightly from one application to the next, but several basic features are standard. Figure 23-24 shows the Paste Special dialog boxes used by Microsoft Word for Windows and Windows Write.

Remember that the Paste Link option is only available if the source drawing has been saved to a file. Selecting AutoCAD r13 Object as the data type maintains the pasted material as AutoCAD drawing data. Selecting Picture brings the information in as a .WMF file and Bitmap converts the incoming data to a .BMP file. Using bitmaps ensures that what you see on the screen is exactly what will print, but tends to make the client files very large and uses more memory. Your choice for the incoming data type has no effect on the original file, and the link is still maintained if the data type supports linking.

Figure 23-24.
The **Paste Special** dialog boxes used by A—Microsoft Word and B—Windows Write.

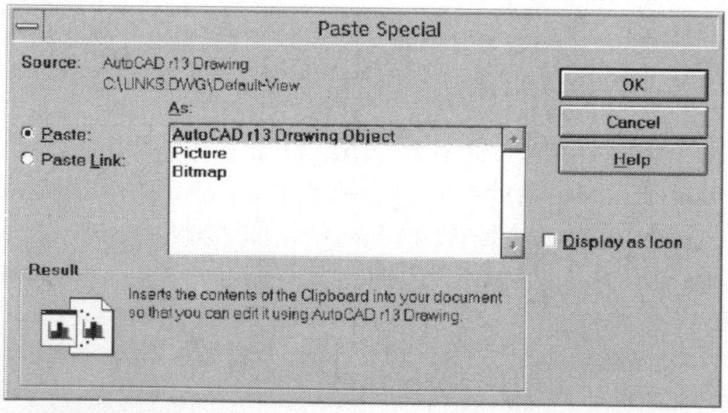

A

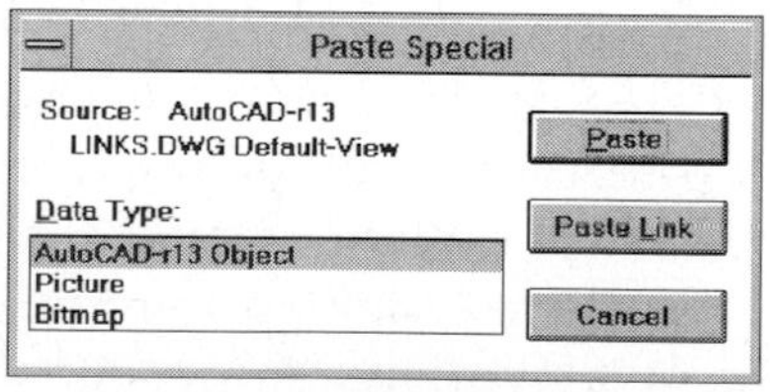

B

Linking and embedding new objects

When you need to embed an object into AutoCAD that has not yet been created, select **Insert Object...** from the **Edit** menu. This allows you to create a completely new OLE object by starting the application associated with the data type you need to create. Selecting this option displays the dialog box shown in Figure 23-25.

The **Object Type:** list box shows the currently-registered applications that support OLE functions. Highlight the desired program that you need to create the new OLE object. Read each selection carefully, because some programs can produce varied types of data. For example, if you have Microsoft Word installed, you may see options for producing a picture or a document. The option you select affects how the specified program is started, and the data type it will be sending back to AutoCAD.

When you are finished creating the OLE object, select the Update option from your File menu or just exit the application. If you do exit before you save, the application will ask you if you want to update the object before you exit.

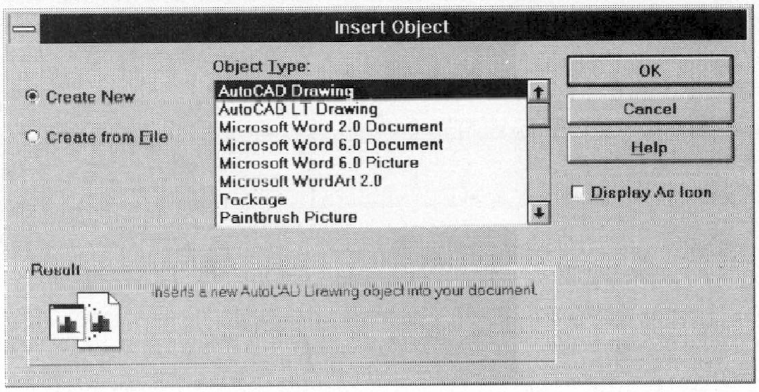

Figure 23-25.
The **Insert Object** dialog box.

USING DYNAMIC DATA EXCHANGE (DDE)

Dynamic Data Exchange, or DDE, is a feature of the Windows operating system that allows you to dynamically share, edit, and exchange data between applications. When a DDE relationship is established, the data being exchanged can be appended, deleted, or modified by either application. For example, you can send your AutoCAD drawing database to a spreadsheet application and then edit your drawing by editing the spreadsheet. This provides the capability to work parametrically with your drawings. *Parametric* refers to creating and editing drawings based on supplying variable values (such as object locations and dimensions) and having the drawing automatically reflect the changes.

This section provides a brief tutorial on establishing a DDE relationship between AutoCAD and a spreadsheet program. Any spreadsheet program that supports DDE may be used; these examples use the Microsoft Excel software.

PROFESSIONAL TIP

A convenient means of managing drawing files is available by pasting links to drawing files into the Windows Cardfile program. The Cardfile application is found in the Accessories group window. It is possible to paste links to some or even all of your drawings into Cardfile, and then to use Cardfile as a front end to AutoCAD.

The concepts and methods for pasting links into a client application are the same here as in other applications. Once you have pasted a link to a drawing into Cardfile, you can browse through the available cards or use a search tool to help you locate a specific drawing file you are looking for. Multiple files can also be maintained, perhaps to keep files from different customers or projects separated.

An image is shown here of the Cardfile application with links to three drawings and comments for each file. Note the convenience of being able to see a preview of the drawing image along with specific text, and then to launch AutoCAD with the desired drawing preloaded all by just double-clicking on the appropriate card.

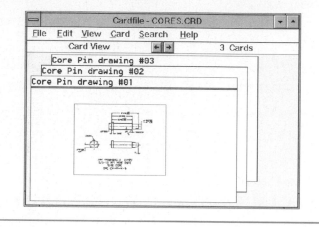

Exporting drawing data to a spreadsheet

The easiest way to initiate the DDE feature in AutoCAD is to load a partial menu file called SHAFT.MNU using the **MENULOAD** command. This custom menu contains macros that automatically load the necessary application files and execute the appropriate commands. Either type MENULOAD at the command prompt or pick **Customize Menus...** from the **Tools** pull-down menu, see Figure 23-26.

Figure 23-26.
Customize Menus... is selected from the **Tools** pull-down menu.

The **MENULOAD** command starts the **Menu Customization** dialog box, where you can load, unload, or adjust the visibility of your menus. When the **Menu Customization** dialog box appears, be certain that the **Menu Groups** panel is showing, as shown in Figure 23-27.

Pick the **Browse...** button to display a file dialog box used to locate the menu file to be loaded. In the **Select Menu File** dialog box, navigate to the \R13\WIN\SAMPLE directory and locate the file named SHAFT.MNU. This is a menu template file for the SHAFT menu. Highlight the filename and pick the **OK** button, see Figure 23-28.

When you return to the **Menu Customization** dialog box, the SHAFT.MNU file should be listed in the **File Name:** edit box. Now, pick the **Load** button, as shown in Figure 23-29. The group name SHAFT should now appear in the **Menu Groups** list box. Highlight it by picking it and then pick the **Menu Bar** tab near the top.

Figure 23-27.
The **Menu Customization** dialog box.

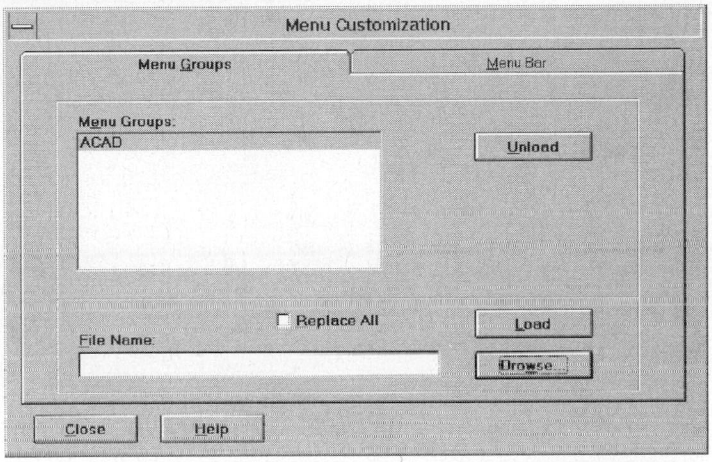

Figure 23-28.
Pick the SHAFT.MNU in the **Select Menu File** dialog box.

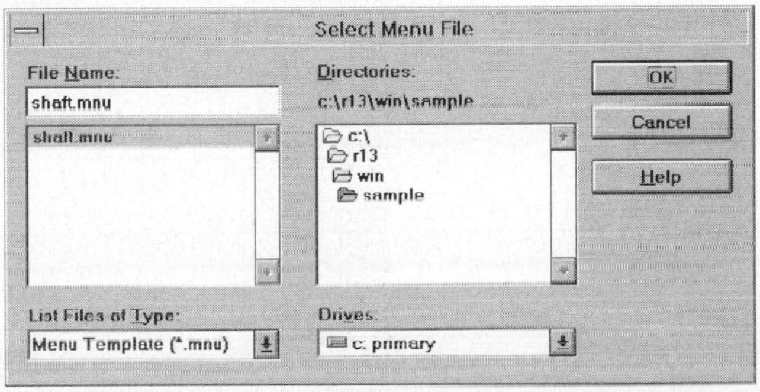

Figure 23-29.
When the menu is selected it will appear in the **Menu Groups** list.

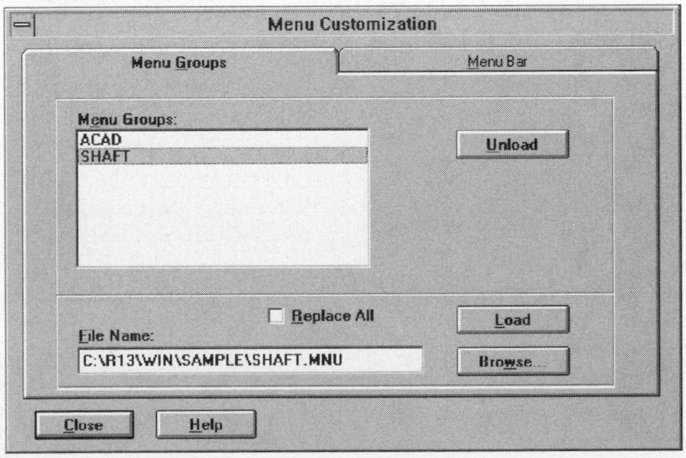

The **Menu Bar** panel of the **Menu Customization** dialog box lets you specify which parts of the loaded menus to display on the pull-down menu bar. In order to add an element from the SHAFT menu, the name SHAFT must appear in the **Menu Group** pop-up list. If the ACAD group is listed, pick the pop-up list and select the SHAFT menu group instead. The SHAFT menu should now be listed in the **Menus:** list box.

In the **Menus:** list box, highlight the SHAFT menu, then pick a menu name in the **Menu Bar:** list where the SHAFT menu is to be inserted and pick the **Insert⟫** button. The existing menus are not affected, but the SHAFT menu is inserted just above the selected menu name. See Figure 23-30. When you are finished, pick the **Close** button. On the menu bar, the newly added SHAFT menu will appear to the left of the selected menu, as shown in Figure 23-31.

Figure 23-30.
The Shaft menu is inserted just above the selected menu name.

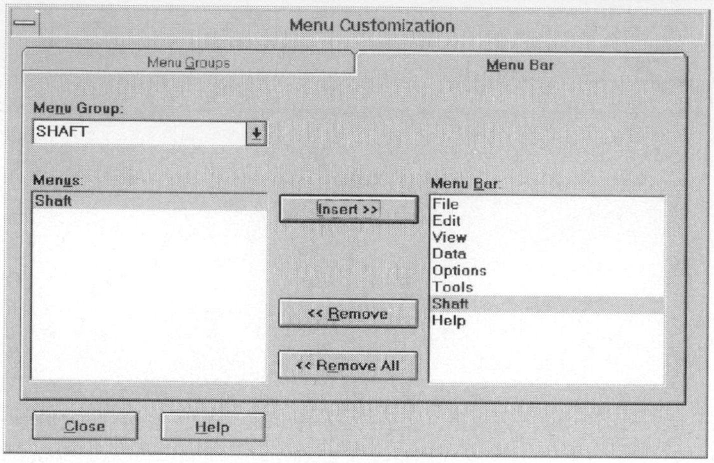

Figure 23-31.
The newly selected **Shaft** menu appears in the menu bar.

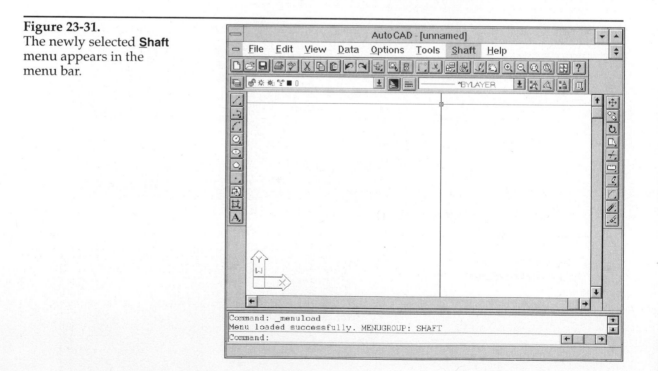

The **Shaft** menu cannot be used until the DDEAD.EXE file is also loaded. This file is found in the \R13\WIN\SAMPLE directory. Use the **APPLOAD** command to load it.

Now, pick the **Shaft** pull-down menu from the menu bar. This menu displays a number of DDE options, as shown in Figure 23-32.

To initiate a DDE conversation between AutoCAD and Excel, pick the **DDE Dialog...** option. This displays the **DDE Initiate Conversation** dialog box as depicted in Figure 23-33. The default item in the **DDE Application:** edit box should be Excel.

Other values in this dialog box will be used with their default values for this example. The **Work file:** should default to Sheet1. The check box in the middle that is labeled **Automatic Update (hot link)** controls whether or not your drawing is automatically updated when you make changes in the spreadsheet file. Leave this box checked. If the **Command Line:** edit box does not indicate the path to your Excel executable file, enter this in the edit box:

C:\EXCEL\EXCEL.EXE

NOTE

Spreadsheets other than Excel may use parameters different than the default values. The **Spreadsheet Parameters** dialog box can be viewed by selecting the **Parameters...** button from the **DDE Initiate Conversation** dialog box. Refer to your spreadsheet documentation for the correct parameters.

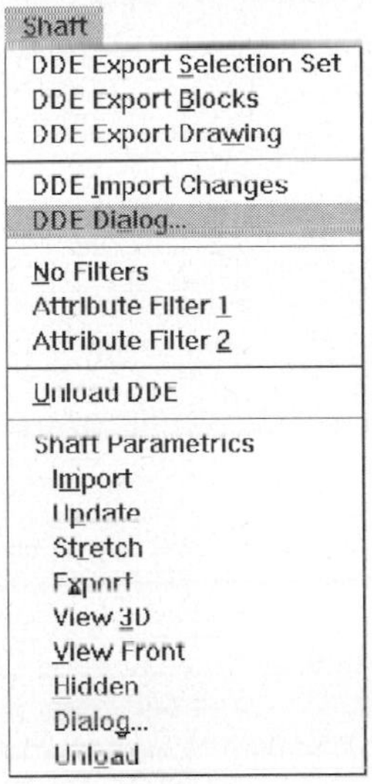

Figure 23-32.
The **Shaft** menu displays several DDE options.

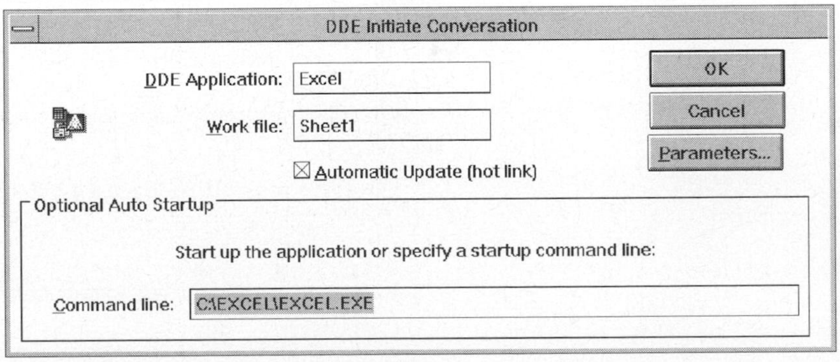

Figure 23-33.
The **DDE Initiate Conversation** dialog box.

Once you have checked and verified the values supplied in the **DDE Initiate Conversation** dialog box, pick the **OK** button. Now, in order to have an object to export the definition data for, draw a 2 unit radius circle using a center point of 4,4:

Command: **CIRCLE**↵
3P/2P/TTR/⟨Center point⟩: **4,4**↵
Diameter/⟨Radius⟩: **2**↵

Now, let's export the drawing data on the circle to the spreadsheet program. To do this, pick the **DDE Export Selection Set** option at the top of the **Shaft** menu, Figure 23-34. If Microsoft Excel was not yet active, it is started automatically now. You will see the Excel start-up banner appear and then the Excel window will appear. Switch to the AutoCAD window if it is no longer active, and you should now be at a Select objects: prompt. See Figure 23-35. Select the circle and press the [Enter] key.

Figure 23-34.
Data is exported with the
DDE Export Selection Set
option.

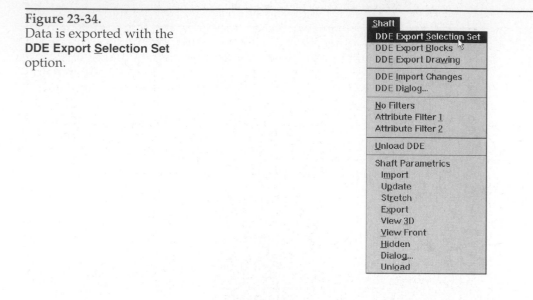

Figure 23-35.
Select the circle at the
Select objects: prompt.

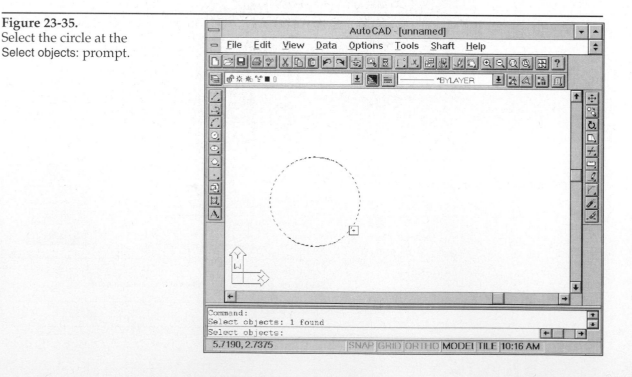

Now, switch to the Excel window to see how your circle looks in a spreadsheet program. The spreadsheet data, as shown in Figure 23-36, uses the DXF format to display drawing information. The DXF format shows a numerical entry in the A column that indicates what the data on the same row in column B is defining. Some data fields require multiple values, such as point coordinates.

Several of the fields should be obvious as to their meaning, for example the 0 field has a value of CIRCLE so the 0 field represents the object type. Note that changing the object type is not permitted, since changing the 0 field to LINE from CIRCLE would generate an incomplete and incorrect listing.

Figure 23-36.
The circle data in the Excel spreadsheet.

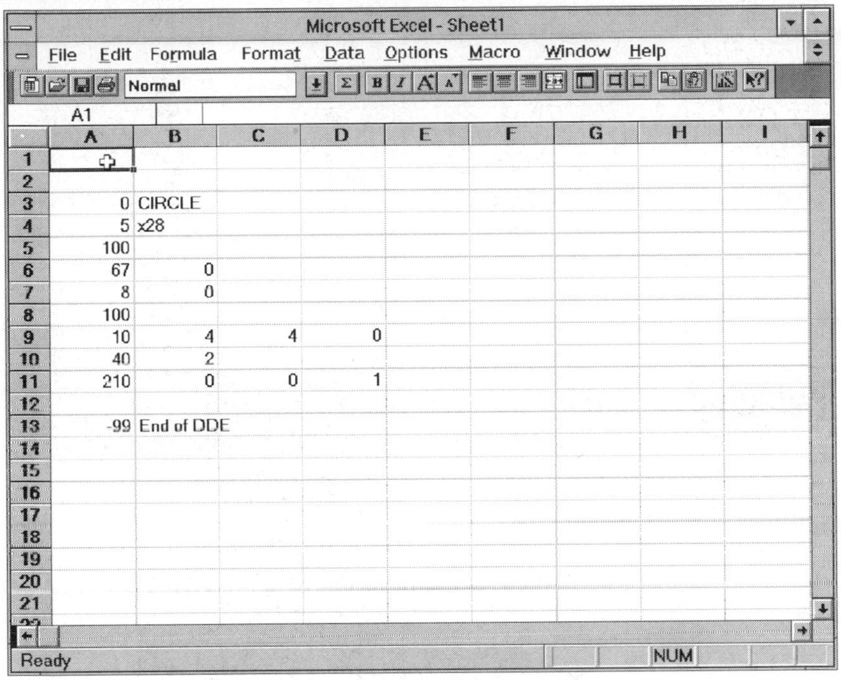

The fields shown in this record are listed below to show their meaning.

Col. A	Col. B	Col. C	Col. D	Description
0	CIRCLE			Object type
5	x28			Entity handler
100				Data marker
67	0			Space where object resides (paper/model)
8	0			Layer object is on
10	4	4	0	X, Y, and Z coordinates of center point
40	2			Radius
210	0	0	1	X, Y, and Z of Extrusion Vector (directional)

To see the drawing update from informational changes in the spreadsheet, we need to first make some changes. In the Excel program, select the field to change by pointing to it with your cursor and pressing the pick button.

For the purposes of this exercise, you will change three fields. The record that begins with the 10 in column A defines the center point of the circle. Change the X value of 4 to 6.25 and the Y value of 4 to 5. Next, change the radius of the circle (listed in field 40) from 2 to 0.125 and then return to the AutoCAD window.

Notice that the changes have not yet been applied. To apply the changes, select **DDE Import Changes** from the **Shaft** menu, see Figure 23-37. The circle is now updated to match the data you supplied in the spreadsheet.

Figure 23-37.
Select **DDE Import Changes** from the **Shaft** menu to apply the changes.

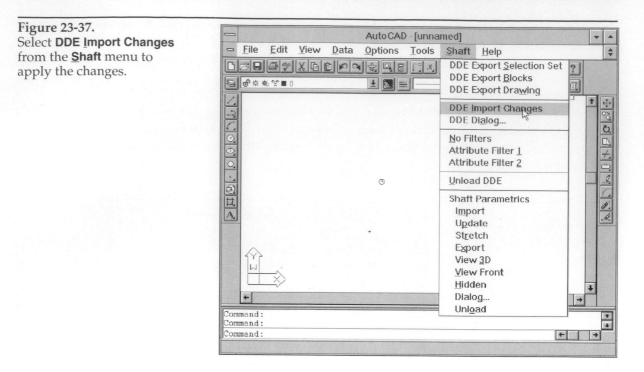

The DDE changes can be supplied in both directions. For example, if upon returning to AutoCAD you found that the changes you made were not appropriate you could then either return to the spreadsheet application or you can directly edit objects within AutoCAD.

For example, select the **Properties** button from the **Object Properties** toolbar to make changes to the circle definition, as shown in Figure 23-38. Change the X and Y coordinates for the center point to 6.25,6.25 and change the radius to 1.5.

Now pick the **DDE Export Selection Set** from the **Shaft** menu, select the circle, and press the [Enter] key. Switch back to Excel and you will see that the changes have been made to match the changes you made in AutoCAD. See Figure 23-39.

Figure 23-38.
Changes made in the **Modify Circle** dialog box.

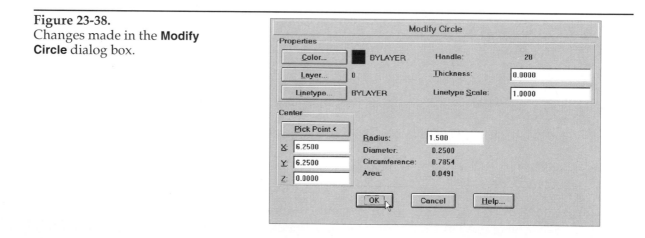

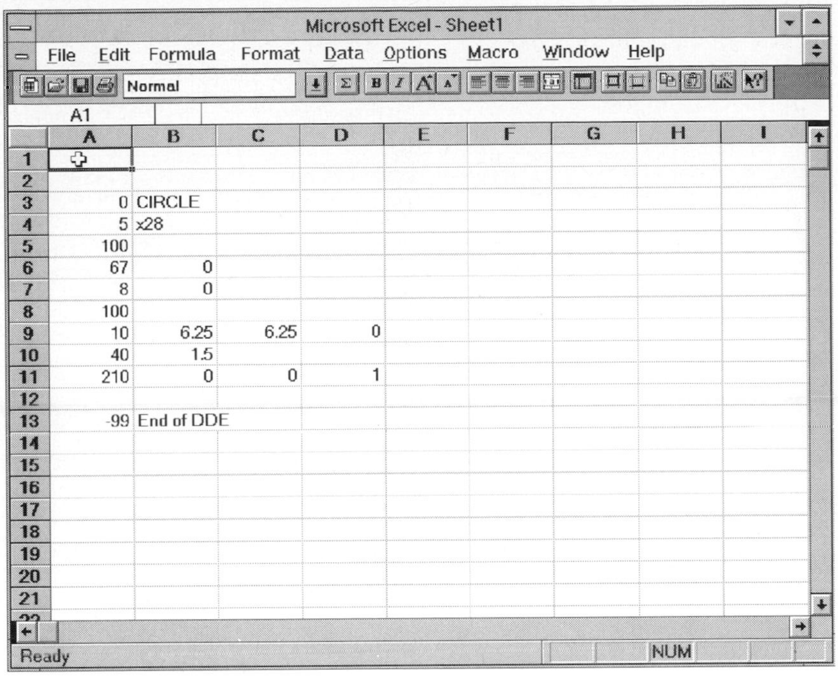

Figure 23-39.
Changes made in AutoCAD can be exported to the spreadsheet.

CHAPTER TEST

Write your answers in the spaces provided.

1. What Windows application assists in copying objects from one software program to another? _____

2. How long does information copied to the application in question 1 remain there? _____

3. What are the five commands in AutoCAD that allow you to work with the application in question 1, and in which menu are they found? _____

4. What are the functions of the [Ctrl]+[C] and [Ctrl]+[V] keystrokes? _____

5. What two commands would be used to copy drawing information from one AutoCAD drawing to another? _____

6. What type of file can be saved from the Clipboard Viewer? _____

7. What does OLE stand for? _____

_____

8. Define the following terms:
   Object— _____

   _____

   OLE Server— _____

   _____

   OLE Client— _____

   _____

9. What does *embedding* mean? _____

   _____

   _____

   _____

10. How can you resize an object that has been pasted into another application? _____

    _____

    _____

    _____

11. How can you edit an object that has been embedding into an application? _____

    _____

    _____

    _____

12. What does *linking* mean? _____

    _____

    _____

    _____

13. How do you insert a new object that has not yet been created into an AutoCAD drawing?

    _____

    _____

    _____

    _____

14. Define the term DDE. _____

    _____

    _____

    _____

CHAPTER PROBLEMS

1. Begin a new drawing and name it P23-1, then do the following:

   General

   A. Insert a title block, or use **MVSETUP** to establish one.

   B. Open the Windows Paintbrush program.

   C. Draw a company logo. Copy the design to the clipboard.

   D. Paste the design into the AutoCAD drawing.

   E. Position the design in the title block.

   F. Save the drawing.

2. Open one of your 3D drawings from a previous chapter, then do the following:

   General

   A. Display the object in a hidden line removed format, or as a rendered image.

   B. Copy the object to the clipboard.

   C. Open a word processing program and paste the clipboard contents to create an embedded object.

   D. Create a memo to a co-worker or instructor in which you describe the process used to create the document.

   E. Save the document as P23-2 but do not close the application. Return to AutoCAD and close the drawing without saving.

   F. Return to the word processor and double-click on the pasted object.

   G. Edit the object in some way and save the drawing.

   H. Return to the document and save.

3. Open one of your 3D drawings from a previous chapter. Perform the same functions outlined in Problem 2, but this time create a link between the AutoCAD drawing and the word processing document. Edit the drawing in AutoCAD and observe the results in the document file. Save the document as P23-3 and close the word processor.

   General

4. Complete this problem if you have access to a spreadsheet program such as Excel.

   General

   A. Create a 2D drawing of the top view of the object in Exercise 12-1 in Chapter 12 of this text. Use the dimensions given.

   B. Export the drawing data to the spreadsheet.

   C. Change the diameter of the two small circles in the spreadsheet. Export the new data to the AutoCAD drawing.

   D. Change the diameter of the large 1.0 diameter circle to .75. Export the change from AutoCAD to the spreadsheet.

   E. Save the drawing as P23-4.

Appendix A

Solid Modeling Tutorial

INTRODUCTION

This tutorial is provided as a supplement to the solid modeling techniques presented in Chapter 10, Chapter 11, and Chapter 12. It is a step-by-step process intended as a guide. Directions are given for each step of the process, but exact details regarding which commands to use, where to find them, and exact coordinate locations are not always given. This allows you to use your knowledge of AutoCAD, use the on-line help files, and to refer to the text for answers. The model for this tutorial is the support base shown in Figure A-1.

Figure A-1.

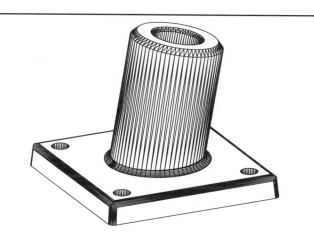

CONSTRUCTING THE BASE OF THE MODEL

The base of the part is first drawn as a region. Then, the region is extruded into the finished height. Finally, holes are added to the base.

1. Draw an 8" square and convert it to a region.
2. Draw a ∅.75" solid cylinder, 1" tall, with its center 1" from each side of the region in the lower-left corner.
3. Create an array so that there is a cylinder in each corner of the region located the exact distance from the corners as the first. Your drawing should look like Figure A-2.
4. Extrude the base to a height of 1" and give a taper angle of 5 degrees.
5. Display the object in a 3D viewpoint. Your drawing should look like Figure A-3.
6. Subtract the four cylinders from the base.
7. Set the **FACETRES** value to 1.0 and remove the hidden lines. Your drawing should look like Figure A-4.

Figure A-2.

Figure A-3.

Figure A-4.

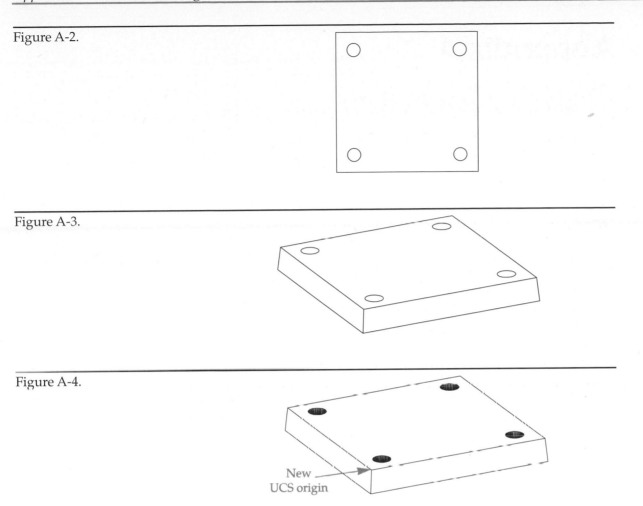

New
UCS origin

CONSTRUCTING THE CYLINDER

First, the large cylinder is constructed and tilted on its axis. Then, holes are constructed inside the cylinder.

1. Create a UCS on the top face of the base with the origin at the lower-left corner as shown in Figure A-4. Display the UCS icon at the origin of the new UCS.
2. Draw a cylinder located at the exact center of the top of the base. Use a diameter of 4″ and a height of 6″.
3. Draw a ∅1.5″ cylinder 1.5″ high with its base centered on the bottom of the large cylinder.
4. Draw a ∅2″ cylinder 4.5″ high with its base centered on the top of the previous cylinder. See Figure A-5.
5. Move all three cylinders down into the base .5″.
6. Rotate all three cylinders 10 degrees on the Y axis. See Figure A-6.
7. Union the two smaller cylinders.
8. Subtract the two small unioned cylinders from the large cylinder.
9. Union the base and large cylinder. Your drawing should look like Figure A-7.

Figure A-5.

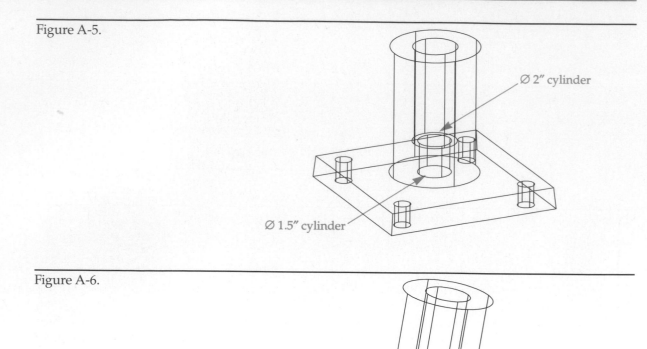

Ø 2″ cylinder

Ø 1.5″ cylinder

Figure A-6.

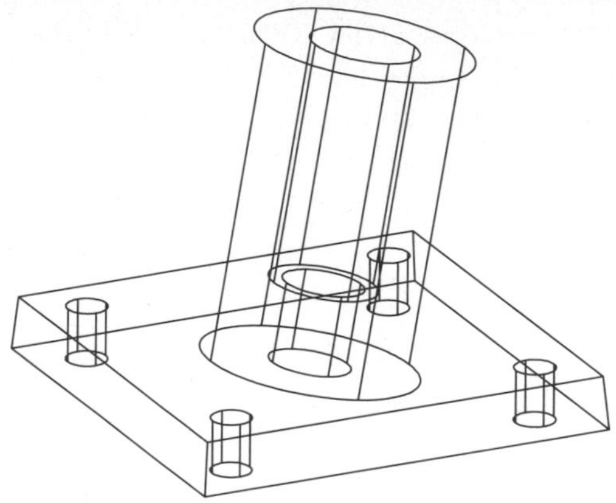

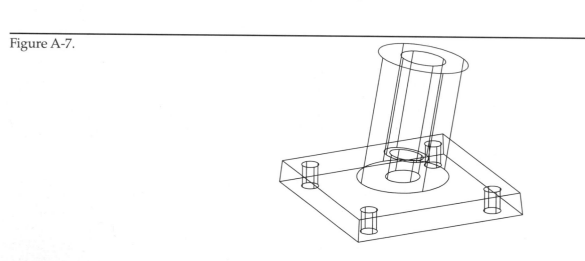

Figure A-7.

ADDING CHAMFERS AND FILLETS

Fillets and chamfers are added to the union of the base and cylinder to complete the object.
1. Fillet the intersection of the cylinder and the base with a .25 radius.
2. Apply a .25″, 45 degree angle chamfer to the top outside edge of the cylinder.
3. Apply a .15″, 45 degree angle chamfer to the top inside edge of the hole in the cylinder. Your drawing should look like Figure A-8.

Figure A-8.

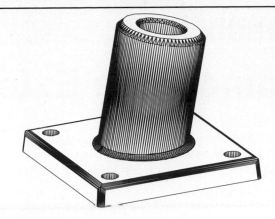

CREATING SLICES AND SECTIONS

To complete the model, you must create a section view. To do this, you must slice the finished object.

1. Rotate the X axis 90 degrees on the current UCS. Move the origin to the center of the cylinders.
2. Create a slice through the center of the model on the current UCS. Select the back side of the object as the part to keep. The remaining part should look like Figure A-9.
3. Create a section through the center of the model on the current UCS. Use the **3point** option of the **SECTION** command.
4. Move the section above and to the left of the model. Add object and section lines, as shown in Figure A-10.
5. Save the drawing as TUTORIAL.

Figure A-9

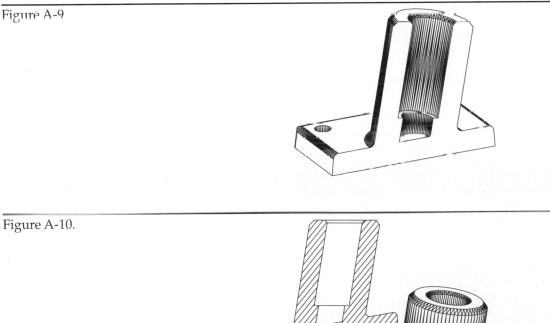

Figure A-10.

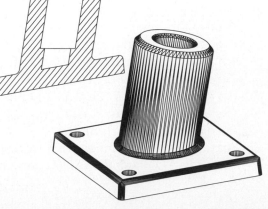

Appendix B
Common File Extensions

The following list gives common file extensions you may encounter when working with AutoCAD. A definition of each file type is also given.

File extension	Description
3DS	This is a native 3D Studio file. They can be created with the **3DSOUT** command and imported with the **3DSIN** command.
AC$	A temporary work file.
ADS	An AutoCAD Development System application. Type (XLOAD *"filename"*) at the **Command:** prompt to load.
ADT	Audit report files created with the **AUDIT** command.
AHP	AutoCAD help files.
ARX	An AutoCAD Runtime Extension application file. These applications run directly through AutoCAD and not through AutoLISP, like ADS applications. Type (ARXLOAD *"filename"*) at the **Command:** prompt to load.
BAK	Backup drawing files created by AutoCAD when the drawing is saved for the second time and anytime thereafter.
BAT	An MS-DOS batch file that executes a series of commands.
BK*n*	Emergency backup files numbered sequentially (BK1, BK2, BK3, etc.) when AutoCAD unexpectedly terminates. These files are numbered in this way to protect the original BAK file.
BMP	A Windows bitmap file. Use the **BMPOUT** command to export this file.
C	An ADS source code file.
CC	An ADS source code file.
CDF	An attribute extract file in the comma delimited format.
CFG	A configuration file.
CUS	A custom dictionary file.
DCC	An ASCII text file that contains color settings for all of the dialog box elements.
DCE	A dialog box error report file. AutoCAD creates the ACAD.DCE text file if errors are found when trying to load a DCL file. It is placed in the current working directory and is deleted when another DCL file is read successfully.
DLL	A platform-specific, dynamic-linked library file.
DWG	The native AutoCAD drawing file extension.
DWK	An AutoCAD drawing lock file.
DWL	A temporary lock file for an externally referenced drawing.
DXB	A drawing interchange file in binary format.
DXF	A drawing interchange file in ASCII format.
DXX	An attribute extract file in DXF format.
EPS	An encapsulated PostScript file.
ERR	An AutoCAD error file that contains diagnostic information. This type of file is created when AutoCAD "crashes."
EXE	An executable program file.
GIF	A graphics interchange format raster file. This type of file can be imported into AutoCAD using the **GIFIN** command.
H	An ADS include file.

File extension	Description
HLP	A Windows help file.
INI	A program initialization file. This is where basic settings for the application are stored.
LIN	A linetype library file.
LOG	This file is a history of all commands and variables used in a drawing session.
LSP	An AutoLISP file.
MID	An identification information file.
MLI	A materials library file.
MNC	A compiled menu file. This file type is for the Windows version of AutoCAD only.
MND	A menu description file created for use with the MC.EXE program.
MNL	A menu AutoLISP file.
MNR	A menu resource file. This file type is for the Windows version of AutoCAD only.
MNS	A menu source file. This file type is for Windows version of AutoCAD only.
MNU	A menu template file in ASCII format.
MSG	An AutoCAD message file that contains information displayed when AutoCAD is opened or when the **ABOUT** command is used.
OLD	The original version of a converted drawing file.
PAT	A hatch pattern library file.
PCP	A plot configuration parameters file.
PCX	A bitmap raster image file. This file can be imported into AutoCAD with the **PCXIN** command.
PFA	A PostScript font file ASCII format.
PFB	A PostScript font file binary format.
PFM	A PostScript font metric file.
PLT	A plot output file. Also called a "plot file."
PS	A PostScript interpreter initialization file.
PSF	A PostScript font file.
SAB	A binary file that stores solid model geometry.
SAT	An ASCII file that stores solid model geometry. Import and export this file type with the **ACISIN** and **ACISOUT** commands.
SCR	A command script file.
SDF	An attribute extract file in the space delimited format.
SHP	This file extension is used for both AutoCAD shape and font source files.
SHX	A compiled AutoCAD shape and font file.
SLB	A slide library file.
SLD	A slide file.
STL	A stereolithography file.
SV$	An automatically saved drawing file.
TGA	A Truevision rendered replay file. Use the **REPLAY** command to display the image in AutoCAD.
TIF	A Tagged Image File format file. Use the **REPLAY** command to display the image in AutoCAD.
TTF	A TrueType font file.
TXT	An attribute extract or template file of SDF or CDF format.
UNT	A units conversion file.
WMF	A Windows Metafile format vector file. Use the **WMFIN** and **WMFOUT** commands to import and export this file type.
XLG	An external references log file.
XMX	An external message file.

Appendix C

AutoCAD Command Aliases

INTRODUCTION

The following aliases for AutoCAD commands are found in the ACAD.PGP file. This file is located in the \R13\COM\SUPPORT subdirectory. The examples given in this file are aliases for the most frequently used commands.

You can easily create your own aliases. The first part of the alias is the character(s) that you type at the keyboard. The second part must begin with an asterisk followed by the name of the command the alias will execute. Do not put a space between the asterisk and the command.

Each alias you create requires a small amount of memory to function. Do not create a lot of aliases if your computer does not have sufficient memory resources. Always consult your instructor or supervisor before altering any file crucial to the operation of AutoCAD.

ALIASES

The following aliases are shown exactly as they appear in the ACAD.PGP file. This file can be opened in any text editor or word processor that can read ASCII files. If you add your own aliases, it is a good idea to add them to the list alphabetically.

```
A,          *ARC
C,          *CIRCLE
CP,         *COPY
DV,         *DVIEW
E,          *ERASE
L,          *LINE
LA,         *LAYER
LT,         *LINETYPE
M,          *MOVE
MS,         *MSPACE
P,          *PAN
PL,         *PLINE
PS,         *PSPACE
R,          *REDRAW
T,          *MTEXT
Z,          *ZOOM


3DLINE,     *LINE


; Give Windows an AV command like DOS has
AV,         *DSVIEWER
; Menu says "Exit", so make an alias
EXIT,       *QUIT
```

(Continued next column)

```
; easy access to _PKSER (serial number)
    system variable
SERIAL,     *_PKSER
; Dimensioning Commands.

DIMALI,     *DIMALIGNED
DIMANG,     *DIMANGULAR
DIMBASE,    *DIMBASELINE
DIMCONT,    *DIMCONTINUE
DIMDIA,     *DIMDIAMETER
DIMED,      *DIMEDIT
DIMTED,     *DIMTEDIT
DIMLIN,     *DIMLINEAR
DIMORD,     *DIMORDINATE
DIMRAD,     *DIMRADIUS
DIMSTY,     *DIMSTYLE
DIMOVER,    *DIMOVERRIDE
LEAD,       *LEADER
TOL,        *TOLERANCE
```

Appendix D
Advanced Application Commands

Command	Description
3D	This command allows you to create the following three-dimensional polygon mesh objects: box, cone, dish, dome, mesh, pyramid, torus, and wedge.
3DARRAY	This command allows you to create a three-dimensional polar or rectangular array.
3DFACE	This command creates a three-dimensional face. The face must have at least three and no more than four vertices.
3DMESH	This command creates a polygon mesh. You must give the coordinate location for each of the vertices in the mesh.
3DPOLY	This command creates a polyline in 3D space.
3DSIN	This command is used to import a 3D Studio into AutoCAD.
3DSOUT	This command is used to save an AutoCAD drawing in the native 3D Studio file format. Only 3D objects are saved. Any 2D objects are lost.
ACISIN	This command allows you to import an ACIS solid model (.SAT) file into AutoCAD.
ACISOUT	This command allows you to save solid objects created in AutoCAD as an ACIS solid model file (.SAT).
ALIGN	This command is used to move and rotate a selected object to align with other objects.
AMECONVERT	This command converts solid models created in AME to AutoCAD R13 solids.
AREA	This command calculates the area and perimeter of selected objects or of defined areas.
ASEADMIN	This command is used to manage external database commands.
ASEEXPORT	This command exports link information for selected objects to an external database file.
ASELINKS	This command is used to manage links between objects and an external database.
ASEROWS	This command displays table data. You can edit data and create links and selection sets.
ASESELECT	This command creates a selection set from rows linked to text and graphic selection sets.
ASESEQLED	This command executes Structured Query Language (SQL) statements.
ASEUNLOAD	This command removes an AutoCAD SQL Environment (ASE) application from system memory (RAM).
BMPOUT	This command saves selected objects as a bitmap (.BMP) format file.
BOX	This command creates a three-dimensional solid box.
CHAMFER	This command is used to bevel the edges of objects. A chamfer can be applied to a 2D or 3D object.
COMPILE	This command compiles shape and PostScript font files.
CONE	This command creates a three-dimensional solid cone.

Command	Description
COPYCLIP	This command copies selected objects to the Windows Clipboard.
COPYLINK	This command copies the current view to the Windows Clipboard for linking to Object Linking and Embedding (OLE) applications.
CUTCLIP	This command removes selected objects from the drawing and places them on the Windows Clipboard.
CYLINDER	This command creates a three-dimensional solid cylinder.
DDUCS	This command is used to manage defined User Coordinate Systems (UCS).
DDUCSP	This command allows you to select from several preset UCSs.
DDVIEW	This command is used to create and restore saved views.
DDVPOINT	This command is used to set the viewing direction.
DSVIEWER	This command allows you to change your view of the drawing using the **Aerial View** window. This command can only be used when your display is configured for a Windows accelerated display driver.
DVIEW	This command allows you to define a parallel projection or perspective view of selected objects.
EDGE	This command is used to make an edge of a 3D face visible or invisible.
EDGESURF	This command creates a three-dimensional polygon mesh using four objects to define the edges.
ELEV	This command is used to set the current elevation and thickness.
EXTRUDE	This command is used to create 3D solid primitives by extruding a two-dimensional region.
FILLET	This command is used to place fillets and rounds on the edges of objects.
GIFIN	This command is used to import a .GIF image file into AutoCAD. A .GIF file is a raster image file.
HIDE	This command is used to display 3D objects with hidden lines removed.
IMPORT	This command is used to import several different types of files into AutoCAD.
INTERFERE	This command is used to create a composite solid from the volume created by the interference of two or more solids.
INTERSECT	This command is used to create a composite solid or region from the intersection of two or more solids or regions.
LIGHT	This command is used to manage lights and lighting effects.
MASSPROP	This command calculates and displays the mass properties of regions or solids.
MATLIB	This command opens the **Materials Library** dialog box. This dialog box is used to import and export materials to and from a library of materials.
MENU	This command is used to load a menu file.
MENULOAD	This command is used to load partial menu files.
MENUUNLOAD	This command is used to unload partial menu files.
MIRROR3D	This command is used to construct a mirror image of selected objects in 3D space using a mirror plane.
MVIEW	This command is used to create floating viewports. It is also used to turn on existing floating viewports.
OLELINKS	This command is used to update, change, and cancel existing links.
PASTECLIP	This command inserts the contents of the Windows Clipboard into the current drawing.
PASTESPEC	This command inserts the contents of the Windows Clipboard and allows you to control the format of what is being inserted.
PCXIN	This command is used to import a .PCX image file into AutoCAD. A .PCX file is a raster image file

Command	Description
PFACE	This command allows you to create a three-dimensional polyface mesh. Each vertex must be individually specified.
PLAN	This command displays a plan view of the current User Coordinate System (UCS), a saved UCS, or the World Coordinate System (WCS).
PSFILL	This command is used to fill a two-dimensional polyline outline with a PostScript pattern.
PSIN	This command is used to import an encapsulated PostScript file into AutoCAD.
PSOUT	This command saves the drawing as an encapsulated PostScript file. You must specify what portion of the drawing is to be saved.
PSPACE	This command switches from model space to paper space.
REGION	This command is used to create a region from selected objects.
REINIT	This command is used to re-initialize the I/O ports, digitizer, display, and program parameters file.
RENDER	This command opens the **Render** dialog box and also initializes the AutoCAD **Render** window. The **Render** dialog box is used to create a realistically shaded image of a three-dimensional object.
RENDERUNLOAD	This command closes the AutoCAD **Render** application. Note: If you use this command, any rendered objects are returned to a wireframe.
RENDSCR	This command displays the last rendering created using the **RENDER** command. This command has no effect if **RENDERUNLOAD** has been used since the last rendering.
REPLAY	This command is used to display a .GIF, .TGA, or .TIF raster image.
REVOLVE	This command is used to create a 3D solid by revolving a closed two-dimensional object about an axis.
REVSURF	This command creates a 3D surface by rotating a 2D object about a selected axis.
RMAT	This command opens the **Materials** dialog box. This dialog box is used to manage materials used for rendering.
ROTATE3D	This command rotates selected objects about an axis in 3D space.
RULESURF	This command creates a 3D ruled surface between two path curves. The curves can be arcs, lines, or points.
SAVEIMG	This command saves a rendered image to a file in .GIF, .TIF, or .TGA format.
SCENE	This command is used to manage scenes.
SECTION	This command creates a region from the intersection of a plane and a solid. The region can then be used to create a section view.
SHADE	This command displays a shaded image of the drawing in the current viewport. This command is faster than the **RENDER** command, but the image quality is not as good.
SLICE	This command "cuts" a set of solids with a plane.
SPHERE	This command creates a three-dimensional solid sphere.
SUBTRACT	This command creates a composite by subtracting the area or volume of one selection set from another selection set. This command can be used for 2D regions and 3D solids.
TABSURF	This command creates a 3D tabulated surface from a path curve and direction vector.
TIFFIN	This command is used to import a .TIF file. A .TIF file is a raster image file.
TORUS	This command creates a 3D solid that resembles a doughnut.
UCS	This command is used to create and manage User Coordinate Systems (UCS).

Command	Description
UCSICON	This command controls the visibility and placement of the UCS and WCS icons.
UNION	This command creates a composite by adding the area or volume of two selection sets. This command can be used with 2D regions or 3D solids.
VPOINT	This command is used to set the viewing direction. This command is commonly used to create a 3D display of the drawing.
VPORTS	This command is used to divide the graphics area into multiple viewports.
WMFIN	This command is used to import a Windows Metafile (.WMF).
WMFOPTS	This command sets the options for using the **WMFIN** command.
WMFOUT	This command saves selected objects as a Windows Metafile (.WMF).

Appendix E

Advanced Application System Variables

Variable	Type	Saved In	Default Value	Description
CHAMFERA	Real	Drawing	0.0000	First chamfer distance.
CHAMFERB	Real	Drawing	0.0000	Second chamfer distance.
CHAMFERC	Real	Drawing	0.0000	Chamfer length.
CHAMFERD	Real	Drawing	0.0000	Chamfer angle.
CHAMMODE	Integer	Not saved	0	Sets the method for creating chamfers. 0 Two chamfer distances are used. 1 One chamfer length and an angle are used.
CVPORT	Integer	Drawing	2	Identification number of the current viewport. The identification number you specify must correspond to an active viewport. Also, the cursor must not be locked in that viewpoint. Tablet mode must be off.
DELOBJ	Integer	Drawing	1	Determines whether objects used to create other objects are deleted from the drawing database. 0 Delete objects. 1 Keep objects.
DISPSILH	Integer	Drawing	0	Display of silhouette curves of body objects in wireframe mode. 0 Off. 1 On.
EDGEMODE	Integer	Not saved	0	Cutting and boundary edges for the **TRIM** and **EXTEND** commands. 0 Uses only the selected edge. 1 Creates an imaginary extension from the selected object.
ELEVATION	Real	Drawing	0.0000	Stores the current 3D elevation relative to the current UCS for the current space.
FACETRES	Real	Drawing	0.5	Adjusts the smoothness of shaded and hidden line-removed objects. Value can range from 0.01 to 10.0.
FILLETRAD	Real	Drawing	0.0000	Fillet radius.
FRONTZ	Real	Drawing	(Read-only)	Stores the front clipping plane offset from the target plane for the current viewport.
ISOLINES	Integer	Drawing	4	Specifies the number of isolines per surface. Values can range from 0 to 2047.
LENSLENGTH	Real	Drawing	(Read-only)	Stores the length of the lens (in millimeters) used in perspective viewing.

Variable	Type	Saved In	Default Value	Description
MAXACTVP	Integer	Not saved	16	Maximum number of viewports that regenerate at one time.
PFACEVMAX	Integer	Not saved	(Read-only)	Maximum number of vertices per face.
PROJMODE	Integer	Config	1	Projection mode for the **Trim** and **Extend** commands. 0 True 3D mode (no projection). 1 Project to the XY plane of the current UCS. 2 Project to the current view plane.
PSPROLOG	String	Config	""	Assigns a name for a prologue section to be read from the ACAD.PSF file when using **PSOUT**.
PSQUALITY	Integer	Drawing	75	Controls drawing of PostScript images. 0 Disables PostScript image generation. < 0 Sets the number of pixels per drawing unit for the PostScript image. > 0 Sets the number of pixels per drawing unit, shows PostScript paths as outlines and does not fill them.
RASTERPREVIEW	Integer	Drawing	0	Sets format of preview image. 0 BMP. 1 BMP and WMF. 2 WMF. 3 No preview image.
RIASPECT	Real	Not saved	0.0000	Image aspect ratio for imported raster images. **RIASPECT** overrides any specification in the imported GIF and TIFF file. PCX files contain no aspect ratio.
RIBACKG	Integer	Not saved	0	Background color number for imported raster images.
RIEDGE	Integer	Not saved	0	Edge detection feature. 0 Disables edge detection. Use when importing an image for viewing but not tracing. > 0 Sets the threshold for **RIEDGE** detection. Values range from 1 to 255.
RIGAMUT	Integer	Not saved	256	Number of colors **GIFIN**, **PCXIN**, and **TIFFIN** used to import an image. Common settings are 8 and 16.
RIGREY	Integer	Not saved	0	Imports an image as a grayscale image. 0 Disables grayscale image importing. > 0 Converts each pixel in the image to a grayscale value.
RITHRESH	Integer	Not saved	0	Controls importing and image based on luminance (brightness). 0 Turns off **RITHRESH**. > 0 Minimum pixel luminance value to be imported.
SHADEDGE	Integer	Drawing	3	Controls shading of edges in rendering. 0 Faces shaded, edges not highlighted. 1 Faces shaded, edges drawn in background color.

Variable	Type	Saved In	Default Value	Description
				2 Faces not filled, edges in object color.
				3 Faces in object color, edges in background color.
SHADEDIF	Integer	Drawing	70	Percent of diffuse reflective light relative to ambient light.
SPLFRAME	Integer	Drawing	0	Controls display of spline-fit polylines.
				0 Does not display the control polygon. Displays the fit surface of a polygon mesh, but not the defining mesh. Does not display the invisible edges of 3D faces or polyface meshes.
				1 Displays the control polygon. Only the defining mesh of a surface-fit polygon mesh is displayed (not the fit surface). Invisible edges of 3D faces and polyface meshes are displayed.
SPLINESEGS	Integer	Drawing	8	Number of line segments for each spline.
SPLINETYPE	Integer	Drawing	6	Type of spline curve to be generated by **PEDIT Spline**.
				5 Quadratic B-spline.
				6 Cubic B-spline.
SURFTAB1	Integer	Drawing	6	Number of tabulations generated for **RULESURF** and **TABSURF**. Mesh density in the M direction for **REVSURF** and **EDGESURF**.
SURFTAB2	Integer	Drawing	6	Mesh density in the N direction for **REVSURF** and **EDGESURF**.
SURFTYPE	Integer	Drawing	6	Controls the surface-fitting done by **PEDIT Smooth**.
				5 Quadratic B-spline surface.
				6 Cubic B-spline surface.
				8 Bezier surface.
SURFU	Integer	Drawing	6	Surface density in the M direction.
SURFV	Integer	Drawing	6	Surface density in the N direction.
TARGET	3D point	Drawing	Read-only	Location of the target point for the current viewpoint in UCS coordinates.
THICKNESS	Real	Drawing	0.0000	Sets 3D thickness.
TILEMODE	Integer	Drawing	1	Controls access to paper space and the behavior of AutoCAD viewports.
				0 Enables paper space and viewport objects (uses **MVIEW**).
				1 Enables Release 10 Compatibility mode (uses **VPORTS**). Returns to Tiled Viewport mode. Paper space objects—including viewport objects—are not displayed, and the **MVIEW**, **MSPACE**, **PSPACE**, and **VPLAYER** commands are disabled.
TRIMMODE	Integer	Not saved	1	Controls edge trimming for chamfers and fillets.
				0 Leaves edges intact.
				1 Trims edges.

Variable	Type	Saved In	Default Value	Description
UCSFOLLOW	Integer	Drawing	0	Generates a plan view whenever you change from one UCS to another. Can be set separately for each viewport. The setting is maintained separately for both spaces, but it is always treated as if set to 0 while in paper space.
				0 UCS does not affect the view.
				1 Any UCS change causes a change to plan view of the new UCS in the current viewport.
UCSICON	Integer	Drawing	1	Displays the Coordinate System icon.
				1 On.
				2 Origin. The icon floats to the UCS origin, if possible.
UCSNAME	String	Drawing	(Read-only)	Stores the name of the current coordinate system. Returns a null string if the current UCS is unnamed.
UCSORG	3D point	Drawing	(Read-only)	Stores the origin point of the current coordinate system, in World coordinates.
UCSXDIR	3D point	Drawing	(Read-only)	Stores the X direction of the current UCS.
UCSYDIR	3D point	Drawing	(Read-only)	Stores the Y direction of the current UCS for the current space.
VIEWCTR	3D point	Drawing	(Read-only)	Stores the center of view in the current viewport, expressed in UCS coordinates.
VIEWDIR	3D vector	Drawing	(Read-only)	Stores the viewing direction in the current viewport expressed in UCS coordinates.
VIEWMODE	Integer	Drawing	(Read-only)	Controls viewing mode for the current viewport using bit-code.
				0 Disabled.
				1 Perspective view active.
				2 Front clipping on.
				4 Back clipping on.
				8 UCS follow mode on.
				16 Front clip not at eye.
VIEWSIZE	Real	Drawing	(Read-only)	Height of view in current viewport.
VIEWTWIST	Real	Drawing	(Read-only)	View twist angle for the current viewport.
VSMAX	3D point	Drawing	(Read-only)	Upper-right corner of the current viewport virtual screen, expressed in UCS coordinates.
VSMIN	3D point	Drawing	(Read-only)	Lower-left corner of the current viewport virtual screen, expressed in UCS coordinates.
WORLDUCS	Integer	Not saved	(Read-only)	Relation between UCS and the World Coordinate System.
				0 UCS and World Coordinate System are different.
				1 UCS and World Coordinate System are the same.
WORLDVIEW	Integer	Drawing	1	Controls whether UCS changes to WCS during **DVIEW** or **VPOINT**.
				0 Current UCS remains unchanged.
				1 Current UCS is changed to the WCS.

Appendix F

Basic AutoLISP Commands

The following is a list of basic AutoLISP commands with a brief definition of each command. These commands are covered in Chapter 21 and Chapter 22 of this text. Detailed definitions of these and all other AutoLISP commands are found in Chapter 13 of the *AutoCAD Customization Guide*.

Command	Description
+ *(addition)*	Adds all of the numbers.
– *(subtraction)*	Subtracts the second and following numbers from the first and returns the difference.
* *(multiplication)*	Multiplies all of the numbers.
/ *(division)*	Divides the first number by the product of the remaining numbers and returns the quotient.
= *(equal to)*	Returns a total if all arguments are equal. Returns *nil* otherwise.
ANGLE	Returns the angle from the X axis of the current UCS to a line defined by two endpoints, as measured counterclockwise. The value is given in radians.
ARXLOAD	Loads an AutoCAD Runtime Extension application.
ARXUNLOAD	Unloads an AutoCAD Runtime Extension application.
CAR	Returns the first element of a list.
CADR	Returns the second element of a list.
CADDR	Returns the third element of a list.
CDR	Returns the second and remaining elements of a list. If the list contains more than two elements, the returned values are placed in a list.
DEFUN	Defines a function.
DISTANCE	Returns the distance between two points. The distance is measured in 3D space.
GETANGLE	Waits for a user-input angle and returns the angle in radians. The user can input the angle at the keyboard or use the pointing device to pick points on-screen.
GETCORNER	Waits for the user to input the second corner of a rectangle using the pointing device.
GETDIST	Waits for a user-input distance. The distance can be entered at the keyboard or use the pointing device to pick points on-screen.
GETORIENT	Waits for a user-input and returns the angle in radians. This is similar to the **GETANGLE** function, but the **ANGBASE** and **ANGDIR** system variables do not affect it.
GETPOINT	Waits for a user-input point and returns the point.
GETREAL	Waits for a user-input real number and returns the real number.
GETSTRING	Waits for a user-input string and returns the string.
GETVAR	Returns the value assigned to a specified AutoCAD system variable.
GRAPHSCR	If the text screen is currently displayed, switches to the AutoCAD graphics screen.
LOAD_DIALOG	Loads a Dialog Control Language file.

Command	Description
NEW_DIALOG	Opens a specified dialog box. This function can also specify a default action of the dialog box.
POLAR	Returns the coordinates of a 3D point a specified angle and distance from a specified point.
PRINC	Prints a specified expression on the command line. This function can also be used to write a specified expression to a file.
PROMPT	Displays a specified string on the command line.
START_DIALOG	Opens a specified dialog box and makes AutoCAD ready to accept user input.
STRLEN	Reports the number of characters in a string.
TERPRI	Prints a new line on the command line.
TEXTSCR	If the graphics screen is currently displayed, switches to the AutoCAD text screen.
UNLOAD_DIALOG	Unloads a Dialog Control Language file.
VMON	Provides virtual function paging. This function is no longer needed in Release 13, but is used for compatibility with previous releases.
XLOAD	Loads an AutoCAD Development System application.
XUNLOAD	Unloads an AutoCAD Development System application.

INDEX